Queens [...]

John Boyle [...]

[...] truly and faithfu[...]

[...] the duties of same

[...]ledged before me

[...] March, 1852.

[...] Resident Magistrate

FROM QUEEN'S COLLEGE TO
NATIONAL UNIVERSITY

From Queen's College to National University

*Essays on the Academic History
of QCG/UCG/NUI, Galway*

TADHG FOLEY

EDITOR

FOUR COURTS PRESS

Set in 10.5 on 12 pt Ehrhardt by
Carrigboy Typesetting Services for
FOUR COURTS PRESS LTD
Fumbally Court, Fumbally Lane, Dublin 8, Ireland
e-mail: info@four-courts-press.ie
website: www.four-courts-press.ie
and in North America for
FOUR COURTS PRESS
c/o ISBS, 5804 N.E. Hassalo Street, Portland, OR 97213.

© the various authors 1999

A catalogue record for this title is available from the British Library.

ISBN 1-85182-527-4

All rights reserved. No part of this publication may be reproduced, stored in or introduced into a retrieval system, or transmitted, in any form or by any means (electronic, mechanical, photocopying, recording or otherwise), without the prior written permission of both the copyright owner and publisher of this book.

Printed in Ireland
by ßetaprint Ltd, Dublin

Contents

	List of Illustrations	vii
	Preface *Tadhg Foley*	ix
1	The Establishment of the Queen's Colleges: Ideological and Political Background *Gearóid Ó Tuathaigh*	1
2	Law *Liam O'Malley*	16
3	Engineering *Paul Duffy*	125
4	Medicine *James P. Murray*	142
5	Mathematics *Seán Tobin*	159
6	Natural Philosophy/Physics *Tom O'Connor*	184
7	Chemistry *R.N. Butler*	218
8	Professor William King and the Establishment of the Geological Sciences in Queen's College Galway *David A.T. Harper*	242
9	Melville, Hart, and Anderson: Early Teachers of Natural History, 1849–1914 *Timothy Collins*	266
10	From Political Economy to Economics and Commerce *Tom Boylan and Tadhg Foley*	303

11	Classics in Victorian Galway *Arthur Keaveney*	326
12	Irish: A Difficult Birth *Breandán Ó Madagáin*	344
13	Modern Languages *Rosaleen O'Neill*	360
14	English, History, and Philosophy *Tadhg Foley and Fiona Bateman*	384
	Notes on Contributors	421
	Index	423

List of Illustrations

2.1	D.C. Heron, Professor of Jurisprudence and Political Economy, 1849–59	45
2.2	H. Law, Professor of English Law, 1849–59	57
2.3	W.B. Campion, Professor of English Law, 1859–1907	77
2.4	J.A. Rentoul LLB (1874), LLD (1875). Judge of the City of London Court and of the Old Bailey	102
3.1	W.B. Blood, Professor of Civil Engineering, 1849–60	128
3.2	E. Townsend, Professor of Civil Engineering, 1860–1910	130
3.3	F.S. Rishworth, Professor of Civil Engineering, 1910–46	133
3.4	W.H. Prendergast, Professor of Civil Engineering, 1947–57	136
3.5	A. Perry BE (1906), first woman engineering graduate in the world	140
4.1	C.C. King, Professor of Anatomy and Physiology, 1849–63	144
4.2	J. Cleland, Professor of Anatomy and Physiology, 1863–77	144
4.3	R. Doherty, Professor of Midwifery, 1849–76	145
4.4	J.P. Pye, Professor of Anatomy and Physiology, 1877–1920	145
4.5	S. McCoy, Professor of Materia Medica, 1849–73	146
4.6	J.V. Browne, Professor of Surgery, 1849–87	146
5.1	G.J. Allman, Professor of Mathematics, 1853–93	163
5.2	M. Power, Professor of Mathematics, 1912–55	170
6.1	A.H. Curtis, Professor of Natural Philosophy, 1857–79	186
6.2	A. Anderson, Professor of Natural Philosophy, 1885–1934 and President, 1899–1934	189
7.1	E. Ronalds, Professor of Chemistry, 1849–56	220
7.2	E. Divers, Assistant, 1854–66, first Professor of Chemistry, University of Tokyo	220
7.3	T.H. Rowney, Professor of Chemistry, 1856–89	223
7.4	A.E. Dixon, Professor of Chemistry, 1889–91	223
7.5	A. Senier, Professor of Chemistry, 1891–1918	225
7.6	R. Clarke, Assistant, 1910–42	225
7.7	T. Dillon, Professor of Chemistry, 1919–54	227
7.8	P.S. Ó Colla, Professor of Chemistry, 1954–81	233
7.9	Group photograph including Elizabeth Lee, Lecturer in Chemistry 1965–76, Associate Professor, 1976–89 and Tony Finan, Lecturer in Chemistry, 1963–98	233
7.10	Seán Ó Cinnéide, Professor of Inorganic Chemistry, 1965–88	233
8.1	W. King, Professor of Mineralogy, Geology, and Natural History, 1849–83	243
8.2	A timetable for the founding of the geological systems	249
8.3	A timetable for major discoveries in palaeontology	249
8.4	Photograph of a typical *Eozoön*	252
8.5	Plastotype of the Neanderthal skull cap in the James Mitchell Museum, NUI, Galway	253
8.6	Part of the 1852 report of the Museum Committee of Queen's College Galway	256

8.7	Frequency of lectures and number of students per annum in Mineralogy and Geology	259
8.8	Examination papers in Mineralogy, etc., 1855	260
8.9	Examination papers in Geology, 1875	261
9.1	A.G. Melville, Professor of Natural History 1849–82	267
9.2	R.J. Anderson, Professor of Natural History, Geology, and Mineralogy 1883–1914	283
9.3	Natural History Museum, Queen's College Galway in the late nineteenth century	284
9.4	Two of Anderson's inventions	287, 289
9.5	H.C. Hart, botanist, explorer, and philologist	293
10.1	J.E. Cairnes, Professor of Jurisprudence and Political Economy, 1859–70	310
10.2	Students at Queen's College Galway, c.1870	315
11.1	W.E. Hearn, Professsor of the Greek Language, 1849–54	327
11.2	W. Nesbitt, Professor of the Latin Language, 1849–54, Professor of the Greek Language, 1854–64	328
11.3	R.B. Bagley, Professor of Latin, 1854–69	328
11.4	D.W. Thompson, Professor of Greek, 1864–1902	331
11.5	J.F. Davies, Professor of Latin, 1880–9	340
11.6	P. Sandford, Professor of Latin, 1890–1903	340
12.1	T. Ó Máille, Professor of Irish Language, Philology, and Literature, 1909–38	355
13.1	A. Bensbach, Professor of Modern Languages, 1849–68	362
13.2	C. Geisler, Professor of Modern Languages, 1868–86	367
13.3	V. Steinberger, Professor of Modern Languages, 1886–1916	369
14.1	J.P. O'Toole, Professor of History and English Literature and Vice-President, 1850–2	387
14.2	Sir T. Moffett, President, 1877–97	391
14.3	W.A. Byrne, Professor of English, 1917–33	403
14.4	M.J. Donovan-O'Sullivan, Professor of History, 1914–57	409
14.5	S. Ní Chinnéide, Associate Professor of History, 1965–70	413
14.6	J.F. Howley, Professor of Philosophy, 1914–36	416

Credits and Sources

2.2	Courtesy of the Benchers of the Honourable Society of King's Inns	57
2.3	From *Memoir of William Bennett Campion, Serjeant-at-Law* (Dublin, 1911)	77
8.4	Courtesy of Dr Eric Robinson, formerly of University College, London	252
9.1	Private Collection	267
9.3	Courtesy of the Department of Geology, NUI, Galway	284
9.4	From a) *Philosophical Magazine*; b) *Monthly Journal of Anatomy and Physiology*	287, 289
9.5	From *Irish Naturalist*	293
14.4	Courtesy of Dr Desmond Donovan, Galway	409

All other illustrations courtesy of NUI, Galway Archives. The portrait of President Alexander Anderson (6.2) is by Charles Lamb RHA and the portrait of Sir Thomas Moffett (14.2) is by Walter Osborne RHA.

Preface

Most older universities, even those of modest antiquity, boast of at least one institutional history. Trinity College Dublin, suitable to its longevity, has several volumes devoted to its history, while Queen's University Belfast has a splendid two-volume work covering its first century of existence. While University College Dublin has, as yet, no systematic history, neither it nor its apostolic predecessor, the Catholic University of Ireland, has lacked scholarly attention. In recent years both the National University of Ireland, Maynooth and University College Cork have been handsomely served by two volumes relating and assessing their respective histories. But, apart from a small number of important articles, virtually nothing has been published on the National University of Ireland, Galway, formerly known as University College Galway but founded as Queen's College Galway in 1845. This is the first book devoted to its academic history. It was commissioned by Professor Gearóid Ó Tuathaigh when he was Vice-President of what was then UCG, and its publication commemorates the sesquicentenary of the opening of QCG on 30 October 1849. Professor Tom Boylan and I were asked to take on the task but Professor Boylan was called to higher things and is now the Dean of Research, having previously given outstanding service as Dean of the Faculty of Arts.

This volume consists of thirteen essays on the academic history of various subject areas, with special emphasis on those disciplines which are in existence since 1849. It begins with an essay on the ideological and political background of the establishment of the Queen's Colleges in Ireland, written by Professor Ó Tuathaigh. Given the very large number of Departments at the present day, some of very recent vintage, it would have been an impossible task to attempt a comprehensive review of their activities. It could be argued that since most of the newer disciplines grew more-or-less organically out of the foundational ones, a study of the more elderly subjects should throw considerable light on their youthful offspring. Even if we had world enough and time, a totally comprehensive treatment would, even in theory, be impossible. For one thing, the history of university education in Galway, or anywhere, is a good deal more than the merely academic. The modest aim of this volume is to be, in some sense, 'representative' of the academic work of this College/University over the past 150 years. The essays are written by authors from within the different disciplines.

Each author was asked to pay some attention to the lives and works of the various professors and lecturers, to the changing nature of the syllabuses, and to the lives and subsequent careers of the students. As this volume was never meant to be a rigidly systematic work, individual contributors had the liberty to concentrate their attention, for reasons of interest or competence, on specific areas, though they were asked to do this in the context of the general aims of the enterprise as a whole. Severe constraints were imposed on the authors by both the lack of adequate archives and the stunningly chaotic nature of existing archives. Abjuring the Procrustean and Draconian modes, the editorial methods of Father O'Flynn had a certain appeal:

> Checking the crazy ones,
> Coaxin' onaisy ones,
> Liftin' the lazy ones on wid the stick.

But avoiding the Scylla of authoritarianism puts an editor in danger of falling foul of the Charybdis of libertarianism. Long before the days of Hayden White, Nennius, the ninth-century compiler of annals, innocently and disarmingly began one of his works with the words: 'I made a heap of everything I could find'. This collection has attempted to avoid the order of the heap, on the one hand, and regimentation, on the other. It is no more than the first word on the subject; it makes no claim to be the last. It provides a database for a more rigorous and ambitious study of the role and function of university education in Ireland over the last century-and-a-half.

In an attempt to alleviate tedium, the generic fate of institutional history (where dullness is seen as the *sine qua non* of serious academic achievement), contributors were encouraged to spice and salt their pious institutional blandishments in order to make their narratives piquant. Just as obituaries find it difficult to speak anything but good of the dead, exercises of this sort struggle in vain to avoid piety. But history has been unkind to the term and if Virgil's Aeneas lived now he would not judge himself honoured to be called pious. A college or university is often fondly seen as an *alma mater*, and it is not always easy to be very critical of one's mother. Indeed the history of these institutions is frequently conceived of in organic terms, either as a human *Bildungsroman* or as an organism of one sort or another, with the inevitable vocabulary of seeds, plants, and growth. Though models such as these may occasionally illuminate, rather more do they serve to darken our counsels, and teleological narratives meet their nemesis in a stubborn and recalcitrant Irish history. Indeed, the Queen's Colleges, like the national schools, were the products of a linear, uni-directional, utilitarian development theory, which sought to bring 'progress' to a society where time was believed to either stand still or (which is more-or-less the same thing) to move in circles. The Irish, previously categorised as ontologically inferior were now deemed to be merely historically backward, a view enabled by contemporary evolutionary thinking. The Duke of Abercorn, for instance, rejoiced to see that 'English literature and English classical works' held their 'fitting place' in the Queen's Colleges and that Milton and Shakespeare were 'honoured as they deserve[d]'. He went on to suggest that these, the 'best models', would act as a 'corrective' to the 'national defects' to be found in the poetry and prose of Moore and Burke. As the west of Ireland, the poorest and most 'backward' part of the country, manifested the 'national character' in a far purer state than the more progressive parts, nowhere was in greater need of a modernising education. Clearly such 'classical' English education would advance the Irish people from the 'Gothic barbarism' and the 'presumptive ignorance of the *hedge*', to the 'bright polish and intellectual refinement of the University', to quote the *Galway Vindicator's* welcome for the new Galway College.

There were important educational consequences to the fact that Ireland, though possessing most of the signs of being a colony, was constitutionally an intrinsic part of the British Empire. In the nineteenth century, even in Ireland, much emphasis was placed on preparing young men to work in the colonies and, for instance, careers in the Indian Civil Service were much sought after. In their continuing efforts to keep their doors open, especially in Galway which was threatened with closure on a number of occasions, College Presidents and others were forever crowing about how much better their students fared in these competitive examinations than those from grander institutions.

But if the first half of the 150-year existence of QCG/UCG was dedicated to the fashioning of colonial masters and imperial subjects, the second half had to address the formation of citizens in the new nation-state. An increasingly confident nationalism struggled with an unionism which was becoming politically residual but which seemed, nonetheless, to still adhere tenaciously, if precariously, to the very structure of the institution itself. The question of the role of the Irish language, especially as set out in the University College Galway Act, 1929, now replaced the equally acrimonious debates on religion which dominated the earlier period.

Much of the research in this volume is devoted to uncovering the lives of the illustrious obscure who taught in Galway and identifying their contributions to scholarship. Some, one could argue, richly deserve the obscurity to which history has, perhaps mercifully, consigned them. But there is always the possibility of discovering some mute inglorious Milton. As these pages will indicate, Galway, for a small, badly-funded, and geographically-peripheral university institution, had many outstanding scholars on the staff and produced an extraordinary number of brilliant students who distinguished themselves in later life. There is space to mention only a representative sample. Sir Joseph Larmor, the distinguished physicist, who was Professor of Natural Philosophy, later became the Lucasian Professor of Mathematics at Cambridge. The concept of gravitational 'black holes' may well have had its origins in a paper published in 1920 by his successor, Alexander Anderson, who eventually became President of the College. His daughter, Emily Anderson, was the first Professor of German and she is celebrated for her *Letters of Mozart and His Family* and her *Letters of Beethoven*, both in three volumes. For its first forty years, Chemistry in Galway was closely linked to von Liebeg's School in Giessen and the Royal College of Chemistry in London. William King, the geologist, both named and established the antiquity of Neanderthal man. He was a distinguished collector of geological specimens and he was forever boasting about the size of his 'Turritella'. And with reason: it was almost a metre long. The work of A.G. Melville, Professor of Natural History, on the dodo and recently-extinct flightless birds, has recently been praised for being one of the first works to identify human beings as the prime cause for the depletion of the planet's biodiversity. John Elliot Cairnes, Professor of Jurisprudence and Political Economy, was regarded as the leading economist in the world at the time of his early death. His pioneering work, *The Slave Power*, was admired by

Abraham Lincoln and Charles Darwin and greatly influenced Marx's analysis of the slave economy. Hugh Law, the first Professor of English Law, subsequently became solicitor-general, attorney-general, and finally lord chancellor of Ireland. W.E. Hearn became a distinguished scholar in later life and was elected Chancellor of the University of Melbourne. Several members of staff in the nineteenth century were elected Fellows of the Royal Society.

Queen's College and University College Galway produced a very impressive array of graduates who distinguished themselves in the arts and sciences, in administration, politics, law, medicine, engineering, teaching, and in many other areas. As details of these careers will be found in the following pages, a few examples will suffice. In medicine, Sir Peter Freyer, who pioneered the prostatectomy, and Sir Alfred Keogh, who directed the medical services of the British Army during the First World War, were both Galway graduates. So also were Edward Divers, who became the first Professor of Chemistry at the University of Tokyo, and George Sigerson, a nationalist activist who is best remembered for his literary activities. In Alice Perry, who graduated in 1906, Galway can claim the first woman engineering graduate in the world. The same school also produced Michael O'Shaughnessy, the engineer responsible for the Golden Gate Bridge and for San Francisco's water supply. One of the most distinguished Galway graduates was Michael McAuliffe, who under the name Max Arthur Macauliffe, translated the sacred book of the Sikhs and wrote what a recent scholar has described as his 'famous and enduring work', *The Sikh Religion*, published in six volumes in 1909. Many MPs and TDs were educated in Galway, among them Frank Hugh O'Donnell and T.P. O'Connor.

I am particularly grateful to Tom Boylan for his help with this volume and for his friendship and support over many years. I want to thank the National Archives, the National Library of Ireland, and, most of all, the extremely helpful staff of the James Hardiman Library, NUI, Galway for granting access to their holdings. I am especially indebted to Kevin Barry, Marie Boran, Fionnuala Byrne, Louis de Paor, Kieran Hoare, Helen Litton (who prepared the index) Seán Mac Íomhair, Séamus Mac Mathúna, Máire Mhic Uidhir, Donna Monroe, Joe O'Halloran, Rosaleen O'Neill, Gearóid Ó Tuathaigh, Lionel Pilkington, Marie Reddan, and Seán Ryder It is my unhappy duty to have to record the recent death of a valued contributor, James P. Murray, a kind and scholarly man. I am very happy to acknowledge the generous financial assistance from the Grant-in-Aid of Publication Fund of NUI, Galway. Vice-President Ruth Curtis and the university management team deserve special acknowledgement for making a researcher available to bring order out of archival chaos. That researcher was Fiona Bateman and I am particularly pleased to thank her for her expertise and her unstinting commitment to the project which went far beyond the call of duty. It is indeed a pleasure to pay tribute to her kindness and generosity. Though this volume has impacted seriously on Molly Fogarty's own work, she has been heroic in her selflessness. Were it appropriate, I would have dedicated this book to our children, Jane and Denis Foley.

TADHG FOLEY
National University of Ireland, Galway

The Establishment of the Queen's Colleges: Ideological and Political Background

GEARÓID Ó TUATHAIGH

The decision to establish the Queen's Colleges at Belfast, Cork, and Galway was essentially a political decision, taken in a very particular set of political circumstances.[1] But, in order to understand why the issue of higher education was deemed a politically appropriate issue for initiative by the government of Sir Robert Peel, and, further, why it aroused a measure of controversy in Ireland, chiefly among the Catholic hierarchy and among the leaders of the nationalist Repeal movement, we need to consider, however briefly, the wider ideological and constitutional framework within which the issue of the 'provincial colleges' emerged as a live political controversy in the 1840s.

The Act of Union of 1801 was enacted in an unsettled atmosphere in which fear and hope were felt by different (and sometimes by the same) elements of the political elite. The fear was the predictable consequence of the traumatic events of 1798 – fear of French invasion, of anarchy and of an assault on all institutions of property and order; fear of bloodshed, of civil strife, of excess.[2] These fears were shared, in varying degrees, by all the propertied classes, across all religious denominations. It was in fearful recoil from the horrific trauma of 1798 that the Irish parliament finally voted itself out of existence, and sought the closer security of the imperial connection in the Union settlement. Fitzgibbon's brutal reminder to the Protestant 'patriots' of the Irish parliament, those opposing the Union, that in the final analysis they held their position and title and privileges in Ireland by right of conquest and continuing superior force (in effect, the imperial army), rather than by the will and loyalty of the 'ruled', was probably the defining moment of the Union debate.[3]

---

1 The definitive account of the high politics (ecclesiastical and lay) of the Colleges (Ireland) Act, 1845 (8 & 9 Vict., c. 66) is Donal A. Kerr, *Peel, Priests and Politics: Sir Robert Peel's Administration and the Roman Catholic Church in Ireland 1841–1846* (Oxford, 1982). For a close reading of one aspect of the episode, see Denis Gwynn, *O'Connell, Davis and the Colleges Bill* (Cork, 1948).
2 Among a recent rich harvest of publications on 1798 and its aftermath, see, in particular: Cathal Póirtéir (ed.), *The Great Irish Rebellion of 1798* (Cork and Dublin, 1998); David Dickson, Daire Keogh, and Kevin Whelan (eds), *The United Irishmen* (Dublin, 1993); Liam Swords (ed.), *Protestant, Catholic and Dissenter: The Clergy and 1798* (Dublin, 1997); Kevin Whelan, *The Tree of Liberty* (Cork, 1996); Daire Keogh, '*The French Disease*': *The Catholic Church and Irish Radicalism 1790–1800* (Dublin, 1993).
3 Excerpts from Fitzgibbon's speech are accessible in James Carty (ed.), *Ireland from Grattan's Parliament to the Great Famine: A Documentary Record* (Dublin, 1949), pp. 53–9. See, also, G.C. Bolton, *The Passing of the Irish Act of Union* (Oxford, 1966).

But others, not directly party to the fateful debate in parliament, also held views and were beset by fears during the years 1798–1800. The Catholic bishops, in general, welcomed the proposed Union. They too were terrified by the excesses of the 1790s, and particularly by the menace to all authority, including their own, presented by the spread of the 'French disease'. Moreover, the momentum of progress for Catholics – in terms of the dismantling of the penal code and the incremental granting of civil and political (and, indeed, economic) rights to Irish Catholics during the final third of the eighteenth century, had often seemed to owe more to the initiatives and insistence of the crown ministers in London than to the instincts or intentions of the leaders of the Protestant parliament in College Green. There was an understanding that the granting of Catholic Emancipation (that is, the removal of the impediments to Catholics becoming Members of Parliament) would accompany or immediately follow the passing of the Union.[4] This expectation, which encouraged the Catholic bishops to support the Union, drove many ultra-Protestants (including leading Orange interests) into opposition to the Union and into firm support for the maintenance of the 'old Protestant parliament' in Dublin.

Whatever the hopes or fears entertained in advance of the Union, by 1801 the deed was done. Henceforth, the legislative authority for Ireland would be the crown and parliament at Westminster. Full fiscal union, critical to complete economic integration, would follow within twenty years of 1801. Yet, the exceptional circumstances of Ireland (and not merely the fact that it was, geographically, a separate island) led to exceptional structures of governance being established.[5] Thus, a viceroy or lord lieutenant would be in residence as the monarch's representative in Dublin (the viceroy was usually a senior political grandee, of independent wealth, the better to be able to maintain that aspect of the office which most gratified the Dublin, and the Irish, loyalists – namely, the social role). In addition, the Irish administration featured an Irish chief secretary (usually a younger 'emerging' politician, with a reputation to make, or, as happened from time to time, one to lose), with a civil service based in Dublin Castle, presided over by the permanent head, the under-secretary for Ireland. The Irish law officers constituted the other vital group in the Irish administration, though a wider circle of 'worthies' (including prelates, judges, and others) were occasionally consulted, as might be deemed necessary or appropriate.

But the special circumstances of the latest addition to the United Kingdom of 1801 demanded more than an exceptional, quasi-colonial administrative structure. They also needed to be properly 'understood', if they were to be effectively managed and administered under the new constitutional dispensation. Accordingly, the first four decades of the Union period saw the establishment of a large number (more than a hundred, by some estimates) of different official enquiries (Select Committees of Parliament or Royal Commissions) into a broad range of Ireland's perceived social and political problems and challenges: including, tithes, poverty,

---

4 See Thomas Bartlett, *The Fall and Rise of the Irish Nation: The Catholic Question 1690–1830* (Dublin, 1992).
5 On the Irish administration, see R.B. McDowell, *The Irish Administration, 1801–1914* (London, 1964).

education, waste lands, railways, law and order, and land occupancy. These enquiries may have been intended as a kind of crash course on 'Irish problems' for the new rulers of Ireland at Westminster, but the investigative binge was also intended to have broader educative benefits for wider circles of the influential and powerful among the thinking classes at the imperial centre.[6]

These 'Irish problems' were, of course, real and urgent in the post-Union decades. The heavy population growth (even if decelerating from the late 1820s) of the pre-famine decades was generated heavily at the base of the social pyramid. Poverty became more widespread and more deep-rooted. The second quarter of the nineteenth century began to see the accelerating de-industrialisation of the economy throughout most of Ireland, with the exception of the north-east. Pressure for access to land became more acute, and the resulting social tensions were sharpened by increasing political mobilisation and excitement and by waves of religious fervour which, in various ways, affected all denominations.[7]

It needs emphasising that the constant objective of government investigations and, over time, of government interventions (legislative, administrative, and military) in Ireland was to render Ireland safe, secure, and 'loyal' within the Union. Tracing and treating the sources of Irish disaffection was, therefore, no abstract matter; it was a pressing political challenge. Of course, there were those who were convinced that the ultimate source of Irish disaffection lay in features ('defects', as they were more commonly described) of Irish 'character', and the adherence of the majority to the superstitions and authority of popery was identified as symptom and source of these defects of national character. But even among those who shared these sentiments (and there were many 'environmentalists' who did not) there was no shortage of enthusiasm for taking steps to deal with Irish backwardness or retardation, whatever its source.[8]

Under the Union, successive governments had recourse to a mixture of policies – or programmes – for dealing with Ireland. Gladstone, it may have been, who explicitly declared in 1867 that his mission was 'to pacify Ireland', but he was by no means the first PM with such an intention. His mentor, Sir Robert Peel, had pursued the same goal in the 1840s and, as we shall see, with some vigour. Likewise, the Conservatives in the later nineteenth century may have devised schemes of 'constructive Unionism' in order to 'kill Home Rule with kindness', but the strategy of taking the sting out of Irish nationalist political demands through a policy of judicious concessions to Ireland (though extended with a firm hand) was already an established strategy of governments in the first half of the century, again, not least during Peel's historic ministry of 1841–6.[9]

---

6 For a lively and unjustly neglected discussion of the political and ideological climate of the pre-famine decades, see R.B. McDowell, *Public Opinion and Government Policy in Ireland, 1801–1846* (London, 1952).
7 For an overview of pre-famine Ireland see Gearóid Ó Tuathaigh, *Ireland before the Famine 1798–1848* (Dublin, 1972); for a recent analysis of economic conditions, see Cormac Ó Gráda, *Ireland before and after the Famine: Explorations in Economic History 1800–1925* (Manchester, 1988).
8 A challenging contribution to the history of ideas in this area is Thomas A. Boylan and Timothy P. Foley, *Political Economy and Colonial Ireland* (London and New York, 1992).
9 While Kerr, *Peel, Priests and Politics* is excellent on Peel's Irish policy, see, for later initiatives,

The content and the timing of concessions – of 'granting justice to Ireland' – were to prove crucial to the political outcome of such concessions. In particular, the failure to grant full Catholic Emancipation at the time of the Union (in effect, completing the process of removing legal discriminations against Catholics and Dissenters) was to prove especially significant. The Catholic bishops in Ireland, overwhelmingly 'legitimist' in outlook and generally anxious to cooperate with and support government efforts at governing Ireland fairly (provided, of course, that Catholic rights of full citizenship were vindicated) were disappointed and felt betrayed in the years following 1801.[10] More significantly, for the bishops, the government and future political developments in Ireland, there emerged in the 1820s a new political force, a mass movement of popular support for Catholic Emancipation, mobilised and led by Daniel O'Connell with a strong cohort of middle-class Catholic lawyers, merchants, and farmers, and increasingly with the vital support of many of the priests (liberal Protestants constituted an important but minority element of the movement).[11]

Through his opposition to the Act of Union at the time of its enactment, O'Connell had already indicated that, however deep his respect for episcopal dignity and authority in the matter of Church teaching, he was determined to work out his own political positions for himself. Already, before the effective relaunch of the Catholic campaign in the 1820s, O'Connell had formed a strong antipathy to Peel during the latter's tenure of the Irish chief secretaryship (1812–18). Peel was resolutely opposed to Catholic Emancipation at this time, and, while anxious to improve the effectiveness of the Irish administration, he was firmly in support (and promoted the interests) of the most unyielding of the Protestant ascendancy talent in Dublin.

The antipathy between O'Connell and Peel was mutual, and enduring.[12] It was a striking irony, therefore, when O'Connell's popular movement for Catholic Emancipation climaxed with his own election for Clare in 1828, that it was Home Secretary Peel (in Wellington's reputedly hard-line Protestant cabinet) who had to advise the king (and cause outrage among his own supporters) that Catholic Emancipation would have to be conceded if Ireland was not to cross the line from popular excitement to disorder and rebellion. The confrontation and brinkmanship of 1828–9 greatly hardened the hostility between Peel and O'Connell.

Andrew Gailey, *Ireland and the Death of Kindness: The Experience of Constructive Unionism 1890–1905* (Cork, 1987), and, from the enormous body of Gladstone studies, Roy Jenkins's recent, *Gladstone* (London, 1995), especially chapter 17.

10 Murray awaits a full-length biography, but see works by Kerr, Whelan, and Bartlett, cited in notes 1, 2, and 4 above. For Crolly, see Ambrose Macauley, *William Crolly, Archbishop of Armagh, 1835–49* (Dublin, 1994). For an overview see, Patrick J. Corish, *The Irish Catholic Experience: A Historical Survey* (Dublin, 1985). Also, Oliver MacDonagh, 'The Politicization of the Irish Catholic Bishops, 1800–1850', *Historical Journal*, 18 (1975), pp. 37–53.

11 Fergus O'Ferrall, *Catholic Emancipation: Daniel O'Connell and the Birth of Irish Democracy 1820–1830* (Dublin, 1985), and Oliver MacDonagh, *O'Connell: The Life of Daniel O'Connell 1775–1847* (London, 1991).

12 On Peel's career, see Norman Gash, *Mr Secretary Peel* (London, 1961), and *Sir Robert Peel: The Life of Sir Robert Peel after 1830* (London, 1972).

During the Whig decade of government – the 1830s – O'Connell, now in parliament with a modest but politically useful following or 'tail' of MPs, first tried his hand at putting the Repeal of the Union on the political agenda. However, even in the post–1832 reformed parliament (and O'Connell had played an energetic part in the Whig-led campaign for the great reform act of 1832) there was no support whatever from British MPs for Repeal. O'Connell, showing what was to be a characteristic brand of pragmatism, promptly put Repeal into abeyance and decided to concentrate on getting justice for Ireland by instalments – in effect through pressing the government for concessions in return for his continued parliamentary support. He supported the Whigs, initially at arm's length, but under a quasi-formal compact arrangement from 1835, after the sympathetic Melbourne had replaced the more politically fastidious Grey as prime minister.

It may be said that O'Connell achieved a modest return on his political support of the Whigs in office, arguably more in the form of administrative changes (in personnel, practice, and attitude) than in strictly legislative terms (though the 'resolution'of the vexatious tithe question and a major municipal reform act were among the legislative boasts of the Melbourne ministry).[13] These administrative initiatives were important. Achieving a Catholic 'presence' in the administration of the law, and some degree of fairness in policing and the magistracy, was not only psychologically important for the mass of the population. It was also, in a sense, creating a potential constituency of 'Catholic unionism', with career lawyers and others increasingly prepared to 'give the system a chance'. O'Connell, it must be said, sought nothing for himself (though government office was offered); but other Catholic lawyers and their connections began to feel optimistic that a career in government service (even in Ireland) was now genuinely open to loyal Catholics with talent.[14]

Among the Whig measures of the 1830s, one which was particularly important was the historic initiative in the field of elementary education – the establishment in 1831 of the national or state system of elementary education. Earlier attempts at state support or endowment, direct or indirect, of elementary education in Ireland had foundered on the rocks of competing confessional demands and accusations of discrimination and of proselytism. The new system launched in 1831 was ambitious, national in scope (at least in a geographical sense), and declaredly non-denominational. Predictably, however, the different denominations in Ireland sought from the outset, by various stratagems, to make it as denominational as possible. In practical terms, the religious leaders succeeded very well, even if some of them remained unreconciled to the formal non-denominational character of the new state system.[15]

---

13 The best account of O'Connell's dealings with the Whig governments and of his Westminster performance in general remains A.D. Macintyre, *The Liberator: Daniel O'Connell and the Irish Party, 1830–1847* (London, 1965).
14 For the administrative and patronage gains, see M.A.G. Ó Tuathaigh, *Thomas Drummond and the Government of Ireland, 1835–41* (Dublin, 1977).
15 D.H. Akenson, *The Irish Education Experiment: The National System of Education in the Nineteenth Century* (London, 1970).

Specifically within the Catholic community, opinions differed on how to respond to the new state system. Among the bishops the view which eventually became the majority view favoured co-operation (albeit cautiously and all the while seeking further concessions and reassurances regarding the religious formation of Catholic children and the milieu of the schools in which they were to be educated). The archbishops of Armagh and Dublin (Crolly and Murray, respectively) were prepared to give the system a chance. Archbishop Murray of Dublin, in particular, was now emerging as the key figure in the post-Union Catholic hierarchy prepared to engage constructively with the government of the day on issues – such as education – where vital Catholic interests were involved.[16]

On the other hand, the archbishop of Tuam, John MacHale, was implacably opposed to the new system, and his refusal to participate in it was symptomatic of a more general political disposition to keep his distance from, if not indeed to actively oppose, a succession of governments throughout much of the nineteenth century. Ironically, in the light of what was to transpire later in the century and which would earn MacHale a Gallican reputation, in these pre-famine years he sought regularly to have Rome issue directives or instructions to the Irish bishops, generally to steel their resolve to defend Catholic interests against the compromising embrace of government initiatives, notably in education.[17] Above all, however, these debates and divisions of the 1830s on the elementary education issue are critical in that, to a significant degree, they anticipate both the terms and the shape of the episcopal divisions on the issue of the Queen's Colleges in the 1840s.

The Irish reform programme of the Whigs had run out of steam some time before the Melbourne government finally surrendered office to Peel, after the latter's triumph in the 1841 general election. O'Connell had anticipated the return to office of his old adversary, and had relaunched his movement to campaign for the Repeal of the Union and the re-establishment of 'the old parliament' in College Green.[18] He faced a formidable task. Some of his fellow professional Catholic lawyers (and others) who had been prominent in the Emancipation campaign of the 1820s, were no longer available for the Repeal campaign: their career prospects having taken a decided turn for the better during the 1830s, and their ambitions for the future in an increasingly bureaucratic state now encouraging greater circumspection in their political activity. Moreover, Rome and several of the Irish bishops had indicated clearly that priests should not become publicly and directly involved in political activity. Most crucial of all, perhaps, was the fact that, whereas there had been significant support for Catholic Emancipation from within the ranks of British parliamentarians (especially on the Whig-Liberal side), there

---

16 See Corish, *The Irish Catholic Experience* and, also, E. Larkin, 'The Quarrel among the Catholic Hierarchy over the National System of Education in Ireland, 1838–41', in R. Browne, J. Roscelli, and R. Loftus (eds), *The Celtic Cross: Studies in Irish Culture and Literature* (New York, 1964), pp. 121–46.
17 For material on MacHale's early career see Pádraig Ó Tuairisg's unpublished MA dissertation, 'Ard-dheoise Thuama agus Cartlann Choláiste na nGael sa Róimh sa Naoú hAois Déag', NUI, Galway, 1979.
18 See MacDonagh, 'Politicization', and Kevin B. Nowlan, *The Politics of Repeal: A Study in the Relations between Great Britain and Ireland, 1841–50* (London, 1965).

was no such support for the cause of Repeal. Apart from O'Connell and his parliamentary 'tail', Repeal was an orphan at Westminster.

Despite these unpromising omens, and his own advancing years, the old campaigner was soon into his stride, building an impressive public campaign through his formidable repertoire of techniques of political agitation, some well-tried, others quite novel. A campaign fund and headquarters, electoral pressure on candidates, resolutions adopted by public bodies, a punishing schedule of public speeches – these were familiar weapons in his political armoury: the latter greatly facilitated by O'Connell's election in 1841 as lord mayor of Dublin by the newly-reformed corporation. Nor was this platform his only stroke of good fortune. Despite official discouragement, many priests gave active support. Repeal 'reading rooms' were opened and Repeal meetings were regularly linked with the temperance movement of Fr Mathew, then gaining momentum. This particular association lent a sober, responsible and resolute edge to many public demonstrations of support for Repeal.[19] The most dramatic public demonstrations were the mass meetings called by O'Connell at historic sites in Ireland, the intention being to rouse the historic memory and thereby strengthen the sentiment for 'the liberty' of Ireland.

Most crucial of all, perhaps, was the success of the Repeal campaign in attracting the support of a cadre of young, gifted intellectuals, Protestant and Catholic, mainly based in Trinity College, who not only gave an injection of new blood, as it were, to the movement, but who also brought a new dimension of argument and propaganda to the cause. In 1842 these young intellectuals (later known as the Young Irelanders) founded a newspaper, the *Nation*, which immediately brought a new and powerful charge to the tone and content of the nationalist propaganda on behalf of Repeal. The *Nation* writers were strongly committed to the tenets of cultural nationalism: poetry, historical essays, folklore, ancient myths and legends, biographies of patriots – these were the materials through which national pride and nationalist sentiment were constructed and strengthened. Of course, the newspaper also reported, at length, the doings, sayings, and fortunes of the Repeal agitation and its leaders. But the most challenging aspect of its agenda was the evocation of a powerful national sentiment. Its intentions were explicitly educative and propagandist: to tell the story of Ireland's past, especially the glorious nature of that past, so as to stir (and to shape and manipulate) popular memory in the interests of nationalist sentiment and pride.[20]

The Repeal movement had gained considerable momentum in Ireland by 1843. In particular, the mass rallies at historic sites were clearly raising the temperature, to say nothing of O'Connell's public declarations that 1843 was to be the 'Repeal

---

19 H.F. Kearney, 'Fr Mathew: Apostle of Modernisation', in A. Cosgrove and D. McCartney (eds), *Studies in Irish History Presented to R. Dudley Edwards* (Dublin, 1979), pp. 164–75. Also, E. Malcolm, 'Temperance and Irish Nationalism', in F.S.L. Lyons and R.A.J. Hawkins (eds), *Ireland under the Union: Varieties of Tension* (Oxford, 1980), pp. 69–114.
20 See Richard Davis, *The Young Ireland Movement* (Dublin, 1987). For a committed view of one of the founders, see C. Gavan Duffy, *Young Ireland. A Fragment of Irish History 1840–50* (London, 1880). Also, John Molony, *A Soul Came into Ireland: Thomas Davis, 1814–1845* (Dublin, 1995).

year'. Peel was determined to face down this challenge, and was confident in so doing, given the bipartisan – indeed virtually unanimous – opposition to Repeal among British parliamentarians at Westminster. (Moreover, the danger of combined Irish Repeal and Chartist pressure was still a legitimate cause for government anxiety.)[21] The Irish policy constructed by Peel to meet the Repeal challenge involved a mixture of carrot and stick. On the one hand, he proposed resolute measures for the suppression of the more threatening and aggressive public aspects of the Repeal campaign. This resulted in the banning of the mass meeting called for Clontarf on 8 October 1843 (which O'Connell obeyed); the arrest, prosecution, and temporary imprisonment of O'Connell and others during 1844; and other emergency measures to curtail public agitation.

These repressive measures proved effective, on their own terms. But the second thrust of Peel's Irish policy was, in its way, equally effective and significant. It had as its objective the detaching of vital constituencies of support from the Repeal cause through a programme of targeted 'concessions'. The establishment of the Devon Commission to enquire into landlord-tenant relations in Ireland demonstrated Peel's recognition of a major issue and source of discontent in Ireland, even if the device of a Commission was cautious and the eventual outcome (the action taken on the report and recommendations of the Commission) disappointing. But Peel's particular objective was to bring forward measures which would earn the support and gratitude of the Irish Catholic bishops and of a larger constituency of 'reasonable' and responsible leaders of Catholic opinion, lay and clerical. The three principal measures of this programme – intended as a Catholic conciliation programme to weaken, divide, and diminish the force of Repeal sentiment – were the Charitable Donations and Bequests Act (Ireland) of 1844, the Maynooth College Act, and the Colleges (Ireland) Act, both of 1845. All three provoked controversy, though the configuration of interests – the outraged and the grateful – varied somewhat from issue to issue.[22]

The intention of the Charitable Bequests Act was to improve and ease the prospects of Catholic charitable causes (including the Church itself and religious orders) receiving the benefit of bequests, an issue encrusted with historical anomalies, prejudices, and prohibitions, all of them unfavourable to Catholic Church interests. The precise terms of the act – and different interpretations and expectations among the Irish bishops as to its likely effects – caused debate and a measure of disagreement among the bishops. Again, as with the system of elementary education and the Board established to supervise it, the decision to accept the act (having availed of all useful channels of persuasion and advice to improve it) and to participate actively in its implementation (through membership of the proposed Board established to administer it) led to robust disagreement among the bishops, with Murray and MacHale inevitably on opposite sides.

---

21 Dorothy Thompson, 'Ireland and the Irish in English Radicalism before 1850', in James Epstein and Dorothy Thompson (eds), *The Chartist Experience* (London, 1982), provides a good starting point for a discussion of this connection.
22 Kerr, *Peel, Priests and Politics* is the definitive account. See, on Maynooth, P.J. Corish, *Maynooth College, 1795–1995* (Dublin, 1995).

On the Charitable Bequests Act, the government – or at least some of the ministers – may have felt a little put out that what was intended, in the overall context of placating moderate Catholics, as a significant concession, was received with less than total gratitude. With the Maynooth grant of 1845, however, there was no such difficulty. Not even the most suspicious and independent of the Irish bishops could seriously look this particular gift horse in the mouth. The provision of a capital grant of £30,000 and the raising of the annual grant from £8,928 to £26,360 (and putting the grant on a permanent footing) was an immense relief and boon to the hierarchy, and indeed to the staff and students of the seriously-underfunded seminary at Maynooth. The aggrieved parties on this occasion were the more ultra-Protestants in Ireland and among the ranks of the Tories, in Peel's own party in parliament and throughout Britain. The government, and Peel in particular, made some enemies because of the Maynooth grant.[23]

The third measure in Peel's package of concessions was the Colleges (Ireland) Act, introduced in the House of Commons on 9 May 1845 and passed into law finally on 31 July 1845. There had been occasional demands for some time for a satisfactory provision of opportunities for university education for middle-class Catholics and, in the case of public opinion in Belfast, for Dissenters.[24] Though entitled to enter and take degrees at Trinity College Dublin, Catholics were still excluded from scholarships and other privileges of that College. Moreover, their minority position within the College involved, in the opinion of the Catholic bishops, a clear danger that Catholics at Trinity would be drawn, by the gravitational pull of the College community and its ethos, into conformity (or conversion) to Protestantism.[25]

Various options had already been canvassed for meeting the needs and the claims of Irish Catholics for a satisfactory system of university education. Changing the structure and complexion of the University of Dublin, through, for example, the establishment within that university of a second college, in addition to Trinity College, or through other means, was one possibility. But, by the 1840s, this was not considered a political runner.[26] Peel and his ministers rightly judged it politically too divisive and damaging to contemplate 'interfering' with Trinity. The state endowment of an explicitly and formally Catholic university was, likewise, politically beyond what Peel was prepared to undertake at this time, especially with Protestant evangelical opinion already outraged by the Maynooth grant.

There was, however, a further option which had already been canvassed and for which there was already some evidence of support in Ireland. This was the suggestion that a number of provincial academies or colleges be established in

---

23 See, for example, E.R. Norman, *Anti-Catholicism in Victorian England* (Cambridge, 1968).
24 See F. McGrath, 'The University Question', in P.J. Corish (ed.), *A History of Irish Catholicism*, v, fascicule 6 (Dublin, 1971).
25 Kerr, *Peel, Priests and Politics*, p. 290, gives figures of 30 Catholics compared to 350 Protestants entering Trinity each year at this time.
26 On Trinity, see C. Maxwell, *A History of Trinity College, Dublin 1591–1892* (Dublin, 1946), and R.B. McDowell and D.A. Webb, *Trinity College, Dublin 1592–1952: An Academic History* (Cambridge, 1982).

Ireland, with state support. A number of independent initiatives had already been taken by interested parties in Belfast (among the Presbyterians) and in Cork.[27] The Cork initiative had involved the establishment of a committee and the start of a public campaign, and it had secured the support of Thomas Wyse, MP for Waterford City and perhaps the most dedicated and consistent advocate of educational causes (and facilities) in pre-famine Ireland, and also the support of William Smith-O'Brien, the Independent (from 1844 Repeal) MP for Limerick, a man who also had a strong interest in education and who gradually moved into close communication and collaboration with Wyse on the issue of 'academic' and university education in provincial Ireland.[28]

O'Brien, it should be said, found himself in something of a dilemma when potential locations for 'provincial' Colleges began to be actively considered. There were strong demands from interested parties in Limerick that the city be selected as the site of a provincial College in the mid-west, and O'Brien gave his firm support to this demand, while yet remaining in close contact with Wyse, for whom Cork was clearly the obvious location for such a College in the south. Indeed, when the government originally agreed the principles and scope of the Colleges bill in November 1844, only Belfast and Cork were firmly identified as locations for the new Colleges. As late as 9 May 1845, when Graham moved the first reading of the Colleges bill in the Commons, Cork was designated as a site of one of the three proposed colleges, together with Galway or Limerick and Belfast or Derry. The possibilities of Tuam being the site for the western College, and of Armagh as the Ulster site, were also briefly canvassed during later public and private discussion of the measure before it finally became law.[29]

However, when the government's proposals were announced on 9 May, it was not the possible locations for the proposed Colleges which provoked the storm of controversy, but the precise nature and character of the institutions being proposed. As proposed, the Colleges were to be strictly non-denominational, with no state funding for theological studies or for specifically religious education or instruction. Neither Peel nor the majority of his cabinet or his party could conceive of any idea of true education that excluded religion. But the issue of state funding of religious education of any kind had become extremely fraught and politically divisive by the second quarter of the nineteenth century, particularly though not exclusively in Ireland. Accordingly, while the government's bill made provision for the private endowment of a chair of theology and also for the use of lecture rooms for religious instruction by clergy of different denominations, the fundamental character of the Colleges was to be non-denominational or 'neutral'.

---

27 T.W. Moody and J.C. Beckett, *Queen's Belfast, 1845–1949: The History of a University*, 2 vols. (London, 1959). John A. Murphy, *The College: A History of Queen's/University College Cork, 1845–1995* (Cork, 1995).
28 For O'Brien, see Richard Davis, *Revolutionary Imperialist: William Smith O'Brien 1803–1864* (Dublin and Darlinghurst, 1998). Also, J.J. Auchmuty, *Sir Thomas Wyse, 1791–1862: The Life and Career of an Educator and Diplomat* (London, 1939).
29 Kerr, *Peel, Priests and Politics*, pp. 317–21.

The Colleges bill, as proposed, faced strong opposition from the outset. While it was the Protestant high churchman, Sir Robert Inglis, who famously denounced the proposed Colleges as 'a gigantic scheme of Godless education', O'Connell (and, more vehemently, his son John) led a chorus of opposition to the proposal within the Repeal movement, taking the more aggressively Catholic and anti-government stance adopted by Archbishop MacHale and, even more trenchantly than MacHale on this occasion, by Archbishop Slattery of Cashel.[30] Presbyterian leaders were also disappointed with the proposed scheme, as the claims of the Belfast group had been for state endowment of a Presbyterian College combining theology and more general studies.

The general response of the Catholic hierarchy to the Colleges proposal was not unanimous, though on this issue there was at all stages a clear majority opposed to the bill. The bishops, while generally unhappy with the original draft of the published bill, were divided on how to respond to it, and, in particular, on what might best be said and done to have the bill amended and rendered more satisfactory and acceptable to them. After a specially convened meeting during 21–23 May, attended by twenty-one prelates, the bishops issued a statement which, while it stopped short of outright condemnation of the bill, declared that 'we cannot give our approbation to the proposed system, as we deem it dangerous to the faith and morals of the Catholic pupils'. The statement went on to set out the terms (and amendments) which the bishops would consider 'fair and reasonable' as the basis for their co-operation with the government on the issue: these, in Donal Kerr's words, included

> a fair proportion of the professors and other office-holders should be Catholic; they should be appointed by a board of trustees who would include bishops; Catholic chaplains should be appointed, paid by the state but dismissible by their bishops. On the central issue of lectures, the bishops declared that 'the Roman Catholic pupils could not attend the lectures on history, logic, metaphysics, moral philosophy, geology or anatomy, without exposing their faith and morals to imminent danger, unless a Roman Catholic professor will be appointed for each of these chairs'.[31]

The bishops may not have unequivocally condemned the Colleges scheme, but this list of changes and preconditions amounted, in effect, to a demand that the government's scheme be fundamentally reconstructed into a virtually denominational system. This was unacceptable to the government, and in the weeks that followed (as the bill moved through its various stages towards the statute book), the gap between government and hierarchy was not closed, much to the government's dismay and, at times, anger. A compromise was not found. The majority of the hierarchy remained unyielding in their opposition to the Colleges. During the decade following the establishment of the Colleges this opposition of the bishops

---

30 Ibid., and Gwynn, *O'Connell*, give a good flavour of the controversy.
31 Kerr, *Peel, Priests and Politics*, pp. 303–4.

to the Colleges was to harden and become more formal, until eventually they embarked on the rival project of a Catholic University in Dublin.

There were many reasons why a compromise was not found between the government and the Catholic prelates on the Colleges issue. The government's tactics (and channels) for consulting the bishops were poor, and the key ministers took umbrage rather promptly at what they perceived (not least in the light of their largesse towards Maynooth) as the rather ungratefully hostile stance being taken by the bishops. However, the factors influencing the bishops constitute the more complex aspect of this political stand-off. In the larger European context, the Catholic Church leaders were sensitive at the encroachments of secular-liberal ideas (and institutions, including the state itself) on such key domains as education. A bitter contest on this issue was already in progress in France.[32]

Moreover, the British state (of which Ireland was an integral part post-1801) was, essentially, a Protestant state. Among the Irish bishops, even several of those who might not have been counted among the ardently nationalist were anxious to keep some distance between themselves and the government of the day (or 'Dublin Castle'), and may have felt that Crolly and Murray, in particular, were becoming too closely (and predictably) aligned with government interventions. Specifically, on the Colleges issue, neither Murray nor Crolly played their cards particularly well, underestimating the strength of opposition among their fellow-bishops and giving to government intermediaries a misleadingly optimistic impression of the prospects for an accommodation.

Two other factors have a special significance in this context. Firstly, there were the exertions in Rome of the then Rector of the Irish College, Paul Cullen, soon to return to assume the leadership role of the hierarchy in Ireland. Cullen was a formidable ally of those Irish bishops opposed to the Colleges. Secondly, there was the 'O'Connell factor'. O'Connell was firmly allied with the anti-Colleges party of the hierarchy. He dominated (many would not consider 'controlled' too strong an alternative) a huge popular movement and his public utterances (praising 'patriotic' bishops and encrypting his criticism of others in language not difficult to decode) undoubtedly created a political climate in which opposition to the government's Colleges scheme seemed to guarantee applause for 'being on the side of the people'. By the 1840s not even prelates could be utterly indifferent to this political climate.

If the government felt offended and annoyed at the reception of the Colleges bill by the Catholic bishops, they had some grounds for consolation in the bitter division on the issue which erupted within the Repeal movement itself – right at the heart of the now somewhat unfortunately named Conciliation Hall. Despite the immediate and sharply hostile response to the bill, on the part of John O'Connell and his father, a robust endorsement of the principle of non-denominational 'academic' education came from Thomas Davis and the *Nation* group within the Repeal camp. This produced serious and bitter debate, despite the best efforts of Smith O'Brien (in close collaboration with Thomas Wyse) to insist that the bishops had

---

32 A. Dansette, *Religious History of Modern France*, 2 vols (Freiburg and Edinburgh, 1961); J. Moody, *French Education since Napoleon* (Syracuse, 1978).

not condemned outright the principle of the measure, and that all Repealers (and others) could honourably join in seeking to amend and to improve the bill in its detail. But, in truth, on this issue there was an unbridgeable chasm between, on the one hand, the O'Connells and their followers – 'Old Ireland' as O'Connell defiantly proclaimed it – and, on the other, Davis and the 'Young Irelanders', who were clearly in favour of young Irishmen of all denominations being educated together. No amount of manoeuvring and tortuous hair-splitting by Smith O'Brien, on the distinction between the principle and details of the bill, could conceal or bridge that chasm.[33]

Davis and O'Connell clashed openly and publicly on the issue at the Repeal headquarters, with Davis breaking into tears during the exchange. And, while there was no formal split or walk-out, on this occasion, and while the old tribune moved immediately and generously to heal the rift, a major political junction had been reached. In particular, the Young Irelanders had openly challenged O'Connell, and the hostility between them and John O'Connell, the Liberator's son and political heir, was deep and very public. In view of the core objective of the government's package of concessions – the weakening of the Repeal support-base – this very public division in the Repeal ranks on the Colleges bill must have brought some consolation for the unexpectedly hostile reception given to the measure by the bishops.

In any case, the government was prepared to press ahead. A few concessions were made, but nothing that came near to meeting the objections and demands of the bill's opponents. O'Connell continued to denounce the measure, MacHale to thunder against 'infidel colleges for the propagation of infidel and revolutionary mania',[34] but the bill passed all stages in parliament comfortably and became law by the end of July 1845. The task of building the Colleges and appointing the first office-holders now began.[35]

Galway was selected as the site of the western College, with Belfast in the north and Cork in the south. Unlike Cork and Belfast, there had not been any particularly strong or forceful campaign launched in Galway during the previous twenty years for the establishment of such an institution. The local MPs, when it became clear that the Colleges would indeed be established, spoke up for Galway as the location of the western College. None of the city's two MPs nor the Galway county MPs were at that time supporters of the government party. The two Galway MPs were Martin Joseph Blake and Sir Valentine Blake, Bt, both nominal Repealers, while the county MPs were John James Bodkin and Thomas Barnewell Martin, both declared Liberals: all four had been returned at the 1841 general election without a contest.[36] Peel's

---

33 See Gwynn, *O'Connell*, and Davis, *Revolutionary Imperialist*.
34 Quoted by Colm Ó hEocha, 'The Queen's College at Galway – Some Memories', in Diarmuid Ó Cearbhaill (ed.), *Galway: Town and Gown 1484–1984* (Dublin, 1984), p. 169.
35 For a fascinating account of the establishment of the Galway College, see James Mitchell, 'Queen's College, Galway 1845–1858: From Site to Structure', *Journal of the Galway Archaeological and Historical Society*, 50 (1998), pp. 49–89.
36 Martin Joseph Blake of Ballyglunin Park, Athenry, was in favour of vote by ballot and of removing the Protestant bishops from the House of Lords. He was an unsuccessful candidate for Galway at the general election of 1832, but gained the seat on petition in 1833, and represented Galway until he retired in 1857. He died in 1861.

decision to establish one of the new Colleges in Galway was not in response to any special urgings from its MPs. Predictably, there was disappointment in Limerick, where a committee and a campaign had been active to secure one of the Colleges for the city. But, in all likelihood, when the notion of 'provincial' Colleges began to take root, then the western province – Connacht – was destined to secure a College, and Galway was the obvious candidate as the host centre for such a College.

The passing of the Colleges Act was welcomed in Galway. This was only to be expected. The town was in sore need of a boost – of morale, employment, and status. The 1840 Municipal Corporations Act, which reformed the corporations of the larger cities and towns of Ireland, did not reform Galway's Corporation; it abolished it, a brutal reduction of civic dignity and status. Yet, there were also encouraging signs of growth, especially in communications, harbour improvement, and links with the hinterland, in the Galway of the 1840s.[37] The building of the Queen's College between 1846 and 1849 was an important boost to the building trade and the general economy of the city and its hinterland, particularly in those harrowing years of the potato famine.

Yet, those who had expressed misgivings as to the numbers likely to enrol in the Galway College seemed, for many decades, to be fully justified in their concern. In the early decades the numbers remained well below one hundred, and would have been lower still but for the presence of a regular supply of northern Presbyterians. No doubt the general economic retardation of Connacht in the post-famine decades was a negative factor in the story of the Galway College's low enrolments in these early decades. More particularly, the dearth of secondary schools in the province contributed significantly to the slow supply of students for the College. The Catholic hierarchy's condemnation of the Queen's Colleges as a system, and particularly MacHale's vehement opposition in Connacht, undoubtedly inhibited participation by such middle-class Catholics in Connacht as might have been available to attend, under different circumstances. It must be remembered that only in the ecclesiastical province of Connacht were the bishops unanimous in 1845 in opposition to Peel's scheme.[38] The Queen's College in Galway would struggle to attract students for many years, though even in the lean years it

---

Sir Valentine Blake, Bt, of Menlo Castle, was born in 1780, the son of the 11th baronet. Married twice, he represented Galway in the pre-Reform parliament. He did not contest the seat again until a by-election in 1838, at which he was defeated. He was elected as a Liberal in 1841 and remained an MP until his death in January 1847.

John James Bodkin of 41 Piccadilly, London, and Kilcloony, Co. Galway, was the son of a former Mayor of Galway, John Bodkin. A reformer, he favoured the ballot. He sat for the town of Galway in 1831 and he was MP for Co. Galway from 1835 to his retirement in 1847. He died in 1882.

Thomas Barnewell Martin of Ballinahinch Castle, was the son of Richard ('Humanity Dick') Martin. He held Whig principles and was MP for county Galway from 1832 until his death in 1847. These profiles are drawn from M. Stenton (ed.), *Who's Who of British Members of Parliament*, vol. i, 1832–85 (Hassocks, Sussex, 1976).

37 For a profile of pre-famine Galway, see Gearóid Ó Tuathaigh, '" … the air of a place of importance": Aspects of Nineteenth-Century Galway', in Ó Cearbhaill (ed.), *Galway*, pp. 129–47.
38 Kerr, *Peel, Priests and Politics*, pp. 328–31.

continued to attract some interesting and lively staff.[39] But, whatever the misgivings expressed or the problems encountered, the College was established and built and received its first cohort of students in 1849.

The political controversy attending the establishment of the Queen's Colleges was soon to be overtaken, in the case of Peel's government, by the seismic impact of the Corn Laws issue, forced to the top of the political agenda in the face of the potato failure in Ireland in 1845 (partial failure) and 1846 (virtually total failure). Likewise, the famine calamity and the final deteriorating days of O'Connell as political ringmaster of nationalist Ireland, witnessed rapid change within the Repeal movement – with splits, new organisations, and a new militancy. By 1847 – 'black '47' – Repeal was as dead as its champion, O'Connell, who died in Genoa on 15 May 1847. The desperate lurches towards the revolutionary gesture of 1848 were well in train. Peel's Irish programme of 1843–6 was soon consigned to history, as he himself lost office and as new men and a new agenda emerged painfully from the shadow of famine in the aftermath of O'Connell's death.

But the Queen's Colleges – established to give the benefits of non-denominational university education outside of Dublin to young middle-class men of promise – may be seen as an early phase of the strategy of 'constructive unionism', which sought to persuade the Irish (notably 'moderate' Irish nationalists) that good government did not necessarily have to be self-government, and, that an indigenous, university-educated Irish professional bourgeoisie could be created under the auspices of and reconciled to the Union. The experiment was undertaken as part of a more general belief in the power of education to shape responsible and loyal citizens of the empire, and to demonstrate to the Irish that there could be genuine justice and equality of opportunity for loyal citizens of all denominations under the Union. Only the future would tell whether these larger assumptions were well-founded, and whether the particular political hopes invested in the Queen's Colleges would be justified.

---

39 Among a number of contributions by Thomas A. Boylan and Timothy P. Foley, see, in particular, chapter 3 of Boylan and Foley, *Political Economy and Colonial Ireland*, pp. 44–66; 'Cairnes, Hearn and Bastable: The Contribution of Queen's College, Galway, to Economic Thought', in Ó Cearbhaill (ed.), *Galway*, pp. 183–205; and Timothy P. Foley, ' "A Nest of Scholars": Biographical Material on Some Early Professors at Queens College Galway', *Journal of the Galway Archaeological and Historical Society*, 42 (1989–90), pp. 72–86.

2

Law

LIAM O'MALLEY

The Law Faculty, under one guise or another, has been in continuous existence for over one hundred and fifty years. It was one of the three original faculties of QCG, when the Queen's Colleges were founded in 1845 for the 'better advancement of learning' in Ireland.[1] Besides Law, there were faculties of Medicine and Arts,[2] the latter having Science and Literary divisions with separate Deans. When the Law Faculty inaugurated its first teaching programme on 30 October 1849, university education was very different from what it is today. Queen's College, Galway began its educational mission, as its first President put it, 'under circumstances of a very discouraging nature'.[3] The original campus building in which teaching took place was then, as now, regarded as very handsome, but there were many other difficulties. Sir Francis B. Head described the building in 1852 as 'one of the

---

1   The construction and endowment of the Queen's Colleges, which came to be situated at Belfast, Cork, and Galway, were authorised by an Act of the UK Parliament of 1845, which was given the short title, the 'Colleges (Ireland) Act', and received the royal assent on 31 July. The purpose of the statute (8 & 9 Vic. c. 66), as given by its long title was: 'An Act to enable her Majesty to endow new Colleges for the advancement of Learning in Ireland'. The policy and statute were the work of the then government of Prime Minister Sir Robert Peel. Letters patent were issued on 30 December 1845 (enrolled in Chancery, 3 January 1846) incorporating Queen's College Galway under the title of 'The President, Vice-President, and Professors of Queen's College, Galway'. On 11 December 1849, Statutes, Rules and Ordinances for the new Colleges were adopted by letters patent. The degree awarding body for the Colleges, the Queen's University in Ireland, was incorporated by letters patent of 13 September 1850 (enrolled on 4 October 1850). For an account of the building of Queen's College Galway, see James Mitchell, 'Queen's College, Galway 1845–1858: From Site to Structure', *Journal of the Galway Archaeological and Historical Society*, 50 (1998), pp. 49–89.
2   It was to be a College, as the letters patent quaintly puts it, 'for students in Arts, Law, and Physic, and other useful learning'. For the text of the Colleges (Ireland) Act and the letters patent, see *The Colleges Act, Letters Patent … of the Queen's Colleges*, printed by John F. Blake (Galway, 1859).
3   Report of Edward Berwick, President, Queen's College, Galway, for 1849–50, in *Reports of the Presidents of the Queen's Colleges in Ireland: Presented to both Houses of Parliament by Command of Her Majesty* (Dublin, 1850), p. 55. (Referred to hereafter as 'President's *Report*'). President Berwick went on to state: 'The town of Galway possesses a population of not more than 20,000 inhabitants, the greater proportion of whom are in a state of the most abject poverty: accordingly, the number of families likely to avail themselves of academic instruction for their children, is, at the present time, very limited. The disastrous occurrences of the last few years have pressed with peculiar severity the Province of Connaught, and the entire of the West of Ireland'. According to a prospectus dated 22 August 1849, matriculation examinations were to be held on Tuesday and Wednesday, 30 and 31 October, scholarship examinations, on 2, 3, and 5 November, and lectures were to begin on Wednesday 7 November.

chastest and handsomest public edifices I have ever seen', but was also struck by the unroofed huts and miserable cabins in the immediate neighbourhood.[4] Black's *Picturesque Tourist of Ireland* (1854) informed the traveller that 'Queen's College is a handsome gothic structure, built of grey mountain lime stone. It is quadrangular in form, the interior quadrangle being 280 feet by 200, and has an elegant cupola in the centre of the chief front facing the town. The architect of the college was Mr J.B. Keane,[5] and it was opened for the admission of students in October 1849'.[6] But appearances were deceptive. The College building, although universally admired, was not fully completed when the College opened;[7] the region was so impoverished that few could avail of the educational opportunity offered; and the whole enterprise was subject to the 'strange and almost unintelligible opposition' of the Roman Catholic hierarchy and clergy who were generally opposed to the whole concept of 'mixed education' – that is, of educating Roman Catholics and Protestants in the same institution.[8]

---

4 Sir Francis B. Head, *A Fortnight in Ireland* (London, 1852), pp. 217–8. He wrote: 'Queen's College just completed on the outside of the town is one of the chastest and handsomest public edifices I have ever seen. It is a pity, however, that the lowness of its position prevents it from contributing as much as it ought to the beauty of the town. In its vicinity is a large poor-house, built eight years ago; and about 100 yards from it, on an elevated plot composed of emerald green turf, stands a school house, resembling very much a modern villa; and yet, in their immediate neighbourhood are to be seen unroofed huts, miserable cabins, a confusion of tottering, crooked stone walls surrounding small enclosures, many of which are so full of rocks that they resemble a rising crop of young tombstones, several, like children's second teeth, coming out all crooked'.
5 John Benjamin Keane, who resided at Dublin, had an extensive practice which included churches, courthouses, and country houses. It appears that the Board of Works was quite dissatisfied with his supervision of the project, and he himself failed to profit by the contract as he became bankrupt shortly afterwards. See Mitchell, 'Queen's College, Galway', pp. 58, 71–2, 82. The contractor, William Brady, also had difficulty in fulfilling his obligations, and one of his guarantors, Francis Burke, a Dublin corn merchant, who was a member of the Burke family of Danesfield, Moycullen, found his general situation so stressful that he committed suicide.
6 *Black's Picturesque Tourist of Ireland* (Edinburgh, 1854), p. 225. Other travellers in later years have remarked on the College as it appeared to them, and the impression seems to have been uniformly favourable. Sir Arthur Grant visited Galway in February 1891. 'Galway possesses', he wrote, 'a most excellent Queen's College, one of the colleges called "godless" by the priests. Here a really good practical education is given, particularly good, I hear, in engineering and cognate subjects. Many of the young fellows now on the new railway lines in the west were educated here'. Sir Arthur Grant, *Eight Hundred Miles on an Outside Irish Car* (Aberdeen, 1891), p. 45.
7 The difficulties encountered in completing the building are described by Mitchell, 'Queen's College, Galway', *passim*. As to the work still unfinished when the College opened, see pp. 78 ff.
8 President's *Report* 1849–50, p. 56. The context of Berwick's remark was as follows: 'Among the difficulties with which the College has had to contend, the strange and almost unintelligible opposition of a portion of the Clergy of that persuasion for whose benefit the Queen's Colleges were mainly founded, must not be lost sight of. In the Province of Connaught it prevails to a very large extent'. The new Colleges went out of their way to support and protect the religious faith of their students, but this was not sufficient. Many Catholic clergy of the period came to regard denominational Catholic education as a fundamental pastoral requirement, and the issue soon devolved into a sectarian-nationalist controversy about the control of education. The issue was not confined to Connacht, and was fuelled by such unfortunate denunciatory tags on the Colleges as O'Connell's 'Godless academies', and Archbishop MacHale's 'Infidel Colleges'. That the issue was not a simple one is shown by MacHale's subsequent opposition to Newman's Catholic University which he refused to support in spite of pressure from Cardinal Cullen.

The social and economic circumstances of mid nineteenth-century Ireland were so different from the present, that it is difficult for us to imagine the environment in which the College first functioned. It was the time immediately following the Great Irish Famine, a period in which economic and social conditions in the west of Ireland, and in Galway, were particularly bad.[9] There were fewer than 2,000 people then living in Galway, 'the greater proportion of whom', as President Berwick put it, were living 'in a state of the most abject poverty'. There was 'an almost total want of schools in the Province',[10] with the result that there were few students who were educationally prepared for university studies. The traditional Irish local self-help schools with their classical curriculum had declined rapidly, and the state's takeover of education had not yet even begun to provide a substitute.[11] These conditions hampered the development of the faculties and the new College as a whole. An additional handicap was the negative attitude and opposition of influential Catholic clergy and politicians, which gave rise to what was called the 'university question'. Government policy at that time supported mixed or 'undenominational' education at university level, a policy which was strenuously opposed by members of the Irish Catholic hierarchy who favoured a denominational education for Catholics which would be consistent with their beliefs, and would act as a counterweight to the essentially Protestant Trinity College Dublin. The founding of the Queen's Colleges was condemned by the Catholic bishops

---

9   A contemporary pen-picture of Galway is given by Head, *A Fortnight in Ireland*, p. 217: 'The town is now a medley of streets and buildings of various dates, forming altogether a strange, incongruous, but very happy family of narrow crooked alleys, broad thoroughfares, docks, churches, dispensaries, chapels, banks, gaols, courthouses, nunneries, barracks, monasteries, storehouses, breweries, a union workhouse, distilleries, flour-mills, docks, bridges, a magnificent railway hotel just constructed, several ancient houses just falling, a number of hovels of the most wretched appearance, evidently destined to be replaced very shortly by mansions of wealth and luxury. There are several streets composed almost entirely of immense warehouses, from four to six stories high, each with a small pent-house covered crane affixed to its upper stratum. These vast receptacles are now nearly all empty; and, on enquiring the reason, I was briefly informed that Galway, which used to import and bond corn in large quantities, now exports it'. Although Part ii of Head's book is mainly an anti-clerical diatribe, the first part, which describes his journey in Ireland, is vivid and appears an accurate account by an inquisitive traveller. He describes (pp. 230–4) his visit to an emigrant ship, *The Albion of Arbroath*, moored in Galway Bay, and the cramped conditions below deck, 'completely thronged with country people, very poorly but clean and decently dressed; in fact, it was evident they were all in their best clothes'. The population of the Ireland dropped from 8,175,124 according to the census of 1841 to 6,551,970 in 1851.

10 President's *Report* 1849–50, p. 55. Berwick wrote: 'Nor must it be forgotten, that there is an almost total want of Schools in the Province, and that no extensive effort has hitherto been made to provide education for the middle and higher classes, to prepare them for Collegiate instruction, or to foster that desire for knowledge which so honorably distinguishes other parts of Ireland'.

11 The decline in these schools was referred to by Professor T. Corcoran SJ, editor, in 'Towards the National University', in *The National University Handbook, 1908–1932* (Dublin, 1932), pp. 13–18. A few schools and teachers survived well into the nineteenth century. Professor Joseph P. Pye, who held the chair of Anatomy and Physiology in the College at a later date, attended a travelling teacher: 'I owe much to Galway. A self-taught student, except for a little elementary teaching from one of the old type of Munster travelling teachers, scholarships and prizes enabled me to live at Galway without any expense to my people'. *Royal Commission on University Education in Ireland* (Dublin, 1902), Appendix to Third Report, Minutes of Evidence, paragraph 7999, p. 149.

and by the Holy See, a condemnation which has been judged to have 'effectively nullified the new colleges as a means of solving the university question'.[12] This rejection was made final and complete when the bishops founded the Catholic University of Ireland in 1854 with John Henry Newman as its first rector.[13] To convince the state to publicly fund or endow the Catholic University, it became important, from the perspective of the Catholic hierarchy, that the Colleges should fail, and be shown to have failed, in meeting the educational needs of Catholics. It was in the face of such obstacles that the newly-appointed professors of Queen's College Galway organised their first teaching programmes.

The Law Faculty was, however, to survive such serious and enduring difficulties, and although the number of students who attended law courses in the College remained low, at least until recent times, many of those who passed through its doors proved successful in later life. The Faculty could be said to have been privileged, to begin with, in the quality of its staff. The first professors, Hugh Law (1849–59) and Denis Caulfield Heron (1849–59), were eminent lawyers in their own right. Hugh Law, as Law Adviser and head of the Irish Liberals, made a major contribution to the Land Acts and was Lord Chancellor of Ireland when he died in 1883. He had also served for a time as law professor at the King's Inns. William Bennett Campion (professor, 1859–1907), who succeeded Hugh Law, had been leader of the Chancery bar and was a much-loved and devoted law teacher at Galway for forty-nine years. He would undoubtedly have moved to the bench had it not been for his total disinclination to involve himself in the politics of his day. Heron's successors to the chair of Jurisprudence and Political Economy included the eminent scholar John Elliot Cairnes (1859–70), who was perhaps the most distinguished economist of his time, and Charles Francis Bastable (1883–1903) who was likewise a highly respected lawyer-economist. The scholarly work of these law professors in the field of economics has been dealt with elsewhere in this volume with much greater ability by colleagues and I do not propose, therefore, to treat of that aspect of the subject in any great detail in this chapter.[14] Other professors at Galway over the years included: James M. Sweetman (1908–13) and Richard J. Sheehy (1913–23) who were successively professors of English Law; William Lupton (1870–76), Robert Cather Donnell (1876–83), John H. Wardell (1903–9), and James Anderson (1910–15) who were professors of Jurisprudence and Political Economy; Patrick Arkins (1924–37), and Patrick J. Gallagher (1937–66) who held the

---

12   Thomas J. Morrissey, *Towards a National University: William Delany S.J. (1835–1924)* (Dublin, 1983), p. 39. For other accounts of the educational issues of the period, see E.R. Norman, *The Catholic Church and Ireland in the Age of Rebellion, 1859–1873* (London, 1965); Fergal McGrath, *Newman's University: Idea and Reality* (Dublin, 1951).

13   Newman was formally invited to become rector of the proposed Catholic University of Ireland in November 1851, but was not formally installed until June 1854. The University began work on 3 November with some twenty students. See D. McCartney and T. O'Loughlin, *Cardinal Newman: The Catholic University* (Dublin, 1990), pp. 129–30.

14   See contribution of Professors Tom Boylan and Tadhg Foley to this volume; see also, by the same authors, *Political Economy and Colonial Ireland* (London, 1992) and 'Cairnes, Hearn and Bastable: The Contribution of Queen's College, Galway to Economic Thought', in Diarmuid Ó Cearbhaill (ed.), *Galway: Town and Gown 1484–1984* (Dublin, 1984), pp. 183–205.

professorship of Law and Jurisprudence. Many graduates will remember Professor J.M.G. Sweeney who followed Professor Gallagher, and whose unstinting efforts helped the Law Faculty to survive in more recent times.[15] The present phase of the Law School's story can be said to have begun with the appointment of Professor Kevin Boyle as the first full-time professor in 1978.[16] As it is much too early to write of the modern 'renaissance' of the Faculty, only a cursory reference is made to its more recent history.

Although most of the Faculty's law students pursued legal careers, a sizable number were to distinguish themselves in a wide variety of other professions. In the earlier period of the Faculty's history, for example, some twenty graduates became judges at various levels of court at home and abroad. Lord Atkinson was the first Irish barrister to go directly from his practice at the bar to the House of Lords as a lord of appeal in ordinary. Graduates appointed to the higher courts in Ireland included John Gordon (King's Bench), John Monroe (Land Court), Richard Edmund Meredith (Judge of the Land Commission Court and Master of the Rolls), Sir Thomas Lopdell O'Shaughnessy (last Recorder of Dublin and High Court judge), and Mr Justice Séamus Henchy (Judge of High and Supreme Courts). Others who became Irish judges included William H. Brown, Michael Drummond, and Andrew Todd. Some, such as William Mulholland, James Mulligan and James Alexander Rentoul, were appointed to judicial office in England. A significant proportion of QCG graduates of the earlier period found fame and fortune in the colonies. These judges included: John T. Donovan (Hooghly and Bakargang, India), Philip C. Fogarty (Burma), Aelian Armstrong King (Ceylon, now Sri Lanka), Walter Llewellyn Lewis (Trinidad), Michael McAuliffe (Punjab), Sir Robert McIlwaine (South Africa and Rhodesia), Bernard Gustavus Norton (British Guiana), James O'Kinealy (Bengal), and Sir Raymond West (Bombay). Other graduates were to find success in professions other than law. Among those who had distinguished careers in the Royal Irish Constabulary were Sir Andrew Reed (Inspector-General), Sir Henry Thynne, and William John Millar. Journalism, politics, and missionary work were to occupy the attentions of others: Joseph R. Fisher was editor of the Belfast *Northern Whig*; the Fenian, James Bryce Killen, combined journalism with revolutionary politics, and was co-founder of the Land League with Michael Davitt; Frank Hugh O'Donnell was a well-known Nationalist MP and author, and Thomas Buckley spent most of his career as a Protestant missionary in Africa. Some graduates were to become law professors themselves: John McKane at Queen's College Belfast, Patrick A. Arkins and Patrick Gallagher at University College Galway. Other distinguished lawyers included George A. Hume KC, Robert A. McCall (serjeant and attorney-general of the Duchy of Lancaster), Robert F. McSwinney KC, Peter O'Kinealy (Advocate-General of Bengal), John Muldoon KC (MP and Registrar to the Chief Justice), and Archibald Smylie (a barrister in

---

15 Professor Sweeney directed the affairs of the Law Faculty following Professor Gallagher's death in 1966 and was appointed Professor of Common Law in 1980. He retired in 1987.
16 Professor Boyle resigned in 1988. He had been on leave of absence for some time prior to his resignation when he was engaged in founding Article 19, the London-based organisation involved in the promotion of freedom of information and press freedom generally.

Australia). John Moran became chief inspector of national schools and Thomas M. Maguire had the unusual distinction of being an outstanding army coach, some of whose charges were later to become distinguished generals.

The First Galway Law Professors

The Colleges (Ireland) Act, 1845 vested the sole power of appointing the President and Vice-President of the Colleges in the crown. The crown was likewise given the right to appoint College professors, at least until the end of the year 1848, but that right was also to continue thereafter if Parliament made no provision to the contrary,[17] which it did not. This meant, in effect, that selection and appointment of senior College staff fell to the Irish executive, and it appears that considerable care was taken, in the early years at least, to recruit the best talent available.[18] The University's Vice-Chancellor, Lord Chancellor Maziere Brady, remarked that Lord Clarendon, who was then Lieutenant-General and General Governor of Ireland, and Chancellor of the Queen's University in Ireland,[19] 'took pains, from all parts of the United Kingdom, to find out men the most eminent in science, men the best qualified in literary attainments, and men of the highest professional station, to undertake the duty of acting as Professors in those Colleges'.[20] The statutes of the College provided for twenty professorships, two of which were in the Law Faculty, namely, the Professorships of 'English Law' and of 'Jurisprudence and Political Economy'.[21] The first holders of these chairs, who were appointed in 1849, appear to have been scholars of exceptional talent, industry, and dedication. Hugh Law was appointed the College's first Professor of English Law, and Denis Caulfield

---

17 Colleges Act, 8 & 9 Vic., c. 66, s. 10.
18 The method of recruitment appears to have varied from time to time. Although the power of appointment was the right of the executive, applications were widely sought and the President was generally given the right to nominate a short list of three applicants from which the successful candidate would be selected. On other occasions, as in the appointment of a professor of 'the Celtic languages' at QCG, appointment was made on the basis of a competitive examination. See account of Vice-Chancellor's address, October 1856, in *Report on the Condition and Progress of the Queen's University in Ireland from 1st September, 1856 to 1st September, 1857*, p. 4. (These Reports are hereafter referred to as '*QUI Report*' followed by the year, for example *QUI Report*, 1856–7, p. 4.)
19 The Queen's University in Ireland, commonly referred to then as the 'Queen's University', was founded in 1850 as the degree-awarding body for the Queen's Colleges. Its role is considered later in the chapter.
20 *QUI Report* 1852–3, p. 66. It is interesting to note how much talent was fostered by the Dublin intellectual revival of the period. Reforms in Trinity College, the stimulus of the Whately Chair of Political Economy, the foundation of the Barrington trust and of the Statistical and Social Inquiry Society, fostered a pool of talent from which Galway acquired such professors as G.J. Allman (Mathematics), Hugh Law and Denis C. Heron (Law), Thomas W. Moffett (Logic and Metaphysics), and William Edward Hearn (Greek).
21 Statutes of Queen's College, Galway (11 December 1849), chapter I entitled: 'Of the Body Politic and Corporate', section 2. The original letters patent of December 1845 set twelve as the upper limit for the number of professors. This was amended to a maximum of thirty by letters patent of 2 November 1849.

Heron (or 'Caulfield Heron', as he was known to his close acquaintances), was the first Professor of Jurisprudence and Political Economy.[22] Both were to have distinguished careers. Professor Law pursued an active and fruitful life as law professor, queen's counsel, Attorney-General, and member of parliament, before finally becoming Lord Chancellor of Ireland. Professor Heron, who was the author of books on jurisprudence and economics, was active in the Dublin Statistical Society (as member, contributor, and Vice-President), was a Serjeant-at-Law, and served as MP for Tipperary. Although his religion may have had nothing to do with his appointment, it is interesting to note that Heron was a Roman Catholic, with family links to Dublin and, possibly, Newry. Some Catholic representation on the overwhelmingly non-Catholic staff of the Colleges was viewed as desirable.[23] Professor Law was born of a Co. Down, Church of Ireland family which later settled in Donegal.

Professors Law and Heron were the only academic members of the College Law Faculty. The Dean of the Faculty was then elected annually, with the right to preside at Faculty meetings and to represent the Faculty on the College Council.[24] Professor Heron acted as Dean, but because of his commitments elsewhere it appears he was not able to attend College Council as often as he wished.[25] Although it was customary to appoint barristers as part-time law professors in Trinity College, Dublin, this practice was not suitable in the Queen's Colleges which were located outside of Dublin and at a considerable distance from the higher courts.

---

22 Heron seems to have been known by the first name 'Caulfield' which is spelt in this manner in the earlier publications and QCG reports. The spelling changed to 'Caulfeild' from about 1860 in both the reports and his published work. See, for example, President's *Report* for 1850–1, p. 59: 'It now only remains to refer to the Reports which ... Messrs. Hugh Law and Caulfield Heron, have given of the progress of their Students'; for 1858–9, p. 23; the letter of Thomas Moffett to William Edward Hearn (August 1887) reproduced in T.P. Foley's '"A Nest of Scholars": Biographical Material on Some Early Professors at Queen's College Galway', in *Journal of the Galway Archaeological and Historical Society*, 42 (1989–90), p. 77: 'Caufield Heron dropped dead while in the act of fishing here in Galway'.

23 The first Presidents at Cork and Galway were Catholics, and the practice of appointing a Catholic president was continued at Cork. In Galway, however, President J.W. Kirwan DD, who had been parish priest of Kilcummin, Oughterard, near Galway, died in 1849 before the College opened, and his successors (until the twentieth century) were Protestants. The influence of Dr Kirwan, had he lived, might have lessened Catholic hostility to the venture. Sir Robert Kane of Cork is thought to have had a major role in shaping the policy of the new Colleges. See Thomas Dillon, 'The Origin and Early History of the National University', pt i, *University Review*, no. v, 1 (1955) pp. 43–51 (especially pp. 45–6); and pt ii, no. vi, 1 (1955), pp. 12–28.

24 *College Statutes* (Dublin, 1849), chapter ii, paragraphs 5, 6.

25 This is clear from Professor Heron's testimony given to the Queen's Colleges Commission in 1857: '4252. [Mr Bonamy Price:] You have been pretty constantly on the Council? – [Heron:] I have been on the Council since the commencement. 4254. [Price:] Do you see any Objection, practically, to dividing the Faculties into two, and giving a certain number to the Faculty of Arts and Law? – [Heron:] If the want of a representative be felt by the other Professors, the Commissioners should regard that. I may mention another reason. The Professors of Law are non-resident, and are, therefore, unable to attend on the Council as frequently as the other Professors'. *Report of Her Majesty's Commissioners Appointed to Inquire into the Progress and Condition of the Queen's Colleges at Belfast, Cork, and Galway* (Dublin, 1858), Minutes of Evidence, p. 289. (This Report is hereafter referred to as the '*Queen's Colleges Commission Report*, 1858'.)

Nevertheless, it was settled at an early stage that the Law professorships were to be part-time appointments which permitted the holders to pursue other paid employment. This was probably a pragmatic response to inadequate funding, as law professors could combine academic work with practice at the bar, and competent applicants could be prevailed upon to take part-time professorial positions at a lower salary.[26] Thus, the designated salaries of £150 per annum for law professors were relatively low compared with £250 per annum for the professors of Greek and Latin, £500 for the Vice-President, and £800 for the President. A fee could in addition be charged to students taking lectures. The Law professors, in addition to the £150 by way of salary from the College, were entitled to two pounds from every matriculated and non-matriculated student who attended a course of lectures in the Faculty.[27]

The organisation of the College in those days was relatively simple and straightforward. There were three faculties, Law, Medicine, and Arts, the latter being divided into Science and Literary divisions. There were also Schools of Civil Engineering and Agriculture which drew on the staff of the three faculties. The modern division of academic subjects had not yet taken place. Students studying the physical sciences read these subjects as part of the Arts programme and were awarded Arts degrees (then designated AB or AM degrees as opposed to BA and MA). The Queen's University introduced a predominantly science curriculum, leading to science degrees (BSc and DSc) in 1870,[28] but it was not until the establishment of UCG and the National University of Ireland in the period 1909–10 that a separate Science Faculty was organised. The year 1870 also saw the first university examinations for women, which were held in Galway and Belfast in June. Diplomas in Engineering and Agriculture were available in the Faculty of Arts, and the Professors of Agriculture and Engineering were members of the science division of that Faculty.[29] The Bachelor in Engineering degree was introduced in 1868 'for the greater encouragement of the study of engineering', and to reward students with a 'more strictly academic designation'.[30] The

---

26 The low level of salaries became a major issue for all the Colleges as appears in the Minutes of Evidence gathered in the course of the Inquiry by the Queen's Colleges Commission (1857–8). It appears the salaries were intended to be much higher. Sir James Graham was reported as stating in Parliament that no professorial salary would be less than £300 a year (*Queen's Colleges Commission Report*, 1858, paragraph 946). It had been generally accepted (see, for example, Berwick's evidence, paragraphs 3397–3401) that when the number of professorships was raised from twelve to twenty, extra remuneration would be provided, but this was never done, thus diluting all salaries. Law provided a convenient opportunity to save money by recruiting practicing barristers as academics on relatively low salaries. There is no doubt that this had a major adverse effect on the development of legal study and research in the universities.
27 *College Statutes and Rules* (Galway, 1859), chapter xix, p. 30; Rules Regulating Fees in the Faculty of Law, p. 34.
28 *QUI Report* 1870–1, p. 5. To inaugurate the new science degrees, a DSc degree, *honoris causa*, was conferred on Professor William King, QCG, for his distinguished work in Geology.
29 The initial University ordinances (30 June 1850) governing courses of study were printed in Appendix iii of *QUI Report*, 1851–2, pp. 8–10. The organisation of Faculties and Professors was formulated in Chapter ii of the College Statutes.
30 *QUI Report* 1868–9, p. 5, Vice-Chancellor, Sir Maziere Brady.

engineering discipline was organised as a 'Department' or 'School' until the introduction of new faculties on the establishment of the NUI.[31] The original Arts Faculty had two Deans, elected from the Literary and Science divisions, to represent their respective interests on the College Council. College governance was a relatively simple affair: the President, Vice-President, and the four Deans constituted the College Council which was vested with 'the general government and administration of the College'.[32] While the Council was responsible for all College matters not entrusted to others by the statutes, its resolutions were not operative until signed by or on the authority of the President, a power of veto which could be potentially divisive.[33] The College was subject, in addition, to indirect outside regulation both by the government and the University Senate, and the President had to report annually to Parliament which funded the institution. Although the College had control over the setting and administration of examinations for matriculation, scholarships, and the sessional examinations which allowed progression to the later years of courses, it did not confer degrees. The degrees and diplomas of the three sister Colleges were awarded by the Queen's University in Ireland (more commonly referred to as the 'Queen's University') to students who had taken the prescribed courses of education in the Colleges and passed the University's examinations. The Queen's University, which was founded by royal charter of 3 September 1850, was situated in Dublin, and was controlled and governed by a Chancellor, and a Senate which included the Presidents of the three Colleges as *ex officio* members.[34]

Legal Education in the Mid-Nineteenth Century

The Law Schools of the Queen's Colleges were founded at a time when there was a great need for quality legal education. There is no doubt that by 1845, the standards of legal instruction in Ireland and England had declined to an alarming

---

31 Statute A, chapter 10, made for UCG by the Dublin Commissioners, 15 May 1909, provided that: 'The Professors and Lecturers within the College shall be constituted into the following Faculties: Arts – including Philosophy, Celtic Studies, Science, Law, Medicine, Engineering'. Students were distributed across these Faculties from 1909–10, at least in the President's *Reports*. (See *Report* for period 1909–10 to 1912–13, Appendix A, p. 12.) The Faculty of Commerce was added shortly after. Commerce had its roots in what was called a 'practical course for commercial and general pursuits' introduced in 1862–3, which led to a diploma called the 'Licentiate in Arts'. (See President's *Report*, 1863, Appendix, pp. 22–3.)
32 *College Statutes* (1849), chapter iii, paragraph 1.
33 Ibid., paragraph 11. A conflict between the President and Council in Queen's College Cork arose as early as 1852 and was submitted both to the Visitors and to the Crown (in the form of a Memorial). The issue was considered by the Queen's Colleges Commission, which favoured the retention of the 'veto' power of the President but recommended that, where the President refused to sign a Council resolution within fourteen days, that he be obliged to enter in the Council minute book the reasons for not doing so. (*Queen's Colleges Commission Report*, 1858, pp. 4–5, 10, 347–8.)
34 A copy of the Queen's University in Ireland Charter (1850) and Supplemental Charter (1852) are to be found in Appendix 1 (pp. 5–7) and Appendix xiii (pp. 27–9), respectively, of *QUI Report*, 1851–2. *Queen's College Galway Rules and Regulations for Matriculation and Scholarships* were first published in Dublin, 1849; see pp. 34 ff.

degree. Almost no legal education existed in Ireland in any meaningful sense. The situation in England was almost equally bad.[35] With minor exceptions, neither Oxford or Cambridge provided courses on the common law.[36] The London Inns of Court required term dinners rather than lectures, and its students were not required to take or pass examinations. Even the promising new law courses, established in the 1830s at the University of London, quickly fell into decline.[37] In Ireland, the King's Inns in Dublin provided no formal legal education for persons wishing to enter the barrister's profession, and the first tentative steps in that direction were not taken until 1851. The University of Dublin (Trinity College) had two part-time Law professors, but the legal education provided there was only nominally better than at Oxford and Cambridge. The part-time professorship in Civil Law was described by the Select Committee on Legal Education, 1846, as a 'perfect sinecure', and its holder gave no lectures. The second, the professorship in 'Feudal and English Law', was occasionally given some temporary vitality by an enthusiastic holder,[38] but was otherwise equally ineffective. There was no obligation on students to attend the law lectures when offered, and law degrees were conferred on graduates on the payment of fees, following the completion of mere formal exercises.

A major factor in this decline in legal education was undoubtedly the low standards required for admission to the practice of law. To qualify as a barrister in England, a candidate had neither to attend lectures nor pass examinations. The student sought admission to one of the four Inns of Court and remained on the books for five years, or for three years in the case of specified graduates. A system evolved whereby the student could pay a fee for the privilege of attending at the chambers of an attorney, pleader, or conveyancer, where he might learn something of the law, depending on the good will of his master. '[A]nything more entirely nugatory, and more of a mockery', as Lord Brougham put it, 'as a test of legal acquirements, cannot possibly be imagined'.[39]

---

35 For an account of the inadequate state of legal education at the time, see Colum Kenny, *Tristram Kennedy and the Revival of Irish Legal Training, 1835–1885* (Dublin, 1996), particularly chapters 6 and 7. 'Overall', he concludes, 'apart from certain modest exceptions in the case of both Oxford and Dublin, training in the common law had been utterly neglected by the universities and the inns of court', p. 148.

36 Although there were promising initiatives in introducing common law teaching to Oxford and Trinity College, they were not sustained. Charles Viner founded a chair in Common Law at Oxford in 1758 which was held with remarkable distinction by William Blackstone. Francis Stoughton Sullivan was appointed first Regius Professor of Feudal and English Law at Trinity College in 1761. See V.T.H. Delaney, 'The History of Legal Education in Ireland', in *Journal of Legal Education*, 12 (1960), pp. 396–406.

37 The episodic but short-lived successes in common law education depended on the enthusiasm of individuals such as Sullivan (TCD), Blackstone (Oxford), and Andrew Amos (London). In the absence of compulsory standards set by the legal profession and state support, such efforts were doomed to failure. The first law professorship at King's College was established in 1831 (Professor Park), but by the 1840s it was only University College, London that offered substantial legal courses. The parent body, the University of London, was an examining and degree-awarding body only.

38 One such was Mountifort Longfield in the 1830s. See Kenny, *Tristram Kennedy*, pp. 158–9.

39 Evidence to the Select Committee on Legal Education, questions 3771–4.

In Ireland, the situation was worse. There is no evidence that the King's Inns in Dublin had ever offered formal legal education of any kind prior to the mid-nineteenth century. Those who wished to practise as barristers in Ireland were required, by an ancient statute, to attend at one of the Inns of Court in London.[40] This compulsory residence requirement was introduced by the Statute of Jeofailles, passed at a meeting of the Irish Parliament in Limerick in 1542.[41] The intending Irish barrister was faced with the burden and expense of keeping a number of dining terms at a London Inn of Court, as well as taking chambers, but could expect very little benefit in return, the more so as Irish law differed in important respects from that in England. Many Irish students did not enter London chambers but preferred, if they had the right connections, to get the assistance of Dublin practitioners who provided advice and the opportunity to read over suitable briefs. Legal education for the other branch, at that time called the 'lower branch' of the legal profession (it then consisted of attorneys of the superior courts of common law, and solicitors of the high court of Chancery) was equally deficient.[42] In essence, preparation for the 'lower branch' of the profession, required 'students' to become articled clerks or apprentices in order to learn what they could while helping out in the office of their masters or by attending them in the offices of the courts. In Professor Hugh Law's opinion, not only was it an unsuccessful system, but it made legal learning generally unpalatable:

> To this preposterous and mischievous system – the only form in which legal education has for many generations appeared, 'if form it can be called, which form hath none', I believe we must attribute in a great measure if not altogether the strange disrelish for legal knowledge which unhappily has hitherto prevailed amongst the public.[43]

Although an examination requirement for articled clerks was introduced in 1843 in England, the first obligatory courses for Irish clerks were only introduced after the Incorporated Law Society of Ireland became independent of the King's Inns in 1866. Prior to that date, the only 'examination' was one of a judicial nature which verified that the candidate had been apprenticed for the proper period and had paid the correct fees. W.F. Littledale, a member of the Council of the Incorporated Law Society of Ireland, who later sought the support of the Queen's Colleges in educating apprentices, concluded that:

40 For a recent account of the education of Irish barristers at that time, see Kenny, *Tristram Kennedy*, pp. 149–54.
41 For an account of the adoption of the Statute of Jeofailles, see Colum Kenny, *King's Inns and the Kingdom of Ireland: The Irish 'Inn of Court' 1541–1800* (Dublin, 1992), pp. 40–8. The obligation to attend an English Inn was finally removed by the Barristers' Admission (Ireland) Act 1885 (48 & 49 Vict., c. 20).
42 An account of the development and education of the so called 'lower branch' comprising solicitors and attorneys can be found in: Kenny, *Tristram Kennedy*, pp. 154–60; W.N. Osborough, 'The Regulation of the Admission of Attorneys and Solicitors', in D. Hogan, W.N. Osborough (eds), *Brehons, Serjeants and Attorneys* (Dublin, 1990), pp. 101–51, especially pp. 132–40; Daire Hogan, *The Legal Profession in Ireland 1789–1922* (Dublin, 1986), pp. 91–143.
43 Public lecture given at QCG in May 1851 as reported in the *Galway Vindicator*, 24 and 28 May 1851.

> It is quite certain that the profession of the Law cannot much longer be left in its present state, where the payment of fees is the sole test of competency for admission to practise, and that speedy means must be adopted to afford to the public some degree of protection from the ignorance of incompetent practitioners.[44]

The apprenticeship system was likewise convincingly condemned by Professor Law in a public lecture given at QCG in May 1851. The system, which introduced students, as he put it, 'into the mystical technicalities of practice by seeing the routine of business in the chambers of a special pleader, or conveyancer, or equity draftsman', was a wasteful drudgery:

> But what copying of precedents, what writing of common forms, what perpetual round of mechanical drudgery was here! 'Hic labor ille domus et inextricabilis error!' For here instruction, if given at all, has been, and indeed must of necessity ever be subordinate and ancillary merely to the practice of the teacher himself. And, from my own observations I can safely say that at least nine tenths of the time and money so spent has been wholly wasted.[45]

Hugh Law's argument was based on the folly of having young people learn practice skills in a specialist jargon they did not understand because no one taught them the underlying principles of law. The pupil attempted, he said, 'most preposterously, to act as practitioner, under his master's direction certainly, but still to practice without having acquired any knowledge of the *principles*, of which practice is but the application. This, surely, is beginning at the wrong end'. He acknowledged that there was value in on-the-job training, but no real advantage could be so gained without first having mastered the principles of the law:

> High as is the privilege of being admitted into the chamber of an eminent lawyer, still if the student imagine he will gain any elementary knowledge of his profession there, he will find himself most lamentably mistaken. The benefits of admission into this kind of pupilage consists in this – that the student having once mastered the principles of law may thus acquire a dexterity and readiness in applying them, by having all the advantage of extensive practice without any of the responsibility. The value of this to the intended lawyer is indeed great; but he only who has qualified himself by

---

44 Document XXXIX, presented as evidence to the Queen's Colleges Commission, 1858, See *Report*, p. 347. In the course of this document, Littledale stated: 'The only qualifications at present required from a person seeking to be articled to a solicitor are, that he should make an affidavit stating his parentage, place of education, and what Latin books he has read. Two other affidavits in support of this are also necessary, and the payment of certain fees. Having served an apprenticeship of five years, he is "examined" previous to admission as an Attorney, pursuant to the 13th and 14th Geo. III. chap. 23, by the Examiners of the Law Courts; but this Examination now consists in a mere formal investigation of the facts of the proper duration of his apprenticeship, and that he has paid all necessary fees and stamp duties. For this investigation the Examiners receive £3 3s'.
45 *Galway Vindicator*, 24 and 28 May 1851, reference is to issue of 28 May.

previous study can reap the benefit. Few, however, of the number of professional students have been used to take this precaution, and the natural result has inevitably followed. Ignorant of the terms daily ringing in their ears, seeing no signification or utility in the forms which must ever be necessary for bringing down an abstract science to practical use, especially when abstract truths are to be applied to a subject so complex and restless as human society – toiling at precedents – grasping at fictions and technicalities, which thus could not fail to bewilder their understandings and disgust their tastes; above all, the law thus made to assume in their eyes the revolting form of a mere instrument [of] quarreling and chicanery, a thing of 'litigious terms, fat contentions, and flowing fees', instead of as it is a transcript of those eternal principles of right and justice, which bind man to man, and promote the peace and happiness of all.[46]

Why a Law Programme in the Queen's Colleges?

As the *Report* of the Queen's Colleges Commission noted, 'It appears from the Colleges' Act and the First Letters Patent, that an education in Law for Students in the Queen's Colleges formed part of the original Plan'.[47] When considered in the light of the scant resources devoted to legal education at that time, the creation of six law professorships in the Queen's Colleges in Ireland (two in each of the Colleges at Galway, Belfast, and Cork) represents an extraordinary development which requires some explanation. The policy decision to establish Law Faculties in the Queen's Colleges in the mid-nineteenth century, appears to have had very little to do with local demand. The need to improve legal education was an obvious justification, as there was considerable criticism of the low level to which legal education had descended. It does not, however, adequately explain the founding of these chairs. The creation of these Law faculties, like the foundation of the Colleges themselves, appears to have resulted more from a combination of specific events and the favourable climate which was provided by the cultural beliefs of the policy makers of the time.

A strong argument can be made that the political pressure for university education in Ireland was greatly assisted by the prevailing intellectual views, which facilitated and validated the investment in the Colleges and in the law faculties in particular.[48] There was an unshakable belief particularly, but not exclusively,

---

46   Ibid., 28 May 1851.
47   *President's Report*, 1858, p. 27.
48   The political circumstances surrounding the founding of the Queen's Colleges are well established, and relate mainly to the policy of Sir Robert Peel who devised a conciliatory policy towards Irish Catholics with a view to dissuading them from backing the campaign for repeal of the Act of Union. University reform was adopted as part of that policy in great measure due to the campaigning of the Catholic educational reformer, Thomas Wyse MP. For an account of the political background see: T.W. Moody, 'The Irish University Question of the Nineteenth Century', *History*, 42 (1958), pp. 90–109; T.W. Moody and J.C. Beckett, *Queen's Belfast, 1845–1949: The History of a University*, 2 vols (London, 1959), vol. i, Introduction, pp. 1–45; G.

among the Whigs or Liberals, in the sustainable 'progress' of society which resulted mainly from science in the broadest sense, and from the wealth and employment-creation potential of commerce and free enterprise. Education, training, and preferment based on the objective examination of ability and attainment, were valued as means of achieving such social progress. Legal education was seen, not only as a means of achieving enhanced professional standards and status, but as providing a necessary training for the proper execution of a wide variety of administrative and clerical functions at home and in the colonies. In the socio-political sphere, there was a belief that a better-educated middle class was an important element in securing peaceful allegiance to the governing authorities in Ireland, and there were even fears that the United Kingdom was being left behind by educational developments in continental Europe. Such social and cultural beliefs, which are reflected repeatedly in the evidence given to inquiries of the period, help explain the support given to both the establishment of the Queen's Colleges and the relatively radical investment in legal education.

The actual idea underlying the Colleges can be traced back at least to an 1838 Report of the Select Committee on Foundation Schools and Education in Ireland. This committee was the result of a petition of the educational reformer, Thomas Wyse, MP for Waterford. It recommended, among other things, the establishment in Ireland of four provincial colleges for higher education, together with law schools either founded separately or in connection with them.[49] Wyse was well versed in the arguments which favoured enhanced legal education. As Colum Kenny has shown, Wyse collaborated closely with the legal education reformer Tristram Kennedy, and their efforts were to have, directly and indirectly, a major effect on legal education in both Ireland and England.[50] Kennedy, who was of Protestant Scots-Irish descent, was a barrister who was so concerned by the absence of adequate legal training that he set up a Dublin Law Institute in 1839, with part-time professors who offered lectures in law. He had hoped that the initiative would be backed financially by the King's Inns and that the government would grant it a permanent charter with a statutory role in professional legal education. The conservative Unionist Benchers of the Inns were not prepared to divest themselves of their powers as the elite controllers of legal affairs. Although a modest financial contribution of £400 had been made in 1841, the Benchers refused to make a second grant. With this and other setbacks, the experiment effectively came to an end the following year.[51]

Ó Tuathaigh, *Ireland before the Famine 1798–1848* (Dublin, 1972), pp. 107–8; McGrath, *Newman's University*, especially chapter 2, 'The Godless Colleges', pp. 43–83; Thomas Dillon, 'The Origin'; Charles Murray, 'The Founding of a University', *University Review*, nos. iii and iv, 2 (1958), pp. 11–22; Conor O'Malley, 'University Education in Galway', *University Review*, nos. iii and iv, 2 (1958), pp. 59–65.

49 *Report from the Select Committee on Foundation Schools and Education in Ireland*, HC 1838 (701), vii. 345, p. 78.
50 See Kenny, *Tristram Kennedy*, pp. 10–16, 79–82, and chapter 6, *passim*.
51 Ibid., chapter 4. '"A Queer Compound of Individuals": The Rise and Fall of the Dublin Law Institute', pp. 83–92.

Wyse and Kennedy did not, however, give up the struggle for legal educational reform. In May 1843, Kennedy instigated Wyse to table a petition in the House of Commons on the regulation of the Irish legal profession. By the following year, the need for better university education in Ireland had become a political issue, and the concept of Provincial Colleges was effectively promoted. Wyse was intimately concerned with the Colleges (Ireland) bill which became the focus of intense debate and controversy in 1845,[52] and in April 1846 he renewed his efforts at legal educational reform by successfully moving in the Commons for a select committee to inquire into the state of legal education in Ireland.[53] Shortly before the inquiry was due to begin, its terms of reference were widened to include the state of English legal education. With Wyse himself as chairman, the committee completed its inquiry and agreed its report within the remarkably short period of three months. The findings of the Wyse committee confirmed the unsatisfactory state of legal education and, in formulating a solution, recommended a principal role for the universities which, with professional colleges of law, would provide a comprehensive training for lawyers. But the Committee went a stage further: the members were convinced of the general value of law as a preparation for a wide variety of administrative and professional careers, and recommended that the universities should also provide legal education for future administrators, magistrates and legislators. It also advocated proper lecture programmes and examinations – a radical recommendation in those times.[54]

The Creation of the Law Programme

As one would expect, the board appointed to draw up the academic programmes for the Queen's Colleges was influenced by the recommendations of the Wyse Committee.[55] An insight into the construction of the Law programme can be obtained from the evidence given to the Queen's Colleges Commission in 1857 by the Revd Pooley Shuldham Henry DD, President of the Belfast College, who was

---

52 Ibid., pp. 132, 135. In July 1844, Sir Robert Peel committed the government to the creation of provincial colleges in Ireland, and overtures were quickly made by the town commissioners and others to have one of these educational establishments in Galway, together with an extension of the railway to the town. On 9 May 1845, Sir James Graham moved the first reading of the bill, originally called the 'Academical Institutions (Ireland) Bill', with the intention of establishing three provincial Colleges in Ireland. The Catholic bishops decided on 23 May that they could not support the bill without amendment, on the grounds that the 'undenominational' character of the proposed scheme was dangerous to the faith and morals of Catholic students. For Graham and his Liberal colleagues, mixed education was a fundamental principle of the Bill and they moved the second reading, unchanged in that respect, on 30 May. Under its new title, the 'Colleges (Ireland) Bill', it was passed in the Commons on 10 July, by the Lords on 24 July, and it received royal assent on 31 July 1845.
53 Ibid., p. 137.
54 *Select Committee on Legal Education*, pp. xli–iii, xlvii–iii. The recommendation of legal studies for non-professional education clearly influenced the law programmes in the Queen's Colleges, and as a desirable policy, was reaffirmed in the findings of the *Queen's Colleges Commission Report*, 1858. See below.
55 Moody and Beckett, *Queen's Belfast*, vol. i, p. 52.

asked to a give a general history of the foundation of the College.[56] He and his Vice-President were appointed to their senior positions in the Belfast College early in 1846. The then Lord Lieutenant, Lord Heytesbury, called together a board of the Presidents and Vice-Presidents of the Colleges and gave them their instructions. The subjects with which the board were authorised to deal were presented to them in the form of a memorandum, a copy of which was given to the Commissioners and was printed in their *Report*.[57] The board was given the task of planning the programmes in the three faculties. The prevailing idea as to what constituted a sound general education was the taking of the undergraduate course in Arts, which was also viewed as a necessary prerequisite for the more professional education in Law and Medicine. The latter were, therefore, viewed as 'not to be entered upon by students until the basis of their general education has been soundly laid'.[58] The board of Presidents and Vice-Presidents was to begin by devising the system of general education by means of an undergraduate Arts programme and 'endeavour to render it full and satisfactory, and to bring it in advance, if possible, of the systems of Undergraduate education hitherto and elsewhere adopted'.[59] The board was to advise on subjects, but it was instructed to be forward looking. Without sacrificing traditional classical literature and philosophy, it was charged to 'recognise the importance of introducing into the curriculum of studies those branches of modern literature and Science now essential to be known by every well educated man'.[60] When this general programme was approved, the board was to consider the arrangements for Law, Medicine, and postgraduate Arts.

The board, which met frequently over the next few months, drew up statutes and regulations on the assumption that the courses would lead to degrees or other awards in the various faculties. There were delays, however, as Lord Heytesbury had left office before he could consider the board's report, and progress proved impossible during the height of the famine. It was not until the arrival of Lord Clarendon in 1847 that the board was reconvened and instructed, not only to complete the Arts statutes, but to also make provision for degrees in Medicine and Law. The statutes were completed and submitted to Lord Clarendon a short time before the Colleges opened.[61] The courses were adopted subsequently by the Senate of the Queen's University and became the basis of the educational programme in the three Colleges. What input the professors of the various disciplines had is unclear. In the case of Law, the manner in which the subjects were to be taught and the materials used were certainly left to the professors, but

---

56 *Queen's Colleges Commission Report*, 1858, pp. 60–2, questions 947ff.
57 Ibid., pp. 315–6.
58 Ibid., p. 315, paragraph 3 of lord lieutenant's memorandum.
59 Ibid.
60 Ibid., paragraph 4, p. 315.
61 Ibid., p. 61, questions 949, 951. The statutes were apparently approved of by Sir Robert Peel (he died following an accident in 1850), and Sir James Graham, who were the immediate architects of the Queen's Colleges scheme. They were also submitted to the heads of the Churches and were given general approval, although there were some misgivings, for example by the Presbyterian General Assembly, which was concerned about the extent of the courses which they regarded as too heavy for their purposes.

there is no clear evidence that they had any input or choice as to the overall shape of the degrees and diploma. On the contrary, there is evidence that the ordinances for the courses of studies were prepared by the three Presidents.[62] The Law professors, on their appointment in 1849, did meet together to discuss the curriculum, however, as is clear from the evidence given by Professor Heron to the Queen's Colleges Commission:

> [Question] 4241 [Bonamy Price]. Could you sketch for the Commissioners the course of Legal instruction pursued in the Law Faculty here [Galway]?
>
> [Heron] – I was appointed Professor of Jurisprudence and Political Economy; and there being six Professors in the Faulty of Law in the three Colleges, we met in the month of October, 1849, and drew up a course which we considered would be the most useful one, and which is now the course pursued in this College.[63]

At the outset, therefore, both the co-operation of the law professors and the common graduation requirements of the Queen's University ensured that the law programme would be substantially the same in the three Colleges.

The Nature of the Law Programme

The law teaching programme of the Queen's Colleges, which was launched in 1849 was, with the possible exception of Harvard's, the most substantial common law programme of its time. It was pioneering, not only in its carefully-structured and comprehensive curriculum, but also in its emphasis on lecture attendance, regular examinations, and its motivating prizes, scholarships, and awards. As the Vice-Chancellor noted, compared to the practice of other educational institutions, Law and Jurisprudence had been given an enhanced standing: 'In the establishment of the Queen's Colleges, these important branches of learning, – important in some degree to every man entering on a public career, indispensable to the professional student – occupy a higher place'.[64] The educational philosophy, content, and

---

62 See Supplemental Ordinance amending a subject in the LLB to include Colonial and International Law: 'Although it has been stated to the Senate that it was the intention of the Presidents of the three Queen's Colleges, by whom the Ordinances were prepared, that such a course should have been prescribed with that of Constitutional Law, but by some inadvertence that course was not inserted'. *QUI Report* 1852–3, p. 69. Presumably the Vice-Presidents were at least *ex officio* involved in the planning process. Edward Berwick of QCG, who was a barrister and graduate of the University of Dublin, acted as secretary to the Board of Presidents and Vice-Presidents. It is generally accepted that the most influential member of the Board was Sir Robert Kane, President at QCC.
63 *Queen's Colleges Commission Report*, 1858, Minutes of Evidence, p. 288.
64 *QUI Report* 1855–6, Appendix I, p. 6, Public Meeting of the Queen's University in Ireland, held in St Patrick's Hall, Dublin Castle, on 11 October 1855. The Vice-Chancellor, who was also the Lord Chancellor of Ireland said in his graduation address: 'In the first place I will notice that

objectives of the law programme had much in common with the recommendations of the 1846 *Report* of the Select Committee of the House of Commons on Legal Education. There can be little doubt that the *Report* influenced the Queen's College programme. The authors of the *Report* emphasized that legal education could not be of general benefit unless it met the needs of both professional and non-professional law students, and went so far as to suggest a broad range of courses to be provided by any law programmes established in the Queen's Colleges. Significantly, besides Jurisprudence, the *Report* suggested Constitutional Law, Comparative Constitutional Law, and Political Economy.[65] Not only did the Colleges introduce Chairs of Jurisprudence and Political Economy, but the study of Constitutional, Colonial, and International Law was made a compulsory law degree course, and the whole purpose of the law programme was designed to meet the needs of both professional and non-professional students. 'In these new colleges founded by the state', Hugh Law remarked,

> provision has been wisely made for teaching the citizens their legal rights and obligations which it is the great business and special duty of the state to enforce. The Queen's Colleges have been the first practically to recognise and adopt the principle that it is but right to impart to the youth of this country some elementary knowledge of that law from which they cannot escape and by whose rules they must be controlled and guided whatever hereafter may be their walk in life; as well so also to provide assistance to the professional student in his abstruse and more tedious course of labour.[66]

The law courses consisted of three elements: a three-year Diploma in Elementary Law, and the degrees of LLB and LLD. Law subjects featured as part of other courses also. Medical Jurisprudence was a subject required for both the LLB and the MD degrees and was first offered at Galway by the Professor of Materia Medica, Simon McCoy MD. Legal study was also considered desirable for some students of agriculture. An early ordinance of the Queen's University in Ireland recommended the Law of Landlord and Tenant and the Elements of Conveyancing for students who might have a future career in the management of estates or large farms.[67] Admission to University degrees and diplomas, and to College scholar-

---

which more immediately belongs to my own profession – the study of law and jurisprudence. I know that in the older universities of England and Ireland professorships have been founded in those sciences, and lectures given by able and learned men, well deserving the diligent attention of the student and the approbation of the public; but I do not, I think, depreciate those institutions when I observe that these subjects have not hitherto substantially formed part of their normal courses of learning, or been sustained by any special encouragement in the way of collegiate position or university honors. In the establishment of the Queen's Colleges, these important branches of learning, – important in some degree to every man entering on a public career, indispensable to the professional student – occupy a higher place'.

65 *Parliamentary Papers* 1846, x, 1, pp. lvi–lix. Political and Commercial Geography, and Statistics were also suggested but these found some recognition in the Arts rather that in the Law programme.
66 Lecture on the Study of Law, given by Hugh Law, in May 1851 at QCG, *Galway Vindicator*, 24 May 1851.
67 *QUI Report*, 1852, p. 30. Ordinance xiv (31 October 1851) stated in part that 'Students intending

ships and distinctions, was open to matriculated students only. In other words, a person could not be enrolled as a student member of the College, and be entitled thereby to full student privileges, unless the required minimum level of education had been achieved. Whereas today admission to matriculation is automatically given in most cases on the basis of success in secondary school examinations, the students of Queen's College were required to pass special matriculation examinations, unless they were transferring from sister Colleges or institutions of similar standing.[68] Non-matriculated students could attend at lectures and use the library for a fee, but were not eligible for awards, distinctions, or degrees. The matriculation requirements for law students were originally the same, and remained substantially the same, as for students of the Arts faculty.[69] Law students were required to pass examinations in Mathematics, Greek, Latin, History, Geography, and English in order to matriculate and thereby become entitled to pursue College courses leading to university awards and distinctions.[70]

The Diploma of Elementary Law

The Queen's Colleges, by means of the two or three-year Diploma, introduced a novel and flexible award, substantial in itself, but not as demanding as a degree. Whereas the diplomas offered in Agriculture and Engineering were of two years' duration, the Diploma of Elementary Law was a three-year programme which permitted the holders to obtain the LLB degree by an additional year of courses, provided they had also obtained an Arts (AB) degree.[71] The law courses were open to matriculated and non-matriculated students, the former only being eligible for

---

to qualify themselves for the Management of Estates, or of Extensive Farms, are recommended to attend also Sessional Courses of Instruction in – 1st, The Law of Landlord and Tenant, and the Elements of Conveyancing. 2nd, Elements of Political Economy and Statistics, as applied to Agriculture and Farm Finance'.

68 *Statutes, Rules, and Ordinances of the Queen's College, Galway* (Dublin, 1849), p. 44.

69 The requirements were originally the same but within ten years a narrower course for Greek and Latin was prescribed in the case of Law.

70 *Statutes, Rules, and Ordinances of the Queen's College, Galway*, pp. 34–5, 50; *Queen's University in Ireland. Queen's College, Galway ... Degrees and Diplomas, session 1856–57* (Galway, 1856), p. 20. The subjects for matriculation in law are given in the 1856 regulations as follows: 'Candidates for the Diploma of Elementary Law are required to pass a Matriculation Examination in the following subjects:– MATHEMATICS. Arithmetic – including Vulgar and Decimal Fractions, the Rule of Three, Simple Interest, and the Extraction of the Square Root. Algebra – including Fractions, Proportion, and the Solution of Simple Equations. Geometry – Euclid, Books I., II. GREEK. Xenophon– Anabasis, Book 1. Grammar. LATIN. One of the following authors:– Caesar – Gallic War, Book V. Virgil – Æneid, Book 1. Retranslation from English into Latin of portions of Caesar. HISTORY AND THE ENGLISH LANGUAGE. History – Outlines of Grecian and Roman History. Geography – Outlines of Ancient and Modern Geography. English – English Grammar and Composition'.

71 The concept of a diploma in law was sufficiently novel to warrant the attention of Vice-Chancellor, Maziere Brady: 'We have established a diploma of elementary law, to be awarded, on sufficient answering before our examiners, to students of the colleges who shall have pursued there, for three years, courses of study which comprise general jurisprudence, the civil law, and the law of England in its various branches of legal and equitable jurisdiction; and one of our

the award of diploma. Although the law courses were viewed as offering a suitable education for law students preparing for the legal profession, they were also intended for non-professional students of law. This was certainly the view of Professor Law, as already noted, and it was shared by Professor Echlin Molyneux,[72] who informed the Queen's Colleges Commission: 'I understand that the object of these Chairs was to extend the knowledge of Jurisprudence and English Law for general purposes and not for strictly professional purposes'.[73] This was substantially true; a general legal education was the only approach then open to the planners as there were effectively no set educational requirements for the legal profession, and the government was neither willing nor disposed to interfere with the power of the very conservative and Unionist Benchers of the King's Inns. There is no doubt that the intention was also to improve the educational standards of the legal profession, and the policy of providing legal education both for professional and non-professional purposes was in accord with the findings and recommendations of the Wyse Select Committee's Report on Legal Education, 1846.[74] In the early life of the Law Faculty, however, the Colleges received little by way of recognition from the Benchers of the King's Inns, and professional legal education was seen as a secondary role for the Colleges whereby they could provide badly-needed training which was not available elsewhere. Soon, however, it became clear that the number of law students would remain low unless there were inducements for legal study in the form of access to professional or administrative employment.

The 'diploma', because it was a new and unfamiliar type of award, required some 'selling' to the public at large. At the 1853 conferring, the Vice-Chancellor said that these Diplomas in Agriculture, Engineering, and Law

honorary premiums is assigned to the best answerer of the candidates for this diploma on a special honor examination'. *QUI Report*, 1856–7, p. 6, Appendix i, Address of the Vice-Chancellor, Public Meeting of the Queen's University in Ireland, held in St Patrick's Hall, Dublin Castle, on 11 October 1855.

72 As a young barrister in Dublin, Molyneux acted as a part-time professor in, and member of the council of, Tristram Kennedy's Dublin Law Institute, in which he gave a course in Equity in 1839–40. He was later appointed Professor of English Law at Queen's College Belfast. (See Kenny, *Tristram Kennedy*, pp. 89–90, 96–7, 99–100.)

73 I take 'not for strictly professional purposes' as meaning not just for professional purposes, as clearly from his testimony, he took that for granted. *Queen's Colleges Commission Report*, 1858, Minutes of Evidence, p. 98, question 1557. The context of the remark was why more students entering the legal profession did not take the law courses: '1556. *Mr Gibson.*– Are young men admitted to the profession of solicitor before twenty-one? – (*Professor Molyneux*) No. I am not sure that it is generally understood that a privilege is attached to taking the course here. 1557. *Mr Price.*– In estimating the future prospects of the Queen's Colleges, the influence exercised by a special education of this kind forms a large element; and the difficulty I want to have explained is, that though the advantage is held out it is not appreciated? – (*Molyneux*) It does not appear to be appreciated. I have a gentleman who is a solicitor, practising, and a graduate of Dublin College, but I do not think there are more than four in the class who are either in the profession or going to it. But I understand that the object of these Chairs was to extend the knowledge of Jurisprudence and English Law for general purposes and not for strictly professional purposes'.

74 The philosophy and recommendations of the Wyse Committee were reaffirmed as goals for the Queen's College Law Schools in the findings of the *Queen's Colleges Commission Report*, 1858, see pp. 27–8.

> constitute a second class of honors ... They are not titles which confer on the persons who obtain them any special rights or privileges in their profession, or any advancement in it; but I have no doubt that they will constitute, in the eyes of those who may be desirous of employing these individuals, a high recommendation, as well as a valid title in their possessors to the confidence and good reception of the public.[75]

The following year he again raised the issue of the diplomas:

> There is some novelty, but, I believe, sound utility in this arrangement. Though not, technically speaking, degrees, those diplomas are in the nature of them ... I believe these courses of study and examination comprise much of all that practically and theoretically can be suggested for the education of the lawyer and agriculturist.[76]

Not everybody was happy with the Diploma. Professor T.E. Cliffe Leslie of QCB argued that students wishing to take the Diploma of Elementary Law also had to take an Arts degree because the Diploma was of 'little practical value', and less valuable, because the amount of knowledge required for it was much less than for the LLB.[77] He described the Diploma as 'a new sort of Degree', but that it had no historical or social status:

> I do not mean to say it is without value, but more distinction is conferred by the Degree of LLB: which is a thing that a man can put as a title after his name, but the Diploma in Elementary Law he cannot. He has, in fact, no means of showing the latter.[78]

The engineering diploma was eventually replaced by a degree in engineering,[79] and clearly it would have been beneficial to the academic development of legal studies if the law diploma had likewise been replaced at an early stage with an undergraduate law degree. It represents one of many instances of the relative neglect of law teaching within the Colleges, a neglect which was due in part to the absence of full-time staff dedicated to the development of the discipline.

---

75 *QUI Report*, 1852–3, Appendix, p. 65.
76 *QUI Report*, 1853–4, Appendix, p. 78.
77 Professor Cliffe Leslie was Professor of Jurisprudence and Political Economy from 1853 until his death in 1882. Born in Co. Wexford, a graduate of TCD (1847), he was active in the Statistical Society. His main intellectual interests and contributions were in economics. See Boylan and Foley, *Political Economy and Colonial Ireland, passim*, including biographical note at pp. 170–1.
78 *Queen's Colleges Commission Report*, 1858, Minutes of Evidence, questions 1567–9, p. 99.
79 In 1868 the Queen's University substituted degrees for the engineering diplomas: 'The Senate of the University for the greater encouragement of the study of engineering, and to give to the successful students in that most valuable branch of collegiate pursuits a more strictly academic designation, have substituted degrees for the diploma we have heretofore conferred'. (Vice-Chancellor Maziere Brady's conferring address, 14 October 1868, *QUI Report*, 1868–9, p. 5.)

The Diploma of Elementary Law was not in itself a heavy programme. Those students, however, who wished to proceed to the LLB were required to take the BA degree in the Arts Faculty also, and this was generally regarded as an excessively heavy course for the average student. The original QCG regulations for the Diploma were as follows:

> Faculty of Law. The elementary Course of Study prescribed for Students in this Faculty extends through three College Sessions, and is as follows:
>
> FIRST SESSION – The law of Property, and the Principles of Conveyancing. Jurisprudence.
> SECOND SESSION – Equity and Bankruptcy. Civil Law.
> THIRD SESSION – Common and Criminal Law.
>
> Students who shall have passed the Matriculation Examination in Arts, and shall have completed the foregoing course of Study, will be entitled to a Diploma of elementary Law.[80]

One of the most striking aspects of Law teaching at QCG is how closely it resembled a modern academic law programme. There was compulsory attendance at lectures for at least two terms of each of the three Collegiate sessions or academic years – a novelty for many universities of that time. Law students, for example, were required to attend the courses of the Professors of English Law and of Jurisprudence, which were delivered in the first and second terms of each session and, 'at the close of those lectures, in the Second Term, to pass an examination on the subjects lectured upon by the Professors of the Faculty of Law during the Session'.[81] Diploma and degree students were required to take and pass both College and University examinations. The examination timetables were not remarkably different from degree examinations of today. There were written papers with examining sessions at 9.00 a.m. and 2.00 p.m., and students generally had no break between examinations. The University examinations were the same for all three Colleges and were conducted by common examiners. At University level, students were examined in the same subject areas, although some refinements were occasionally introduced. Equity and Bankruptcy, for example, were subsumed as examinable subjects at university level into the broader subject area of Equity, Common and Criminal Law.[82]

---

80 *Statutes, Rules, and Ordinances, of the Queen's College, Galway*, p. 50. The course of studies for the Diploma at University level had been prescribed by Ordinance of 30 June 1850 to the same effect, but with prerequisites: 'Students who shall have passed the Matriculation Examination for the Faculty of Law, in one of the Queen's Colleges, and shall have pursued during three years the following course of Study, shall be admitted to Examination for the Diploma of Elementary Law'. (*QUI Report*, 1851–2, p. 9.) In the same ordinance, there was an error as to one of the LLB subjects – 'Constitutional Law' was prescribed instead of 'Constitutional, Colonial and International Law'. (See *QUI Report*, 1852–3, pp. 4, 69, concerning a supplemental ordinance made in 1852.)
81 President's *Report* 1849–50, p. 71.
82 *QUI Reports* for 1852–3, p. 6; for 1853–4, p. 87, for 1854–5, p. 79.

The University regulations provided for formal written examinations by means of printed papers, the examiners having 'power to add such *viva voce* examination for Diploma as may appear necessary'. The rules required a distinct honours examination in which 'the several subjects will receive a more profound and extensive discussion'. Candidates were required to supply certification of matriculation, and of admission to the Law Faculty of one of the Queen's Colleges, and certification of having pursued 'during at least three years subsequent to Matriculation, the course of studies prescribed ... as qualifying for the Diploma in Elementary Law'.[83] Exhibitions, medals, and prizes were instituted for honours students, and university law examiners were selected from qualified applicants, who might be from one of the Colleges, or an 'outsider'. The first University law examiners were James A. Lawson LLD, for Law,[84] and Denis Caulfield Heron for Jurisprudence and Political Economy.[85] The scholarships were a valuable incentive to needy students of the time, and were distributed throughout the faculties. Three of these were assigned to the annual classes of the Diploma of Elementary Law, and were awarded on the basis of a special examination, the prescribed course for which was set out in the College's regulations. Examination of candidates for honours was confined to students recommended by the examiners, and there were exhibitions or medals for first, second, and third honours, valued at £25, £15, and £5 respectively.[86]

The LLB and LLD Degrees

The Bachelor of Laws or LLB degree, like the law Diploma, was a departure from the prevailing practices in the older universities. As Echlin Molyneux, Professor of English Law at Belfast, put it:

> I may state that the Degree of LLB in the Queen's University is the only Degree in Law that occurs to me, which requires either study or examination.

---

83 *QUI Report*, 1852, pp. 34–5.
84 James Anthony Lawson (1817–87), a native of Waterford, had graduated from TCD (BA, 1831; LLB, 1841; LLB, 1850) and was called to the Irish Bar, 1840, and appointed a QC, 1857. He held the Whately chair of Political Economy at TCD from 1841 to 1846. There followed a very successful legal career as Solicitor-General, 1861, Attorney-General, 1865, justice of the Common Pleas, 1868, English privy councillor, 1870, and justice of the Queen's Bench Division, 1882. See *DNB*; F.E. Ball, *The Judges in Ireland, 1221–1921* (Dublin, 1993), vol. ii, pp. 267–8; Boylan and Foley, *Political Economy and Colonial Ireland*, p. 163.
85 *QUI Report*, 1851–2, p. 35; *QUI Report*, 1852–3, p. 5. There were initial teething problems which included a Mr McMahon, a student in Arts and Law at Galway who was unable to comply with the rules because of an incorrect change as to the year of the course in which Botany was available as a subject.
86 *QUI Report*, 1851–2, Appendix, p. 35. *QCG Statutes, Rules and Ordinances*, ch. ii (3), pp. 21–2: 'Three Junior Scholarships are founded in the Faculty of Law, of the value of Twenty Pounds each, which shall be awarded by Examination, to Undergraduate Students of the Faculty of Law, viz., one to Students of the first year, one to Students of the second year, and one to Students of the third year'.

> It is a mere nominal matter to take the Degree in Law in the Dublin University. I believe in the old Universities in England it is pretty much the same – a matter of pounds, shillings, and pence.[87]

The attainment of the degree in the Queen's Colleges was quite a formidable achievement, as it was awarded only when the candidate had successfully completed the Diploma of Elementary Law, the Bachelor of Arts (AB degree), and an additional year of law courses. The requirements, as described in the College's regulations, were as follows:

> Candidates for the Degree of LLB, will be admitted to Examination for that Degree from the Queen's University in Ireland, provided they shall have proceeded to the Degree of AB, and shall have attended the Lectures, and passed the Examinations prescribed for the elementary Course; and shall also have pursued the following Course of Study: –
>
> FOURTH SESSION –
> A more extended Course of Study of the subjects appointed for the elementary Course, together with a Course of Study of the Law of Evidence and Pleading in the Courts of Common Law and Equity, of Medical Jurisprudence, and of Constitutional, Colonial, and International Law.[88]

The number of students completing the LLB programme always remained low. The difficulty of the programme was a contributory factor. It was not the extent of the law courses themselves, though substantial, which was the problem, but the fact that the student had to complete the undergraduate Arts degree as a prerequisite for the LLB. The extent of the work-load involved in the LLB programme made it a degree which would not be undertaken lightly.[89]

There were many at the time who argued that the Arts degree course itself was too demanding in that it involved an excessively heavy workload, especially for students who had an inadequate second-level education due to the scarcity of quality schools at that period. The undergraduate Arts course endeavoured to embrace the new contemporary fields of study without giving up the traditional classical education of the past. The result was an admirable, but overly-extensive liberal education, which embraced ancient and modern languages, mathematics, the physical sciences, philosophy, and a course in either jurisprudence and political economy or metaphysics. Attendance at lectures was required for at least two of the three terms of each of the three academic years. An LLB student had, therefore, to pursue a minimum of four difficult years of study in both disciplines, assuming that he had the capacity to take and pass both the Arts and Law programmes simultaneously. The first graduates, George Yielding McMahon –

---

87 *Queen's Colleges Commission Report*, 1858, Minutes of Evidence, question 1540, p. 97.
88 *Statutes, Rules and Ordinances of the QCG*, p. 50.
89 Ibid., pp. 46–7, 50.

who later became Professor of Modern Languages at the Royal College, Mauritius – and Dominick Daly Ryan, did in fact study for both the Diploma in Elementary Law and the AB degree in the first three years, as they were conferred with both awards in October 1852. Although the completion of both courses was very difficult for average students, good students were in a position to pursue both courses successfully. Professor Heron rejected any suggestion that the pursuit of a professional discipline interfered with the attainment of a liberal education in Arts, at least in the case of hard-working students:

> The Faculty of Law does not interfere with the general education in Arts. Those who come from the Arts Faculty into the Law Faculty, are generally the hard-working students; and they do not find the slightest difficulty by reason of the additional course. I never heard a complaint from such a student, that he was overworked. I arrange my lectures so as to make it convenient to the students to attend my class; and I have heard no complaints that they are overworked.[90]

The majority opinion was different, however, and Heron did not address the issue of average or weaker students. The reality was that many students taking arts and law courses did not proceed to take the University examinations. From the numbers of matriculated students in the Colleges, the Vice-Chancellor thought that the number of candidates seeking the University's degrees in the early years ought 'to be nearly treble, if not quadruple, the actual sum of them', and he had been assured by many that the University had 'aimed at too high a standard of acquirements'.[91] The extent of the curricular requirement gives some justification to contemporary criticisms. Professor T.E. Cliffe Leslie, who was characteristically forthright in his objections, regarded the Arts/Law programme as burdensome, discouraging, and likely to promote superficial learning due to its excessive breadth. 'I think', he said,

> that in the first instance, without reference to the Law Faculty, there is too much required of the student merely to get the Arts Degree; but when I consider that the student going to take the Degree in Law, has this vast amount of subjects to prepare himself in addition, I believe, the excess becomes more apparent.[92]

---

90 *Queen's Colleges Commission Report*, 1858, question 4247, p. 289.
91 *QUI Report*, 1856–7, pp. 4–5: Vice-Chancellor Maziere Brady said at the October 1856 conferring: 'I am assured by many, whose opinions are of great value, that, in endeavouring to give to our degrees an important character and value in public estimation, as evidences of superior learning in their possessors, we have aimed at too high a standard of acquirements, and involved our students in courses of preparatory study too numerous and oppressive for a complete pursuit of them in the allotted time; so that, having regard to the average capacities of youth, it is by many found to be impossible, within the period of their collegiate term, to attain an adequate stage of preparation for the prescribed examinations'.
92 *Queen's Colleges Commission Report*, 1858, Minutes of Evidence, question 1571, p. 99. Leslie summarised his objections to the AB as follows: 'The Examination, if I may be allowed to offer

The University examination for the LLB was based on advanced papers in the five subjects prescribed for the Diploma and additional papers in the subjects: Pleading, Practice and Evidence, Constitutional, and Colonial and International Law.[93] Medical Jurisprudence was not examined by the University for the purposes of the degree. In line with these programmes, it was proposed to confer the LLD degree 'at the expiration of two years after having obtained the Degree of LLB, on the candidate who shall pass a second examination on the subjects prescribed for the LLB examination, and in addition, in the Admiralty and Ecclesiastical Laws'.[94] Given the low state to which legal education had fallen elsewhere, these programmes were revolutionary and academically demanding. The Vice-Chancellor could rightly claim:

> As regards the degrees of bachelor of laws and doctor of laws, which may be conferred by the Senate of this University, they are not here mere formal steps in the scale of learned titles to be attained by the performance of some trivial and unmeaning exercises at the end of a given term of years from the assumption of a prior degree. On the contrary, special examinations are assigned to the candidates for these distinctions, making them, as all university degrees ought properly to be, true tests of merit and knowledge in their possessors.[95]

It was not just the admiration of a partial commentator, as the system of legal education drew admiring comments from Cambridge. The Regius Professor of Law, Dr Abdey, wrote to Ball, secretary to Queen's University, requesting copies of the law examination papers, and expressing the hope that his university would adopt a similar system. Vice-Chancellor Maziere Brady was pleased to inform his

---

 an opinion, for the Degree in Arts, is, I consider, wholly apart from its operation upon the Law Faculty, excessive. I conceive that an Examination in Classics, English Literature, Modern Languages, Logic, the Mental Sciences, and the Political Sciences, involves a good education; and, when taken for professional purposes, such as that of the Law, it is the best sort of education which can be given; but, I believe, it is impossible to get any thing, but a very superficial amount of knowledge, when you add Law and such subjects as Mathematics and the Physical Sciences. I should suggest, that there should be an option which does not at present exist, of allowing the students either to take the Moral Sciences and Literature, or to take Mathematics and the Physical Sciences, along with Modern Languages'. (Ibid., question 1570, p. 99.)

93 QUI Regulations of 30 June 1850, and 14 December 1852, *QUI Reports*, 1851–2, pp. 8–9; 1852–3, p. 69. There were initially nine subject areas (Property; Jurisprudence; Equity; Common and Criminal Law; Civil Law; Pleading, Practice and Evidence; Constitutional; Colonial; and International Law) examined in four sessions, in ordinary and honours examinations, but there was no University examination in Medical Jurisprudence. See, for example, examination papers, *QUI Report*, 1853–4, pp. 32–8; *QUI Report*, 1854–5, pp. 58–63. In the latter Constitutional, Colonial and International Law were combined into one paper.

94 *Queen's Colleges Commission Report*, 1858, p. 27. The LLD was originally envisaged as a degree awarded on the basis of an examination held three years after the LLB (see Ordinance of 30 June 1850, *QUI Report*, 1851–2, p. 9.

95 *QUI Report*, 1855–6, Appendix, p. 6. Public Meeting of the Queen's University in Ireland, held in St Patrick's Hall, Dublin Castle, on 11 October 1855.

audience of this tribute in the course of the graduation address at St Patrick's Hall, Dublin Castle, on 11 October 1855:

> I have great satisfaction also in referring ... to some letters received by our secretary from the learned gentleman who fills the chair of the Regius Professorship of Law in the University of Cambridge, in the first of which, after alluding to our printed examination papers, and requesting copies of them, and stating that he is a member of a committee appointed for the purpose of entirely remodeling the course of lectures for the faculty of Law in that University, he says, 'The questions in the Queen's Colleges for the degree of LLB, as well as those on jurisprudence, strike me as being so admirably adapted to students of the principles of law, that I should wish to make as much use of them as I can'; and again, in reply to a letter from Dr Ball, with which had been transmitted to him some copies of the University and College papers, containing the examination questions, Dr Abdey says, 'I sincerely trust that in many points we shall imitate the system adopted in the Queen's Colleges in our proposed new Law classes in this University, as I feel no doubt of the benefit we shall derive by so doing. I speak with more boldness on the subject of the questions in Jurisprudence and the Civil Law, as that is my own department here ... But it is not only in the Law papers that your Colleges show their merit and utility. The whole system of education pursued by you is, in my humble opinion, so well suited to the present times that I sincerely trust it may defy all opposition'. [96]

The Queen's College Law Programme and Legal Professional Practice

It was no doubt the quality of its degrees, together with Chancellor Brady's influence (he was Vice-President of Queen's University) which persuaded the King's Inns to grant some educational concessions to graduates studying for the Bar. The Benchers were persuaded to attach the same privileges to the Queen's University BA degree as had already been granted to the BA degrees of Cambridge, Oxford, and Trinity College.[97] Arts graduates of the Queen's University in Ireland would now have to attend fewer terms before being called to the Bar. The holders of an arts or law degree from the Queen's University were also granted the privilege, by statutory enactment, of becoming solicitors after serving a three-year rather than a five-year apprenticeship. A request for other privileges for holders of the Diploma of Elementary Law and the LLB had also been made to the King's Inns, and the President of QCG hoped for a favourable outcome for the Queen's Colleges 'as being the first Collegiate Institutions that have given to the Science of Law its due importance'.[98]

---

96 *QUI Report*, 1855–6, p. 6.
97 This concession was granted as early as 1851, see President's *Report*, 1850–51, p. 60.
98 President's *Report*, 1850–1, paragraphs 35–6, p. 60. The President wrote: 'I have the fullest confidence that every privilege that justice can require will be ceded by that learned body. I hope,

The desire to improve the educational standards of the legal profession in Ireland has had a long and unsatisfactory history and, to some extent, it remains unsatisfactory to this day. The first efforts at raising standards were indirect, in that it was hoped to attract better-educated individuals into the profession by granting concessions to graduates. In 1782, an 'act to regulate the admission of barristers at law' tried to establish a five-year enrollment period in the society of King's Inns as a condition of admission to the Irish bar. Graduates of Oxford, Cambridge and the University of Dublin were, however, granted, among other privileges, the right to be admitted after an enrollment of only three years.[99] This privilege was technically lost when the statute was repealed in 1792, but was continued as a matter of practice.[100] In the following year, the English Inns reduced the obligatory term of membership for admission to the bar in England from five to three years in the case of graduates of Trinity College.[101]

As a result of a similar initiative in 1821, the length of apprenticeship was reduced from five to three years, in the case of graduates of Oxford, Cambridge, and Dublin who wished to qualify as attorneys and solicitors.[102] This concession was extended to graduates in arts and law of the Queen's Colleges at Belfast, Cork, and Galway in 1851,[103] although it was suggested in the early years that very few took advantage of it.[104] The same statute provided that a student who was simultaneously studying for a degree, or who attended prescribed law courses for two years with the Law Professors of Trinity College or any of the Queen's Colleges, would be qualified to be admitted as an attorney or solicitor in four years from the commencement of his apprenticeship, instead of five.[105] Students who

however, it will not be considered improper to observe, that the Queen's Colleges have peculiar claims to the favourable consideration of the heads of the legal profession as being the first Collegiate Institutions that have given to the Science of Law its due importance, and that by introducing into its ordinary courses the study of its noble principles, as well as by the creation of Legal Faculties, and the endowing them with Scholarships, have endeavoured to promote the cultivation of legal knowledge'.

99 Statute 21 & 22 Geo. III, c. 32 (1782). See Kenny, *King's Inns*, pp. 184–6. The statute created the concept of a student of the King's Inns for the first time, but prohibited Catholics from being students.

100 32 Geo. III, c. 18 (Statutes, Ireland, 1792). As the statute also abolished the five-year enrollment requirement, graduates were no worse off. Legislation in the same year (32 Geo. III, c. 21), removed many disabilities on Catholics, and permitted them to join the legal profession, but not to become king's counsel or judges. Trinity College admitted Catholics as students in 1793, although they were not entitled to full membership.

101 See Kenny, *King's Inns*, pp. 252–3. This privilege had been extended to graduates of Oxford and Cambridge in 1762.

102 1 and 2 Geo. IV, c. 48: an act to amend the several acts for the regulation of attorneys and solicitors. See Osborough, 'Attorneys and Solicitors', pp. 134–6.

103 14 and 15 Vict, c. 88, section 1. (An act for amending the several acts for the regulation of attornies and solicitors.)

104 Evidence of Professor Mills, Cork, to the Queen's Colleges Commission, 1858, question 3224, p. 229.

105 14 and 15 Vict. c. 88, section 2, which applied as follows: 'That every person who has Matriculated, or as a Non-Matriculated Student of one of the Queen's Colleges, shall have attended, or shall attend, the prescribed lectures, and shall have passed, or shall pass, the prescribed examinations of the Professors of the Faculty of Law in any of the said Queen's

wished to avail of this privilege at Galway, whether they were matriculated or non-matriculated students, were required to enter their names with the Registrar and pay the course fees before the teaching session began. The College regulations required such students 'intending to proceed for the Certificate of the Law Professors', to attend all the lectures and pass all the examinations prescribed for the first and second years of the course for the Diploma of Elementary Law.[106]

The QCG Careers of Professors Hugh Law and Denis C. Heron, 1849–59

From the evidence given by Professor Heron to the Queen's Colleges Commission, and the somewhat sparse record of the College and University Reports, it is possible to form an impression of the earliest period of the Law Faculty's existence. Both professors Law and Heron were appointed in 1849 and, as previously noted, the six Queen's Colleges law professors (two from each College), met to consider a law teaching programme which had been designed in its essentials by the board of Presidents, and which had been substantially inspired by the Wyse Committee Report on Legal Education. In terms of their own education, both Law and Heron were TCD graduates, but as regards religious and cultural experience, they came from different backgrounds.

Hugh Law, the first Professor of English Law at Queen's College Galway, was born in Woodlawn, Co. Down on 19 June 1818, the only son of John and Margaret Law (fig. 2.2).[107] His mother Margaret was a daughter of Christopher Crawley of Cullaville, Co. Armagh. His father John, who had served as an officer in the 26th Cameronians, became successively a land agent to Lord Annesley and Lord Leitrim, moving to Milford, Co. Donegal, in his latter capacity.[108] Hugh Law received his early education at the Royal School, Dungannon, and entered Trinity

    Colleges for a period of two collegiate years, and who shall have duly served as an apprentice or clerk, by contract in writing, duly stamped at or before the signing thereof, or within six months after, for the term of four years, in like manner as by the said herein-before first-recited Acts is directed respecting the service for the term of five years, shall at any time after the expiration of five years, from the commencement of such attendance on lectures, or of such period of service, which shall first happen, be qualified to be sworn and to be admitted as an attorney or solicitor respectively, according to the nature of his service, of the several and respective superior Courts of Law or Equity in England or Ireland, as fully and effectual to all intents and purposes as any person having been bound and having served five years is qualified to be sworn and to be admitted or enrolled an attorney or solicitor, under or by virtue of any Act or Acts now in force for the regulation of attorneys or solicitors in England or Ireland, anything in the said Acts or any of them to the contrary in anywise notwithstanding'.

106 *Queen's University and Queen's College, Galway ... Degrees and Diplomas*, Session 1856–7 (Galway, 1856), pp. 22–3.
107 Biographical details of Law are to be found in the *DNB;* Frederick Boase, *Modern English Biography; Irish Law Times and Solicitors' Journal*, xvii (15 September 1883), pp. 489–90; *Law Times*, 15 September 1883; *Law Journal*, 15 September 1883; *Times*, 4 September 1883; *Irish Times*, 11 September 1883; *Law Magazine and Law Review*, 1883–4, pp. 95–6; Ball, *The Judges in Ireland*, vol. ii, pp. 273–4; *The Presidents, Vice-Presidents, and Professors of Queen's College, Galway: A List of their Contributions to Science and Literature, 1845–1902* (Dublin, 1902), p. 39; Foley, 'A Nest of Scholars', pp. 81–2.
108 *Irish Law Times and Solicitors' Journal*, xvii (September 1883), p. 489.

College Dublin as a matriculated student in 1834, where he was a companion of the later renowned judge, Lord Cairns.[109] A diligent and able student, Law became an elected scholar of the University in 1837, and graduated BA in 1839, having successfully pursued the honours programme, thereby obtaining a first senior moderatorship and gold medal in classics. He had already applied for, and had been admitted to, Lincoln's Inn, London, in 1838, clearly indicating an interest in a legal career as a barrister. He was duly admitted to the Irish Bar in Easter term 1840. Hugh Law joined the north-east circuit but, as his practice grew, he worked principally in the Courts of Equity in Dublin. Law, like Heron, was very interested in social questions, and both of them were members of the Dublin Statistical Society.[110]

2.1 Denis Caulfield Heron, Professor of Jurisprudence and Political Economy, 1849–59

Denis Caulfield Heron was the first son of William Heron and Mary Maguire (fig. 2.1).[111] He was born on 16 February 1824, probably in Dublin.[112] He received his early education at St Gregory's School, Downside, and later at Trinity College

---

109 Hugh MacCalmont Cairns (1819–85) was admitted to, and practised at, the English Bar. A Conservative MP for Belfast (1852–66), he became successively, solicitor general (1858–9) and attorney general (1866) for England. Appointed first Baron (1866) and lord chancellor of England (1868, 1874–80), he was created first Earl Cairns in 1878.
110 Many of the leading lawyers of the period were actively involved in the Dublin Statistical Society (it merged later with the Social Inquiry Society) which was founded in 1847 by William Neilson Hancock, Whately Professor of Political Economy at TCD and first Professor of Jurisprudence and Political Economy at QCB. Besides Hugh Law and Denis C. Heron, there were other lawyers involved in the early years – James Lawson who became a judge of the Irish Queen's Bench; Joseph Napa and Thomas O'Hagan, who were to occupy the office of Lord Chancellor. See R.D.C. Black, *The Statistical and Social Inquiry Society of Ireland Centenary Volume, 1847–1947* (Dublin, 1947), pp. 25–6; J.F. McEldowney and Paul O'Higgins, 'Irish Legal History and the Nineteenth Century', in J.F. McEldowney and Paul O'Higgins (eds), *The Common Law Tradition: Essays in Irish Legal History* (Dublin, 1990), pp. 203–30.
111 Biographical details of Heron are to be found in Boase, *Modern English Biography; Irish Law Times and Solicitors' Journal*, xvii, p. 219 (23 April 1881); *Law Magazine and Law Review*, (1880–1), p. 291; *The Presidents, Vice-Presidents*, pp. 39–40; Foley, 'A Nest of Scholars', p. 81; Boylan and Foley, *Political Economy and Colonial Ireland*, pp. 172–3.
112 Some accounts state that he was born in 1826 (*Boase; Thom's Almanac*, 1871–3; *Law Magazine and Review*, 1880–1). An obituary in the *Irish Law Times and Solicitors' Journal* (23 April 1881) states that he was born in Newry. The entry in Burtchaell and Sadleir's *Alumni Dublinensis* states that he was sixteen when he registered at TCD on 16 October 1840, that he was born in Dublin, and describes his father as 'scriba' – a gentleman professional of some kind.

Dublin, where he lived for 'six or seven years',[113] and where he was auditor of the Historical Society. He received the BA degree in 1845 as Senior Moderator, or honours graduate, in Classics,[114] a subject for which he also won a gold medal. His time at Trinity College was marked by controversy. He had originally entered TCD as a 'pensioner' – a non-foundation scholar who paid for his own commons – but had obtained a 'sizarship' in 1842, which could last as long as four years, and under which the recipient had free commons and was exempted from annual fees. In the following year, Heron, who was a Catholic, applied for one of sixteen Trinity College foundation scholarships. Although he came fifth in order of merit, he was deemed ineligible as he was not a member of the established Church of Ireland, and refused to make the then mandatory religious declaration against transubstantiation. He appealed to the Visitors of the University against the decision of the Provost and senior fellows which denied him a scholarship. Although the Visitors first refused to hear his appeal, they were forced to do so when Heron successfully applied for, and obtained, an order of mandamus from the Queen's Bench in June 1844 – an order which directed them to hear his case.[115]

Beyond the narrow issue of scholarship entitlement, the case had potentially major implications for the character, ethos, and even the long-term control of TCD. Not surprisingly, the College employed experienced barristers to defend its interests. The Visitors, who were the Church of Ireland archbishops of Armagh and Dublin, nominated Justice Richard Keatinge, Judge of the Prerogative Court, as 'assessor' to advise them, but in effect to rule on the merits. The hearing before the Visitors took place in the Dining Hall at TCD on 11 and 12 December 1845 with heavy legal representation.[116] After hearing the arguments, the assessor

---

113 In his evidence to the Queen's Colleges Commission, Heron expressed his dissatisfaction with the lack of accommodation for students in Galway: 'The College in this respect is just as if it was placed in a desert'. In extolling the virtues of the unfurnished accommodation at Trinity he said: 'I lived in Trinity College for six or seven years, and I think the arrangements there in this respect are very good. The bare walls are given to the student on the payment of a deposit'. *Queen's Colleges Commission Report*, 1858, Minutes of Evidence, questions 4277–8, p. 290.

114 Five persons entered for the Classical Moderatorship out of 300 (ibid., question 4278, p. 290). In his evidence to the Commissioners, Heron said: 'In reference to the Senior Scholarships, there is no competition, which arises from this, that the best man is known. In Trinity College, for the Gold Medal Examination, there is no competition in point of numbers. When I took my Degree only five persons went in for the Classical Moderatorship, out of a class of 300. Four got gold medals; but there was no competition because the best men were known'.

115 *R. (Heron) v. Visitors of Trinity College* (1845–46), *Irish Law Reports*, vol. 9, p. 41. See A.R. Hart, 'The King's Serjeant at Law in Ireland: A Short History', in W.N. Osborough (ed.), *Explorations in Law and History* (Dublin, 1995), pp. 56–7. See also H.H.G. McDonnell and William Neilson Hancock, *Report of the Case of Denis Caulfield Heron against the Provost and Senior Fellows, in the Visitorial Court of Appeal, Trinity College Dublin* (Dublin, 1846), and J.F. Waller, *Report of the Case of D.C. Heron (Appellant) v. The Provost and Senior Fellows of Trinity College, Dublin (Respondents)* (Dublin, 1847).

116 David Richard Pigott QC and Stephen Woulfe Flanagan, both Liberal Catholics, represented Heron as appellant. Pigot was appointed Chief Baron of the Exchequer the following year and Flanagan was later to become a judge of the Landed Estates Court and Chancery judge, as well as a privy councillor successively in Ireland and England. Richard Moore QC and Mountifort Longfield QC represented the Provost and Senior Fellows of TCD who were the respondents.

advised the Visitors to dismiss Heron's appeal, which they did. Although Catholics had been admitted to Trinity College since 1793,[117] and could be conferred with its degrees, the assessor ruled that under section 13 of the Relief Act and the relevant College statute of 1794, Catholics (or Protestant Dissenters) were not eligible for foundation scholarships. The statutory intent was to extend access to liberal education and grant the right to obtain degrees only, 'but without allowing them to become members of the corporation of Trinity College, Dublin, or in any manner changing its Protestant character'.[118] The College as corporation had retained its Established Church character, and Heron was not eligible to be elected a member scholar. Heron's case, however, proved sufficiently embarrassing to prompt the University to endow some non-foundation scholarships for which Catholics could compete. Foundation scholarships or 'fellowships', as such, were not open to Catholics until 1873.

Heron, who appears to have been intelligent,[119] determined, and resourceful, was not quite yet finished with his campaign. His skirmish with the College authorities appears to have raised his standing among his student colleagues. After two enjoyable years as member of the Historical Society, where he had passed his time, as he said, 'in honourable rivalry with my fellow students', he was elected auditor. His inaugural address, before a distinguished gathering, was given in the Dining Hall on 4 November 1846, and was published at the Society's expense by a unanimous vote of its members.[120] In the following year, at the early age of twenty-four, he published *The Constitutional History of the University of Dublin*,[121] a work in which he demanded the reform of the whole position of Catholics in the university, and argued that the University's stance was illegal.

Moore was appointed Justice of the Queen's Bench in 1847 and Longfield was later an Encumbered Estates Commissioner and judge of the Landed Estates Court. Isaac Butt QC, the distinguished barrister and politician, represented the interests of TCD as a corporation.

117 A provision of the Relief Act 1793 permitted Catholics to enter and graduate from the University of Dublin, and provided that any future College founded within the University (besides the existing TCD) should be free from religious tests. A substantial number of middle-class Catholics entered TCD after 1793 without any obvious Catholic Church disapproval until the Queen's Colleges controversy in 1845. See V.T.H. Delany, *Christopher Palles* (Dublin, 1960), pp. 20–1.

118 Waller, *Report*, p. 110.

119 The entry in *Thom's Directory* (1871) states that Heron also took first prizes in history and political economy and the Historical Society's gold and silver medals for history and oratory.

120 Heron's *An Address Delivered before the College Historical Society* was published in Dublin in 1846. He took as his object to defend student debating against the charges of the archbishop of Dublin who had apparently condemned debating societies 'as injurious to mental health'. The Address reveals a very capable public speaker who gave a sophisticated and polished performance which, if somewhat formal and stilted by today's tastes, seemed to have been a model of formal, gentlemanly, discourse at that time. The College Historical Society had been effectively disbanded in 1815 and very successfully revived again in 1843.

121 D.C. Heron, *The Constitutional History of the University of Dublin. With some Account of Its Present Condition, and Suggestions for Improvement* (Dublin, 1847), 2nd ed., revised, 1848. There is a 2nd. ed. copy in the library of NUI, Galway, with the hand-written inscription: 'Presented to the Library of Queen's College, Galway by the author'. The book was published at the expense of the university reform activist, James Heywood, MP for North Lancashire.

Heron was called to the Irish Bar in 1848 and subsequently joined the Munster circuit. Given his interest in educational reform, it was natural for him to be concerned with other social and economic issues of the day. He became an original member of the Dublin Statistical Society, and served as a member of its Council in 1850. For an able young man such as Heron, without major family fortune or influential connections, an academic career represented an attractive option, suited to his intellectual abilities and interests. Although he distinguished himself as a professorial candidate for the Whately Chair of Political Economy at Trinity College, for which he was unsuccessful, he had the consolation of being appointed as Barrington Lecturer in that subject in 1849.[122] His excellent academic record, and the prominence and notice he had earned in intellectual and political circles did, however, lead to a successful application for the new Chair of Jurisprudence and Political Economy at Galway.

One of the great defects of the new law schools was undoubtedly that the law professors were non-resident. There was nothing in the constitution of the Colleges which required such an arrangement, and what little evidence there is, strongly suggests that the recruitment of part-time non-resident professors was a pragmatic response to the inadequate funding of the Colleges, which had to be stretched even more thinly when the number of professors was raised without any increase in the overall endowment. Unlike disciplines such as medicine, in which a part-time professor could carry on his medical practice near the College, the law professor who was also a barrister had to attend his circuit and the Dublin courts during the law terms. That the implications were understood and consented to, there is no doubt, and the College authorities must be implicated in the failure to adequately resource the law schools from the beginning. The issue was put to Heron by the Queen's College Commissioners and he naturally defended the practice:

> 4256. *Mr. Gibson*– When you state the Professors in Law are non-resident, that arises from the circumstances of these Professors having other pursuits to attend to? –
> [*Heron*] They are practising barristers.
>
> 4257. [*Mr. Gibson*] – Keeping your Terms here, does not interfere with the terms in Dublin –
> [*Heron*] It does not.
>
> 4258. [*Mr. Gibson*] – At the time you were appointed, it was known you had other pursuits to attend to? –
> [*Heron*] It was well known. The arrangements as regards College lectures were left to the good sense of the Professors and the College Council, and no inconvenience has ever arisen in this respect.[123]

---

122 *Transactions of the Dublin Statistical Society*, 1 (1847–9), p. 22; see also McEldowney and O'Higgins, 'Irish Legal History', in McEldowney and O'Higgins, *The Common Law Tradition*, pp. 206–7; Black, *Centenary Volume*, footnote 1, pp. 25–6.
123 *Queen's Colleges Commission Report*, 1858, Minutes of Evidence, questions 4256–8, p. 289.

The division of academic duties as between the Professor of English Law and the Professor of Jurisprudence and Political Economy seems to have evolved more or less uniformly in the three Colleges, partly based on the functional titles of the chairs. From the minute of the evidence given by Heron to the Queen's College Commission in 1857, we know that the law course given at Galway was as agreed by all the law professors in October 1849 which they 'considered would be the most useful one'. Professor Heron described to the commissioners the division of labour between himself and Hugh Law:

> Accordingly, in the First-year course you will find the Law of Property and the Principles of Convevancing, – Professor Law takes that department; you will also find Jurisprudence, which is my department. In the Second year Professor Law takes Equity and Bankruptcy, and I take Civil Law. In this subject I give the students instruction in the *Institutes of Justinian*, and in the History of the Civil Law ... In the Third year Common and Criminal Law come in, which is taught by Professor Law. In the Fourth year, there is an extended course of study on the subjects I have mentioned, a course on the Law of Evidence and Pleading, and I take up Constitutional Law, the book I use being, Hallam's *Constitutional History of England*. I also put the students very briefly over International Law from Wheaton's *Elements*. I give a very short course on Colonial Law; but I do not find that it is practically of any use.[124]

He explained also that he gave the course of lectures on Jurisprudence and Political Economy to the third year Faculty of Arts students. When it was suggested that he and Professor Law together gave 'a complete professional education to the students of Law', Professor Heron agreed that they did.[125]

Some indication of the content of legal education provided at that time can be gleaned from the surviving materials. These include the formal law examination papers for scholarships and for University awards, which were by printed examination papers that were later published in the College and University reports. An indication of syllabus and required reading is also available, as these were printed, in the case of scholarship examinations, and were occasionally referred to in the professors' reports. A similar division of subjects was adopted in all the Colleges.[126] The Professor of Jurisprudence and Political Economy gave the

---

124 Ibid., Minutes of Evidence, questions 4241–2, p. 288. (Italics have been added, otherwise capitalisation is left unchanged.)
125 Ibid., Minutes of Evidence, question 4243 p. 288: 'By your combined efforts, you and the Professor of English Law give a complete professional education to the students in Law? – The Faculty of Law gives a complete course of education in Law'.
126 Ibid., evidence of Echlin Molyneux, Professor of English Law, Belfast. As regards the Professor of Jurisprudence and Political Economy, he stated: 'My colleague will state what courses he is bound to deliver, embracing the subject of Jurisprudence, Civil Law, International Law, Constitutional Law, and Colonial Law'. A supplemental written statement by Professor Leslie indicates that he gave twenty-four lectures in these subjects, and a like number on Political Economy, but regarded the field to be so vast as to be oppressive and unfair to students (ibid., p. 327). Professor Horner Mills, in Cork, appears to have had a lighter burden: 'Roman Law and

courses in Jurisprudence, Civil Law (that is, Roman Law), Political Economy (the forerunner of modern economics, and intended primarily for third-year Arts students), and Constitutional, International and Colonial Law. The Professor of English Law gave the courses in the Law of Property and Conveyancing, Equity and Bankruptcy, Common and Criminal Law, and the Law of Evidence and Pleading. Common Law apparently consisted of Contract Law for the most part. The procedural aspects of Equity and Criminal Law were also covered in these courses.[127] Thus, the more professionally-oriented law subjects tended to be the province of the Professor of English Law, whereas subjects of a more philosophical, historical and comparative nature were assigned to the Professor of Jurisprudence and Political Economy. The syllabi, examinations, and courses, suggest that a high standard was expected of students. Limits on space in this volume do not, unfortunately, allow for a detailed exploration of these materials on this occasion, and only the more problematic subjects will be considered.

Although Heron, who had a scholarly interest in the subject, satisfactorily addressed the problem of teaching Jurisprudence at QCG, the subject presented difficulties in the other Queen's Colleges. Professor Mills at Cork was particularly unhappy with the then state of the subject. He could find no general principles or anything scientific in Jurisprudence, and he clearly found it a subject which was very difficult to teach. When asked to 'favor' the commissioners with a statement of what he taught in Jurisprudence, Mills, having informed them that he found the subject vague and indefinite, continued:

> There are almost no books upon Jurisprudence. There is such a variety of subjects comprised under the term Jurisprudence, that it is not very easy to know what to teach. The London University, so indefinite is the subject, calls it the Science of Legislation, and the book they examine on is Bentham. In other Colleges they take selections from Whewell's Elements of Morality, parts of Justinian, and some German authors. In the Queen's Colleges there is greatly in use a book called Reddie's Inquiries in the Science of Law, but none of us think it a very desirable book if better could be had ... I do not mean to disparage the importance of the subjects which may be embraced in Jurisprudence; but it has no fixed general principles, and I speak from experience, that in attempting to reduce it to any thing like the shape of a Science, I have never been able to lay down general principles, and draw conclusions with any reasonable degree of probability.[128]

Professor Cliffe Leslie at QCB was closer to Heron in his views on the subject. He informed the Queen's Colleges Commission that he endeavoured to combine the historical and philosophical methods of teaching Jurisprudence:

Jurisprudence are the portions of instruction in the Law School with which I am charged'. (Ibid., question 2311, p. 228.)
127 Ibid., Professor Molyneux's evidence, questions 1552, 1558.
128 Ibid., Minutes of Evidence, question 3230, p. 229.

> 1574. *Mr. Price.* – What do you teach under the head of Jurisprudence?–
> [*Leslie:*] I have endeavoured to combine the historical method, with what is called the Philosophical method of teaching the subject. I treat of the various views which have been taken of Law by the greatest philosophers, from time to time; but more especially, I trace the formation of our own Legal system. I trace the origin of the Court of Chancery, show how the division between Law and Equity arose, and what the results of the present system are, and what the facilities for fusion may be.[129]

When asked what was the philosophical branch of Jurisprudence, Leslie replied: 'I go into the general principles of Law, and I briefly do that with reference to Political Philosophy, as that is one of the subjects of examination for Writerships'. He was of the view, however, that 'Suitable and sufficient text-books, upon the general principles of Jurisprudence do not exist',[130] – a problem which may be said to continue to the present day.[131] Such differences had practical implications because the University awards of the Law Diploma and LLB degree were based on common exams. Where the examiner's views were different from those of a College professor, the students were at a disadvantage in that they were not adequately prepared for the examinations. In his more carefully-crafted remarks in a supplementary statement to the Commissioners, Cliffe Leslie, who was just completing a two-year stint as university examiner, emphasised the need for a uniform syllabus, and specifically recommended Bacon and Bentham as texts in Jurisprudence:

> And it is further necessary that the Professors of the three Colleges should be required to teach the principles of Jurisprudence upon a common system, since the students are examined in common in the University; The history of the principal changes that have taken place in the laws relating to property and the mode of administering justice, is a subject to which the Professor's lectures might with great advantage be principally directed; while definite selections from the writings of Lord Bacon, Bentham, and other authors, might be agreed on as text-books for the students.[132]

Civil or Roman Law also presented difficulties as a curricular subject. The problem did not arise at Galway, perhaps in part, because both Law and Heron had

---

129 Ibid., questions 1574–5, p. 99.
130 Ibid., supplementary statement by Leslie, p. 327.
131 The late Professor J.M. Kelly, as he explained in the preface to his book, *A Short History of Western Legal Theory* (Oxford, 1992), was prompted to write that work by the lack of an appropriate text for his Jurisprudence classes. Among the problems he identified were the differences in approach and subject matter by other authors, an over-concentration on more recent writers by Anglo-American scholars, and the mutual ignorance of each other's scholarship by the common law and civil law traditions. In a letter to Tony Honoré he wrote: 'Perhaps there is too much sailing under the flag of "jurisprudence" and it might more rationally be divided into two subjects: (a) history of legal theory; (b) modern philosophy of law. At any rate I think law students should not graduate without knowing a little about how we arrived where we are'. (Preface, p. xvi).
132 *Queen's Colleges Commission Report*, 1858, supplementary statement by Leslie, p. 327.

taken Classics at TCD. The situation was very different at Cork and Belfast. The role of the subject, and whether it should be on the curriculum at all, were the troubling issues rather than the matter of texts. Cliffe Leslie considered the subject too broad: 'Civil Law, alone, opens a field of unlimited extent for laborious study'.[133] From his evidence to the Queen's Colleges Commissioners, it is clear that he considered it a subject of little practical use:

> 1577. What do you teach under the head of Civil Law? –
> [*Leslie*:] It is a most important element in the formation of the Court of Chancery, and I take that as the means of giving a history of the Civil Law – not only tracing its general history and present condition over the world, but also showing how gradually it worked its way into the doctrine of Equity.
>
> 1578. Have you courts in Ireland at all corresponding to Doctors' Commons? –
> [*Leslie*:] Yes; but no Degree is necessary for practising there.
>
> 1579. Is there no field for the study of Civil Law? –
> [*Leslie*:] The class of persons living by it is so limited, that I cannot say any instruction would be of much use at present.

As far as Cliffe Leslie was concerned it would, he wrote, be a 'most desirable alteration' to omit Civil Law entirely from the legal curriculum.[134] Professor Mills at QCC held similar views. He was clearly disappointed at the low number of students taking courses in both Civil Law and Jurisprudence, and suggested abolishing that portion of the law programme entirely. He pointed out that Civil or Roman Law was required by the Bar only in the case of non-graduates. As regards the other branch, the attorneys: 'I certainly do not conceive that the attorney profession would at all value, nor do I say, in a strictly professional School, ought they value a knowledge of Roman Law and of Jurisprudence'.[135] Although a knowledge of Civil Law was necessary for practice in the Ecclesiastical Courts, 'the practice in them' was, he said, 'very limited, and the general feeling is that they will soon be removed'.[136] As an exponent of purely practical professional law teaching, he could see no benefit in teaching either Jurisprudence or Civil Law.

The subject which caused the most difficulty in the LLB programme was probably Colonial Law, which Heron regarded as of little use. 'In the Fourth year', he explained,[137] 'I take up Constitutional Law, the book I use being, Hallam's *Constitutional History of England*. I also put the students very briefly over International Law from Wheaton's *Elements*. I give a very short course on Colonial Law; but I do not find that it is practically of any use'. None of the professors were happy with Colonial Law as a subject. Cliffe Leslie who had 'considerable

---

133 Ibid.
134 Ibid.
135 Ibid., *Minutes of Evidence*, question 3211, p. 288.
136 Ibid., question 3215, p. 229.
137 Ibid., question 4242, p. 288.

difficulty' with both Colonial and International Law, admitted that there were no means of 'keeping up' his knowledge of these subjects and he was 'not prepared to give lectures on the laws of all our Dependencies',[138] 'All hitherto done', he said, 'has been to give a sketch of the different Colonial Constitutions';[139] He considered it 'a most desirable alteration' to omit both Colonial Law as well as Civil Law from the programme.[140] Not surprisingly, Colonial Law was taken off the curriculum in the 1860s.

In a 'Supplementary Statement' to the Queen's Colleges Commissioners, Cliffe Leslie set out his views on 'The Necessity for some Alterations in the Department of Jurisprudence and Political Economy'. In this document, he took the opportunity to criticise the excessive content of the Arts course, and the injustice of the Benchers in giving preferential recognition and status to the law lectures at Trinity College: 'It is', he argued, 'only just that attendance on the lectures in the Law Schools of the Queen's Colleges should be equally recognised'. His first three objections to the arrangements for the Chair of Jurisprudence and Political Economy summarise the main criticisms of the new law programme and give us an insight into the problems of the law professor of that period:

> First; it would require the devotion of the whole time of a Professor of extraordinary attainments to give instruction, in a suitable manner, upon such a variety of subjects; while the Chair does not offer advantages which can by possibility secure such services. The present emoluments of the Chair were settled upon the supposition that its occupant would always be a practising barrister.
>
> Secondly; the course is oppressive, and operates unfairly upon the Law students. Civil Law, alone, opens a field of unlimited extent for laborious study. Suitable and sufficient text-books, upon the general principles of Jurisprudence do not exist. The Professor must be nearly as much puzzled as the student how to deal with Colonial Law; so that, when the latter is about to proceed for his Diploma or Degree in the University, he must be quite at a loss how to prepare for an Examination conducted by a Professor of a different College from his own.
>
> Thirdly; however great may be the value of Roman Law, as part of a complete education in Scientific Jurisprudence, it is unlikely that it will ever be regarded as useful or interesting by the class of young men who may be expected to join the Law classes in the Queen's Colleges.[141]

If there was any serious dissatisfaction in the Law Faculty at Galway in the very early years, it is not evident from surviving records. The impression given is one of serious academic endeavour by a small, intimate group of students and staff. The College session began in the third week of October and ended on the second

---

138 Ibid., question 1581, pp. 99–100.
139 Ibid., question 1582, p. 100.
140 Ibid., supplementary statement, xvi, p. 327.
141 Ibid.

Saturday in June, with recesses at Christmas and Easter. The Law courses consisted typically of 24 lectures per subject, delivered in the months of October, December, and February. There were three examining periods: one for scholarships in October, another in February for prizes, and the general sessional examinations in June.[142] The reports of the law professors reveal very small, but attentive, well-disciplined, and hard-working classes. In 1851, for example, Professor Heron was able to report that 'The conduct, attendance, and answering of the Students at the Lectures and Examinations have been most satisfactory'.[143] Professor Law's satisfaction with his students is also evident from his entry in the President's Report:

> The attendance of the Students has been throughout as regular as could be expected, considering the extent to which their time has hitherto been occupied with their other studies; and their attention and anxiety to receive instruction during the Lectures has been always highly satisfactory and encouraging. The answering too of *all* of them, both at the examinations for scholarships and at those held for prizes, was exceedingly good; evincing not only a substantially accurate recollection of the Lectures previously delivered, but also a very careful study of those books which the Professor had recommended for their private reading.[144]

In the following year, Professor Law was again pleased with his students, but his report provides further evidence of the extent of their courses, and suggests the need for an occasional motivational 'push':

> As to the attention and progress of all, I think it but just to say, that although, perhaps, more rapid progress might have been made, still, considering the variety of subjects which occupy the time of the Students in their other courses, I cannot but commend their industry and attention while prosecuting their legal studies; and I may add, that it has *very* seldom, indeed, been necessary for me to urge them to greater exertion.[145]

His report for 1852–3 reveals a similar story. After listing the number of his students, Professor Law reported his great pleasure in testifying to the 'industry and attention uniformly exhibited by all these gentlemen in the prosecution of their legal studies'. Professor Heron's comments for these years were similar but more reserved and impersonal. He reported in 1852: 'The Professor of Jurisprudence and Political Economy, in conclusion, begs to speak in the highest terms of the diligence and conduct of his Classes during the Session'. In the following year, after listing his student class numbers, he wrote: 'The Classes were attentive and diligent. The 13 Students above-mentioned passed their Sessional Examinations. Other Students attended the above courses without so doing'.[146]

---

142 QCG *Calendar*, 1851, pp. 23, 54; President's *Report*, 1850–1, p. 59.
143 President's *Report*, 1850–1, p. 59.
144 Ibid.
145 President's *Report*, 1851–2, p. 12.
146 President's *Report*, 1852–3, p. 9. That same year, Simon McCoy reported giving thirty lectures

Liam O'Malley *on Law*

The Subsequent Career of Professor Hugh Law

Professor Hugh Law had been called to the Irish Bar in 1840 but only for actions in the Court of Chancery (fig. 2.2). It was a court where advocates were 'not brought prominently before the public' and Law, 'undistinguished by those powers of oratory not rare at the Irish Bar', did not gain the same reputation as men of 'far less professional conceit'.[147] Law took no obvious interest in politics in his earlier career and appeared to have surprised contemporaries by coming out as a firm Liberal in later life. That he was already well established as a barrister while a professor at QCG is shown by the fact that he was, soon after, appointed a Queen's Counsel on 4 July 1860. His professional practice had grown to such an extent by the late 1850s that he could no longer successfully fulfill his duties at QCG. He resigned his post as Professor of English Law 'with great reluctance' on 1 December 1858, finding it 'now impossible to devote the time required for the proper discharge of its duties', and leaving it to be filled, as he put it, 'by someone whose professional engagements are less engrossing'.[148]

There is indirect evidence that pressure of legal work at the Bar may have forced him to compress his lectures into shorter time periods, and that this did not meet with the approval of the College. Two resolutions of the Council were passed in November 1858 which may have either led to Professor Law's resignation or, more likely, may have been made in the knowledge of his impending resignation, with a view to the binding of his successor. The Council resolved, firstly, that 'in order to secure the efficient working of the Law School in this College it will be quite necessary to provide that the lectures be delivered during a period of at least eight weeks in each Session', and secondly, that the 'lectures should be distributed through two terms, but is anxious to meet the wishes of the Professors as to the times which should be selected within the specified limits'. Professor Law's letter of resignation, together with copies of the Council's resolutions, were sent to the Lord Lieutenant's office by the President on 10 December 1858. President Berwick expressed the Council's earnest wish that, if approved, the resolutions should be brought to the attention of the candidates for the vacant professorship. He informed the Lord Lieutenant's office that, as the first term ended on 18 December, a new appointment need not be made until 'about the 7th or 10th of January'.[149] That the law lecture times had become a serious issue is also evidenced by a letter sent to the Secretary for Ireland, by Augustus Bensbach MD, Professor of Modern Languages and Dean of the Literary Division of the Arts Faculty. As

---

to medical and law students, but complained of the lack of resources: 'The want of any special fund to procure the necessary materials to illustrate those Lectures, threw a great deal of additional labour and some expense on me, as I had to make most of the tests for the analysis or poisons, to provide suitable apparatus, and various other matters necessary to a proper demonstration of the different parts of the course'.

147 Obituary, *Annual Register*, 1883 (London, 1884), pp. 168–9.
148 National Archives, MS CSORP 1858/19725. Hugh Law to Edmund Berwick, 1 December 1858. Law's address is given as 4 Great Denmark Street, Dublin.
149 Ibid., Berwick to the Chief Secretary's Office with Law's letter of resignation and the resolutions as enclosures.

a member of the Council he considered it his duty, he wrote, 'to inform you that the Law School of this College is not working well and that you should make some inquiries before you fill up the office of the Chair now vacant through the resignation of Professor Law'.[150] Whether the attendance at College of one or both of the law professors was the full extent of the problem is unclear. It probably was, as Bensbach appears to have been something of an interfering busybody. When William B. Campion BA was appointed as the new Professor of English Law in February 1859, he found himself immediately accosted by Bensbach in an unreasonable and interfering manner as soon as he had arrived in the College.[151]

After taking silk in 1860, Hugh Law quickly rose to prominence in legal and political circles. He retained his interest in legal education for a time, and accepted a three-year appointment as part-time Law Professor at the King's Inns.[152] In 1863 he married Ellen Maria or 'Helen',[153] youngest daughter of William White of Shrubs, Co. Dublin. 'Mr Law', it was noted, 'had not at that time appeared upon the surface of political life, and was known only as a lawyer, more sound than showy, whose business, except on circuit, was almost exclusively at the Chancery Bar'.[154] He continued to build up a very successful practice on the north-east circuit, however, and openly declared himself for the Liberals. His ability and support were soon officially recognised when, following William Gladstone's appointment as Prime Minister in 1868, he was appointed Law Adviser to the Government in Ireland, and was elected a Bencher of the King's Inns in 1870. Gladstone, who received and needed Irish support, had committed himself to the redress of Irish grievances.[155] As part of his policy for Ireland, he had pledged three measures in particular: the disestablishment and disendowment of the Church of Ireland, a land reform bill to assist hard-pressed Irish tenants, and a Universities bill to meet the demands of the Catholic hierarchy for Catholic education. Law was intimately associated with the resolution of the first two of these issues.

Both disestablishment and land reform had been on the Liberal agenda for many years, and had been effectively promoted by the advocacy of John Bright.[156]

---

150 National Archives, MS CSORP, 1858/30304.
151 Anon., *Memoir of William Bennett Campion, Serjeant-at-Law* (Dublin, 1911), pp. 51–3.
152 The holders of the King's Inns professorships up to 1872 are listed by Professor Mark S. O'Shaughnessy, 'On Legal Education in Ireland', *Journal of the Statistical and Social Inquiry Society of Ireland*, 6 (1871–6), p. 132 (paper read in November 1872).
153 The name is given as 'Helen' in various numbers of *Thom's Directory*. Their residence is given as 9 Fitzwilliam Square.
154 Obituary, *Annual Register*, 1883, p. 168.
155 On hearing that he was to lead the Government in 1868, Gladstone is supposed to have said 'My mission is to pacify Ireland'. (See Stephen J. Lee, *Aspects of British Political History, 1815–1914* [London and New York, 1994], p. 167.) By tackling Irish grievances he hoped to make Fenianism redundant: 'our purpose & duty is to endeavour to draw a line between the Fenians & the people of Ireland, & to make the people of Ireland indisposed to cross it'. (This is from a letter to General C. Grey, quoted by H.C.G. Matthew, *Gladstone, 1809–1974* (Oxford, 1988), p. 192.)
156 Bright (1811–89) was the son of a Quaker miller of Rochdale who served successively as MP for Durham, Manchester, and Birmingham. He advocated far-reaching reforms in Ireland following a post-famine visit in 1849. He was president of the Board of Trade, 1868–71, when he contributed to the Irish Church Disestablishment bill (a policy he had long supported) and to

2.2 Hugh Law, Professor of English Law, 1849–59

Disestablishment, the notion of a free Church in a free State, helped maintain an alliance between Irish Catholics and English and Scottish Dissenters as it was an issue on which they could readily agree. Gladstone had come out in favour of disestablishment even before the election of 1868 and, following his election with a strong majority, he pushed ahead with the Irish Church Disestablishment bill in the 1869 parliamentary session.[157] Hugh Law is usually credited with having drafted the legislation – 'a monument of his knowledge and skill' – although, according to one account, he prepared the initial draft, and the bill was then

the Landlord and Tenant bill, 1870. He was responsible for the inclusion of land-purchase provisions in the Land bill which were referred to as the 'Bright clauses'.

157 33 & 34 Vict. c. 42. Although the Act was a tremendous shock to the establishment, it was extremely generous. The Church of Ireland became a voluntary body from 1871, with its investment resources held by Commissioners. A large proportion of its wealth was paid out in compensation, most of the remainder given over to charitable purposes. Thus, the Church was substantially re-endowed but on a private basis. It was nevertheless a major political undertaking, given the central constitutional importance of the Anglican Church.

completed, on the instructions of a Cabinet committee, by the Parliamentary counsel who was assisted by Law and Sir Edward Sullivan.[158] The obituary in the *Annual Register* of 1883 states:

> To Mr Law was entrusted the task of drafting the Irish Church Bill, and the comparative ease with which it has been interpreted and worked bears testimony to the technical skill and legal knowledge of its framer. Even those who were most bitterly opposed to the policy of the Bill, and were filled with resentment against all who assisted in securing its enactment, felt constrained to pay the tribute of their admiration to the counsel who had drawn the measure so well.

Law is also credited[159] with the drafting of the 'equally astute',[160] and landmark Bill which became Gladstone's Landlord and Tenant Act, 1870, generally known as the Irish Land Act, 1870.[161] The Act was the first serious attempt to redress the appalling problems of land tenure in Ireland by curtailing the absolute ownership of landlords.[162] Given the prevailing economic philosophy of free trade in land, and the political power of the landlord class, the legislation had to be drafted with pragmatic sensitivity and subtlety. Its three principal objects were security of tenure for tenants, the encouragement of agricultural improvements, and the

---

158 *Irish Law Times and Solicitors' Journal*, 15 September 1883, pp. 489–90. The *DNB* attributes the bill to Law alone: 'Until the disestablishment of the Irish church was proposed, he took little part in politics, though generally he was believed to be a conservative, but he then sided with the liberal party, drafted the Irish Church Act, a monument of his knowledge and skill; he was also the draftsman of the Irish Land Act of 1870'. Matthew, in his *Gladstone* (pp. 191–3) states that Gladstone personally 'prepared' the Bill in consultation with selected advisers, and Thring, the parliamentary draftsman. It would appear that the policy and heads of the Bill were negotiated and agreed under his personal supervision and Law did the crucial drafting.

159 See for example, *Irish Times*, 11 September 1883; obituary in the *Annual Register* 1883 (London, 1884), p. 168.

160 R.F. Foster, *Modern Ireland 1600–1972* (London, 1989), p. 396. Foster writes that: 'This cautiously introduced some principles of tenant protection – about one and a half of the "3 F's" ... Little changed in practice. Tenants grumbled, and landlords were outraged. But the reasons for their outrage were significant. However tentatively, Gladstone had interfered with property rights; his theoretical principles of compensation implicitly admitted the Irish tenant's moral property in the holding' (pp. 396–7).

161 33 & 34 Vict. c. 46. The Act legalized, or at least confirmed the legality of, the Ulster tenant right custom which had long recognised the tenant's right to compensation for goodwill in, and improvement made to, land held by him when the landlord resumed possession. The Act also gave a new statutory tenant right to all tenants in the form of compensation for disturbance, which could be assessed by County Court Judges and was subject to a statutory maximum. Tenants entitled to the benefit of the Ulster Custom could choose to claim under the Custom or under the new statutory tenant right to compensation for disturbance.

162 A number of limited tenant-right bills had been privately introduced in the Commons since 1835 without success. For an account of these bills, see D.C. Heron, 'On the Landlord and Tenant (Ireland) Act, 1870', *Journal of the Statistical and Social Inquiry Society of Ireland*, 6 (1871–6), p. 64 (paper read 22 December 1871). A growing political interest on the part of the Liberals, together with the pressure of tenant right meetings, especially in Ulster, from 1867 on, help explain Gladstone's land policy. The Irish land problem had, however, a long and complex

creation of a peasant proprietorship.[163] In endeavouring to achieve these ends, the framers, as Richey put it, 'dared not to state openly (and it was constantly denied) that the object of this statute was to give the tenant any estate in the land, or to transfer to him any portion of the absolute ownership'.[164] If a landlord attempted to disturb the tenant, however, the Act empowered the tenant to refuse to give up possession without compensation – the absolute property right of the landlord no longer existed:

> Under this statute the tenant did not acquire any 'estate' in the land, if the term 'estate' is used in its technical English meaning; but of the ownership of the land, whether the word be used in its popular or proper meaning, he did acquire a share; for if a man cannot be put out of possession by the rightful owner without the payment of a certain sum of money, he is an owner to the extent of the sum requisite to buy him out.[165]

Although the Act was too limited in scope to solve the land problem, it was perhaps as much as could be then achieved, and has been judged important as 'the precursor of the great remedial measures on behalf of the tenants which were to follow'.[166] A more radical bill was enacted in 1881, and Hugh Law was also

---

      background. The Devon Commission (1843–5) had considered Irish land tenure problems, and had recommended, among other improvements, compensation for disturbance (*Parliamentary Papers* 1845 xix–xxii). A variety of developments had increased the number of evictions and made legislative intervention to alleviate the distress of tenants imperative. There were pressures and incentives to consolidate the size of farms – of a political nature in the case of the abolition of the 40 shilling freehold franchise in 1829 (replaced by a £10 freehold franchise); of an economic nature in the case of the poor-law rates, after 1838, where the burden fell wholly on the landlord where the tenant valuation was at or under £4; and as a result of the repeal of the Corn Law in 1846 by Peel, partly as an anti-Famine measure. The latter measure made tillage by tenants on small, often marginal land, economically non-viable. Both the Act to facilitate the Sale of Encumbered Estates, 1848, and the Landlord and Tenant Act, 1860 which put the relationship of landlord and tenant on a contractual basis, promoted free and unfettered trade in land, and consequent disregard for tenants. Cf. J.C. Brady, 'English Law and Irish Land in the Nineteenth Century', *Northern Ireland Legal Quarterly*, 23 (1972), pp. 24–47; E.D. Steele, *Irish Land and British Politics: Tenant Right and Nationality, 1865–1870* (Cambridge, 1974).

163 For a contemporary account of the Act's provisions see Robert Donnell (holder of the chair of Jurisprudence and Political Economy at QCG, 1876–83), *A Practical Guide to the Law of Tenant Compensation and Farm Purchase under the Irish Land Act* (Dublin, 1871); *Reports of One Hundred and Ninety Cases in the Irish Land Courts with Preliminary Tenant Right Chapters* (Dublin, 1876). For a contemporary view of the Act's 'success', see Heron 'On the Landlord and Tenant (Ireland) Act'. Some of the intellectual analysis and economic thinking behind the Act came from William Neilson Hancock, founder of the Dublin Statistical Society and first holder of the Chair of Jurisprudence and Political Economy at QCB. Hancock, who was very interested in practical problems, published *The Tenant Right of Ulster; Considered Economically* (Dublin, 1845), and *Report on the Landlord and Tenant Question in Ireland* (Dublin, 1866). Chichester Fortescue, the Irish Secretary, had himself been involved with the failed Irish Land Bill of 1866.

164 Alexander G. Richey, *The Irish Land Laws* (London, 1880), p. 64.

165 Ibid., p. 65.

166 C. F. Kolbert and T. O'Brien, *Land Reform in Ireland* (Cambridge, 1975). The Catholic hierarchy was moderately satisfied with it but there was division within the National Association as to its merits. With the continued dominance of the propertied classes in Parliament, and the rise of

intimately connected with it. During his period as Law Adviser, he chaired a Commission of inquiry into alleged electoral corruption, which was reported by Judge Keogh to have taken place among the Freemen voters of the City of Dublin, during the 1868 election which returned Sir Arthur Guinness and Mr Pim to Parliament. In recognition of his standing, Law was elected a Bencher of the Honorable Society of King's Inns in 1870.[167]

In January 1872, Richard Dowse QC vacated the office of Solicitor-General to become the new Attorney-General, the latter office having become vacant when the holder, Charles Robert Barry QC was appointed judge of the Court of Queen's Bench. Although Hugh Law was in line for the vacant post of Solicitor-General, he was passed over in favour of the more junior but very able Christopher Palles, probably because there was a need for a Catholic appointment. In November, however, he succeeded to the post when Palles became Attorney-General, Dowse having vacated the latter office to become Baron in the Court of Exchequer. There was a tradition that one or both of the senior law officers should be Members of Parliament to enable them to deal with the Irish Government's legislative and legal business in the House of Commons. As neither Law nor Palles were Members of Parliament, Palles was chosen by the Liberals to contest the Londonderry seat vacated by Dowse, but was unsuccessful. Palles and Law spent much of their time going back and forth to London to advise the Government on Irish legal affairs.[168]

The third element of Gladstone's Irish policy, the university issue, turned out to be a disaster for the Government party. The most important issue, as far as the Irish Catholic hierarchy was concerned, was education. In August 1869 the bishops, meeting at Maynooth, once more condemned mixed education and set out their demands in a series of resolutions. Unable to deal with other aspects of the problem, Gladstone's cabinet took up the unsettled university issue in November 1872, resulting in a University Bill which came before the Commons in February 1873. It was proposed to separate the University of Dublin from TCD and transform it into a federal, degree-awarding, Irish National University, to which the Colleges would be affiliated. These Colleges were to include TCD, QCB, QCC, the Catholic College in Dublin, and Magee College in Derry. Unhappily, Queen's College Galway was not to be included. The Bill did not propose to do away with mixed education, nor did it endow Catholic university education. It was condemned but not totally rejected by the hierarchy. Luckily for QCG, most of the Irish members and some of the Liberals sided with the

---

anti-Catholic feeling in England, it is doubtful if anything more radical could be then achieved. The rise of the Home Rule party after 1870 and the later pressures of the Land League, would, of course, facilitate more radical changes.

167 *Irish Law Times and Solicitors' Journal*, 15 September 1883, pp. 489–90.

168 Delany, *Christopher Palles*, pp. 56–8, 65–6. The story of Palles's election campaign for Derry is narrated at pp. 67–74. Among his difficulties were his unpopularity for having to prosecute, as Attorney-General, thirty-six persons for undue influence under the Corrupt Practices Act, 1854, arising out of Judge Keogh's finding of clerical interference in the election of Captain Nolan at Galway in February 1872. Among the accused were the bishop of Clonfert and nineteen Catholic clergy. Palles was also unpopular with non-Catholics for his stand on Catholic education – he was a close friend of Cardinal Cullen.

Conservatives in opposing the measure. Even though Gladstone made the vote on the Bill a matter of confidence in the Government, it was defeated by three votes on 11 March 1873.[169] Gladstone resigned, but had to resume and complete his term of office when Disraeli and the Conservatives refused to form a government. In the following election in February 1874, Gladstone and the Liberals lost their majority in the Commons, and the Conservatives temporarily took power. Hugh Law did, however, secure a seat for the Liberals, having been elected MP for Londonderry, a seat he held until he became Irish lord chancellor in 1881. A mere matter of hours before Gladstone surrendered his seals of office to the Queen, he appointed Palles as the new lord chief baron of the court of exchequer. For a brief period, Hugh Law succeeded him as attorney-general. He was appointed a member of the Irish Privy Council in 1874,[170] and became the recognised head of the Irish Liberals.

With his party out of office during Disraeli's second administration, Law returned to his work as a barrister. Although a leading barrister on the north-east circuit, he practised principally in the Courts of Chancery (Equity) in Dublin and in Irish appeals in the House of Lords.[171] It is said of him that 'he won the reputation of being a keen cross-examiner', and 'held briefs in many ... *causes célèbres*, such as *Bagot v. Bagot*, and the great Blackwater Fishery case'. Above all, he was 'distinguished as a real property lawyer of pre-eminent ability'.[172] When Gladstone became once more prime minister in 1880, Law was re-appointed attorney-general[173] and member of the privy council in Ireland. (He had been re-elected member for Londonderry the same year.) As Irish attorney-general and MP, Law was closely involved with two of the most contentious issues of that period: the 'State Trials' brought against Parnell and other Land League members, and the Land Act, 1881.

The Parnell trial (the case against the 'Traversers') began on the 28 December 1880. The counsel for the crown, led by Law as attorney-general included, among others, Serjeant Denis C. Heron, and Constantine Molloy QC, who was the greatest authority on the criminal law at the time. Law's opening of the case lasted three days. Precautions were taken to counter disturbances in the city, but these were found unnecessary and, although the move to prosecute was bold and sensational, the hearing itself was not found particularly exciting:

> The dramatic effect of the 'State Trials' was not striking. A small room, hot and crowded. Mr Law with his back to us making his speech, which went on for three days – Traversers in a semi-circle opposite (Mr Parnell I did not

---

169 For an account of the events surrounding the University Bill, see Norman, *The Catholic Church and Ireland*, chapter 9, 'Episcopal Agitation: A Last Phase 1870–3', pp. 409–62, particularly pp. 446–53.
170 Delany, *Christopher Palles*, pp. 82–5; *Irish Law Times and Solicitors' Journal*, 15 September 1883, p. 489; *DNB*. One account states that Law was attorney-general from January to March 1874, but as Palles's appointment dated from 16 February, Law must have held the office at that time for only a few weeks in February and March, until the establishment of the Disraeli administration.
171 *DNB*.
172 *Irish Law Times and Solicitors' Journal*, 15 September 1883, p. 489.
173 10 May 1880.

recognise at first from his having shaved off his light-brown beard) – Mr Dillon reading the *Pall Mall* – above, the two Judges in scarlet – on the right the Jury – a throng of lawyers going in and out – a number of people standing about in the fine central hall of the Four Courts waiting to find room – perfect indifference apparently on all sides.[174]

After Law had opened the case, the prosecution witnesses, mainly constabulary note-takers, gave their evidence of Land League meetings, and the speeches of the traversers and others. In opening for the defence, Francis McDonagh QC side-stepped the issues by characterising the prosecution as 'a landlord's indictment against the tenants, nothing more or less',[175] and by suggesting that there were no contracts in equity to be interfered with as there was a total absence of equality and freedom of contract as between the powerful landlord and powerless tenant. The defence had intended to use the nineteenth count to introduce extensive evidence of evictions back in 1848–9 and turn the proceedings into an indictment of landlordism. The crown side put an end to this and substantially shortened the proceedings by abandoning the count entirely.[176] The defence fell back on the argument that the primary intent of the Land League was to prevent the hardship of evictions and not the injury of the landlords. Heron, who had examined many of the prosecution witnesses, gave the closing address for the crown. In spite of a well-presented case which ran for over twenty days, and Law's opening address, which was said to be 'a model of masterly clearness, order, and argumentative force', the jury in *The Queen v. Parnell and others* had to be discharged without agreeing a verdict.[177] It was well known that two jurors, one of them a Quaker, refused to join the majority in an acquittal. It was said of Law that 'he displayed so much tact and moderation in the task as to escape altogether the popular odium which fell so heavily on those responsible for the maintenance of law and order'.[178]

---

174 T.W. Moody and Richard Hawkins (eds), *Florence Arnold-Forster's Irish Journal* (Oxford, 1988), p. 47. (Journal entry for 29 December 1880). The judges were John David Fitzgerald and Charles Robert Barry. The court room scene was captured by W.T. Parkes who depicts counsel, presumably Law, addressing the court. A print of the original, which is in the Dublin Civic Museum, is to be found in Noel Kissane, *Parnell: A Documentary History* (Dublin, 1991), p. 34.

175 For a summary account of the trial, see J. McDonnel Bodkin, *Famous Irish Trials* (Dublin and London, 1918), pp. 157–70.

176 Molloy had been consulted on the indictments, but the dropping of the nineteenth count gave scope for the Bar wits. Verse which circulated on the issue, written by Jack Humphreys, included the lines: 'In the Library he sat, // Someone cried "Ahoy" // Holy Saints, what name was that ? // Constantine Molloy!! // But the nineteenth count was bad, // Would not do, my boy; // This is very, very sad, // Constantine Molloy'. Quoted by Sir John Ross, *The Years of My Pilgrimage* (London, 1924), p. 39.

177 A full report of the trial was published in 1881 as *The State Trials ... Report of the Trial of The Queen ... against Charles Stewart Parnell* (Dublin, 1881).

178 Obituary, *Annual Register*, 1883, p. 168. The writer continued: 'No one doubted the ability which he displayed in the general management of the trials, and the calm but clear, impressive, and forcible manner in which he presented the case to the Court. The proceedings were carried out without any hitch or flaw, though the evidence was complex and voluminous, requiring the utmost skill in the grouping and application of it. The jury disagreed, but the failure was in no respect due to the law officers engaged for the Crown'.

The complex and controversial Land bill, 1881, which appears to have been drafted principally by Hugh Law who was the main Government spokesman on the bill,[179] was introduced on 7 April.[180] It was regarded as so complicated that 'ninety-nine out of every hundred of the Members of Parliament were floundering in the mazes of that extraordinary measure'. 'The saying of the time is well known', O'Connor wrote, 'that but three men in the House of Commons knew the Land bill – Mr Gladstone, Mr Law, and Mr Healy'.[181] The bill eventually received the royal assent on August 22, and another revolutionary step had been taken along the difficult road of land reform. In the context of those times, and having regard to its objects, it was, as A.M. Sullivan called it, 'a great and noble measure'.[182] He gave due recognition to Gladstone's personal commitment to Irish land reform, praising the 'indomitable spirit, the unwearied attention, and the marvellous grasp of his subject' which he displayed. He was equally fulsome in his praise of Law:

> There was, moreover, by his side one faithful colleague, on whom fell the brunt of the work, and whose brave spirit and sympathetic nature left their imprint indelibly on the Bill; and to him there went up from the whole body of the Irish popular representatives, without distinction of creed or section, a hearty tribute of respect and admiration. This was the Right Hon. Hugh Law, MP, then Attorney-General, at present Lord-Chancellor of Ireland.[183]

---

179 Law's obituary in the *Irish Law Times and Solicitors' Journal* (15 September 1883) states: 'He it was, too, who drafted the Bill by which the recent revolution in the relation of landlord and tenant in Ireland has been accomplished'. Presumably this refers to the more recent 1881 bill rather than that of 1870. Both he as Attorney-General, and William Moore Johnson (Solicitor-General) spent much of their time in London on Irish Parliamentary business. It was Law, however, who handled the complexities of the Land Bill in the Commons.

180 The policy underlying the bill was formulated under Gladstone's direction with input from Forster, who had sent memoranda to the cabinet on the subject at the end of December 1880, and again in early March 1881 when Forster seemed pleased to be told that some re-drafting had been done 'in the direction he wished'. Gladstone decided that it was desirable to have very little time for criticism of the bill before the debates began in the Commons, and it was not until the 21 March that he announced his intention of introducing the Land bill on 7 April, which was the day before the House was to rise for the Easter vacation. See Moody and Hawkins (eds), *Arnold-Forster*, pp. 86, 89, 99.

181 Ibid., p. 402. Healy was greatly assisted by his brother Maurice, a lawyer, who corresponded with him on a regular basis on the Bill and its amendment.

182 A.M. Sullivan, *New Ireland: Political Sketches and Personal Reminiscences of Thirty Years of Irish Public Life* (Glasgow, 1882), pp. 457–8.

183 Ibid., pp. 459–60. Sullivan considered the Land Act an outstanding piece of legislation which was misrepresented by nationalists for political reasons and out of hatred for the coercion legislation. Although requiring some amendment, he wrote of it (p. 458): 'seldom in the history of the world had the course of human legislation witnessed a more wise and elevated purpose than that proclaimed in every page of this scheme. Short of the compulsory expropriation of a landlord class at a swoop, it would be difficult to devise a bolder proposition in the interests of justice and equity; nor could any man suggest on the whole a more prudent compromise of a question involved and complicated beyond all precedent. That is to say, if it was not now too late for a joint-interest or landlord-and-tenant system, on even the most just and liberal basis, here surely was its best form'.

In spite of Law's success with the Land Act, it was nevertheless a very difficult time for him as Irish attorney-general because of the demands of his political superiors for more stringent legal powers to deal with the crisis of lawlessness in Ireland. The Irish law officers were not generally in favour of overly repressive measures – probably realising that these could lead to greater trouble. In late May, for example, Forster was contemplating a general proclamation announcing that police and soldiers could open fire if attacked while enforcing the law. Sir Edward Sullivan, Master of the Rolls since 1870, supported the measure, but Hugh Law opposed it, and it was abandoned in favour of lesser measures. Both Law and Solicitor-General Johnson counselled a moderate and conservative approach, but were away from the turmoil in Ireland as they spent much of their time on government business in London. Chief Justice O'Hagan, who was old and unwilling to take responsibility, exerted little influence in the Irish privy council, and the Government increasingly yielded to the advice of the hawkish Sullivan who exercised considerable influence on the Government. It had fallen to Sullivan, who was attorney-general at the time, to successfully prosecute the Fenian leaders in 1865.

When O'Hagan was prevailed upon to retire in November 1881, there was uncertainty as to which of the two contenders, Law or Sullivan, would get the lord chancellorship. Forster favoured Sullivan and recommended his appointment.[184] It appears that Gladstone was, at first, reluctantly inclined to accept the recommendation. In a letter of 21 October 1881, he informed Lord Granville: 'O'Hagan retires – and I have agreed, not without difficulty, that Sullivan *not* Law shall be Chancellor. It is a question of the greater capacity against *far* the greater service'.[185] In spite of this apparent resolve, however, the decision was reversed, and Law was appointed Lord Chancellor, the highest judicial office in Ireland.[186] As a con-

---

184 Forster to Gladstone, 19 October 1881, announcing O'Hagan's resignation and recommending Sullivan (Add. MS 44159, folio 66); Cowper's endorsement, 19 October (Add. MS 44472, folio 124); Gladstone to Forster, 20 October, accepting the recommendation (Add. MS 44159, folio 69). See Agatha Ramm (ed.), *The Political Correspondence of Mr Gladstone and Lord Granville, 1976–1886*, vol. i, 1876–1882 (Oxford, 1962).
185 Ramm (ed.), *Political Correspondence*, vol. i, no. 559, pp. 304–5. Gladstone to Granville, PRO 30/29/124, emphasis as in the original. In his reply on 25 October, Granville remarked: 'I suppose Sullivan is a stronger man than Law'. Ibid., no. 561, p. 306; Add. MS. 44173, folio 194.
186 Moody and Hawkins (eds.), *Arnold-Forster*, pp. 155, 157, 158, 303, 306. The editors quote (p. 159) from a letter to Gladstone at the end of May, in which Forster complained that Cowper gave no leadership: 'Cowper does attempt to steer the ship ... Questions then which ought to be decided without delay and on the spot, are referred to London for my decision guided by the law officers. Here again the difficulty is increased; were I here I should almost always feel I could act on the opinion of the law adviser ... But in London I must be guided by Law and Johnson, & they, away from the facts, can hardly avoid taking a *dangerously safe* side. With all this O'Hagan our Chancellor is useless. He does nothing & if he did anything he would probably be worse than useless ... O'Hagan is rich, tired of work & in poor health, & above all he is shy of responsibility'. From September 1880, the Dublin authorities considered the use of the old Whiteboy Acts (1 & 2 Wm. IV c 44 and 15 & 16 Geo. III) to prohibit meetings called specifically to intimidate individual landlords, and by December these Acts were being used, with some reluctance on the part of the law officers (although the legal adviser, John Naish, seemed more in favour). The Under-Secretary, Thomas H. Burke, was 'in a white heat of indignation' against the hesitation of the Law Officers in banning a meeting on 17 December 1880. (See ibid., pp. 17, 35, 40.)

solation to Sullivan, Forster succeeded in having him made a baron,[187] and he was eventually to become chancellor following Law's early death. A downside of Law's advancement was that he was no longer available to the government party in the Commons, as he was required to resign his seat on moving to the bench. By all accounts, Law was a most friendly, urbane, and respected man. He was Florence Arnold-Forster's 'favourite of all the Irish officials', and she anticipated his loss to the Government: 'Of all our official friends Mr Law is the most amiable. We shall miss him greatly during the coming Session, as a man even more than a politician, and in this capacity too, he was very helpful to the Govt'.[188]

His honesty, integrity, and desire to contribute to the well-being of society were known and appreciated in parliament and in legal circles. In the Commons he had apparently earned the nickname 'honest Hugh Law'. As the writer of his obituary put it:

> by no member of his party was the Government served with more loyal and unflagging zeal than by 'honest Hugh Law' – the sobriquet by which he was known, and fitly described, in the House of Commons. In November, 1881, the highest judicial preferment in Ireland was awarded to him, his acceptance of the custody of the Great Seal being universally hailed with unalloyed satisfaction. Too brief has been his tenure of that lofty and well-won position, yet long enough to display judicial abilities of a high order, especially in cases dealing with the new law of landlord and tenant, such as *Adams* v. *Dunseath*, *Chaine* v. *Nelson*, and *Killeen* v. *Lambert*, his quick and masterly grasp of complicated facts, in particular, being remarkable. Nor alone was he possessed of a keener penetration into the essence of individual facts, but he was gifted with a great power of generalising; and, above all, he was comprehensively impartial, and judged 'righteously between every man and his brother, and the stranger that is with him'. In the very prime of his powers, at the age of 65, he has suddenly passed away, and widespread indeed is the regret of all who were either socially, professionally, or politically connected with the sound and assiduous lawyer, the firm, unbiased and conscientious judge.[189]

The Right Hon. Hugh Law, Lord Chancellor of Ireland, after a brief illness, had died on Monday morning, 10 September 1883, at Rathmullen House, Milford, on the shores of Lough Swilly, Co. Donegal. His death was unexpected although he had been in delicate health for some time. He had travelled through Derry on his way to Rathmullen on the previous Friday and had spent the greater part of the afternoon fishing on the Lough close to his residence. He developed an inflammation and congestion of the lungs during the night. Sir George Porter, Surgeon to the Queen in Ireland, was sent for but Law's symptoms were grave by Sunday

---

187 In a letter to Granville on 22 November, Gladstone wrote: 'Forster wishes a Baronetcy for Sullivan. It is rare to make legal Baronets: but it seems a reasonable thing in proper cases'. Ramm (ed.), *Political Correspondence*, vol. i, no. 574, p. 312.
188 Ibid., pp. 34, 359.
189 *Irish Law Times and Solicitors' Journal*, 15 September 1883, pp. 489–90.

and he died the following morning, the disease having by then caused an 'infection of the heart'. The remains were taken by the mail train from Derry to Amiens Street station on the following Friday, and from there by hearse to his residence at 9 Fitzwilliam Square. The funeral, attended by the Lord Lieutenant, members of the nobility, the judiciary, the legal profession, and others, took place on Saturday morning to the mortuary chapel, Harold's Cross, and was followed by interment in the family vault at Mount St Jerome Cemetery. The chief mourners included his sons John and Hugh Alexander.[190] His wife, Ellen Maria, died in 1875. Law's second son, Hugh Alexander,[191] also qualified as a barrister and like his father pursued a political career. A rare Unionist of nationalist leanings, he served as MP for Donegal in the UK (1902–18) and Free State Parliaments (1927–32).

Professor Heron's Later Career

In 1859, within months of Hugh Law's resignation from his post at QCG, Denis Caulfield Heron also resigned from the chair of Jurisprudence and Political Economy. He was succeeded by the renowned scholar, John E. Cairnes, who took political economy as his special interest, and earned a well-deserved reputation as one of the foremost economists of his day. Heron's subsequent career was similar to that of his colleague, Hugh Law. Called to the Irish Bar in 1848, he joined the Munster circuit where he quickly developed a large practice as a junior counsel, mainly in the Bankruptcy Court and as a commercial lawyer. He was awarded the LLD by TCD in 1857 and was made a QC, 'taking silk' on 4 July 1860. It seems he earned early distinction by his success in the Tipperary Bank litigation, bringing to his work 'the conscientiousness and careful reading that were his characteristic',[192] and rapidly earned a strong professional reputation as a leading barrister. In 1854 Heron had married Emily Fitzgerald, the youngest daughter of David and Catherine Fitzgerald of Dublin.[193] It may have been through his wife's family connections, that Heron went into practice on the Munster circuit. The Fitzgerald family, who were Catholics, were strongly represented in legal circles. Two of Emily's brothers were lawyers. Thomas Fitzgerald was a solicitor, and John

---

190 *Irish Times*, 11, 15, 17 September 1883.
191 Hugh Alexander Law was resident, in later life, at Marble Hill, Ballymore, Co. Donegal. He died in April, 1943, leaving one son and three daughters. He was educated at Rugby and Oxford, and married Charlotte Stuart, daughter of the Revd Alexander George Stuart of Bogay, Co. Donegal. He was called to the Bar in both England and Ireland, and he served in the secretariat of the Ministry of Munitions (1915–16), and in the news department of the Foreign Office (1916–18). He was made a Knight, Military Order of Malta. He served as member of the Congested Districts Board, 1919, and of the Housing Committee, Local Government Board for Ireland, 1919–22; he was active in the co-operative movement. He served as MP for West Donegal (1902–18), and as a member of the Free State Parliament (1927–32). He wrote on Irish literature and history: *Why Is Ireland at War?* (Dublin, 1915 and 1916) and *Anglo-Irish Literature* (London, 1926).
192 Obituary in the *Irish Times*, 16 April 1881.
193 Catherine Fitzgerald was a daughter of a David Leahy of Dublin. Heron's wife appears to have died in 1863. He had a Dublin residence in later years at 7 Upper Fitzwilliam Street.

David Fitzgerald, who had practised as a barrister on the Munster circuit, was elected MP for Ennis in 1852, and ended his career as a Justice of the Queen's Bench and a Lord Justice of Appeal (a law lord in the House of Lords).[194] Her sister Kate married Charles Robert Barry (1823–97) who, like his brother-in-law, became a Justice of the Queen's Bench and Lord Justice of Appeal. He was elected MP for Dungarvan in 1865.[195] Barry and Fitzgerald were Liberal Party supporters and, not surprisingly, Heron was drawn towards politics. He went forward as a liberal candidate, at the invitation of the local clergy, in the 1869 Tipperary by-election caused by the death of Charles Moore of Mooresfort. His opponent was the dedicated Fenian activist Jeremiah O'Donovan Rossa who, following his arrest in 1865, had been tried by Judge Keogh and sentenced to penal servitude for life. His co-accused included other Fenian leaders such as John O'Leary, who had been a student at QCC and QCG, and Charles J. Kickham. General sympathy for the manner in which Fenians were treated, and support for an amnesty for Fenian prisoners, increased substantially after the abortive Rising in March 1867, and the execution of the so-called 'Manchester Martyrs' in the following November.

In spite of these extraordinary circumstances which helped his opponent, Heron had much to recommend him as a candidate, and was expected to win the election. He was not only a staunch nationalist and Catholic, but had defended prominent Fenians accused of high treason in 1867 and 1868. Some of Heron's speeches for the defence in these state trials were published,[196] and they reveal a capable and persuasive advocate at the height of his career. Heron was also engaged as defence counsel in one of the most extraordinary cases arising out of the 1867 Rising – the trial of the Fenian crew of the brigatine, *The Jacknell*,[197] which had sailed out of New York in April 1867 under the name *Erin's Hope*, and arrived in Sligo Bay in May with munitions intended for insurgents who did not then exist. Before sailing back to the USA, some thirty of the party came ashore near Dungarvan with the assistance of a local fishing boat, but they were quickly rounded up and imprisoned. In the ensuing trials, Heron represented Colonel John Warren and W.J. Nagle at the first hearing,[198] a case which raised important legal issues, one of

---

194 Ball, *Judges in Ireland*, vol. ii, p. 363. John David Fitzgerald (1816–89), was appointed successively, Solicitor-General (1855), Attorney-General (1856–8, 1859–60), and Justice of the Queen's Bench (1860). He was appointed a Lord Justice of Appeal in 1882.
195 Ibid., p. 369. *Irish Law Times and Solicitors' Journal*, xvii (23 April 1881), p. 219. Charles Robert Barry (1823–97) was the eldest son of James Barry, a Limerick solicitor, who rose through the legal ranks to become Third Serjeant (1866), Solicitor-General (1868), and Attorney-General (1870). He was appointed a Justice of the Queen's Bench in 1872, and a Lord Justice of Appeal in 1883. Barry and Fitzgerald had presided at the state trial of Parnell and others which began at the end of December 1880 and continued into early January 1881.
196 D.C. Heron, *Irish State Trials, 1867: Special Commission for the County of Cork. The Speeches of Denis Caufeild Heron, QC* (London and Dublin, 1867). The defence succeeded in securing an acquittal in the case of the *Queen v. Captain Patrick Joseph Condon and Dominick O'Mahony*, to the delight of local supporters. D.C. Heron, *Irish State Trials, 1868: The Speeches of Denis Caufeild Heron, QC* (London and Dublin, 1868).
197 The name is given as 'Jacknel' by Sullivan, but appears as 'Jackmel' in Heron, *Irish State Trials, 1868*, p. 83.
198 For an account of the trials, see William G. Chamney, *Report of the Trial for Treason-Felony at The County Dublin Commission ... 1867* (Dublin, 1867).

which led to a dispute between the UK and US governments, and a change in the law. As A.M. Sullivan wrote:

> Two important legal points were raised on the trials which ensued. Firstly, whether any hostile act had been committed within British jurisdiction; secondly, whether American citizens of Irish birth would have their American status recognised, and be allowed a mixed jury. Colonel John Warren, a native of Clonakilty, in Cork county, but a duly naturalised citizen of the United States, was the first put on his trial. When the jury came to be impaneled, Mr. Heron, QC, produced the prisoner's naturalisation papers, and claimed for him a jury *mediatate linguae*. The presiding judge fully realised the gravity of the point which he was about to decide: but the law as it then stood was clear; no subject of the British Crown could divest himself of allegiance; and so he ruled.[199]

Warren protested his arraignment as a US citizen to no avail and, having instructed Heron to withdraw as his defence counsel, insisted that the US government was now principal. He, as well as Lieutenant Augustine Costello, was tried and convicted. The jury disagreed at Costello's first trial for treason-felony but, in spite of Heron's efforts, he was convicted on the second trial and received twelve years' penal servitude.[200] Although the US government abandoned the accused to their fate, it did take issue on the allegiance question, as the 'whole fabric of American power stood upon that doctrine'. The issue was peacefully resolved by negotiation, and in 1870, as Sullivan wrote, 'the Act 33 and 34 Vict. cap. 14, known (in Ireland, at least) as the "Warren and Costello Act", was passed through Parliament; and now a British-born subject may, by certain formalities, divest himself of his birth-allegiance, and adopt another citizenship'.[201]

Another prominent case in which Heron featured arose out of a fracas which developed following a provocative Orange march in Monaghan town on 12 July 1868.[202] Death and injury ensued when the Orangemen boarded themselves in Baird's public house and fired on their assailants. Although Monaghan was three-quarters Catholic, the sub-sheriff, who was an Orangeman, had rigged the jury panel so that there was less than ten per cent chance of a Catholic being chosen as a juror. Not surprisingly, Baird was found not guilty of murder, and cases against other Orangemen failed. When a Catholic was tried for murder, however, his chances of a fair trial were slim. Isaac Butt and Heron were his lawyers and they decided to challenge the jury panel. The legality of the panel was tried by a special jury consisting of the two jurors who were at the top of the list, and they quashed it. In his attack on William Mitchell, the sub-sheriff, Heron was forthright: 'Men whose every feeling was poisoned with prejudice and with hatred of their fellow

---

199 Sullivan, *New Ireland*, p. 283.
200 Heron's address to the jury appears in *Irish State Trials, 1868*, pp. 83–98.
201 Sullivan, *New Ireland*, pp. 283–4.
202 An account of the incident is given in Frank Wright, *Two Lands on One Soil: Ulster Politics before Home Rule* (Dublin, 1996), pp. 272–4.

men, and who lived as foreigners in a land which they should love as their native land, were unfit for such positions'.[203] Although no move was made to dismiss Mitchell or rectify the panel, he was later dismissed by the Chief Secretary when the High Sheriff had the audacity to publicly challenge the credibility of one of the two special jurors who had quashed the panel.

Heron's public profile as a Liberal nationalist was countered, however, by the unusual circumstances of the Tipperary by-election. There had been delay in choosing a candidate, and after Heron had been approached and had consented to stand, a suggestion was made that the election of a gaoled Fenian would be an effective answer to the government's refusal to grant amnesty to political prisoners. The matter was taken up seriously by ardent nationalists. Although the clergy opposed the move as a fruitless and absurd proceeding, sufficient support and sympathy was roused to cause a major electoral upset. To vote against Rossa, as Sullivan put it, 'seemed like a stroke at amnesty', and Rossa was elected:

> the bulk of the electors decided to abstain or else cast a voice for 'the prisoner-candidate'. Out of twelve thousand on the register only about two thousand came to the poll; but of these a decided majority – 1054 to 898 – voted for Rossa.[204]

Although Heron and the local Catholic-Liberal alliance were defeated, O'Donovan Rossa's success was the result of the peculiarities of the moment and proved a fruitless triumph. He was subsequently disqualified from holding a seat in parliament as an undischarged felon. Heron won the new election which was held in 1870, defeating the Fenian Charles Kickham by a mere four votes, and held the seat until 1874. He showed a particular interest in the Irish land question during his time in parliament, and had previously contributed a number of papers on land reform to the Statistical Society. As a strong advocate of tenant-right, he had supported the Land Act of 1870, and in the same year had proposed a bill of his own which, however, was not adopted.

Heron's professional practice at the Bar continued to flourish. He was briefly appointed Law Adviser at Dublin Castle in 1866 by the Gladstone administration and, in testimony to his growing legal and personal reputation, he was elected a Bencher of the King's Inns in Michaelmas Term, 1872.[205] He was appointed a Justice of the Peace for the counties Armagh and Down, and with the advent of Gladstone's second administration, Heron was appointed Third Serjeant-at-Law in October, 1880 – a key position for future elevation to the Bench.[206] He was

---

203 Quoted in ibid., p. 273.
204 Sullivan, *New Ireland*, p. 330.
205 Heron's obituary reads, in part, 'at the time of the Fenian conspiracy he was appointed Law Adviser at Dublin Castle during Mr Gladstone's Administration'. According to *Thom's Directory*, however, he was Law Adviser at Dublin Castle from April to July 1866.
206 T. Rice Henn, Recorder of Galway, when addressing the Grand Jury, adverted to Heron's sudden death and noted that 'had his life been spared, his advanced and rapidly advancing career must inevitably have placed him upon the judicial bench, and he, too, like his distinguished judicial relatives, would have served his country as a great magistrate'. (*Irish Times*, 18 April 1881)

viewed favourably in Liberal circles, and was on friendly terms with Forster's family even before Forster became Chief Secretary in 1880. Florence Arnold-Forster refers to him in her Journal as 'our old Danube friend' which suggests an acquaintance going back at least to 1876. It was in September of that year that the Forsters visited Hungary where, presumably, they met Heron.[207] He had been Vice-President of the Dublin Statistical Society from 1871 and wrote an account of his impressions in 'A Visit to Russia' which was his last published contribution to appear in the *Transactions* of the Society.[208] His friendship with the Forsters deepened after he became Serjeant, and he appears at various social functions at the Vice-Regal Lodge and elsewhere.[209] His career was cut short, however, by his untimely death on Good Friday, 15 April 1881. He collapsed in the early morning while salmon fishing on the banks of the Corrib river in Galway, and died at 3.30 p.m. He was aged fifty-seven.[210] On Saturday in Dublin, 'a cold dreary morning with a dense sea fog over everything', the Forsters, as Florence wrote, were genuinely upset to read of his death:

> We were sincerely grieved and shocked to see in the papers the sudden death of our old Danube friend, Sergeant Heron. He was a man whom we all liked, and to Father his personal friendship and bright cheery ways were a real refreshment amongst the crowd of strangers and official acquaintance with whom he has been so constantly surrounded during his time at the Castle.[211]

Heron's wife had also died suddenly some years before as she was returning to Ireland on board the Holyhead packet just as it was nearing Kingstown. Denis Caulfield Heron was buried in Glasnevin Cemetery. An obituary in the *Irish Law Times* recorded his passing:

207 Moody and Hawkins (eds.), *Arnold-Forster*, p. xxi.
208 Heron had travelled to Russia as a delegate to the eight International Statistical Congress at St Petersburg.
209 Florence Arnold-Forster records his presence as dinner guest (17 December 1880), '5 o'clock tea' (26 December 1880), walk in the Park (6 March 1881). Moody and Hawkins (eds.), *Arnold-Forster*, pp. 40, 45, 88.
210 The *Irish Times* correspondent reported on 16 April 1881: 'Galway, Friday. While Serjeant Heron was playing a salmon this morning on the river he had an attack of apoplexy, to which he succumbed in about two hours and a half. Yesterday evening he was in excellent health and spirits, and dined at the County Club with the Recorder of Galway and several gentlemen. He was a devoted sportsman, and was out on the river this morning at six o'clock. He had landed two salmon, and was playing a third when he suddenly fell back, and would have fallen into the river, which is very rapid at this place, had he not been caught by a man named Lyden, who was attending him. Brown, another attendant, took Mr Heron's rod and killed the salmon'. The reporter also wrote that Major Trench and John Pollok (the High Sheriff), who were also fishing the river, had Heron carried to the weir-house where Dr Browne and Dr Colohan tried in vain to save him. The last sacraments were administered by Fr Greaven PP. His remains were taken to the railway terminus at 7.30 p.m. on Saturday to be conveyed on the night train to the Broadstone Terminus, Dublin, and were taken from there by his brothers-in-law to Heron's residence at 7 Upper Fitzwilliam Street. The burial took place on Tuesday morning, 19 April in the family vault at Glasnevin Cemetery.
211 Moody and Hawkins (eds.), *Arnold-Forster*, p. 121. Notice of Heron's death appeared in the *Freeman's Journal*, and in the *Irish Times* on the 16 April 1881.

> The leader of the Munster Bar, he was an able and effective nisi prius lawyer, a fluent speaker to whom his scholarship and literary attainments supplied an ever ready fund of illustration (which often served him in good stead even in law arguments e.g., *Lawler* v. *Linden*, 10 Ir. L. T. Rep. 86); above all, a perfect gentleman in the truest sense, whose kindly and genial companionship won the cherished regards of his circle, while his higher attributes commanded its respect.[212]

All accounts suggest that Heron was very popular with all shades of opinion, a fact evidenced also by the genuine sorrow at his sudden death and the distinguished attendance at his funeral. The *Irish Times* noted that:

> The Irish Bar has thus lost one of its most eminent men, and on every side of politics, persons of every faith and opinion will be saddened by his melancholy removal. Heron was more than a lawyer of great learning and experience ... It was also no small praise deserved by him that he gave his whole mind to the cases entrusted to him, and was therefore a safe counsel for suiters, and enjoyed the respect equally of the bench and the jury, and the confidence of solicitors and his brethren ... His politics were Liberal, and throughout his career consistent. His sympathies were with the people in all reforms, but he was never extreme in his views or conduct, or gave any support to revolutionary principles. Had he been willing to do so he could have retained his seat for Tipperary.[213]

The Recorders at Cork and Galway were moved to note his passing in court. Judge Hamilton at the Quarter Session Court at Cork related how he had spent a part of a recent summer with Heron in Donegal and said of him: 'in that close association it was impossible not to become acquainted most intimately with him; and I will say now that a kinder, a more sincere, simple, or more generous nature never existed than that which my late lamented friend possessed'.[214] It appears that Heron preferred the law courts over the political arena and was intent on achieving a judicial appointment when his career came to a sudden an unexpected end.

The Contribution of Law, Heron, and William Edward Hearn

In assessing the academic careers of Law and Heron, credit is due to both of them as pioneers in establishing the initial law programme at Galway. In reviewing the

---

212 *Irish Law Times and Solicitors' Journal*, xvii (23 April 1881), p. 219.
213 Under the headline 'Sudden Death of Serjeant Heron', 16 April 1881.
214 *Irish Times*, 18 April 1881. The Recorder, Judge Hamilton, also said of Heron: 'The position he occupied on the Munster circuit is well known to the public of Cork, and of Ireland. A more eminent position no one could occupy at the Irish Bar. Of his great literary and scientific information, with which he so often delighted a large circle of friends, everyone is aware, but the dearer qualities of his kindly nature were best known to those who were intimately acquainted with him, and of that number I had the happiness to be one'.

evidence, there is the unmistakable sense that both endeavoured to establish a Faculty with the highest possible standards in circumstances which were far from ideal. That said, Heron appears to have played the fuller academic role – perhaps because his career at the Bar was less well established. It was Heron who took on the duties of Dean, who gave evidence to the Queen's Colleges Commission, and who put himself forward as University examiner.[215] He had a strong interest in the intellectual and academic development of his students, and he continued to expand his own intellectual horizons. He was awarded the LLB and LLD degrees in 1857,[216] and retained a life-long, active interest in intellectual affairs by his writings and his contribution to the work of the Statistical Society, of which he was a distinguished office-holder. His concern for his students is evident from the time and effort he devoted to the provision of suitable texts, particularly in the problem field of Jurisprudence. He supplemented his lecture materials on Jurisprudence with a translation of Lord Bacon's *Tract on Universal Justice*,[217] and his own article, 'Discourse on the Study of Jurisprudence',[218] which was published in the *Law Review*.

The lack of an intellectual consensus on the nature and content of Jurisprudence, and the absence of suitable texts in the subject, prompted Heron to write and publish his book, *An Introduction to the History of Jurisprudence*.[219] As he stated in the preface, a great portion of the book was a 'compilation', in the sense that it was an account of the work and ideas of the great writers of the past. Although published in 1860, it clearly represented the fruit of his teaching at Galway, as it mirrored his Jurisprudence syllabus. This large volume, of some eight hundred

215 Heron was appointed University examiner for the subjects taught by the professors of Jurisprudence and Political Economy for the sessions 1852–3 and 1853–4; he was succeeded by William Neilson Hancock, for the 1854–5 session, and by Cliffe Leslie for the period 1855–7. Heron was re-appointed in July, 1857. Heron's appointments (with James A. Lawson for the Law subjects) were made on 17 July 1852 and 16 July 1853, (*QUI Report*, 1852–3, pp. 5, 76). Hancock and Professor Michael Barry, QCC (Law), were appointed on 17 July 1854, (*QUI Report*, 1853–4, p. 88). Leslie, and Barry were appointed on 16 July 1855, (*QUI Report*, 1854–5, p. 83). Leslie and William B. Drury Barrister-at-Law, (Law), were appointed on 16 July 1856, (*QUI Report*, 1855–6, p. 99). Heron was re-appointed, with Drury, on 16 July 1857 (*QUI Report*, 1856–7, p. 49). The Vice-Chancellor explained the importance of, and care given to, the selection of competent examiners, so as to inspire public confidence in the merits of the degrees and the integrity of the examining process: 'Accordingly, searching among the candidates who presented themselves to be Examiners in this University, and selecting from among them those who were most highly qualified in their respective departments, we did not confine the selection to any particular institution or college. Some were taken from the Queen's Colleges of Belfast, Cork and Galway; some were taken from the Professors of Trinity College, Dublin; and some were selected from the general ranks of scientific and professional men'. Address, October 1853, *QUI Report*, Appendix, pp. 65–6.

216 These degrees were awarded by TCD, the University of Dublin. In his evidence to the Queen's Colleges Commission in 1857, he expressed regret that the Queen's University could not award doctorates to its own deserving staff as was the case in other universities.

217 See Heron's reports in the Presidents' *Reports*, 1850–1, p. 59, and Appendix, p. 77, and President's *Report*, 1851–2, p. 12. The translation of Lord Bacon's tract was published in Dublin, 1852.

218 *Law Review*, vol. xiv, no. 28.

219 London, 1860. Heron's address, as given in the Preface, was 7 Upper Fitzwilliam Street, Dublin.

and fifty pages, mainly consisted of an historical survey of the outstanding writers and schools of Jurisprudence, with some thoughts on the nature of Jurisprudence and its principles, which he considered to be evolving, if they had not already evolved, into a 'science' by the mid-nineteenth century. In regard to its structure, the main body of the work is preceded by some one hundred and fifty pages of rather haphazard analysis of the nature of Jurisprudence and its relation to the social sciences. The analytical section, edited with minor updating, formed the substance of Heron's *The Principles of Jurisprudence*, which was published as a separate volume in 1873. He had a strong belief in an underlying natural law which should act as a guide to positive law. 'Jurisprudence', he wrote, 'is the Science of Positive Laws'. Very much influenced by the Victorian belief that there was an underlying order governing all phenomena, including those in the social sphere, he could write with certitude that 'There are natural and fixed principles of legal Right and illegal Wrong, as there are natural and fixed principles of Gravitation'. In his view, the object of the 'Science of Jurisprudence', was 'the discovery of the relations which ought to be established by the Positive Law, and the best means to enforce such relations'.[220] Although these works are wide-ranging, they are not particularly well organised or presented.

Heron's other intellectual interest was in the field of economics, particularly in relation to taxation and land tenure. In addition to a work entitled *Three Lectures on the Principles of Taxation, Delivered at Queen's College, Galway, in Hilary Term, 1850*,[221] he contributed a number of papers to the *Transactions* on the land question and other issues, some of which, such as 'Historical Statistics of Ireland' and 'Ireland in 1864', proved quite controversial at the time.[222] His earlier work, *Constitutional History of the University of Dublin*,[223] which was very much the work of the young graduate, was polemical and controversial. Although coloured by Heron's nationalist and Catholic views, and his personal grievance at being denied a scholarship, it did raise a legitimate issue which fuelled wider debate. Rather unfortunately for the new Queen's Colleges, both the book and the controversial law case taken against the University of Dublin, heightened and sharpened the controversial issue of denominational higher education for Catholics.[224]

---

220 Denis Caulfield Heron, *The Principles of Jurisprudence* (London, 1873), pp. 1, 7–8. He wrote: 'Jurisprudence is the Science of Positive Laws, and, as such, is the theory of those duties which are capable of being enforced by the public authority. Jurisprudence, so treated, may take its place as one of those inductive sciences in which, by the observation of facts and the use of reason, systems of doctrine have been established which are universally received as truths among thoughtful men' (p. 32).

221 Published in Dublin 1850. The book was based on public lectures, an abridged account of which appeared in the *Galway Vindicator*.

222 Papers which were printed include: *Should the Tenant of Land Possess the Property on the Improvement Made by Him?* (Dublin, 1852); *Celtic Migrations: A Paper Read before the Dublin Statistical Society* (Dublin, 1853). Among the papers contributed to the Transactions of the Statistical Society were: 'Historical Statistics of Ireland', 'Ireland in 1864', and 'A Visit to Russia'.

223 First published in 1847, a second edition appeared in 1848.

224 A piece entitled 'Reform in Dublin University – The Scholarship Question', appeared in *Dublin Review*, October 1847, and a polemical review of Heron's book entitled 'University Reform – Trinity College', appeared in *Dublin University Magazine*, 30 (1847), pp. 609–30. Heron himself had published an *Address Delivered before the College Historical Society* (Dublin, 1846).

The intellectual interests of both Law and Heron centred on law, economics, and politics. These interests were shared by another remarkable contemporary at QCG, William Edward Hearn (see fig. 11.1). Although Hearn held the chair of Greek, his background, interests, and work were virtually identical with those of Law and Heron, and it is easy to imagine that he might have been more content to have been appointed to the chair of Jurisprudence and Political Economy. Like the law professors, he had been a senior moderator in classics at TCD, was called to the Irish bar, and was an active member of the Dublin Statistical Society. Like Heron and Professor Moffett (later to become President of QCG), he was one of the first Barrington Lecturers – scholars appointed under the Barrington Trust to promote the knowledge of Political Economy (Economics). After some five active years at QCG, W.E. Hearn resigned from the chair of Greek to take up a professorship at the recently-established University of Melbourne. Although his professorial duties embraced History and Literature, Political Economy and Logic, he was also a lawyer and had been called to the Bar of both Ireland and Victoria. In 1873, he became the first Dean of a newly-created Faculty of Law, and his intellectual work was primarily in the fields of economics and law. Like Law and Heron, he too became active in politics, and from 1878 until his death in 1888, he was a member of Victoria's Legislative Council. As unofficial 'leader' of the House, his task was to critically assess proposed Bills and to advise members on them. He was particularly concerned with land reform and codification of the law.

W.E. Hearn's intellectual work was pioneering and influential. His book, *The Government of England: Its Structure and Its Development*,[225] was long considered a classic and authoritative work in constitutional law. A.V. Dicey and Sir John Marriott acknowledged their indebtedness to it, and it was regarded as having anticipated Bagehot. In 1879, Hearn published *The Aryan Household: Its Structure and Its Development*, which was presented to the reader as 'an introduction to Comparative Jurisprudence'. This highly original treatment of the evolution of social structures, focuses on the development of sophisticated societies, using historical, anthropological, and sociological data. There are some parallels with Heron's work on Jurisprudence but, fundamentally, the approaches are very different. Many of the insights of both come from their common background – a deep knowledge of classical literature, combined with the new learning of the Victorian era, especially in economics, history, and comparative culture. Whereas Heron, however, looked at the phenomenon of law from an analytical perspective in which he reviewed the theories of other jurists, W.E. Hearn took a mainly historical approach. He boldly developed a unifying evolutionary model of society which attempted to explain, primarily from an historical perspective, how law reflected the underlying social and economic structure of societies. The archaic form of Aryan societies, he argued, consisted of an amalgam of family-clan units, which occupied common property, were bound together by ties of blood and common worship, and obeyed a common head who was the male descendant of a revered 'founder'. Societies evolved different kinds of groupings, including forms

---

225 London, 1867, 569 pages; second edition, 1886.

of association that we can recognise as the primitive state, itself a form of the non-genealogical clan or tribe, bound together on the basis of characteristics analogous to those which bound the family or clan unit.[226] Its constituent elements were 'individuals in groups'. The true political society of the modern world only emerged with 'the complete subordination of the clan, and the direct communication of the State with each individual citizen'.[227] The form of law in archaic society was custom, transforming itself into law as we know it when archaic society evolved into the 'state' structure.

Thus, in the approaches taken by the two authors, Heron relies on the analytical, W. E. Hearn on the historical method in Jurisprudence. Although Heron shows a staggering knowledge of works of jurisprudence down through the ages, W. E. Hearn's work is far more original and thoughtful, is better organised and presented, and shows a better command of a more diverse range of sources. Not content with this excursion into historical jurisprudence, he also explored the subject from the analytical perspective in *The Theory of Legal Duties and Rights: An Introduction to Analytical Jurisprudence*.[228] Hearn's major work in economics was *Plutology, or the Theory of the Efforts to Satisfy Human Wants*, 1864, which won for him an international reputation as one of the foremost economists of his day. It was an important work in that it elaborated a novel analysis in economics which broke from the dominant tradition of Ricardo and Mill. Hearn put wants and the means of satisfying them at the centre of his analysis, a novel approach which provided an insight into economic behaviour that was to command the admiration, and influence the work, of economists such as William Stanley Jevons and Alfred Marshall.

Although long absent from Galway, Hearn was not forgotten in his old College. In a letter dated August 1887, President Moffett, who had himself been active in the Dublin Statistical Society in the old days, informed him that he frequently referred to two of his books in his lectures, and he wrote of the passing of most of their old colleagues at QCG, including Law and Heron: 'Hugh Law, who had reached the highest eminence at the Bar, and was highly respected in the House of Commons died Lord Chancellor of Ireland. Caulfield Heron dropped dead in the act of fishing here in Galway'.[229] So it went on – most of the founding professors had died, and although that bond which is often forged in the excitement and challenge of a new venture had survived the years, the College itself had by then entered a steady maturity, but was soon, under the Royal University of Ireland, to enter upon a period which, if not of decline, was certainly one of stagnant frustration.

Cairnes and Campion – A Settled System

It can be said that the system of legal education initiated at QCG by Hugh Law and Denis Caulfield Heron became the established pattern under their successors,

---

226 These characteristics are listed in *The Aryan Household*, pp. 321–2.
227 Ibid., p. 335.
228 Melbourne, 1883, 401 pages.
229 University of Melbourne archives – quoted in Foley, 'A Nest of Scholars', pp. 75, 76–7.

and remained substantially unchanged for the remainder of the nineteenth century. William Bennett Campion succeeded Law as the new Professor of English Law at Galway in February 1859. John Elliot Cairnes replaced Heron as Professor of Jurisprudence and Political Economy later in the same year, and held that post until he resigned, due to ill health, in 1870. Campion taught the practice-oriented courses, whereas Cairnes took responsibility for the more academic courses, such as Jurisprudence, Civil Law, and Political Economy.

John E. Cairnes was born the sixth child and eldest surviving son of William Cairnes and his wife Mary Anne Wolsey, on 26 December 1823 at Castlebellingham, Co. Louth (see fig. 10.1).[230] His father was then a partner in a brewery in Castlebellingham, but shortly afterwards he moved to Drogheda to run his own highly-successful brewery business. The Cairnes family traced its ancestry to an Alexander Cairnes from Cultons, Wigton, who settled in Donegal in 1610. This man's great-grandson, William, was a captain in King William's army and was one of those who rushed to shut the gates of Derry against Lord Antrim. William's grand-nephew, John Elliot, succeeded to his estates and adopted the arms and surname of Cairnes. This gentleman was Professor Cairnes's great-grandfather.[231] Cairnes himself was educated at a boarding school at Kingstown, and was later sent to a Mr Hutton, a clergyman tutor at Bristol, who assessed him as a dull boy, unfit for college. It seemed then that he was destined to enter his father's business, and he spent three years at home where he learned some chemistry, dabbled in religion, and began to read widely.[232] In those years, however, Cairnes had developed academic interests and insisted on going to college against the wishes of his father, who reluctantly granted him a small allowance which enabled him to attend TCD. He was clearly a very able student as he graduated BA in 1848 as a first senior moderator (honours), and took his MA in 1854.

Unsettled as to his career, Cairnes moved from one occupation to another for several years. Having tried journalism, he came to Galway where he entered an engineer's office for a time, and where he resumed his study of chemistry as an occasional student. It was during his time in Galway that he developed a life-long friendship with Professor William Nesbitt, who successively held the chairs of Latin and Greek at QCG, before taking up the chair of Latin at QCB later in his career.[233]

---

230 See *DNB*; Foley, ibid., pp. 83–4; Boylan and Foley, *Political Economy and Colonial Ireland*, pp. 166–7; and Boylan and Foley, 'Cairnes, Hearn and Bastable', in Ó Cearbhaill (ed.), *Galway*, pp. 194–205.
231 H.C. Lawlor, *A History of the Family of Cairnes* (Dublin, 1906), pp. 128–35, table iv.
232 Leslie Stephen, who wrote his biographical summary in the *DNB*, and who had personal knowledge of Cairnes, wrote that he came under the influence of a young man named La Bart who: 'drew him for a time towards Calvinism, and the young men held prayer meetings together, while Cairnes also began to develop intellectual tastes. He read Gibbon and many other books, and gradually took a dislike to business'.
233 William Nesbitt (1824–81), who was born the son of a Methodist minister in Enniskillen, took his BA at TCD in 1845 and was appointed to the chair of Latin at QCG in 1849. He succeeded W.E. Hearn as Professor of Greek in 1854, and moved to Belfast in 1864 to take up the chair of Greek there. He took on the additional burden of Librarian in 1880, to supplement his meagre professorial salary. Active in College administration, he published principally on the educational issues of his day.

2.3 William B. Campion, Professor of English Law, 1859–1907

Nesbitt directed his interest towards economic issues, and convinced him to apply for the Whately Professorship in Political Economy at TCD. Cairnes successfully competed for the post by examination in 1854, and held it for the prescribed period of five years. He had found what was to be his intellectual passion for the remainder of his life, a passion he could more readily pursue after he succeeded to the Moor Park estate on his father's death in 1854, an inheritance which provided some £1,000 a year by way of additional income. Although he was called to the Irish Bar in Michaelmas term 1857, he devoted his energies primarily to the study of political economy and never seriously practised law. Cairnes delivered his first series of lectures as Whately Professor in Hilary term of 1857, and published them under the title of *The Character and Logical Method of Political Economy*.[234] Cairnes was keen to secure the Galway professorship. As soon as he heard that Heron was resigning from his chair, he determined to secure the post and conducted an extensive canvass. Through his friend Professor Nesbitt, he got the

---

234 London 1857, 2nd ed. 1875. The work was highly praised by Walter Bagehot and Professor R.D. Collison Black. The latter said of it that it 'stands as the definitive statement of the methodology of the English classical school'.

support of QCG President, Edward Berwick, which proved to be decisive in his success.[235]

William Bennett Campion was born about the year 1813 at the Rectory, Knockmorne, Co. Cork (fig. 2.3).[236] His father, the rector, was the Revd Thomas Spread Campion DD, a well-educated clergyman with literary interests.[237] The Campion family were well-known Co. Cork landed gentry, whose family burial place was at Leitrim, Co. Cork. They traced their ancestry to the Suffolk family of Champaigne, a family of Norman origin, some of whom received grants of land in Kerry and Meath in Elizabethan times. The ancestor of this branch of the family was said to be an officer of Charles I who opted to join Cromwell's successful Parliamentary side in 1649, and was later rewarded by the grant of the Leitrim estate on the banks of the Blackwater under the Act of Settlement, 1660. Although Captain Campion became an early Quaker, his descendants reverted to the Episcopal Church. William Bennett Campion's mother was Anna Johnston, daughter of Alderman Johnston of Cork.

In spite of a quiet rural upbringing in his father's rectory at Knockmorne on the banks of the river Bride, young William was lucky to survive to become a law professor. The story is told that as a young boy he was lost in Dublin due to the negligence of his country nursemaid who was charged with minding the children while his parents visited London. Luckily for him, they missed the boat and his sharp-eyed mother, while returning to temporary accommodation in St Stephen's Green, recognised her white-faced son being dragged along the street by a sooty chimney-sweep. The new recruit was rescued for a future legal career. Worse was to come, however, when William got caught up in a Cork tithe riot. He was about fourteen years of age when he was met by rioters while riding to Fermoy. The wretched and starving mob vented their anger at the tithe laws by attacking and almost killing the parson's son. He was found unconscious in a ditch some hours later, and apparently he carried the marks of the assault all his life.

Campion was educated in a local school which he remembered as having a brutal headmaster and then, in October 1829, he travelled to Dublin at the early age of sixteen to become a student at TCD.[238] He remembered his university days as amongst the happiest of his life. He took honours at his entrance examination, and graduated BA in 1834. Following a few years spent at home, apparently

---

235 An account of Cairnes's campaign for the professorship is given by Boylan and Foley in 'Cairnes, Hearn and Bastable', in Ó Cearbhaill (ed.), *Galway*, p. 195. Cairnes sought the support of James Anthony Lawson, Lord Carlisle, Archbishop Whately, Professors Moffett, and G. Johnstone Stoney among others. Heron, however, was not a supporter. Cairnes refers in his correspondence to 'some unhandsome dodges' practised against him by Heron and his associates.

236 Details of Campion's life are taken mainly from the posthumous biography *Memoir of William Bennett Campion, Serjeant-at-Law* (Dublin, 1911) referred to hereafter as *Memoir*, and the *Irish Times* obituary, 21 September 1907. The obituary and *Memoir* state that Campion was born in Co. Cork. Rather curiously, the meagre three lines on Campion in *The Presidents, Vice-Presidents, and Professors of Queen's College, Galway*, p. 39, states that 'Professor Campion is a native of Waterford'. TCD records give Cork as his place of birth. G.D. Burtchaell and T. U. Sadleir (eds.), *Alumni Dublinenses* (London, 1824), p. 131.

237 The name is given as 'Thomas Brett Campion' in the *Irish Times* obituary.

238 Formally admitted to TCD on 2 November 1929. Burtchaell and Sadleir, *Alumni Dublinenses*, p. 131.

because of delicate health, the young Campion returned to Dublin to study law under Professor Longfield and went to London to complete the then obligatory attendance at the Inns of Court.[239] He became a pupil of John Hastings Otway, a leading junior counsel who was later to become a QC, an Assistant Barrister (the equivalent to a County Court Judge of later years), and Recorder of Belfast. A strict and conscientious tutor, Otway insisted on neatness and accuracy in his pupils' work. Campion himself was to develop similar habits, devoting careful attention to the minutest details, polishing his prepared speeches, and exercising the greatest care with his written opinions. In contrast, and perhaps as a subconscious reaction to this precision, he was notorious for toppling his ink bottles. Out of embarrassment he would hastily endeavour to mop up the spill with anything that came to hand, even using his wig for the purpose on occasion.[240]

Following his call to the Irish Bar in Easter term of 1840, he joined the Munster circuit, and after many lean years, earned an unrivalled reputation in Equity and Real Property Law. The key to a very unusual, but highly successful and lucrative legal career, was Campion's ability to master Chancery practice and to keep abreast of rapid change. The old procedure was swept away by the Chancery (Ireland) Regulation Act 1850 and the new Court of Appeal in Chancery was established in 1856. Campion's careful, honest, and conscientious approach earned him the confidence of solicitors and the admiration of the Masters in Chancery. When the Masters were replaced by chief clerks in 1867, the legislation prohibited representation by counsel, but Campion was equally successful in Chancery cases which were then tried before the Master of the Rolls and the Vice-Chancellor. The new procedure was based almost exclusively on affidavit evidence with the option of cross-examining witnesses on notice given. Success depended on a thorough mastery of the evidence, and convincing argument on the authorities.[241] This could be laborious work, but it suited Campion's abilities and he offered, in addition, a professional and conscientious concern for the welfare of his client. His practice thrived: 'Mr Campion was singularly successful in this work, and from the time he took silk, was for many years engaged in every Chancery action of importance in Ireland'.[242] His talents were equally well suited to the new Court of Appeal which dealt with all the most important Chancery cases.[243] Campion, who was already well established as a successful junior barrister when he succeeded Hugh Law in February 1859, subsequently became one of the best Chancery and Real Property lawyers of his day. A kind, caring, and conscientious man, who was deeply religious in a non-doctrinaire way, he carried out his teaching duties at QCG in a careful and conscientious manner for almost fifty years.

---

239 The *Memoir* records that he stayed at the Strand Hotel and that: 'The Law Students' dinners were of the most primitive description. The knives and forks were chained to the table, and the food was coarse and roughly served, amidst dirty surroundings'.
240 Both his wig and the seat he used in the 'Little Room' of the old Four Courts Library were apparently identifiable by traces of ink. *Memoir*, p. 41.
241 Ibid., pp. 44–8, 57–60.
242 Ibid., p. 58.
243 Master Brooke wrote that 'He has more than common learning as an advocate, strong reasoning powers, clearness and candour'. Master FitzGibbon described him as 'an accomplished lawyer,

The Law programme taught by Campion and Cairnes consisted, as before, of a three-year Diploma of Elementary Law, the postgraduate LLB, and the taught LLD degree. Some changes were made to the QUI regulations which resulted from a commission of enquiry into the Colleges held in 1858, and the changes made to the Arts programme, in particular, did help to lessen the burden on law students. The most significant changes, however, arose outside the College walls. By the 1860s, the political influence of the Catholic Church in Irish educational matters, which was partly exercised through sympathetic Irish MPs, had become so strong that no UK government could complete the Queen's Colleges system. The Colleges were left to struggle with insurmountable difficulties, which resulted in declining student numbers and almost no innovation. In legal education, also, the most critical constraints came from without. Both TCD and the King's Inns were controlled by members of an establishment which had traditionally controlled the professions. These Benchers and Fellows moved to ensure that they would remain the dominant and controlling force as regards entry to the Bar, thereby exercising a stranglehold on the development of professional legal education elsewhere. Because the Colleges were state-funded, there was also the constant pressure of parliamentary scrutiny.

The Queen's Colleges Commission Report, 1858

The colleges were scarcely seven years in operation, in February 1857, when a Parliamentary Commission was established to make a diligent and full enquiry into 'the progress and condition of the Queen's Colleges'. It was called 'a measure of some severity' by QCG's President Berwick, who attributed it to the unjustified allegations of opponents that the Colleges were a failure.[244] The Commissioners consisted of Charles William FitzGerald (Marquis of Kildare), Sir Thomas Redington, who was born at Oranmore and was the first Catholic under-secretary, Bonamy Price MA, who was later to hold the chair of Political Economy at Oxford, and James Gibson BL.[245] The Commissioners held 'courts of inquiry' in each College, at which sworn evidence was taken from office holders and professors, and they completed their *Report* at the end of June 1858. There were problems which the rigorous inquiry brought to light, including disappointment with the slow growth in student numbers, yet the Commissioners generally approved the work and progress of the Colleges. 'We should be glad to be able to report', they wrote,

and a gentleman in the best sense', and said of him 'I know of very few of equal and none of superior qualities'. Otway wrote of him that he was 'one of the best lawyers I know, with a most felicitous power of expression, and in every thought and feeling a perfect gentleman'. See *Memoir*, pp. 36–7, 47.

244 Berwick pointed out in his *Report* for 1857–8, p. 5, that QCG had in that year had its third triennial visitation. To order such an additional inquiry into the Colleges after seven years, he wrote, 'was to submit them to a trial of no ordinary kind'.

245 *Queen's Colleges Commission Report*, 1858. The commissioners were appointed on 6 February 1857. Sir Thomas Nicholas Redington KCB was born at Kilcornan, Oranmore, Co. Galway in

a larger number of students availing themselves of the great advantages held out to them in the Queen's Colleges; but, we think, that the Colleges cannot be regarded as otherwise than successful, when, notwithstanding opposing causes, to which we shall presently allude, they have in their Halls, attending lectures, nearly 450 students.[246]

The 'opposing causes', which constituted a formidable array of obstacles, included the following: 'the severity of the College training'; the prestige of TCD which attracted the sons of the higher classes; the difficulty of obtaining an elementary classical education in Ireland which was an obstacle to College entry for middle-class families; school exhibitions in, and associations with, TCD which drew most students of the Royal Schools to that College in preference to the Queen's Colleges; the 'opposition of the Roman Catholic Church' (although the Commission could find no basis that Queen's College education would in any way be dangerous to faith and morals); the residency requirements in the Queen's Colleges given the scarcity and expense of student accommodation, particularly in Cork and Galway, whereas almost half of the students at TCD were non-resident; the disadvantage of being unable to take divinity students, who went to TCD and Maynooth; and the general lack of practical motivation to take degrees and diplomas, in that few privileges of importance attached to them. In light of such factors, the Commission's endorsement and approval of the progress made in the Colleges was not surprising. Of the quality of education in the Colleges, they had no doubt:

> We are able to report with unqualified satisfaction of the educational progress of the Colleges. Although but a short time in operation, they have distinguished themselves in those great public contests in which even the most distinguished students of the old universities are proud of success.

There was also the hope, not unfounded, that mixed education operated 'to soften those feelings of party antagonism and sectarian animosity which have heretofore unhappily had too extended an existence in Ireland'.[247]

The Commissioners made a number of recommendations in relation to the Colleges, some of which had been consistently pressed upon the Government by President Berwick. In most cases, the difficulties experienced at QCC and QCB were felt more acutely in Galway. Berwick again and again in his *Reports*, explained that three factors in particular made it excessively difficult for middle-class parents

---

1815 and died at London in 1862. Educated at Oscott College, Birmingham, and Cambridge, he was MP for Dundalk (1837–46), and the first Catholic under-secretary (1846–52). His eldest son, Christopher Talbot Redington (1847–9), who served as privy councillor, JP, and High Sheriff of Co. Galway, was Vice-Chancellor of the Royal University from 1894–9. Gibson, who was elevated to a QC, was a staunch Presbyterian and a trustee of Magee College. He was later an influential member of the QUI Senate until his death in 1880.

246 *Queen's Colleges Commission Report*, p. 35.
247 Ibid., pp. 35–7.

to educate their sons at QCG: the expense of accommodation for students who had to reside in the town; the lack of suitable second-level schools to prepare students for university studies,[248] and the exceptional difficulty of the Arts degree for students in general, and for those with inadequate pre-university schooling in particular.[249] While these factors affected all three Colleges, they had a more serious impact in Galway. The town's population was less than 24,000 (Cork and Belfast had more than three and four times that population respectively).[250] Because of the relatively small size of the town, an increase in QCG student numbers would have to come from families who could afford the accommodation costs of residing at Galway, which were twice as expensive as in Belfast. Similarly, the general population of Munster and Ulster were almost twice that of the Connacht region, and the numbers attending classical schools in those provinces, though low by the standards of Leinster, were proportionately three and four times higher than in Connacht, which had a mere seven hundred such students – about the equivalent of one large secondary school today.[251] Although the Commissioners adopted Berwick's recommendation for the establishment of Halls of Residence, the Government was unable to fund the project, and the problem was left unsolved.[252]

As regards the other difficulties, there was very little that could be done in the short term. The problem of poor second-level schooling might be countered by lowering the standard of the matriculation examination, but such a proposal could certainly not be entertained publicly. The Commissioners recommended that the original high standard be maintained and 'if any change be hereafter made therein, that the tendency of such should always be to elevate, and never to depress, the general standard of school education throughout the country'.[253] Although a 'great majority' of the Presidents and professors 'advocated a more or less diminution' in the Arts course, the Commissioners stood by the policy of a broad general education. 'We are of opinion', they reported, 'that the Queen's University, and consequently the Colleges, should not make any radical change in their curriculum of Studies for the Bachelor of Arts Degree, though we think that some important modifications may be made in their arrangements'.[254] In that regard, it was

---

248 This was also recognised later by the Catholic bishops who realised that even with their own university, Catholics would be at a disadvantage in the competition for higher education unless they too had a system of endowed intermediate education.
249 President Berwick gives an elaborate analysis of some of these difficulties in his *Report* for 1856, pp. 4–10, although they had been brought to the government's attention in earlier *Reports*.
250 The Census Report of 1851 gives the following population figures: Galway – 23,605; Cork – 83,745; Belfast – 100,301; Dublin – 258,361.
251 Berwick examined the implications of these population figures, taken from the 1851 Census, in his *Report* for 1856.
252 According to the *Queen's Colleges Commission Report*, p. 30, the President of Galway College stated: 'that the want of a Hall of Residence has proved a great obstruction to the progress of the College, and that, in fact, such a building is absolutely necessary, as it is extremely difficult to find suitable premises for Licensed Boarding-houses. The respectable householders will not take charge of the Students unless they derive a very large profit from them which puts these residences out of the reach of a large class of Students'.
253 Ibid., p. 18.
254 Ibid., p. 19.

suggested that there should be a University examination at the end of second year which would be final for all subjects not chosen for the third-year degree examination itself. This would provide an independent test of the knowledge attained in the first two years, and lighten the examination burden in the third-year degree examination. The Senate of the Queen's University was also left free to modify the curriculum in minor respects, and a proposal, first mooted in 1854, for what the *Report* called a 'New School in Arts' was approved by the Commissioners. This proposal recommended the introduction of a more limited educational programme than the Arts degree, which would take the form of a predominantly science-based diploma, with a small liberal element. This diploma would provide a more 'real' or practical education to meet the needs of the more pragmatic middle class, especially those interested in commerce, manufacturing, and the public service.[255] From these beginnings there developed the modern commerce and business programmes, and eventually a separate Commerce Faculty.

The Senate of the Queen's University acted promptly on these recommendations by introducing ordinances to modify the Arts programme in the Colleges. More flexibility was introduced. Students were allowed to choose modern languages instead of the Classics at the end of first year; the recommended post-second year University examination was introduced, which allowed students to focus on subjects which suited their aptitudes in the final year; and a new two-year Diploma of 'Licentiate in Arts' was begun. Whereas Greek and Latin were obligatory subjects in the BA degree, the Licentiate in Arts could be conferred on members of what Berwick called 'the trading and commercial classes', after they had spent two years studying a curriculum 'in which the dead languages are not made compulsory'.[256] It was against this background that Campion and Cairnes conducted their law teaching at QCG. Given their respective backgrounds, they must have found teaching in Galway a new and unusual experience.

Bright Students and Successful Lawyers

In the 1859–60 session, Cairnes took over the courses previously taught by Heron. He did not move permanently to Galway on his appointment, but kept house in Dublin, where he was still Whately professor at TCD, or he resided at the family home, Stameen, in Drogheda. With the help of Nesbitt, he found lodgings in Galway with a Mrs Gill and came to town to give his courses, bringing with him his servant Brown and his horse.[257] In the following year, aged thirty-six years, and settled in his career, Cairnes married Eliza Charlotte Alexander, whose sister was married to Nesbitt. She was a daughter of George Henry Minto Alexander,

---

255 Ibid., pp. 19–21.
256 Appendix to QCG President's *Report*, 1858–9, p. 9.
257 Although Mrs Gill was an agreeable landlady, he had to persuade her not to boil the turnips for the pigs in the kitchen due to the most unpleasant smell it caused. Brown caused consternation by mislaying one of Cairnes's manuscripts on one occasion. Boylan and Foley, 'Cairnes, Hearn and Bastable', in Ó Cearbhaill (ed.), *Galway*, p. 196.

officiating judge at Banda, India. They were to have three children.[258] That same year (1860) brought its share of trouble when he injured his knee in a hunting accident. An apparent cure, resulting from a visit that year to Aix-les-Bains, proved illusory, and the injury eventually left him crippled and in a weak and painful state of health.

Campion's teaching career had an inauspicious beginning.[259] It took two weary days to get to Galway, first travelling by canal-boat from Portobello Bridge, Dublin, to Mullingar, and then by coach to the town. He went straight to the College and just outside the gates was 'gruffly accosted by a stout old person, whom he afterwards discovered to be the German Professor of Modern Languages' who is reported to have said: 'Are you de new Law Professor? Den instantly dis minute to de class you must go! You are late and he wait you'![260] Although the travel-weary Campion explained that he was not lecturing that day, the narrow path by the stream where they stood continued to be blocked by the Languages Professor until Campion's patience ran out:

> At last the Law Professor, though the gentlest of men, could stand no more, wearied as he was from the long journey. 'Do you see the mill-stream down there?' he asked, as he stood towering above the little man. 'Well, if you say another word to me—' He advanced threateningly, and the German fled.[261]

They later became the best of friends, Campion patiently enduring Bensbach's favourite subject – the injustice of the law and how he himself suffered from its defects. On his appointment as Professor of English Law at QCG, he ceased to go on circuit, but continued to practice in the Dublin courts. He was appointed QC on 9 May 1868, and was married in the same year to a Miss Wilson of Scartbarry, Co. Cork, whom he had first met as they travelled together to a country house at which they were both guests. Their very happy life together was cut short by his wife's death fifteen years later. Campion was devasted, became ill for a time, and tried to deal with his grief by excessive work. Years later, a bundle of uncashed cheques for work done at this time was found amongst his papers. He enjoyed law teaching at QCG in his earlier career and took a personal interest in each of his students. He lived in Salthill during term time and enjoyed the informal entertaining of a 'pleasant little social circle in or near Galway'. Professor and Mrs Charles Croker King were at the centre of this circle in the early years and, in addition to local society folk, there were the officers of the Connaught Rangers, such as Colonel O'Hara.[262] Although Campion continued his work at QCG after

---

258 William Elliot (1863–1902), a captain in the Royal Irish Fusiliers, Frederick, and Anna Alexander (Mrs Brinkman).
259 According to the *Irish Times* obituary, Campion had lectured in law at TCD although this is not referred to in the *Memoir*.
260 *Memoir*, pp. 51–2. The professor was apparently Augustus Bensbach MD, then Dean of the literary division of the Arts Faculty.
261 Ibid., p. 52.
262 Ibid., pp. 54–5.

his wife's death in the early 1880s, he appears to have found it very burdensome. Instead of residing in at Salthill in term time, he stayed in what is now the Great Southern Hotel:

> He shunned the seaside home where he had spent so many happy months, and stayed at the big railway hotel, in those days the dreariest spot in winter. It was but half lighted and half heated, and, during one term, to increase the gloom, the only other inmate was the half-witted member of some local family, who had been crazed by a lawsuit.

This unfortunate man followed Campion around, hopelessly begging him for advice on old deeds and law papers in a legal suit disposed of over twenty years before.[263]

Although the changes made to the curriculum were of some help to law students, especially those who had to complete the Arts programme as a prerequisite to the LLB, the number of students who graduated in Law remained low. The student classes were small, but typically had at their core bright, diligent students who simultaneously took the Law and Arts programmes. In his first year of teaching (1858–9), Campion reported that the number of students who attended his lectures on English Law throughout the session was seven, and that he delivered forty-eight lectures in that session.[264] 'The subjects of these lectures were', he wrote, 'for one class, various branches of Common Law; for the other class, the principles of Equity and the several grounds of equitable jurisdiction. The general attendance at lectures was satisfactory'. He found that the performance of those students who competed at the annual occasional examinations for prizes was 'highly creditable'. Nevertheless the number of students prepared to take the law programme was unacceptably low, and this is also reflected in Heron's final report. In the following year, Campion wrote that the 'number of students whose names were entered for the Law Class for the above session was 7, divided into two classes', to which he gave an aggregate of forty-six lectures. The students were very good, however, and one of them had the unusual distinction of being commended in the professor's report by name:

> The students who intend pursuing the legal profession were most attentive during the session. The answering of one Gentleman educated in this College, and now preparing for the Bar (Mr. Munroe), [*sic*] may justify my specially noticing his name, as the extent of his information and his accurate knowledge of the principles of Law are extremely creditable to him.[265]

The Monroe referred to by Campion was John Monroe from Moira, Co. Down, who had won four annual law scholarships, and who was in later life to become a

---

263 Ibid., p. 69.
264 Appendix to QCG President's *Report*, 1858–9, p. 23.
265 Ibid., 1859–60, p. 11.

judge of the High Court in Ireland.²⁶⁶ In an age when governments appointed lawyers of their own political persuasion Monroe, fearing that no other suitable opportunity would arise, accepted a judicial appointment to the Chancery Division for the Landed Estates Court in 1885. He was an excellent judge, though considered wasted in that particular court. Cairnes's classes were scarcely much larger. In the same year he reported that he delivered thirty-four lectures in Jurisprudence and fifteen in Political Economy, and that the 'number of students in the former subjects was 7; the number in the latter, 6'. He could, however, report that the 'progress of the students was, on the whole, satisfactory, and their general deportment exceedingly good'. This pattern was to be repeated in the decades to come: small classes of very able students, most of whom would have taken the Arts degree.

Many other students at QCG during Monroe's time were also to have distinguished careers in later life. These included: James O'Kinealy, the Thynne brothers, Andrew Reed, John McKane, Michael McAuliffe, Bernard Gustavus Norton, John Atkinson, Aelian Armstrong King, and William Mulholland. O'Kinealy went out to India in 1861 and served in the judicial branch of the civil service in Lower Bengal.²⁶⁷ He ended his career as a puisne judge of the Calcutta High Court, but he is also remembered as an Arabic scholar and editor of law books. The Thynnes (Henry and Andrew Joseph) were natives of Ennistymon, Co. Clare. The sons of Edward Thynne, farmer, and his wife Bridget Stuart (born Fitzgerald), they were educated at the local Christian Brothers' school and both attended QCG. Andrew Joseph does not appear to have completed the degree programme – a not uncommon proceeding, as some law students merely attended for two years to acquire a King's Inns exemption.²⁶⁸ He emigrated to Queensland with his parents in 1864 and after a short time as a civil servant became a successful solicitor. He was elected to the Legislative Council, and served successively as

---

266 John Monroe was born in 1839, the son of John Monroe of Moira in Co. Down. He matriculated in QCG where he read for the BA, MA, and LLB degrees. He entered the Inner Temple in 1860 and was called to the Irish bar in 1863. He married Lizzy, daughter of John Watkins Moule of Elmley-Lovett in Worcestershire in 1867. He was appointed QC in 1877 and was awarded the LLD in 1882. A follower of the Conservatives, he was appointed Solicitor-General 1885 and a justice of the Chancery Division for the Landed Estates Court in the same year. Monroe was made a privy councillor in 1886. He retired in 1896 and died in 1899.
267 For a biographical note on James O'Kinealy (1837–1903), see C.E. Buckland, *Dictionary of Indian Biography* (London, 1906), pp. 321–2. He graduated BA at QCG in 1858, taking a first honours, medal, and prize in mathematics, a second and third in Chemistry and Natural Science respectively. He was given an honorary LLD by QUI on the occasion of its dissolution. O'Kinealy went to India in 1861 and served in the judicial branch of the Civil Service in Lower Bengal. He worked as a legal remembrancer, District Judge, and was a member of the Rent Commission and of the Bengal Legislative Council. He was appointed acting Secretary to the Government of India, Home Department. From 1883 to 1899 he served as puisne judge of the Calcutta High Court. He was president of the Board of Examiners. Noted as a good Arabic scholar, he also edited law books. He died on 14 January 1903.
268 For biographical summary, see *Dictionary of Australian Biography*, p. 467; *Australian Dictionary of Biography, 1891–1939*, pp. 228–9. Andrew Thynne is named as a successful candidate for a first year junior scholarship (literary division, Arts Faculty) for 1861–2 in the UCG *Calendar*, 1915–16, p. 302.

Minister of Justice, Minister without portfolio, Postmaster-General, and Secretary for Agriculture. He was appointed to the first senate of the University of Queensland in April 1910, and was elected vice-chancellor in 1916 and chancellor in 1925. His brother, Sir Henry Thynne,[269] who was awarded the BA (1859) and LLB (1873) degrees, was a resident magistrate from 1878 to 1886, and Deputy-Inspector General of the RIC from 1886 to 1900.

Andrew Reed, who was born in Galway, was educated at the local Erasmus Smith School and QCG.[270] He was awarded the BA (1859) and the LLB (1873) degrees and entered the RIC as a career cadet. The Earl of Carlisle, who visited Galway in 1859, is said to have informed President Berwick that he wished to give a public appointment to a promising Galway student. Reed, we are told, 'was brought to his notice, and was offered a nomination for a cadetship in the Constabulary'.[271] Noted for his efficiency, he received rapid promotion and rose to the highest post, to become the only police officer to fill the office of Inspector-General (1885–1900). He was called to the Irish Bar in 1873 and was awarded the LLB with first honours – he was also a gold medalist – in 1877. He was author of books and pamphlets on topics such as the Irish liquor laws, and wrote the *Irish Constable's Guide*. In 1886 he was thanked by the Government in the House of Commons for his services in controlling riots in Belfast. John McKane, the son of J. McKane of Belfast, a linen manufacturer at Ballymena, Co. Antrim, was educated at QCB and QCG.[272] He obtained a first-year law scholarship (1858–9 session) at QCG. He

---

269 See *Who Was Who, 1897–1915*. Sir Henry Thynne was born in 1839. He appears to have spent some time in QCC as well as QCG (QUI *Calendar*, 1882, p. 323). He was awarded three junior scholarships in QCG, 1855–6 to 1857–8 (science division of the Arts Faculty), and two senior scholarships, Natural Philosophy in 1859–60, and Mathematics in 1860–1. He was awarded the BA in 1859, and gained first-class honours in Mathematics, Mathematical Physics, and Experimental Physics. He was awarded first-class honours in the LLB in 1873 and received a gold medal. He was awarded an honorary MA and LLD by QUI in 1882. In the course of his career, he was a Resident Magistrate (1878–86) and Deputy Inspector-General of the Royal Irish Constabulary (1886–1900). He was appointed CB (1890) and knighted (1898). Both he and his brother were expert, competitive rifle marksmen. He resided at Plantation, Donnybrook, Co. Dublin and died on 11 December 1915.
270 See *Who Was Who, 1897–1916*. Sir Andrew Reed, son of John Reed and Mary Adamson, was born in Galway on 26 September 1837. He was educated at the Erasmus Smith School and QCG. He was awarded the BA, 1859 and the LLB with first honours and gold medal in 1877. Reed graduated LLB in 1878 and was awarded the MA, 1882 (honorary, on recommendation of QUI senate committee). He was called to the Irish Bar in 1873. He entered the Royal Irish Constabulary as a cadet, in 1859, and became, successively, District Inspector, County Inspector, and Assistant Inspector-General. Reed was Divisional Commissioner (1883–5) in charge of police in the counties of Clare, Galway, Mayo, and Roscommon. He was appointed Inspector-General of RIC (1885–1900) and received the special thanks of the Government in Parliament in connection with the suppression of riots in Belfast, 1880. He was knighted in 1889, and received the KCB (1897) and CVO (1900). He married Elizabeth Mary Lyster (she died in 1913). Reed published *Liquor Laws of Ireland; Irish Constable's Guide; Policeman's Manual;* and various pamphlets on reformation of criminals, probation of offenders, and reform of liquor licensing laws. He resided at 23 Fitzwilliam Square, Dublin. He died on 7 November 1914.
271 Notice of Sir Andrew Reed's death in *UCG College Annual*, 1915, p. 59.
272 See Boase; Moody and Beckett, *Queen's Belfast*, vol. ii, p. 588; QUI *Calendar*, 1882, p. 319. McKane's 1858–9 scholarship appears in two categories – law, and first medicine (literary

graduated BA with first-class honours in Logic and Metaphysics (1860), and MA with a first in Logic, Metaphysics and Political Economy (1862). He was called to the Irish Bar in 1864 and was Barrington Lecturer in Political Economy in 1867. McKane was Professor of English Law at QCB from 1875 to 1885. He was elected conservative MP for Mid-Armagh in December 1885, but died in Dublin on 11 January 1886, without taking his seat.

Norton, King, and McAuliffe were all lawyers who served as judges in the colonies. Bernard G. Norton (BA 1860), who entered the Inner Temple, London, was appointed solicitor-general of British Guiana in 1863, and held the post of first puisne judge from 1868 to 1871.[273] Aelian A. King held scholarships throughout his student years at QCG (1859–63), and graduated BA in 1862 in Mathematics and Modern Languages.[274] He served first, as assistant government agent, and later as district judge in Ceylon. Michael McAuliffe graduated BA (1860) with a first in Modern languages.[275] He entered the Indian civil service and was later appointed divisional judge of the Punjab. He is also remembered as a scholar who translated the sacred book of the Sikhs. Atkinson and Mulholland also entered the legal profession and ended their careers as judges. William Mulholland,[276] the son of a Belfast doctor, was a student at QCG from 1860–1 to 1865–6, where he graduated BA with second honours in 1863, and was a senior scholar (Metaphysical and Economic Science). He took up legal studies on graduation and gained third-year and senior law scholarships (1864–5 to 1865–6). He was called to the Bar in Ireland (1865) and England (1875). Appointed QC (1894), he was made Bencher of Lincoln's Inn, and judge of the County Courts (England).

    division), see, for example, UCG *Calendar* 1915–16. He was awarded an honorary LLD by the QUI in 1882.

273 Bernard Gustavus Norton, attended QCG and graduated BA in 1860. In the 1858–9 session he was a third-year junior scholar in the literary division of the Arts Faculty. He qualified as a barrister and was a member of the Inner Temple (6 June 1855). Norton was appointed solicitor general of British Guiana in March 1863, and was first puisne judge of the supreme court of British Guiana from 1868 until his death. He died at Norwood, Surrey, on 13 April 1871. See *Irish Law Times and Solicitors' Journal*, vol. xv, 478 (1871); Boase.

274 Aelian A. King attended at QCG from 1859–60 to 1864–5, and graduated BA in 1862 with a third honours in Mathematical Science and Modern Languages. He held junior scholarships in his three undergraduate years, and senior scholarships in Mathematics (1862–3) and Modern Languages and Modern History (1863–4). He was awarded an honorary MA in 1882 on the occasion of the dissolution of the QUI, on the recommendation of the Committee of the Senate. He made his career in the civil service of Ceylon where he was appointed successively Assistant Government Agent and District Judge.

275 Michael McAuliffe attended QCG from 1857–8 to 1862–3. He graduated BA with first honours in modern languages in 1860. He held a scholarship in each year of his course: Junior scholarships in the literary division of the Arts Faculty for the years 1857–8, 1858–9, 1859–60; Senior scholarships in Ancient classics (1860–1) and in Modern Languages and History (1861–2). He was awarded an honorary MA by the QUI in 1882 on the occasion of its dissolution. He was appointed a divisional Judge of the Punjab. He translated the sacred book of the Sikhs.

276 See *Who Was Who*. William Mulholland was born on 19 January 1843, the eldest son of J.S. Mulholland MD, of Belfast, and Rosa, daughter of Charles MacMahon, Brookfield, Dundalk. He was educated at QCG (1860–1 to 1865–6), where he was a second and third-year junior scholar (literary division, Arts Faculty), and a senior scholar (in Metaphysical and Economic Science). Following his graduation (BA with second honours in 1863), he continued his legal

John Atkinson was the son of Edward Atkinson, a physician, of Glenwilliam Castle, Co. Limerick, and Skea House, Enniskillen.[277] He was born at Drogheda, Co. Louth and educated at the Royal Belfast Academical Institution and at QCG (1858–9 to 1864–5). He gained junior scholarships (science division of Arts) in his first three years at Galway and senior scholarships in his fourth and fifth years in Mathematics, and Natural Philosophy. He graduated BA with first-class honours in 1861, and in the following year registered as a student both in King's Inns, Dublin, and at the Inner Temple. Like Mulholland, he too was a third-year and senior law scholar (1863–4 to 1864–5), but unlike him, he sat for and gained firsts in both the Diploma in Elementary Law (1864), and the LLB (1865). He joined the Munster circuit, of which he remained a member until his appointment as a law officer. Appointed QC in 1880 at the early age of 36, he was elected Bencher of King's Inns in 1885. Atkinson became solicitor-general for Ireland in 1889, attorney-general, and Irish privy councillor in 1892, and was elected Conservative MP for North Derry in 1895. For the next ten years he was again attorney-general, and in 1905 he was the first Irish barrister to be appointed directly from his practice to the House of Lords. As a lord of appeal in ordinary, he took the title of Lord Atkinson, of Glenwilliam, Co. Limerick, and served until his retirement in 1928. He was as valuable to the government as much for his political as legal abilities, and was also sworn a member of the English privy council. Although not as insightful a lawyer as Lord Lindley, whose place he filled in the Lords, he was a courageous, active, and productive lord of appeal until his retirement. Theodore C. Tobias wrote of Atkinson:

>studies and was third year and senior law scholar in the years, 1864–5 and 1865–6. He was called to the Bar in Ireland (1865) and in England (1875). He joined the English Northern Circuit. He became a QC in 1894 and was elected a Bencher of Lincoln's Inn in 1897. Mulholland was appointed a Judge of the County Courts in 1899. He resided in London where he died on 21 August 1907.

277 See *DNB*. John Atkinson (Baron Atkinson of Glenwilliam) (1844–1932) (Life Peer, 1905), was born on 13 December 1844 at Drogheda, Co. Louth, the eldest son of Edward Atkinson, physician, of Glenwilliam Castle, Co. Limerick, and Skea House, Enniskillen, and Rosetta (his first wife), the daughter of John Shaw McCulloch. He was educated at the Royal Belfast Academical Institution and at QCG (1858–9 to 1864–5). He gained junior scholarships (science division of Arts) in his first three years at Galway and senior scholarships in his fourth and fifth years (Mathematics, and Natural Philosophy). He graduated BA with first honours in 1861, and in the following year he registered as a student both in King's Inns, Dublin, and at the Inner Temple. Atkinson was a third-year and senior law scholar (1863–4 to 1864–5), and gained firsts in both the Diploma in Elementary Law (1864), and the LLB (1865). The QUI awarded him an honorary LLD in 1882. He married Rowena, daughter of Richard Chute MD, of Tralee, Co. Kerry, and they had four sons, the three elder of whom predeceased their father. He joined the Munster circuit, of which he remained a member until his appointment as a law officer. Appointed QC in 1880 at the early age of 36, he was elected bencher of King's Inns in 1885. Atkinson became solicitor-general for Ireland in 1889, attorney-general and Irish privy councillor in 1892, and was elected Conservative MP for North Derry in 1895. For the next ten years he was again attorney-general, and in 1905 he was the first Irish barrister to be appointed directly from his practice at the bar to the House of Lords. As a lord of appeal in ordinary, he took the title of Lord Atkinson of Glenwilliam, and served until his retirement in 1928. He was as valuable to the government as much for his political as legal abilities, and was also sworn a member of the English privy council. His intimate knowledge of Irish land and social problems

> In office his knowledge of land and social problems in Ireland rendered him a highly valued adviser to the chief secretary for Ireland, Gerald Balfour ... in the framing and passing of the Irish Land Act of 1896 and the Local Government Act of 1898 ... he was a ready speaker, an energetic worker possessing an instinctive and sincere passion for justice, and, above all, endowed with the gifts of courage both physical and moral, and an inflexible sense of duty, which enabled him to steer undaunted a straight course through the stormy seas of Irish political life during a period when navigation was by no means easy, and to resist the strong pressure put upon him to resign by the first coalition government in order to satisfy the requirements of the political party leaders.[278]

In spite of the quality of the students, there remained the problem of low numbers, a problem which was considered by the Queen's Colleges Commissioners in the course of their review of the Law programme as a whole. Although impressed with the study arrangements in Law – which the Commissioners described as 'a very lengthened, extensive, and complete course of legal study' – they expressed regret that so few students had taken advantage of it, as the average annual attendances for all three Colleges had only been about twenty students. They attributed the low numbers of law students to the fact that there was no incentive to take law courses, as there were no worthwhile privileges conferred on law students by the legal professions for so doing. 'We are of opinion', they wrote,

> that the small attendance in the Law Schools of the Queen's Colleges is fairly attributable to the want of motives to induce Students to go through a systematic course of Legal Study. The only privilege at present conferred on Students in the Law School of the Queen's Colleges is that given by 14 and 15 Vic., chap. 88, which provides that the Student who has attended the Law Professors of any of the Queen's Colleges shall be qualified to be admitted as an attorney or solicitor in four years from the Commencement of his apprenticeship, instead of five. This privilege seems not to be much valued, as, from Returns obtained from the officers of the Courts of Law, only one apprentice appears to have availed himself of it.[279]

In the course of their inquiries, the commissioners had put the issue to the law professors interviewed. In Galway, Heron explained that he had nine students, four in the Law Faculty and five in Arts. On the numbers issue, he said:

---

made him highly valuable to chief secretary Balfour, particularly in framing and passing the Irish Land Act, 1896 and the Local Government Act. He was an active, energetic and deeply concerned lord of appeal until his retirement in 1928. He resided at 39 Hyde Park Gate, and died in London on 13 March 1932. His portrait, by John St Helier Lander, hangs in the dining-hall of King's Inns, Dublin.

278 *DNB*.
279 *Queen's Colleges Commission Report*, p. 27.

> It never could have been anticipated that there would be a very large number of students in the Faculty of Law. I may mention, as regards the number of students, that when I was in Trinity College, attending the lectures of Dr. Longfield, his number was limited to eight or nine. These were men who were going to the bar, or Scholars who wanted, by attending his lectures, to keep up a course of lectures which is compulsory on Scholars on the foundation.[280]

He was of the view that large numbers were never envisaged, and the reason the Law Faculty had been given disproportionate representation on the College Council was not in anticipation of large student numbers, but because the Law Dean was always a lawyer.

There were other factors at work as the total number of students going to the Irish Bar had apparently fallen off in any event. This decline was variously attributed to the introduction of the Common Law Procedure Act,[281] and to increased opportunities in the civil service.[282] Heron supported the compulsory education of apprentices which he knew was greatly desired by the Dublin attorneys, and which would probably greatly increase the size of law classes in Belfast and Cork where there were respectable numbers of attorneys. There were only some ten attorneys resident in Galway.[283] But even without compulsory education, he believed, the Faculty of Law should continue its work:

> There will always be some three or four students, at least, in each of the Colleges going to the bar. These will be generally among the most distinguished students – the men who work most, and are most distinguished in other departments. It is most important that they should be furnished with the best means of being educated, in both the Science and Practice of Law. I could, if necessary, mention the names of many students who have derived great advantage from the Law School.[284]

Professor Mills in Cork was of the view that attorneys and solicitors wanted a simple, practical, vocational education, and he recommended the abolition of Jurisprudence and Roman Law (Civil Law) which he maintained were not valued,

---

280 Ibid., question 4255, p. 289. See also Kenny, *Tristram Kennedy*, pp. 90–2. In the 1840s there were some four or five candidates annually for the London LLB, and a typical TCD law class was about seven students, and although there were some four hundred students registered at the King's Inns, relatively few attended the Dublin Law Institute's courses.
281 Presumably the 'Act to Amend the Procedure in the Superior Courts of Common Law in Ireland', 16 & 17 Vic., c. 13. Daire Hogan, *The Legal Profession in Ireland*, argued that the Chancery Regulation Act, 1850, and the Common Law Procedure Act, 1853, did result in a decline in legal business by getting rid of a large amount of useless, cumbersome, and artificial procedural work (p. 83).
282 *Queen's Colleges Commission Report*, Minutes of Evidence, question 1572, p. 99 (Cliffe Leslie); question 4260, p. 289 (Heron).
283 Ibid., Minutes of Evidence, questions 4243, 4235, p. 289.
284 Ibid., Minutes of Evidence, question 4246, p. 289.

and therefore not attended by them. While he regarded a more liberal education as vital to those professions, he was of opinion that they would not voluntarily avail of it:

> That is proved by the present state of things. The value of the Diploma is not sufficient to induce him to undergo a course of Roman Law, and would not be sufficient to induce him to take both a professional and a general education.[285]

Professor Heron also supported the case for compulsory education for attorneys.[286] There may have been other reasons for the low uptake of the apprenticeship privilege. Professor Molyneux at Belfast was of the view that the privilege attached to studying law was not widely known and appreciated. The picture presented may also have been too bleak. Some solicitors and apprentices living near the Colleges attended lectures on a more casual basis as evidenced by Professor Molyneux who testified to having four in his classes.[287] There may have been more in earlier years, as he told the Commission: 'There have been a good many local solicitors practising in this town in all the classes, at least in the first classes. I have had a number either of solicitors or those who were serving their apprenticeships'.[288]

Cairnes's Later Career and the Supplemental Charter Débâcle

John Elliot Cairnes was the quintessential scholar and shortly after his arrival in Galway rose to the height of his fame. The success of his book, *The Slave Power* (1862), which was a powerful defence of the cause of the Northern States in opposing black slavery in America, gave him an international reputation. It made a great impression both in England and America, and a second edition, 'greatly enlarged, with a new preface', appeared in 1863. He was enabled, because of his private income, to pursue a full-time academic career. His work displayed great breadth and depth. Although known mainly as an economist, his intellectual interests covered political and social theory, international law, history, and education. He was, for example, a strong supporter of non-denominational or 'mixed' education, and was active in supporting the Queen's Colleges, as Leslie Stephen noted:

> He was deeply interested in questions of national education in Ireland, being always a strong advocate of united education. He took an energetic part in the opposition to the supplementary charter of the Queen's Colleges in 1865–6, which was ultimately pronounced invalid by the master of the rolls. He also did much to inspire the successful opposition to Mr. Gladstone's scheme of an Irish University in 1873.[289]

---

285 Ibid., Minutes of Evidence, questions 4246, p. 289; 3320–5, p. 229.
286 Ibid., question 4245, p. 289.
287 Ibid., questions 1556–7, p. 97.
288 Ibid., question 1539, p. 97.
289 *DNB*.

The supplementary charter issue arose out of the Catholic hierarchy's campaign for a state-supported and funded Catholic university. This campaign, vigorously pursued under the leadership of Cardinal Cullen, at first focused on getting a charter for the Catholic University which was ailing and in financial difficulties. The charter issue was revived in June 1865, when Daniel O'Donoghue MP (known as 'The O'Donoghue') put a motion before the Commons seeking a charter of incorporation for the Catholic University.[290] Although the government felt unable to grant a charter, it was prepared to be conciliatory.[291] Sir George Grey on the government's behalf proposed a solution similar to that adopted by the University of London, namely, the extension of the powers of the Queen's University (a change of name to the more acceptable 'Royal University' was first suggested at this stage) so that it could also grant degrees to students outside of the Queen's Colleges.

President Berwick of QCG, who lived in close proximity to two formidable opponents of mixed education, Archbishop MacHale of Tuam and Bishop MacEvilly of Galway, foresaw grave danger in the proposal for his College. If students could get their degrees from a central examining body without the need of attendance, then, he believed, the Church would move from active discouragement to a total ban on Catholics attending the Queen's Colleges. His report for 1885–6, which blames the Charter proposal for a fall-off in student attendance, bears an undertone of incredulous anger at the policy shift implicit in the government's announcement, which appeared to accommodate both sectarian and non-residential education at third level. Worse still, he clearly realised that it was a capitulation to pressure brought by the Catholic Church hierarchy, which in his view had used or misused its authority to frustrate the Colleges in every way possible. He pointed out that the Catholic Deans had been forced to retire on pain of suspension; that Cardinal Cullen who had recommended that the sacraments be denied to parents who sent their children to TCD had, in the same sentence, ranked the Colleges as more pernicious; and that a local bishop had in fact proclaimed 'that henceforth the sacraments should be refused to all who entered the Queen's Colleges'.[292]

While the bishops argued for greater concessions, however, growing opposition to the proposal came from a variety of influential people, including Cairnes. Cardinal Cullen was prepared at first to settle for a 'closed system' in which

---

290 O'Donoghue (1883–9), who was born in Kerry and educated at Stonyhurst, had been MP for Tipperary (1857–65) and Tralee (1865–85), first as a Liberal and, after 1880, as a 'home ruler'. A prominent nationalist politician, he was a strong advocate of a Catholic university and tenant right. A colourful character, he challenged Sir Robert Peel to a duel in 1862 for having called him 'a mannikin traitor'.

291 It was at the end of Lord Palmerston's ministry (1859–65), in which Lord John Russell was foreign secretary (he had succeeded Peel as prime minister in 1850) and William Gladstone was chancellor of the exchequer. Russell led the government after Palmerston's death (October 1859), but was defeated on a parliamentary reform motion in June 1886. Derby assumed office on 9 July with Disraeli as chancellor, and although the 'Conservative' Disraeli claimed credit for the Reform Act 1867 which was imposed upon him, he lost the subsequent election, which was based on the Act's principles, to the Liberal Gladstone.

292 President's *Report*, 1865–6, p. 7.

Catholic students could be educated in a chartered Catholic College which would be associated with the Queen's University. As negotiations progressed, however, he changed his mind. He feared that such a system would validate the Queen's Colleges, and would inadequately guarantee Church control of both the new Catholic College and any altered University Senate. Cullen opted instead for the freedom and independence of an 'open system', analogous to the University of London, with powers to associate Colleges at a later date. Such an initiative required both a modification of the Queen's University Charter and supplementing legislation.

Letters patent for a supplementary charter were issued and enrolled in June 1866, and were accepted by a two-vote majority of the Queen's University Senate especially called for the purpose on 6 October. Although the plan survived a change of government, and a committee of the Senate had prepared appropriate regulations (approved on 15 November 1866) to implement it, the scheme came to an abrupt end when the Charter was first rejected by the University members meeting in Convocation, and then challenged in court by three Queen's graduates.[293] Although the plaintiffs were held to have no *locus standi*, and were therefore not entitled to bring the case, it was clear that the Master of the Rolls believed there was substantive merit in their objection.[294] A perpetual injunction was indeed granted against the Charter on 1 February 1868 as a result of subsequent legal proceedings. It is believed that Cairnes played a major role in campaigning against the Charter and that he also did much to inspire the successful opposition to Gladstone's University Bill of 1873 which could have led to the dissolution of QCG had it secured parliamentary approval.

Gladstone's bill, as already noted, proposed to transform the University of Dublin into a federal Irish National University to which TCD, the Catholic College in Dublin, and the other Colleges would be associated, except of course for QCG which was to be suppressed. The bill, which was introduced at the time Hugh Law was Legal Adviser to the government in Ireland, was defeated by a mere three votes. So it was that the Queen's Colleges, though constantly subject to attack, and forced to operate in a state of anxious uncertainty as to their future, without further significant support from the government, continued their academic work, more or less unchanged, until the establishment of the Royal University in 1882.

---

293 The letters patent for a Supplemental Charter was dated 13 June 1866 and enrolled on 25 June. Its purpose was to extend the powers of the Queen's University to allow it to confer its degrees and awards on qualifying candidates who had not matriculated in, or attended at, the Queen's Colleges. A new charter, dated 8 October 1864, was issued to the QUI to allow for an annual assembly of members in Convocation. This power took effect by royal warrant of 25 September 1866 and Convocation met on 12 October following. See *QUI Reports*, 1865–6 and 1866–7.

294 *MacCormack v. The Queen's University, Irish Reports* (1867), 1 Equity series 160. Law (presumably Hugh Law) and Kane represented members of the Senate who voted against acceptance of the Charter, but made no argument. It was in their interests that the petitioners should succeed. At the end of his judgement, John Edward Walsh MR said: 'It is certainly not free from difficulty; but my present impression is in favour of the view pressed by the Petitioners, that the Charter of 1864 does not vest the power of accepting or rejecting the new Charter in the senate exclusively'.

Towards the end of his life, Professor Cairnes was in very bad health. He had settled at Mill Hill near London in 1865 and was appointed Professor of Political Economy at University College London in the following year, a post he held concurrently with his professorship at QCG. His health, according to Stephen, in his *DNB* entry on Cairnes, deteriorated rapidly:

> Renewed attacks of ill health in the shape of rheumatic gout forced him to pay several visits to foreign baths. A severe operation in 1868 gave him some relief, but he was in time completely crippled. In the spring of 1870 he settled at Lee, near Blackheath, and two years later at Kidbrooke Road, Blackheath. Here he remained for the rest of his life, becoming by degrees a more hopeless invalid, but never losing his cheerfulness or his intellectual vigour.

He kept up a close personal and intellectual friendship with his near neighbour, J.S. Mill, and he had the companionship and the stimulating company of Henry Fawcett and L.H. Courtney who regularly visited him in his later years. Cairnes's poor health made it impossible for him to fulfill his teaching duties at Galway. William Lupton, a lawyer and the Registrar at QCG, fulfilled Cairnes's teaching commitments and this time, and his name appears on the examination papers in Jurisprudence and Political Economy from 1865 onwards. Cairnes resigned his professorship at Galway in 1870 due to ill health, and was forced to resign his London professorship in 1872 for the same reason. President Berwick, in his *Report* for 1869–70, felt obliged to note his resignation:

> I regret to add that, in consequence of his continued ill-health, the College has been deprived of the services of one of its ablest Professors – Mr. J.E. Cairnes. I cannot conclude this report without bearing testimony to the zeal and eminent ability manifested by him during his connexion with the College.

Although he was called to the Irish Bar, he never seriously practised. His contribution was undoubtedly in the field of economics rather than in law. He was conferred with an honorary LLD degree by the University of Dublin in 1874. Cairnes was described as 'a man of singular charm of conversation, even when quite disabled physically'. He died, 'after long suffering, borne with public patience', at his home in London on 8 July 1875 leaving a widow and three children.

Professors William Lupton and Robert Cather Donnell

William Lupton (1830–76), who took over Cairnes's teaching, had received his university education at Queen's College Belfast, where he was a member of the first graduating class in 1852.[295] He was an able student who graduated BA with

---

295 For biographical notes see Boylan and Foley, *Political Economy and Colonial Ireland*, p. 173; *Presidents, Vice-Presidents, and Professors of Queen's College, Galway*, p. 41.

first-class honours in Mathematics (taking an exhibition valued at £25) and a second-class honours in Natural Philosophy for which he was awarded a medal.[296] In 1853 he was awarded an honours MA in Mathematical and Physical Sciences, wining an exhibition of £15 and a gold medal.[297] He immediately moved to Galway where he had secured the post of Registrar at QCG, a post he held until 1870. Lupton developed an interest in the law and was admitted a member of the Inner Temple. When Cairnes resigned his post in 1870, Lupton successfully applied for the professorship and quit the office of Registrar. He held the Chair of Jurisprudence and Political Economy until his death in 1876. He had a particular interest in the university question and was the author of *The Reform Bill and the Queen's University in Ireland* (Dublin, 1860). He also wrote a series of articles on economic issues, which were published in the *Irish Industrial Magazine* (1866).

Professor Lupton was too ill in the 1875–6 College session to take his classes, and a colleague, Professor Maguire, was employed to act as *locum tenens* to do his teaching. President Berwick noted in his report for the year:

> I deeply lament to state that Mr. Lupton, the able Professor of Jurisprudence and Political Economy, has been prevented by severe illness, from attending at the College during the present session. The College is fortunate in possessing the services of a Professor, who, in addition to the ardous duties of his own chair – the chair of the Latin language – is fully competent to fill the chair of Jurisprudence. With the consent of the Lord Lieutenant, the College has appointed Professor Maguire to perform, during the continuance of Mr Lupton's illness, the duties of his Chair.[298]

On Lupton's death in 1876, Robert Cather Donnell MA, LLD (1839–83) became Professor of Jurisprudence and Political Economy.[299] The second son of William Donnell and Isabella Cather, he was born at Ballinamallard, County Tyrone, and educated at Queen's College Belfast where he graduated BA in 1860. Donnell received the QUI gold medal in Jurisprudence and Political Economy. He was awarded the MA degree in 1863 and was called to the Irish Bar in the following year. He maintained a life-long interest in economics and law. Following his appointment as Barrington lecturer (1871–3), he successfully applied for the Whately Professorship of Political Economy at Trinity College Dublin (1872–7). Following the death of William Lupton in 1876, Donnell secured the post of Professor of Jurisprudence and Political Economy at QCG, a post he held until his death in 1883. His major scholarly contribution was in the field of landlord and tenant law. He had, he states, 'been engaged into inquiries into the Ulster tenant-right, and to the general relations of landlord and tenant in Ireland' when it was

---

296 Appendix to *QUI Report*, 1852–3, pp. 63–4.
297 Ibid., 1853–4, pp. 74–5.
298 President's *Report*, 1875–6, p. 9. In this regard, Berwick quoted the minute of an earlier report given to the Visitors (the Duke of Leinster, who was Chancellor, Justice Fitzgerald, and Edward Hamilton MD), who had made a triennial visitation to QCG on 6 April 1876.
299 See biographical note in Boylan and Foley, *Political Economy and Colonial Ireland*, pp. 167–8.

suggested to him that he might produce a work on the novel Irish Land Act, 1870 – the Act drafted by Hugh Law. The result was his first major publication, *Practical Guide to the Law of Tenant Compensation and Farm Purchase under the Irish Land Act* (Dublin, 1871). This was followed by a detailed analysis of the Ulster tenant-right custom which was at the heart of the Act in *Chapters on the Leaseholder's Claim to Tenant-Right, and Other Tenant-Right Questions* (Dublin, 1873). Although Donnell wrote mainly on legal matters, he applied his economic training to his subject, giving remarkable insights into this branch of the law. In some respects he anticipates the 'law in context' approach to legal study used in more recent times. He produced a new addition of the book in 1876 with the cumbersome title: *Reports of One Hundred and Ninety Cases in the Irish Land Courts; with Preliminary Tenant-right Chapters* (Dublin, 1876). *A Scheme of Land Transfer for Small Proprietors, by Local Registry of Title* appeared two years earlier, which was also published in Dublin.

The Success of the Law School under the Queen's University

By the time of Donnell's death, the old Queen's University in Ireland had been replaced by the less successful Royal University. The period of the Queen's University (1850–82), in spite of its difficulties, was probably the most successful for the Galway Law School – at least until modern times. Those years saw a succession of very able law students pass through the College gates. In spite of lower student numbers and greater local difficulties, the Galway law students outperformed those of its sister Colleges in that period – at least as regards honours obtained in the LLB and Diploma in Elementary Law. Galway students secured 18 firsts, 5 seconds, and 1 third; Belfast students had to their credit 14 firsts, 6 seconds, and 2 thirds, while Cork students obtained 4 firsts, 3 seconds, and 1 third.[300] In addition to those Galway students – some of whose careers have been mentioned above – there were also students who took legal studies and had successful legal careers without taking out any academic qualifications in law. Richard Edmund Meredith, for example, who was to become Master of the Rolls in Ireland for the period 1906–12, matriculated at Galway in 1875.[301] Born in November 1855, he was the fourth son of a Dublin solicitor, William Rice Meredith. He registered in the Middle Temple in 1876 and was called to the Irish Bar in 1879. Sir Thomas Lopdell O'Shaughnessy (1850–1933) was also educated at QCG although he too does not appear on the graduate list.[302] His father, Thomas, was a solicitor, and his mother, Marion, was daughter of Charles Lopdell of Castle Lodge, Gort, Co. Galway. O'Shaughnessy, one of the more colourful

---

300 Data taken from *QUI Calendar*, 1882, pp. 275–7. Where students attended more than one College, the honour was attributed to all Colleges attended.
301 See *Who Was Who*; Ball, *The Judges in Ireland*, vol. ii, p. 382; list of matriculated students as in *QUI Calendar*, for example, 1880. See also J.B. Hall, *Random Records of a Reporter* (London and Dublin, n.d.), pp. 99–101. (Includes a portrait illustration of O'Shaughnessy.)
302 *Who Was Who*.

characters of the Irish Bar and Bench, was Recorder of Dublin (1905–24) and Judge of the High Court (1924–5). He was elected Bencher of the King's Inns (1895), made a KC (1901), and privy councillor (1912), and received a knighthood (1927). The Recordership of Dublin was regarded as a most important office and was filled by a lawyer of high standing. It was Maurice Healy's opinion that it had never been 'more efficiently occupied than by the ... the Right Hon. T.L. O'Shaughnessy'.[303] J.B. Hall wrote that

> The retirement of 'Tommy O'Shaughnessy', the last of the Recorders, from the Bench, removed one of whom it might be said that no man in Dublin was more universally known, and that in his long occupancy of the historic position in Green Street, he distinguished himself by his rare judicial qualities.[304]

Although O'Shaughnessy had been a past master in the art of brow-beating witnesses, he did not, according to Eugene Sheehy, tolerate histrionics in his own court:

> The stories told of the Recorder are legion; and his court was a scene of abundant comedy. He often dealt with sixty or eighty cases in a day. I met him in the street one day after his retirement, and he assured me that 'what the public required was cheap and quick law'. He certainly provided it at a fast gallop. Very often, after a few questions had been addressed to the plaintiff, he would tell the solicitor or counsel acting for the defendant to put his client in the witness box; and he would then decide as to where the truth lay without the necessity of hearing further evidence. This was 'form at a glance' with a vengeance. He was a very shrewd judge of men and evidence, and his judgments were usually sound, but the unsuccessful litigant could hardly be blamed if he left the Court with the feeling that his case had not been properly heard.[305]

In Hall's view he was 'an ideal Recorder, indefatigable, fair and just', and he remarked of him that in his private life 'he was a genial gentleman with two fads – snuff boxes and Airedales'.[306]

QCG students such as O'Shaughnessy are difficult to track, and there appear to have been others. Judge Rentoul, in writing of his student days at Galway refers to Sir Henry Blake as a student at QCG.[307] Blake, who was the son of an RIC

---

[303] Maurice Healy, *The Old Munster Circuit: A Book of Memories and Traditions* (London, 1939), p. 206.
[304] Hall, *Random Records*, p. 99. Apparently O'Shaughnessy was responsible for giving the name 'Court of Appeal' to a local pub called 'Barney's'. When a well-known solicitor failed to answer the Crier's call in Green Street Court, he said: 'Try the Court of Appeal', and the name stuck (p. 86).
[305] Eugene Sheehy, *May It Please the Court* (Dublin, 1951), pp. 80–1.
[306] Hall, *Random Records*, p. 101.
[307] James A. Rentoul, *Stray Thoughts and Memories* (London, 1920), p. 83; Judge J. A. Rentoul LLD, KC, 'Old Galway', *Q.C.G.*, November 1905, pp. 4–7; *Who Was Who, 1916–28*.

county Inspector, was born in Limerick, and rose from being an RIC cadet and magistrate, to become successively the Governor of Bahamas (1884–7), Newfoundland (1887–8), Jamaica (1889–97), Hong Kong (1897–1903) and Ceylon (1903–7).

Among the students who attended QCG in those years was Sir Raymond West (1852–6), who became an outstanding Indian civil servant, judge, and jurist. He was born at Ballyloughrane, Co. Kerry, in September 1832, the son of Frederick Henry West, a journalist. A brilliant student, he secured three Junior scholarships, a first-class honours BA, and exhibitions and gold medals in two degree subjects. Having won both a King's Inns studentship and an Indian civil service competition, he chose to go to India, arriving there in September 1856 to join the judicial department. He progressed from Registrar of the High Court to positions as district judge, judicial commissioner, and Judge of the High Court of Bombay (1873–86). He returned to Ireland for two year's leave (1868–70), but instead of taking a well-deserved rest, he read for the MA degree, absorbed himself in 'omnivorous legal study', and was called to the Irish Bar. He was appointed a member of executive council of the Governor of Bombay (1886–92) and was made Vice-Chancellor of the University of Bombay. West published an annotated edition of the Bombay code (1867–8) and, with Dr J.G. Bühler, produced an important *Digest of Hindu Law* (1867–9). Knighted in 1888, he was appointed, on his retirement, a lecturer in Indian law at Cambridge (1895–1907). Of his contribution, it has been written:

> The long series of his judgments enjoys an authority in India not exceeded by that of any other judge; and the ultra-conservatism of some of them, which has recently evoked criticism from Hindu reformers, is perhaps a judicial virtue ... West deserves to be remembered not only for his own judicial eminence, but also for his guidance of the subordinate judiciary. English law and justice in India were exotics which required personal explanation and example to render them workable or even intelligible. It was an even greater task to build up a sound tradition, an esprit-de-corps, and, above all, an efficient system of inspection and control.[308]

Other notables who had studied at Galway in this period include: Judge John Gordon, Justice of the King's Bench (1916–22); Sir Walter Llewellyn Lewis, Chief Justice, British Honduras; James Alexander Rentoul, Judge of the City of London Court; Michael Drummond, County Court Judge; the journalist and author, Joseph R. Fisher, and the O'Donnell brothers, Frank Hugh and Charles.

John Gordon (1849–1922) was the eldest son of Samuel Gordon of Shankill House in Co. Down.[309] He held scholarships throughout his student years at QCG

---

308 *DNB*.
309 Ball, *The Judges in Ireland*, vol. ii, p. 385; *Who Was Who, 1916–28*. He was an unassuming, reliable, and conservative judge. John Gordon was awarded the BA in 1873 (he gained third-class honours in Mathematical Science), and gained a second-class honours LLB in 1876. He was conferred with an LLD in 1882 (honorary on dissolution of the QUI). He was a Junior scholar, science division of the Arts Faculty from 1870–1 to 1872–3, and a Senior Scholar in

(1870–7), and graduated BA in 1873 and LLB in 1876. He was called to the Bar in the following year and made a QC in 1892. He was elected MP for South Derry as a Liberal Unionist in 1900, and held his seat until 1915 when he became attorney-general. He was appointed judge of the King's Bench the following year. Sir Walter Llewellyn Lewis, who specialised in science at QCG, chose a legal career on graduation.[310] Although he gained firsts in Experimental Science in his BA (1869) and MA (1871), he entered the Middle Temple, London. He was called to the English Bar in 1876 and joined the South Wales and Chester Circuit. He was successively appointed, stipendary magistrate (1885) and puisne Judge of the Supreme Court of Trinidad (1893), and Chief Justice of British Honduras (1900).

Frank Hugh O'Donnell, had a distinguished record as a law student at Galway, where he was first and third-year law scholar, and took the senior law scholarship in 1868–9.[311] A prolific writer, he was one of Parnell's early supporters, famous for his ability to obstruct parliament. He was described in action in the Commons by Florence Arnold-Forster as:

> A jovial eloquent young man who is hail fellow well met with all parties in the lobby, and in the House – can render valuable assistance to his friends by turning on a copious stream of oratory, pathetic, indignant or derisive, on any subject at a moment's notice. This evening he was mainly derisive, the chief object of his wrath being the Liberal Ministers.[312]

Mathematics in 1873–4. He took both a third-year (1874–5) and a Senior Law (1874–5) scholarship.

310 *Who Was Who, 1929–40*. Lewis was born in Banbury, Oxfordshire, on 13 November 1849. He was a Junior Scholar, science division, Arts, 1867–8 and 1868–9; a Senior Scholar in Natural Philosophy 1869–70; and Senior Scholar in Chemistry (1870–1).

311 Frank Hugh O'Donnell entered QCG as Francis McDonald, but changed his name to the more 'Irish' Francis Hugh O'Donnell. He was born in Co. Donegal in 1848 and his father was apparently from Carndonagh. He was awarded a second-class honours BA (QCG) in 1865, and gained a first-class honours in the MA in 1868. He was first-year Law scholar (1865–6), third-year Law scholar (1867–8), and Senior Law scholar (1868–9) as well as a gold medalist. For an account of his life and work see Áine Ní Chonghaile, *F.H. O'Donnell 1848–1916: A Shaol agus a Shaothar* (Dublin, 1920). O'Donnell joined the staff of the *Morning Post*, and became MP for Galway, in 1874. He joined the IRB and was elected home rule MP for Dungarvan, 1877–85, and was a noted obstructionist in the Commons. He was somewhat erratic and eccentric in his views. He argued strongly against the educational policy of the Queen's Colleges in the early years, and argued in favour of mixed education later. He left the Parnellites over their Land League policy, and his unsuccessful action for libel against the *Times* led to the Parnell Commission. A man of immense knowledge, he was an entertaining companion and a fine speaker. He wrote many works, for example, *The History of the Irish Parliamentary Party* (London, 1910). He died in London in 1916. His brother, Charles J. O'Donnell (formerly Charles McDonald), also attended QCG where he received the BA (1868) and MA (1870). He joined the Indian civil service and became MP for Walworth in 1906.

312 Moody and Hawkins (eds.), *Arnold-Forster*, p. 80. It was a debate on the 'Coercion' Bill (Protection of Person and Property Bill) on the night of 24 February 1881. Another QCG man, T.P. O'Connor, was equally famous as an obstructionist. In an earlier entry of the 6 January Arnold-Forster describes the opening of the Parliamentary session: 'The Traversers present in person, there being no legal objection ... I went down to the House in the evening – the first and familiar sight that met my eyes on looking down from the Gallery being Mr T.P. O'Connor declaiming against the Government' (Ibid., p. 49).

Even as a student debater he provoked controversy, causing Professor Moffett to leave the chair at a debate in which he referred to Queen Elizabeth as 'Elizabeth the Infamous'.[313] Another QCG man, James Bryce Killen,[314] got into similar difficulties. He had just graduated in May 1869 when he caused controversy at QCB for reading a paper entitled 'The Spirit of Irish History' which was clearly contrary to the ban on political subjects being discussed in the Colleges. His allegedly 'very questionable expressions' were the subject of a Parliamentary question, but the Chief Secretary was able to assure the House that no seditious or treasonable language was used.[315] Killen was a radical nationalist who was later active in forming the Land League. Michael Davitt, James Daly, editor of the *Connaught Telegraph*, and Killen, who was then editor of the Belfast *Northern Star*, were arrested in November 1879, and charged with sedition in respect of speeches made at a land agitation meeting on the second day of that month, at Gurteen, Co. Sligo. The resulting trial involved the unusual circumstance of a prosecution by one QCG man against another.[316] The Crown was represented by one of QCG's ablest law graduates, John Monroe QC, who was then Law Adviser at Dublin Castle, and was later to become a Chancery Judge on the Landed Estates Court.[317] Killen had also been a QCG man, but had taken a very different political course.

James Alexander Rentoul was the eldest son of the Revd Alexander Rentoul of Manor Cunningham, Co. Donegal (fig. 2.4).[318] A family ancestor had fled from France to Scotland as a religious refugee, and his grandfather, who had been sent by his Scottish Presbytery to undertake two years' work in Ireland, had settled in Donegal. After attending Cookstown Academy, Rentoul entered QCC so as to be at the same College as his companions, but left early owing to the death of his father. Two relatively unsuccessful years followed at QCB, where he shared a room with a cousin, and he went thereafter, first to Brussels, and then to the University of Berlin. He graduated BA on his return (1869) and secured a senior scholarship in modern languages at QCG. In his memoir, *Stray Thoughts and Memories*, he recounts that he chose Galway because of romantic associations created by reading J.F. Smith's *Substance and Shadow*, serialised in the weekly *Cassell's Family Paper*, the only light reading admitted to his father's strict Presbyterian household. He

---

313 Rentoul, *Stray Thoughts and Memories*, p. 78.
314 James Bryce Killen (1845–1916) was born at Kells, Co. Antrim. He was awarded a Queen's University BA in 1863 and took both the MA and LLB degrees in 1868. He was called to the Irish Bar in 1869. Killen was an active nationalist who was a co-founder of the Mayo Land League with Davitt, a fellow Fenian. He acted as editor of the Belfast *Northern Star*, and was arrested while acting editor of *United Ireland* at the beginning of December 1881. In her Journal, Florence Arnold-Forster remarked: 'Considering that the paper was one broadsheet of direct "incitement not to pay rent" it was not surprising that the authorities felt bound to take notice of him'. (Moody and Hawkins (eds), *Arnold-Forster*, p. 328.) Killen worked for many years as a journalist in Dublin.
315 Moody and Beckett, *Queen's Belfast*, vol. i, p. 205.
316 See the account given by J. McDonnel Bodkin, *Famous Irish Trials* (Dublin and London, 1918), pp. 129–43.
317 BA 1857; MA 1859; LLB 1862; LLB 1882. See above, footnote 266.
318 *Who Was Who, 1916–38*; Rentoul, *Stray Thoughts and Memories;* and Rentoul, 'Old Galway', pp. 4–7.

2.4 James A. Rentoul LLB (1874), LLD (1875). Judge of the City of London Court and of the Old Bailey

turned to legal study, secured law scholarships in each of the following three years, and successfully read for the LLB (1874) and the LLD (1875) degrees. Rentoul drifted into a clerical career, in part from a sense that he should fill his father's vacant pulpit, although he was advised that he should take up law:

> Professor Campion, Professor of Law, paid me a most surprising compliment, when, after an examination, he sent for me and said, 'I have scarcely ever taken the responsibility of advising a student about his future, but I have no hesitation in advising you to go on for the Bar.' I replied that I had decided on the Church. Professor Campion's answer was, 'God forbid that I should advise any one to choose a worldly calling in preference'.[319]

Rentoul initially chose the church and studied Divinity at Magee College and Assembly's College, Belfast. After some ten years of service, the attractions of a legal career having proved irresistible, he went to London and was called to the English Bar in 1884. He obtained first place in his examination and a scholarship of one hundred guineas. Success came quickly. He was made a QC in 1895, and Judge of the City of London Court and of the Central Criminal Court (as a Commissioner at the Old Bailey) in 1902.

---

319 Rentoul, *Stray Thoughts and Memories*, p. 75.

Rentoul was also a very successful parliamentary representative. He had at first no political ambitions, but was recruited by the Unionist party whose leaders were impressed by a fund-raising lecture he had given in October 1889 at the Ulster Hall, Belfast, on the subject of 'The British Empire'. Captain Ker was eager to resign the safe seat of East Down and Rentoul was returned as his successor without opposition. He held the seat as a Conservative MP without a contest from 1890 until he was raised to the bench in 1902. Rentoul was also elected a member of the first London County Council. Highly regarded as a moderate Unionist, he fulfilled the role expected of him by selling the positive side of Unionism at numerous meetings around Britain. Although convinced in his early career that Ireland's true advantage lay within the Union, he had grave misgivings towards the end, and blamed the divisions in Ireland on the Unionist extremist leaders who exploited the covenant and shaped the physical force policies of the Ulster movement. But, of course, not all Unionists were fanatical. Rentoul recounts how he had been asked by William Redmond to oppose a plan to erect a statue to Oliver Cromwell in the Palace Yard on the grounds that it would be, and was intended to be, offensive to Catholics. Rentoul agreed. On his next visit to East Down, a grim deputation of 'Orange friends' felt duty bound to call him to account on the issue. 'Who was Oliver Cromwell'? Rentoul asked, and getting no satisfactory reply, he hit on a means of defusing the situation:

> Suddenly I asked, 'Was he the man who said he would send all the papists in Ireland to hell or Connaught?'
> Satisfaction shone on their faces, and the spokesman said, 'The very man, sir.'
> 'Well,' I replied, 'I certainly voted against his statue, for I am no believer in alternatives, and he should have given them no choice.'
> That the men were neither fanatical, nor lacking in a sense of humour, is shown by the fact that they made some laughing reply and left me apparently with a sense of a duty duly performed, and I heard no more in my constituency of the Protector or his statue.[320]

Rentoul clearly enjoyed his time at QCG and held its teachers, its educational success, and its students in the highest regard. Some of the professors who were greatly admired were: Thomas W. Moffett, Professor of History, English Literature, and Mental Science who was later President; D'Arcy W. Thompson, Professor of Greek; Edward Townsend, Professor of Civil Engineering, and William Campion. In a whimsical piece written for *Q.C.G.*, the College magazine, he fondly recalled his time at Galway and the friends he made there. The picture, somewhat tinged, no doubt, by the rose colour of fond memory, is that of a small, friendly, intellectually-vibrant, community of dedicated scholars and bright, eager, students. He recalled how they planned to snowball the professors at the College gate. The student names of the culprits reads like an extract from a *Who Is Who* of later years: 'The leaders of the enterprise were: – Drummond, Pye, Colahan,

---

320 Ibid. pp. 141–2.

O'Donnell, Freyer, Maxwell, Rentoul, Ievers, Maguire, Moorehead, McSwinney, McCall, Mulligan, Harrison, Shiel, Gordon, and others'. Those they liked best were paid the doubtful compliment of being the target of the most snowballs:

> In my day we snow-balled most those Professors whom we liked best. I remember Townsend got it hot; Campion had to run for his life, and D'Arcy Thompson had no 'day Dreams' for several hours after. Moffett alone passed through untouched; but we never included him in any category. We spoke of the Professors and Moffett. I think we would have almost spoken of the angels and Moffett.

The Queen's University period at QCG (1845–82) was undoubtedly the high point of the College's history until the modern era. In Rentoul's opinion, it was in Galway in particular that the ideal of mixed education was fully realised. There was for many years a roughly equal number of Catholic and Protestant students at QCG. There was, of course, some taunting and argument, but it appeared to be of an acceptable and creative kind. 'The man', he wrote, 'who lived the life of a Galway Student for some years, and who could ever be a religious bigot, or who could ever cease to feel as Irish as they make them, would be a poor thing indeed'.[321] Professor Joseph P. Pye, who was a Catholic fellow-student, stated many years later in evidence that 'There were many Presbyterians from Ulster, and there was much clash of opinion in our debating Society and elsewhere ... The mixture of North and West, was a good thing for both'. The small and intimate nature of the institution was part of its attractiveness. That, however, would be nothing without the efforts and abilities of staff and students. Graduates made successful careers in all walks of life and were, as Rentoul pointed out, well represented in Parliament:

> Long after my College days had ended, when some question regarding Irish University education was being discussed in the House of Commons, seven members, formerly Galway students, rose to reply. I stated that I believed no other College had ever at one time been so largely represented in the House, but it was pointed out that by Christ Church, Oxford, and also by Trinity College, Cambridge, this number had been exceeded.
>
> No doubt this may have been so, but the honour of Galway is not lessened but rather increased if we remember how very small was Galway's average number of students, and ... to the average Galway student the House of Commons seemed an almost impossible goal, and each man who reached it had to work his own way every inch of the road.[322]

---

321 Rentoul, 'Old Galway', p. 7.
322 Rentoul, *Stray Thoughts and Memories*, p. 76.

Changing Times: The Royal University and after

The success of the Law Faculty in the early years was intimately connected with the varying fortunes of the College as a whole. QCG achieved remarkable success given the problems of the time and the almost constant opposition and hostility directed against the Colleges, particularly by the Catholic Church. There was the additional problem that no provincial College had ever been established in Dublin, as it was apparently hoped that TCD would prove an acceptable university institution for Catholics. This hope receded in the face of the Catholic Church's objection to mixed education, and the determination of the Board of Trinity to preserve TCD's Protestant character. Leinster was by far the wealthiest province, with the most advanced infrastructure, and any third level education system which did not cater for its Catholic population was seriously deficient. University educational planning for the remainder of the century was almost totally Dublin-oriented, and focused on meeting the demands for Catholic denominational education. It was clear that QCG, in the poorest part of the country, could be easily sacrificed in a bid to find an acceptable solution in the capital.

As a result of the entrenched Church opposition to mixed education and the influence of the hierarchy under Cardinal Cullen, there was little the government could do to perfect the Queen's Colleges system. It seems that where the problems of the Colleges required to be redressed by substantial public investment, the government was simply unable to act. Financial crisis in the Colleges was averted in the early 1860s by readjusting expenditure to increase the inadequate pay of professors, and by money raised in a very successful public appeal which was led by Sir Robert Peel, the son of the founder, who had been appointed Chief Secretary of Ireland.[323] Peel's efforts represent the last serious governmental attempt to resolve the university question by means of supporting and completing the Queen's Colleges scheme. In spite of the boost given to the Colleges by Peel, the difficulties facing QCG became worse and the government was politically unable to help. Unlike Belfast, which grew rapidly, the population of Galway had declined below 17,000 by 1861. Residential costs continued to make university education expensive in a relatively poor province. Second-level schools remained inadequate, and students in the new Catholic private schools were encouraged to go to the Catholic University of Ireland in Dublin (later effectively replaced by University College, St. Stephen's Green) rather than to the 'godless Colleges'. Although QCG survived enormous practical difficulties, and continuous parliamentary monitoring, it was the dissolution of the Queen's University and its replacement by the Royal University which caused the greatest damage.[324]

---

[323] See President Berwick's QCG *Report*, 1861–2, pp. 8–9. The result was apparently achieved by diverting £600 which was saved by suppressing some chairs, and by making College professors serve as the University examiners. To achieve this purpose, new Charters were granted in August 1863.

[324] Yet another investigation was undertaken by the Queen's College (Ireland) Commission; see *Report to His Excellency John Poyntz, Earl Spencer, KG, Lord Lieutenant and General Governor of Ireland* (Dublin, 1885).

The creation of the Royal University was another attempt to meet the demands for state-supported denominational university education for Catholics.[325] Following the successful introduction of the Intermediate Education Act, 1878, which addressed denominational education at second level, there was widespread anticipation that the Government would endeavour to resolve the university question on the same lines. The Act had used an indirect means of subsidising denominational education without abandoning the undenominational principle. Money prizes based on the results of competitive public examinations formed the basis of indirect subsidies for denominational secondary education. Although not ideal, it proved a feasible system in practice. With a general election due, nothing seemed to be happening until the educationalist, William Delany SJ, in March 1879, prompted the O'Conor Don to bring forward a bill, and also wrote to Arthur Kavanagh the leader of the Irish Tories requesting his support.[326] A bill was drafted which proposed the creation of a new 'St Patrick's University' financed from the surplus church fund, with associated Colleges eligible for results fees, exhibitions, and scholarships. Professors of the university could be engaged to teach in the Colleges which could also be given financial support for equipment and libraries. Perhaps because of the coming election, unexpected support came from the opposition in May, and O'Conor Don withdrew the bill when the Home Secretary announced at the end of June that the government intended to bring in its own bill.[327]

Although the Royal University bill appeared to be limited to the establishment of a mere examining and degree-awarding university, it was soon evident that the government were open to the notion of making results-fees available to Catholic colleges. On 1 August, James Lowther, the chief secretary, announced a clause which would empower the Senate to draw up a scheme of exhibitions, prizes, and scholarships, leaving matters intentionally vague and confused to avoid an intolerant and hostile rejection by unsympathetic elements in the Commons and the country. The significant detail was left to the recommendations of the future Senate. The Irish members of the Commons accepted the Bill and it passed on 5 August. The Charter appeared on 27 April 1880 and the Senate contained eighteen Catholic and eighteen non-Catholic senators. At its meeting on 24 June, the Senate appointed a committee, which included Moffett, to draw up a financial scheme.[328] Although forty-eight fellowships of £400 each were first proposed, the number was eventually reduced to twenty-six when the government allocated only £20,000 a year to the Royal University. It was finally agreed that half the fellowships, examinerships, and other appointments would go to Catholics, and it was accepted that the thirteen Catholic fellows would teach at the Catholic University at

---

325 For an account of the establishment of the Royal University scheme, see Thomas J. Morrissey SJ, *Towards a National University: William Delaney SJ (1835–1924)* (Dublin, 1983), chapter 2.
326 Principal of St Stanislaus College, Tullabeg, Co. Offaly; later President of University College, St Stephen's Green.
327 Ibid., pp. 51–3.
328 Ibid., pp. 56–9. Delaney was quite content, if necessary, to see the dissolution of QCC and especially QCG if public money had to be saved.

Stephen's Green, and also act as examiners. Indirect state support for Catholic education was thus achieved, but at a high price. A secondary, indirect consequence was that the Jesuits agreed to run the Catholic-controlled University College, Stephen's Green, which formed the nucleus of the future University College Dublin.

The Law School after the Foundation of the Royal University

By the time of Robert Cather Donnell's death in 1883, the Royal University of Ireland had been founded by Royal Charter of 27 April 1879, under the terms of the University Education (Ireland) Act, 1879.[329] The Act provided for the dissolution of the Queen's University, which took place on 3 February 1882, and made all Queen's graduates and matriculated students at the time of dissolution, graduates and students of the new Royal University. All existing Queen's professors continued to be university professors. On the dissolution of the old university, many of its successful former graduates were conferred with honorary degrees.[330] The Act which, in the words of President Moffett, 'established the Examinational system, as distinguished from the Collegiate, on the broadest possible basis', proved another major obstacle to the College.[331] Except in the case of medicine, students did not need to attend at any campus, but could prepare for Royal examinations and degrees privately if they wished.

After the establishment of the Royal, QCG and its Law Faculty continued its work as before. The Colleges, as the President put it,

> had entered a new era, their corporate unity lost; but what is past is well stored; their position is changed, but their duty remains the same. The established discipline of lectures and instruction in common will not be relaxed, and it is to be hoped that no change in the University system will tend to impair the substantial benefits conferred by the Colleges.[332]

The new system, however, proved highly detrimental. Student numbers at QCG declined successively from 201 to 144 to 103 in the three years from 1881–2 to 1883–4.[333] When conditions were almost at their worst another commission of enquiry into the Colleges was established in the on-going war concerning university education in Ireland. Variously known as the 'Poyntz', 'Earl Spencer', or 'Queen's Colleges (Ireland) Commission', it held its enquiries in 1884 and issued majority and minority reports in the following year.[334] The conflicting reports reflect the

---

329 42 & 43 Vict., ch. 65. The Charter was enrolled on 31 May 1880.
330 A list of former QCG students who were so honoured is given in the President's *Report* for 1881–2.
331 Ibid., 1882–3, p. 4.
332 Ibid., 1881–2, p. 4.
333 Ibid., 1884–5, pp. 7–8.
334 *Queen's Colleges (Ireland) Commission, Reports* (Dublin, 1885).

unhappy mix of educational, religious and political divisions which made a resolution of the university question so difficult. The Commissioners had very little of substance to say about legal education, as Arts and Medicine were the main battlegrounds, and Law did not seriously count in the wider educational debate. The analysis of legal education was peripheral and superficial, and focused once more on the lack of inducements from the legal professions to encourage legal studies. The main report concluded that:

> Apart from a desire to acquire legal knowledge, the only substantial inducement to a student to attend the law classes in the Queen's Colleges is in the scholarship alloted to that faculty, or in the prospect of obtaining the degrees of LLB, or LLD, as distinctions in after life.[335]

As a degree-awarding body, the Royal University proved a useful examining and certifying body for students emerging from the new intermediate schools. Its positive effects are easy to exaggerate, however, partly because, other than the University of Dublin which was not a real choice for many students, the Royal had a monopoly in the grant of higer education awards in Ireland. There was also a greater number of students capable of taking higher university level studies. In any event, it failed to satisfy any of the parties in the end. The *Report of Royal Commission on University Education* (the Robertson Commission, 1903) gives us a sense that university education in the best sense had declined under the Royal:

> Apart from internal defects of organisation, the Royal University has brought about one result which was doubtless unforeseen by its founders. It has seriously impaired the value of the University education which was previously in existence. On this side its influence has been one of positive, destruction. Since it came into being, the growth of the Queen's Colleges has been arrested. The Queen's University at the time of its dissolution was doing academical work of undoubted excellence. The number of students was not very large, but the Colleges were working on true, academical lines. College residence was required from all candidates for a Degree. The Professors were *ex officio* Examiners in the University, and all in rotation took their share in this duty. Examination was kept in close touch with teaching. Each College felt itself to be a self-contained academical community; nothing was needed for the development of a more vigorous life save an increase in numbers. The growth of the Royal University has depleted the classes of the Queen's Colleges.[336]

Professor Campion continued to teach under the new regime in his capacity as Professor of English Law. He had outlived Cairnes, Lupton, and Donnell. In a long career that ended with his death in 1907, he was to work with two other holders of the Professorship of Jurisprudence and Political Economy: Bastable

---
335 Ibid., p. 3.
336 *Royal Commission on University Education in Ireland, Final Report*, 1903, p. 24.

(1883–1903) and Wardell (1903–9). In Hilary term 1884, Campion had been elected a Bencher of the King's Inns and in the following year he was appointed Serjeant-at-Law by Lord Ashbourne. Utterly non-political, he made no effort to obtain that position, and the honour was seen as a well-deserved recognition of his talent and position as leading Chancery barrister. The appointment was warmly welcomed.[337] He acted as counsel to distinguished clients such as the Synod of the Church of Ireland, TCD, the Guinness family, and the Royal Dublin Society, and he advised on appeals to, and argued cases in, the House of Lords.

As a lawyer he was said to have assisted the College to extricate itself from legal difficulties. On one occasion when he had helped it to narrowly escape a lawsuit, he remarked to a difficult member of College Council: 'Really, one would imagine you all enjoyed these difficulties!' 'Why, of course we do,' was the reply, 'sure, isn't it the only little excitement we have down here!' One of his well-known and respected opinions proved to be of assistance to President Moffett. Although he felt unable as a serjeant to take a brief against the crown, he had advised Sir Thomas Brady, Senior Inspector of Fisheries, that a government order compelling him to retire at sixty-five was unlawful. Although this opinion was in direct conflict with that of the crown law officers, it survived a petition of right hearing in the Court of Appeal.[338] A similar attempt to retire President Moffett was abandoned by the government on the strength of Campion's opinion.[339]

Charles Francis Bastable LLD, BL (1855–1945) became Professor of Political Economy and Jurisprudence in 1883.[340] He was born in Charleville, Co. Cork in 1855. His father was an Episcopalian clergyman and young Bastable received his early education at Fermoy College, Co. Cork. He entered TCD in 1873 and graduated as First Senior Moderator (equivalent to first-class honours) in Modern History and Political Science in 1878. Although he immediately began his legal studies, he also appears to have read political economy as part of the programme. He won first prizes in International Law, Political Economy, and in Feudal and English Law in 1879, and first prize in Roman Law in 1880. He received his call to the Irish Bar in 1881, having again distinguished himself as a scholar.[341] In the following year he proceeded to the degree of MA and was elected to the Whately Chair of Political Economy at TCD for the then statutory five-year period. In 1887, however, Bastable was re-elected to the Chair on new, altered, conditions, and retained it until he retired in 1932.

The remuneration attached to the Whately Chair was not adequate in itself, but Bastable succeeded in obtaining the chair of Jurisprudence and Political Economy at QCG following Professor Donnell's death in 1883. The combination of these

---

337 *Memoir*, pp. 65, 76.
338 See *New Irish Jurist*, vol iii, p. 279.
339 *Memoir*, pp. 74–5.
340 For biographical notes see G.A. Duncan, 'Charles Francis Bastable 1855–1945', *Proceedings of the British Academy*, 31 (1946), pp. 1–4; Boylan and Foley, *Political Economy and Colonal Ireland*, pp. 169–70; *Presidents, Vice-Presidents, and Professors of Queen's College, Galway*, pp. 42–3.
341 He held the First Senior Studentship in Jurisprudence, International and Roman Law, Inns of Court, London, 1881, and the Benchers' Exhibition (3 years) at King's Inns, Dublin, in 1882.

two part-time appointments gave him a firm academic base. He at once embarked on a long, energetic, and prolific academic career. Although he took his LLD degree in 1990, and fulfilled his role as a law professor, at least as regards the teaching duties, his research interests were almost exclusively in economics rather than in law.[342] His principal publications were in public finance and international trade theory, and it was in this field that he earned an international reputation as an outstanding scholar. Some of his finest works were produced while he was a professor at Galway. These included, *The Theory of International Trade; With Some of Its Applications to Economic Policy* (Dublin, 1887), *The Commerce of Nations* (London, 1892), and *Public Finance* (London, 1892). In 1902 TCD, recognising the importance of Bastable, appointed him to the revived chair of Civil Law and General Jurisprudence, and he resigned from the law chair at QCG in 1903. He was appointed Regius Professor of Laws in the University of Dublin in 1908, and continued as an active academic until he retired, aged 77, in 1932. Thereafter, as his health declined, he lived a cheerful but secluded life until he died at his residence in Rathgar, Dublin, on 3 January 1945.

In the course of his work at QCG, Bastable wrote a short report in 1902 on the state of his Department at QCG for the benefit of the Royal Commission on University Education in Ireland which was then taking evidence. The Commission's *Report* provided the raw material of agreed fact which was to help finally resolve the vexed question of university education in Ireland. Within a few years, the Irish Universities Act, 1908 had provided for the creation of an independent Queen's University of Belfast and the creation of a state-funded University College, Dublin (UCD).[343] The Queen's Colleges at Cork and Galway became University College Cork (UCC) and University College Galway (UCG) respectively, and together with UCD were constituted (and until recently remained), constituent Colleges of a new 'National University of Ireland' (NUI), a university to which Maynooth was also affiliated as a 'recognised' College. These Colleges are now, of course, independent universities, and the old QCG, which became UCG in 1908, has been once more transformed into today's National University of Ireland, Galway (NUI, Galway).

In the evidence given in 1902, Bastable pointed out that, whereas he was a professor in the Law Faculty, he taught on both the Law and Arts programmes. He was in no doubt that the Law programme had 'suffered most seriously' from the withdrawal of King's Inns' privileges[344] and from the dissolution of the Queen's University:

---

342 His purely law writings are scant: 'Homestead Laws', *Journal of the Statistical and Social Inquiry Society of Ireland*, 9 (1887–8); an article on 'Ulster Tenant Right' (Palgrave's *Dictionary of Political Economy*); 'Adam Smith's Lectures on Jurisprudence', *Hermathena*, 10 (1898), pp. 200–11; and a review of *Roman Private Law in the Times of Cicero and of the Antonines*, by H. J. Roby, *Hermathena*, 12 (1903), pp. 512–17.
343 8 Edw. 7. c. 38.
344 Campion had earlier expressed similar complaints about the King's Inns. In his report for the session 1875–6, he wrote: 'I regret to say that the last rules of the Benchers, rendering it to a great extent compulsory on law students to attend their school in Dublin, have necessarily had an injurious effect on the law schools in the Queen's Colleges as regards the number of students'. President's *Report*, 1875–6, p. 19.

> The recognition of two years' attendance on Law lectures in Galway, in substitution for a similar period in Dublin, in order to qualify for call to the Bar, has been reduced to that of one year, while the requirement that the student, to obtain even this privilege, must be a graduate of the Royal University, has operated as a further restriction. The practical result has been that students of the Queen's College have actually had to attend courses of lectures in the same subjects in Galway, and again in Dublin. Nothing could be more effective in hindering students from taking their Law courses in Galway.[345]

He believed that if a similar rule was applied in medicine it would 'certainly drive away a large percentage of the members of the Galway Medical School'. But the establishment of the Royal had, he believed, been even more damaging. Bastable complained that in place of the 'well-ordered arrangement' of the Queen's University, the Senate of the Royal University substituted a single examination, and prescribed it as an elementary course in law, in which the subjects of Jurisprudence, Roman Law, and International Law were practically ignored. This 'strange proceeding', he wrote,

> made the teaching given in the Jurisprudence departments of the Queen's Colleges quite useless for the purpose of obtaining a degree in Law in the Royal University and it therefore discouraged attendance even on the Professors of English Law, as the College regulations still required attendance on the lectures of both the Professors of the faculty. The character of the Royal University Law courses was, moreover, such as to allow of their being 'made up' by private study, with, in the case of inferior students, a little 'coaching'.[346]

Even when the Royal recognised the weakness of the law programme and introduced an 'Intermediate Examination in Law', they still completely disregarded, according to Bastable, the the long-established system of the Queen's Colleges by placing all the subjects connected with Jurisprudence in the 'Intermediate' course, and all the English Law subjects in the LLB degree course. He believed that this 'most unsuitable division of subjects' was probably copied from the University of London, but the Royal failed to copy that University as regards its standards:

> The examinations in Jurisprudence, Roman Law, and International Law, in London University, are conducted by experts, and the papers are of high standard. In the Royal University two Examiners conduct all the Law examinations, and no representative of Jurisprudence and the connected subjects has ever been chosen to examine. As a necessary result, the examinations on those subjects have suffered in quality, and students who

---

345 *Royal Commission on University Education in Ireland, Third Report*, Appendix, Minutes of Evidence (Dublin, 1902), pp. 10–11: 'Report by Professor Bastable, LLB, on the Department of Jurisprudence and Political Economy, Queen's College, Galway'.
346 Ibid.

have been carefully trained in principles are discouraged by finding that mere book knowledge is the necessary and sufficient condition of success at their examinations. Under these circumstances, the wonder is, not that so few students from the Queen's Colleges present themselves at the Royal University Law examinations, but rather that any should continue to do so.[347]

There was another difficulty according to Bastable. When College statutes had to be revised on the dissolution of the Queen's University, the Law Faculty, which had no full-time resident staff to fight for its interests, was the easy victim:

> Eligibility for the Senior Scholarship in Law was made to depend, not, as previously, on the possession of a BA Degree, but on qualifying within 'six years from Matriculation.' Since the adoption of this limitation in time in 1882, no Law student has been eligible for Senior Scholarship, as the Arts and Law courses took up somewhat more than the six years' period.[348]

Worse was to come in 1895 when a College statute abolished the Senior Scholarship entirely, and reduced the Junior Law Scholarships from three to two, instead of (as had been done in Belfast and Cork) increasing them to four. By way of conclusion, Bastable noted:

> It is thus plain that the Galway Law School suffers from all the evils that have affected the other departments of the College, and has besides to meet difficulties peculiar to itself. Unlike the Medical School, its students obtain hardly any professional advantage from certificates of attendance on lectures, or of having passed examinations. Unlike the Engineering School, it has not the benefit of University examinations (which qualify for degrees) conducted in harmony with its courses, and by Boards of Examiners on which it is represented.
>
> The attempt made before the Commission to compare the work of the different schools on the basis of figures is altogether misleading, and suggests complete ignorance of the facts on the part of those using it.
>
> It must also be remembered that the endowment of the Law Faculties in the Queen's Colleges is very small, and that, while the Medical and Engineering Schools are assisted in their work by several Arts Professors, the Law Schools obtain no such assistance; on the contrary, about half the time of one of the 'Law' Professors is given to classes in the Faculty of Arts.[349]

On Bastable's resignation, Henry Lloyd Cowdy was appointed as temporary lecturer in Jurisprudence and Political Economy by the College Council. He was a graduate of TCD who had obtained a moderatorship and gold medal in political economy and had recently graduated LLB. Although Cowdy applied for the

---

347 Ibid.
348 Ibid.
349 Ibid.

position, it was John Henry Wardell MA (1878–1957), however, who was appointed to the chair, a position he held from 1903 until his resignation in 1908.[350] Educated at Wellington and TCD, he had been a senior moderator and gold medallist at university where he won prizes for his economics papers.[351] Wardell was appointed Reader at TCD in 1902, and was elected Barrington lecturer in 1903. He was appointed Professor of Modern History in the University of Dublin, a post he held until 1911.

The last person to hold the professorship was James Anderson who succeeded Wardell in 1910. Anderson (1881–1915) was born in Derry, the son of Thomas Anderson, a local merchant.[352] On leaving the Derry National School he entered the bank at fifteen. He continued his education, however, by matriculating in the Royal University (1902), and graduating as the top first-class honours BA examination candidate in 1905. He was law scholar and McKane gold medallist at QCB the following year, and graduated MA with a top first in 1907, thereby gaining a well-deserved studentship. He was called to the Irish Bar in the same year and was appointed acting Professor of Jurisprudence and Political Economy at QCB for the session 1907-8. Following his appointment as a full professor at Galway, he joined the Connacht Circuit. This highly promising young man became Reid Professor of Criminal and Constitutional Law at TCD in 1914, but tragically died at an early age in June 1915. The chair was not filled on Anderson's death. A UCG statute provided for the amalgamation into one professorship of Economics, Commerce, and Accountancy, and for the creation of a single chair of Law and Jurisprudence. By then QCG had been reconstituted as UCG and was one of the NUI Colleges.

Professor Campion's death on Thursday 19 September 1907, and the establishment of the NUI shortly after, mark the end of an era for the Galway Law School. Campion had travelled back and forth from Dublin to Galway on the train with typical dedication to duty, and a strong sense of loyalty to the College and its students. Although his colleagues at the Bar teased him on the subject, they knew well how seriously he took his teaching duties:

> He used to be much chaffed about the 'Condensed essence of Law' administered at the College – his disappearances at Dublin being so short. They used to declare at the Library that he carried his class backward and forwards in the train to save time by lecturing on the way, but they knew that

---

350 *Who Was Who, 1951–60.*
351 *Q.C.G.*, November 1903, p. 35.
352 The *Tuam Herald* of 12 June 1915 carried the news of Anderson's death: 'Universal and deep regret is felt throughout Galway at the untimely death of Mr James Anderson BL, LLB, Professor of Law, University College. He died very suddenly on Friday morning at Dalysfort Road, Galway. Deceased was quite a young man, but was a brilliant advocate and in several intricate cases was warmly complimented by the Recorder for the brilliancy of his arguments. He held the Law Professor's chair at Galway University for some years, and was most popular with the students. Mr Anderson was a native of the North – a Presbyterian, but universally liked. He held more distinctions and honours than any young man at the Irish Bar'. Anderson's photograph appeared in *U.C.G.*, no. 4, 1 (1916), p. 6.

he not only performed all his professional duties conscientiously, but also found time to lend a helping hand again and again to the College in the numerous difficulties that beset it.[353]

In spite of attacks of influenza over the winter of 1906–7, Campion continued to fulfill his teaching obligations at Galway. When he arrived for the start of the final term in March 1907 he was overcome with weakness. He got progressively more feeble over the summer and autumn and contracted bronchitis towards the end. He died at 'Beaconsfield', his summer residence at Delgany, Co. Wicklow, and after a burial service at the Church of St Mathias, he was buried in the family burial place in the ruined church of Leitrim, Co. Cork.

The tribute to Campion printed in the student magazine, Q.C.G., captures some of the spirit and character of the professor in his older years – that tall, kindly, gentleman, with a spare figure, and gently considerate face:

> there was a quality in the Serjeant which was not a product of any special study; something inherent – personal to the man which we, who have had the privilege of knowing him, will recall with affection so long as memory shall last – his delightful old-world courtesy and chivalrous consideration.
>
> Students' answers to Serjeant Campion's questions might be as far wide of settled law as misplaced student ingenuity could make them – I regret to say they frequently were so – yet our gentle Professor would approach the consideration of them with as much deference as if they were engrossed on fifty-guinea briefs; would (very probably) deprecatingly suggest that his own clear precise language did not sufficiently indicate the points he wished to elucidate, and would finally leave his class in full possession of his views together with a pleasant (if erroneous) impression that they had helped this grave, dignified old gentleman to unravel knotty legal conundrums.

He almost never spoke disapprovingly of anybody or anything – other than the College Council which, without consultation, stripped the law programme of some of its most important subjects. Then there was at the end,

> his daily search for those elusive spectacles which were found carefully deposited between the leaves of 'Mr. Williams' or used to mark some maxim of equity which 'I do not think gentlemen, I can better explain than by quoting the admirably clear and precise statement of Mr. Snell'.[354]

Many tributes to Campion reflect the fondness and regard with which he was held. He was known among his friends by the sobriquet 'First Jurist Old Series'. He was, it was said:

---

353 *Memoir*, p. 70.
354 *Q.C.G.*, March 1908, pp. 4–5.

> a great jurist, and the most charming of men. Among English lawyers he had no superior in knowledge of Real Property Law. His opinion has been sought by English clients, and in Ireland by all who desired the highest guidance in any intricate question of the devolution of property and the construction of family settlements. He was master of equity case law. None but himself could deal familiarly with the old and now obsolete law of fines and recoveries; the equities of ecclesiastical levies and the *toties quoties* covenants for renewal as affected by the Church Temporalities Act. He knew everything connected with the law of property in the most thorough way.[355]

Although noted for his classic and elegant diction, and the logic of his argument, he had hearing difficulties towards the end of his life which made court work difficult, and his voice was beginning to lose its strength.

> Still, such was his clearness, his erudition, his soundness of view and transparent sincerity and integrity that there were few really big cases at the Equity side of the Court in which his services were not requisitioned.[356]

It was remembered of him that he was for many years one of the most knowledgeable Chancery lawyers in Ireland and was highly valued for his legal expertise:

> Serjeant Campion's arena lay in the gentler waters of Chancery, and up to his last working hours his opinion on every branch of the law was as highly valued as that of any leader of the Bar … Serjeant Campion's gentle personality was wholly foreign to cases of the sensational type, hence to the ordinary man in the street his name might during all these years have been comparatively unfamiliar. But in the course of his career he was engaged in a vast number of highly important suits. These he would argue with a gentleness and courtliness of style, a considerateness for every opponent no matter how junior, and a sense of the honour and dignity of his profession, which constituted a blend of the very highest forensic ideals. He on three occasions argued cases in the House of Lords.[357]

James M. Sweetman succeeded Campion as Professor of English Law in 1908, and when he resigned the post in 1913,[358] Richard J. Sheehy became the new 'Professor of Law', a post he held until his death in 1923. A Mr Flood BA, BL had been employed for a time as locum for Professor Sheehy.[359] The opportunity was then taken to merge the chairs into a single professorship of 'Law and Jurisprudence',

---

355 *Irish Law Times and Solicitors' Journal*, xvi, 28 September 1907, pp. 246–7.
356 Ibid., p. 247.
357 Obituary, *Irish Times*, 21 September 1907.
358 A notice of Serjeant Campion's death appeared in *Q.C.G.* no. I, 6 (1908), pp. 4–5.
359 A note in *Galway University College Magazine*, no. 9, 2 (1922–3), reads: 'we regret Mr Flood has now left us – to take up a District justiceship somewhere in Leinster. We offer him our hearty congratulations, and we wish him the best of luck. His place is taken here by Mr Patrick A.

a post held successively by Patrick Arkins BA, LLB (1924–37)[360] and Patrick J. Gallagher BA, LLB (1937–66). Some graduates will remember Professor J.M.G. Sweeney whose dedication kept the Faculty going until the first full-time Law appointments were made with the advent of Professor Kevin Boyle and Mr Dennis Driscoll. These appointments mark the beginning of the modern, and hopefully the most vibrant phase, of the Faculty's history. But that is a different story, and for another time.

APPENDIX

Graduates in Law 1849–1953, and Graduates who had a Legal Career

(Note that this list is not intended to be fully comprehensive, and that * signifies First-Class Honours, † signifies Second-Class Honours, + signifies that the student is known to have also attended another College.)

Atkinson, John, (Rt Hon. Lord), (1858–9 to 1864–5); *BA 1861; *LLB 1865; MA, LLD 1882 (honorary on dissolution of QUI); Third-year Law scholar 1863–64; Senior Law scholar 1864–65. John Atkinson (1844–1932) was born on 13 December 1844 at Drogheda. He was educated at the Royal Belfast Academical Institution and at QCG where he gained scholarships in every year of his courses. Following his call to the Bar (Ireland), he practised on the Munster Circuit and was appointed QC in 1880 at 36 years of age. He was made a Bencher of the Honorable Society of King's Inns (1885) and elected a Conservative MP for North Derry (1895). He served as Attorney-General for Ireland from 1895 to 1905, at which latter date he was appointed to the House of Lords as Lord of Appeal in Ordinary, and was made a Life Peer (baron), taking the name 'Lord Atkinson of Glenwilliam' (his father was born in Glenwilliam Castle, Co. Limerick). He died on 13 March 1932. *DNB*; *Who Was Who, 1929–40*.

Atkinson, Nicholas, First-year Law scholar 1863–4; Second-year Law scholar 1864–5; Third-year Law scholar 1865–6.

Arkins, Patrick A.+, *LLB 1918; Second-year Law scholar 1916–17; Exhibitioner 1918–19; Professor of Law and Jurisprudence UCG, 1924–37.

> Arkins BA, LLB, of the firm of O'Dea and Arkins, solicitors, of Dublin and Galway. Mr Arkins' appointment was a very popular one. He had a distinguished career as a student in our College, having obtained First Class honours in all his examinations'.

360 Professor Arkins was born in County Clare, near Kilfenora. He graduated at UCD where he read for the BA (Legal and Political Science). Having secured a Faculty of Law second-year scholarship at UCG in 1916–17, he was awarded the LLB with first-class honours in 1918, gaining a College exhibition (1918–19). After Arkins qualified as a solicitor, he began to practise as a lawyer in Galway in the firm O'Dea and Arkins. The Professorship was a part-time post, and the duties were not very onerous, and could easily be combined with the practice of law. Before he married, Professor Arkins resided at the Eglinton Hotel in Salthill. The number of students reading law was then very small. It is said that he sometimes took his classes at the hotel, as there often were no more than half-a-dozen law students in a particular class. The procedures were often friendly and informal. Professor Arkins was known to have given legal advice to the Governing Body on occasion. When the chair of English fell vacant, he advised that the 1929 Act did not apply to the appointment. His advice was not, however, accepted. The successful applicant was Jeremiah Murphy, and a number of other candidates, including a Mr Shakespeare, were unsuccessful.

Bodkin, Leo F., First-year Law scholar 1898–9.
Brown, James, First-year Law scholar 1879–80; Second-year Law scholar 1880–1.
Brown, William Herbert, †BA 1879; MA 1882 (honorary on dissolution of QUI); *LLB 1887; First in First university examination in Arts, October 1878; Junior scholar, science division, Arts, 1876–7 to 1878–9; Senior scholar in Natural Philosophy 1879–80; First-year Law scholar 1885–6 (under the name 'Brown, William'); Second-year Law scholar 1886–7 (under the name 'Brown, William, MA'). Judge William H. Brown (c. 1856–1927); County Court Judge; Died 7 Feb. 1927. *Who Was Who, 1916–28.*
Buckley, Thomas, BA 1882; LLB 1889; First-year Law scholar 1886–7; Second-year Law scholar 1887–8; Third-year Law scholar 1888–9. Venerable Thomas Richard Buckley (1859–1936); Missionary in Uganda; Curate of All Souls', Eastbourne, 1925; Died 16 February 1936. *Who Was Who, 1929–40.*
Caldwell, John, First-year Law scholar 1892–3.
Card, Thomas D., BA, First-year Law scholar 1875–6; Second-year Law scholar 1876–7.
Clancy, John J., BA 1866; †MA 1868 (Ancient Classics). John Joseph Clancy, (1847–1928), was born at Carragh Lodge, Claregalway; appointed Classics Master, Holy Cross School, Tralee 1867–70; worked as newspaper editor; KC (Ireland), 1906; MP for North Dublin County; Died 25 November 1928; *Who Was Who, 1916–28.*
Clarke, William A., BA 1886; LLB 1890.
Concannon, Patrick, *BA 1871; †MA 1874; Second in First university examination in Arts, October 1869; Junior scholar, science division Arts, 1868–9 to 1869–70; First-year Law scholar 1870–1. (Apparently died young, see J.A. Rentoul, *Q.C.G.*, November 1905, p. 6.)
Concannon, William, BA 1918; *LLB 1924.
Conroy, John C., First-year Law scholar 1890–1; Second-year Law scholar 1891–2; Third-year Law scholar 1892–3.
Conroy, John S., †BA 1918; First-year Law scholar 1915–16.
Costigan, Thomas J., First-year Law scholar 1860–1; Second-year Law scholar 1861–2; Third-year Law scholar 1862–3.
Crooks, William, BA 1865; First-year Arts scholar 1860–1; Second in First university examination in Arts under the name William Crooke, October 1862; First-year Law scholar 1864–5.
Cusack, Patrick J., First-year Law scholar 1901–2; Second-year Law scholar 1902–3.
Donnell, William, BA, First-year Law scholar 1878–9; Second-year Law scholar 1879–80; Third-year Law scholar 1880–1.
Donovan, John T., BA 1906: First-year Law scholar 1909–10; Obtained a high place in the examination for the Indian Civil Service and accepted an appointment; (UCG, President's *Report*, 1913, p. 3.) John Thomas Donovan (1885–1973) BL (Ireland); son of William Donovan of Galway; joined Indian Civil Service, 1910; Member of the Legislative Assembly of India and District Magistrate Hooghly and Bakarganj, India; Died 2 March 1973. *Who Was Who, 1971–1980.*
Dooley, John L., BA 1873; Second-year Law scholar 1869–70.
Drummond, Michael, †BA 1869 ; †MA 1870 (Ancient Classics); First in First university examination in Arts, October 1868; Third-year Law scholar 1870–71; Junior scholar, literary division, Arts, 1866–7 to 1868–9. Judge Michael Drummond (1850–1921); KC (Ireland); Bencher of the Honorable Society of King's Inns; County Court Judge and Chairman of Quarter Sessions of the Counties of Cavan and Leitrim; *Who Was Who, 1929–40.*
England, William G., BA 1880; First-year Law scholar 1877–8; Second-year Law scholar 1878–9; BL (Ireland).

Fahy, John V., First-year Law scholar 1903–4; Second–year Law scholar 1904–5.
Farrell, Gerald P., †BA 1911; Second-year Law scholar 1910–11.
Farrelly, Michael J., (1872–3 to 1876–7; 1878–9 to 1881–2); †BA 1876; MA 1882 (honorary on dissolution of QUI); *LLB 1890; LLD 1892; First in First university examination in Arts, October 1875; Junior scholar, literary division Arts, 1875; Senior scholar in Ancient Classics 1876–7; Senior Law scholar 1881–2; BL (Ireland); Member of Senate of the Royal University; Law adviser to the Transvaal Government.
Fisher, Joseph R., BA 1876; (1855–1939); Journalist, member of the Irish Boundary Commission; Author of *Finland and the Tsars* and *The End of the Irish Parliament*; co-author of Fisher and Strahan's *Law of the Press*; BL (England); Editor of the Belfast *Northern Whig*; Died 26 October 1939. *Who Was Who, 1929–40*.
Flack, Isaac, First-year Law scholar 1904–5; Second-year Law scholar 1905–6.
Flanagan, Stanislaus, First-year Law scholar 1908–9; Second-year Law scholar 1909–10.
Fogarty, Philip C., †BA, 1905; LLB 1920; First-year Law scholar 1906–7. Appointed additional judge of the Prome township, and President of the Paung-deh Municipality, Burma. (UCG, President's *Report*, 1913, p. 3.)
Fogarty, William G., First-year Law scholar 1905–6; Second-year Law scholar 1906–7.
Gaffney, Michael P.K., †H Dip in Ed 1940; *LLB 1945.
Gallagher, Patrick, *BA, †LLB 1929. Professor of Law and Jurisprudence (1937–66) at University College Galway.
Garvey, John C.+, BA; *LLB 1915; First-year Law scholar 1913–14; Second-year Law scholar 1914–15.
Garvin, John,+ *BA, †B Comm 1925; LLB (UCD) 1930; DLitt.; Born in Sligo; Secretary, Department of Local Government 1948–66; Dublin City Commissioner 1969; wrote and lectured widely on Anglo-Irish literature, Irish local history, and on local government; international authority on James Joyce.
Gordon, John, BA 1873; †LLB 1876; LLD 1882 (honorary on dissolution of QUI); Third-year Law scholar 1874–5; Senior Law scholar 1876–7. Hon. Mr Justice John Gordon (1849–1922); KC (Ireland) ; Bencher of the Honourable Society of King's Inns; MP for South Derry; Justice of the King's Bench, 1916; Died 26 September 1922. *Who Was Who, 1916–1928*.
Greenfield, John K., BA. 1875; First-year Law scholar 1873–4; Second-year Law scholar 1874–5.
Hanna, James, †BA 1874; MA 1876; First-year Law scholar 1872–3; Second-year Law scholar 1873–4 (Peter O'Kinealy, BA, is named as Second-year Law scholar in the 1893–4 *Calendar*.)
Henchy, James A., *BA, *MA 1940; PhD 1943; Judge Séamus Henchy, judge of the High and Supreme courts in Ireland; Son of Patrick Henchy of Corofin Co Clare; Attended St Mary's College, Galway, UCG, and UCD; Called to the Bar 1943; called to the Inner Bar 1959; Professor of Roman Law, Jurisprudence, and Legal History in UCD 1948–62; Chairman of commissions (Mental Illness 1962–6; Mentally Ill and Maladjusted Persons 1972; Racial Problems in British Guiana 1966); Awarded honorary LLD at NUI, Galway, 1999.
Heneghan, Thomas F., *BA 1920; H Dip in Ed 1921; MA 1925; LLB 1927.
Hession, James M., LLB 1937.
Hooper, Charles J.,+ *BA 1855 (QCG); †MA 1856 (QCG); *LLB 1858; LLD 1862; Junior scholar, literary division Arts, 1851–2–1853–4; Senior scholar in Metaphysical and Economic Science 1855–6; First-year Law scholar 1854–5; Senior Law scholar 1858–9; (Also attended at QCC); Exhibition and gold medal in Jurisprudence and Political Economy (BA); Exhibition and gold medal (Metaphysical and Economic Science) in MA. The Revd Charles J. Hooper became a minister of the Church.

Horgan, [née Hannon], Bridget W., LLB 1935.

Hume, George A., *BA 1878; *MA 1879; *LLB 1880; LLD 1882 (honorary on dissolution of QUI); Second-class in First university examination in Arts, October 1877; Junior scholar literary division Arts, 1875–6 to 1877–8; Senior scholar in Metaphysical and Economic Science 1878–9; Third-year Law scholar 1879–80; Senior Law scholar 1880–1. George Hume (1860–1905), born at Crumlin, Co. Antrim; Educated at the Royal Belfast Academical Institution and QCG; called to the Bar (Ireland) 1881; made KC (Ireland) 1899; died 10 Jan 1905; *Who Was Who, 1897–1916*.

Hynes, John A., †BA 1946; LLB 1948.

Jones, James, †BA 1894; MA 1895; First-year Law scholar 1895–6.

Jordon, Michael J., †BA 1886, First-year Law scholar 1888–9.

Joyce, James B., LLB 1945.

Keane, Christopher Marceet (or Marcus), BA 1853; *Diploma in Elementary Law, 1853 (with exhibition and gold medal); First-year Law scholar 1850–51; Second-year Law scholar 1851–2; Third-year Law scholar 1852–3; Senior Law scholar 1853–4.

Keary, Flan James, Diploma in Elementary Law, 1865.

Keys, Patrick J.G., BA 1935; LLB 1939.

Killen, James B., †BA 1863; MA 1868 with Third honours in Logic, Metaphysics and Political Economy (QCG); *LLB 1868 (at QCG); Born in Kells, Co. Antrim; Co-founder of Land League in Mayo with Davitt; journalist; editor of *Northern Star*; called to the Bar (Ireland) 1879; worked as a journalist in Dublin.

King, Aelian A., (1859–60 to 1864–5); BA 1862; MA 1882 (honorary on dissolution of QUI); Entered the Ceylon Civil Service by competition; Appointed successively Assistant Government Agent and District Judge.

Lawson, Charles H., Appears as both First-year Law and Arts (Science division) scholar in 1856–7.

Leitch, Andrew C., First-year Law scholar 1889–90; Second-year Law scholar 1890–1; Third-year Law scholar 1891–2.

Lewis, Walter Llewellyn, *BA 1869; *MA 1871; BA First in Experimental Science, 1869; MA First in Experimental Science, 1871; Junior Scholar, science division Arts, 1867–8 to 1868–9; Senior Scholar in Natural Philosophy 1869–70; Senior Scholar in Chemistry 1870–1; Sir Walter Llewellyn Lewis (1849–1930) was born in Banbury. Called to the Bar (Middle Temple), 1876; joined South Wales and Chester Circuit; Stipendiary Magistrate, Trinidad, 1885; Puisne Judge of the Supreme Court, 1893; Chief Justice of British Honduras, 1900; *Who Was Who, 1929–40*.

Louden, John J., First-year Law scholar 1859–0; Second-year Law scholar 1860–1; Third-year Law scholar 1861–2.

Lydon, Patrick J., BA 1902; Second-year Law scholar 1908–9.

Lynch, John B., †BA 1904; First-year Law scholar 1902–3; Second-year Law scholar 1903–4;

McAuliffe, Michael, (1857–8 to 1862–3); BA* 1860; MA 1882 (honorary on dissolution of QUI); Entered the Indian civil service and became a divisional Judge of the Punjab; Translated the Sacred Book of the Sikhs.

McAuliffe, Michael J., First-year Law scholar 1893–4.

McCall, Robert A., BA 1867; MA 1868; LLD 1882 (honorary on dissolution of QUI). Sir Robert Alfred McCall (1849–1934), born Lisburn, Co. Antrim, 9 July 1849 – his mother was Alice, daughter of James MacSwinney of Galway. Called to the Bar, Middle Temple, 1871; Joined the Northern Circuit; Made QC 1891 and Bencher of the Middle Temple, 1894; Treasurer, 1918; Was Senator of London University and Vice-Chairman of the Council of Legal Education (1917); Appointed Attorney-General and Queen's Serjeant of the Duchy of Lancaster, 1899–1921; Died 6 April 1934; *Who Was Who, 1929–1940*.

McConnell, John K., BA, Second-year Law scholar 1889–90; Third-year Law scholar 1890–1.

McCoy, Sarah M.M., †BA, BComm, H Dip in Ed, MA, LLB 1929; PhD 1937.

McDermott, Brian, First-year Law scholar 1861–2; Second-year Law scholar 1862–3; Second honors, First university examination in Arts, May, 1861; Brian Patrick Sarsfield McDermott, (1858–9 to 1863–4); BA, MD, staff-surgeon.

McDonagh, Patrick E., †BA, †B Comm 1923; *LLB 1925.

McDonagh, Redmond, †BA, 1882; MA 1883; First-year Law scholar 1882–3; Second-year Law scholar 1883–4; Third-year Law scholar 1884–5.

McDonald, Francis, see O'Donnell, Francis (Frank) Hugh.

McElroy, Peter, *LLB 1940.

McFarlane, Robert A., *B.A 1867; †MA 1869; First-year Law scholar 1866-7; Second in First university examination in Arts, October 1864; Junior scholar Arts, literary division 1862–3 to 1864–5; Senior scholar, Metaphysical and Economic Science, 1867–8.

MacGiollarnáth, Proinnsias, *BA, 1948; *MA 1952; †LLB 1953; BL (Ireland); Professor of Romance Languages, UCG, (1959–87); served as Dean of Law Faculty.

MacGregor, William, †BA 1893; MA 1894; *LLB 1897; LLD 1901; Second-year Law scholar 1895–6; Senior exhibition, Law, 1897–8. From Raphoe, County Donegal, he qualified as a solicitor 1904.

McGuane, Hugh J., *BA 1932; H Dip in Ed 1933; *MA 1940; †LLB 1946.

McIlwaine, Robert, BA 1893; MA 1894; LLB 1895; First-year Law scholar 1894–5; Sir Robert Alfred McIlwaine (1871–1943), born in Larne, Co. Antrim; Joined the Civil Service of Cape Colony, 1895; transferred to Rhodesian Service, 1898; held many offices: Solicitor-General, official member of Legislative Council, Water Court Judge and Judge of High Court Rhodesia, Assistant Magistrate, Salisbury and British South Africa; Died October 1943; *Who Was Who, 1941–1950*.

McIntyre, Patrick J.W., BA 1935; †LLB 1940.

McKane, John,+ (1858–9); *BA 1860; *MA 1862; LLD 1882 (honorary on dissolution of QUI); First-year Law scholar 1858–9; also attended QCB; Barrington Lecturer; Professor of English Law, Queen's College, Belfast; BL (Ireland); MP for Mid-Armagh.

McMahon, George Y.,+ (1849–50 to 1850–1; 1857–8 to 1859–60); BA 1852; †Diploma in Elementary Law 1852: †MA 1860; Junior scholar, literary division Arts, 1849–50 to 1850–51; Senior scholar Metaphysical and Economic Science 1857–8; Senior scholar in Ancient Classics, 1859–60; Also attended at QCB; Professor of Modern Languages, Royal College, Mauritius.

McMullan, Hugh S., BA 1892; MA First-year Law scholar 1899–90.

Macnamara, Michael A., First-year Law scholar 1891–92; Second-year Law scholar 1892–3; Third-year Law scholar 1893–4; Senior Exhibition, Law, 1895–6.

McSwinney, Robert F., (1863–4 to 1869–70); †BA(Ancient Classics) 1866; MA 1868; *LLB 1870; LLD 1882 (honorary on dissolution of QUI); Second-year Law scholar 1867–8; Third-year Law scholar 1868–9; Senior Law scholar 1869–70; First-class exhibition in Law of Real Property, Inns of Court, London, 1871 ('against 51 competitors from all the leading Universities of the Empire' – QCG President's *Report*, 1870–72, p. 10); BL (England); Bencher of the Inner Temple.

Madill, Thomas, BA 1861; LLB, 1878; LLD 1879; Second-year Law scholar 1857–8.

Maguire, Thomas M., †BA 1867; †MA 1870 (English, History and Political Economy); LLB 1870 (third honours); LLD 1874; First-year Law scholar 1867–8; Second-year Law scholar 1868–9; Third-year Law scholar 1869–70; Senior Law scholar 1870–1; Third honours in First university examination in Arts, October 1866; University undergraduate essay prize, 1867. Thomas Millar Maguire (1849–1920) was born in Bray; became a barrister; a successful army 'coach'who wrote on strategy and great campaigners; had as pupils famous generals such as Allenby, Byng, Gough, and Wilson.

Malone, John, First-year Law scholar 1884–5.

Marshall, Robert L., BA 1907; LLB 1909; MA 1910; LLD 1912.

Marshall, William F., BA 1908; LLB 1910.

Mason, William, Diploma in Elementary Law 1855. Second-year Law scholar 1853–4; Third-year Law scholar 1854–5.

Megaw, Robert T., BA 1877; LLB 1885; LLD 1887.

Meredith, Richard Edmund, matriculated QCG; Appointed QC 1892; elected a Bencher of King's Inns, 1894; Judge of the Supreme Court of Judicature in Ireland, and Judicial Commissioner of the Irish Land Commission, 1898–1906; Master of the Rolls in Ireland, 1906–12; *Who Was Who, 1897–1916*.

Millar, William J., (1878–9 to 1881–82); †BA 1881; MA 1882 (honorary on dissolution of QUI); †LLB 1887; Third-year Law scholar 1882–83; District Inspector, RIC.

Molloy, Mark, †BA 1881; MA, LLB 1882 (honorary on dissolution of QUI); LLD 1883.

Monroe, John, (1854–5 to 1861–2); *BA 1857; *MA 1859; *LLB 1862; LLD 1882 (honorary on dissolution of QUI); First-year Law scholar 1858–9; Second-year Law scholar 1859–60; Third-year Law scholar 1860–1; Senior Law scholar 1861–2; Law studentship, Inns of Court, London; Barrington Lecturer; Examiner in Jurisprudence and Political Economy, QUI; Entered King's Inns, Dublin 1863; Bencher April 1885; QC 16 February 1877; law adviser to Irish government 1879–80; solicitor general for Ireland June to November 1885; Judge of Landed Estates Court, November 1885; resigned 24 March 1896; PC Ireland 1886. *Who Was Who, 1897–1916*.

Monroe, Samuel H., *BA 1873; MA 1882 (honorary on dissolution of QUI); Second in First university examination in Arts, October 1872; Junior scholar, science division Arts, 1871–2 to 1872–3; Sessional Crown Solicitor, Armagh.

Moorhead, John R., BA, 1881; *LLB 1886; First-year Law scholar 1883–4; Second-year Law scholar 1884–5; Third-year Law scholar 1885–6.

Moran, John, (1867–8 to 1875–6); *BA 1870; *MA 1872; †LLB 1878; LLD 1879; Third honours in First university examination in Arts, October 1869; Junior scholar, science division Arts, 1867–8 to 1869–70; Senior scholar Modern Languages and Modern History 1870–1; Second-year Law scholar 1872–73; Head Inspector of National Schools; Member, Royal Irish Academy.

Muldoon, John, (1865–1938), Third-year Law scholar 1889–90; Born in Co. Tyrone, 1865; BL (Ireland) 1894; KC (England); MP (Nationalist) Donegal 1905–6; East Wicklow, 1907–11; East Cork, 1911–18; Registrar in Lunacy, 1921; Registrar to Chief Justice, 1926; retired, 1935. *Who Was Who, 1929–1940*.

Mulholland, William, (1860–61 to 1865–6); †BA 1863; MA 1882 (honorary on dissolution of QUI); Third-year Law scholar 1864–5; Senior Law scholar 1865–6; First in First university examination in Arts October 1862; born 19 January 1843; son of J.S. Mulholland MD, Belfast; Barrington Lecturer; BL (Ireland) 1865; BL (England) 1875; Joined Northern Circuit; QC (England) 1894; Bencher, Lincoln's Inn, 1897; Judge of County Courts (North Staffordshire) 1899; Died 21 August 1927; *Who Was Who, 1916–1928*.

Mullally, Michael, (1867–8 to 1873–74); *BA 1871; †MA 1873; First honours in the First university examination in Arts, October 1870; Junior scholar, science division Arts, 1868–9 to 1870–71; Senior Scholar in Modern Languages and Modern History 1871–2; Senior Law scholar, 1873–4; Inspector of national schools, Ireland. (Deceased by 1905 – See Rentoul, *Q.C.G.* November 1905, p. 6.)

Mulligan, James,+ (1868–9 to 1871–2); †BA 1869; *MA 1871; First-year Law scholar 1868–9; Senior Law scholar 1871–2; Exhibition; Also attended at QCB; Judge James Mulligan (1847–1937) was born in Annaclone, Co. Down; Judge of Norfolk County Court 1906–21; BL (England); Senior Bencher of Gray's Inn; Treasurer, 1896–7; Wrote *The Riddle of Justice* (1925); *Justice in the After-life* (1927); *Thoughts of an Octogenarian on Overcrowding* (1929); *Notes on Bacon's Historia Vitae et Mortis* (1932); Died 15 December 1937; *Who Was Who, 1929–1940*.

Mullins, Richard, BA 1945; H Dip in Ed 1946; BComm, LLB 1948.

Murphy, Lindsay P., BA 1911 [or 1912?]; *LLB 1914; First-year Law scholar 1912–13; Second-year Law scholar 1913–14

Nelson, Thomas E., BA 1880; MA 1881; *LLB 1884; LLD 1886; First-year law scholar 1881–8; Second-year Law scholar 1882–3; Third-year Law scholar 1883–4.

Norton, Bernard G., (1849–0, 1858–9); BA 1860; Junior scholar, literary division Arts, 1849–50, 1858–9; Barrister and member of the Inner Temple (6 June 1855); Appointed solicitor general of British Guiana, March 1863, and was first puisne judge of the Supreme Court of British Guiana (Demerara) from 1868 until his death; Died at Norwood, Surrey, 13 April 1871.

O'Beirn, Fionnguala, †BA 1931; †LLB 1934.

O'Connor, Francis, Second-year Law scholar 1888–9.

O'Connor, Thomas V., †LLB 1940.

O'Donnell, Francis (Frank) Hugh, alias McDonald, Francis, (1862–3 to 1868–9); †BA, 1865; *MA 1868; First-year Law scholar 1865–6; Third-year Law scholar 1867–8; Senior Law scholar 1868–9; Joined staff of the *Morning Post*, obstructionist MP returned for Galway and Dungarvan; Wrote *History of the Irish Parliamentary Party* and other works. (His brother Charles J. O'Donnell, formerly Charles McDonald, (at QCG from 1865–6 to 1869–70), joined the Indian civil service and was MP for Walworth 1906.)

O'Feely, Timothy O'Brien, BA 1856; *Dip. El. Law 1856; *LLB 1857; LLD 1860; Exhibition and gold medal in Elementary Law; Junior scholar, science division Arts, 1849–50 to 1850–1; Second-year Law scholar 1852–3; Third-year Law scholar 1855–6; Senior Arts scholar in Metaphysical and Economic Science 1856–7; Senior Law scholar 1857–8.

O'Grady, Patrick F., †B Comm 1935; †BA, H Dip in Ed 1936; *LLB 1946.

O'Hara, Thomas, (1849–50 to 1860–61); Diploma in Agriculture 1852; †BA 1860; MA 1882 (honorary on dissolution of QUI); First and Second-year scholar, School of Agriculture, 1849–50 to 1850–51; First-year Law scholar 1856–7; Senior scholar in Metaphysical and Economic Science, 1860–1; Inspector of national schools, Ireland.

O'Hara, Robert F., BA 1873; BL (Ireland).

O'Keeffe, James D., First-year law scholar 1887–8.

O'Kennedy, Gerard, †LLB 1945; †MA 1949.

O'Kinealy, James, *BA 1858; MA and LLD 1882 (honorary on dissolution of QUI); Judge; writer, Arabic scholar; Judge of the High Court of Judicature, Fort William, Bengal.

O'Kinealy, Peter, (1871–2 to 1875–6); *BA 1874 ; †MA, †LLB 1875; LLD 1882 (honorary on dissolution of QUI); First honours in First university examination in Arts, October 1873; Junior scholar science division Arts, 1871–2 to 1873–4; Senior scholar in Mathematics 1874–5; Senior Law scholar 1875–6; Advocate-General of Bengal; BL (England).

O'Neill, George F., (1855–6 to 1859–60, 1871–2, 1873–4); *BA 1858; MA 1862; First-year Law scholar 1871–2; Inspector of national schools, Ireland.

O'Neill, Peter J., BA 1872; Third-year Law scholar 1872–3; BL (Ireland).

Parker, James D.,+ BA 1854; Diploma in Elementary Law 1855 (QCB); LLB 1857; LLD 1864; Senior Law scholar 1856–7; Also attended at QUB.

Perrin, Patrick, First-year Arts scholar, 1850–1; Law scholar, 1853–4; Second-year Law scholar 1854–5; Third-year Law scholar 1856–7.

Pierce, Arnold, First-year Law scholar 1855–6.

Reed, Sir Andrew,+ (1856–7 to 1859–60); BA 1859; *LLB 1877 (QCG and QCB); LLD 1878; MA 1882 (honorary on dissolution of QUI); Junior scholar science division, Arts, 1856–7 to 1858–9; KCB, CVO; Special resident magistrate; Inspector-General, RIC.

Rentoul, James Alex.,+ (1869–70 to 1872–3), BA 1869; †LLB 1874; LLD 1875; Senior scholar in Modern Languages and Modern History 1869–70; Second-year Law scholar 1870–71; Third-year Law scholar 1871–72; Senior Law scholar 1872–73; Also attended at QCC; KC (England); Judge of the City of London Court and Old Bailey, 1901; MP for East Down.

Rice, James P., Second-year Law scholar 1893–4.

Rutledge, John G., BA, 1893; MA, 1894; Second-year Law scholar 1894–5; Third-year Law scholar 1895–6; Senior exhibition, Law, 1896–7.

Ryan, Dominic D., †BA 1852; Medal for modern foreign languages; Diploma in Elementary Law 1852; MA 1882 (honorary on dissolution of QUI); First-year Arts scholar, science division 1849–50; Second-year Law scholar 1850–1; Third-year Law scholar 1851–2; Senior Law scholar 1852–3.

Sheehy, John F., First-year Law scholar 1911–12.

Shiel, Joseph R., BA 1871; †MA 1873; *L.L.B. 1874; LLD 1882 (honorary on dissolution of QUI); Second in First university examination in Arts, October 1870; Junior scholar, literary division Arts, 1868–9 to 1870–71; Second-year Law scholar 1871–2; Senior scholar in Metaphysical and Economic Science, 1872–3; Third-year Law scholar 1873–4; Senior Law scholar 1874–5.

Smith, Henry, BA 1863; MD, MCh MAO, 1888; Second-year Law scholar 1885–6.

Smith, Joseph, BA 1884; LLB 1887; Third-year Law scholar 1886–7.

Smylie, Archibald,+ BA 1864; †MA 1874; LLB, LLD 1877; BL (Australia); Second honours in First university examination in Arts (Galway) October 1863; Junior scholar, literary division of Arts, QCG, 1861–2 to 1863–4; Also attended at QCB.

Smyth, Charles, BA, 1910; First-year Law scholar 1910–11; (Under name 'Charles J. Smyth' Second-year Law scholar 1911–12?)

Stephens, Robert, First-year Law scholar 1851–2; Third-year Law scholar 1853–4.

Thornton, John A., LLB 1948.

Thynne, Henry,+ (1854–5 to 1860–1); *BA 1859; *LLB 1873; MA, LLD 1882 (honorary on dissolution of QUI); CB (Knighthood – Companion of the Bath); Resident magistrate; Deputy Inspector-General, RIC; Also attended at QCC.

Todd, Andrew, †BA 1876; *LLB 1879; MA, LLD 1882 (honorary on dissolution of QUI); Junior scholar literary division, Arts, 1874–5 to 1875–6; First-year Law scholar 1876–7; Third-year Law scholar 1878–9; Senior Law scholar 1879–80; KC (Ireland); Senior Crown Counsel for County Longford.

Todd, Robert Henderson,+ BA 1870; MA 1871, †LLB 1873; LLD 1875; First-year Law scholar 1869–70; Senior scholar in Metaphysical and Economic Science 1870–1; Also attended at QCB.

Turner, Alexander K., First-year Law scholar 1900–1; Second-year Law scholar 1901–2.

Walkinshaw, Robert, Junior scholar, Science division Arts, 1849–50 to 1851–52; First-year Law scholar 1852–3.

Walsh, Daniel, BA 1940; H Dip in Ed 1941; †MA., LLB 1942.

Webb, Patrick J., First-year Law scholar 1914–15; (May be the same student who studied medicine at QCG from 1921–3.)

West, John D., *BA 1859; First-year Law scholar 1857–8; Second-year Law scholar 1858–9.

West, Sir Raymond, (1852–3 to 1855–6); *BA 1855; †MA 1869; LLD 1882 (honorary on dissolution of QUI); Obtained a first, exhibition, and gold medal in Ancient Classical Languages and Literature; Exhibition and gold medal in Experimental Physics (Natural Philosophy); Junior scholar, literary division Arts, 1852–3 to 1854–5 (also qualified in Science division and First medicine.); KCIE; Judge of the High Court of Bombay; Vice-Chancellor, University of Bombay; Member of the Council of the Government of Bombay; Teacher of Indian Law in the University of Cambridge; Honorary doctorate, University of Bombay.

3

Engineering

PAUL DUFFY

This is not a systematic history of the Engineering School at NUI, Galway; rather it is a view by a forensic engineer, from the trackbed of a long-vanished railway, of one aspect of that School's rich and varied heritage. Whilst the Galway-Clifden railway might seem a strange, or perhaps eccentric, vantage point from which to view the trajectory of an academic discipline, it should be borne in mind that Edward Townsend, the School's longest serving Professor, was directly involved in its design and construction. Indeed, as all of the Professors of Civil Engineering since the foundation of the College have had some involvement with railways, it is proposed to view the School's history from the point of view of railway engineering, including ancillary services.

Prior to the opening of the Engineering School in Galway, technological education was provided by apprenticeship. The aspirant engineer or surveyor paid a fee to a recognised master in return for a practical and theoretical training. Henry Clements, Galway's first County Surveyor, advertised for a pupil shortly after taking up his appointment. The pupil was to be well educated, be 'of respectable connections' and would have the choice of living in or not. He 'would have an opportunity of acquiring a knowledge of the various branches of the business, as also the practical part of building and architecture'. The fee was to be 'moderate'. Clements headed his advertisement '*Engineer, Surveying*', obviously intending to show that the emerging profession of civil engineering was more advanced, and indeed had subsumed that of the Land Surveyor.[1] Some surveyors extended their work beyond land measurement and mapping to include road-making, canal and bridge works, and so forth. Possibly, the most notable of these in the western area was Alexander Nimmo – the most famous of the three Nimmos who worked in Co. Galway.[2] Others, like Michael Logan, best remembered for his map of Galway drawn for James Hardiman's *History*, were content to remain land surveyors and to make only the occasional foray into the realms of engineering.[3] He was paid ninety shillings in 1832 for a map survey of Threadneedle Road – then a new line

---

[1] *Tuam Herald*, 18 July 1839.
[2] For a recent account of Alexander Nimmo's life, see Seán de Courcey, 'Alexander Nimmo: Engineer Extraordinary', *Connemara*, 2 (1995), pp. 47–56.
[3] James Hardiman, *A History of the Town and the County of the Town of Galway* (Dublin, 1820).

of road.[4] Logan, who had set up in practice in Galway in 1817, and had taken up residence in the city in 1822, expanded his business to such an extent that, in 1825, he advertised for an apprentice.[5] Galway did, however, have at least one Mathematical Academy, where some technological education was given. John Reynolds, 'Professor of Mathematics', taught mensuration, gauging, surveying, and navigation, amongst other subjects, at this school in Back Street, Galway, in 1793.[6] This seemingly short-lived Academy may have been the source of the three surveying instruments offered for sale by Peter Martin, 'Kelp Inspector', in June 1795.[7] The advent of work on the Ballinasloe Canal brought another mathematics master into print.[8] Nicholas Smith posed a problem on estimating quantities for excavation in canal work, supplying the answer in the next issue of the newspaper.[9] This form of advertising was practised by several mathematics masters around the country, some of whom were land surveyors and, quite probably, taught surveying as part of their curriculum.[10] A Mr Gregory CE, of 9 Holles Street, Dublin, in an advertisement headed 'ENGINEERING', announced that as he was now 'unconnected with the college', that is, Trinity College Dublin, he was ready to take on a limited number of outdoor pupils and one indoor pupil. Gregory described himself as the author of a new work on engineering and surveying and of various scientific works. He also announced that he would be glad to undertake large surveys, estate improvement by drainage, together 'with every description of other works' connnected with the profession.[11] Obviously, the training was in the realms of surveying, drainage, land reclamation, and agricultural engineering.

The advent of the railway age brought new schools into the public arena. One such school was run by Thomas Fannin (or Fanning) at 9 Lower Mount Street, Dublin, where, it was claimed, gentlemen would be 'expeditiously and practically prepared' in 'Railway Engineering and Levelling'. The school had a valuable engineering library and a 'full' supply of instruments including, for example,

---

4   Patrick J. Kennedy, 'The County of the Town of Galway', *Journal of the Galway Archaeological and Historical Society*, 30 (1963), pp. 98–9.
5   *Connaught Journal*, 17 April 1817 and 25 March 1825.
6   Ibid., 25 March 1793.
7   Ibid., 1 June 1795.
8   For an account of the canal construction, see M.B. Mullins, 'On the Origin and Reclamation of Peat Bogs', *Transactions of the Institution of Civil Engineers of Ireland*, 2 (1847), pp. 37–48.
9   Smith posed the following problem in the *Connaught Journal*, answering it in the issue of 23 June 1825:
    Q. It is required to investigate a rule, whereby the solidity of an Angular Canal, whose opposite banks are unequally inclined to the horizon, may be found.
    Solution: Let ABC and DEF represent the opposite banks of the canal, which are equal in length and parallel to one another. Conceive a vertical section of the canal passing the angular points BE: the product arising by multiplying the area of this section by the sum of the perpendiculars let fall from the points AC to the lines BE will be the content of the canal. The area of said sections will be found by multiplying the sum of its breadths at top and bottom by half the depth of the canal.
    From the description the reader may supply the diagram.
10 James Irwin of Limerick published his method of determining the areas of right-lined figures in *Anthologia Hibernica*, 4 (1794), pp. 133–6.
11 *Galway Vindicator*, 28 December 1842.

theodolite, spirit levels, sextant, and staffs. Theodolites were always expensive so the listing of equipment implies a limited number of places available for practical training. The advertisement alludes to this: 'some of the students are engaged in actual field practice, others in mapping, drawing or mathematics'. Obviously the school was a practice nursery and the students were given 'hands on' training as junior unpaid assistants. The training must have been to a reasonably acceptable standard, as Fannin's advertisement stated that several pupils from the school had 'lately received situations on Railways, and for the Board of Works'.[12] The school had vacancies for three boarders in October 1846.[13]

The formation of the Office of Public Works (1831), County Surveyorships (1835), and the progress of major developments, such as railway construction, created a demand for highly skilled engineers. The Institution of Civil Engineers of Ireland was formed in 1835 to promote the professional development of engineers and the general advancement of engineering science and knowledge.[14] The Engineering School of Trinity College Dublin was founded in 1841 and, when the Queen's Colleges were established, it was decided that they too should have Engineering Schools.[15] However, as late as October 1844, private colleges were still in the market for students. The *Galway Vindicator* of 26 October 1844, carried an advertisement for the 'College for Civil Engineers', based in Putney, London. The courses were intended to equip young men for the professions of architect, civil, mining, and mechanical engineers, surveyors, and estate managers. The syllabus included mathematics, chemistry, architecture, and general construction, surveying, mineralogy, and geology. Surveying was to be taught by 'Practical' professors and through site visits 'to public works and actual surveys'. The College had its own machinery room, powered by a steam engine, a foundry, and a smithy. Classical instruction and courses in modern languages and drawing were available for the junior students. As well as the professions listed above, the College claimed to prepare students for careers in mining and in 'the superintendence of works carried out by machinery'. The education provided would be useful for emigrants or those proceeding to the colonies with naval or military appointments. Strict attention was paid to the moral habits of the students by the Resident Principal, the Revd Morgan Lowie MA, who had 'a careful regard to orderly, reverential behaviour' and who also provided religious instruction. It still remains to be seen whether this institution was a truly academic one, or a forcing ground to supply trained staff for the vested interests of its sponsors and promoters. Within a few months of the advertisement appearing, Galway had been selected as the site for one of the new Queen's Colleges.[16] The building of the College would appear to have put an end to the private training of engineers in the west of Ireland.

---

12 *Western Star and Ballinasloe Advertiser*, 17 October 1846, where the name is given as Fannin.
13 Ibid., 14 November 1846, where the name is given as Fanning.
14 Ronald C. Cox, *Engineering Ireland 1778–1878* (Dublin, 1978), p. 5.
15 Ronald Cox, *Engineering at Trinity* (Dublin, 1993).
16 For an account of the selection of Galway as the site for one of the Queen's Colleges, see James Mitchell, 'Queen's College, Galway, 1845–1858: From Site to Structure', *Journal of the Galway Archaeological and Historical Society*, 50 (1998), pp. 49–89.

3.1 William Bindon Blood, Professor of Civil Engineering, 1849–60

When Queen's College Galway (QCG) opened for students in October 1849, the Engineering course was of two year's duration, leading to a Diploma in Civil Engineering. The fee was £11.10.0 for the first year and £10 for the second. The School formed part of the Faculty of Arts at that time.[17] The appointment of the first Professor was noted in the *Galway Mercury* of 11 August 1849: 'Civil Engineering: Thomas Drane of St Peter's [sic] College, Cambridge, formerly engineer to the Ceylon Railway Co.'. The tenure of the felicitously-named Drane was brief. On his resignation, he was succeeded, in April 1850, by William Bindon Blood, Resident Engineer to the Birmingham and Oxford Railway (fig. 3.1).[18] Blood had been educated at Edinburgh and Trinity College Dublin, where he obtained a BA degree in 1839 – the Engineering course did not begin until 1841.[19] He obtained the College Gold Medal in Mathematics and Physics in 1838. He was the third son of Bindon Blood of Rockforest, Co. Clare, by his second wife, Harriet Bagot, of Nurney, Co. Kildare. After graduation, Blood began his railway career in the south of Scotland where he met and married a Miss Stewart in 1841. Blood subsequently moved to Harberry Hall, Warwickshire where he worked under Brunel on the Birmingham-Oxford section of the London to Birmingham Railway. His wife died in 1849 and the following year he returned to Ireland to take up the vacant Professorship of Civil Engineering in Galway.[20]

After his appointment, Blood carried out 'a very elegant analysis' on the stresses in continuous girders in three spans.[21] According to William Anderson, Blood was the first to show the possibility of determining the strains in the diagonal braces in beams. He also made a scale model to illustrate and prove the correctness of his views. Anderson exhibited a copy of the model at a meeting of the Institution of Civil Engineers of Ireland on 14 December 1858.[22] Blood presented a paper on

---

17 S.J. Maguire, 'Galway Scrap Book', *Galway Reader*, nos i and ii, 3 (1950), pp. 44–76. Reference is on p. 61.
18 *Galway Vindicator*, 17 April 1850. I am indebted to the Revd James Mitchell for this reference and for information on Drane.
19 Ronald Cox, personal communication.
20 *Galway Vindicator*, 17 April 1850.
21 General Sir Bindon Blood, *Four Score Years and Ten* (London, 1933), pp. 13, 14, 19. See, also, Frank Brew, *The Parish of Kilkeedy: A Local History* (Tubber, Co. Clare, 1998), pp. 98–102.
22 William Anderson, 'On Beams and Girder Bridges', pt iii, *Transactions of the Institution of Civil Engineers of Ireland*, 5 (1857), p.154.

stresses in girders to the (British) Institution of Civil Engineers in London.[23] Prior to this, he furnished his friend, Samuel Downing, with his formulae, calculations, and a description of the model. Downing used, with full acknowledgement, a portion of Blood's work and a full description of this model, 'which was devised ingeniously to admit the actual measurement of ... strains'.[24] Blood's intellectual generosity and Downing's professional courtesy stand out in sharp contrast to the unseemly controversy between MacNeill and Barton over credit for the design of the ironwork for the Boyne Viaduct.[25] Indeed, Bindon Stoney, the Resident Engineer on that viaduct, confirmed the importance of his kinsman Blood's contribution to bridge design. In a discussion following Barton's paper on the Boyne Viaduct, presented to a meeting of the British Association in Dublin on 1 September 1857, Stoney observed that the abstruse mathematical analysis necessary for design purposes had been carried out by Professor Blood of Queen's College Galway.[26] The Boyne Viaduct would appear to have been the first bridge designed in accordance with stress calculations and to have had the longest span in the world when first constructed – its central span had a length of 269 feet. It was also one of the earliest examples of a continuous truss girder bridge anywhere.[27] The ironwork on the viaduct was replaced in a major reconstruction project in 1933.[28] Blood also had some experience in road-making, being credited for much of the work carried out on the road from New Quay and Burren to Tubber, Co. Clare. The road was variously known as 'The New Line', 'Bindon's Line', or 'The Oyster Road'. The seemingly unoriginal 'New Line' was merely a convenience name in any locality where a new road had been built. 'Bindon's Line', no doubt, was applied to credit Blood's father with obtaining the necessary presentments to finance its construction, from both the Galway and Clare Grand Juries. 'The Oyster Road' indicates the 'why' rather than the 'who' behind its construction – the Road was built to open up the oyster trade. Bindon Blood appeared to have had some interest in the development of the area as he also engaged in the planting of broad leaf trees.[29] Some of this interest in local development seems to have passed on to his son, for the professor acted on the Industrial Committee set up by the Royal Galway Institution. This Committee was set up to promote the National Exhibition of 1852, which was held in Cork.[30] There is no evidence, however, to suggest that William Blood inherited his father's interest in antiquities.[31]

23 *The Presidents, Vice-Presidents and Professors of Queens College, Galway* (Dublin, 1902), p. 52
24 Samuel Downing, 'On a Demonstrative Model, Showing the Diagonal Strains in Wrought Iron Girders', *Transactions of the Institution of Civil Engineers of Ireland*, 4 (1851), p. 58.
25 Canice O'Mahony, 'Iron Rails and Harbour Walls: James Barton of Farnderg', *County Louth Archaeological and Historical Journal*, 22 (1990), pp. 134–49; see especially pp. 140–2.
26 Ibid., p. 139.
27 Martin Heydon, *The Book of Bridges* (London, 1976), p. 102. See also K.A. Murray, 'The Boyne Viaduct', *Irish Railway Record Society Journal*, no. 5, July 1949, pp. 141–7, reprinted in *Journal of the Old Drogheda Society*, no. 6 (1989), pp. 5–18.
28 G.B. Howden, 'Reconstruction of the Boyne Viaduct, Drogheda', *Transactions of the Institution of Civil Engineers of Ireland*, 60 (1934), pp. 71–111.
29 Brew, *Kilkeedy*, pp. 101–2.
30 John Francis Maguire, *The Industrial Movement in Ireland* (Cork, 1853), p. 457.
31 His father's collections were auctioned by Sotheby's after Bindon's death in 1855 and realised £17,000. See Brew, *Kilkeedy*, p. 100.

Pioneering work by Blood, and others, led to major girder bridges becoming commonplace on railways. Indeed, the most prominent landmark on the Galway-Clifden Railway was the Corrib Viaduct in Galway City. This bridge provided a useful training model during Professor Rishworth's tenure of office; final-year students were often sent out to measure up the ironwork in the bridge and to work out the design in reverse – that is, to start with the finished product and 'progress' backwards through the various design stages. After the demolition of the superstructure in 1935, both F.S. Rishworth and his successor W.H. Prendergast, often set the problem of designing a replacement structure, using the surviving piers. This structure could be a railroad or pedestrian bridge.[32] Indeed, in the recent past, a German postgraduate student came up with two different designs for a timber footbridge at this location.[33] The construction of one or other of these designs would make a stunning millennium statement, would enhance the reputation of Irish wood products and help to carry on a 1,200-year-old tradition of major bridge construction using timber.

3.2 Edward Townsend, Professor of Civil Engineering, 1860–1910

The Clifden railway was designed by Edward Townsend and J.H. Ryan.[34] Townsend, who succeeded Blood, combined his professorship with a long career as a railway engineer (fig. 3.2). His two published papers might seem slim by today's standards but they reveal a strong, practical mind which could identify a problem and impose a solution without superfluous twaddle. Both papers display a keen sense of the financial value of applying practical engineering solutions to the problem at hand. Townsend's first paper, which rejoiced in the title 'A New Method of Finding the Angles between the Face Joints and Cousing Spirals on the Soffit in a Skew Arch' runs to all of two-and-a-half pages of text and one page of graphics. Its short introductory paragraph gives a very good insight into the man's approach to things technical:

32 William (Bill) Glynn BE, personal communication.
33 Bernhard Brummer, 'Structural Engineering in Ireland', Diplomarbeit, Bayern Technische Universität, Munich 1993.
34 J.H. Ryan, 'The Galway and Clifden Railway', *Transactions of the Institution of Civil Engineers of Ireland*, 28 (1902), pp. 203–35.

The methods which have been given in the works on engineering for finding those angles which are necessary for cutting the Voussoirs in a skew arch, are rather long and cumbrous, and are attended with much trouble and difficulty in their practical application. I was, therefore, led to search for an easy practical method for working this problem, and arrived at the following solution, which is so simple in its application as to lie within the scope of the most ordinary draughtsman.[35]

The arrival of the railway age called for a change in bridge-building techniques. Skew bridges became a necessity. Railways, by their nature, cannot be 'dog-legged' or 'double-bended' over rivers or roads but have to be carried over at whatever angle is required – hence the need for skew bridges. Skew or oblique arch bridges were first developed by Richard Chapman during the construction of the Kildare Canal in 1788.[36] The problem with skew masonry bridges was that the faces of the voussoirs or wedge-shaped arch stones had to be cut to particular angles to fit in particular locations in the arch. This was a time-consuming process, requiring precise calculations for the angles to be correctly marked out on templates for the masons who would subsequently cut the stones. Any error in an angle would mean that the voussoir faces would not fit together leaving the arch liable to collapse. Townsend's work, by simplifying the design process, greatly reduced both the possibility of error and also the costs of the operation. Townsend, through his connection with the Midland Great Western Railway, was no doubt familiar with the major bridge carrying the Ballinasloe Station over the Deerpark River. The bridge is 304 feet long, with each end constructed in the spiral or skew manner.[37] He was certainly familiar with the construction methods used by Hemans when building the section of the Midland Railway from Enfield to Mullingar.[38] Hemans's method of bog drainage and consolidation derived, in its ultimate form, from that followed in the construction of the Ballinasloe extension of the Grand Canal.[39] This method was followed in the construction of the Clifden line through the soft bogs west of Maam.[40] Indeed, the Ballinasloe canal has another link with Townsend. His second paper to the Institution of Engineers of Ireland, on estimating quantities in excavation, has an echo of Nicholas Smith's problem of 1824.[41] It is also worth noting that the earliest proposal for a railway into

---

35   *Transactions of the Institution of Civil Engineers of Ireland*, 8 (1868), pp. 116–18.
36   Ruth Delaney, *The Grand Canal of Ireland*, 2nd ed. (Dublin, 1995), pp. 58, 59, and illustration p. 56.
37   R.V. Boyle, 'Description of a Model of a Skew Bridge, on the Midland Great Western Railway of Ireland, near Ballinasloe', *Transactions of the Institution of Civil Engineers of Ireland*, 4 (1851), pp. 26–8.
38   G.W. Hemans, 'Account of the Construction of the Midland Great Western Railway of Ireland over a Tract of Bog in the Counties of Meath and Westmeath', *Transactions of the Institution of Civil Engineers of Ireland*, 4 (1851), pp. 48–60.
39   Mullins, 'Peat Bogs', *passim*.
40   Ryan, 'The Galway and Clifden Railway', pp. 209–10.
41   E. Townsend, 'An Easy Proof of the Prismoidal Formula, with an Accurate Method of Taking out the Quantities of Earth, and of Setting out the Half Breadth in a Cutting with a Steep Gradient', *Transactions of the Institution of Civil Engineers of Ireland*, 9 (1868), pp. 28–31.

Connemara arose out of a series of canal proposals put forward in the 1830s. The Ballinasloe canal played a prominent part in some of these. Thomas Bermingham was the originator of these ideas; realising the importance of the new mode of transport, railways, he proposed a Dublin-Galway-Bertroughboy Bay railway line some seventeen years before Galway was connected to Dublin by rail.[42]

Edward Townsend had an extended role in the saga of the Galway-Clifden Railway. In 1881, he was appointed by the Office of Public Works (OPW) to hold a public enquiry into the merits of the proposed Galway, Oughterard, and Clifden Railway. He was later appointed by the Board of the OPW to enquire into the West of Ireland Rail Company. He was Design Engineer for the proposed Guaranteed Light Railways and Tramways Company who put forward plans for a Clifden Line. In June 1887, he gave evidence before the Royal Commission when they met in Galway to enquire into the railway question.[43] As well as designing, with J.H. Ryan as a partner, the line that was constructed, Townsend also co-designed a rival scheme. Along with Arthur E. Joyce, he prepared plans for the Galway and Clifden 'via Oughterard' Light Railway, Recess and Killary Branch. This proposed line started at the north-western corner of Galway docks and terminated at Clifden quay, with a branch-line running down the Inagh Valley to the deep water at Killary.[44] No doubt this proposal was influenced by the British Admiralty's interest in Killary as a safe haven for the North Atlantic Fleet. Townsend had previously worked with Joyce on the design for the Attymon and Loughrea Railway in 1883-4.[45] In 1895, he supervised the surveying of the route for a proposed railway to link Oranmore and Ballyvaughan, which was never built.[46]

Townsend had the reputation of being a very good lecturer and he was also an examiner at the Royal University. In his later years, he was also the Registrar at the College. During his time, he firmly established the reputation of the Galway Engineering School, retiring in 1910, having served fifty years as professor.[47] He died in 1919 and he is buried in the New Cemetery, Bohermore, Galway. His son, Sir John Townsend FRS, a graduate of Trinity College Dublin, was appointed Wykeham Professor of Physics in the University of Oxford in 1900. Even though Sir John did not follow his father into Engineering, he had an interest in the profession. It was largely due to his influence that the Oxford Engineering School was founded.[48]

Townsend's successor was a former student of his, Frank Sharman Rishworth (fig. 3.3). Rishworth, born in Tuam in 1876, was educated at the Ranelagh School

---

42 Paul Duffy,'The Galway-Clifden Railway', *Council Signpost*, no. 2, 1999. See also Paul Duffy, 'A Dublin-Galway Ship Canal', *Inland Waterways News*, no. iv, 23 (1996), p. 10.
43 Pádraic Ó Cuimin, personal communication.
44 Parliamentary plans for this proposed line are in the author's collection.
45 Pádraic Ó Cuimin, *The Baronial Lines of the M.G.W.R.* (Dublin, 1972), p. 17.
46 Jimmy O'Connor, 'The Campaign for the Oranmore-Ballyvaughan Railway', *Trácht*, 1990, pp. 25–9. Reference is on p. 25.
47 Michael George O'Malley, 'Memories of Queen's College Galway, 1904–1906', *Journal of the Galway Archaeological and Historical Society*, 50 (1998), pp. 112–17. References at pp. 112, 114.
48 Obituary Notice, 'Sir John Townsend FRS', *Times*, 18 February 1957, reprinted in the *Engineers Journal*, April 1957, p. 175.

3.3 Frank Sharman Rishworth, Professor of Civil Engineering, 1910–46

in Athlone and entered Queen's College Galway in 1899. He graduated with the BE and BA degrees in 1898 and 1899 respectively, having taken first place in both the science and engineering examinations each year. Rishworth began his professional career on the construction of railways in Derbyshire in England and he also worked on designs for the London Underground railway system. He joined the Egyptian Public Service in 1902, lecturing in irrigation, railway construction, and public works in the Ghizeh School of Engineering. He was actively involved with experiments carried out in connection with the Aswan Dam project and other irrigation works; and there can be no doubt but that it was here that he developed a keen appreciation of the Theory of Models and the benefits of its application for large-scale engineering works. When he retired from Ghizeh in 1910 to take up his new post in Galway, he was decorated by the Khedive of Egypt for his engineering services to that country.[49] During his tenure of office, Rishworth consolidated and

---

49 Obituary Notice, F.S. Rishworth, *Transactions of the Institution of Civil Engineers of Ireland*, 86 (1960), pp. 175–7.

enhanced the reputation of the Engineering School. In 1925, he was seconded by the government and appointed Chief Engineer on the Shannon Hydro-Electric Scheme.[50] Galway folklore credits Rishworth with instilling into Dr Thomas McLaughlin the idea of harnessing the Shannon. Rishworth, however, never claimed this honour. But he did have an input into McLaughlin's plans. In March 1944, speaking in the discussion following a paper by J.A. O'Riordan, Rishworth stated:

> It might be of interest to record that the Shannon Scheme was more or less the result of an accident. One of his pupils (Dr McLaughlin) went to Germany and in 1923, he wrote asking for information with reference to the flow of various Irish rivers for the use of an eminent German engineer.

Rishworth sent on volume forty-five of the *Transactions of the Institution of Engineers of Ireland*, containing Chaloner-Smith's paper on the duration of stated flows in the Shannon. According to Rishworth, the Shannon Hydro-Electric Scheme started in that small way.[51] For the record, Chaloner-Smith concluded that the 'Great Shannon Myth' (that is, large-scale harnessing of the river) was not economically feasible and many of those present at his lecture concurred.[52] It would seem that engineers differ and the country prospers!

A major problem facing the Government at the start of the Shannon Scheme was the recruitment of high-calibre technical staff capable of dealing with the contractors. Patrick McGilligan, the then Minister for Industry and Commerce, persuaded University College Galway to release Rishworth to act as Chief Civil Engineer on the job. No doubt his experience in Egypt on dam works was of major benefit to him. As well as bringing his considerable technical skills to the Shannon Scheme, Rishworth also applied his strong sense of fair play when appropriate. When the Department of Finance attempted to short-change J.F. Sothman, an eminent American engineer recruited for the Shannon Scheme, Rishworth intervened directly, securing some degree of fair treatment.[53] This same attitude surfaces in his presidential address to the Institution of Engineers of Ireland on 2 November 1936. He argued that the young graduate engineer was worthy of a fair salary and he was highly critical of the practice of long-term temporary employment for engineers in the public sector. This system was adopted by the public sector as a cost-cutting measure, resulting in many engineers losing out on pension entitlements. Rishworth's concern was also of a very practical nature. He wanted to make it compulsory for students to undergo a minimum of three months work experience before graduation. Some sixty years on, this suggestion

---

50 Maurice Manning and Moore McDowell, *Electricity Supply in Ireland: The History of the ESB* (Dublin, 1984), p. 44.
51 *Transactions of the Institution of Civil Engineers of Ireland*, 70 (1944). Rishworth's contribution is on pp. 131–3.
52 J. Chaloner-Smith, 'Notes on the Average Volume of Flow from Large Catchment Areas in Ireland ... Deduced from Gaugings on the River Shannon', *Transactions of the Institution of Civil Engineers of Ireland*, 45 (1921), pp. 41–118. See pp. 79, 85–7, and 114–15 in particular.
53 Manning and McDowell, *Electricity Supply*, pp. 44–5.

is still under consideration. One area where he was able to achieve concrete results immediately was in the setting up of a benevolent fund to assist engineers who had fallen on hard times and the bereaved families of engineers. Rishworth laid down the guiding rule of the fund: it was to operate without publicity or ostentation. In other words, it was to do good by stealth. He was a regular contributor to the fund until his death. Two proposals put forward by Rishworth to help alleviate the chronic transport problems of Dublin in 1936 were prophetic. He called for the electrification of the Amiens Street-Bray line, which has now been accomplished as part of the DART system. He also advocated the electrification of the Harcourt Street-Bray line. This line was subsequently ripped up but it is now proposed to re-lay it and electrify the track as part of the proposed LUAS system.[54]

On completion of the Shannon Scheme, Rishworth returned to UCG but he was retained as a consultant by the Department of Industry and Commerce. His report of 1932 paved the way for the expansion of Ardnacrusha by the addition of an extra turbine.[55] He engaged in consultancy work for several local authorities, particularly in relation to water supply and sewerage schemes. He also designed a number of reinforced concrete bridges. On several of these, he worked in association with E. Ralph Ryan, consulting engineer, who lectured part-time in the College. Amongst these were the three fixed road bridges across the Eglington Canal in Galway.[56] Their construction meant the closure of the canal for navigation purposes. It is worth noting that Rishworth's predecessor, Townsend, was for many years Engineer to the Corrib Navigation Trustees, having succeeded Samuel U. Roberts in that post.[57] Roberts had been the engineer in charge of the first Corrib drainage works at Galway and he was also in charge of the construction of the canal. On his retirement from the Board of Works, he became County Surveyor for the Western Division of Galway.

Prior to the Shannon Scheme, Rishworth lived at 'Gort Ard', Rockbarton, Galway, a house built by Blood. After the completion of the scheme, he resided in Dublin, commuting to Galway during the week.[58] He died at his residence, 29 Leeson Park, Dublin, on 31 March 1960, and is buried in Enniskerry Churchyard, Co. Wicklow.

True to form, Rishworth's successor, William Hillary Prendergast, was engaged in railway work before his appointment to Galway (fig. 3.4). Of all the permanent professors in the Engineering School, he had undoubtedly the most colourful career. He obtained his degrees in Engineering and Science, from UCG, in 1915 with first-class honours. In 1916 he joined the Royal Engineers and he returned from service in the Middle East, with the rank of major, in 1918. In 1919 he was

---

54 F.S. Rishworth, 'Presidential Address', *Transactions of the Institution of Civil Engineers of Ireland*, 63 (1937), pp. 1–17.
55 Manning and McDowell, *Electricity Supply*, p. 94.
56 Specification for the works in author's possession.
57 Townsend's reports on the Corrib Navigation of 1891, 1892, 1899, 1902, 1903, in author's possession, as is Roberts' report of 1873. For a summary of these reports, see Paul Duffy, 'Random Notes on the Corrib', *Inland Waterways News*, no. iii, 23 (1996), p. 15.
58 Tom O'Connor, personal communication.

3.4 William H. Prendergast, Professor of Civil Engineering, 1947–57

working on irrigation in Mesopotamia and, in 1920, he took up duty with the Bengal-Assam Railway. His decision to take up the appointment was prompted by waking up one morning to a cold, dense fog overhanging London. As the railway company's policy was to provide all its own ancillary services, Prendergast's work involved not only the construction and maintenance of the permanent way but also residential units, workshops, power houses, hospitals, roads, and water supply schemes. In 1940, he was seconded to the British Army, commissioned as a lieutenant-colonel in the Royal Indian Engineers, and promptly set about raising and training a number of railway construction companies. He planned and organised the doubling of the railway line between Basra and Baghdad. When the Japanese invaded Burma, he was sent, with a small volunteer party of railway men, to organise the evacuation of Rangoon. He travelled on the locomotive of the last train to leave Rangoon, with the 'last Ditchers', who had blown up the port and harbour installations and set alight the oil refinery. The train was derailed in an evening attack on a bridge and Prendergast led 'an orderly withdrawal of civil and military passengers during the night and the following day under continual enemy attacks which were repulsed'. He was awarded the DSO and was twice mentioned in dispatches. After leading his party safely to India, he became engineer-in-chief of the Assam lines. The railway had to be developed to seven times its peace-time capacity to supply the front line and the Allied 'Hump' airlift to China. This was done in record time. At the end of the war, he had to organise the removal of the redundant track and the dismantling of the 750-mile-long petroleum pipeline he had laid from Calcutta to the Burma Road. In 1947, he resigned his post as general manager of the Bengal-Assam Railway and returned to Galway to take up the professorship vacated, on age grounds, by Rishworth.[59]

One Galway engineering graduate, who saw active service in the Far East during the war, was not as fortunate as Prendergast. Joseph Fitzgerald, who obtained his BE degree in 1937 was in Malaya when the war broke out. He was

---

59 Considerable detail about Prendergast can be found in the following: Obituary Notice, *Transactions of the Institution of Civil Engineers of Ireland*, 84 (1958), pp. 232–3; appreciation notices by Patrick Tobin and Con Buckley, *Engineers Journal*, September 1957, pp. 374–5; 'Profile', *Engineers Journal*, April 1958, pp. 142–5; W.H. Prendergast, 'A Galway Engineer in Assam', *Galway Reader*, no. 1, 4 (1953), pp. 102–12.

commissioned in the Indian Army and saw active service throughout the Malayan campaign. He was taken prisoner at the fall of Singapore in 1942 and spent the next three-and-a-half years working as slave labour on the Burma-Siam railway for the Japanese.[60] There were other graduates in engineering who had some military involvement. They included George Lee, Galway's last County Surveyor and first County Engineer, who began his professional career in the Galway Shell Factory,[61] and Hubert O'Connor (BE 1916, ME 1920) who also worked in munitions briefly, before becoming a lecturer in the College. He subsequently founded his own firm of consultant engineers, H.G.L. O'Connor and Co.[62] The Shell Factory later became part of the IMI Complex, which was subsequently subsumed into the campus. Two other graduates deserve mention in this regard also. Thomas P. Flanagan of Mayo, on graduating, deferred taking up a professional career, joined the Mayo Brigade of the IRA, and saw active service in the War of Independence. He later became a major organisational figure in the 'Turf Campaign' during the 'emergency' years of the Second World War.[63] Maurice Sweeney was working as an Assistant County Surveyor in the Western Division of Galway when he was interned by the Free State Government on suspicion of supplying the Republican forces with information on bridges which were blown up in Connemara.[64] Sweeney was a pioneer in the development of wind-powered public water supplies in a number of areas in western Galway in the 1920s and 1930s. Some of his schemes were still in use up to the 1950s.

Prior to dieselisation, an essential ingredient for the efficient running of a steam railway was a plentiful supply of clean water – no water, no steam. One of the many problems Prendergast had to contend with during his wartime railway work was the laying on of an adequate water supply.[65] A similar problem, albeit on a much smaller scale, faced the Midland Great Western Railway in Galway in the late 1880s. The City Waterworks at Terryland, which was designed by Samuel Roberts, opened in 1867. It had two water wheels which powered the pumps. The rising and distribution mains were made of cast iron. With the growth in demand and leakage due to corrosion of the mains, the water wheels were proving inadequate and so an auxiliary steam engine was installed, about 1895, to boost the pumping capacity.[66] This however, did not cure the leaks. Periodically, there was insufficient water, which was at a very low pressure, in the feeder main to the railway station. This meant that the Midland's Water Tower would run dry and, accordingly, engines would have to steam to Athenry, tank up with water, and

---

60 *Engineers Journal*, February 1967, p. 44.
61 Institution of Engineers of Ireland Archives, membership records.
62 Obituary Notice, *Transactions of the Institution of Civil Engineers of Ireland*, 83 (1957), p. 159.
63 'Profile', *Engineers Journal*, January 1952, pp. 20-1.
64 Kathleen Villiers-Tuthill, *Beyond the Twelve Bens* (Galway, 1986), p. 236.
65 Prendergast, 'Galway Engineer', p. 110.
66 James Perry, *Report on Galway Waterworks* (Galway, 1902); J.H. Swiney, *Report on Galway Waterworks* (Galway, 1901); an undated broadside entitled, *Galway Waterworks*, gives further reports from Perry (26 May 1903, 23 December 1903, 6 August 1906) and Swiney (6 August 1906), and detailed replies from Perry to questions raised at Galway Urban District Council meetings. Copies in author's possession.

return to Galway to carry on working. The situation had become so serious in 1892, that the Midland sought parliamentary powers to lay a watermain from the former Persse Distillery at Newcastle to the railway station. The water was to be pumped from the old Roberts wheel pit which still survives on campus.[67] The Roberts water wheel, both in its design and construction, was a major triumph in the development of water-power resources in this country.[68] Roberts' work on the Corrib drainage certainly affected the physical outline of the present campus along the river front. However, his contribution to hydrology, and that of his protégé, Robert Manning (of Manning's Law fame), had an impact on hydrology education everywhere. In Galway, Professor J.E. Nash gained an international reputation for the College in applied hydrology, and this tradition of excellence has been carried on by Professors Con Cunnane and Kieran O'Connor. By 1906, with the re-laying of the city watermains and the substitution of turbines for the water wheels and steam engine, the problem had eased for the railway company. The City Waterworks was electrified by the Electricity Supply Board in 1934 – one of their first major pumping-station installations. Subsequently, enlargements and improvements to the city supply were carried out to designs prepared by the companies of H.G.L. O'Connor and P.J. Tobin. The founders of both of these firms were closely involved with the Engineering School for many years. Indeed, P.J. Tobin's paper on water-supply practice was considered an essential reference by many local authority engineers up until the early 1970s.[69]

As well as strengthening the courses in public health engineering, Prendergast also re-organised the School's laboratory facilities and introduced special courses in Soil Mechanics. He appears to have been immensely popular with his students and, in appreciation of the work done in the School of Engineering, a number of overseas graduates decided to purchase some equipment for the Soils Laboratory. Unfortunately, Prendergast died suddenly on 22 July 1957. However, the fund-raising went on and, at Christmas 1957, the proceeds were presented to Pádraic Ó Lochlainn, Acting Professor of Engineering. The money collected was to go towards the purchase of a soil consolidation apparatus.[70] Ó Lochlainn, who lectured for many years in Soil Mechanics, was Associate Professor of Engineering when he retired in 1981.

Prendergast's successor, John Declan O'Keeffe (Déaglán Ó Caoimh), a Corkman, arrived in Galway shortly after the dawn of the prestressed concrete era in the west of Ireland. Flannery Bridge, a single-span, prestressed concrete bridge, and a landmark in early prestressed concrete bridge-building in Ireland, was erected near Kilkerrin, Carna, Co. Galway, in 1954. It had a clear span of 171 feet between abutments. It has recently been demolished. O'Keeffe brought the concrete technology courses in Galway right up to date. He had obtained his PhD

---

67 Parliamentary plans entitled 'Midland Great Western Railway of Ireland. Additional Lands and Water Supply', Session 1891–2. Copy in author's possession.
68 S. Roberts, 'An Account of an Iron Breast Wheel, 36 H.P., Recently Erected at the Newcastle Distillery in Galway', *Transactions of the Institution of Civil Engineers of Ireland*, 4 (1851), pp. 53–7.
69 P.J. Tobin, 'Contemporary Irish Water Supply Practice', *Transactions of the Institution of Civil Engineers of Ireland*, 78 (1953), pp. 108–58.
70 John Silke, 'West Region Notes and News', *Engineers Journal*, February 1958, p. 63.

degree at the University of Leeds after three years research into prestressed concrete. He worked in Paris for Saintrap et Brice, a design construction firm, which was involved in the design of an underground hydro-electric scheme in the Pyrenees and also in the underground railway in Haifa. He subsequently worked with J.L. Kier, Civil Engineering contractors, on mining projects in Britain. After a stint as Assistant Lecturer in Civil Engineering in University College Cork, he was appointed to the Professorship of Civil Engineering in Galway in 1958.[71] O'Keeffe added enormously to the content of the concrete technology courses available at Galway and he introduced a very strong structural design element into the curriculum.

The School had, for very many years, a valuable course in concrete technology. John P. Glynn ME, who was Acting Professor during Rishworth's tenure on the Shannon Scheme, lectured in reinforced concrete design and subsequently published a short manual on the design and construction of small reinforced concrete bridges and footbridges.[72] Rishworth had considerable experience in the use of concrete in large engineering works, not only on the Shannon Scheme but also in Egypt prior to 1910.[73] Finally, it is worth noting that Townsend used precast concrete units in the construction of the passenger platforms on the Clifden Railway. These were, quite probably, the first precast units to be used in the west of Ireland.[74]

O'Keeffe set out to recruit women students into the Engineering School in the late 1950s, visiting many convent schools to persuade them to take up the teaching of honours mathematics at Leaving Certificate level. Finally, almost sixty years after the world's first woman engineering graduate, Alice Perry (BE 1906; fig. 3.5), qualified at Galway, the College's second female engineering student, Anne Woods, entered the faculty.[75] Alice Perry also had the distinction of being Ireland's only woman County Surveyor. On the death of her father, James Perry ME, County Surveyor for Galway West, she was appointed as Temporary County Surveyor in his stead, until a permanent appointment was made in April 1907. Having emigrated to London, Perry joined the Factory Inspectorate, pursuing a career in Industrial Safety, until she retired in 1922. The scientific study of accidents can be said to have begun with the various investigations into railway accidents. These procedures were later applied to workshop and factory accidents and, when the motorised transport industry arrived, with its ever-increasing toll of death and mayhem, it too became the object of such scientific scrutiny. The Galway Engineering School has not been found wanting in this regard. One of the best case studies of urban traffic accidents was published recently by Michael Brennan and D. Connolly.[76] Brennan, who lectures in Highway Engineering, had a brief

---

71 Anon., 'Professor John Declan O'Keeffe', *Engineers Journal*, October 1958, p. 365.
72 John P. Glynn, *Bridges (Minor Roads) and Footbridges* (Galway, 1937).
73 For a brief account of the engineering works, see Paul Duffy, *Ardnacrusha: Birthplace of the ESB* (Dublin, 1991).
74 Ryan, 'The Galway and Clifden Railway', pp. 215–6.
75 Sidney Geraghty, 'The First Woman Engineer', *Engineers Journal*, no. iii, 52 (1998), pp. 31–3.
76 M.J. Brennan and D. Connolly, 'The Pattern of Urban Traffic Accidents: A Case-Study', *Traffic Engineering and Control*, no. vi, 39 (1998), pp. 366–9.

3.5 Alice Perry BE (1906), first woman engineering graduate in the world

career spell with Córas Iompair Éireann, being involved in a bridge clearance survey on the rail system in 1969. No doubt Townsend, a keen cyclist, would have approved of an early publication of his entitled 'Bicycle Travel in Galway City'.[77]

O'Keeffe's successor, Pádraic O'Donoghue, another Cork graduate, obtained his PhD in Civil Engineering at the Georgia Institute of Technology in the United States in 1985. His primary area of interest is in structural engineering, particularly in relation to problems of structural integrity and durability with application to gas pipelines, aircraft, offshore structures, and bridges, which obviously involves safety. Over the past few years, a number of fracture mechanics procedures have been successfully used to investigate the integrity and durability of aerospace transportation vehicles. One of the most topical of his projects

---

[77] M.D. O'Sullivan, 'The Centenary of Galway College: The Text of a Centenary Lecture Delivered on the 19th November, 1949', *Journal of the Galway Archaeological and Historical Society*, 51 (1999), pp. 24–42. The reference is at p. 37. This article was prepared for publication by Joe O'Halloran. Michael Brennan's article, 'Bicycle Travel in Galway City', was published by An Foras Forbartha in Dublin in 1979.

involved the assessment of the structural integrity of space stations subject to debris impact.[78] At the present time (1999), a large space station is currently being assembled in orbit. O'Donoghue has also carried out investigations into the fracture of railroad rails. So, strange as it may seem, all permanent Professors of Civil Engineering in Galway, from the opening of the College until the present, have had some railway involvement. O'Donoghue's appointment marks a new departure for the Engineering School. As we enter the new millennium, truly it can be said that Engineering in Galway has steamed into space.[79]

78 Personal communication.
79 The author would like to acknowledge the assistance, and the patience, of Tadhg Foley and Tom Boylan. He is very grateful to Mary McGann for her skills in transforming his manuscript and to Pádraig Ó Cuimin for information on Townsend's early involvement with the proposed rail line to Clifden. The Revd Dr James Mitchell listened patiently to several oral renditions of this paper and of him it can be truly said: without him was written nothing that was written.

4

Medicine

JAMES P. MURRAY

Queen's College Galway, 1849–1908

'A shameful squandering of public money', was the opinion in 1889 of the then Catholic archbishop of Dublin concerning the annual grant of £1,790 for the support of the Medical faculty of Queen's College Galway (QCG). He also quoted figures relating to honours awarded at the medical examinations of the Royal University, purporting to show the superiority of the candidates from the Catholic School of Medicine in Dublin over the students from the Queen's Colleges, but especially Galway. His figures were highly selective and conveniently omitted four out of the previous seven years in which Galway students were placed first in the final examinations.[1]

The merits of a medical education in Galway should have been evident to the archbishop if he had only cast a cursory glance around the Dublin medical scene at the time. Five graduates from Galway held prestigious positions in Dublin hospitals: Edward Dillon Mapother was senior surgeon to the archbishop's own hospital, St Vincent's; William Roe was in charge of the Lying-In Hospital in Holles Street; Anthony Corley, William Thornley Stoker, and William Thomson were senior surgeons at the Richmond Hospital. They all held high academic positions in the Royal College of Surgeons; four had been elected President of the College, indicating the esteem in which they were held by their fellow surgeons.[2]

All of our Dublin luminaries had careers of which any medical school would have been proud, but were they reasonably representative of the graduates produced by the Galway school at that time? QCG calendars indicate that they were 'run-of-the-mill' students while in Galway: their names do not appear amongst the scholarship winners and only one, Thomson, had taken an Arts degree, as many of their contemporaries did. They did graduate from the Queen's University whereas about two thirds of their contemporaries were content with licentiates from a surgical or medical corporation which could be taken after only

---

[1] William Walsh, *The Irish University Question: The Catholic Case* (Dublin, 1897), pp. 176, 180.
[2] Charles Cameron, *History of the Royal College of Surgeons in Ireland*, 2nd ed. (Dublin, 1916), Corley, pp. 563–4; Mapother, pp. 435–6; Roe, p. 498; Thornley Stoker, pp. 500–1; and Thomson, pp. 669–70.

three years study instead of the four required for university graduation. The fact that each had acquired a university degree suggests that already, as medical students, they aspired to academically-oriented careers.[3]

But that is not to disparage those who opted to qualify in the shorter time: many who did so figured prominently in the scholarship lists and were obviously not lacking in intellectual capacity. Many of those scholarship winners found their vocation in isolated dispensaries in Connemara and Mayo and some paid the supreme sacrifice for their dedication. Had it not been for them, the poor and destitute would have been bereft of medical attention, but perhaps the good archbishop in Dublin was too far removed from the harsh reality of life in the west of Ireland to realise this.

Our five examples were pre-eminent in medicine in Dublin but many of their contemporaries at Galway also reached the heights in their chosen branches of medicine. Christopher Joynt, one of the first two medical graduates from QCG (in 1855), ultimately retired as Deputy Surgeon-General of the Indian Medical Service and Alfred Keogh, who graduated in 1878, established such a reputation that he was recalled from retirement to direct the medical services of the British Army during World War I. Galway graduates were always prominently placed in the entrance examinations to the British Army Medical Services and their successes and subsequent careers were important in establishing and maintaining the reputation of the College. Undoubtedly they were responsible for attracting students to Galway, and not just to Medicine. At that time, the sons of many middle-class families in Ireland aspired to careers in the public service at home and abroad. There was a special social cachet attached to a career in the Indian Medical and Civil Services.

Many graduates were appointed to university chairs in Ireland, England, and abroad, such as the five already mentioned in the College of Surgeons and William H. Thompson at Trinity College Dublin. Many Galway graduates distinguished themselves in England: Sinclair White was Professor of Surgery at Sheffield, Henry Lawson was on the staff of St Mary's Hospital in London, Peter Freyer pioneered urological surgery at St Peter's, and Felix Vinrace founded St Paul's Hospital, later to merge with St Peter's to form the Institute of Urology in London. Even today the link with Galway, that started with Freyer and Vinrace, is maintained by a Galway graduate, Niall O'Donoghue, who is on the consultant staff of the Institute. Edward Divers, who graduated MD from Galway in 1860, was the first Professor of Chemistry at the University of Tokyo.

The second half of the nineteenth century was a difficult period for medical schools generally, but especially so for small schools, such as Galway, with meagre resources and an administrative structure not responsive to rapid change. There were fundamental advances in medical knowledge, such as anaesthesia, antiseptic and aseptic surgery, the discovery of micro-organisms as causes of disease and the clarification of physiological and pathological factors affecting the internal environment of the body, all of which demanded continuous change in medical practice. Those changes gathered momentum in the last quarter of the century

---

3   See James Murray, *Galway: A Medico-Social History* (Galway, 1994), chapters 9 and 14, *passim.*

4.1 Charles Croker King, Professor of Anatomy and Physiology, 1849–63

4.2 John Cleland, Professor of Anatomy and Physiology, 1863–77

and it must be admitted that Galway was tardy in adapting to some of those changes. For instance, although the importance of pathology in the curriculum was emphasised by the General Medical Council as early as 1886, a chair in the subject was not established in Galway until 1910. But Galway's forte had been and remained the pre-clinical subjects of anatomy, physiology, and materia medica and its reputation in those subjects was undoubtedly responsible for attracting students from outside its expected catchment area and ensuring its survival.

The Medical School was well served by its teachers in those disciplines from its foundation. The reputations of Charles Croker King (fig. 4.1) and John Cleland (fig. 4.2) must have been, at least partly, responsible for attracting students to Galway. During his time in Galway from 1849 to 1863, Croker King, the foundation Professor of Anatomy and Physiology, organised an excellent Anatomy Department which included a useful Museum of Human and Comparative Anatomy; the emphasis in his teaching was on surgical anatomy and he made special arrangements with the Surgeon at the County Infirmary to enable him to conduct bedside teaching in surgery and demonstrate operative surgery there.

This private arrangement was necessary because the government, in drafting the legislation, had not ensured access to the local hospitals for the clinical teachers, an oversight which also embarrassed Richard Doherty, the foundation Professor of Midwifery, who had to make a similar arrangement to the surgeon (fig. 4.3). This anomaly was not corrected until the Galway Hospitals Act of 1892.

Until the middle of the present century, anatomy was the fundamental science of medical education and the reputation of any medical school was largely determined by the standard of its teaching in this subject. The Anatomy Department

4.3 Richard Doherty, Professor of Midwifery, 1849–76

4.4 Joseph P. Pye, Professor of Anatomy and Physiology, 1877–1920

was also, in effect, the social centre of the School. Dissecting sessions were informal, with easy rapport between professors, demonstrators, and students. Students tended to congregate around the Anatomy Room fire during their free time and the discussions there were as much part of the learning process as the formal lectures, though no doubt earthy at times before the advent of lady students in 1902. Relations between the individual professors of anatomy and the students were relaxed and informal and this has persisted in Galway up to the present day. It was not surprising that James Mullin, who was a student in Arts and Medicine in Galway from 1871 to 1880, held Joseph Pye, Professor of Anatomy, in the highest regard (fig. 4.4).[4]

It was generally recognised that the museum and laboratory facilities in all three Queen's Colleges were better than in any other medical school in Ireland at the time. In 1862 the President of QCG reported that, in addition to the Anatomy Museum, the Pathological Section of the Medical Museum contained a valuable collection of specimens and preparations illustrating skin and surgical conditions before and after operation; the Materia Medica Museum was said to contain all relevant apparatus and a complete range of the medicines in the British Pharmacopoeia, thanks, no doubt, to Simon McCoy, the first Professor of Materia Medica, who held office from 1849 until 1873 (fig. 4.5). The Montgomery Collection, purchased in 1859, consisted of over 600 specimens relating to the pathology, anatomy, and physiology of the reproductive system. With the exception of the Montgomery Collection, all the collections had been assembled

4 James Mullin, *The Story of a Toiler's Life* (Dublin and London, 1921), p. 144.

4.5 Simon McCoy, Professor of Materia Medica, 1849–73

4.6 James V. Browne, Professor of Surgery, 1849–87

by the staff, which does them great credit and shows that they were concerned with the development of the institution.[5]

In the last century, criticism was repeatedly levelled at the Galway School concerning the inadequacy of the clinical teaching, and with justification, although the staff and successive presidents repeatedly took issue with the adverse comments. In 1870, the Presidents of the Royal Colleges of Surgeons and Physicians in Dublin inspected the three Galway hospitals as a result of an official complaint made by a student (Andrew Melville), regarding the deficiency in clinical teaching: they reported favourably on the condition of the hospitals and considered that the range of patients and practice were suitable for clinical teaching in medicine and surgery.[6] However the College authorities were conscious of the problems caused by lack of proper access to the local hospitals. In December 1879, the President made a strong and earnest plea to the chief secretary to introduce legislation giving the clinical professors rights of access to the hospitals without remuneration; but was told that 'His Grace is not prepared to recommend the introduction of a Bill upon the subject'.[7] The three Galway hospitals were recognised by the Royal Colleges and by the Royal University as a single teaching clinical unit which provided about 200 beds in constant occupation; in practice, Galway students

[5] Appendix no. 1 (dated 1865–6), to the *Report of the President of Queen's College, Galway, for the Academic Year 1863–64*, p. 30.
[6] *Report of an Extraordinary Visitation of QCG Held in Dublin Castle on 30th and 31st March 1870* (Dublin, 1870).
[7] NUI, Galway Archives, courtesy of Dr Séamus Mac Mathúna, Secretary for Academic Affairs.

sought their main hospital training in Dublin, London, or Edinburgh. Attendance at the Galway hospitals alone would not have complied with the requirements for admission to the degree examinations of the Queen's or Royal University.

The professors of medicine, Nicholas W. Colahan and John Isaac Lynham, had good reputations as physicians and teachers but the lack of a maternity hospital severely limited the scope of Doherty, and his successor Richard J. Kinkead, in midwifery. The most serious deficiency was undoubtedly in surgery and remained so until the arrival of Michael O'Malley in 1915. The foundation professor, James V. Browne (fig. 4.6), who held the chair from 1849 to 1887, was ultimately shown to be an impostor, masquerading as his dead cousin, and his successor, William W. Brereton who was professor until his death in 1924, is better remembered as a spiritualist than a surgeon!

Considering the dubious quality of the teaching in surgery, it is remarkable and surprising that so many Galway graduates achieved such high reputations and took pioneering roles in surgery. Four presidents of the Royal College of Surgeons in Dublin in the last century were Galway graduates and others are recognised for their pioneering achievements, such as Thornley Stoker in neurosurgery, Sinclair White in childhood surgery, Freyer in prostate surgery, and Henry Smith in cataract surgery. Perhaps their success can be attributed, in part, to a good grounding in anatomy obtained in Galway.

The standard of clinical instruction may have been dubious but we can feel reasonably assured that those qualifying from Galway reached the standard acceptable at the time for entry to the medical profession. All the degree examinations were conducted in Dublin by the Queen's, and later the Royal, University and about two-thirds of the Galway students qualified via a Royal College or Conjoint Board licentiate, obtainable only in Dublin, London, or Edinburgh. From 1866, the General Medical Council operated a system of visitations at medical examinations conducted by all bodies in the United Kingdom intended to maintain a uniform standard in all centres. Comments on the candidates from the Queen's Colleges were uniformly favourable.

During the sixty years of Queen's College Galway, scientific publications from members of the medical faculty were meagre, with two notable exceptions. The most important contributions were from John Cleland in anatomy, who also edited the 1867 edition of *Quain's Anatomy* while in Galway. His contributions merited his election to a Fellowship of the Royal Society, though he was not unique amongst the staff in gaining such an honour; four other members were also elected FRS – an amazing achievement for a small college as remote as Galway. Richard Kinkead published papers relating to diseases of women and children, and problems in medical jurisprudence. His *Guide for Irish Medical Practitioners*, published in 1889, was particularly useful for doctors in the public service.[8] It should be remembered that research funding was virtually unavailable in Galway in the last century, except for the 1851 Exhibition Scholarships which enabled a few graduates to pursue research projects at home or abroad.

---

8   *The Presidents, Vice-Presidents, and Professors of Queen's College, Galway: A List of Their Contributions to Science and Literature, 1845–1902* (Dublin, 1902).

The publications from graduates are more impressive and many were important landmarks in medical literature. Mapother was a prolific contributor of papers on a diversity of subjects: public health and sanitation, diet, and the circulation of blood. His *Manual of Physiology*, published in 1862, was the standard text at the time and went into a third edition after his death; his paper on 'Shock' in 1879 is a classic on the subject. Over forty publications are attributed to Mapother in Hayes's *Sources for the History of Irish Civilisation*. Henry Smith's publications on the treatment of cataract brought ophthalmologists from all parts of the world to see him operate in Jullandar; his textbook on cataract extraction went into three editions and the Smith-Indian method of cataract extraction became the standard procedure for over forty years.[9] Freyer's papers on bladder surgery, particularly his paper on 'One Thousand Cases of Prostatectomy' revolutionised the management of prostatic enlargement; his method of prostatectomy was the standard for over half a century and is still used in some circumstances.[10] Sinclair White, through his publications on childhood surgery and his position on the staff of the Children's Hospital, Sheffield, was in the vanguard of paediatric surgery.[11] Sir Alfred Keogh's papers in the first decade of this century on the structure of military medical services were responsible for many improvements in the British Army Medical Services, including the medical organisation of the Territorial Force, the foundation of the School of Army Sanitation, and the establishment of the Royal Army Medical Corps College at Millbank in London.[12]

Even the last class to graduate in 1908 from the old Queen's College included one of its most distinguished graduates, Arthur Compton, though he is not as well known as he deserves. He was a pioneering bacteriologist and immunologist and a prolific contributor to the scientific literature in both English and French on a diversity of subjects including bacteriophage, bacterial variants, and tissue cultures. His long association with the Pasteur Institute in Paris earned him the decoration of Officier d'Academie in 1948.[13]

Medical graduates of QCG also showed literary talents. James Mullin, a largely self-educated orphan from Co. Tyrone, has left an interesting account of his student days in Galway from 1871 to 1880 and his subsequent life in South Wales, in his autobiography published in 1921.[14] Tom Garry also published his autobiography, *An African Doctor*, in 1939. Séamas O'Beirn, who graduated in 1905, was noted as a dramatist even as a student and was a founder of Taibhdhearc na Gaillimhe; but his greater claim to fame was in pioneering health education, a crusade which inspired the Tuberculosis Prevention Act of 1908.

---

9 D. Vail, 'The Man and His Cigar', *American Journal of Ophthalmology*, 75 (1947), pp. 1–5.
10 Davis Coakley, *Irish Masters of Medicine* (Dublin, 1992), pp. 304–8.
11 Victor Gustave Plarr, *Plarr's Lives of the Fellows of the Royal College of Surgeons of England* (Bristol, 1930), vol. ii.
12 J.P. Murray, 'Sir Alfred Keogh: Doctor and General', *Irish Medical Journal*, no. 12, 80 (1987), pp. 427–32.
13 Obituaries of A.J.W. Compton, *British Medical Journal*, 2(1967), p. 708 and *Lancet*, 1(1967), p. 1281. See also *NUI Handbook 1908–1932* (Dublin, 1932), pp. 220–4.
14 Mullin, *The Story of a Toiler's Life*.

What if the government had yielded to the archbishop's pressure in 1889 and extinguished the Medical Faculty? Without the medical students, the total enrolment would have been less than 80 each year, over the next twenty years, and it is doubtful whether the College would have survived. The result would have been catastrophic for Galway and the west. There can be no doubt that if the Medical Faculty had been extinguished, even had the College survived, the Medical School would never have been revived.

Admittedly the Medical School was ailing in 1889 with only 40 students on the rolls. After a shaky start in 1849, it had gone from strength to strength under the Queen's University with numbers reaching 122 in 1881, indicating the growing reputation of the School. The transition to the Royal University proved almost catastrophic for Galway. The new enrolments in the Medical Faculty dropped from 59 in 1881 to only 11 in 1882 and continued at about this level until 1908. It was the lowest and most precarious time in the School's history but, fortunately, students continued to come from the north of Ireland, though in fewer numbers. The western bishops no longer voiced their opposition to the College and, with the improvement of second-level education in Connacht, more Catholic parents were encouraged to send their sons to QCG, to the advantage of the Medical Faculty. In all, 1,254 students attended the Galway Medical School during the life of Queen's College and, of those, 437 graduated from the Queen's or Royal University of Ireland but this low graduation rate of 35 per cent was only slightly below the average for all university medical schools in the United Kingdom in that period. The bulk of medical students qualified by taking a licentiate from one of the Surgical or Medical Corporations of Conjoint Boards. The records at UCG do not indicate the number who qualified by a route other than graduation but a review of the membership lists of the Medical Alumni Association and Medical Directories indicates that at least 1,000 doctors were produced by QCG between 1849 and 1908. About 40 per cent of those who qualified from QCG were from Connacht and were critical to the maintenance of a reasonable level of health care along the western seaboard.

By any criterion, the QCG Medical School served Ireland well. It played a crucial role in developing and maintaining a good standard of health care in the west; it was responsible for expanding and replenishing the 'medical stock' and its graduates provided medical cover in the isolated and deprived districts that otherwise would have had none. Galway medical graduates, including the many who entered the Services, made significant contributions to medicine and medical education in Ireland, England, and further afield.

University College Galway, 1908–1948

With the transition to University College Galway in 1908, a new breath of life was instilled into the Galway Medical School. The Catholic condemnation, which had inhibited its well-being for sixty years, was removed and immediately the future looked brighter. There was a progressive increase in the number of medical students from 37 in 1909 to 102 in 1916. There was even a welcome injection of capital for badly needed teaching facilities: a major extension of the Anatomy Department was built in 1911 and the Pathology Department transferred to more commodious accommodation in the new Civil Engineering building in 1914. This latter was a significant precedent. For the first time designated research facilities were incorporated in a new department.[15]

There were also a number of new appointments which augured well for the future. Thomas Walsh was appointed to a newly-established chair of Pathology in 1911 and organised a more satisfactory course, ending the dependence on temporary lecturers in such an important subject. Ralph Bodkin Mahon succeeded Lynham as Professor of Medicine in 1913. Though Mahon was a practising surgeon, his appointment was considered appropriate and met with general approval. He was a good all-round clinician with special interests in dermatology and neurology and his tenure of the chair until his retirement in 1932 was apparently satisfactory.

But undoubtedly the most propitious and badly needed arrival was Michael O'Malley in 1915. Although his initial appointment was as Demonstrator in Anatomy, his influence in Surgery was felt immediately both in the hospital and Medical School. Brereton was elderly and ineffectual at the time and O'Malley, in effect, acted as Professor of Surgery. He was an automatic choice to succeed Brereton when he died in 1924. Seaghan Mac Énrí was appointed Professor of Ophthalmology and Otology in 1916, another timely addition to the clinical teaching staff. Dennis Morris, first as assistant to Kinkead from 1919, and then as Professor of Obstetrics from 1928, was another fortunate addition to the staff. His influence was not confined to obstetrics; he founded the Galway Clinical Club in 1919 which provided a common forum for university staff and other doctors.

When Pye died in 1920, his combined chair was divided and again the Medical School was fortunate in the choice of the new professors; Joseph Donegan in Physiology and Stephen Shea in Anatomy continued the high standard maintained by the school in those subjects from its foundation. Both were excellent teachers and each gave over forty years' exemplary service to the College. Donegan was on friendly terms with all the great names in physiology such as Starling, Warburg, and Krebs and spent his vacations and sabbaticals working in their laboratories and participating in their researches. It was a period of important discoveries in physiology relevant to medical practice, and Donegan incorporated those advances in his teaching often before they appeared in standard textbooks. Consequently his teaching was always interesting and pertinent to clinical practice.[16] As Dean of the Medical Faculty for forty years, Shea was a worthy advocate of the Galway School in the many debates on medical education and manpower, especially in the decade after World War II.

The 1920s marked a significant change in the Galway Medical School. Instruction in anatomy and physiology had always been beyond censure but, for the first time in its history, the finger of reproach could not be pointed at the clinical teaching. The commissioning of the Central Hospital in 1924 provided a wide range of clinical material in one institution and residential hospital experience was available to the students in addition to the required attendance in

---

15 *College Handbook* (Dublin, 1915), pp. 29–30.
16 Obituary of J.F. Donegan, by P.F. and C. McC., *Irish Medical Journal*, no. 10, 78 (1985), p. 302.

Dublin. All the clinical teachers had appointments in the hospital and, without exception, all were excellent teachers. Bedside teaching became the forte of the Medical School and remains so to this day.

Between the World Wars, scientific publications with a clinical orientation from Galway were meagre. The part-time clinical professors were dependent on private practice to make a reasonable living and were completely overwhelmed by the service requirements of the Central Hospital with inadequate support staff and facilities. Funding for research was non-existent at that time and laboratory facilities barely sufficient for teaching and service commitments. Even if funds for research had been available, the needs of teaching were paramount in a small understaffed medical school such as Galway.

The publications from the Departments of Anatomy and Physiology reflected the personal interests of the professors. Anatomical studies by Shea on skeletons unearthed at local archaeological digs, yielded interesting information about prehistoric social conditions in the west of Ireland and his studies in comparative anatomy of the pulmonary alveolar wall were important. Donegan made significant contributions to the understanding of acid-base mechanisms, the physiology of muscle and veins, especially the influence of venous return on output in heart-lung preparations.[17]

The austerities of the war years deferred any development of the Medical School, other than the transfer of the Pathology Department to more spacious accommodation in the Royal Galway Yacht Club on Earls Island, and travel difficulties accentuated the remoteness of Galway from the mainstream of academic affairs. Career options and access to postgraduate training were also limited for medical graduates.

University College Galway: 1948 to the Present

As occurred after the first World War, there was a post-war decline in the number of medical students in Ireland and Britain but in the case of Galway it was obscured by an unexpected influx of Polish students, from 1946 to 1955, due to the closure of the Polish Medical School in Edinburgh. During the 1960s there was a rapidly progressing increase in enrolments to reach the staggering total of 147 at pre-medical level in 1969–70.[18] The numbers overwhelmed the facilities available and had to be curtailed to 70 each year at pre-medical level. Later, entry was reduced to 55 from Ireland with a small number of places for Third World candidates and for specially qualified and vocationally-motivated students at first medical level. Another striking feature has been the progressively increasing proportion of female students enrolling in medicine; they now comprise more than half the number in each class.

In recent years it was decided to admit a limited number of additional students from abroad who would pay full economic fees and now some 20 such students are

---

17 *NUI Handbook*, p. 229.
18 President's *Reports* 1969–70 to 1990–2.

admitted at pre-medical level each year, most are Malaysians sponsored by their Government through arrangements negotiated in 1989. The fees are a welcome addition to the resources of the Medical Faculty and they add a cosmopolitan aura to the Medical Faculty which can only be to the benefit of all students.

In the aftermath of World War II, medical education and manpower requirements were the subjects of much debate in Ireland and Britain. Most worrying for the Galway Medical School were the opinions being expressed that Ireland was producing more doctors than the country needed (which it was) and there were frequent comments that the number of medical schools in the country should be reduced. It was a crucial time for the Galway School with its very survival at stake. Fortunately the essential role of the Medical School in the development of health care services in the west was recognised by the planners in the Department of Health. The post-war hospital developments in Galway and the fate of the Medical School were interdependent: were it not for the Medical School, it is doubtful whether the Department of Health would have invested so heavily in the hospital building programme and, without the new hospitals and laboratories, the Medical School could not have met the requirements of modern medical education.

The modernisation of the Medical School really started with the decision, in 1948-9, to develop a Regional Laboratory in Galway and to combine service and academic facilities in the grounds of the proposed Regional Hospital. This resulted in a closer integration of laboratory disciplines with clinical teaching, another strength of the Galway School which has persisted to the present. Happily this coincided with the return of John Kennedy to Galway in 1948 to take up his appointment as Professor of Pathology in UCG and Pathologist to the Central Hospital. He was to play a formative role in the adaptation of the Medical School to modern requirements. Kennedy provided academic leadership and a fresh perspective badly needed in a staff then overwhelmed by heavy service loads and adverse conditions. But the older members of the faculty also played their part and were not found wanting in supporting and encouraging change.

The Visitation, in August 1955, by Inspectors from the American Medical Association gave added stimulus and direction to the changes necessary to meet the rapidly evolving trends in medical education. The critical comments of the Inspectors were salutary, if unpalatable, but the favourable comments were encouraging and put an official stamp on the inherent advantages that the Galway School enjoyed. The Inspectors praised the close association of university and teaching hospital, especially the clinical professors being also on the staff of the hospital. They were severely critical of the poor ancillary facilities and the paucity of junior staff and research workers. They noted that the Regional Hospital, then under construction, would result in a big improvement in the facilities for clinical teaching and agreed with the proposed legislation to give UCG a stronger voice in the selection of staff for the hospital. Similar comments were made by Inspectors from the General Medical Council in the following year.[19]

The 1953 Health Act formalised the relationships between the Medical School and the Regional Hospital. The Hospital was declared a 'teaching institution'

---

19 'The American Visitors' Report', *Journal of the Irish Medical Association*, 33 (1953), pp. 183–5.

which meant the local authority was required to provide teaching facilities as the Minister for Health might direct, and UCG was given representation on the selection boards for permanent medical staff in the hospital, whether they had immediate teaching functions or not. This facilitated the formal linking of hospital and university appointments and the terms of appointment of most clinical teaching staff were changed from part-time to a full-time commitment in college and hospital, to the advantage of both.

Medicine was entering an era of important discoveries in molecular biology which were rapidly changing medical practice. Radical alterations in the medical curriculum were necessary to conform with the changing needs in medical education. Anatomy, formerly the fundamental science of medical education, was being over-shadowed by physiology and biochemistry in the pre-clinical years; bedside instruction, clinical clerking and surgical dressing, though still important, were no longer adequate to prepare the student for entry to practice; he or she had to become familiar with the changing concepts of disease and know how to apply laboratory and other diagnostic facilities then rapidly evolving. With the growth of specialities, new subjects, and even new examinations, had to be introduced into the teaching programme. Within a decade, the curriculum was crowded and it became increasingly difficult to ensure that the new graduate had a good all-round knowledge of fundamentals and the training that would enable him or her to acquire further knowledge and skills after graduation. Admittedly, the introduction of postgraduate internships in 1953 helped to relieve the pressure at undergraduate level.

The establishment of the large multi-disciplinary Regional Laboratory complex, with a commitment to both service and academic functions, facilitated the closer integration of laboratory subjects with clinical teaching; the commissioning of the large Regional (now University College) and Merlin Park Hospitals, with their specialised departments, greatly increased the breadth and variety of clinical material available locally and it was no longer necessary for Galway students to spend a year in metropolitan hospitals. Elective periods spent in County Hospitals and general practice attachments provided valuable experience for the students.

At a repeat Visitation in 1963, the Inspectors from the General Medical Council could report that the clinical teaching was very much improved since their previous inspection in 1954. They also expressed the opinion that the Medical School was integral to the maintenance of adequate health care in the west.

In line with the increasing specialisation in the new Regional Hospitals, a number of special lectureships were established which broadened the curriculum. Lecturers were appointed in Medical Therapeutics, Paediatrics, and Preventative Medicine in 1959, in ENT, Ophthalmology and Radiology, Cardiology, Chest Surgery, Gastroenterology, and Rheumatology between 1964 and 1969.

The 1960s saw the establishment of new departments. A Department of Experimental Medicine and Practical Pharmacology was established in 1960 with Seán Lavelle as Professor. It was innovative at the time and was to prove its worth in training students to cope with the rapidly evolving trends in medical practice, especially in the application of computers in clinical problem solving and in research methods. The establishment of an independent Department of Biochemistry, under Colm Ó hEocha in 1963, reflected the growing importance of that discipline in medical and scientific education and research.

Recognising the special importance of child health in medical practice, and consequently in the curriculum, the Lectureship in Paediatrics was upgraded in 1967 to a Department of Paediatrics separate from Medicine. Brian McNicholl initiated a programme of research into metabolic and developmental conditions which had important results, especially in the field of coeliac disease.

The 1970s were marked by the struggle to bring the facilities into line with the requirements of increasing student numbers and the changing pattern of medicine. The old traditional departments of Medicine, Surgery and Obstetrics were all expanded with additional lecturers, some with specialised commitments, such as Respiratory Medicine and Gastroenterology. The newer departments established in the 1960s were also expanded and some of the independent lectureships were upgraded to professorships with the establishment of the new departments of Psychiatry and Radiology.

The overriding consideration was how to provide physical facilities adequate for the increased number of students and for the expanding clinical departments. As early as 1964, a Clinical Sciences building in the grounds of the Regional Hospital was proposed and appropriate space was offered by Galway County Council but the College did not proceed with the project at that time. Temporary pre-fabricated accommodation (which was patently inadequate) was provided instead and rapidly deteriorated. In 1973–4 a full schedule of the requirements of the various clinical departments was prepared and the project was accorded top priority in UCG and ostensibly also at higher levels. But, despite constant pressure on the Higher Education Authority, no progress was made and indeed similar projects leapfrogged the Galway proposal, though they had been proposed later and appeared of less urgency.

Finally in 1987, John Flynn, then Dean of the Medical Faculty, embarked on a fund-raising campaign to build a Clinical Sciences Institute. It was a daunting task in the west of Ireland with its meagre resources but it was entirely successful due to John Flynn's initiative and powers of persuasion. Graduates, both at home and abroad, the medical profession, and commercial firms in the west subscribed over £1.2 million; the Department of Education promised £1 million and the balance was derived from 75 per cent of the fees of full-fee paying overseas students. The new Clinical Sciences Institute was opened for students in September 1992; its estimated cost was over £4.2 million. It provides badly needed lecturing and library facilities, seminar and study areas, teaching and research laboratories, and office accommodation for the Dean and all clinical departments. It heralded a new era in the development of the Galway Medical School and it augurs well for its future.[20]

Until recent years, the Medical Faculty had little more than a peripheral interest in postgraduate medical education. Intercalary BSc degrees in a wide variety of biological subjects were available and UCG awarded a Diploma and BSc in Public Health until 1939. The Medical Faculty also had to approve the eligibility of candidates for higher degrees and advise on the preparation of theses. Graduates aspiring to consultant or specialist status had to seek out appropriate

---

20 Ibid., p. 207.

short-term hospital appointments acceptable to the Royal Colleges and other bodies awarding higher qualifications. During the 1970s this old haphazard system was replaced by structured training programmes approved by relevant committees under the general umbrella of the Council for Postgraduate Medical and Dental Education. In 1977, the Medical Faculty nominated John Flynn for appointment by the Council as Co-ordinator for Postgraduate Medical Education for the West of Ireland. An active and co-ordinated programme of postgraduate education was set up covering virtually all specialities with formal lectures, workshops, and rotating appointments in the Western Health Board hospitals.

In 1983, a postgraduate course leading to a degree of Master in Medical Sciences was established. The course consists of a core module in advanced research techniques and a module oriented towards the candidate's chosen speciality with attachments to the appropriate hospital and university departments. The candidate prepares a thesis on a research project completed during the course. The course is intended to provide tuition in the academic, research, and experimental aspects of medical science and complements the specialist qualifications awarded by other bodies.[21]

The output of scientific publications from the Medical School may have been meagre until about 1960 but since then the output has been prolific and has contributed significantly to medical knowledge. Admittedly, it was a period when funding for research became more readily available, from local sources, from the Medical Research Council, commercial firms, agencies abroad, and later from the European Commission, but it was necessary to actively seek out those research grants which were usually obtainable only against stiff opposition. Local conditions were hardly conducive to research: laboratory and other facilities were barely adequate for teaching and service commitments, junior and ancillary staff were few in number, and pressures on senior staff left little time for non-essential interests. Consequently research had to be clinically oriented and likely to be of immediate local importance, and this was so even in the non-clinical departments. Now the various projects form a highly desirable element in the postgraduate training of junior staff as well as initiating an interest and involvement by undergraduates in research.

A striking feature of the research has been the co-operation and collaboration between departments, including between clinical and non-clinical departments. For instance, important research in coeliac disease, initiated in the Department of Paediatrics by Brian McNicholl in the early 1960s, has also involved the Departments of Biochemistry, Pathology, and Medicine for more than thirty years. Initial studies indicated that the west of Ireland had the highest incidence of the disease in the world and the sensitising fraction of gluten was identified in the Department of Biochemistry. Later the research was continued into adulthood under Ciarán McCarthy with important findings relating to the natural history of the disease, especially the related incidence of malignancies. The importance of the research was recognised internationally and attracted the Third International

---

21 UCG *Calendar* 1992–3.

Conference on Coeliac Disease to Galway in 1977. The long-lasting collaboration between the departments led to the formation of the Centre for Study of Digestive Diseases in 1979.[22] More recently the Department of Paediatrics, under Gerry Loftus, has been especially interested in asthma.

From its inception in 1960, the Department of Experimental Medicine, directed by Seán Lavelle, has conducted research into thrombosis, carcinogenesis and anti-cancer agents, artificially-induced arthritis, and clinical applications of computers, funded by various agencies and later by the European Commission. Much of the research, especially into computer-aided diagnostic programmes, has been conducted in collaboration with clinical departments in the local hospitals or with centres throughout Europe. The Department of Pharmacology, under Brian Leonard, has been very active in research into the neuropharmacology of mental diseases, especially depression, Alzheimer's, and Parkinson's diseases.

Collaborative research has been carried out by the Departments of Obstetrics and Gynaecology and Biochemistry into the pharmacokinetics of hormone replacement therapy in post-menopausal women and into salivary hormones in relation to ovulatory function, funded by grants from the Medical Research Council. Biochemistry has been active in developing diagnostic kits for HIV testing, the presence of drugs, and prediction of osteoporosis, and the Department of Microbiology has made significant contributions involving health care and food production leading to the establishment of the National Diagnostics Centre at UCG.

Important research in breast cancer has been carried out in the Department of Surgery under Fred Given, which involves collaboration with the Departments of Pathology, Immunology, Biochemistry, and Radiology. This programme has led to the establishment of the National Breast Cancer Research Institute, based in the Breast Clinic and Surgical Research Unit at University College Hospital, Galway. The research is oriented towards the early diagnosis of breast cancer and the recognition of women at increased risk. Already a break-through has been achieved in recognising a genetic predisposition to the cancer and in developing a diagnostic kit to identify such women. The Institute attracts research funds from a variety of sources and conducts a broad range of molecular, biochemical, and immunological research projects.

The Department of Plastic Surgery has already shown that the incidence of skin cancers in Galway is over eight times that in Britain and three times that in Cork and Kerry. It is hoped that the Western Skin Cancer Registry set up by the Departments of Plastic Surgery and Histopathology may help to clarify the risk factors. Important research into cardiovascular conditions is being carried out in the Department of Cardiology, funded mainly by CROÍ, the West of Ireland Cardiology Foundation. There is ongoing research in the Department of Psychiatry under Tom Fahy into panic and seasonal affective disorders, biological markers for lithium in mania and childhood emotional problems. The Laboratory Departments are all actively engaged in research usually in association with clinical

---

22 C.F. McCarthy, 'Coeliac Disease', *Journal of the Irish Colleges of Physicians and Surgeons*, 19 (1990), pp. 45–7.

departments, but also independently, for example Histopathology in multifocal breast cancer and Haematology in the management of leukaemias.[23]

Research projects carried out in the Departments of Anatomy and Physiology are published in specialised journals and do not attract publicity but are important contributions to scientific knowledge, concerning, for example stress, renal amino acid metabolism, and proteases. Turlough Fitzgerald's *Textbook on Neuroanatomy*, published in 1985, has gained world-wide recognition as the standard text on the subject. Many other members of the Medical Faculty have published scientific texts and contributed sections or chapters to such books.

The publications emanating from Galway in the last thirty years have established an international reputation for the Galway Medical School and have helped attract further research funds from a diversity of sources. In recent years, the grants obtained have shown a progressive increase and now generally exceed £150,000 per annum, not including those won by departments primarily in the Faculty of Science. Many of the grants are committed for a number of years and enable the departments to employ designated researchers and acquire sophisticated equipment which they could not otherwise afford. Research is important and contributes to the prestige of a medical school but it is clear that in Galway it does not detract in any way from teaching. In the main, the research is immediately relevant to local medical problems and, as such, is integrated with the service commitments of the academic staff.

Difficulties in funding have often meant that developments are delayed long after their need is perceived. The Departments of Health Promotion, established in 1990 and the first such department in Ireland, and of General Practice established in 1995, had both been incubating for some years. Diploma and degree courses in Occupational Health, Hygiene and Ergonomics, Health Promotion, and Nursing are all noteworthy additions in recent years to the range of studies available in Galway.

As NUI, Galway celebrates the 150th anniversary of its opening, it is appropriate to assess if the original decision to include a Faculty of Medicine was correct, if not entirely obvious. There was no tradition of medical education in Galway as there was in Belfast and Cork, but Sir Robert Peel, then Prime Minister, was evidently determined to be absolutely impartial in allocating funds and facilities between the three colleges. Perhaps he appreciated that a fully comprehensive third-level institution was needed to maximise the benefits to the west. He was more conscious of the social needs of Ireland than he is generally given credit for and, already in 1845, he was making arrangements to counter the impending famine.

Until about 1948, the bulk of Galway graduates went into general practice in Ireland and Britain but, in the two decades between 1950 and 1970, there was a stream of medical emigrants from Galway to North America. This diminished after 1970 but many still pursue their careers in America. Galway medical graduates are to be found in many parts of the world, in general practice in Ireland or England, in Irish and British teaching hospitals, in the United States and Canada and, of course, the overseas students back in their own countries.

---

23 And *passim*, President's *Reports* UCG 1969–70 to 1990–2.

The records show that 2,500 students graduated in medicine from UCG between 1908 and 1994 which means, with the estimated 1,000 produced from QCG, that approximately 3,500 students have entered the medical profession from the Galway Medical School. That alone would have justified its existence. I estimate that about 1,500 of those were from Connacht and it is doubtful if many of those would have been able to study medicine were it not for the School in Galway. The presence of such a school in Galway has been integral to the development and maintenance of a high standard of health care in the west of Ireland and its graduates have made significant contributions to medicine and medical education in Ireland and Britain and, in recent decades, in America.

While its survival may not be in doubt, the Galway Medical School faces formidable challenges in the future. With its overwhelming dependence on public funding, the resources available will inevitably fall short of its aspirations to develop and adapt to the changing trends in medical education. The guidelines concerning a core curriculum outlined by the General Medical Council in 1991 and the series of discussion papers in the *British Medical Journal* in 1992–3 forecast radical changes in the future.[24] The establishment of Departments of Health Promotion and of General Practice means that Galway is poised to adapt its curriculum to the reduction of suitable clinical material in the main teaching hospitals and the need to have the teaching more community oriented. But it will all require more resources and financial investment in staff and facilities such as clinical skills, laboratories, and community-based teaching centres.[25] Ironically, its small size may be to the advantage of the Galway Medical School, as there is a growing recognition that a strong rapport and personal relationships between teachers and students is highly desirable in medical education, which cannot be achieved in large, and inevitably impersonal, medical schools.

---

24 General Medical Council, *Undergraduate Medical Education: A Consultation Document* (London, 1991).
25 L. Rees and J. Wass, 'Undergraduate Medical Education', *British Medical Journal*, 306 (1993), pp. 258–61.

Mathematics

SEÁN TOBIN

John Mulcahy, 1849–53

The Mathematics Department was one of the original departments which formed the fledgling Queen's College Galway (QCG) in 1845. Various officers were appointed, but the College did not open its doors to students until 1849; and the first Professor of Mathematics, appointed in that year, was John Mulcahy, who was a native of Cork city and had gained the degree of AB from Trinity College Dublin (TCD) in 1830. He was welcomed with extraordinary acclaim by local newspapers, and the *Galway Vindicator* of 11 August 1849 published an enthusiastic tribute from the Provost, Vice-Provost, and Fellows of Trinity College, noting that in 1829 Mulcahy had won the Pensioner's Science Gold Medal, 'the highest honour which can be bestowed on an Undergraduate, equivalent to the Senior Wranglership in the University of Cambridge'.[1] As this would normally result in the conferring of a Fellowship in TCD, the statement goes on to explain that as John Mulcahy was a Catholic he could not legally hold such an office. However, he had devoted himself with outstanding success to instruction in the various branches of science in Trinity and had given such assistance to the Fellows that his colleagues were 'happy to declare as our opinion that his talents, his acquirements, his long experience, and his character, eminently qualify him to fit one of the highest offices in connection with the Colleges proposed to be established in this country'. He was one of the two Roman Catholics appointed to the Faculty of Arts in Galway,[2] and soon afterwards the high opinion of his TCD colleagues was confirmed by the award of Trinity's LLB degree in 1850 and the LLD in 1851.

Such was the man who established the Department of Mathematics in QCG, who quickly became Dean of the Science Division of the Faculty of Arts there, and who was the first Examiner in Mathematics for the three colleges of the Queen's University. On 19 December 1849 the *Galway Vindicator* published the text of a public lecture delivered by Professor Mulcahy in which he gave a long and thoughtful commentary on the benefits of education, the new features of the

---

1 Senior Wrangler was the title given to the candidate who came first in the degree (Tripos) examination in Cambridge.
2 Timothy P. Foley, '"A Nest of Scholars": Biographical Material on Some Early Professors at Queen's College Galway', *Journal of the Galway Archaeological and Historical Society*, 42 (1989–90), p. 79.

Queen's Colleges, the importance and utility of mathematical studies, and on some interesting discoveries in the physical sciences, concluding with 'a few suggestions on the temper and spirit proper for philosophical pursuits'. He remarked that 'I am filled with the most hopeful anticipations ... we shall confer the benefits of a university education upon many, by whom otherwise they would be unobtainable ... benefits open in every particular to all, without distinction of sect or creed'. It is a most interesting lecture, and well worth reading even today for its modern outlook on abstract mathematics, as well as for its warning that 'purely Mathematical pursuits, when too exclusively followed, may possibly have an injurious tendency even in an intellectual point of view'.

Indeed the lecture is worth reading for its general good sense, even if the language is a little old-fashioned. As an example of his style, here are the opening sentences of his concluding remarks, on the proper approach to 'philosophical pursuits':

> It is said by Pope that a little learning is a dangerous thing, an expression which, although true in a certain sense, is apt to be misunderstood. A little learning is indeed a dangerous thing if it be mistaken by the possessor for a great deal; or if that to which the name of learning is applied be not worthy of the name. On the other hand, a little real learning is an acquisition of the highest value, inasmuch as it may be made the groundwork of larger accumulations. Besides the epithet, little, is in this case entirely relative, and men of the most exalted acquirements should be the readiest to admit the vastness of their ignorance; however it is well remarked by Locke at the commencement of his celebrated essay, that although our faculties are not adapted to the knowledge of all things we are enabled to attain, in the words of the apostle, all things 'requisite for the conveniences of life and the information of virtue'.

In July 1852 the Senate of the Queen's University, having advertised the positions and having received numerous applications, appointed nine examiners in addition to eleven re-appointed from 1851; there were no examinations in Arts or Law until 1852, since no students had completed the necessary courses until then. Mulcahy was appointed Examiner in Mathematics for the Queen's University, and perhaps to make allowances for the different emphases of the Colleges his examination papers in mathematics were quite long. The annual *Reports* to the lord lieutenant, on the 'Condition and Progress of the Queen's University in Ireland', made in the early years by the vice-chancellor the Right Hon. Maziere Brady, contain these papers. In 1852, for example, there were five papers, each containing eighteen questions, for the honours Arts degree. It is evident that Professor Mulcahy was quite demanding in his honours-level examinations, while the pass examinations were rather elementary. Mathematics was an obligatory subject in the first year of the three-year AB degree course, and in both years of the two-year course for the 'Diploma of Civil Engineering'. In addition, Mathematics was a main group for the Honours AB and AM courses, and the University instituted Senior Scholarships in these groups, as well as cash exhibitions of £25 and £15, and medals valued at £5 for the earlier honours examinations. Mulcahy designed the original curricula in mathematics; indeed his successor George Johnston

Allman, in giving evidence to the Commission of 1858, remarked that the syllabus had been drawn up by 'a man who, perhaps of all others in this country, had the most experience in teaching mathematics and was well acquainted with the capabilities of the students'.[3]

Whatever about the capabilities of the students, the original undergraduate syllabus seems to have been followed with some modifications and additions for the next one hundred years; the major addition during that time was the theory of functions of a complex variable. This is not to say that mathematics stagnated in the College, rather that Mulcahy had been quite ambitious and up-to-date in his drafting of the courses. Geometry of two and three dimensions – both Euclidean and Cartesian; plane and spherical Trigonometry; integral and differential Calculus; and Algebra were all given a place in the curriculum, but the greatest of these was Geometry and so it remained for most of a century. A later professor, Martin J. Newell, was wont to remark that 'Geometry is the subject that separates the men from the boys' and one could certainly make a good case for this assertion in relation to the challenge of the discipline, its usefulness for training students in logical thought, and its role in demonstrating the nature of (and the necessity for) careful proofs.

Mulcahy wrote a textbook, *Principles of Modern Geometry*, which was published in Dublin in 1852. It was 'for many years the only systematic treatise on Modern elementary geometry adapted to the requirements of students unacquainted with higher algebraic analysis'.[4] It is recorded that George Boole ordered a copy for the Library at Queen's College Cork. A second, revised edition appeared in 1862. Incidentally, Boole had been of the opinion that there was too much emphasis on Geometry in Trinity College Dublin; however, he went on to say that his views had in some degree changed as to the importance of the study of Geometry 'with a view to intellectual benefit'.[5]

In his *Report* for the year ending June 1852, Maziere Brady remarked that 'The payments of salaries on the part of the University not having commenced until a late period of the year [1851] there remains a balance of the grant'. This delay cannot have helped Mulcahy's finances, but his is a really tragic story; he was not long in Galway when his wife died, and in the following year, in late November 1853, he himself died leaving a family of young children. The *Galway Packet* of 30 November 1853 carried a very full obituary, attributing his death to a 'malignant fever of only eight or nine days duration', but also referring darkly to 'a most cruel and galling injustice' which coming soon after the death of his wife affected his strength and health.

The funeral procession through the town was accompanied by the President, staff, and students in their academic robes, and 'a large number of the respectable inhabitants of the town', to the railway station where the body was put on board a train for Ballinasloe, to be buried there.

---

3   *The Queen's Colleges Commission: Report of Her Majesty's Commissioners Appointed to Inquire into the Progress and Condition of the Queen's Colleges at Belfast, Cork, and Galway* (Dublin, 1858), evidence 3925.
4   *The Presidents, Vice-Presidents and Professors of Queen's College, Galway* (Dublin, 1902), p. 8.
5   *The Queen's Colleges Commission*, 1858, evidence 2293 and 2728.

George Johnston Allman, 1853–93

The chair was very quickly filled with the appointment of George Johnston Allman (1824–1904) in December of that same year (fig. 5.1). He had studied in Trinity College Dublin, where his father William Allman MD was Professor of Botany from 1809 to 1844, and was himself author of three mathematical works one of which, 'On the Mathematical Relations of the Forms of the Cells of Plants', was published in the *British Association Report* for 1833. G.J. Allman graduated in 1844 as Senior Moderator and Gold Medallist in Mathematics and was a Bishop Law Mathematical Prizeman; he received the degree LLB in 1853 and the LLD in 1854. He lived in TCD until 1853 when he moved to QCG, where he became Bursar in 1864, holding both posts until his retirement in 1893. He was elected a member of the Senate of the Queen's University in Ireland in 1877 and, when the Royal University replaced the Queen's, Allman was nominated by the crown as a life senator. The Queen's University conferred an honorary DSc on him in 1882, and in 1884 he was elected a Fellow of the Royal Society (FRS). He married Louisa Taylor in 1853; unfortunately she died in 1864, leaving him to care for their young family of a son and two daughters.

He edited Professor James MacCullagh's lectures, *The Attraction of Ellipsoids*, for the Royal Irish Academy,[6] and he contributed a number of articles to such journals as the *Quarterly Journal of Pure and Applied Mathematics*, for example 'On Some Properties of the Paraboloids' in 1874. He had a great interest in the mathematics of antiquity; he contributed the articles on Ptolemy and several other ancient Greek mathematicians to the ninth edition of the *Encyclopaedia Brittanica*. Articles which he wrote for the TCD journal, *Hermathena*, in 1878 and 1887 were subsequently published, in 1889, as the *History of Greek Geometry from Thales to Euclid* in the Dublin University Press series, a book which, according to the *Dictionary of National Biography*, 'threw new light on the ... early development of mathematics'.

Allman gave evidence twice to the Commission of 1858.[7] At the first interview (in March 1857) he was questioned pretty closely on the standards achieved by students in Galway; he maintained stoutly that the standards there were comparable with those in his *alma mater*, Trinity, or indeed further afield, and he made much of the achievements of students who after one year in QCG had enough mathematics to become teachers in schools, for instance in the Erasmus Smith Grammar School in Galway.[8] Allman stated in his evidence that there were thirty-four students taking courses in mathematics in 1856–7 but that in his opinion students were actually leaving QCG for two reasons; firstly because of the 'weight of the curriculum' – he thought that the course of studies for the three-year Arts degree was heavy enough to require five years – and secondly because the Science courses were 'not arranged in logical order'. As an afterthought he added that some students were leaving because of 'the high Mathematical

---

6   *Transactions of the Royal Irish Academy*, 22 (1853), pp. 379–95.
7   Actually the interviews took place in 1857, but the *Report* was published in 1858.
8   This may not have been such a great achievement, for it is clear that the standard of mathematics in schools was rather low at the time.

5.1 George Johnston Allman, Professor of Mathematics, 1853–93

education they get in the first year'. He claimed that 'In one year here, by close attention, they get an education which is, in many respects, superior to that given in four years in any other University or College'. What the Commissioners thought of this amazing claim is not recorded – but they went on to question him about the mathematics courses, and in describing them he paid notable tribute to his predecessor, Mulcahy.

Later, Allman and Richard Doherty MD, the Professor of Midwifery, acting as a delegation from the professors, gave evidence to the Commission on the inadequacy of College salaries. On this occasion Allman made much the shorter of the two contributions, but attached great significance to the number of resignations which had occurred since 1849 – five in Belfast, seven in Cork, and five in Galway.

Twenty-seven years later, in June 1884, Allman gave evidence to another commission, the Queen's Colleges (Ireland) Commission, whose *Report* was published in 1885. Incidentally, Allman's signature appears on the title-page of a copy of this *Report* in the James Hardiman Library, NUI, Galway. Before commencing, he was congratulated by the Commissioners on being elected a Fellow of the Royal

Society on the previous day. Allman blamed deficiencies in the syllabus of the new Royal University for the poor knowledge of trigonometry among matriculated students, and went on to say that his colleagues in Galway allowed him to have an absolute veto on the entry of students who did not meet a sufficient standard in the examinations which covered Books I and II of Euclid, some arithmetic, and algebra as far as the solution of simple equations. He said that in 1883–4 there were just 23 students in mathematics courses, spread over three years, and remarked that because of the decline in student numbers his class fees – which supplemented his salary of £300 – had fallen from £80 in 1880 to £40. We may contrast this with the salary of £600 for W. Burnside, the newly-appointed Professor of Mathematics at the Royal Naval College in Greenwich. We may note also that the number of students attending lectures in Queen's College Galway had risen fairly steadily from 68 in 1849-50 to a peak of 208 in 1880–1; this had collapsed to 103 in 1883–4, a year in which only 28 new students entered. The numbers taking mathematics had started bravely with 54 in 1849–50, but had soon settled down to a reasonably steady pattern averaging a College total of 36 up to and including 1882–3. The number in 1880–1 was 47, so by 1883–4 Mathematics suffered exactly the same *pro rata* decline as the whole College. It is clear from Allman's remarks above that his colleagues did not envisage any lowering of entry requirements in order to enhance student numbers.

Allman stated that, on the whole, he approved of the mathematics courses prescribed for the Royal University, but thought that they should be 'toned up a little more'. In reply to queries about the honours courses in Galway, he stated that the second-year honours course dealt with analytical geometry (conic sections) and with differential and integral calculus *ab initio*; in fact it appears that the students must have been pushed quite hard if they were to cover a course which involved the theorems of Taylor and Maclaurin, maxima and minima in one variable, applications of differential calculus to the geometry of plane curves; and the standard methods of integration and applications to area and length. The texts were by Todhunter or Williamson, while geometry was taken from Salmon's *Conic Sections*, chapters x to xiv. The third-year honours course covered three-dimensional geometry, applications of calculus to the study of second-order surfaces and higher-plane curves, differential equations, and more advanced theory of equations. As proof of the excellence of the mathematics training in Galway, he mentioned *inter alia* a former student, John Atkinson, who had become a Queen's Counsel, and of whom Professor Boole (appointed Examiner in Mathematics for the Queen's University in 1856) said that his answering in mathematics surpassed anything previously seen in the University. For good measure, Allman also mentioned another Galway graduate, T.H. Harrison, who in the 1872 examinations for the Indian Civil Service (at the time keenly contested by ambitious young men) had merited the highest marks ever awarded in mathematics. Harrison himself actually attended and gave evidence to the Commission, to refute a 'mis-statement' made in the House of Commons in 1873 about the credit for his success, which, he believed, should be ascribed in large part to the tuition he had received in Galway.

Another, independent, witness was Alexander Anderson who, in 1881, was awarded the MA degree in QCG, with first-class honours in Mathematics and second-class honours in Experimental Science. After additional coaching by Joseph Larmor (who, in his early twenties, held the chair of Natural Philosophy in the College, and later held the Lucasian Chair of Mathematics at Cambridge for almost thirty years),[9] Anderson went to Sidney Sussex College in Cambridge as a Foundation Scholar in June 1884, and was placed 6th Wrangler and awarded the Mathematical Tripos in 1885. He returned to Galway in 1885 to succeed Larmor in the Chair of Natural Philosophy, and eventually to become President in 1889. His opinion, in testimony to the Commission, was that mathematical education in Galway compared more than favourably with that available at the time in Cambridge.

Allman continued to hold his Chair and the Bursarship until 1893 when, in his 69th year, he resigned from both posts. By that time the student numbers in Mathematics had averaged 39 over the five years from 1888–9 to 1892–3, although the College total was still fluctuating around the 110 mark. So he could reflect that Mathematics was in comparatively good shape when he left QCG. He died of pneumonia ten years later, in Finglas, Dublin.

Alfred Cardew Dixon, 1893–1901

Alfred Cardew Dixon ScD, MA (1865–1936) was born in Yorkshire. He went to Trinity College, Cambridge as a major scholar and graduated in the Mathematical Tripos of 1886 as Senior Wrangler; in 1888 he was awarded a Smith's Prize, and was elected a Fellow of Trinity. He also taught in the Leys School in Cambridge, and his textbook *Elementary Properties of Elliptic Functions* was published by Macmillan in 1894. He succeeded Allman as Professor in Galway in 1893.

In his *Report* for the year 1893–4, the President of QCG, Thomas William Moffett (who was also Professor of History, English Literature, and Mental Science) reported that the Professor of Mathematics had delivered 238 lectures to 48 students (from a total College enrolment of 120) and that the Senior Scholar had given 41 lectures to the Junior Class; he also stated that a paper by Professor Dixon, 'On the Singular Solution of Simultaneous Ordinary Differential Equations and the Theory of Congruences', would appear shortly in the *Philosophical Transactions of the Royal Society*. In the following year the President's report shows that Dixon gave 347 lectures; there were 35 mathematics students in a College total of 114; the total number of professors was 17 – a staff to student ratio that has probably never been bettered! The President took the opportunity to remark that the dissolution of the Queen's University in 1881 had checked the steady growth of QCG, since in the Royal University which replaced it any candidates could sit the examinations whether or not they had attended lectures. He also mentioned that by a recent change in the statutes all the prizes and scholarships were now

---

9 D'Arcy W. Thompson, the famous biologist, whose father was Professor of Greek in QCG, wrote, in an obituary of Larmor, in 1942: 'Galway was then a nest of scholars, like one of the little old German Universities – as Larmor said, looking backward later on. My father was there ... Allman was there, writing his small but famous book on the Greek Geometers'. Cited by Colm Ó hEocha, 'The Queen's College at Galway – Some Memories', in Diarmuid Ó Cearbhaill (ed.), *Galway: Town and Gown 1484–1984* (Dublin, 1984), p. 174.

open to women as well as men. Moffett, in his 1897 *Report*, complimented Dixon on his research work, citing five papers in analysis and differential equations; the two submitted to the Cambridge Philosophical Society bore the titles 'On a Method of Discussing the Plane Sections of Surfaces' and 'On Lie's Method of Solution of Partial Differential Equations'. Incidentally, he stated that for the Professor of Mathematics the class fees amounted to £70, while the salary was £330.

The new President, Alexander Anderson, in his *Report* for the year 1898–9, mentioned that a former Senior Scholar in Mathematics in Galway, F.W. Lyons BA, had been appointed to an Inspectorship in the Imperial Chinese Customs at Swatow; it would appear that Galway graduates in mathematics were ready to support more than one empire! His *Report* for the following year refers to five papers by Dixon, one submitted to the *Philosophical Transactions of the Royal Society* and the others to the *Proceedings of the London Mathematical Society*; one of these, 'On the Reduction of a Linear Substitution to Its Canonical Form', deals with an important basic problem in matrix theory, treated by different methods in a paper by T.J. l'A. Bromwich and in one by W. Burnside in the previous issue.[10]

In 1901 Dixon resigned his post in Galway to become Professor of Mathematics in Queen's College Belfast. Like Allman before him he was elected FRS (in 1904) and also became a Fellow of the Royal University. He retired in 1930 from what by then had become the Queen's University; his wife had died in 1926 and they had no children. He continued his interest in mathematics, and from 1931 to 1933 he was President of the London Mathematical Society. His other main interests throughout his life were singing in (Methodist) church choirs, and golf. He died in 1936, and in an obituary published in the Society's Journal, the eminent mathematician E.T. Whittaker speculated that possibly the life of a prize fellow combined with teaching and private coaching was not conducive to work of distinction; and he said that it was really from the time of his appointment in Galway that Dixon became 'a most productive original worker'.[11]

Thomas John l'Anson Bromwich, 1902–7

The next Professor, appointed in 1902, was Thomas John l'Anson Bromwich MA (1875–1929), a Fellow of St John's College, Cambridge. He was born in Wolverhampton but spent his youth in Natal, where he was educated in Durban. In 1892 he went to Cambridge as a Pensioner in St John's College, and he was Senior Wrangler in the Tripos of 1895, and was elected a Fellow in 1897. According to the obituary by G.H. Hardy, the famous analyst, from which this account is taken, Bromwich was very popular in Cambridge, being an active lawn tennis player, fond of music, and an accomplished dancer. He married in 1901, and on his death in 1929 was survived by his widow and one son.[12]

---

10 *Proceedings of the London Mathematical Society*, 30 (1898–9) pp. 180–94 and ibid., 31 (1899), pp. 170–6 [Dixon] and p. 289 [Bromwich].
11 *Journal of the London Mathematical Society*, 12 (1937), pp. 145–55.
12 Ibid., 5 (1930), pp. 209–20.

In his *Report* for 1902–3, President Anderson remarked that the total enrolment, which had fallen as low as 83 in 1898–9, was again increasing and stressed that half of the 118 students came from Connacht, with 33 from Ulster. He was at pains to contradict testimony given to 'the recent Royal Commission on University Education' that the majority of students at Galway were really 'clever young fellows' from Ulster coming to Galway to avail of Bursaries there. He gave various examples of distinctions won in open competition by Galway students including Agnes M. Perry who was awarded First Place in the competition of 1901 for Scholarships in Mathematics of the Royal University of Ireland, and Thomas Stuart MA, who had been a University Scholar in Mathematics in 1891, had 'gained the high distinction of the Junior Fellowship in Mathematical Science (of the Royal University of Ireland) in 1900 and been awarded a Special Prize of £100 a year for two years' on account of the excellence of his original thesis, culminating in the award of the DSc in 1902. Anderson then spoke of the excellent research work being pursued in the College, and cited five papers published by Bromwich in 1902–3.[13]

Bromwich published a book, *Quadratic Forms and Their Classification by Means of Invariant Factors*, in 1906, and in that same year he was elected FRS. His best-known work is his book *An Introduction to Infinite Series*, based on lectures delivered in Galway and published by Macmillan in 1908. A second, revised, edition was published in 1926, and has been reprinted several times. As a student in UCG, I consulted the Library copy of Bromwich on many occasions and found it always clear and helpful.

In 1907, Bromwich, by then the author of over fifty published papers, resigned from Galway to take up a permanent Lectureship in St John's College, Cambridge. He continued to work in both pure and applied mathematics, a characteristic of mathematicians trained in Cambridge in that era. He died by suicide in 1929; G.H. Hardy published an obituary in the *Proceedings of the Royal Society* in 1930, as well as in the *Journal of the London Mathematical Society*, cited above. Hardy considered Bromwich to be 'one of the most accomplished and most versatile among English mathematicians of the last fifty years'. He remarked that in later life Bromwich was greatly overworked, but that 'he would have had a happier life, and been a greater mathematician, if his mind had worked with less precision ... he lacked the power of thinking vaguely'. Curiously enough, in the light of Whittaker's remark about Dixon in Galway, Hardy was of the opinion that Bromwich's best work had been completed by the year 1908, shortly after he left Galway. Thus it would appear that three mathematicians, Allman, Dixon, and Bromwich, successively professors in Galway, were elected Fellows of the Royal Society, the

---

13 'The Discriminant of a Family of Curves or Surfaces', *Quarterly Journal of Mathematics*, 34–35 (1903–4), pp. 98–116 (a joint paper with R.W.H.T. Hudson); 'The Line of Inflexions of a Plane Unicursal Cubic', *Messenger of Mathematics*, 32–33 (1902–4), pp. 113–15; 'The Caustic by Reflection of a Circle', *American Journal of Mathematics*, 26 (1904), pp. 33–44; 'Note on Double Limits and on the Inversion of a Repeated Infinite Integral', *Proceedings of the London Mathematical Society*, ser. 2, 1 (1903–4), pp. 176–201; 'On Similar Conics through Three Points', *Transactions of the American Mathematical Society*, 4 (1903), pp. 489–92.

highest accolade available to mathematicians in Great Britain and Ireland, largely on the strength of the work they carried out while in Queen's College Galway.

W.A. Houston, 1908–12

William Anderson Houston MA, who was appointed to succeed Bromwich in 1908, was a Fellow of St John's College, Cambridge, to which Bromwich had just returned. It is interesting to note that three consecutive Professors of Mathematics in Galway came from Cambridge; of course that was the most influential centre for mathematics in these islands, and the fact that Larmor was now Professor in Cambridge and President Anderson had studied mathematics in Cambridge points to a strong mathematical link between the old university and the young college in Galway.

We know rather little about Houston but a number of letters and other documents in the National Archives relating to his appointment throw an interesting light on the procedures of the time.[14] A birth certificate, included among these documents, shows that he was born in 1871 at The Manse, Ballyclabber, Coleraine, where his father was a clergyman.

In October 1907 President Anderson sent a letter to the under-secretary at Dublin Castle 'for the information of His Excellency the lord lieutenant' to report on the qualifications of the candidates for the Chair. He emphasised that the subject of the Chair was '*Pure* and not *Mixed*, or *Applied*, Mathematics' and he thought it should remain so as the study of advanced pure mathematics was not making progress elsewhere in this country. He ranked first a former Fellow of Trinity College, Cambridge, J.E. Wright MA; but Wright was by then at Bryn Mawr College in Pennsylvania, and would not be free until June 1908. Anderson discussed two other candidates, T. Stuart MA, DSc and W.A. Houston MA; either would be suitable, both were Irishmen, both had distinguished and more-or-less parallel careers in mathematics in the Royal University of Ireland and in Cambridge. He placed Stuart's name before Houston's, 'because he was a student of this College, probably the best Mathematician which it has produced' (an intriguing pronouncement), and because of his publications.

There followed an extensive series of memoranda, letters, and telegrams, mainly concerning Wright and attempting to get him to take up the post much earlier than June 1908. Wright had suggested the employment of a substitute until that date – Anderson was not entirely opposed – but the view in Dublin Castle was that 'this would seem an arrangement of doubtful expediency'. The under-secretary suggested that he could himself interview Wright in Washington in early November, and pursue further enquiries as to his qualifications as a teacher. The chief secretary agreed to this proposal, but added that he had no preference for a Senior Wrangler (which Wright had been in Cambridge), and thought it '*essential* to get a first rate teacher', though also most desirable to secure a mathematician 'of real distinction'.

---

14 National Archives of Ireland, MS CSORP 1908/3801. My thanks to Fiona Bateman for copies of these documents.

In mid-November, subsequent to the interview, Wright wrote to the under-secretary to say that Bryn Mawr would not release him in January, and went on to ask several questions about salary, fees, and duties in Galway. In a similar letter to Anderson, he expressed uncertainty about accepting an offer of the chair for October 1908, in the event of its being made. Writing to the under-secretary about it on 1 December 1907, Anderson commented 'I don't like this letter'. He added that he had reason to think now 'that it would be risky' to appoint Stuart, and that the best course would be to offer the chair to Houston 'and ask him to come at once'.

The officials acted swiftly: the proposal was put before the lord lieutenant on 4 December, and he approved it on the same day. Houston was at the time in Cairo, working in the Ministry of Education where he was, according to Anderson, 'charged with the oversight of the Mathematical and Science Teaching' in Egypt. On 6 December, in response to a telegram from Dublin, Houston sent a wire saying, 'Can accept work commencing January'; and in reply to a following letter wrote that he expected 'to catch an early boat in January'.

Houston had been Fifth Wrangler in Cambridge in 1896 and Second Smith's Prizeman in 1898. He also obtained first class honours in Part II of the Mathematical Tripos, and as mentioned above was, for a time, a Fellow of St John's College. However it would seem that he had become increasingly interested in general educational matters, and when he was appointed Assistant Commissioner to the Board of Intermediate Education in Ireland in 1912, he resigned his chair.

Meanwhile, in 1909, the Royal University had been dissolved as of 1 November, and the National University of Ireland established; thus sixty years after first opening its doors to students, Queen's College Galway became University College Galway.

Michael Power, 1912–55

The next professor, appointed in 1912, was Michael Power (1885–1974; fig. 5.2). His third-level education commenced in the seminary in Maynooth, but after a year there (which, he told his family later, had been a most enjoyable and carefree time) he realised that he did not have a vocation for the priesthood and left to study in Dublin for degrees of the Royal University. He graduated with the degree of BA in 1907, gaining the MA in 1908 and an MSc in 1909. He came from a farming family beside the village of Piltown in south-west Kilkenny. His brother John, who lived to be just a few months short of one hundred years of age, was a member of a famous Kilkenny senior hurling team.

President Anderson waited until 1913 before making a *Report*, this time a four-year report, on the progress of UCG. He made a very sharp attack on the unequal financial treatment of UCG, saying that '[t]here was no such difference in [respect of] the Colleges of the Queen's University'. The number of students taking mathematics courses averaged 53 out of a student total averaging 143, both enrolments remaining fairly steady, and the number of lectures delivered annually varied between 230 and 315. In the next three-year *Report*, the mathematics numbers had fallen to 42 in 1915–16 but the number of lectures given jumped

5.2 Michael Power, Professor of Mathematics, 1912–55

enormously to 491 in that year, which suggests an increase in the number of courses offered (presumably to quite small classes). The increase to a College total of 214 students in 1915–16 was ascribed by Anderson, in large measure, to increased numbers of medical students, but he pointed out the very rapid and very large increase in the proportion of students coming from Connacht (almost 90 per cent of the total enrolment in 1915–16).

Michael Power held the chair for forty-three years until his retirement in 1955, thus exceeding Allman's record by three years. He was a sturdily-built man of middle height, with a very strong voice, and equally strong views. In the mid 1950s Professor M.H.A. Newman, the internationally-renowned head of the Mathematics Department at the University of Manchester, was appointed External Examiner in Mathematics by the NUI. This involved visiting all three NUI Colleges (Galway, Cork, and Dublin) twice a year; and on one occasion Newman wrote to Power suggesting that in view of the distance from Dublin to Galway, Power might consider bringing the scripts to Dublin to discuss them there with Newman. Power replied that, by his calculations, the distance from Galway to Dublin was just as great as the distance from Dublin to Galway and insisted that Newman make the journey. Newman, although himself quite a touchy individual, took it in good part and in later life remarked that he had greatly enjoyed all his visits to Galway. Incidentally, Newman was a wonderful external examiner: careful, helpful, decisive – and quick!

Power, was from time to time, a member of the Governing Body of UCG, and also of the Senate of the NUI. He was deeply committed to the UCG branch of the Society of St Vincent de Paul, and he attended their regular meetings in the College; no doubt their practical approach to charitable work appealed to his straightforward nature. He also acted at one time as Secretary of an Academic Staff Association in UCG, and there is extant an extract from a draft letter of his to the Secretary of the day in Dublin Castle, complaining about the salaries in the College and listing the various disadvantages under which the staff in Galway laboured.

Power suffered a domestic tragedy similar to that of two earlier professors, Mulcahy and Allman, in that his wife died prematurely in 1930, leaving him to bring up a relatively young family of five daughters and one son; this included two sets of twins, the youngest children being eleven years old. Power was deeply affected by her death, but fortunately had relatives in Galway city who could help him to care for his family. His son Patrick studied medicine, and ultimately became Medical Officer of Health for Galway. A daughter, Sheila, showed exceptional mathematical talent and eventually became Associate Professor of Mathematical Physics in University College Dublin; her children showed great musical talent, her son Hugh Tinney is a world-renowned concert pianist while her daughter Eithne is well-known as a conductor of orchestras and choirs.

Power's main interest in mathematics was the theory of complex functions, and he preferred to teach from the works of French mathematicians – he maintained that there was no good English text on the subject. This opinion might not be universally held, but his students found it expedient to purchase the English translation of Goursat's *Mathematical Analysis*.

Michael Power developed an abiding passion for golf and fishing; the main occasion for the latter was the annual appearance of the mayfly on Lough Corrib, while golf outings were a regular feature of his life in Galway. An old photograph from 1924 (reproduced in the *Galway Advertiser* in October 1981) shows seventeen members of the Galway Golf Club including 'Professor Power (Captain)' at about the time the club moved from its course near the Barna Road to its present site in Blackrock. Power found a kindred spirit when Monsignor Pádraig de Brún arrived in 1945 as President of UCG. Pádraig de Brún (1889–1960) was a man of extraordinary talents, with a deep knowledge of the Classics, a wonderful command of the Irish language, and as well as that he was a mathematician. In 1910 he won a Travelling Studentship in Mathematical Science, the first one awarded by the newly-established NUI and studied at the Sorbonne where his doctoral thesis concerned problems in Integral Equations. Before coming to Galway he had been Professor of Mathematics and Mathematical Physics in St Patrick's College, Maynooth since 1914, and he was Chairman of the Council of the Dublin Institute for Advanced Studies from its foundation in 1940. It is also worthy of note that de

Brún's family home was at Grangemockler in the shadow of Slievenamon in the southeast of Co. Tipperary, not far distant from Power's family home in Piltown. He and Power played golf together very frequently, but they also journeyed together to Mathematical Colloquia at St Andrews, and in 1936 attended the International Congress of Mathematicians in Oslo. It is reported that at these meetings there was always great competition to share a table with them at meal times, to enjoy the lively wit and conversation of both men, which allied the urbane erudition of de Brún with the brisk pragmatism of Power.

In 1929 the Oireachtas passed an Act which placed a special responsibility on UCG to provide courses through the medium of the Irish language and to encourage, in every way possible, the use and development of the native language. To support this endeavour, four new lectureships were set up to provide courses solely in Irish; one of these was a Lectureship in Mathematics through Irish, and the first holder of that office was Eoghan Mac Cionnaith. He set to work enthusiastically, and produced for the summer examinations the first ever papers in mathematics in the Irish language. He found it necessary to translate a number of mathematical terms into Irish, and had the self-confidence to do so. He held the post until 1935, when he was appointed Professor of Mathematical Physics. His daughter Siobhán McKenna, the celebrated actress, recounted in later life how her father tried hard to persuade her to study mathematical science but – fortunately for the Irish theatre – to no avail.

During this time also, Ralph Ryan, a very bright young graduate in Engineering, was appointed to a part-time post in UCG, as Assistant in Mathematics. He remained in that capacity for many years, even after he had established a flourishing firm of consulting engineers in Galway. In fact it has been suggested that he found this useful, not for the small fees he received from the College, but because it enabled him to meet and evaluate promising young engineering students.

One of the students from Connacht was a young Galway city man who entered UCG in 1926, taking first places in the County Council and University Entrance scholarship examinations, and during that year winning the College's Peel Prize in Geometry. This was Martin J. Newell, who in 1930 gained the degree of MSc with first-class honours and won the Travelling Studentship of the NUI. He used this to study for two years at St John's College, Cambridge, the college associated with Professors Bromwich and Houston, where he sat the Tripos examinations.

After leaving Cambridge he taught for two years at St Michael's Secondary College in Listowel and in 1935 returned to Galway as Lecturer in Mathematics (through Irish), as successor to Eoghan Mac Cionnaith. Martin Newell, as Máirtín Ó Tnúthail, took his responsibilities as Lecturer through Irish very seriously; he prepared textbooks on algebra, calculus, and geometry, which were offered to An Gúm, the government agency for the publication of books in Irish. The calculus text was prepared in collaboration with the Professor, Michael Power, and was quite conventional; wartime exigencies delayed publication, and Mr Christopher Townley who worked in the college library (and later became Librarian) prepared roneod copies of the manuscript draft which were made available to students at a very modest cost. The geometry text may have been too unconventional for An Gúm; it was never published. The most noteworthy book was the algebra text,

Algébar Iolscoile, which appeared in 1947 and was used regularly thereafter by honours classes in UCG. It is an introduction to classical algebra, concisely and elegantly written, containing a wealth of information in a very condensed presentation.

In 1947 the Minister for Education, Frank Aiken, introduced new scholarships to encourage students to take University degrees through the medium of Irish at UCG; at £150 per annum they were 50 per cent more valuable than any existing scholarships and were eagerly contested. The first cohort of 'Aiken Scholars' arrived in UCG in 1947, in the Faculties of Arts, Commerce, and Science. The conditions for retention of these scholarships were initially quite severe, and there was great emphasis on taking honours courses. One outcome was a strong honours class in mathematics, which put Máirtín Ó Tnúthail on his mettle. He had beautiful Irish but suffered from increasing deafness; this occasionally caused great merriment in class when students tried to alert him to some slip in his work on the blackboard. In those days the staff wore black academic gowns, and he had a very ancient one, the tail of which he would seize and use when he could not spot the regular eraser; often in his haste he failed to spot the error and rubbed out perfectly correct material. This naturally led to further attempts to redress the situation. However, he himself was perfectly good-humoured about the matter, and indeed was unfailingly charming and courteous to his students. Consequently, they were not suspicious when each year, in early May, he would tell them gravely that he was about to give them a couple of weeks to reflect on their year's work, and that after that he would be back to deal with any difficulties they were unable to resolve. It was only in later years that they realised that the extension of this facility to them coincided with the news that 'the mayfly was up' on Lough Corrib. Professor Power too would vanish and thus did an annual metamorphosis of insect life determine the intellectual biorythm of the UCG Mathematics Department in those golden days!

Incidentally, in those days the honours mathematics classes were entirely male, so much so that in the early fifties when one woman did take the honours courses she became known throughout the College not by her given names but as 'Honours Maths'.

One of the first band of Aiken Scholars, who arrived in UCG in October 1947, was John Joseph (Seán) Tobin, in other words, gentle reader, the present writer. I also won a County Tipperary (South Riding) university scholarship, but could not avail of both. My family lived in Carrick-on-Suir in southeast Tipperary, not far from Grangemockler and Piltown. Students from that part of the country usually went to university in Cork or Dublin, so I was regarded with some interest by the President and the Professor of Mathematics in Galway. Born in 1930 in Dublin, I was educated by the Christian Brothers in Carrick-on-Suir, except for the final two years of secondary school which I spent as a boarder in the Irish-speaking A-school of the Augustinian Fathers in New Ross. I graduated in UCG in 1950, and was awarded the MSc with first-class honours in Mathematical Science in 1951. On the advice of the External Examiner, W.H. McCrea, I was awarded a grant to enable me to study for a doctorate in Manchester, which at the time was the foremost centre for Algebra in Britain, if not in Europe. Influenced by the courses

I had taken from M.J. Newell, and some papers of his which I had helped to proof-read, I elected to study group theory and was assigned as a research student to Dr Graham Higman who gave me a problem concerning 'exponent four' groups. I was awarded the degree of PhD by Manchester University in 1954; and even more importantly, in Manchester I met Lois Brown, a Yorkshire girl then studying at the College of Domestic Science, who later became my wife. I spent the academic year 1954–5 in Columbus, Ohio as an Instructor in the mathematics department, where I worked with the noted group theorist Professor Marshall Hall.

In 1950, Martin Newell was appointed a member of the Governing Body of the School of Theoretical Physics at the Dublin Institute for Advanced Studies and acted in that capacity until 1965. Despite his inclinations towards classical geometry, his own forte was in combinatorial algebra. In 1952 he was awarded the degree DSc by the NUI for his published work on Schur Functions and on Orthogonal and Symmetric Groups; in that year also he was elected a member of the Royal Irish Academy. His researches on Schur functions were referred to by the celebrated group theorist Philip Hall of Cambridge in his lectures to the 1955 St Andrews Colloquium. Hall was discussing the proof of certain key properties of Schur functions and remarked that 'a particularly elegant derivation of the central theorem, and of many other important formulae' had been given in Newell's papers.[15] Again, in his monograph, *The Orthogonal and Symplectic Groups*, published by the Dublin Institute for Advanced Studies in 1958, F.D. Murnaghan (who had in his time been the second person to win a Travelling Studentship in Mathematics from the NUI) ascribed considerable improvements upon part of the exposition in his classic book, *Theory of Group Representations* (Baltimore, 1938) to his being 'able to use with great profit the ideas of Professor M.J. Newell'.

Martin J. Newell (Máirtín Ó Tnúthail), 1955–60

In 1955 Michael Power retired from the Chair of Mathematics, and was succeeded by Martin Newell. On Newell's recommendation, the lectureship in mathematics through Irish was extinguished, and a new unrestricted statutory lectureship in mathematics was established. His idea in making this proposal was that students in all the classes whether through Irish or English should share the same teachers, and accordingly be seen to share the same instruction.

About this time also, a successful operation restored Newell's hearing and so he entered on a new phase of life just as the Irish university system – dormant during World War II and its aftermath – was itself quickening to a new life.

In 1955 I returned to UCG as an Assistant in Mathematics, and in 1956 I was appointed to the newly-established Lectureship. Shortly after that I was elected a member of the Academic Council, probably because I inherited the mantle of the semi-independent Lectureship through Irish.

---

15 Which had appeared, in 1951, in the *Proceedings of the London Mathematical Society*, ser. 2, 53 (1951), pp. 345–55; in the *Quarterly Journal of Mathematics*, ser. 2, 2 (1951), pp. 161–6; and in the *Proceedings of the Royal Irish Academy*, section A, 54 (1951–2), pp. 143–52 and 153–63.

The courses on offer in mathematics at that time in UCG were the standard ones of the day: a three-year course in calculus, algebra, and geometry leading to the Pass degree in Arts, Science, or Commerce; three years of mathematics for engineers; three years of a separate honours degree course in the Arts and Science Faculties; and a one-year graduate course leading (together with a corresponding course in mathematical physics) to the master's degree in mathematical science. In addition, Newell had introduced a brief course in statistics each year for second-year students of Agricultural Science. Then, as now, the Department gave lectures to more than a quarter of the entire student body. The honours courses involved real and complex analysis, algebra (mainly matrices and theory of equations), and geometry (including projective geometry and areal coordinates). The pass courses were given in both Irish and English, the Engineering courses in English only, and the honours courses in Irish. Problems of terminology arose of course, and both Newell and I took part in a project of the State Department of Education to compile a dictionary of mathematical terms in Irish.

In 1955 the Department of Mathematics had one small office-cum-lecture room for the professor, furnished with a small bookcase, a small table, some collapsible desks, chairs, and a miniature blackboard. Most of the lectures were given in other larger lecture rooms which 'belonged' to other departments and could only be used for lectures by the grace and favour of the professors concerned. It is said that the English mathematician G.H. Hardy (who wrote the obituary of Bromwich in 1930) abhorred the use of fountain pens, typewriters, and telephones. Whatever about fountain pens, he would not have been troubled by any other modern aids in the mathematics department in Galway twenty five years later!

Through the efforts of President de Brún and the Governing Body, UCG got a new building, which was designed by de Brún's friend Michael Scott. It was built in the 1950s, and later named Árus de Brún. This had, apart from lecture rooms and laboratories, eight offices for staff; one of these was assigned to the Professor of Mathematics but in return the Department lost the previous office, so the Lecturer still had no place in which to work.

Seán (John J.) Tobin, 1961–95

In the autumn of 1959, Monsignor de Brún, having reached the age of seventy, retired from the presidency of the College. Martin Newell, much to his surprise, came under intense pressure from both de Brún and the Registrar, Professor James Mitchell, to enter the lists for the vacant office. Both men were on the Senate of the NUI, and exerted their considerable influence to ensure the success of their somewhat reluctant candidate. He was appointed President of UCG by the Senate in 1960, and resigned the professorship and also his seat on the Governing Body of the School of Theoretical Physics. In the following year I succeeded to the chair, and also to the other – honorary – position. I later became, for some years, a member of the Governing Body of UCG.

In earlier days, when no thought of occupying the post had entered his mind, Newell had strongly expressed the opinion that a President should always reside in the College (as all previous ones had in fact done). Now he felt obliged to live up to that ideal, so he moved into the presidential quarters with his wife Noreen, a daughter, and four sons. This was not an easy move for his wife, who loved the home which they had built (in upper Newcastle, not far from UCG) and occupied for only seven years; nor was their corner of the original Quadrangle the easiest place in which to rear a young family. But she was a capable mother, blessed with great energy and a lively sense of humour, and was undoubtedly a wonderful support for the new President. I and my wife Lois bought the Newell's family home when it was put up for sale by tender; and to add yet another coincidence, we also eventually had a family of one daughter and four sons.

The research work on which I had embarked in Manchester University was an attempt to elucidate the structure and, if possible, the order of certain finite groups of 'Exponent Four' which belong to a celebrated class of easily-defined but rather mysterious objects known as Burnside Groups. Results reached in the thesis submitted for the PhD degree in 1954 in Manchester, which concerned problems of derived length and class, were used subsequently by myself and other authors in studying these groups; the definitive result was found twenty-five years later by the Russian mathematician Y. Razymyslov. One result in the thesis caused much surprise and some amusement in group theoretic circles, because it showed that Philip Hall had incorrectly calculated the structure, and consequently the size, of a certain group and Hall was a Homer who had never seemed to nod. Both Hall and I were working without benefit of computers, which can construct the group in question (now that its structure is known) in a matter of minutes. My main paper was the long survey article, 'Groups of Exponent Four', in the *Proceedings of the St Andrews Group Theory Conference 1981*. This augmented the course of lectures which I gave at the Conference, and contained many new results as well as improvements on several already known. The chief outcome of my research work might be said to be a new interest in, and development of, commutator calculations in combinatorial group theory. Incidentally, a joke which I made about these procedures during a talk to the 1967 British Mathematical Colloquium, to the effect that such calculations 'should only be performed in private, by consenting adults', a phrase much in the news at the time because of proposed new legislation on homosexuality in Britain, was regarded by some of the audience as rather risqué but has now passed into the mathematical folklore.

The lectureship which I vacated was filled by the appointment of Dr Donald L. McQuillan, another Aiken Scholar who had been awarded the MSc with first-class honours in UCG, and had gone to Johns Hopkins University to study for his PhD. His area of research was algebraic number theory. His stay in UCG was very brief, as he resigned in 1963 to return to the US; but, brief as it was, he contributed significantly to the education of three Travelling Studentship winners, John P.J. McDermott (1963) (of whom more anon) and both Thomas P. McDonough and John F. Mulhern (1964). Dr McDonough is now a Senior Lecturer in Aberystwyth; Dr Mulhern returned to UCG in 1968 as Lecturer in Mathematical Physics but sadly he died prematurely in 1977, leaving his wife Colette to rear their young family. Don McQuillan eventually became a tenured full professor at the University of Wisconsin; he later returned to a full professorship in UCD, which he still holds.

There was a hiatus of a year before Dr Seán McDonagh was appointed to the Lectureship in 1964. He also was a UCG graduate, and had won a Prize in the 1960 Studentship examination. In 1966 he resigned in order to study in the United States; however in 1967 he applied for the still vacant lectureship, and was re-appointed. Apart from mathematics he had a strong interest in general educational problems: when the Regional Technical Colleges (RTCs, now Institutes of Technology) were set up, he resigned from UCG in 1970 to become the principal of the newly-established College in Dundalk. Since then several mathematics graduates from Galway have joined the Dundalk staff.

Things were occasionally very difficult, especially in the two years when I was the only full-time staff member; demands on the Department were growing, and Mr Ralph Ryan decided that he had laboured long enough in the academic vineyard. I was lucky, then and later, to have assistance from some excellent graduate students; and apart from those who are now on the staff in NUI, Galway, I should like in particular to mention two Mayo men: Des MacHale who is now a professor in NUI, Cork; and Tom Laffey who was awarded a Prize on the Studentship examination in 1965, got his PhD in record time with Professor Lederman in Southampton, and is now a professor in NUI, Dublin.

In 1965–6 I took sabbatical leave to work as a Visiting Fellow in the School of Advanced Studies at the Australian National University in Canberra, at the invitation of Professor Bernard Neumann. This resulted in the publication of two joint papers, one with Narain Gupta on groups of exponent four, and one with Gupta and Michael Newman on groups with prime-power exponents. My absence was made possible by the advent of a young Greek mathematician, Anthony Christofides, who had been educated in Alexandria before taking his PhD in London, and then teaching in Magee College in Derry and in UCD. Tony, who is a talented linguist, fell in love with the Irish language and the way of life in Connemara. This prompted him, after further study in the Mathematics Department in Yale, to apply for a permanent post in UCG. He was appointed to a Statutory Lectureship in 1968 and has always taken his full share of the courses given through Irish.

I took subsequent sabbaticals at eight-yearly intervals, and spent time in the Mathematics Departments at the Universities of Freiburg, Würzburg, Oxford, Winnipeg, and Padua, and in the California Institute of Technology. I also encouraged all the staff in the Department, as the numbers grew, to avail of their sabbatical opportunities – this was made possible, in the absence of College financing, by the willingness of staff members to take on extra work to cover the absence of a colleague. I was also fortunately able, at a fairly early stage, to persuade the College authorities to support visits by mathematicians to give seminar talks here; my wife very kindly invited them always to stay as guests in our home, so that only travel costs were involved and we could have more talks on a very limited budget. This contributed to the high output of good research work by members of the department, who also speak at national and international conferences, and lecture to seminar audiences at home and abroad. In fact, despite its relatively small numbers the NUI, Galway Department of Mathematics is widely recognised abroad for the excellence of its staff and graduates.

The foundation of the RTCs at the end of the 1960s was an indication that the government was about to take heed of the growing need for higher education in the 1970s, and the university sector made plans to expand. But funds remained very tight, and there was much debate about the allocation of scarce resources within the individual colleges. An attempt was made in UCG to establish an objective formula to determine the allocation of new posts among the Departments; this formula soon became known as the 'Misery Index' and was very effective when arguing the case for Mathematics.

The arguments bore fruit, and the Department was assigned a second Lectureship: thus at the same time that Christofides was appointed in 1968, a young man from Ring in Co. Waterford, Michael P.J. (Bobby) Curran, also became a Lecturer. He had graduated from UCG with Honours in Mathematical Science, and had gone to London for further study; there he became interested in the new discipline of computing and worked in that field – returning with much valuable theoretical and practical knowledge of computers. As soon as it could be agreed by the Board of Studies, Bobby Curran set up a course in numerical analysis. This meant that the NUI Senate had to appoint a special external examiner, and they chose Professor Fox from Oxford. The course was intended for advanced students in mathematics, and Fox later reported to the Senate of NUI that he had never encountered better standards of answering from students of the subject. The course was subsequently modified for other classes; Bobby Curran resigned in 1978 to take up the new position of Director of Computing Services at UCG and the courses were taken over by other staff members. Incidentally, it is departmental policy to assign members to different courses on a regular basis in the belief that this encourages the interest of the lecturer and consequently of the students.

In 1970 the Mathematics Department was granted another badly-needed lectureship, but at the same time I urged the establishment of a Department of Statistics. This proposal was not accepted, so the new lectureship was sacrificed for one in Statistics, since it seemed clear that the College should have a professional statistician to instruct the students. Statisticians were being snapped up by industry at the time; to illustrate this, the statistics department in Manchester University could not find a professor and was being run at a distance by the Professor of Statistics in Sheffield. I went to visit him in Sheffield to discuss the possibilities, and indeed the outlook seemed bleak; but eventually a young statistician from the Central Statistics Office, Iognáid Ó Muircheartaigh, who had graduated from UCD and obtained his PhD in Glasgow, applied and was appointed to the Lectureship. He then set up our courses in statistics, and these attracted a large number of students from several Faculties. He was promoted to an associate professorship in 1984. A long-time member of the Governing Body, he is now Registrar and Senior Vice President of NUI, Galway. A noted runner as a UCD undergraduate, Ó Muircheartaigh has been deeply involved with the Galway tennis and golf clubs during his time here. More recently, in 1992, a second statistician has been appointed, Dr Jerome Sheahan, a champion chess-player, a graduate of UCC and the University of Calgary, who was formerly a professor at the University of Alberta.

I was lucky to be in charge of the Department of Mathematics at a time when the Irish education system as a whole began to expand. My predecessors had to cope with the most meagre of resources, and I salute them for their achievements under conditions which cannot nowadays even be imagined. It appeared that an opportunity was presenting itself to establish a worthwhile Department, and this posed a problem of strategy. One might try to get an expert in each one of a number of mathematical disciplines or one might try to assemble a number of experts in one area initially who could provide a critical mass of research workers. I determined to follow the second option.

Dr Christofides is an algebraist and so am I, so I decided, not unnaturally, that the Department specialism would be group theory, which was my own interest and in which the two Lecturers could join. This policy was quite successful, largely because of a period of rapid expansion in the university sector overall, coupled with the fact that a number of very able mathematics graduates of UCG were already studying abroad in some of the prime centres for group theory in Europe. One of these was Martin L. Newell, an Aiken Scholar, who won a Prize in the 1962 Studentship examination and was also awarded a grant from the German Academic Exchange Service. He studied for his DPhilNat in Reinhold Baer's Department in Frankfurt. He was appointed Lecturer in UCG in 1969, but given permission to defer taking up his appointment until 1970; in 1976 he was promoted to an Associate Professorship. He was later elected to membership of the Royal Irish Academy. He is a son of the previous professor, and had won fame as one of the Galway senior football team which won the All-Ireland Championships in three successive years. Indeed the GAA continued to call on his services while he was in Germany, leading Baer to ask me, when I met him at a conference, to 'remonstrate with Mr Newell' about his excessive zeal for football! Another native of Galway, John McDermott, won a Travelling Studentship in 1963 and studied for his DPhil in Oxford. He was appointed to a statutory lectureship in UCG in 1973 and he in turn was allowed to defer commencement until 1974. Already in 1970 I was allocated a new Junior Lectureship; the first appointee was Dr Donal Hurley, a graduate of UCC, whose research interests were in analysis. He resigned in 1973 to return to Cork; his successor in the post, chosen from a very strong field, was a young Cambridge group theorist, Dr Rex Dark, who became a statutory lecturer in 1979.

Thus in 1973 we were able to organise an international conference on 'Group Theory and Computing' in Galway. Through personal contacts I assembled an impressive panel of expert speakers from the US, Canada, and Britain, while Bobby Curran showed a flair for garnering financial sponsorship and organised the publication of the Proceedings. The other staff members and graduate students helped so well in making the meeting a success that for years afterwards at mathematical meetings abroad I was eagerly questioned about holding another such conference in Galway. That did not happen until 1993; but in the meantime Christofides, Dark, McDermott, and Newell set up a small two-day meeting which has run in May each year for twenty consecutive years. We believe this to be a world record, and it is now (1998) well-established as 'Groups in Galway'.

Conditions were improving in UCG at this juncture; Árus de Brún had been extended and we were able to bring staff members together into one building (although this is no longer the case due to increased numbers) and we even got a room for seminars and a room for use as a departmental office. In 1974 our first departmental secretary, Catherine Coote, was appointed and cheerfully set about establishing an office with, it must be said, very meagre resources. Catherine was succeeded in turn by Fionnuala Concannon, Carol Conroy, and the present secretary, Geraldine Byrne. The furniture and equipment of the office have improved greatly over the years, but what remained constant were the efficiency, hard work, and general good humour of our secretaries under the continually increasing demands of a growing department. They have contributed greatly to its development, and I take this opportunity to pay them a well-deserved tribute.

As the College developed, and student numbers grew, recruitment continued in the Department of Mathematics, and the range of interests was broadened. Our graduates continued to perform well in the Studentship examinations. The following were awarded Studentships: M.J. Fitzgerald (1975), P.G. Scallan (1978), F.J. Rooney (1980), and Anne F. O'Halloran (1993); and prizes were won by T.C. Hurley (1966), J.D. Fanning (1972), Olivia M. Fagan (1974), J.J. Ward (1978), R. O'D. Johnstone (1979), A.J. Bent (1980), Mary A. McDonough (1982), D.M. Ryan (1984), P.R. McManus (1987), S. Ó Catháin (1989), P.J. Gillen (1991), Caroline M. McCarthy and J.J. McDermott (1992), J.A. Cruikshank, C.J. Houghton, and Maria G. Meehan (1993), and N.P. Friel and D.P. McInerney (1996). It may be noted that in earlier years the students received half of their courses in their BSc and MSc years from the Department of Mathematical Physics; but as the staff numbers increased students were given a wider choice in the postgraduate year so that, for example, in the case of Francis J. Rooney above, the main interest (and preparation) was in mathematical physics whereas for Anne F. O'Halloran it was in mathematics.

The Department continued to expand with the following appointments: John Sheil (Statistics), 1977; Ray Ryan (Functional Analysis), 1978; Thaddeus (Ted) Hurley (Group Theory), 1980; John Hannah (Ring Theory), 1982; James Ward (Algebra), 1984; Graham Ellis (Algebraic Topology), 1987; Donal O'Regan (Differential Equations), 1990; John Burns (Differential Geometry), 1990; Aisling McCluskey (Topology), 1992; Dane Flannery (Group Theory) and Götz Pfeiffer (Computer Algebra), 1996. Of these, Sheil, Hurley, Ward, and Burns had graduated with first-class honours MSc degrees in Mathematical Science in UCG; Dr Sheil studied for his PhD in UCG under the direction of Ó Muircheartaigh; and the other three went abroad to study for their doctorates in the universities of London, Freiburg, and Notre Dame (USA) respectively.

Ray Ryan studied in Dublin and Warwick, and holds his PhD from TCD; John Hannah came from New Zealand with a doctorate from Canterbury; Graham Ellis studied in Bangor and his PhD is from the University of Wales; Donal O'Regan studied for the doctorate in Oregon; and Aisling McCluskey studied in Queen's University Belfast, where she was awarded her DPhil.

In addition there were several temporary full-time staff who came and went in the course of the years, including Dr Gertrude Stanley, Professor Helen Sullivan (a Benedictine nun from the USA), Drs James MacMahon, Paul McGill, Alan Williamson, Johannes Siemons, Martin Wood, Mark Leeny, David Hughes, Mark Jones, Brendan McCann (a UCG graduate, who got his doctorate in Würzburg and is now a lecturer in the Waterford Institute of Technology), and Cora Stack (also a graduate of UCG, who studied for her doctorate at Reading and is now a lecturer in Tallaght Institute of Technology).

Several visitors came to spend a year, or a semester, in the UCG Mathematics Department, on Fulbright grants and other arrangements. Some came purely for research, while others taught courses, with some interesting results!

The revision of syllabi and the introduction of new core courses in discrete mathematics, linear algebra, group and ring theory, topology and metric spaces, differential equations, and functional analysis has gone on steadily over the last forty years. Of course this has necessitated the removal of older and less relevant material; in particular there is now very little classical geometry, a sad but necessary excision. An early useful innovation was the introduction of a four-year honours degree in Mathematics, and later a Higher Diploma in Mathematics. We have introduced a new denominated degree in 'Mathematical Science and Computing' for which the prime mover was Ted Hurley, and this has led to several new options for students in the honours degree courses, for instance fractals, cryptography, artificial intelligence, automated reasoning, and expert systems.

In 1971, in order to introduce a course in the 'History and Philosophy of Mathematics' for Arts undergraduates, I enlisted the help of James Callagy MA, HDipEd, a well-known teacher of mathematics in Coláiste Éinde in Galway, and a great enthusiast for the history of the subject. He had been a fellow student in UCG with Martin J. Newell, the subsequent Professor and eventual President of the College. This innovation proved quite successful, although regarded at the time as somewhat eccentric; but twenty-five years later the introduction of similar courses in a number of British universities was hailed as a welcome step forward. Jim Callagy remained on the staff as Assistant until 1985; during that time, upon retiring from Coláiste Éinde, he participated in the teaching of mathematics classes through Irish. Jim has now gone to his eternal reward; the many students whom he influenced will remember him not only for the concern he showed for their progress but also for his very interesting notes on the history of mathematics, written in a beautifully clear copperplate hand.

Since then Mr Séamas McNena BSc, HDipEd, has taken some of our Irish classes. The demand for these classes fell off considerably during the 1980s and early 1990s, but is now increasing again. Following a suggestion of Martin L. Newell, a special outing to the Irish centre in Carraroe takes place each year for the first-year Irish class accompanied by staff members, and this has proved very popular with the students.

In addition to the 1973 Conference and the annual May meetings already mentioned, in 1993 we hosted the Galway-St Andrews International Group Theory Conference which was the biggest, the most successful – and the longest – meeting on groups ever held up to that time. The bulk of the work at the Galway end was carried out most efficiently by Ted Hurley and James Ward.

In 1994 I secured a grant of European funds from the Higher Education Authority which enabled us to hold a three-day Instructional Conference on the teaching of mathematics at university level. This was the first of its kind in Ireland, and was very well received.

Since then the department has hosted three international conferences, in Statistics – organised by Ó Muircheartaigh, in Algebra – organised by Newell, and in Topology – organised by McCluskey.

Thaddeus C. (Ted) Hurley, 1996–

At the end of the academic year 1995, having reached the age of 65, I retired from office and Dr Christofides was chosen as Acting Head. Already, in late 1963, I had requested the Mathematics staff to consider the future management of the Department. As a result of their deliberations, the College set up a new statutory arrangement to provide for a rotating headship, based on a model already operating in the Physics Department. The first Head under the new dispensation is Professor Ted Hurley MSc, PhD, who was appointed to the chair in 1996.

Born in Tuam, Co. Galway in 1944, he graduated from UCG in 1966 with a first-class honours MSc in Mathematical Science and he was awarded a Prize on the Studentship examination. He went as a research student to London University at Queen Mary College, widely celebrated for its strength in group theory, where he obtained his doctorate with Dr Karl Gruenberg as his supervisor. Ted taught subsequently for some years in Sheffield University and UCD, before returning to Galway as a Lecturer in 1980. Back in Galway, he has always shown a deep concern for the welfare of students and is keen to help them find careers with a mathematical dimension. The degree in Mathematical Science and Computing has proven very worthwhile in this connection.

Innovation in the Department continues, with proposals (made initially by Dr Jerome Sheahan) for a course in the mathematics of finance being brought to fruition through discussions with the Department of Economics, with an offer of assistance from the Department of Mathematical Physics. Consideration is being given also to the introduction of a new 'undifferentiated' mathematics degree in the Arts Faculty; the original impetus for this came from Dr Tony Christofides.

Two new Junior Lectureships were filled in 1997, with the appointment of Dr Götz Pfeiffer, formerly at St Andrews, and Dr Dane Flannery from Australia. Out of twenty valuable post-doctoral Fellowships instituted to mark the Irish presidency of the European Union in 1996, three were won by mathematicians who elected to come to study in Galway: in 1996–7 Dr Chris Boyd came to work with Ray Ryan, and is now employed in UCD; while in 1997–8 Dr Paul Gartside and Dr Niamh O'Sullivan worked with Aisling McCluskey and Ted Hurley respectively.

Furthermore, some postgraduate students have successfully completed, or are about to complete, work for doctorates : Maria Meehan, supervised by Donal O'Regan and currently employed in UCD; Páraic Kirwan, supervised by Ray Ryan; Seán Connolly, supervised by Jerome Sheahan; and Aidan McDermott supervised by Graham Ellis.

At the outset of this account it seemed best to describe the history of the Department by considering events during the tenure of each Professor individually; but the latter half of this century has seen a continuous development of mathematical activity of all kinds, and another essay would be needed to do justice to the research output, teaching successes, and personal achievements of all the staff named above. At this point I could go on to write at length about fruitful research partnerships in the Department and also about working relationships established with foreign mathematicians and foreign universities; about books written or edited; about papers and books reviewed; about the many research publications and talks at learned conferences by members of the staff; about their great success in attracting research grants now that such funds have at last become available in pure mathematics; about their outside interests and about their contributions to College life in general. And indeed I would like to say something about the level of wit and the conversational fun we enjoyed over the years (so much so that Des MacHale was prompted to collect jokes and study humour, with results well-known to Kerrymen). But I hope that at this point my colleagues will agree that these are matters for a future writer to cope with. Suffice it, for the moment, to say that the Department of Mathematics at NUI, Galway, has developed as a well-functioning, well-regarded, university department of international status.[16]

---

16 I should like to thank Professors Tom Boylan and Tadhg Foley for inviting me to write this article, and for providing me with guidance as to the existence and location of records. The unbounded enthusiasm of Tadhg, in particular, encouraged me to persevere, and I should like to express my thanks also to Fiona Bateman for her assistance in tracking down references. In addition, I owe special thanks to our former Librarian Christy Townley, and to Dr Paddy Power and his wife Mary, for conversations about the Power/de Brún era. I am grateful to Professor Marty Newell for permission to use material from his (as yet) unpublished article 'Matamaitic tré Ghaeilge'. Finally, I thank him and Dr John McDermott who each read a draft of this essay carefully and made several very helpful comments.

Natural Philosophy/Physics

TOM O'CONNOR

Natural Philosophy, which was one of the twenty foundational chairs in Queen's College Galway (QCG) when it opened its doors in 1849, dealt with the areas of knowledge which today are covered by the Departments of Experimental Physics and Mathematical Physics. This chapter outlines the development of the subject in Galway up to 1996, the professors who filled the chair, the courses they taught, the growth and migration of the Department, some details about the other people who taught and studied in it, and the contributions which they made to knowledge while in Galway and elsewhere. Because of limitations of time and space, this account must be selective and only aims to record some of the activities in the Department over its first 150 years. As a protagonist in the story for the last 40 years, my selection may reflect my personal interests and experience, but I am grateful for all of the help so readily given by my colleagues in the Department and by the editor of this volume.

The Professors

The professors who held the chair of Natural Philosophy in Galway all came to it as young men. For some it was a stepping stone to an illustrious career elsewhere, while others spent the greater part of their careers in Galway. In the earlier years, from 1849 to 1879, the professors were graduates of Trinity College Dublin (TCD). In the middle years, from 1880 to 1934, they were graduates of the Queen's University and the University of Cambridge. This was followed by the era of University College Dublin graduates which links to the present times when the professional staff of the Department come from a variety of universities in Ireland and abroad.

The first holder of the Chair of Natural Philosophy, from 1849 to 1852, was Morgan William Crofton. Professor Crofton, a scion of the Crofton family of Mohill, Co. Leitrim, was born in Dublin on 27 June 1826. His father was the Rector of Skrene, Co. Sligo. He was educated at Trinity College Dublin, where he was first senior moderator in Mathematics and Mathematical Physics in 1847. He came to Galway in 1849 to set up the Department of Natural Philosophy in the new college and he resigned in 1852. He subsequently went on to a distinguished academic career, first teaching mathematics in a number of Jesuit educational institutions in France while later in Britain, in 1856, he was appointed to the mathematical staff of the Royal Military Academy at Woolwich. In 1870 he succeeded Professor J.J. Sylvester as the Professor of Mathematics at this institution. He was elected Fellow of the Royal Society (FRS) in 1868. He was the author of many papers dealing with the calculus of operations, differential equations, and theory of probability, and was the joint author of *Tracts on Mathematics* and the article on 'Probability' in the ninth edition of the *Encyclopaedia Britannica*. His biographer was a successor to his chair in Galway, Sir Joseph Larmor. In his retirement Morgan Crofton lived off and on in Monkstown, Co. Dublin, and died in Brighton on 13 May 1915 in his 89th year.[1]

Professor Crofton was succeeded by his classmate, George Johnstone Stoney, who had been the second senior moderator in Mathematics and Mathematical Physics in 1847 at Trinity College Dublin. Although born in Kingstown, now Dun Laoghaire, on 15 February 1826, his family were from Oakley Park, Clareen in King's County, now Co. Offaly. Before coming to Galway in 1852, Stoney was employed by the earl of Rosse as an astronomer at what was, for many years, the world's largest telescope in Birr Castle, Birr (then Parsonstown), Co. Offaly. During his tenure of the chair in Galway, he published a paper 'On a Collimator for Completing the Adjustments of a Reflecting Telescope',[2] and another on a 'Description of an Arrangement of Grove's Battery',[3] thus beginning in Galway a tradition of the study of astronomy and applied physics which continues to the present day. He was also deeply interested in the progress of university education, and made a detailed submission to the Queen's Colleges Commission in 1857 proposing changes in the curriculum, more flexibility in the employment of support staff, and the provision of suitable accommodation for students.[4] He resigned from the Galway College in 1857 and went to Dublin to become Secretary of the Queen's University until its dissolution in 1882. He was Honorary Secretary of the Royal Dublin Society for twenty years and used their laboratories for much of his scientific work. He was the first recipient of that Society's Boyle Medal. He remained very active in scientific circles in Ireland and Britain and contributed significantly to many branches of physics and astronomy. He was a prominent participant in the British Association for the Advancement of Science and was President of its Section A – Mathematical and Physical Sciences – in 1879. He is credited with making the first reasonable estimate for the natural unit of electricity in 1874 and with coining the word 'electron' for it at a meeting of the Royal Dublin Society in 1891.[5] He was elected Fellow of the Royal Society in 1861 and, on his

---

1 Obituary by J. B., *Irish Book Lover*, 7 (1915), pp. 35–6.
2 *British Association Report* (London,1856), pp. 30–1.
3 *British Association Report* (London,1857), pp. 20–1.
4 *Report of Her Majesty's Commissioners Appointed to Enquire into the Progress and Condition of the Queen's Colleges at Belfast, Cork, and Galway; with Minutes of Evidence, Documents, and Tables and Returns* (Dublin, 1858), evidence 3978–4054, pp. 266–71, and documents pp. 329–30.
5 P.A. Wayman, 'Stoney's Electron', *Europhysics News*, September 1997, p. 159; G. Squires, 'J.J. Thomson and the Discovery of the Electron', *Physics World*, 10 (1997), p. 35; *The Scientific Transactions of the Royal Dublin Society*, 4 (1891), p. 583; J. O'Hara, 'George Johnstone Stoney: Physicist and Educationalist', in R.C. Mollan et al. (eds), *Some People and Places in Irish Science and Technology* (Dublin, 1985), pp. 50–1.

6.1 Arthur Hill Curtis, Professor of Natural Philosophy, 1857–79

retirement to London, he became a Vice-President of the Society in 1898. He died on 5 July 1911 after a long illness and his ashes rest in the little cemetery in Dundrum, Co. Dublin. The large first-year laboratory in the present Department of Physics is named in his honour and a commemorative plaque has recently been placed in the archway of the Quadrangle.

The next Professor, Arthur Hill Curtis, was the first senior moderator in Mathematics and Mathematical Physics of Trinity College Dublin in 1849 (fig. 6.1). He became a tutor in Mathematics in Trinity College and won many honours such as Bishop Law's mathematical premium and the McCullagh prize in physical optics. On coming to Galway, he lived for a while in The Retreat on Revagh Road, Salthill. He published works on a variety of topics and compiled a manuscript describing the textbooks used in the Department with an illustrated list of the extensive range of 'philosophical' apparatus which was used to demonstrate physical principles in his lectures. This manuscript was also used to record the purchase of other apparatus and it gives a rare insight into the range of suppliers and the cost of such items in the second half of the nineteenth century.

Some of his theorems relating to centres of pressure were important in engineering for understanding the forces on dams, and a paper, 'On the Freezing of Water at Temperatures Lower than 32° F', is of interest in the light of current work on ice nucleation in the Department.[6] In 1861 he also initiated the systematic study of the weather in Galway and established a climatological observing station in the President's garden, close to where Árus de Brún now stands. These observations have been continued by the Department of Physics, with a few interruptions, to the present day and help to quantify the weather experienced in Galway over the years. He became Registrar of the College in 1877. He subsequently resigned in 1879 and went to Dublin to become the Assistant Commissioner of Intermediate Education in Ireland. This career move may have been associated with dissatisfaction at the transition from the Queen's University to the Royal University of Ireland (RUI) at this time. He held the position of Assistant Commissioner until 1886.

The appointment in 1880 of Joseph Larmor to the chair of Natural Philosophy in Galway marked the change from the links with Trinity College Dublin to those with the Queen's University and the University of Cambridge, but the strong emphasis on the more mathematical approach to physics continued. Larmor was born in Magheragal, Co. Antrim, on 11 July 1857. He was educated in Queen's College Belfast from 1871 to 1875 and then in St John's College, Cambridge, where he took the Mathematical Tripos in 1880. He was the Senior Wrangler, with the distinguished physicist J.J. Thomson being Second Wrangler. During the five years of his tenure of the Professorship of Natural Philosophy in Galway, he published eleven papers, mainly in mathematical journals.

The idea of practical classes for students of physics had been introduced in Cambridge by James Clerk Maxwell with the opening of the Cavendish Laboratory there in 1875. Larmor may have had similar plans for Galway, where he is reputed to have made a wooden compound pendulum. He was also involved in the purchase of modern physical apparatus, such as a Wheatstone microphone and phonograph, as shown by the entries in the stock book for that period. After five happy years in Galway he returned, not without reluctance, to a distinguished career in Cambridge as a fellow of St John's College.[7] He became a Fellow of the Royal Society in 1892 and the Lucasian Professor of Mathematics at Cambridge, in succession to the Sligo-born G.G. Stokes, in 1903. He received a knighthood in 1909, and was an MP for the University from 1911 until 1922. He always kept fond memories of Galway until his death at Hollywood, Co. Down, on 19 May 1942. He donated a sum of £750 to the College to endow the Larmor Prize for the first place in the BSc examination in Mathematics, Mathematical Physics, or Experimental Physics. His memory is also perpetuated in Galway by the Larmor lecture theatre in the Department of Physics.

One of Larmor's first students in Galway was a fellow Ulsterman, Alexander Anderson, who was born in Coleraine on 12 May 1858 (fig. 6.2). He took the first

---

6   *Philosophical Magazine*, series v, 32 (1866), pp. 422–4.
7   C. Ó hEocha in D. Ó Cearbhaill (ed.), *Galway: Town and Gown 1484–1984* (Dublin, 1984), p. 175.

place and gold medal in the BA examination in 1880 and the MA in 1881. He then entered Sidney Sussex College in Cambridge University, taking first place in the open scholarship examination; he was a Goldsmith's exhibitioner in 1882 and he graduated as Sixth Wrangler in 1884. He returned to Galway as the Professor of Natural Philosophy in 1885 and set about the development of proper laboratories for practical physics. After persistent efforts he succeeded, and the records first show practical Physics classes for students in the session 1890–1. The growth of teaching and research in the Department will be described in more detail later on in this chapter.

As well as his duties of running what were essentially two Departments, Experimental Physics and Mathematical Physics, Anderson assumed the Presidency of the College in 1899 in succession to Professor Starkie. He was an able university administrator who guided the College through a period of major changes in the University and in Ireland until his retirement in 1934. Among these changes were the incorporation in 1908 of the old Queen's College into the new National University of Ireland, the establishment of the Irish Free State, and the beginning of the Gaelicisation of the College at the end of the 1920s. In an anonymous appreciation, which appeared in the *U.C.G. Annual* following his retirement, we read:

> During these developments, the position of President of University College, Galway, was often a very invidious one, but his tact and broadminded attitude avoided many a difficulty and solved many a problem. When, about 1925, the very existence of the Galway College was at stake, his great reputation and skilful direction were, to a large extent, responsible for averting the danger. When the Gaelicisation of the College was begun, he guided the first years of the new development with the same skill and interest in the College which he had always shown and many were surprised to realise the depth of his knowledge of the Irish language.[8]

He married Emily Binns of Galway and they had a son and three daughters, one of whom, Emily, was Professor of German in Galway from 1917 until she resigned in 1920. On his retirement he went to live at 7 Pembroke Park, Dublin, where he died on 5 September 1936. He is buried in Dean's Grange Cemetery.

One of Anderson's more distinguished students was a fellow Coleraine man, John A. McClelland, who received his BA with first-class honours and gold medal in Physics in 1893 and his MA in 1894. He also obtained an 1851 Exhibition scholarship, and went to Cambridge University in 1895 to pursue further research. He worked under J.J. Thomson and C.T.R. Wilson on the discharge of electricity through gases and on atmospheric electricity. In 1900, before the setting up of the National University of Ireland, McClelland returned to Dublin as Professor of Physics in what was then University College Dublin (UCD). He continued his line of research there on the behaviour of electricity in gases, which had a profound

---

8 'Lough Corrib', *U.C.G. Annual*, 1935, pp. 37–9.

6.2 Alexander Anderson, Professor of Natural Philosophy, 1885–1934 and President, 1899–1934

influence on the development of physics in Ireland. One of his students, J.J. McHenry, after qualifying in UCD and later in Cambridge, came to Galway in 1922 as an assistant and, later, a lecturer in Physics. In 1932 McHenry moved to University College Cork to become Professor of Physics and, later, President of that College.

Another graduate in Physics from UCD was Cilian Ó Brolcháin, who received his BSc in 1925 and his MSc in 1926 for work, under the brothers J.J. and P.J. Nolan, on ions in the atmosphere. He later went on a travelling studentship to Graz University in Austria for two years to work for a PhD degree under the Nobel laureate V.F. Hess. In 1932 he came to Galway to replace McHenry. As an Irish speaker 'ón gcliabhán' he took a special interest in the development of university courses through Irish which was taking place in Galway at that time.

On the retirement of President Anderson in 1934, his chair of Natural Philosophy was divided into the Chairs of Experimental Physics and Mathematical Physics. The first holders of these chairs were Cilian Ó Brolcháin and Eoghan Mac Cionnaith, respectively. Although the lecture loads were considerable, the number of students taking advanced courses in Science to BSc level in Galway in these years was small. Most of the students taking higher degrees by research were in Chemistry and, by courses and examinations, in Mathematical Science. Besides the scarcity of students, there was also the scarcity of resources, which was exacerbated by 'the Emergency' during World War Two. During this period, Professor Ó Brolcháin devoted a major portion of his time to service as an officer in the Local Defence Force.

After the War, the advent of the Aiken (or '£150') scholars from All-Irish or 'A' schools all over the country, as well as the provision of scholarships for students from Gaeltacht areas, led to a significant increase in the number of students taking their courses through Irish. These courses and the use of Irish in the business of the College were of special concern to Professor Ó Brolcháin. He presided over the expansion of the Department, which will be described later. As Dean of the Science Faculty, he took a keen interest in the planning of the new Science building and of his own Department. Ill health caused him to retire in 1973, just before the opening of the new building, and he died in Galway in 1976.

The statutory staff of the Department doubled in 1947 with the arrival to a lectureship of Declan M. Larkin, another Dubliner, and graduate in Physics from UCD, who had served in the Irish Meteorological Service and the Post Office Engineering Branch. He took a career break from 1958 to 1960 to obtain a PhD in Physics from Duke University in North Carolina in the field of microwave spectroscopy. He was appointed Professor of Electron Physics in 1965 and served as Registrar and Supervisor of Examinations from 1974 to 1980. He retired in 1986.

In 1973 the Department of Physics, in an innovative move to maintain unity and cohesion in a growing Department, made statutory arrangements for the headship of the Department to rotate among its Professors and Associate Professors on a three-year cycle. The first Professor of Experimental Physics to be appointed under this scheme was George F. Imbusch. He was born and educated in Limerick city, and came to Galway as a student in 1953. He graduated in Physics in 1956 and went on to take an MSc by research in optical spectroscopy in 1958. He obtained one of the first Joseph P. Kennedy Jr Foundation fellowships which enabled him to study in the USA for a PhD degree at Stanford University in laser-related research under the Nobel laureate Arthur Schawlow. After a distinguished career in Stanford, he spent some years at the Bell Telephones Central Research Laboratories at Murray Hill, New Jersey, before returning to a lectureship in Galway in 1967. He obtained an Associate Professorship in Physics in 1969. In 1973, he became Professor of Experimental Physics and the first head of the Department for three years under the new scheme. He was appointed as one of the two Vice-Presidents of the College, with special responsibilities for human and physical resources, when the new College management structure was initiated in 1992.

In 1978, with the appointment of Philip W. Walton to a new chair of Applied Physics within the Department, the early links with Trinity College Dublin were re-established. Professor Walton is a Dubliner who took his BA (Mod) in Physics from TCD in 1962 and his PhD in 1968 with a thesis on the statistics of secondary electron emission. After a period as a medical physicist in Scotland and in Virginia,

USA, he returned to Ireland to take up this chair and to pioneer the development of degree courses and research in Applied Physics.

In recent times two Galway graduates have been appointed to associate professorships in the Department. Stephen Gerard Jennings, a native of Ballinasloe, graduated in 1965 and was awarded an MSc for research in aerosol physics in 1967. He did research for his PhD in the Atmospheric Physics group in the University of Manchester Institute of Science and Technology on the interaction of falling water drops, and spent some time pursuing research in the University of Durham, UK, and in the Atmospheric Sciences Laboratory at White Sands in New Mexico, USA, before returning to Galway in 1980. His research interests are in the field of Atmospheric Physics. He was appointed an associate professor in 1991.

Thomas J. Glynn is a Galwegian who obtained his BSc in 1968. After obtaining his MSc for research in optical spectroscopy he went to Queen's University in Belfast to carry out research for the PhD degree, under Professor D.J. Bradley, on 'Saturable Absorbers for High Power Lasers'. He spent some time in the Universities of Oxford and Munich before returning to Galway in 1976. He is the founder and current director of the National Centre for Laser Applications which is based in the Department. He became an associate professor in 1995, and is currently head of the Department.

Students and Courses

From its inception, Queen's College Galway sought to give its students a broadly-based education as well as a solid preparation for the professions of law, medicine, and engineering. The faculty of Arts contained both an Arts and a Science division, and courses for the BA degree involved over ten subjects ranging from classical languages to Natural History. The Department of Natural Philosophy played a major role in both aspects of the College's programme. It provided a large amount of service teaching to various faculties and also a large amount of teaching to a much smaller number of students who were taking honours courses at an advanced level for scholarships and exhibitions or for a career in science. The fundamental importance of physics to human knowledge, as well as for every career in science and technology, has meant that the role of the Department, and indeed the basic concepts of its elementary courses, have remained relevant over the 150 years of the College's existence.

In the nineteenth century, in the President's annual *Report*, the professors gave an account of the number of lectures which they delivered, the number of students attending their courses, how they performed in examinations, and other items on the development of their departments. Many of their remarks on student performance could apply equally to the students of today, showing that human nature remains fairly constant, even as academic circumstances evolve and change.

In the 1850–1 session, Professor Crofton delivered 154 lectures to eleven students. These belonged to the Faculty of Medicine and the School of Engineering and Agriculture, since students in Arts were not required to study Natural Philosophy until the third session from matriculation. Two of the students were attending second-year lectures. In general their attendance and answering at examinations was satisfactory, with a few exceptions, which he attributed 'entirely to their uneducated state on entering College, particularly to their imperfect knowledge of Mathematics, which rendered it very difficult for them to form correct physical notions, even of the most fundamental description'.[9] Regarding the state of education of the average entrant to College, it must be remembered that the recent catastrophic potato famine had devastated the west of Ireland. While more than a million people then lived in the province of Connacht, only 625 were attending classical schools.[10]

In the President's *Report* for 1853, Professor G.J. Stoney records that, in all, 207 lectures were delivered in Natural Philosophy. These were distributed into three courses, each extending throughout the entire session; an elementary course in Natural Philosophy, an honours course in Mathematical Physics, and an Engineering course in Practical Mechanics. It is interesting to note in his remarks that

> The elementary course was fully illustrated by experiments, and was attended by 19 students, in most cases with great regularity and attention, their answering at sessional examinations evinced a competent knowledge of the subjects, so far as they were treated in the lectures, but did not in most cases indicate as much independent study of the text-books as seems desirable.[11]

The common misconception of students that if an item is not covered in lectures then it is not on the course or will not be examined seems to have been prevalent in Galway from its earliest years. The textbooks which described the syllabus in Natural Philosophy for the senior scholarships on the BA examination at that time were Walton's *Mechanical Problems*; Walton's *Hydrostatic Problems*; Parkinson's *Optics*; Hymer's *Astronomy*; Jamin's *Trait de Physique*; Lloyd's *Lectures on the Wave Theory of Light*; selections from Duhamel's *Course de Mécanique*, and the Professor's lectures to the honours class of the third year.

The emphasis on the mathematical and mechanical aspects of Physics reflected the education received by the first two professors as classmates in TCD and the general state of knowledge of Physics at that time. There was then in the curriculum of the College a subject called 'Mixed Mathematics' which included such topics as heat, light, and astronomy. It is interesting to note that the title Mathematical Physics was in use for some courses in the Department and that the lectures in the elementary course were illustrated by experiments. The demonstration apparatus and the experimental side of natural Philosophy will be dealt with later in this chapter. Professor Stoney expressed his views in his Presidential address to the Mathematical and Physical Section of the British Association in 1879. For, he claimed,

---

9 *Report* of the President, 1851, p. 56.
10 *Report* of the President, 1856, p. 9.
11 *Report* of the President, 1853, p. 8.

an investigator of Nature, the great science of mechanics must be studied by him in its own best form, and not degraded by the vile expedient of evading the legitimate use of infinitesimal calculus, to comply, perhaps, with the ill-judged requirements of some examining body.[12]

The latter remark may have been prompted in part by his disappointment that the Queen's University in Ireland, in which he had played a prominent part for twenty-five years as Secretary, was being wound up and replaced by the Royal University of Ireland, which was mainly an examining body.

While the students for the BA degree took courses in a wide variety of subjects, they did show some specialisation. In the list of BA graduates, Science Division, the first name we find is that of Charles W. Dugan, who obtained a first honours in Natural Sciences in 1852. In 1857 the BA degree of Richard C. Bateman was described as a first in Physics, while a year later John Moorhead was awarded the BA with a first in Mixed Mathematics and a first in Physics. Natural Philosophy does not appear as an area of specialisation within the BA, and the degree of Henry Thynne in 1859 shows a first in Mathematics, a first in Mathematical Physics, and a first in Experimental Physics. In 1860 Charles O'Hara got a first in Experimental Physics and a second in Chemistry. While the names of individual subjects were sometimes mentioned, most of the degrees were classified as Mathematical Science, Experimental Science, Natural Science, and a few as Biological Science. In all, forty BA degrees in the Science Division were awarded to students of the College up to 1880 by the Queen's University of Ireland.

The pattern of teaching continued with the number of students attending lectures in Natural Philosophy being about 30 per cent of the College's total student population. In the President's *Report* for the session 1859–60, we find the future Professor of Engineering, Edward Townsend, acting as Professor of Natural Philosophy and teaching four courses. He gave 64 lectures to 32 students in the general class in Mixed Mathematics and Experimental Physics; 35 lectures to 9 students in the honours class in Experimental Physics; 46 lectures to 3 students in the honours class in Mixed Mathematics; and 27 lectures to 1 student in the Engineering class in Practical Mechanics. Townsend added:

> I am happy to state that throughout the entire session the students attending my lectures were both gentlemanlike and orderly in their conduct, punctual in their attendance, and diligent in their study. It is a matter of regret that a few of the medical and agricultural men were unable to keep pace with the rest of the class, owing to their slight acquaintance with mathematics, a certain amount of which is indispensable to the acquisition of a fair knowledge of Natural Philosophy.[13]

In the following session the number of students of Natural Philosophy jumped to a peak of 48.6 per cent or 70 out of a total of 144 in the College, and these received

---

12 *British Association Report* (London, 1879), p. 246.
13 *Report* of the President, 1859–60, p. 9.

213 lectures in all from Professor Curtis. The percentage of College students attending Natural Philosophy lectures remained around 40 per cent during Professor Curtis's tenure of the chair until 1879, and the 'disturbance' caused by the change from the Queen's to the Royal University.

The Department was frequently teaching over half of the students of the College in a given session despite a falling-off for a time in the Medical students, who preferred, under the Royal University of Ireland (RUI) scheme of examinations, to take their instruction in Physics from 'grinders' in Dublin. These gentlemen, to quote Professor Larmor, 'conduct[ed] their instruction with reference to examination papers'.[14] The Department also frequently topped the tables for students attending, and lectures given, per session. Over the period 1880 to 1899 on average 46.4 per cent of the students in College attended lectures in Natural Philosophy. During the session 1883–4, we find Professor Larmor giving a total of 294 lectures to 35 of the College's 103 students. This was a greater number of lectures than that given by any other department in the College. A feeling for the workload involved may be gathered from Larmor's report to the Queen's Colleges (Ireland) Commission in June 1884:

> Under present arrangements, the work of this department consists of the following courses:
> 1. A general course of lectures on Experimental Physics, of a preliminary character, for first year students. This course is attended by first year arts and engineering students, together with a portion of the first year medical students. The medical part of the class is chiefly composed of scholars and exhibitioners of the College, who are required to attend some non-professional classes.
> 2. An advanced course of Experimental Physics, attended by second arts students. This is an honour course, and includes all topics connected with heat and sound that are within the range of the mathematical knowledge of the students.
> 3. An honour course in Mathematical Physics, which corresponds to the second university examination for honours in the Royal University. It is not, however, confined to these limits, but frequently extends beyond them, when it is thought such an extension would be profitable to the students.
> 4. An honour course of Experimental Physics for third year students, the subjects being electricity and magnetism and light. These students re-attend class 2, as part of this course. The course includes the use of physical instruments, and the making and working out of exact physical measurements by the students. This latter is included as part of the requirements for the senior scholarship, but as it is not at present exacted in the honour examinations of the Royal University, it is only in some years that there are students who are willing to devote to it the large amount of time necessary for a *complete* course.

---

14 *Queen's Colleges (Ireland) Commission Report* (Dublin, 1885), evidence 6435–6, p. 220.

5. An honour course of Mathematical Physics for third year students, which corresponds to the honour degree examinations of the Royal University. [This class does not exist in the *present* session]
6. A course, theoretical and experimental, of Applied Natural Philosophy, for engineering students reading for their degrees. The other courses are also attended by engineering students.

The subjects of these courses overlap, and students are frequently recommended to attend parts of courses different from the ones they have taken up, when by doing so they can fill up deficiencies in their knowledge.[15]

About a century ago, in the session 1894–5, we again find Natural Philosophy at the top of the table with Professor Anderson giving 351 lectures to 62 of the College's 114 students. In addition, in that year the Senior Scholar delivered 20 lectures to the junior class, and there were 51 lectures to 14 students in Practical Physics. This was a considerable reduction on the 439 lectures and 108 Practical Physics lectures given to a total of 58 students in the session 1892–3! There were also some students, such as Anderson himself, who took courses for the MA degree and undertook teaching and research. Several won '1851 Exhibition' scholarships worth £150 per year for two years for postgraduate study. Mention could be made of William J. Gannon who obtained his MA in 1892, J.A. McClelland in 1893, and John Henry in 1894.

The number of students specialising in Science subjects remained small and only around thirty took the BA degree under the regime of the Royal University of Ireland between 1880 and 1910. The BSc degree had been introduced as a postgraduate qualification similar to the MA, but was taken by very few people. With the advent of the National University of Ireland in 1908, the numbers remained small. Much of the work of the Department of Natural Philosophy consisted of servicing the medical and engineering students. It is worth noting that Medical students during the period 1925 to 1941 took the usual introductory course in Physics in their pre-medical year and a course in Applied Physics, with special practicals, in what was then their first medical year. Courses were also given in Mathematical Physics up to degree level in Engineering until the division of the Department in 1934, as well as a course on 'Physics and Meteorology' for the Diploma in Public Health in the 1920s.

The total number of students taking Physics as a subject of their degree examination in the period 1911 to 1940 was 37. From 1941 to 1950 it was also 37. These were mainly for the BSc general degree while a few were for major or minor honours in Physics. As mentioned above, on the retirement of President Anderson from the chair of Natural Philosophy in 1934, the Department was divided into the Departments of Mathematical Physics and Experimental Physics. The honours BSc degree at that time was a three-year course with students of Mathematical Science taking equal honours in Mathematics and Mathematical Physics while those in Experimental Physics took the honours examination in their

---

15   Ibid., submission 44, re. evidence 6722, p. 484.

minor subject in the summer of their third year and in the major subject in the autumn.

In the early 1950s the number of students taking Physics to degree level began to increase, and there were students presenting for the honours BSc every year from 1951 to 1980. The number per year varied from 1 to 12, with a total of 132 during that period. During the same period the number taking Physics in the BSc General or minor Physics in the BSc Honours was around three or four times those doing honours Physics. This was due in part to a general increase in the total number of students in the College and probably also to the increased awareness of physics in the popular mind as an exciting field of study. This was the era when developments in electronics spurred revolutionary changes in communications and entertainment, the era which held the promise of nuclear power, and which ushered in the exploration of space. Two quite dissimilar events in 1957 caused a major increase in the number of students taking Physics: the launching of the Sputnik satellite by the USSR and the change of the Civil Engineering degree from three to four years. With over 70 students in the second year during the 1958–9 session, all available space, including the lecture theatre itself, was pressed into service for laboratory work. The change from three to four years for the honours BSc in Physics occurred in 1964, contributing also to the workload of the Department.

Around this time the number of students taking Physics through Irish justified having a first-year practical class through Irish and classes through Irish up to the BSc degree level. The fact that the first-year lectures through Irish were at the traditional time for long-established European universities of noon to 1.00 p.m. on Mondays, Wednesdays, and Fridays while the same lectures through English were on Tuesdays, Thursdays, and Saturdays from 1.00 to 2.00 p.m. may have been a factor with students who did not like a late lunch. In later years however, as the number of the local authority university scholarships increased and their value improved, the advantages of the scholarships through Irish, apart from the absence of a means test, were eroded. Consequently, numbers fell and courses through Irish were taken only in the first two years of Physics, and more recently, in the first year only.

The period 1950–80 also saw the revival of higher degrees by research in optical and microwave spectroscopy supervised by Declan Larkin and Frank Imbusch and in atmospheric and aerosol physics supervised by myself. In fact, in 1961 I was the recipient of the first PhD degree to be awarded in Physics in Galway. Despite the time and effort that went into the planning, building, and occupation of the new Department in the period 1965–74, the number of higher degrees awarded to students of the Department between 1954 and 1980 was 9 PhDs and 28 MScs. With the addition of the BSc in Applied Physics and Electronics, under the leadership of Professor Philip Walton, the corresponding figures for the period 1981 to 1995 were 8 PhDs, 24 MScs and 7 Diplomas in Electronics. Since 1991, the Department has had a considerable input into the Occupational Hygiene content of a Higher Diploma in Applied Science (Occupational Health and Hygiene) and the MSc in Occupational Health and Ergonomics. In the five years up to 1996, of the 56 students who have taken the MSc course, 19 have specialised in Occupational Hygiene while 78 have obtained the Higher Diploma.

With the appointment of Philip Walton as Professor of Applied Physics in 1978, the scope of the Physics teaching in the Department expanded. Courses leading to the degree of BSc in Applied Physics and Electronics were introduced into the third and fourth years of the programme. The new degree had the added novelty of the students doing a major project instead of set practical classes in their final year. It received some encouragement at the time from the Government's so-called 'Manpower programme' which was introduced to increase the number of graduates in technological fields to meet the growing demands of the country's industrial expansion programme. The first fruit of this programme was a group of seven graduates who received the BSc in Applied Physics and Electronics in 1981. In the period 1981 to 1995 the majority of a total of 207 honours Physics graduates have taken this degree and over half of these are working in industry in Ireland. The appointment of two lecturers in Applied Physics and Electronics, Dr Joseph Martin in 1980 and Dr Michael Redfern in 1981, saw the introduction of a number of new courses in electronics and the practical aspects of computing. These were taken by students for the Physics BSc degree as well as by students taking the BE degree in the newly created Department of Electronic Engineering.

Although the Department was offering two distinct honours degrees since 1980, its essential unity was always maintained by the rotation of the headship among the professors every three years and by all of the staff working on either programme, as required. Familiarity with the use of computers had become increasingly essential for graduates in almost all disciplines, and the use of personal computers in undergraduate laboratories and research projects was encouraged. The Department of Physics provided the first Local Area Network (LAN) in the College with an Aethernet around the Department. It also installed and operated an Econet LAN in the first-year laboratory to provide an introductory computing facility for all students of the Faculty of Science in 1984 and continued to do so until 1994. Mainly at the initiative of Dr Joe Martin, it also provided courses in Computing Studies which were availed of by Science students of various Departments and, since 1990, has been offering courses leading to an honours BSc degree in Physics and Computing.

In addition to teaching courses leading to degrees in Physics, service teaching, and research work, staff of the Department have been active over the years in contributing to the College's extramural and continuing education programmes. In the early years of the College, the professors contributed to the Barrington lectures at venues around the country or to the learned circles of the city with lectures at the Royal Galway Institution. In 1855 the *Sligo Chronicle* reported on a course of lectures being given in Sligo by Professor G. Johnstone Stoney of QCG on various branches of Science. One of the lectures on 'Heat as a Source of Power' illustrated the working of the steam engine with a beautiful sectional model of an engine brought from the Galway College.[16] In the 1960s and 1970s there were contributions to the Science component of the College's Diploma in Extramural Studies, which were held in various towns in the west of Ireland.

---

16   Ó hEocha, in Ó Cearbhaill (ed.), *Galway*, p. 171.

More recently, the emphasis has been on more specialised short courses for technological transfer or in-service training either in the Department or at the premises of clients. Among these were the Radiological Safety courses for users of radioactive isotopes, in-service courses for secondary school teachers, applications of lasers in industry, applied optics, measurement of air pollution, occupational hygiene, and aspects of health and safety at work. In addition, staff of the Department have organised national and international conferences and workshops on topics related to their research activities.

A summary of the teaching activities of the Department, its staff and students, 150 years after its official foundation, may be gathered from the entries in the UCG *Calendar* for 1995–6. The Department offered courses leading to four degrees with a large Physics component. These are the three-year BSc General degree, the BSc Honours degree in Experimental Physics, the BSc Honours degree in Applied Physics and Electronics, and the denominated BSc Honours degrees in Experimental Physics, in Applied Physics and Electronics, or in Physics and Computing. All students take four subjects in their first year, three in their second year, ten modules in their third year, and eight modules in their fourth year. In the denominated degree programmes all students choose their courses from a definite list of options, while in the undenominated or traditional degree programme their choice can be somewhat wider.

The Premises

The location and extent of the Department of Natural Philosophy has changed several times during the history of the College. The original architectural plans for the College allocated to it some 2,000 square feet (186m^2) of the ground floor of the Quadrangle building from the Archway to the north-east corner. The lecture theatre, originally called the Mechanical and Philosophical theatre was known to later generations of students as the Greek Hall. It was the scene of many historic meetings and debates until its demise about 1980 when it was converted into a board room. It now houses the computer centre and data management system for the administration of the College. Adjacent to the theatre, in the area currently occupied by the Physiology lecture room (A141), there was a mechanical apparatus room, another room for apparatus and the professor's room. The latter had an en suite toilet, a convenience which few professors enjoy in these modern times! The Department of Chemistry occupied a similar area on the other side of the Archway and had, from the start, a laboratory with bench space for eight students.

We have already noted that the trend away from practical demonstrations in lectures towards students doing a set of experiments themselves took a step forward in 1880 with the arrival of Larmor from the Cavendish Laboratory in Cambridge to the chair of Natural Philosophy in Galway. With his replacement in 1885 by Anderson, who had also spent some years in Cambridge, the search for space for laboratories was intensified. After repeated letters to the Board of Works, which was charged with the material care of the College buildings, the Department moved to occupy some 2,500 square feet (238m^2) on the ground floor of the south side of the quadrangle building, with its original premises going to Classical Languages. Some of the Literary lecture rooms on the south side of the quadrangle were converted into a Physics lecture room, a museum, and a laboratory. This latter room remained virtually unchanged, from what it had been early in the twentieth century, until about 1960. It corresponds to what is today the new board room (A 114) and the Vice-President's office (A 116). In the President's *Report* for the session 1894–5 we read that 'the introduction of electric power into the Physical Laboratories, and the extension of these laboratories by the Board of Works, are important additions to the efficiency of a growing department'.[17] A workshop and other laboratories occupied the space which is currently the Staff Club premises (A108 and A109).

As the number of students taking Chemistry increased in the twentieth century, the lack of laboratory space became critical. About the time of the foundation of the National University, the government supplemented this accommodation by handing over to the College a room in the Galway Model School (on the Newcastle Road, adjacent to the hospital) where a laboratory for the teaching of first year students was set up.[18] In 1932 the government granted the College a long-term lease of the building and grounds of the Model School. Lecture rooms, a library, and laboratories for research and advanced classes were gradually provided and the whole Department moved out of the quadrangle. In 1937 the Department of Physics took over the area vacated by Chemistry, which included a lecture hall that became known as the Physics theatre and is now occupied by Applied Geophysics and an office (A106 and A103).

In 1960, when Professor Máirtín Ó Tnúthail became President, the western third of the first year Physics laboratory was partitioned off to provide a more spacious office for the President, and the remainder of the laboratory was used to accommodate the larger second-year Physics classes. The first-year Physics Practicals moved out to the top floor of the old Royal Yacht Club on the banks of the Eglinton canal (currently Block Q). These premises had been vacated by the Department of Pathology which had moved to new laboratories in the grounds of the Regional Hospital.

To accommodate the growing research activities of the Department, a small World War II coastal observation post on Mace Head, west of Carna, was hired and renovated in 1958 for studies on the marine atmosphere, and in 1965 Block R was built behind the Men's Club and boat house as research laboratories and staff offices. This building is currently used by Engineering Hydrology. A Philips nitrogen liquefier and a Collins helium liquefier were acquired in 1968 and 1970 respectively, with financial help from the Irish Hospitals Sweepstakes, and installed in the ground floor of Block Q.

When the Department of Experimental Medicine moved out of rooms at the centre of the north side of the quadrangle in 1969 to block G1, one of the rooms (A 136B, currently part of the Accounts Office) was used as a Physics laboratory

---

17 *Report* of the President, 1894–5, p. 6.
18 UCG *Calendar*, 1939–40, p. 46.

for third-year experiments. This dispersal of the Department around five sites on campus ended in 1973 when the Department moved into some 4,600m² of purpose built space in the new Science Building.

The layout of the new Department was the result of extensive discussions between the architectural team (Scott Tallon Walker Architects) and the staff of the Department led by Professor Ó Brolcháin. The building, in line with the general architectural plan, consists of eleven square two-storey 'cells', or modules, each 14m x 14m with a pre-stressed concrete frame and largely steel-framed tinted glass walls. The 'public' space is situated on the upper floor to cater for the larger numbers of undergraduate students. The 'private' space on the ground floor is reserved more for postgraduate research laboratories, staff offices, and workshops. An 88–seat tiered lecture theatre opening off the main concourse area was named the Larmor Theatre in memory of the fourth professor of Natural Philosophy. A large laboratory for first-year students, comprising of two rooms each catering for forty students, is known as the Johnstone Stoney Laboratory in memory of the second professor. The rest of the upper floor is devoted to laboratories for second and third-year students, two lecture rooms, administrative offices for the head of the Department, and a research suite for the Atmospheric Physics group.

When the new Department was planned in the late 1960s, provisions were made for four research suites and an academic staff of twelve. The research groups were for optical spectroscopy, low temperature Physics, atmospheric Physics, and the future Applied Physics option. The Department provided space for two College facilities, a new suite of X-ray research apparatus, and the existing cryogenics facility with nitrogen and helium liquifying plants. The promised increase in staff did not come at the rate that was promised and the Department was able to offer suitable space for the expanding computer services within the College for nearly twenty years. With the gradual growth in the numbers of staff, expanding research activities, and increasing numbers of honours students in the Experimental, Applied, and Computing options the Department has reached its envisaged size and space is now at a premium.

Mention should also be made of the workshops in the Department. There was always a need for workshop facilities in the Department for the construction and repair of apparatus for teaching and research. Prior to 1973 there was a mechanical workshop in the central porch in the south side of the Quadrangle building (A115) which is now part of the staff club. In the current Department, there is a special electronics workshop and a suite of workshops for wood and metal working, located along the service road under the concourse. There are also stores for raw materials, for spare parts, and for antique apparatus of historical interest or pedagogical use.

Equipment and Apparatus

Natural Philosophy involves the study of the physical universe and the formulation of theories and models to describe and explain the observations made and to elucidate the laws of nature. This requires special apparatus to make accurate measurements, to demonstrate phenomena, to arouse interest, and to illustrate lectures. The Galway College from its inception strove to provide such facilities for its students. The Department of Physics is fortunate that much of what it acquired over the years survives in various degrees of repair and the nature of the subject means that the unchanging principles and laws of Physics can still be demonstrated by apparatus purchased almost 150 years ago.

An idea of the way in which the financial resources of the College were dispensed at the beginning may be gained from the following excerpt from the *Report* of the President for 1850:

> A sum of £3,000 has been allocated to each College, to provide it with Libraries, Specimens, Apparatus for illustrating lectures, etc. Of this sum, £1,500 has been expended in the purchase of books. We have endeavoured as far as the limited sum permitted, to provide the Library with those works most essentially necessary in the different branches of learning. Many departments, however, are still most inadequately provided.
>
> The remaining sum has been distributed in the purchase of apparatus and instruments for illustrating the lectures of the Professors, and Specimens for the Museum. It is enough to enumerate the different branches of science to which this sum has been applied to show how very inadequate it is to the end proposed. These branches are as follows:- Mechanics, Optics, Hydrostatics, Acoustics, Astronomical and Optical Instruments, Electricity, Magnetism and Electro-Magnetism, Chemistry, Heat and Meteorology, Natural History, Mineralogy and Geology, Agriculture, Engineering, etc.[19]

It may be noted that the Department of Natural Philosophy as such is not included in this list of subjects but that eight of the seventeen headings given relate to this Department. Whether this creative approach was to increase the benefits coming to the Department or to impress some Treasury official is not clear at this remove.

A few years later, in the *Report* of the President for the session 1859–60, the Acting Professor of Natural Philosophy, Edward Townsend, wrote that 'from the very large amount of apparatus added this year to the departments of Heat, Electricity, Magnetism and Light, I have not the least hesitation in saying that the school is now in a very high order of efficiency'.[20] Perhaps it was this growth in the amount of demonstration apparatus in the department that prompted the professor, A.H. Curtis, to compile a book, in 1861, in which he recorded the apparatus and books held in the department and the syllabus of the courses given. Many of the items listed were illustrated by sticking in diagrams cut from contemporary catalogues and occasionally by comments on the care of the apparatus and how to make it work effectively. All of this is very useful in identifying the many items that survive to this day and some of which are still used to teach the principles of physics. This book is also a mine of interesting information, as it was

19 *Report* of the President, 1850, p. 57.
20 *Report* of the President, 1860, p. 9.

used to record the date of purchase, price, and supplier of many other instruments acquired in the nineteenth century. Another source of information on the department's holdings of physical apparatus, after about fifty years of existence, is a catalogue compiled and printed in 1902. This shows that the College was keeping up to date with recent developments in Physics as it lists, for instance, five Röntgen ray tubes of one pattern and three of another, a Marconi's coherer on a stand, and a Braun's cathodic ray tube. All of these were invented just a few years previously.

In its purchase of apparatus, the Department has always striven to meet the requirements of the day and to strike a balance between items to illustrate lectures, equipment for training students in experimental techniques in laboratories, and items for advanced training and research. In the President's *Report* for the session 1855–6 we read:

> The Museum of Physical Apparatus belonging in this College has been formed solely with the view to its educational uses. Accordingly, the instruments selected have been such as will, in the opinion of the Professor, most fully illustrate the lectures given on the mechanics of solids and fluids, on astronomy, and on the properties and effects of heat, light, and electricity.
>
> The collection embraces a beautiful series of optical apparatus, by Dubosq of Paris; a serviceable collection of electrical apparatus; a fine air pump, with its usual accessories; some good educational models; most of the ordinary mechanical and hydrostatical apparatus; and some minor instruments.
>
> The collection owes many of its most useful parts to the recent liberality of the Legislature; and so efficient an auxiliary has it become to the teaching of the Professor, as to have enabled him to give extensive courses of instruction in physical research to such of the more diligent students as wished to attain proficiency in that branch of knowledge.[21]

It has already been noted that Professor Larmor told the Queen's Colleges (Ireland) Commission in 1884 that his honours course in Experimental Physics for third-year students 'includes the use of physical instruments, and the making and working out of exact physical measurements by the students'. As the latter was not a requirement of the RUI examinations not all students were 'willing to devote to it the large amount of time necessary for a *complete* course'.[22]

Professor Anderson developed the first laboratories for Physics and introduced formal practical classes in the 1890s. The support given to these developments by the College may be judged from the entries in the accounts of the College for the year ending 31 March 1895. Of a total of £397 8s. 6d. expended on 'Apparatus, Diagrams, Materials for Laboratory, &c' for Chemistry, Physics, Engineering and the Medical Faculty, £115 7s. 10d. or about 30 per cent was spent on the 'Physical Cabinet'. In the same year from a total grant to the Library of £286 0s. 10d. almost a quarter (in fact £68 15s. 8d.) was devoted to the Mathematical and Physical Sciences.

---

21 *Report* of the President, 1856, p. 11.
22 *Queen's Colleges (Ireland) Commission Report* (Dublin, 1885), p. 484.

Today, one hundred years later, when the total budget for the activities of the College has increased from £10,000 to over £40,000,000 per annum, the financial resources for the Department have decreased drastically in percentage terms. The proliferation and increasing specialisation of scientific journals in the last fifty years has meant that the grant to the Library is no longer adequate to meet the needs of a growing Department. It is regrettable that journals such as the *Philosophical Magazine*, of which the College holds a complete run from its inception in 1798, had to be terminated in 1983. Advances in modern telecommunications, photocopying, electronic mail, and computerised data storage have gone some way towards alleviating this problem and the Department is making good use of such facilities as well as the inter-library loan schemes. The costs of providing apparatus for teaching and research have escalated at a rate well above that of inflation, and careful husbandry of capital and recurrent grants is necessary to provide adequate facilities for students. The growing trend towards individual project work in undergraduate training is putting an extra strain on resources. Much of the research work of the Department is now dependent on outside sources for support, and participation in various national and international collaborative research projects has added new dimensions to the activities of its staff and students.

Research

Research and the advancement of knowledge is an integral part of university activity, along with the dissemination of this knowledge through teaching and publications. This has always been the practice in the Department of Physics in Galway. The work of the first professors, often theoretical studies, has already been mentioned at the beginning of this chapter. During his tenure of the chair in Galway, Larmor published eleven papers including the first of an important series on electromagnetism entitled 'Electromagnetic Induction in Conducting Sheets and Solid Bodies',[23] and two of a series on the application of the Principle of Least Action as the fundamental formulation of dynamics and Physics. The latter was a subject of which he never tired; it was 'a confession of his scientific faith'.[24]

His successor, Anderson, continued this interest in electromagnetic induction and developed the 'Anderson Bridge', a widely-accepted method of measuring coefficients of self induction. As already noted, Anderson was responsible for the development of Physics laboratories and practical Physics classes in the 1890s. He also had Senior Scholars employed as demonstrators, to assist him with the practical classes, especially after he had assumed the additional duties of President of the College in 1899. Many of these assistants went on to undertake experimental research projects which led to joint publications.

Anderson had wide research interests, both theoretical and applied, and published twenty-nine papers, mainly in the *Philosophical Magazine*, up to 1923,

---

23 *Philosophical Magazine*, January 1884, pp. 1–24.
24 D'Arcy W. Thompson jun. cited by Ó hEocha, in Ó Cearbhaill (ed.), *Galway*, p. 174.

when presumably his Presidential duties (ensuring the survival and growth of the College) took precedence over his scientific interests. Some of his earlier papers were in the area of optics and the focometry of lens systems and he had a continuing interest in the working of quadrant electrometers and their use in the study of contact potential difference. His prowess as a teacher was shown by his publication of simpler methods of deducing several theoretical formulae.

He also participated in contemporary debates in science and took a special interest in Einstein's General Theory of Relativity which was published in 1916 as an attempt to link or unify electromagnetic and gravitational phenomena. He submitted a paper 'On the Advancement of the Perihelion of a Planet (Mercury) and the Path of a Ray of Light in the Gravitational Field of the Sun', to the *Philosophical Magazine* on 13 February 1920.[25] In it, after deriving the necessary formulae, he wrote as follows:

> We may remark, though perhaps the assumption is very violent, that if the mass of the sun were concentrated in a sphere of diameter of 1.47 kilometres, the index of refraction near it would become infinitely great, and we should have a very powerful condensing lens, too powerful indeed, for the light emitted by the sun itself would have no velocity at its surface. Thus if, in accordance with the suggestion of Helmholtz, the body of the sun should go on contracting, there will come a time when it will be shrouded in darkness, not because it has no light to emit, but because its gravitational field will become impermeable to light.

This seems to be the first published suggestion of the possibility of 'black holes' which is correct in the relativistic sense. Although this paper is cited in a historical review entitled 'Dark Stars' which appeared in the book *Three Hundred Years of Gravitation*,[26] Anderson's bold and prescient description of Einsteinian black holes deserves wider recognition. It is interesting to note that the concept of gravitational 'black holes', which has so excited many of the scientific community and the general public in recent years, had its origin in Galway some seventy-five years ago and may become Anderson's main claim to fame.

At present Anderson is remembered mainly for his contributions to practical physics. A widely-used textbook, *Practical Physics* by Worsnop and Flint, in its ninth edition,[27] included four entries under Anderson for the measurement of 'Surface Tension and Angles of Contact',[28] 'Viscosity of Air',[29] 'Coefficients of Induction',[30] and 'On the Theory of the Quadrant Electrometer'.[31]

---

25 *Philosophical Magazine*, series vi, 39 (1920), pp. 626–8.
26 S. Hawking and W. Israel (eds), *Three Hundred Years of Gravitation* (Cambridge, 1987), p. 204.
27 B.L. Worsnop and H.T. Flint, *Practical Physics*, 9th ed. (London, 1957), pp. 129, 161, 617, and 649.
28 A. Anderson and J.E. Bowen, *Philosophical Magazine*, series vi, 31 (1916), pp. 143–8, 285–9.
29 Anderson, ibid., series vi, 42 (1921), pp. 1022–3.
30 Ibid., series v, 31 (1891), pp. 329–37.
31 Ibid., series vi, 23 (1912), pp. 380–5.

An interesting example of Applied Physics research and the provision by the College of a service to the people of Galway was the use of the newly-discovered X-Rays for medical diagnostic purposes. In November 1895, in Göttingen, the discovery by Professor W.C. Röntgen of a mysterious or X-type of radiation, which could 'look through' the human body and reveal the skeleton, quickly caught the imagination of the general public and the popular press when it was published in December 1895. The use of X-rays soon became widespread as the necessary apparatus – an evacuated discharge tube, a high voltage induction coil and a fluorescent screen or photographic plate – were readily available in most Physics Departments. Galway was no exception, and Anderson produced X-ray photographs experimentally in 1896. By 1898, one of his research assistants, John Henry MA, BE, was providing an X-ray service to doctors in the Galway area. In an interesting early example of industry-university collaborative research, the Eastman-Kodak Company provided a grant and scholarship for research on X-ray photography around 1898–1900. In 1900 this service was provided by William Hare, the instrument technician in the Department, who was trained by Anderson. He took over 50 radiographs between 1900 and 1902.

One of these, in December 1902, led to what is believed to be the first court action claiming damages for the misuse of Röntgen rays or ionizing radiations in these islands. The case, which was heard in Dublin in February 1904, attracted considerable public and scientific attention. Lord Kelvin and Sir Oliver Lodge were among the scientific experts and observers who came from Britain. The case involved a seven-year old boy who was sent to QCG for an X-ray of a knee in which part of a steel needle was thought to have lodged. Repeated exposures using photographic plates and fluorescent screens did not show the needle present. However, the extent of the exposures damaged some of the flesh of the knee and led to the development of a painful sore and later scar tissue. After hearing evidence for several days, the jury found that the doctors had not been negligent in the use of X-rays and dismissed the claim. After the case the service in QCG was discontinued and the apparatus transferred to the County Infirmary. Hare continued to operate it, on the basis of a fee of 5 shillings per item, until the hospital closed in 1924.[32]

John E. Bowen MA was an assistant in Natural Philosophy from 1908 until 1921 when he obtained his MB degree and left to pursue a career in medicine. When he and the technician, Hare, helped Professor Anderson demonstrate the clinical applications of X-rays the standard student complaint was that all they could see was 'bone and hair'! He was involved in the development of the Anderson and Bowen method, already mentioned, for measuring the surface tension of a liquid.[33]

When J.J. McHenry came to Galway in 1922, he used the quadrant electrometers to continue an existing line of research into the properties of contact potentials

---

32 A more detailed account of the case is given by Professor J.P. Murray in his book *Galway: A Medico–Social History* (Galway, 1994), pp. 68–9. A report of the trial appeared in the *Freeman's Journal*, 5–12 February 1904.
33 *Philosophical Magazine*, series vi, 31 (1916), pp. 143–8, 285–9.

and the variation of the electromotive force with the operating temperature. The results of this work were published in two papers, 'On the Temperature Coefficient of Contact Electromotive Force',[34] and 'On the Variation with Temperature of Contact Electromotive Forces'.[35] The NUI awarded him a DSc degree in 1931. Another paper, 'On the Effective Capacity of a Quadrant Electrometer',[36] which also extended the work of Anderson, was written before he left Galway to take up the post of Professor of Physics in University College Cork in 1932.

The lack of postgraduate students in Physics and of modern equipment and resources, severely curtailed research in UCG in the 1930s and 1940s. The advent of D.M. Larkin in 1947 and the purchase in 1951 of a Hilger constant deviation prism spectrometer with Fabry-Perot interferometers saw the beginning of a new line of research in optical spectrometry. The first MSc by research in Physics in UCG for many years was awarded to Br J.F. Casey for a thesis entitled 'The High Frequency Oscillator in the Excitation of Spectra and in the Investigation of Hyperfine Structure'. This was followed in 1958 by G.F. Imbusch with a thesis entitled 'An Attempt to Produce a Mercury Atomic Beam Light Source Suitable for Spectroscopic Use: Excitation and hfs Analysis of Mercury Using a hf Oscillator'.

This line of research then diversified into new areas. In 1958 Larkin went to Duke University, North Carolina, USA where he worked under Professor Walter Gordy for a PhD degree in microwave physics and spectroscopy. After his return in the 1960s he set up a successful research group on microwave spectroscopy in the newly-built laboratory in Block R. With the acquisition of the nitrogen and helium liquefiers and the purchase of new research equipment on moving into the new Department in 1973, he developed research in cryogenics and very low temperature physics especially the applications of SQUID (Superconducting Quantum Interference Device) technology to the measurement of weak magnetic fields, such as those produced by a beating heart.

In 1959 G.F. Imbusch went to the USA and, as already mentioned, obtained a PhD from Stanford University in California and spent some time at the Bell Telephones' Central Research Laboratories at Murray Hill, New Jersey. On his return to Galway in 1967, he set up a research programme on optical spectroscopy and energy transfer processes in solid state insulating materials doped with rare earth and transition metal ions. Much of this work required investigations to be done in liquid helium at temperatures close to absolute zero.

In setting up the necessary facilities he was greatly assisted by the return of Jim Larkin, a fellow Limerick man, who graduated in 1960 and completed an MSc in microwave spectroscopy in 1962. He then travelled to many parts of the world on seismic exploration work for the Shell Oil Company before returning to the College in 1969 as a lecturer. He brought a wealth of practical mechanical skill and experience to the Department which was invaluable for installing and operating the liquid helium plant, first in the ground floor of Block Q and later for its

---

34 Ibid., series vii, 4 (1927), pp. 857–63.
35 Ibid., series vii, 8 (1929), pp. 474–91.
36 Ibid., series vii, 13 (1932), pp. 650–64.

transfer to the cryogenic facility in the new Department building in 1973. He also contributed significantly to the development of electronic data acquisition systems for the spectrometers and obtained his PhD degree in 1973 for a thesis on 'Relaxation Effects in Optical Spectra of Solids'.

In 1978 Imbusch spent a sabbatical period in the University of Wisconsin at Madison. His contacts with prestigious research establishments led to fruitful collaboration and many Galway graduates followed similar career paths. Several have established successful research groups at other universities in Ireland and contribute to the Optronics Ireland organisation. Here in Galway, T.J. Glynn and G.P. Morgan have continued the research in solid state optical spectroscopy. New techniques of fluorescence line narrowing and Raman scattering were introduced, laboratories were expanded, and work concentrated on the commercially-important semiconductor materials. From 1989 onwards Tom Glynn was instrumental, with support from Forbairt,[37] in establishing and developing a National Centre for Laser Applications to provide research, training, and technology transfer services to Irish industry. By the end of 1995 this Centre was supporting four research personnel. Gerard Morgan is currently collaborating with the Department of Biochemistry on the biological applications of optics and lasers. Since 1954 eleven PhD students and thirty-six MSc students have graduated through the spectroscopy, cryogenic, and laser groups.

Research on aspects of atmospheric physics and meteorology has a long history in Galway. Mention has already been made of the weather records initiated in 1861 by Professor Curtis and his paper in 1866 'On the Freezing of Water at Temperatures Lower than 32° F'.[38] In 1912 Professor Anderson and his postgraduate student H.N. Morrison published 'On Electric Currents in Air at Atmospheric Pressure, with Remarks on Induced Contact Electromotive Forces'.[39] Both J.J. McHenry and Ó Brolcháin did postgraduate research on ions in the atmosphere before coming to Galway. In more recent times, in 1944, one notes that J.P. Deignan obtained an honours BSc in Physics in Galway and went on to UCD to work under P.J. Nolan for an MSc with a thesis on 'Observations on Atmospheric Condensation Nuclei in Stored Air'.[40] In Galway D.G. McLaughlin obtained an MSc in 1954 for a thesis on 'Atmospheric Electrical Conductivity and Ionic Mobility'.

In January 1956, the Revd T.P.G. McGreevy and I were appointed as assistants in Physics. Fr McGreevy, who was from Emyvale in Co. Monaghan in the Clogher diocese, resigned in 1958 to teach in Enniskillen and in 1960 he was appointed Professor of Physics in St Patrick's College, Maynooth. He continued his studies of aerosol particle counters and was awarded a PhD degree from UCG in 1965 for a thesis entitled 'Methods of Measuring the Time Variation of the Size Distribution of Stored Condensation Nuclei'.

A native of Kildare, I attended University College Dublin and obtained my

---

37 Forbairt, now Enterprise Ireland, was the national development agency responsible for indigenous industry.
38 *Philosophical Magazine*, series v, 32 (1866), pp. 422–4.
39 Ibid., series vi, 23 (1912), pp. 750–2.
40 P.J. Nolan and J.P. Deignan, *Proceedings of the Royal Irish Academy*, 51A (1948), pp. 239–49.

honours BSc in Physics there in 1952. I did my MSc research work, also in UCD, under Professor P.J. Nolan on 'The Size and Mobility of Ions Produced by Bubbling'. I then spent two years as a research assistant with Professor L.W. Pollak in the School of Cosmic Physics of the Dublin Institute for Advanced Studies, working mainly on the development of the Nolan-Pollak photo-electric condensation nucleus counters. On moving to Galway, I obtained two nucleus counters from Professor Pollak and initiated a research programme on the ionization equilibrium between aerosol particles and small ions in the atmosphere. The conditions over the ocean are of special interest so I decided to use the unique advantages of Galway's location on the Atlantic coast of Europe to undertake such investigations.

In the summer of 1957 I cycled around the coast of Connemara looking for a site for a research station that would receive air from the Atlantic ocean which had not crossed over local sources of contamination such as roads or houses. An excellent site was located at Mace Head on the Ard peninsula west of Carna looking out at the uninhabited MacDara's Island and across the mouth of Bertraughboy Bay towards Roundstone to the northwest. Winds from the sector 180°N to 300°N reach the site without passing over any local sources of man-made pollution. A disused World War II coastal lookout post was leased and renovated, electricity was installed, and measurements of ionisation equilibrium in maritime air began there in 1958. This work was strengthened and expanded when I was awarded the first research contract between University College Galway and an Office of the US Forces in Europe. Research began on the origin of very small particles or condensation nuclei in the atmosphere as a result of photochemical reactions of trace gases from natural sources. This led to the invitation to Fr McGreevy and myself to spend the summers of 1960 and 1961 in collaborative research with Professor Verzar of Basle at the Klima-physiologisches Forschung Station at St Moritz in Switzerland.

This international collaboration has continued to be a feature of the research at the Mace Head and research groups from three continents, and over fifty universities and institutions abroad, have come to make measurements there. In the 1960s the original station was used by groups from University College Dublin and the University of Mainz. Its use by UCG became intermittent due to the scarcity of funding and the switch of research to laboratory experiments and to man-made pollution. For the latter the University collaborated with Galway Corporation and the newly appointed Public Analyst, Dr P.P. O'Donovan, to measure smoke and SO_2 at sites in Galway city, at Mace Head, and at a remote site in Cloosh Forest above Oughterard. This work was used in a joint research project with the Department of Botany to look at lichens as an indicator of air pollution in Galway city. An automated Nolan-Pollak condensation nucleus counter was constructed and used to show that the air pollution in Galway was strongly linked with the traffic.

Postgraduate students who contributed to this work included W.P.F. Sharkey, V.P. Flanagan, A.F. Ó Rodaighe, S.G. Jennings, J.J. O'Dea, and J.G. McCurtin. Áodhagán Ó Rodaighe completed an MSc on 'The Production of Condensation Nuclei by Heated Wires and by Electromagnetic Radiation' in 1963 and went on to gain a PhD from Edinburgh University with a thesis entitled 'The Formation of Condensation Nuclei in City Air by Ultra-violet Radiation of Wavelength > 290 nm'. During a spell as a post-doctoral research assistant to Professor Lou Grant at the University of Colorado in Fort Collins, he developed an interest in ice nucleation in the atmosphere. On his return to Galway, as a lecturer in Physics in 1969, he developed a research group on sources of ice nuclei which in later times has extended its research to study the properties of noctilucent clouds. Besides his administrative work as the Dean of the Faculty of Science (1986–92) and as a member of the Governing Body of the College, he has taught an undergraduate course in Meteorology and developed a meteorological satellite facility in the Martin Ryan Institute of Marine Science. He is currently collaborating in an international project on the biogeochemical cycle of methane in the global atmosphere.

Gerard Jennings completed his MSc thesis on 'Studies in Electrically Charged Aerosols' in 1967 and then studied in the University of Manchester Institute for Science and Technology (UMIST) where he received a PhD for research on 'The Interaction of Falling Water Drops' in 1971. He spent three years in the Atmospheric Physics group in the University of Durham before going to the USA in 1976, where he carried out post-doctoral research at the Atmospheric Sciences Laboratory at White Sands, New Mexico, on the interaction of electromagnetic radiation with aerosol particles. In 1980 on his return to Galway, as a lecturer in Physics, he continued these studies and has expanded them to include the volatility of aerosol particles and the role of black carbon in the global radiation balance. He was the principal investigator and co-ordinator of a European Union funded project involving atmospheric research at Atlantic coastal stations similar to Mace Head in Portugal, France, Scotland, Norway, and Sweden. He is currently involved in several international projects connected with global climate change and air-sea exchange studies in which the Mace Head station plays an important part.

During the period 1954–95 some six PhD and eighteen MSc degrees have been awarded to students working in the atmospheric physics and aerosol fields. Two important international conferences were also organised by staff of the Department. In September 1977 the Ninth International Conference on Atmospheric Aerosols, Condensation, and Ice Nuclei was held in the College. It was the ninth in a series of conferences begun in Dublin in 1955 and was attended by one hundred-and-forty-two scientists from twenty-two countries. The proceedings were published by Galway University Press.[41] In June 1989, an International Conference on Aerosols and Background Pollution took place in the College under the auspices of the College and the European Association for the Science of Air Pollution. About one hundred scientists from seventeen countries around the world participated. The proceedings, with guest editors T.C. O'Connor and S.G. Jennings, were published in the journal *Atmospheric Environment*.[42]

---

41 A.F. Roddy and T.C. O'Connor (eds), *Atmospheric Aerosols and Nuclei* (Galway, 1981).
42 *Atmospheric Environment*, 25A (1991), pp. 533–824.

I was asked to lead a group in the Department investigating another aspect of atmospheric physics, renewable energy sources. In 1973 the sharp rise in the price of oil led to an 'energy crisis' in the western world and stimulated research into alternative sources of energy. Again making use of the location of Galway on the Atlantic coast of Europe, where nature provides abundant sources of renewable energy in the form of winds, waves, and mild moist air, research was begun to quantify the resources and to develop wind energy conversion systems. In collaboration with commercial interests, the ESB, and the University of Ulster at Coleraine, a Renewable Energy Research Group was set up in UCG in 1974. A vertical axis Darrieus wind mill was constructed to harness the kinetic energy of the wind and a series of air-to-water heat pumps were developed to extract thermal energy from the atmosphere for domestic space and water heating. The efforts of the Physics Department were helped by John Kenny, a visiting professor of Physics from Bradley University, Peoria, Illinois and a number of mechanical engineers, M.A. Hynes, M.F. Kyne, and J.G. McGovern.

A national seminar on some aspect of renewable energy was organised, in collaboration with the Solar Energy Society of Ireland, each year from 1976 to 1991. These seminars, together with the research in the Department and in other Departments in the College, helped to establish UCG as an important centre for renewable energy research in Ireland.

Another development, which originated in the atmospheric physics and aerosol research interests in the Department, was the study of air quality in the workplace and other aspects of occupational hygiene. This story began back in 1963 when I, already appointed to a statutory lectureship in Physics in 1962, was awarded a Cultural Exchange (Fulbright) scholarship to study for a year in the United States. The College at that time had not established a regular sabbatical leave scheme so in order to get leave of absence from a Department that was pressing for an increase in staff, it was agreed that I would resign from my lectureship and take the chance of reapplying for appointment to it again a year later. This was, in fact, what happened. During my time in the USA, I held a post-doctoral research post under Professor Leslie Silverman in the Department of Industrial Hygiene in the Harvard University School of Public Health in Boston, MA. One of the doctoral students in that department in 1963–4 was Parker C. Reist. In 1984 Reist, by then a Professor of Industrial Hygiene and Air Engineering at the University of North Carolina (UNC) at Chapel Hill, was awarded a Fulbright Scholarship to study in Europe. He chose to spend the year 1984–5 in the Department of Physics in UCG where he contributed to several short courses and seminars on various aspects of occupational hygiene. He and his family fell in love with Ireland in general and Galway in particular and have managed to return for a spell almost every summer since then. This has led to an informal but very real collaboration between UCG and UNC and the holding of a series of Summer Institute courses on topics in occupational hygiene such as the design of ventilating systems, clean room technology, and air quality measurements.

These developments were very timely as the arrival in Ireland of industries using clean room technologies, such as microelectronics and health care, brought a demand for such courses. Around this time, the Barrington Report on Safety,

Health and Welfare at Work and various items of European legislation had raised the awareness of the need for expertise in occupational hygiene. With the passage of the comprehensive Safety, Health and Welfare at Work Act in 1989 and the establishment of the new National Authority for Occupational Health and Safety (HSA) there was a clear need for more professionals in this field. This led to the establishment by the College in 1992 of full-time postgraduate courses leading to an MSc in Occupational Health and Ergonomics and a Higher Diploma in Applied Science (Occupational Health and Hygiene). The Department of Physics contributes the Occupational Hygiene component of these courses and also collaborates with the National Irish Safety Organisation (NISO) in running seminars and their Foundation Course in Occupational Health and Safety at various centres in the west of Ireland.

Returning briefly to the history of the Atmospheric Research Station on Mace Head we may note that the College in 1975 purchased a small cottage, that lay uninhabited and derelict on a strip of land between the road and the coast on the side of Mace Head at Leath-Mhás or Half Mace. It was not until 1985 that resources were available to refurbish the cottage as a two-room laboratory and install water and a sewage system. In 1986 Professor Bob Duce of the University of Rhode Island and then President of the International Commission on Atmospheric Chemistry and Global Pollution, came to Ireland seeking a coastal site for the Atmosphere-Ocean Chemical Experiment (AEROCE), a large study of the biogeochemical cycles in the North Atlantic. He was immediately impressed by the potential of the Mace Head site and the logistical support that the UCG could supply. At the same time the recently recognised 'hole' in the ozone layer over the Antarctic stimulated the Global Atmospheric Gases Experiment (GAGE) to seek a site in Ireland to replace that operated for a while by J.E. Lovelock in Adrigole on Bantry Bay for the measurement of the concentrations of certain chlorofluorocarbons (CFC) gases in the atmosphere away from local sources of pollution. With the collaboration of Dr Peter G. Simmonds of the University of Bristol, a gas chromatograph was installed in the cottage on Mace Head in December 1986 and regular measurements have continued since January 1987. It is of interest to note that these results from Mace Head were being cited at the Meeting of the International Geosphere Biosphere Programme on Global Change (IGBP) in Beijing in 1995 as evidence of the success of the Montreal Convention on the banning of some CFCs in reducing their loading in the world's atmosphere.[43]

A change in the European Union's laws on the exemption from external import duty and VAT on scientific equipment imported for collaborative research was necessary before the AEROCE programme could bring their equipment to Mace Head.[44] With financial help from the US National Science Foundation (NSF)

---

43 P.G. Simmonds, R.G. Derwent, A. McCulloch, S. O'Doherty, and A. Gaudry, 'Long-term Trends in Concentrations of Halocarbons and Radiatively Active Trace Gases in Atlantic and European Air Masses Monitored at Mace Head, Ireland from 1987–1994', *Atmospheric Environment*, 30 (1996), pp. 4041–63.

44 Council regulation (EEC) No. 4235/88 of 21 December 1988 amending Regulation (EEC) No. 918/83 setting up a Community system of reliefs from duty, *Official Journal of the European Communities* no. L 373/1–2, 31 December 1988.

through AEROCE and from the Max Planck Institute for Atmospheric Chemistry in Mainz a road was built to the shore at Mace Head and a laboratory with about 65m² of floor space and a 20m walk-up sampling tower was erected near the shore in 1989. A grant of £60,000 from the European Regional Development Fund (ERDF) through the Government's Office for Science and Technology enabled the building of a 40m² extension to the Cottage and a second laboratory of about 90m² near the shore in 1990. The Electricity Supply Board contributed the free installation of an enhanced three-phase supply to the installations. These facilities have been used by many groups in Europe and America, and by the CSIRO in Australia, and the station has hosted two international workshops. The latest, on 'mercury in the atmosphere', was held in September 1995. Mace Head is now a part of many global and regional observing networks and is recognised as one of the most important stations for atmospheric science in the northern hemisphere. In 1993 it was accepted by the World Meteorological Organisation as one of the three baseline stations in Europe in its Global Atmospheric Watch (GAW) programme.

The applications of Physics to medicine has long been of interest to personnel of the Department. Besides the earlier work on providing an X-ray service in Galway there was some research undertaken by graduates on the use of ionising radiation in nuclear medicine units outside Galway. In 1972 James F. Malone was awarded a PhD for a thesis on 'The Kinetics of Recovery of Cellular Proliferation after Irradiation' and in 1978 Laurence P. Clarke was also awarded a PhD for a thesis on 'Measurement of Organ Function in Vivo by External Detection of Collimated Gamma Rays'.

The appointment of Philip W. Walton to the newly-created chair of Applied Physics in 1978 led to the development of several new lines of research in the Department. Because of his research background in Medical Physics there has been considerable emphasis on developing instrumentation for bio-medical research. A Sensor Applications and Research Unit (SARU) was established in 1992 as part of UCG's Manufacturing Research Centre. This is a contact centre for industrial projects related to sensors and also to broader areas. Work that has been undertaken includes research on piezoelectric-based sensors, an inexpensive microtitre plate reader for immunoassays, a quantitative method for diagnostic agglutination assays and a quantitative method for diagnostic strip tests. Recently the major effort is to devise a digital radiographic sensor for use in mammography. Group members have also worked with industry on the modelling of the radiation dose distributions for a gamma ray sterilisation plant, on the provision of courses and advice on ionising radiation and on the provision of advice on the safety of non-ionising radiation (for example, from cellular phone systems and Loran C navigational masts).

Another research field has been developed by Michael Redfern, in which aspects of imaging (ranging from the very pure to the very applied) have progressed in conjunction with one another. The different projects – pure and applied – share many techniques and use similar equipment so that they assist each other. The very pure aspects concern astronomical imaging with high space and time resolution. The applied research ranges, for example, from the development of airborne 3–D LIDAR imaging for incorporation into aircraft safety equipment, to an optical reconstruction method for sounds on antique (wax cylinder) records.

The high resolution astronomy project has concentrated upon producing a partial correction for the effects of the turbulent atmosphere, in order to improve spatial resolution by a factor of about 3 or 4 (from 0".5 to 0".15 arc-seconds in the best cases). This has enabled deep imaging studies of extremely densely-packed regions of the sky, such as the cores of globular clusters, to be made, and a hitherto unknown population of variable stars in them has been identified. Alternatively, the high resolution camera has been used to search for extremely faint pulsating stars, which are the optical counterparts of the well-known radio and X-ray pulsars. More than fifty per cent of all known optical pulsars have been identified by this method. Very large telescopes are needed for this work because of the extreme faintness of optical pulsars – the optical pulsar 'Geminga' produces about the same amount of light as would a candle at the distance of the moon. The Galway camera has been used on large telescopes in Spain, Chile, and Russia for this work.

The LIDAR project is called MFLAME (Multi Function Laser Atmospheric Measurement Equipment). A European consortium aims to produce an airborne laser radar to measure wind speed 1–3 km in front of passenger aircraft, to identify potential hazards, such as turbulence, windshear, and wake vortices. In the latter case, vortices shed from the wing tips of preceding large aircraft pose a hazard to smaller aircraft, especially during take off or landing. The Galway group has the responsibility for the signal processing and analysis of the LIDAR signals, analysis of the test data and artificial intelligence to provide a timely warning of hazards to the cockpit.

More recently appointed members of staff with an interest in research in high energy astrophysics are Gary Gillanders and Mark Lang. Both are graduates of University College Dublin where they conducted their PhD research under Professor D.J. Fegan, and were Harvard-Smithsonian pre-doctoral fellows based at the Whipple Observatory in Arizona. Since joining the Department in Galway in the early nineties, they have continued collaborative work in the area of high-energy gamma-ray astronomy in conjunction with the Smithsonian Institution and a number of other American, British, and Irish universities. Recently, the collaboration has secured major funding in the USA to build the next generation of ground-based gamma-ray telescope arrays.

Support Staff

An account of the development of Physics in Galway over the first 150 years would be incomplete without some mention of the support staff who have contributed so much in various ways over the years. These include the technicians, secretaries, porters, cleaners, as well as post-doctoral fellows, research assistants, part time assistants, and demonstrators who helped to run the laboratory classes, particularly those for the first-year students.

The need for assistance in running the Department was apparent from the beginning of the College. In his lengthy submission to the Queen's Colleges Commission in 1857 Professor G.J. Stoney said:

There is an item on the College accounts that I would like to mention. There is a fund allocated to Porters and Servants, which we have been drawing on for the payment of salaries. Now there is very much wanted a provision for the Demonstrator in Anatomy, for a Drawing Master in the Engineering Department, and for Assistants to the Professor of Chemistry, to myself, and to the Museum. From want of sufficient funds these Assistants are brought under the title Porters and Servants. They should be placed on the foundation, and provision made for them, so as always to procure competent men. With reference to my own department, it has been found necessary to supplement the small sum, which can be devoted to the payment of an Assistant out of the Porter's fund, by purchasing some of the apparatus made by him, which are paid for out of the annual Parliamentary grant of £1,600. I think that it would be a more desirable way that the Assistants should be made permanent officers of the College, and provision made for them distinct from that for Porters and Servants.[45]

The response from Her Majesty's government does not seem to have been overwhelming. In the list of minor officers, porters, and servants appointed for the year commencing 1 April 1898 we find that William Hare, Assistant in Natural Philosophy, had an annual salary of £40.10s.0d., paid monthly, from the Endowment Fund. For the year commencing April 1901 this salary had increased to £46.10s. per annum and he also had an allowance of a suit of plain clothes (£3) annually and an overcoat (£2.10s.) every second year. The fact that Hare was getting five shillings for operating the X-ray equipment in the County Infirmary on a fee per item of service basis in 1913 shows that it was a welcome way to supplement his income.[46] At the same dates the Demonstrator in Natural Philosophy, R.J. Cummins BE, was getting £25 per annum, payable in three instalments, and no clothes allowance. Meanwhile a College charwoman, Mary Naughton, was getting nine shillings per week and thirty shillings worth of clothing at Christmas.

William Hare continued with the Department until 1927. He was succeeded by Jack O'Donnell who served as the technician in Physics until he resigned in 1952. He subsequently returned to the College staff in the Porters' Office (1972–9). He was succeeded as the Physics technician for six years by Michael Healy. In 1958 Frank Gaffney came to the College, after training and service with the Irish Air Corps, and served with distinction until his retirement in 1993. During that time there was considerable expansion in the number of technicians employed in the Department and in the range of technical services supplied. Among these was the provision of liquid nitrogen and later liquid helium to users in the Department, to other Departments of the College, and to medical and other practitioners in the west of Ireland. Among those who trained and served for a while in the mechanical workshops were Colm Walsh, Michael Myles and Máirtín Davey Ó Coisdealla. Pádraic Ó Droighneáin, who came in 1968, and Pádraig Breathnach, who came in 1970, are still providing a splendid service in the mechanical workshops.

45 *Report of Her Majesty's Commissioners*, 1858, evidence, 4052.
46 The late Professor J.P. Murray, in a private communication.

With the constant growth and sophistication of electronics in all aspects of Physics, the Department acquired a special electronics workshop on moving into its new premises in 1973, and John Goode was appointed as an electronics technician. On his resignation in 1980, he was replaced by Peter O'Kane who greatly facilitated the development of computer applications in the Department. Subsequently P.J. Walsh and Bridget Cullagh joined the electronic technical team. Walsh was appointed Chief Technician on Frank Gaffney's retirement.

With the growth in student numbers at undergraduate and postgraduate levels, the workload for the academic and technical staff has increased greatly in the past forty years. While the work in the laboratory classes was shared by all, the task of catering for around six hundred students each week in the first-year practicals fell mainly to another technician, Paddy Reilly. From his arrival from Maynooth in 1974 until his resignation and departure for Australia in 1989, Pat Hogan worked mainly in the cryogenic area and the second-year laboratories. The support for the lecture theatres and audio-visual aids, as well as photocopying and other services have been provided in the Department since 1975 by Richie McDermott.

Secretarial services in the College were meagre and confined to the administrative offices until the expansion of the 1960s. The Department of Physics acquired its first IBM 'golf ball' typewriter in 1966 as well as a part-time secretary while Professor Ó Brolcháin was Dean of the Faculty of Science. The duplication of notes, reports, and manuals at that time was carried out with the Gestetner stencil system. Since then, the Department has benefited from the services of several very efficient secretaries but pride of place must go to Máire Ní Dhireáin, Mai Wims, and Tess Mahoney for smoothing its operations and keeping its accounts in order.

Academic assistance to the Professor came from graduate students of the Department for the first century of its existence. The Queen's University had a prize of about twenty guineas almost every year for the Senior Scholar in Natural Philosophy which was awarded on the results of the final BA examination. There were special postgraduate lectures for the MA degree. The profits from the Great Exhibition, held in London in 1851, provided scholarships for students to pursue postgraduate studies in British universities and graduates of the Galway College were often successful in obtaining them in open competition. In 1894 the Royal University of Ireland instituted junior fellowships worth £200 per year for four years. Regarding rewards for students it is interesting to note part of the address of the Vice-Chancellor, the Right Hon. C.T. Redington MA to the fourteenth annual meeting of the University held in St Patrick's Hall in Dublin Castle on 25 October 1895:

> In Natural Philosophy the Junior Fellowship has been won by Mr J.A. M'Clelland, M.A. (1893) of Queen's College Galway. He, also, has had a distinguished university career, having gained honours at his B.A. Examination, first class honours in his M.A. Examination in Mathematical and Experimental Physics, and a Gold Medal. The Senate, to show their appreciation of the Thesis which he wrote for the examination, have ordered it to be printed and circulated, and I think that such an exceptional honour must be a source of great satisfaction to the distinguished Professors of the Galway College, and to its most honoured President.[47]

47 *Fourteenth Report of the Royal University of Ireland (for 1895)* (Dublin, 1896), p. 7.

McClelland used his scholarship to go to Cambridge University, as already mentioned. John Henry followed the same path a year later.

The post of Demonstrator in Physics, generally held by a graduate student, made its first appearance in the report of the President for the session 1898–9. It was held then by the same John Henry who was also engaged in the fledgling work on X-rays. John E. Bowen held the senior scholarship in Natural Philosophy in the session 1907–8 and stayed with the Department until 1920; he qualified in medicine in 1921. William G. Griffith was an assistant in the Department from 1910 to 1912. He was Professor of Electrical Engineering from 1909 until his death in 1932. A BSc in Electrical Engineering was available in the College between 1913 and 1946. Another person who worked in the Department and became a founding father of the ESB was Thomas A. McLaughlin. He qualified in Physics in UCD with a BSc in 1916 and an MSc in 1918. During his time in Galway, 1920–2, he took a BE degree and obtained a PhD in 1923 with a thesis on the 'Calaphoresis of Air Bubbles in Various Liquids and Deleterious Effect of Fibres on Insulating Power of Oils'. He was succeeded by John J. McHenry (1922–32) and Cilian Ó Brolcháin (1932–4).

Among the many people who have served the Department as assistants, some have done so for a number of years. Pádraic Ó Lochlainn served from 1939 to 1945 and went on to become a Lecturer in and Associate Professor of Civil Engineering. Mrs J.J. Burke (née McGowan) was there in the 1940s and afterwards her private tuition helped many a student through their first-year examinations. Jim Horgan came from his teaching in St Joseph's School (the 'Bish') to take the first-year practical classes each afternoon from 3.30 to 6.30 p.m. from 1945 until 1962. Besides the growing number of full-time staff and graduate students who have shared the teaching load in the practical classes in the past thirty years there were a number of part-time assistants. Among them were J. Oliver Ryan, Séamus Gallagher, Richard Lee, John Cunningham, and Alasdar MacCana. Between 1975 and 1980, Denis O'Sullivan came from the Dublin Institute for Advanced Studies as a guest lecturer in high-energy nuclear particle Physics.

Sources for the funding of research have diversified over the past forty years. The College has always tried to support the research efforts of its staff from its less than adequate resources. To supplement this income, members of the staff of the Department have sought and won contracts for research from funding agencies in Ireland, America, and Europe and from national and multi-national industries. Forbairt and its predecessors (EOLAS, National Science Council, Institute for Industrial Research and Standards) has provided funds through a variety of schemes which has allowed full-time graduate research assistants and postdoctoral fellows to be hired for research projects. The Commission of the European Communities has also provided funds for research which involves collaboration with groups in other European countries. Among the visiting postdoctoral and Fulbright fellows and academics spending some sabbatical leave in the Department have been Peter Scott, John Kenny, Parker Reist, Wil Graben, and Cathy Cahill from America; Graham Walker from England; Franco Zappa from Italy; Brendt Georgi from Germany; In-Ho Kim from Korea; and Brendan McGann from Australia.

Present and Future

This article has dealt mainly with developments in Physics within what is now the National University of Ireland, Galway. Space does not permit a survey of achievements of our graduates and their contributions to Physics, administration, education, and industry in the greater world outside our walls. The growth in international collaboration in research, the participation of staff in international committees, and the dispersal of our students around the world means that the Department in Galway has active participation in research all over the world and is no longer a rather isolated centre of learning on the perimeter of Europe. It is also making important contributions on the local, regional, and national levels with innovative courses, active research groups, collaboration with industry and public authorities, and increased interaction with second-level schools and the general public.

This brief historical review has only given a selective flavour of the proud tradition which we inherit today. The Department at present is alive to its responsibilities and looks forward to continued progress and contributions to NUI, Galway in the next millennium.[48]

---

[48] I would like to acknowledge all the assistance given readily by my colleagues in the Department, the staff of the James Hardiman Library, and the editorial team for this volume, in providing information and suggesting improvements in the text. The final version is my responsibility as regards content and presentation. The history of the Department deserves a more detailed treatment. Corrections, suggestions, and further information and anecdotes would be a valuable contribution to such a history. This article is just a beginning.

Chemistry

R.N. BUTLER

In 1845 when the Queen's Colleges in Belfast, Cork, and Galway were incorporated, Chemistry was both a mature and a primitive science. Primitive because, when the Galway College opened in 1849, twenty years were yet to pass before Mendeleev was to classify the elements in the first Periodic Table in 1869, and over fifty years of scientific endeavour were required before Thompson discovered the electron and the beginnings of atomic structure in 1897. It is difficult to imagine such a world nowadays.

The maturity of chemistry at that time is illustrated by the fact that in 1822 the Irish Linen Board in Dublin, subjected to a government economy drive, decided to abolish the posts of clerk of works, messenger, watchman, and of course the 'chymist'.[1] The chemist had served them well with work on bleaching and the finding of cheaper materials for their processes. However, it is to the credit of that Board that they had realised the importance of employing a chemist. This particular chemist was none other than William Higgins, Fellow of the Royal Society (FRS), who was born at Collooney, Co. Sligo (in 1762 or 1763), and who, having worked and studied in Oxford and London, published a book, in 1789, entitled *A Comparative View of the Phlogistic and Antiphlogistic Theories with Inductions*. It sold a thousand copies within two years. This book was later claimed by Higgins to have superceded Dalton's atomic theory (1802), a debate which was still controverial in the 1940s and 1950s.[2] In it, it is clear that Higgins was thinking in terms of atoms. He was the first to use letters to represent elements, for example S for Sulphur, P for phlogisticated air (Nitrogen), C for Copper, I for Iron and so on, and he drew single lines between the letters to indicate chemical links.

In 1795 Higgins had been helped in gaining employment, from the Council of the Dublin Society (later RDS), by Richard Kirwan who thought highly of him. Higgins was familiar with Kirwan's work on chemical affinity. He had received early instruction from his uncle, Dr Bryan Higgins, in Co. Sligo on the false phlogiston theory championed by Kirwan but his experiments in support of the principles of Lavoisier helped to refute this and did much to persuade Kirwan and

---

[1] T.S. Wheeler, *Endeavour*, no. 41, 11 (1952).
[2] For an extensive account of the controversy, see E.R. Atkinson, *Journal of Chemical Education*, January 1940, p. 3. Lecture presented to the Division of the History of Chemistry, 98th meeting, ACS, Boston, Mass., USA, 12 September 1939.

other phlogistians to recant. By 1849 chemistry had matured to a sound experimental discipline based on accurate measurements of weights, and having passed through the furnace of a bitter major international controversy it possessed a significant community of leading personalities. It was producing economic benefit to those capable of using it and it was bringing new knowledge of and insight into nature to those capable of exploring it. The Great Exhibition of 1851 in London was only two years away. It was logical that any worthy university should teach and explore the subject of chemistry and hence a Professorship of Chemistry was instituted in Queen's College Galway from the beginning. There was no Science Faculty and while chemistry was not yet a subject suitable for first-year courses, it was available as a subject in second and third-year arts courses. The following extract from a book published in 1850 by Thomas Graham FRS, famous for his law of diffusion, illustrates the intellectual level of chemistry when the Galway College was opened:

> Chemical combination takes place between the atoms of bodies, which then come into juxtaposition; and in decomposition the simple atoms separate again from each other, in possession of their original properties. The atom or integrant particle of a compound body is an aggregation of simple atoms, and must therefore have a weight equal to the sum of their weights; as will be obvious from the exhibition of the atomic constitution of a few compounds.
>
> | | Atom | Weight |
> | --- | --- | --- |
> | Water | HO | 1 + 8 = 9 |
> | Protoxide | NO | 4 + 8 = 12 |
> | Deutoxide of nitrogen | NOO | 14 + 16 = 30 |
> | Sulphuric Acid | SOOO | 16 + 24 = 40 |
>
> It is unnecessary to make any assumption as to the nature, size, form, or even actual weight of the atoms of elementary bodies, or as to the mode in which they are grouped or arranged in compounds. All that is known or likely ever to be known respecting them is their relative weight. The atom of oxygen is eight times heavier than that of hydrogen, but their actual weights are undetermined.[3]

The First Fifty Years

In the early and mid–1800s, Germany was the main centre of advancement for chemistry and Liebig's School of Practical Chemistry at Giessen had acquired a world-wide reputation. Following the publication, in 1840, of Baron von Liebig's *Chemistry of Agriculture and Physiology*, his students came to occupy many senior positions in chemistry. In 1842 Liebig made 'a sort of triumphal' tour of England

---

[3] T. Graham, *Elements of Chemistry* (London, 1850), vol. i, p. 134.

7.1 Edmond Ronalds, Professor of Chemistry, 1849–56

7.2 Edward Divers, Assistant, 1854–66, first Professor of Chemistry, University of Tokyo

during which he met Sir Robert Peel and other leading persons.[4] Following this tour, chemistry immediately became a popular science in England and developments ensued which led to the setting up of the Royal College of Chemistry in London in 1845 as the focal point of an English School of Practical Chemistry based on Liebig's School. A.W. von Hofmann, from Liebig's School at Giessen, was appointed Professor and for over seventy years the great Hofmann was to have an enormous influence on the development of chemistry in Great Britain and Ireland generally, and Galway in particular. In his Hofmann memorial lecture of 1896, Sir F.A. Abel, a student of Hofmann at this time, recalls his first meeting with Thomas H. Rowney, a fellow student whom Hofmann appointed as his first lecture-assistant.[5] In 1850, at the age of thirteen, a young man named Edward Divers entered the City of London School and became a classmate of W.H. Perkin, both working under Thomas Hall who had been a student of Hofmann at the Royal College of Chemistry. Hall was an inspiring teacher who directed Divers and W.H. Perkin to Hofmann at the Royal College. Divers spent a year with Hofmann (1852–3) at the Royal College and later ascribed much of the value of his training there to Sir William Crookes who was an assistant. In 1853–4 Divers worked as a junior assistant at St Bartholomew's Hospital Medical School in Stenhouse's laboratory where, at this time, August Kekulé was also working. In 1854 Divers became a full assistant to the Professor of Chemistry at Queen's College Galway where he stayed for twelve years until 1866. That Professor was Edmond Ronalds who had been an assistant to Liebig and who had also worked

---

4   Lord Playfair, 'Hofmann Memorial Lectures', *Journal of the Chemical Society*, 69 (1896), p. 577.
5   F.A. Abel, 'The History of the Royal College of Chemistry and Reminiscences of Hofmann's Professorship', ibid., p. 580.

with Hofmann (fig. 7.1).[6] His father, Edmond Ronalds, was a London merchant and a brother of Sir Francis Ronalds, who was knighted in the late 1880s for work on the origin of the electric telegraph. Ronalds received chemical training in Jena, Giessen, Berlin, Heidelberg, Zurich, and Paris. He was Secretary of the London Chemical Society from 1848 to 1850 and he was the editor of the first two volumes of the *Journal of the Chemical Society* in 1848 and 1849. He was appointed first Professor of Chemistry in Galway in 1849 when the College opened. Few university chemistry departments could have had more distinguished academic staff at their beginnings. Ronalds published papers with the titles 'On the Oxidation of Waxes with Nitric Acid'; 'Excretion of Phosphorus'; and 'The Most Volatile Constituents of American Petroleum'.[7] With Thomas Richardson he translated and edited Friedrich Ludwig Knapp's *Chemical Technology: Or, Chemistry Applied to the Arts and Manufacturers*.[8] In 1856 Ronalds left Galway and took over the Bonnington Chemical Works in Edinburgh where the products of the Edinburgh Gasworks were worked up. About twenty years later he gave up business and set up a private chemical laboratory where he made welcome any chemist who needed laboratory space. He was married to Barbara Tennent, a grand-daughter of John Tennent, founder of the Scottish Tennent Caledonian Breweries.[9]

Edward Divers was both a medical student and Assistant in Chemistry at the Galway College where he took an MD degree in 1860 (fig. 7.2).[10] He delivered popular lectures on his work as a chemist, in Ballina and other centres at the request of the Committee of the Council on Education. In 1862 he published a paper on the action of ammonium carbonate on magnesium salts followed by another in 1863 on the conversion of gun-cotton into pectic and parapectic acids.[11] In 1865 he married Margaret Theresa Fitzgerald of Mayfield, Co. Cork and they moved to London in 1866. In July 1873 Divers took up an initial five-year contract in Japan, where he stayed for the next twenty-six years. Japan, at that time, had issued invitations to all nations that could give her assistance in acquiring the material civilisation of the west. Divers was immensely successful and he became the first Professor of Chemistry at the University of Tokyo. He published a large number of papers on the chemistry of sulphur-nitrogen compounds. In the years 1884–5 alone, twenty-four papers appeared in the *Journal of the Chemical Society*.

6   D. Ó Raghallaigh, 'Three Centuries of Irish Chemists', *Historical and Archaeological Papers*, no. ii (Cork, 1941). This paper contains some errors about Ronalds, not least of which is giving his name as 'Rolands'. See also obituary, 'Dr Edmond Ronalds (1819–1889)', *Journal of the Chemical Society Transactions*, 57 (1890), p. 456.
7   'On the Oxidation of Waxes with Nitric Acid', *Liebig Annual* (1842) (in German); 'Excretion of Phosphorus', *Philosophical Transactions* (1853); and 'The Most Volatile Constituents of American Petroleum', *Journal of the Chemical Society Transactions*, 18 (1865), p. 54.
8   London, 1848–51.
9   On 24 March 1984, the Registrar of the College received a letter from the successor of this company seeking descendants of the couple, although there appear to be none living in Galway or among the list of Galway graduates. Letter to Registrar (Professor J.D. O'Keeffe), from D.I.H. Johnstone, Quality Control Manager, Tennent Caledonian Breweries Ltd.
10 Edward Divers FRS (1837–1912), Obituary, *Journal of the Chemical Society Transactions*, 103 (1913), p. 746.
11 Ibid., 1862, p. 196 and 1863, p. 91.

His studies on oxides of nitrogen showed that in the metal salts the metal is bonded to the oxygen atom, and led to significant understanding of the hyponitrites. Among the many honours awarded to him were a Fellowship of the Royal Society, in 1885, and a DSc (*honoris causa*), in 1898, by his old University, the Royal University of Ireland. The loss of his son to an illness contacted in China and the death of his wife in 1897 were severe blows to him. An attack of inflammation of the eyes in infancy had left him with seriously impaired vision and, on 24 November 1884, he suffered severe damage to his right eye when a bottle, in which phosphorus oxychloride had been kept, exploded in his face.[12] (This is described as a test-tube explosion in the Royal Society obituary.) He is reported in later life as visiting his old laboratory in Galway and feeling his way around the benches which he could not see. He was highly honoured in Japan and, after he left in 1899, a bust of him was presented to the Imperial University of Tokyo by his former pupils and unveiled on 17 November 1900. His memory is still honoured there and this led to an invitation to the former College President, the late Dr Colm Ó hEocha, to visit Divers's old Department in Tokyo. The metal bust still remains there, it having been concealed by chemistry staff during the second World War when such mementos were being melted down for military use. Divers was a remarkable person and his twelve years in Galway brought considerable distinction to the College.

In 1856 Ronalds was succeeded as Professor of Chemistry in Galway by Thomas Rowney who had been an Assistant to Hofmann at the Royal College of Chemistry in London (fig. 7.3). Rowney served as Professor for thirty-three years until 1889, with Divers as Assistant up to 1866. Thus the first forty years of chemistry in Galway were closely linked to chemistry at the Royal College of Chemistry in London and to Liebig's Laboratory at Giessen. Rowney's early papers with F.A. Abel included 'Analysis of the Waters of Artesian Wells, Trafalgar Square' and 'Mineral Waters of Cheltenham'.[13] In the 1850s he was studying the reactions of ammonia with organic acids and produced the following papers: 'The Action of Ammonia on the Oils and Fats', 'Action of Ammonia on Sebacic Ether', and 'Solid Compounds Obtained by Distilling Stearic Acid with Lime'.[14]

The Second Fifty Years

Rowney resigned from the Professorship of Chemistry in Galway in 1889 and he was succeeded by Augustus E. Dixon MD (fig. 7.4). Dixon was born in Belfast in 1860. He was educated at the Royal Academical Institute, Belfast, Trinity College Dublin (TCD), and the University of Berlin where he worked with Hofmann. He was an Assistant Lecturer in Chemistry at TCD. Dixon was studying the action of isothiocyanates on 'aldehyde ammonias'.[15] He stayed in Galway less than two

---

12 Ronalds, Obituary, ibid., 57 (1890), p. 456.
13 Divers, Obituary, ibid., p. 746.
14 Ibid., 1854, p. 200; 1851, p. 334; 1853, p. 97.
15 Ibid., 1888, p. 411.

7.3 Thomas H. Rowney, Professor of Chemistry, 1856–89

7.4 Augustus E. Dixon, Professor of Chemistry, 1889–91

years, resigning in 1891 when he moved to the Professorship of Chemistry in Queen's College Cork (QCC). At that time, Alfred Senier had been appointed as a locum for Maxwell Simpson, Professor of Chemistry, at QCC. On the resignation of Simpson, Dixon from Galway was appointed to the Professorship of Chemistry in QCC, and Senier, who had been in Cork, was appointed to the Professorship of Chemistry in Galway (fig. 7.5). With the completion of these chemical musical chairs, things appear to have settled down in both Departments. Dixon went on to publish substantial work on sulphur-nitrogen compounds with nineteen papers in the *Journal of the Chemistry Society* between 1893 and 1903. There is the distinct impression that times were poor for chemistry in Galway in the 1880s. There are no published works from Rowney, and as well as Dixon's brief stay we find the following statement about Senier's beginning in Galway: 'Meanwhile, the problem of continuing his researches had to be faced ... at first little progress could be made, as Galway offered but a poor field for creating and maintaining an advanced chemical atmosphere'. Elsewhere we are told that since

> the dissolution of the Queen's University in 1879 the three Colleges at Belfast, Galway and Cork had been reduced from the status of integral members of a University to that of Colleges where students were able to study for the examinations of an external institution – the Royal University. In addition to this loss of prestige, the College at Galway suffered through lack of active support by the people of Connaught. It was therefore not in close sympathy with its environment.

The existence of the College had often been threatened, but it had survived and indeed had 'attained a flourishing condition'.[16] This last quotation refers to the

16 Alfred Senier (1853–1918), Obituary, ibid., 115 (1919), p. 447.

benefits brought about by the 1908 Act setting up the National University of Ireland (NUI) which, of course, was seventeen years away when Senier was appointed Professor of Chemistry in 1891. By 1891 it appears that the effects of the famine and the social deprivation in Connaught was threatening the survival of the College, bringing an insecurity to the College psyche, echoes of which still remain.

The Chemistry Department was fortunate to have got Senier. He proved to be the right man in the right place. Senier was born in 1853 at Burnley, Lancashire but the family moved to Mazomanie in the USA shortly after his birth. He graduated with a medical degree from the University of Michigan in 1874 and returned to London shortly afterwards where he was employed as assistant to Professor Attfield at the school of the Pharmaceutical Society. In 1881 he took charge of teaching chemistry at St John's College, Battersea where he remained for three years. In 1884 he went to Berlin to study under A.W. von Hofmann who had returned to Berlin in 1865 to set up the Chemistry Department of the Frederick William University of Berlin. Senier became a close friend of Hofmann who inspired him enormously in the chemistry of organic nitrogen systems which he later went on to develop with great success in Galway. He must have heard at first hand from Hofmann of the work of his great students Perkin and Griess on azo and diazo chemistry and this influence is clearly visible in the work on heterocyclic rings and Schiff bases which he later published from Galway. Through Senier the direct influence of Hofmann on chemistry in Galway was extended, from 1849 until 1918. After obtaining his PhD degree in 1887 under Hofmann, he returned to London where he worked on chemical dictionaries until his arrival in Cork in 1890 and Galway in 1891. During his time in London, Senier also showed a strong interest in philosophical questions and he was honorary secretary and treasurer of the Aristotelian Society when it was formed in 1880. In 1877 he wrote a strong letter to the Pharmaceutical Journal advocating the admission of women pharmacists to the Pharmaceutical Society. As well as holding the Professorship of Chemistry, Senier was lecturer in Medical Jurisprudence and Hygiene. In the period 1885–6 Senier published a number of papers on cyanuric acid and its derivatives. Further papers on this topic appeared from Galway in 1902, co-authored with Thomas Walsh.[17]

It is of interest to follow the story of one female student in the Galway College during Senier's time. Rosalind Clarke, daughter of the Revd Dr Courtney Clarke, Minister of the Presbyterian Church in Galway city, joined the College as a sixteen-year-old student in 1900 choosing from the 'First Arts' syllabus of English, Latin, Greek or a Modern Language, Mathematics, and Experimental Physics (fig. 7.6). She had won scholarships in both the literary and science divisions and she opted for the science scholarship. In her second year (1901–2) she took Mathematics (with Professor Bromwich), Experimental Physics (with Professor Anderson), and Chemistry with Senier. There were three lectures per week in Chemistry on Monday, Wednesday, and Friday at 12.00 noon. Chemistry practical

---

17   Ibid., 1985, p. 762; 1986, pp. 311, 693; and 1902, p. 280.

7.5 Alfred Senier, Professor of Chemistry, 1891–1918

7.6 Rosalind Clarke, Assistant, 1910–42

classes were held on the same afternoons at 3.00 p.m. and the same timetable covered Chemistry for Engineering students where the lectures were part of the first-year Engineering course, and the Chemistry Practicals were part of the second-year Engineering course. The fees for practical chemistry were £3, chemistry lectures £2, and the College fee was 10s. In the third year of the course, lecture times in Chemistry were by arrangement with the Professor. Chemistry consisted of theory of Chemistry – inorganic and organic and laboratory experiments – qualitative and simple quantitative (volumetric and gravimetric) analysis. Rosalind Clarke was inspired by Senier's approach to chemistry and she won first place in Chemistry and second place in Experimental Physics and Mathematics. In 1904 she took the honours BA degree of the Royal University in Chemistry and Experimental Physics with an Exhibition to the value of £21. She was appointed Demonstrator in Chemistry in the College and in 1905 she was awarded the 1851 Exhibition Scholarship. She used this to study for two years at the University of Bonn under Professor Anschutz. In 1908 she published a paper on 'phenylmesaconates', from her work with Anschutz.[18] On her return to Ireland she taught at Rochelle Seminary in Cork until 1910 when she was appointed Assistant to Professor Senier in University College Galway. Since 1908 the Royal University had been abolished and the NUI and UCG, with a separate Science Faculty, had been born. Rosalind Clarke remained on the academic staff of the Chemistry Department until 1942. She was awarded the DSc degree of the NUI for her researches in 1914. In 1905 she was co-author with Senier and Percy C. Austin of a paper entitled 'The Interaction of Acridines with Magnesium Alkyl Haloids'.[19]

18   *Annalen*, 359 (1908), p. 188; *Journal of the Chemical Society Abstracts*, 1 (1908), p. 335.
19   *Journal of the Chemical Society Transactions*, 1905, p. 1469.

By 1910 Senier was a leading figure examining phototropic compounds including many nitrogen Schiff bases which changed colour on exposure to sunlight. The colour changes were observed with some compounds under the influence of heat instead of light and Senier coined the term 'thermotropy'. In the period from 1903 to 1912 Senier published a series of papers with co-authors P.C. Austin, A. Compton (Demonstrator), and F.G. Shepheard (Assistant).[20] Rosalind Clarke begins to appear on these papers from 1911 onwards.[21] Up to 1918 Senier published four more major papers on phototropy and thermotropy.[22] Some of Senier's work presaged the modern liquid crystal work which has produced many useful products as well as trivia such as T-shirts which change colour with temperature. Senier died on 29 June 1918 and is buried in the New Cemetery, Bohermore, Galway. The Department's link with London was over. The world outside the walls of UCG was about to catch up on the Chemistry Department.

Around this time Thomas Dillon (fig. 7.7) was employed by University College Dublin where he carried out research under the prolific Professor Hugh Ryan. In 1909 Ryan and Dillon published a paper on 'Montana (montan) and Montanin Waxes'.[23] Further papers by Ryan and Dillon appeared in 1913 and 1916.[24] At this time there was a flourishing research school in Dublin and Hugh Ryan was publishing a large amount of work with a range of co-authors of whom Dillon was one. Dillon had obtained a BA degree in Chemistry and Physics in University College Cork in 1904 having at first been a medical student on a scholarship. His secondary schooling was at St Nathy's Diocesan College, Ballaghadereen, Co. Roscommon and Clongowes Wood College. After his BA degree he joined Hugh Ryan at the Catholic University School of Medicine in Cecilia Street, Dublin where he studied for an MA degree and worked as an assistant to Ryan. He also taught science at the Loreto Convent, Dalkey to people studying for degrees of the Royal University. With the foundation of the NUI in 1908, Ryan was appointed Professor of Chemistry in UCD with Dillon as his assistant. Dillon was awarded the DSc degree by the NUI in 1912. He was born in Inniscrone, Co. Sligo on 15 January 1884, the son of John Blake Dillon a nephew of the Young Irelander of the same name. His mother was a daughter of W.K. Sullivan, Professor of Chemistry and President of Queen's College Cork. His uncle, Valentine Dillon, was Parnell's solicitor and a lord mayor of Dublin. At UCD, Dillon was trained as an analytical organic chemist and, at this time, Geraldine Plunkett was also studying

---

20 A. Senier, P.C. Austin, and R. Clarke, *Journal of Chemical Society Transactions*, 1905, p. 1469; A. Senier and R. Clarke, ibid., 1911, p. 2081; ibid., 1912, p. 1950; A. Senier and A. Compton, ibid., 1907, p. 1927; ibid., 1909, p. 1623; A. Senier and F. G. Shepheard, ibid., 1909, pp. 441, 494, 1943.
21 For example A. Senier and (Miss) R. Clarke, 'Studies in Phototropy and Thermotropy, part ii, Naphthylideneamines', *Journal of the Chemical Society Transactions*, 1911, p. 2081. The last paper by Senier and Clarke was 'Phototropy and Thermotropy, part iv, o-Nitrobenzylidene-arylamines and their Photoisomeric Change', ibid., 1914, p. 1917.
22 A. Senier and R.B. Forstar, *Journal of the Chemical Society Transactions*, 1914, p. 2462; idem., ibid., 1915, pp. 452, 1168; A. Senier and P. H. Gallagher, ibid., 1918, p. 28.
23 *Journal of the Chemical Society Abstracts*, 1(i) (1909), p. 629.
24 'Higher Tertiary Alcohols Derived from Palmitic and Stearic Esters', ibid., 1 (1913), p. 583, and 'The Hydrocarbons of Beeswax', ibid., 1 (1916), p. 706.

7.7 Thomas Dillon, Professor of Chemistry, 1919–54

chemistry under Hugh Ryan. In 1916, along with Ryan, she published a paper on unsaturated ß-diketones.[25] On Easter Sunday morning 1916, Dillon and Geraldine Plunkett were married. She was a sister of Joseph Plunkett, a signatory of the Proclamation of the Irish Republic. Dillon had been acting as a chemical adviser to the Volunteers on the production of simple explosives and hand grenades, and he was sworn in as a member of the IRA. He was aware that a rising was planned for Easter Sunday 1916 but not of the details. After his wedding that morning he took a room in the Imperial Hotel opposite the GPO in Dublin without realising that this was to be the battle-ground. He was told to await instructions to take charge of chemical works that it was intended to commandeer. The rising did not take place as expected on Sunday owing to a hitch, but the action started on Monday. On the Monday evening a messenger was sent from the GPO to Dillon in the Imperial Hotel to tell him that, owing to another hitch, no chemical factories had yet been taken over and he could go home and await orders.[26] Dillon escaped

25 Ibid., 1 (1916), p. 656.
26 J.A. Schufle, 'Thomas Dillon: Chemist and Revolutionary', *Chemistry (ACS)*, 43 (1970), pp. 18–21.

the subsequent arrests and executions because two friends, one a medical officer in the British army and the other the attorney-general of Ireland, had sincerely vouched that they knew he would not be involved in a military uprising. In 1917 Dillon assisted his father-in-law, Count Plunkett, in organising a meeting in Dublin of about a thousand delegates from country-wide local bodies. To prevent dissension from splitting the national movement, the 'Mansion House Committee' was formed with the object of freeing the country with Dillon as its secretary. Representatives of the Volunteers were brought onto the Council of Sinn Féin as were W.T. Cosgrave and Éamon de Valera, who had recently escaped from prison. In October 1917 a Sinn Féin convention was held in which Arthur Griffith proposed de Valera as President. Dillon was nominated as Secretary. This must have been a moment of truth for Dillon, one faced by politically-active scientists in many countries, whether or not to become a full-time politician-administrator on behalf of the political movement. Dillon refused the nomination and stayed with Chemistry, but agreed to serve on the Executive Council to which he was elected. In May 1918 all the members of the Sinn Féin Council were arrested except for a few who escaped. Dillon was imprisoned in the City of Gloucester Gaol until March 1919. During his time in jail in England he was retained on full pay by Professor Hugh Ryan at UCD where his teaching duties were voluntarily undertaken by George Ebrill and Joseph Algar. He states that he managed to do some limited reading of a few chemistry books there. After his release in 1919 Dillon was appointed to the Professorship of Chemistry at University College Galway to succeed Senier. Like many of that generation his attributes included stamina and longevity. He served as Professor of Chemistry until 1954 and the roots he put down were strong and deep.

In Dillon's first years in Galway he must have experienced significant difficulties, since by 1920 the crown forces were operating martial law and were essentially behaving as state terrorists. The litany of destruction of homes, communities, and properties in Galway and the list of people murdered by them in Galway in 1920 has recently been documented.[27] Three named *agents provocateurs* who were implicated in the murder of Fr Michael Griffin, on the night of his kidnap in November 1920, entered the house of Michael Kennedy, the Galway County Engineer, in Rockbarton where they said they were looking for a certain professor. Dillon lived on the seafront opposite the Eglinton Hotel and he, as well as Professors Liam Ó Briain and Tomás Ó Máille, were alerted by a Dr O'Malley who had been a visitor at the Kennedy home during the intrusion. At this time Dillon was acting as a judge in the Sinn Féin Courts in Galway. These courts competed with, and eventually supplanted, the British legal system in the country. Dillon was also obviously exploring new chemical ideas probably seeking out the future path for his researches. His first paper from UCG, in collaboration with Rosalind Clarke, was on the topic of the isotopes of lead, which was fashionable at the time. In it they reacted lead dichloride with the Grignard reagent ethyl-magnesium iodide and separated the 'lead tetraethyl' from the remaining metallic

---

27   P. Ó Laoi, *Fr Griffin: 1892–1920* (Galway, 1994), pp. 62, 84–5.

lead. Dillon wisely did not pursue this further but the paper suggests that he was trying to develop new research interests divorced from his original training.[28] His natural instinct, however, was to try to do research which would be of some economic use to the country and particularly the west of Ireland. When he turned his attention to the copious amounts of seaweed to be found along the west coast he hit a chemical jackpot. No longer could the Chemistry Department of UCG be said to be 'not in close sympathy with its environment'.

By Dillon's first year in UCG, 1919–20, the BSc degree of the Science Faculty had been well established. Most science subjects were still first arts subjects but not BA examination subjects. In the first science course, the subjects were divided into two groups, Group A: Mathematics, Mathematical Physics, Experimental Physics, Chemistry, Botany, Zoology, Logic, and Physical Geography; and Group B: Irish, Greek, Latin, English, French, German, and Italian. Science students had to present for examination in five subjects including four from Group A and one from Group B or in four subjects including Mathematics, Mathematical Physics, Experimental Physics or Chemistry, and one subject from Group B. The first-year Chemistry lectures were at 12.00–1.00 p.m. on Tuesday, Thursday, and Saturday and the second-year lectures were at the same time on Monday, Wednesday, and Friday. First-year and second-year practical classes were held at 3.30–6.30 p.m. on Monday, Wednesday, and Friday and all students of both years took six hours of practical work per week. The third-year timetable was by arrangement with the professor. The first-year course, as described in the 1919–20 *Calendar*, was an introduction to general chemistry. The second and third-year courses as described were almost completely organic chemistry but they each contain the statement 'A Review of Physical and General Chemistry'. At this time the staff of the Chemistry Department consisted of Dillon and Clarke. The latter is described in the 1919–20 *Calendar* as a 'Demonstrator in Chemistry'. The teaching load was heavy and in Dillon's own words,

> Dr Clarke took on a great part of the burden, teaching Organic Chemistry to science students and helping to supervise their practical work as well as conducting practical classes for first year students, including those of medicine, engineering and agriculture. In the laboratory she was a strict disciplinarian. First year students were not allowed to smoke during practical classes ... the gentle and friendly manner in which she enforced such regulations completely removed any irritation they might have caused.[29]

During the 1920s Dillon was developing his approach to the chemistry of seaweed. In 1928 in his first paper, 'A Suggested Method for the Utilization of Seaweed', he describes some of the materials arising from the decomposition of seaweed in a tub for seventeen weeks.[30] A year later he had found the presence of

---

28 T. Dillon, R. Clarke, and V.M. Hinchy, *Scientific Proceedings of the Royal Dublin Society*, 17 (1922), pp. 53–7; *Journal of the Chemical Society Abstracts*, 2 (1922), p. 710.
29 *Journal of the Institute of Chemistry of Ireland*, 1953–4, p. 8.
30 T. Dillon and E.F. Lavelle, *Economic Proceedings of the Royal Dublin Society*, 2 (1928), p. 407 and *Chemical Abstracts*, 23 (1929), p. 4780.

oxidising compounds in fresh fronds of *Laminaria digitate* (seaweed) which liberate iodine from potassium iodide.[31] By 1931 Dillon was discussing the occurrence and structure of alginic acid in plants; by 1934 he was discussing the chemistry of red and brown algae.[32] He had derivatised some of the sugar units in the cellulose obtained from seaweeds (laminariae) as phenylglucosazones. By the mid 1930s there was a strong and growing research school in the Chemistry Department. The first higher degrees in chemistry were coming out as well-trained laboratory chemists. Up to the present time, about 250 such graduates (see Appendix) have been trained in the UCG Chemistry Department and they are to be found in senior positions throughout the private and public sectors in the country. The period 1935 to 1965 was the era of the MSc degree and there are many famous names to be found in the appendix. Many of the early MSc theses were concerned with the chemistry of Laminarin and, from 1950 on, many are written in Irish, beginning with that of Colm Ó hEocha. In 1929–30 Vincent C. Barry from Cork joined Dillon as an Assistant and his name appears prominently on the research in Galway until 1943, when he went to UCD. In the early thirties, Tadhg Twomey was also an Assistant in the Chemistry Department. In 1936 the first of a series of papers on alginic acid appeared, 'Acetylation of Alginic Acid', and by 1939 the structure of laminarin was beginning to be elucidated.[33] Barry suggested that laminarin consisted of a chain of ß-glucopyranose units twisted into a spiral. In 1939 Dillon and co-authors took out two patents on the use of seaweed. One dealt with the use of digested seaweed for making pulp for wallboard and paper, the other dealt with the production of iodine from digested seaweed and the use of the remaining liquor as a fertiliser.[34] A state-sponsored unit was attached to the Department, employing P. Moynihan (Ó Muineacháin), and D.T. Flood, to explore the applications of seaweed. By 1940 the seaweed research included carrageen moss and at this time another Assistant, P.S. Ó Colla, had joined Dillon. In 1940 their first joint paper appeared on the acetolysis of carrageen mucilage.[35] By the end of the 1930s the group had established that seaweed (laminariae) was predominantly made up of carbohydrates. The complicated carbohydrate compounds which had been isolated were alginic acid, mannitol, fucoidin, cellulose, and laminarin. Laminarin was present in seaweed fronds harvested in late autumn. It was particularly easy to extract as it appeared as a white deposit on leaves left overnight immersed in dilute hydrochloric acid. Two types of laminarin were

---

31 T. Dillon, *Nature*, 123 (1929), p. 161 and *Chemical Abstracts*, 23 (1929), p. 2465.
32 T. Dillon and Annie McGuinness, *Scientific Proceedings of the Royal Dublin Society*, 20 (1931), p. 129 and *Chemical Abstracts*, 26 (1932), p. 975; T. Dillon and T. Ó Tuama, *Nature*, 133 (1934), p. 837 and *Chemical Abstracts*, 28 (1934), p. 5100; T. Dillon and T. Ó Tuama, *Scientific Proceedings of the Royal Dublin Society*, 21 (1935), p. 147 and *Chemical Abstracts*, 29 (1935), p. 2735.
33 V.C. Barry, T. Dillon, and P. Ó Muineacháin, *Scientific Proceedings of the Royal Dublin Society*, 21 (1936), p. 289 and *Chemical Abstracts*, 30 (1936), p. 4162; V.C. Barry, *Scientific Proceedings of the Royal Dublin Society*, 22 (1939), p. 59 and *Chemical Abstracts*, 33 (1939), p. 3339.
34 T. Dillon, D.T. Flood, V.C. Barry, and P. Ó Muineacháin, *Br.Pat*. 508671 (1939) and *Chemical Abstracts*, 34 (1940), p. 3088; T. Dillon, D.T. Flood, V.C. Barry, and P. Ó Muineacháin, *Br.Pat*, 508715 (1939) and *Chemical Abstracts*, 34 (1940), p. 2544.
35 T. Dillon and P. Ó Colla, *Nature*, 145 (1940), p. 749 and *Chemical Abstracts*, 34 (1940), p. 5416.

found, soluble and insoluble in dilute acid, and the insoluble form was particular to a single species of seaweed. In 1940 the occurrence of xylans in marine algae was also reported.[36] Between 1940 and 1943 a number of papers appeared on hydrolysis and oxidative degradation of laminarin with periodic acid.[37] These culminated in the so-called Barry Degradation in which periodic acid was used to oxidise the end groups of Laminarin introducing two aldehyde groups with loss of one carbon. The aldehydes were oxidised to carboxylic acids with bromine giving a polysaccharide with two end-carboxylic acid groups and Barry concluded that laminarin consisted of 16 glucose units linked from the aldehyde carbon of one to carbon atom 3– of the adjacent unit (as opposed to the 1, 4–ether linkages of cellulose).[38] At this stage the fine details of complicated carbohydrate structures had been penetrated and a rich school of analytical and synthetic carbohydrate chemistry had developed in the Department, traditions which continue to this day. Ever seeking practical applications for seaweed, in 1943, Dillon proposed the stiff jelly which arises from absorption of water by seaweed as a food for livestock and discussed its nutritive value in comparison to potatoes. The proposed feed was tested on two pigs of approximate weight 235 lb each.[39] In the period 1942–3 the degradation procedures with periodic acid were extended by Dillon and Barry to starch, cellulose, and the glucan polysaccharide obtained from yeast.[40] In these papers the aldehyde groups generated were converted into osazones with phenylhydrazine. In 1943 Barry was a key figure in the Galway group and when he left to join UCD it must have been quite a loss for Dillon. In 1944 and 1945 they still published joint papers on the formula for agar and a galactan sulphuric ester which they suggested contained a repeating unit of four galactopyranose units linked through the 1, 3–positions.[41] Barry went on to UCD where he carried out fine work on anti-tubercular compounds before eventually moving into medical research at TCD.[42] The legacy of his work still lives on in what is part of the history of these Colleges. No publications appeared from UCG between 1947 and

36 V.C. Barry and T. Dillon, *Nature*, 146 (1940), p. 620 and *Chemical Abstracts*, 35 (1941), p. 1092.
37 V.C. Barry, *Scientific Proceedings of the Royal Dublin Society*, 22 (1941), p. 423 and *Chemical Abstracts*, 35 (1941), p. 7985; V.C. Barry, T. Dillon, and W. McGettrick, *Journal of the Chemical Society*, 1942, p.183.
38 V.C. Barry, 'A New Method of End-group Assay for Laminarin and Similarly Constituted Polysaccharides', *Journal of the Chemical Society*, 1942, p. 578.
39 E.J. Sheehy, J. Brophy, T. Dillon, and P. O Muineacháin, *Economic Proceedings of the Royal Dublin Society*, no. 12, 3 (1942), p. 150 and *Chemical Abstracts*, 37 (1943), p. 694.
40 T. Dillon, *Nature*, 155 (1945), p. 546 and *Chemical Abstracts*, 39 (1945), p. 4318; V.C. Barry, *Nature*, 152 (1943), p. 537 and *Chemical Abstracts*, 38 (1944), p. 760; V.C. Barry and T. Dillon, *Proceedings of the Royal Irish Academy*, 49B (1943), p. 177 and *Chemical Abstracts*, 38 (1944), p. 956.
41 V.C. Barry and T. Dillon, *Chemistry and Industry*, London, 1944, p. 167; V.C. Barry and T. Dillon, *Proceedings of the Royal Irish Academy*, 50B (1945), p. 349 and *Chemical Abstracts*, 40 (1946), p. 3728.
42 V.C. Barry, *Nature*, 158 (1946), p. 863 and *Chemical Abstracts*, 41 (1947), p. 1312; V.C. Barry and P.A. McNally, *Nature*, 156 (1945), p. 48 and *Chemical Abstracts*, 39 (1945), p. 5283, V.C. Barry, *Nature*, 158 (1946), p. 131 and *Chemical Abstracts*, 40 (1946), p. 7381; V.C. Barry and D. Twomey, *Proceedings of the Royal Irish Academy*, 51B (1947), p. 137 and *Chemical Abstracts*, 41 (1947), p. 4453.

1949 but in 1950 Barry's replacement, J. McKenna, reported with Dillon on the carbohydrates in the mucilage extracted from red algae.[43] McKenna was an able UCD graduate who was on the staff of the Department from 1943 until 1946 when he left to become a lecturer at the University of Sheffield. By 1949, after one hundred years, the Chemistry Department in UCG was well established and it had built up a distinguished national and international reputation. For the second fifty years of its existence, Dillon dominated the Department. I never met Dillon but there are many still living who knew him well. Remarkably, considering all that I have heard about Dillon, no one has ever had a bad word to say about him. He seems to have had a charming, friendly personality with a roguish sense of humour which could be disturbing, insofar as people were unsure whether or not he was joking. Although he was an excellent teacher of the Bohr Theory, folklore says he enjoyed telling English professors, tongue-in-cheek, that he did not believe in the electron and some of them did not know what to make of this. Dillon was a founder member of the Cumann Ceimicidhe in 1923, the forerunner of the current Institute of Chemistry of Ireland. He believed strongly in a separate Institution of Irish Chemists and in the obituary he wrote for Rosalind Clarke, who died in 1954, he highlighted her strong support for the Cumann and the fact that she was a member of the Council of the original Cumann. She joined it again on its revival in 1936 and thereafter attended many meetings of the Institute in Dublin where she retired in 1942.

In 1942 the staff of the Department consisted of Dillon with Barry, Ó Colla, and Clarke as Assistants. There were three students (including Seán Ó Cinnéide) taking the three-year honours chemistry degree and eight taking the pass degree. The numbers of students in 1993–4 were about ten times higher. The honours degree has been of four years' duration since 1964. Following the University College Galway Act, 1929, which gave UCG a special responsibility with regard to the Irish language, Dillon encouraged the teaching of chemistry through Irish. In the early 1940s, the first-year and parts of the second and third-year courses were taught through Irish as well as English. The courses through Irish were given by Barry and Ó Colla. By 1976 Ó Colla was still teaching part of the second-year course through Irish but with only one student the course was no longer viable. However, the first-year course is still given through Irish, and thirty-four students took the course in 1993–4.

The Third Fifty Years: The Modern Era

Dillon's research continued well into the 1950s. He retired in 1954 and the torch was passed on to Proinnsias S. Ó Colla who was appointed the sixth Professor of Chemistry in 1954 (fig. 7.8).[44] Ó Colla, from Gweedore, Co. Donegal, was an

43 T. Dillon and J. McKenna, *Proceedings of the Royal Irish Academy*, 53B (1950), p. 45 and *Chemical Abstracts*, 44 (1950), p. 7782.
44 In 1981, P.S. Ó Colla passed on to me some memorabilia of the Department among which I found a photograph of Dillon. This I had made into a portrait to hang in the Dillon Theatre, with a simple typed caption, 'Scholar and Patriot', which, I felt, described him accurately and which

7.8 Proinnsias S. Ó Colla, Professor of Chemistry, 1954–81

7.10 Seán Ó Cinnéide, Professor of Inorganic Chemistry, 1965–88

outstanding student who had graduated in 1936 and obtained the MSc degree in 1937, winning a special prize in the NUI travelling studentship examination of that year. In 1937–8 he studied under Professor Freudenberg at the University of Heidelberg. Having returned to UCG as Assistant in Chemistry from 1938–40, he was science master at Coláiste Éinde, Galway from 1940 to 1942 when he again returned to UCG as Senior Assistant. He was appointed Statutory Lecturer in 1947. He obtained the PhD degree in 1950 and DSc degree in 1954. From the late 1940s, he played a major supervisory role in the research of the Department. He introduced paper chromatography which became widely used in the Department since it allowed the separation of complicated branched polysaccharides.

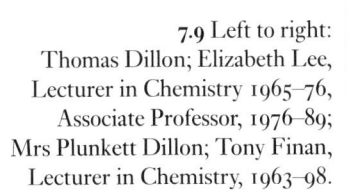

7.9 Left to right: Thomas Dillon; Elizabeth Lee, Lecturer in Chemistry 1965–76, Associate Professor, 1976–89; Mrs Plunkett Dillon; Tony Finan, Lecturer in Chemistry, 1963–98.

probably would have been to his liking. In the era we live in now, I was afraid it would be vandalised as was a picture of Divers. Fortunately it has not been and someone, presumably from the Buildings Office, provided it with a proper metal plaque with the same inscription. I hope that many generations of students will see this in the future.

Ó Colla co-authored numerous papers with Dillon and some of the younger chemists of the time such as Tony Finan and Elizabeth Lee (fig. 7.9). Many of these papers were concerned with the degradation and constitution of complicated carbohydrates such as carrageenin, arabic acid, and xylans from various sources.[45] Enzymes extracted from oats, barley, and potatoes were also used for the hydrolysis of 1, 3–linked polyglucosans.[46] In other work Ó Colla was developing analytical chromatographic techniques for chlorinated organic insecticides and hexachlorocyclohexanes as well as studying the degradation of snail galactogen and Floridean starch.[47] In 1954 Dillon published a review on the polysaccharides of the red algae.[48] The previous year he had published a major paper in the *Journal of the American Chemical Society* on the action of phenylhydrazine on the periodate degradation products of ß-D-glucopyranosyl sulfones.[49] In 1956 in the *Journal of the Institute of Chemistry of Ireland*, he published a review entitled 'Adventures in Carbohydrate Chemistry'.[50] This was his swan-song and it was fitting that he chose the Institute of Chemistry of Ireland (having served as President of Cumann Ceimicí na hÉireann, its predecessor, in 1936, and again as President of the Institute from 1952 to 1954) which he had helped to found. After his retirement he was given some space in Trinity College Dublin from where he kept in touch. The last paper which he co-authored was published in 1960 and was concerned with the structure of the gelatinous polysaccharide of *Furcellaria fastigiate*.[51] This, it was suggested, had a core consisting of a 1, 3–linked galactan with branching on C–6 with the remainder consisting of galactose sulfate and 3,6–anhydrogalactose residues. On 12 February 1969, at a dinner in the College a presentation was made to mark his eighty-fifth birthday. Vincent Barry, Boyle medallist of the Institute, delivered a lecture to honour Dillon. The title was 'Synthetic Phenazine Derivatives and Mycobacterial Disease: A Twenty Year Investigation'. Dillon expressed great pleasure in seeing so many former students

---

45 T. Dillon and P.S. Ó Colla, *Proceedings of the Royal Irish Academy*, 54B (1951), p. 51 and *Chemical Abstracts*, 46 (1952), p. 439; T. Dillon, D.F. Ó Ceallacháin, and P.S. Ó Colla, *Proceedings of the Royal Irish Academy*, 55B (1953), p. 331 and *Chemical Abstracts*, 49 (1955), p. 877; T. Dillon, D.F. Ó Ceallacháin, and P.S. Ó Colla, *Proceedings of the Royal Irish Academy*, 57B (1954), p. 31 and *Chemical Abstracts*, 50 (1956), p. 193; V.C. Barry, T. Dillon, B. Hawkins, and P.S. Ó Colla, *Nature*, 166 (1950), p. 788 and *Chemical Abstracts*, 45 (1951), p. 8461.
46 T. Dillon and P.S. Ó Colla, *Chemistry and Industry*, London, 1951, p. 111 and *Chemical Abstracts*, 45 (1951), p. 5206.
47 P. Moynihan and P.S. Ó Colla, *Chemistry and Industry*, London, 1951, p. 407 and *Chemical Abstracts*, 45 (1951), p. 10205; P.S. Ó Colla, *Journal of the Science of Food and Agriculture*, 3 (1952), p. 130 and *Chemical Abstracts*, 46 (1952), p. 8802; P.S. Ó Colla and J. O'Sullivan, *Journal of the Chemical Society*, 1954, p. 3735; P.S. Ó Colla, *Proceedings of the Royal Irish Academy*, 55B (1953), p. 165 and *Chemical Abstracts*, 48 (1954), p. 165; P.S. Ó Colla, *Proceedings of the Royal Irish Academy*, 55B (1953), p. 321 and *Chemical Abstracts*, 47 (1953), p. 10880.
48 T. Dillon, 'Polysaccharides of the Red Algae', *Congr. Intern. Botan., Paris Rapps et Communs*, Section 17, 8 (1954), p. 29 and *Chemical Abstracts*, 48 (1954), p. 11568.
49 E. Blanchfield and T. Dillon, *Journal of the American Chemical Society*, 75 (1953), p. 647.
50 T. Dillon, 'Adventures in Carbohydrate Chemistry', *Journal of the Institute of Chemistry of Ireland*, 4 (1955–6), pp. 49–63 and *Chemical Abstracts*, 52 (1958), p. 1068.
51 M.J. Clancy, K. Walsh, T. Dillon, and P.S. Ó Colla, *Scientific Proceedings of the Royal Dublin Society*, series A, 1 (1960), p. 197 and *Chemical Abstracts*, 55 (1961), p. 16698.

who had achieved distinction as professional chemists coming from all over the country to celebrate his birthday fifteen years after his retirement. He died on 11 December 1971 aged eighty-seven years.

All of the references to be found in the *Chemical Abstracts of the American Chemical Society* and the *Abstracts of the London Chemical Society* for papers from the Galway Chemistry Department for the period 1849–1960, including all of Dillon's papers, are included in the footnotes to this article. More work was, of course, produced in non-published project reports which have now become obscure. From 1960 only selected references are included. All of the publications from the Department are, of course, quoted in the annual *Reports* of the President of the College. History is the story of the doings and adventures of those who have lived and died. When it is written about those who are still alive it becomes politics. The remainder of the major players in this story are happily still alive and hence the remainder of this article is but a record of broad facts and there can be no special mentions of individuals. It is for another generation to assess what was done and to place their value on it.

Many years ago, Dillon drew attention to the increased teaching load due to the growth in the numbers of students after the First World War. In the early 1950s history was repeating itself. Student numbers were increasing, and chemistry as a subject had become revolutionised after the Second World War. No longer could a group of organic chemists working in a single field run a university chemistry degree course. Most American and European university chemistry departments had branches of Physical, Inorganic, Organic, and Analytical chemistry by the mid 1950s. Ireland lagged behind and it was not till the late sixties that new science buildings, including Chemistry Departments, appeared in UCC and UCD, and 1973 in UCG. Meanwhile the Galway carbohydrate research group was continuing to flourish in both teaching and research. Cation exchange resins were being used for both carbohydrate synthesis and degradation by Ó Colla, Lee, and Finan, and the Barry degradation was extended to beet araban and Yeast Mannan.[52] Students from the Department were publishing in universities overseas such as Ó hEocha at the University of California, at La Jolla, and Finan on the application of mass spectrometry to carbohydrates, in the University of Glasgow.[53] Ó hEocha was appointed Lecturer in Chemistry in 1955. His work was biochemical in nature, being concerned with chromatography and acid hydrolysis of Phycoerythrins and

---

52 P.S. Ó Colla and E.E. Lee, *Chemistry and Industry*, London, 1956, p. 522 and *Chemical Abstracts*, 51 (1957), p. 3466; P.A. Finan and P.S. Ó Colla, *Chemistry and Industry*, 1955, p. 1387 and *Chemical Abstracts*, 50 (1956), p. 10012; P.A. Finan and P.S. Ó Colla, *Chemistry and Industry*, 1958, p. 493 and *Chemical Abstracts*, 53 (1959), p. 235; P.A. Finan, A. Nolan, and P.S. Ó Colla, *Chemistry and. Industry*, 1958, p. 1404 and *Chemical Abstracts*, 54 (1960), p. 6563.

53 C. Ó hEocha, *Congr. Intern. Biochem. Résumés Communs, 3e Congr.*, Brussels, 1955, p. 106 and *Chemical Abstracts*, 51 (1957), p. 3757; *Archives of Biochemistry and Biophysics*, 73 (1958), p. 207 and *Chemical Abstracts*, 52 (1958), p. 9254; P.A. Finan, R.I. Reed, and W. Snedden, *Chemistry and Industry*, London, 1958, p. 1172 and *Chemical Abstracts*, 53 (1959), p. 11243; P.A. Finan and R.I. Reed, *Nature*, supplement no. 24, 184 (1959), p. 1866 and *Chemical Abstracts*, 54 (1960), p. 10498.

Phycocyanins of cryptomonads.[54] Along with Professor Máirín de Valera, he organised the Third International Seaweed Symposium which was held in the Department in August 1958. He left Chemistry in 1963 to become the first Professor of Biochemistry and subsequently President of the College. Dr Finan, who was appointed to the Lectureship vacated by Ó hEocha in 1963, still supervises an active research group in carbohydrate chemistry and was, until his recent retirement, Dean of the Science Faculty.

Up until the early 1930s, the Chemistry Department was in the main College building, then it was moved to the Model School on the Newcastle Road about 300 yards from the main campus. By the early 1960s the available space was no longer adequate and the College relinquished the Model School. Ó Colla was offered the top storey of Árus de Brún but he held out for a new Department and decided to opt for temporary wooden huts located behind the old civil engineering building. The move out of the Model School in 1963 was traumatic for Ó Colla and for the next ten years the situation was unsatisfactory with the lecture halls, laboratories, stores, library, and offices scattered widely through these huts. Ó Colla, however, had read the situation well for the long-term welfare of chemistry and the present generation in the new Department, occupied in 1972, are the beneficiaries of his judgement. He had the satisfaction of occupying the new Department from 1972 to 1981. The first major international Conference, a EUCHEM Conference on Carbohydrate Chemistry, was held in the new Department in 1976, organised by Ó Colla and Finan.

Meanwhile, in the 1960s, the increased numbers of students and the changed nature of the subject required expansion of the academic staff. Elizabeth Lee, who had been an assistant since 1947, was appointed to an NUI Statutory Lectureship in 1963 and Seán Ó Cinnéide was appointed first Professor of Inorganic Chemistry in 1965 (fig. 7.10). Ó Cinnéide brought a new dimension of inorganic and nuclear chemistry to the Department. After obtaining a first-class honours BSc (1945) and MSc degrees (1946) at UCG, and working in some teaching and industrial posts until 1950, he joined the Atomic Energy Research Establishment at Harwell, Oxfordshire as a Scientific Officer. By 1965 he had been promoted through a number of grades to Principal Scientific Officer. His research up to 1961 led to forty-five research papers and he was awarded the DSc degree of the NUI in that year. He set up a vigorous Inorganic section in the Chemistry Department in 1965 and the first higher degrees in Inorganic Chemistry were awarded in the late sixties. Research was concerned with metal complexes and uranium chemistry. The interactions of humic acid from peat with metals were also analysed.[55] Ó Cinnéide supervised many PhD and MSc degrees. He developed and reorganised the teaching of

---

54 C. Ó hEocha and M. Raftery, *Nature*, 184 (1959), p. 1047 and *Chemical Abstracts*, 54 (1960), p. 11163; C. Ó hEocha and F.T. Haxo, *Biochimica et Biophysica Acta*, 41 (1960), p. 516 and *Chemical Abstracts*, 54 (1960), p. 25085.

55 S. Ó Cinnéide, J. Scanlon, and M.J. Hynes, *Chemistry and Industry*, London, 1972, p. 340; C. Ó Nualláin and S. Ó Cinnéide, *Journal of Inorganic and Nuclear Chemistry*, 35 (1973), p. 2871; S. Ó Cinnéide, *Ceimic Bunúsach*, pt. ii (Dublin, 1973); C. Ó Nualláin and S. Ó Cinnéide, *Journal of Inorganic Chemistry*, 36 (1974), p. 1420.

inorganic chemistry and he contributed immensely to the teaching of chemistry through Irish. He wrote two textbooks, in Irish, for undergraduates. He retired in 1992. Financial constraints have to date delayed the filling of the vacant professorship.

In 1962–3 when the Department moved into temporary accommodation, the number of students taking chemistry were: First Science, 85; First Agricultural Science, 19; First Engineering, 32; Pre-medical, 74; total first year, 210. In Second Science there were 57 students and 13 in Second Agricultural Science. There were 22 taking the third-year BSc pass course and 15 in the fourth-year honours BSc group as well as five postgraduates. The overall total coming to 374. These numbers were typical of the early to mid 1960s. The corresponding total numbers for 1993–4 were: first-year total 560; second-year total 138; third-year total 74; fourth-year honours BSc, 29; postgraduates, 52. An overall total of 853 students. Dr Elizabeth Lee supervised an active research group and contributed to the teaching of Organic Chemistry. In the years since 1947, when she was appointed Assistant, she had undertaken a heavy teaching load in all branches of the subject. In her research she synthesised a wide range of new derivatives of carbohydrates and carried out detailed structural analysis using nuclear magnetic resonance and x-ray crystallography. Her work led to fourteen PhD and six MSc degrees and a wide range of publications.[56] She was appointed Associate Professor in 1976. She retired officially in 1989 but she served for a further three years in an acting capacity. The late sixties and seventies saw the appointment of the current staff as follows: B. Ó Cochláin (1969), the first physical chemist; M. Hynes, Inorganic (1971); W.J. Spillane, Organic (1970); R.N. Butler, Organic (1971); P. McArdle, Inorganic (1972); D. Cunningham, Inorganic (1972); J. Simmie, Physical (1972); Wm Carroll, Physical (1976); N.W.A. Geraghty, Organic (1979); A. Savage, Organic (1983); T. Higgins, Inorganic (1989); and F. Heaney, Organic (1992). Mr John Muldoon was appointed Chief Technician in 1980. Prior to that, in a remarkable record, the O'Healy family from Galway filled the post of Chief Technician from the time of Rowney (1886) to Ó Colla (1979). Mr Ronan O'Healy was Technician from 1927 to 1979 and his father John O'Healy served as Technician from 1886 until 1934. In these early years the post was not designated as Chief Technician, but it was the equivalent of the modern post. In 1995 the technical staff of the Department were: J. Muldoon, P. Naughton, T. Killeen, J. Cotter, S. Collier, S. Kelehan, Ms B. Conroy, D. McGrath, G. O'Reilly and the secretarial staff were Ms B. Stewart and Ms Y. Egan.

The Chemistry Department in 1995

In 1981 I was appointed to succeed P.S. Ó Colla. Since then the academic staff have developed the Department with an increased emphasis on modern analytical instrumentation. In 1984 the Department opened the first highfield nuclear

---

56 A few examples are: D. McGrath, E.E. Lee, and P.S. Ó Colla, *Carbohydrate Research*, 11 (1969), p. 461; *idem*, ibid., 11 (1969), p. 453; P.S. Ó Colla, E.E. Lee, and S. McGrath, *Scientific Proceedings of the Royal Dublin Society*, series A, 1 (13) (1963), p. 337; E.E. Lee, P. Browne, P. McArdle, and D. Cunningham, *Carbohydrate Research*, 224 (1992), p. 285; E.E. Lee, P. McArdle, D. Cunningham, and M. O'Gara, ibid., 241 (1993), p. 261; E.E. Lee, A. Bruzzi, E. O'Brien, and P.S. Ó Colla, ibid., 35 (1974), p. 103.

magnetic resonance laboratory in the country which until 1987–8 provided a service to the other universities until they acquired similar facilities. The NMR laboratory acquired a new 400 MHz machine in 1996. The Inorganic Section of the Department has developed a unique x-ray crystallography and x-ray powder diffraction laboratory. A special high performance liquid chromatography (HPLC) laboratory has been set up and this, as well as all other forms of chromatography, feature prominently in the BSc courses. A new honours BSc degree in Chemistry and Applied Chemistry, containing applied and industrial chemistry in addition to the core fundamental chemistry of the honours BSc degree, began in 1990. A two-unit course on Analytical and Industrial Chemistry was set up when the Science Faculty unitised the BSc degree and this third-year course is heavily subscribed each year. After assessments by the Royal Society of Chemistry, London and the Institute of Chemistry of Ireland in 1993 and 1998, both of the degree courses in the Department have been recognised for professional membership of these bodies for five-year periods. Over the past ten years the Department has collaborated with the Biochemistry Department in running the very successful postgraduate Higher Diploma in Applied Science – Biochemistry/Chemistry – following the realisation by the Science Faculty in the late 1970s of the need for Applied Diplomas to parallel the Higher Diploma in Education for science graduates seeking industrial employment. The postgraduate research school of the Department accommodates on average about forty-five research students. Over a hundred PhD degrees and approximately fifteen MSc degrees have been conferred for research since 1981 (see Appendix). Most of these graduates are employed in Ireland and provide a major source of support and goodwill for the Department. The academic staff are all active in research, with each supervising a research group. Every year approximately thirty research papers from the Department are published in prestigious refereed journals, in many cases the *Journal of the Chemical Society London*. Over the past decade numerous conferences have been held in the Department, including two Congresses of the Institute of Chemistry of Ireland and two Irish Universities Chemistry Research Colloquia, and a major EUCHEM Conference on '1, 3–Dipoles in Organic Synthesis' in July 1990. Collaboration with industrial companies has been strongly encouraged and a number of companies have been given special assistance and laboratory access (when laboratories are free from practicals) which helped them to get into production. The approach adopted is 'tuigeann ceimiceoir ceimiceoir eile'; the encounters between university chemists and chemists in industry have been mutually productive. I feel Thomas Dillon would approve. Many chemists from industrial companies have been invited to give lectures on their work in the Chemistry Department over the past decade.

At the present time in the research fields of the academic staff, the Department is well-known, it participates internationally and it operates at the forefront. The task now is to keep it there. As Victor Hugo declared: 'Scientists have searched for a perpetuum mobile; they have found it: it is science itself'. The quest is forever.[57]

---

57 When I was asked to do this work by Tom Boylan and Tadhg Foley, I was happy to undertake it as an obvious duty, but I was all too aware of the difficulty of the task. I knew that nothing I would write could do justice to the people involved. The story is too large and all-embracing.

Addendum

This paper was written during the period July–September 1995, on the occasion of the 150th anniversary of the foundation of the College, and it reflects the Chemistry Department as it was at that time. Much has changed in the past four years and some of the main changes are briefly listed here. Dr Colm Ó hEocha, the then President of the College, retired in 1996 and sadly passed away in May 1997. Mr T. Killeen, technician in the organic laboratory, sadly died unexpectedly in August 1997. Dr Tony Finan, having completed six years as Dean of the Faculty of Science, retired in September 1998 and happily still graces the Department with his knowledge and wisdom. New appointments include Dr Donal P. Leech (Lecturer, Physical Chemistry), Mr Gerard Fahy (Organic Laboratory Technician), Ms Karen Costello (Secretary), Ms Keelin McKenna (temporary part-time Technician). Academic staff promoted include Michael Hynes (Associate Professor), Angela Savage (Statutory Lecturer), and William Carroll (Statutory Lecturer). Conference activity in the Department increased significantly and major conferences held include the 50th Irish University Chemistry Research Colloquium (1998), a world conference on Carbohydrate Chemistry (1999), a Euroconference on Bioactive Molecules (1999), an International Conference on Heterocyclic Chemistry, jointly with the Royal Society of Chemistry, London (1998), and an International Conference on Carbohydrate Chemistry, jointly with the Royal Society of Chemistry, London (1997). The development of the equipment, facilities, courses, and published research record of the Department continues apace.

Since 1981 it has been my good fortune to have the co-operation of a first-rate team of academic staff who are leaders in their profession. The Department is fortunate in being served by a group of technicians who, led by the Chief Technician, share our pride in the high standard of teaching and research which has now endured for 150 years, and who demonstrate this pride by the consistent high quality of their work. In preparing this paper I have had many helpful discussions with Tony Finan, Elizabeth Lee, and Seán Ó Cinneide, and I thank them for their recollections, anecdotes, and the documentation they have given me. Finally I wish to acknowledge the assistance I received from Professor Ó Colla and the late President, Dr Colm Ó hEocha.

APPENDIX
PhD and MSc Degrees by Research in Chemistry
(asterisk denotes MSc by Research)

1923 to 1947

1923: E.F. Lavelle*
1929: Annie McGuinness*
1934: Mary B. Gallagher*
1936: P. Moynihan*
1937: Eva Ryder,* P.S. Ó Colla,*
Ann Tinney,* T. Ó Tuama
1939: Mary Tully*
1940: Mary B. Folan*
1941: Winifred McGettrick*
1944: B.M. Hawkins*
1945: D. Ó Tuama,* Sarah Forde,*
Mary F. Jordan*
1946: S. Ó Cinnéide,* J. McKenna,*
M.T. Jordan*
1947: E.E. Lee*

1950 to 1969

1950: C.B. Ní Gairneir,* P.S. Ó Colla,
P.J. Haran,* C. Ó hEocha*
P. Canavan,* F. Ní Choluim,*
P. Horan,* J.J. O'Sullivan,*
Maire B. Ní Uaildrich,*
Máire de Paor,* Eilis Ní Chonaire
1951: P.M. Ó hIceadha,* Mary P. Foy,*
Caitlin Breathnach,* M.M. Devitt,*
Margaret Devane,*
D.F. Ó Ceallacháin*
1952: B. Ní Fhiaich,* M.J. Clancy,*
Johanna T. O'Sullivan,*
J.P. McGlynn,* E. Blanchfield,* P.S. Clerkin*
1953: K.P. Eames,* B.C. Slattery,*
M.A. Duane*
1954: P.A. Finan,* P.K. Hanley*
1955: M.B. Golden,* J.D. Holland,*
J.J. O'Donnell,* P.A. Kearney,*
D.F. Ó Ceallacháin
1956: T.M. Feeley,* R.A. Rutledge,*
A.C. Nolan,* M.M. Scanlan*
1957: Rosemary Holland,*
M.A. Hayes,*
P.S. Ó Donnchadha*
1958: M. Manning,* P. O'Hare,*
Daithi McCraith,*
Elizabeth Conroy*
1959: C.N. Ó Ceallacháin*
1960: E.E. Lee, F. Ó Muirthile,*
Kathleen D. Gardner*
1961: Margaret A.C. Birmingham,*
D. Mac An Fhailí*
1962: J.A. Molloy,* R.F Lambe,*
A. Kenny,* D.A. Curley,*
D.A. MacDaeid,* D. McGrath,*
Donal Carroll,* Adrian Kilbane*
1963: P.J. Connolly,* B. Ó hUadaigh,*
T.M.D. Feeley,* T.A. Kenny,*
F.R. Lambe,* E. MacErlane,*
P. Ó Carra
1964: D. O'Hare,* C.C. Ó Murchu*
1965: Mary R. McInerney,*
Ann U. Egan,* M.A. Raftery
1967: M.P.J. Little*
1968: P.P. Canavan,* H. Lawless,*
U.B. Ó Ceallacháin,* Grainne Finan,* Ellen Cleary*
1969: D. MacDaeid, J.P. Garvey,
T.M.D. Feeley

1970 to 1979

1970: S. Kilmartin,* J.G. Brennan,
M.J. Hynes, H. Stynes,* J. Scanlon*
1971: A.P. Dunbar,* P. McCarthy,*
C. O'Donnell
1972: Sr A. Hartigan, K.B. Nolan,
R. O'Toole,* J. Scanlon
1973: T.A. Costelloe, J.M.B. Hanniffy,
J. McCarthy, A.J. Moran,*
E. O'Brien, A.A.M. Corless,
N. Regan*
1974: J. Blunnie,* A. Bruzzi, J.J. McEntee,
R.G. Shaw

1975: Mrs J.P. Carroll,* W.M. Carroll, J.N. Cassidy, J. Finnegan,* P.J. Hennelly
1976: G.A. Benson, W.B. King, J.A. McKeon
1977: Ann Hanahoe,* P.M. Larkin, Mrs. B. O'Regan, P. Firtear,* G. Keaveney, N. Sherlock
1978: P.F. Brannick, W.A. McCann, K. McLoughlin
1979: S.K. Chopra,* M.G. Cunningham,* Ann O'Donoghue, J.O. Wood

1980 to 1994

1980: T. Kelly, G. McGlinchey
1981: S.K. Chopra, T. Higgins, P. Kavanagh, T.M. McEvoy, G.M. Mooney,* G. Moran, J. Nunan, P. O'Malley, C. O'Regan
1982: E.P. Coffey,* T. Hannigan, G.M. Morris, J.P. O'Reilly, M.T. O'Shea*
1983: R. Benson,* D. Lenihan,* M. McNeela,* J. Brennan, V. Garvin, S. McDermott, J. O'Callaghan, Ann Taheny, Eilis O'Donoghue, Denis O'Donoghue, J.P. James
1984: Sean Johnston, B. Kneafsey, J. Thornton,* A. Abuhalguma, M. Kearns,* C. O'Meara*
1985: M. Little, J. Walshe 1986: J. McGinley,* Noreen Hanly, J. Kavanagh, D.P. Shelly, M. O'Dowd, T. Walshe, P. Burke
1987: J. Ferry, Mary Mahon, N. Hallinan, Ann M. Evans,* Joan Fitzgerald, John Lally, Noel Gavin, John Reidy
1988: Patricia Browne, Ann Gillan, P. Patterson, Frank Falls, Gerard O'Halloran, M. Keane, F. McHugh, M. Monaghan
1989: Mary Casey, Noreen Morris, D. Kelly, Eilis Marren, Paul O'Shea, K. Fitzgerald, Brenda Cashin, Carmel Donoghue, Sinead D'Arcy, M.A. Sheahan
1990: M. Dunphy, B. Howley, John McGinley, E.M. McNeela,* Ann Kenny*
1991: Carmel Breslin, M. Boyce, N. Melody, J.J. Donoghue, D. McHale, John Gallagher, C. Blanco,* Jim Garvey, Fiona Lysaght
1992: T. Mooney, Jean Keenan, D. Sheerin, Paul Duffy, M. Doody*
1993: K.F. Quinn, H.A. Gavin, N. Clarke, M. O'Gara, J. Keely
1994: E.P. Ní Bhradaigh, Mary A. Flynn, Geraldine B.M. Hogan, S.C.G. Ó Domhnaill, Donal F. O'Shea, Mary T. Rabbitte, Alan G. Ryder, C. Ann Ryder, Carmel S. Pyne, J. Wurmel,* Karen Daly,* J.G. Sharkey,* D.J. Claffey, H.J. Curran, E.E. Lynskey, C.P. Munnelly, M.A.I. Murphy, P.V. Murphy, M.A. Walsh

Professor William King and the Establishment of the Geological Sciences in Queen's College Galway

DAVID A.T. HARPER

William King was appointed to the chair of Mineralogy and Geology at the opening of Queen's College Galway on 30 October 1849, at the age of forty, with no formal qualifications (fig. 8.1). He arrived in Galway, already surrounded by the controversy attending his rapid departure from the Hancock Museum, Newcastle-upon-Tyne, and was armed with substantial collections of fossils including the future type and figured material for his classic monograph on the Permian fossils of England. King quickly accumulated collections from the Silurian rocks of north Connemara and South Mayo and the Carboniferous rocks around Lough Corrib and Lough Mask together with the Burren. A teaching programme, initially mainly for agriculture and engineering students, was soon up and running. Nevertheless, from a position of relative isolation, King participated in a number of high-profile debates and research programmes together with projects currently occupying the centre stage of European science. His Permian monograph formed an important basis for the description and identification of the Permian System and its fossils whereas his many taxonomic papers helped set the agenda for several future animal and plant classifications. King, together with Thomas Henry Rowney, debunked the so-called dawn creature *Eozoön* and, based largely on geological evidence, King established the antiquity of Neanderthal Man; not surprisingly, his modified support for Darwin's *On the Origin of Species* was not popular locally. But his interests ranged far outside palaeontology; he discussed, with variable degrees of success, the economic geology of Ireland, the development of cleavage in Donegal, and the uplift of the Burren, and he acted as a consultant for the route of transatlantic cables. His remarkable career undoubtedly brought considerable honour to Gladstone's 'derelict college in a decaying town'; his wide-ranging experience and knowledge also formed the basis for a top-quality undergraduate programme in the geological sciences. Despite his considerable international reputation he remained a relatively anonymous figure in the vigorous and colourful Irish geological community of the nineteenth century.

Professor William King DSc died peacefully at his home in Glenoir, Galway, on 24 June 1886 at the age of seventy-eight and a few days later was buried in the New Cemetery in Galway. His death ended a remarkable career, spanning nearly

8.1 William King, Professor of Mineralogy, Geology, and Natural History, 1849–83

fifty years, and documented in over seventy scientific papers.[1] King established an international reputation through a vigorous and sometimes controversial research programme, often with far-reaching consequences for the advancement of nineteenth century science. He developed a teaching curriculum that apparently included a wide range of contemporary developments in the science, and accumulated and maintained collections that have instructed generations of students, which now as part of the James Mitchell Museum, educate, inform, and entertain the public at large. He participated in a number of high-profile, international debates from one of the then most isolated and poorest parts of Europe. His legacy can be physically measured by the breadth of his collections and publications. Relatively few students followed courses in Mineralogy and Geology and perhaps

1 D.A.T. Harper, '"The King of Queen's College": William King D.Sc., First Professor of Geology at Galway', in D.A.T. Harper (ed.), *William King D.Sc. (1809–1886): A Palaeontological Tribute* (Galway, 1988), pp. 1–24.

his most notable graduate was his own son, William King jun. who graduated in October 1853 with a BA and directed the Geological Survey of India from 1887 until 1894.[2]

But above all King's tenure demonstrated the close links between teaching, research, and museology within the university system. His curriculum, extant in examination papers, his research profile documented in scientific papers, and the importance of the practical side of the science manifest in the collections and displays of the geological museum, were remarkable achievements. He was at the heart of Sir D'Arcy W. Thompson's 'Nest of Scholars' in Queen's College Galway.[3]

Life in Sunderland

King was born in a small cottage in Low Row, Bishopswearmouth, Sunderland, on 22 April 1809. His father was a coal caster of probable Scottish origin, although this has been debated; his mother was a genteel lady who kept a confectionery shop in the town.[4] The young William was educated in the best of the local schools, developing a keen interest in books and natural history together with a desire to collect. Apprenticed to an ironmonger, he gradually accumulated sufficient capital to open a book shop where soon the literati of Sunderland gathered and held court. In the quest to advance his scientific knowledge he attracted the attention of Sir William Jackson Hooker, later director of the Royal Botanic Gardens at Kew. In fact King's first papers, published in 1843 and 1844, concerned some Carboniferous plant genera based on his own collections from the Westphalian rocks of north-east England; these collections were later to arrive in Galway as part of the foundation for the Geological Museum. Posts as the secretary and librarian of the Sunderland Literary and Philosophical Society were followed by a position as the first curator of the collections of the Sunderland Natural History and Antiquarian Society.[5] Grants from the Society permitted him to collect in Yorkshire, Germany, and the Alps. In 1839 William King married Jane Nicholson, a native of Newcastle-upon-Tyne. Ironically his marriage would later, in 1842, disqualify him from the vacant post of editor and curator in the Geological Society of London, a position reserved for bachelors.[6]

---

2   G.L. Herries Davies, 'William King and the Irish Geological Community', in Harper (ed.), *William King*, pp. 25–32.
3   C. Ó hEocha, 'The Queen's College at Galway: Some Memories', in D. Ó Cearbhaill (ed.), *Galway: Town and Gown 1484–1984* (Dublin, 1984), p. 174. See also T.P. Foley, '"A Nest of Scholars": Biographical Material on Some Early Professors at Queen's College Galway', *Journal of the Galway Archaeological and Historical Society*, 42 (1989–90), pp. 72–86.
4   W. Brockie, 'Sunderland Worthies: No. 8, Professor William King', *Sunderland Public Library Circular*, 10 (1901), pp. 206–10.
5   T. Pettigrew, 'William King (1808–1886): A Biographical Note', *GCG: Newsletter of the Geological Curators' Group*, 3 (1980), pp. 327–9.
6   Harper, 'The King of Queen's College', pp. 1–24.

Hancock Museum

In 1840 King was appointed curator of what is now the Hancock Museum in Newcastle-upon-Tyne. His annual salary of £100 not only sustained himself and his family; it also financed his rooms, additional staff, and collecting trips. King had no obvious private means, which made him quite distinct from the prosperous, gentlemanly culture of Victorian geologists. Soon King would be locked in battle with his employer, the Committee of the Natural History Society of Northumberland. Undoubtedly King traded in fossils and moreover retained for his own collections material acquired during his expeditions for the Hancock Museum. The circumstances surrounding these disagreements and his ultimate departure have become known as the 'King Affair',[7] which is documented by lengthy correspondence.[8] By 1847 the Management Committee of the Hancock Museum had invited King to resign. The locks were changed but not before King removed a very substantial part of his collections.

Nevertheless the major beneficiary of the affair was to be the Geological Museum in Queen's College Galway. During the next two years King was actively preparing his Permian monograph for publication and attracted the notice of Sir Henry De la Beche. De la Beche, through his friendship with Sir Robert Peel, was determined to establish a Geological Survey in Britain and Ireland with specialists competent to compete with the best in Europe.[9] The survey in Ireland was founded in 1845, the same year as the Queen's Colleges; De la Beche also had a major role to play in the appointment of the first professors in Mineralogy and Geology.

Queen's College Galway

In a brief statement the *Galway Vindicator* announced, on Saturday 11 August 1849, that William King, late Curator of the Newcastle Museum, lecturer on Geology, and author of several memoirs on Palaeontology and Geology, had been appointed to the chair of Mineralogy and Geology.[10] The Department was part of the Science division of the Faculty of Arts, located in the Main Quadrangle of the College. The course offered initially, catered for second-year agriculture and engineering students and the first four students attended over fifty lectures during the 1850–1 academic year.

King's salary was £200 per annum, but in addition to the duties of a professor, the chair of Mineralogy and Geology also had responsibility for the museum.[11] The curator had to attend the museum when necessary, catalogue and present

---

7 S. Turner, 'Collections and Collectors of Note: 26, William King 1808–1886', *GCG: Newsletter of the Geological Curators' Group*, 3 (1980), pp. 322–6.
8 William King correspondence, Archives of the Natural History Museum, London, England and Hancock Museum, Newcastle-upon-Tyne, England.
9 P.J. McCartney, *Henry De la Beche: Observations on an Observer* (Cardiff, 1977).
10 *Galway Vindicator*, 11 August 1849.
11 The Colleges Act Letters and Patent (1859).

specimens, supply and record material, and revise the museum catalogue annually; moreover the curator undertook to preserve from loss and injury all museum specimens. Teaching loads, however, were relatively light; three lectures per week, one each on Monday, Wednesday, and Friday formed the basis of the course.[12] Apparently no practicals or fieldwork were scheduled.

Professor King's inaugural lecture, in the presence of the Vice-President, covered a wide range of contemporary topics in the geological sciences and in some respects set the agenda for much of King's subsequent career in the Queen's College.[13] King operated within the widest possible definition of geology. Drawing on his already comprehensive knowledge of local geology, King cited the spectacular diversity of rocks nearby, including the Carboniferous limestones stretching east from Lough Corrib, the older greenstones forming the foundations of the city, and the granites, marbles, mica slates, and serpentinites of Connemara. Sediments such as the conglomerates north of Killary were derived from the destruction of huge mountains, limestones accumulated in ancient seas, and coal deposits were the remains of decomposed ancient vegetation. And whereas many rocks have been baked by volcanic activity, the granites around the northern part of Galway Bay were once a liquid. Metals and minerals associated with these rocks and relevant to the human economy should not be overlooked.

Many sedimentary rocks contain rich accumulations of fossil animals and plants. King recognised the simplicity of very ancient life and the apparent complexity and diversity of living animal and plant communities. 'Seaweeds' had already been reported from rocks the same age as the ancient slates (Silurian) around Oughterard, while higher plants such as the tracheophytes arrived later. There was clearly an order of creation with the consecutive appearance on the planet of biotas from the simplest to the most complex against a background of increasing diversity.

The concept of deep time was a recurrent theme in King's address. Niels Stensen, during the late 1600s, had established the fundamental principle of superposition of strata, that younger rocks generally overlie older rocks. Giovanni Arduino's research a century later, in northern Italy, indicated that the rocks in the Apennines at least could be classified into three main temporal divisions: primary or basement rocks, secondary or stratified rocks, and tertiary or poorly consolidated strata. Although Desnoyer added a fourth division in the 1820s, the Quaternary, the first two terms were later discarded. By 1815, however, William Smith had developed the crucial role of evolving life in the identification and correlation of rock strata. Smith, an engineer engaged in canal construction, sketched in vivid detail, from the top of horse-drawn coaches, the stratigraphical succession from eastern England to north Wales, based on a series of traverses across country. These traverses formed the basis for the first geological map of England and Wales published in 1815.

Equipped with the techniques of superposition and correlation by fossils together with a broad chronostratigraphic-type classification, King adopted a

---

12 Queen's College Galway, *Calendar* (1852).
13 *Galway Vindicator*, 22 December 1849.

similar strategy to illustrate the geological history of eastern England and Scotland together with the west of Ireland. Two traverses, one centred on his native northeast of England and one from his adopted home on the western seaboard of Europe, extravagantly displayed some snapshots from the long and varied geological history of these islands. King's transect from the Southern Uplands of Scotland first encountered Silurian slates overlain unconformably by the Old Red Sandstone, Carboniferous limestones, sandstones, and carbonaceous shales; rocks of the Permian System formed the summit of the primary division, cropping out around King's native Wearside and forming the basis for much of his lifetime's work. Middle England was the site of secondary rocks where the Triassic, Jurassic, and Cretaceous systems preserved the age of reptiles. Tertiary clays and sandstones in the London Basin with both molluscs and mammal faunas were overlain by superficial Quaternary deposits. Could the same type of section be constructed for King's adopted home? In simple terms, a traverse from Galway Bay to north of Killary Harbour encounters first the igneous rocks of the Galway Granite and the adjacent metamorphic belt of Dalradian rocks centred on the quartzites of the Twelve Bens; these were apparently overlain by Silurian slates and, north of Killary Harbour, the Old Red Sandstone (now recognised as an Ordovician conglomerate sequence); these units in turn were overlain by the Mountain Limestone (Carboniferous) which occupies great tracts of County Galway east of Lough Corrib and Lough Mask.

King devoted some time to aspects of economic and engineering geology and to the relevance of geology to agriculture with a view to the needs of his students. Those involved in agriculture and civil engineering must study geology; projects such as canal and harbour engineering, tunnelling and railway construction, drainage and mining schemes together with the quarrying of building stones, directly involve geology. His strong emphasis on these aspects of the geological sciences was undoubtedly client driven; the majority of his students were initially from these backgrounds.

The final part of King's lecture was devoted to the planet's changing biotas and reflected the professor's own research interests which would be developed in later teaching programmes to Arts students. King paused first to note, with a sense of wonder, the anatomy of the Jurassic fish-lizard, the ichthyosaur, quite distinct and quite different from any living animal.[14] His discourse, however, concentrated on the development of terrestrial vertebrate life. The early nineteenth-century discoveries of marine reptiles and the first dinosaurs, although sparse, were understandably the focus of much attention. The primary period was dominated by marine life; the seas swarmed with all manner of shells and fishes. But the discovery of *Cheirotherium*, the hand-shaped footprints of a tetrapod, in Triassic sandstones in England, signalled the rocks and fossils of the secondary period and the first definitive evidence of life on land. Later during the Jurassic and early Cretaceous periods, the dinosaurs such as the carnivore *Megalosaurus* and the herbivore *Iguanodon* appeared. By the tertiary period extraordinary mammals such as the

---

14 S.R. Howe, T. Sharpe, and H.S. Torrens, *Ichthyosaurs: A History of Fossil 'Sea Dragons'* (Cardiff, 1981).

giant sloth *Megatherium*, together with large carnivorous birds such as *Dinornis*, populated the planet. The mid nineteenth-century fossil database was still small, and many extraordinary discoveries were yet to be made. Nevertheless enough information existed to formulate models for the origin and development of life on earth.

King's inaugural lecture was a magnificent exposition of the developing techniques and wisdom of mid nineteenth-century geological science. The clear appreciation of deep time, developing life, and the dynamism of the planet's systems formed the basis of King's philosophy. Although it was not until this century that the true enormity of deep time was defined and plate tectonics provided a model through which to describe the planet's dynamics, a paradigm for developing life, evolution by natural selection, was just around the corner. King's style was imaginative and upbeat; despite his working-class background he was in the vanguard of nineteenth-century geological science, was very much aware of and involved in current developments, and was not afraid to engage in controversy.

Nineteenth-Century Palaeontology and Stratigraphy

During the late 1700s and early to mid 1800s the search was on to find, describe, and establish new major stratigraphical units, the geological systems; each system would represent a period of geological time, and at its type section, could function as a standard reference or yardstick for that particular time interval. By the end of the century all the main stratigraphical divisions were in place and with the aid of careful mapping and fossil data all the geological systems had been assembled in stratigraphical order (fig. 8.2). The development of a global stratigraphy together with relatively robust animal and plant classifications provided the basis for broader studies on the development and evolution of life on the planet.[15]

Although fossils had been recognised as the remains of living organisms by Greeks such as Xenophanes and Herodotus, many medieval scholars were in favour of more magical and mystical interpretations. Nevertheless Leonardo da Vinci (1452–1519), Niels Stensen (1638–86), and Robert Hooke (1625–1703) established without doubt the organic nature of fossils.[16] During the mid 1700s the discovery of the North American mastodons, quite different from living elephants, indicated not only the reality of fossils but also the probability of extinction. The late 1700s and early 1800s, however, saw an escalation in the discovery of many significant fossil remains (fig. 8.3). During the later 1700s Collini described the extinct flying lizard *Pterodactylus* while during the early 1800s the first fragmentary remains of dinosaurs, *Iguanodon* and *Megalosaurus* were discovered in the Mesozoic rocks of England. The reports of ancient marine reptiles, such as Fajau's Maastricht *Mosasaur* and ichthyosaurs and plesiosaurs from the Dorset coast, formed the basis for a radically new interpretation of life in the Mesozoic seas. These and other exciting discoveries promoted a sustained interest in fossils with

---

15 M.J.S. Rudwick, *The Meaning of Fossils: Episodes in the History of Palaeontology* (London, 1972).
16 M.J. Benton and D.A.T. Harper, *Basic Palaeontology* (Harlow, 1997).

David A.T. Harper *on the Geological Sciences*

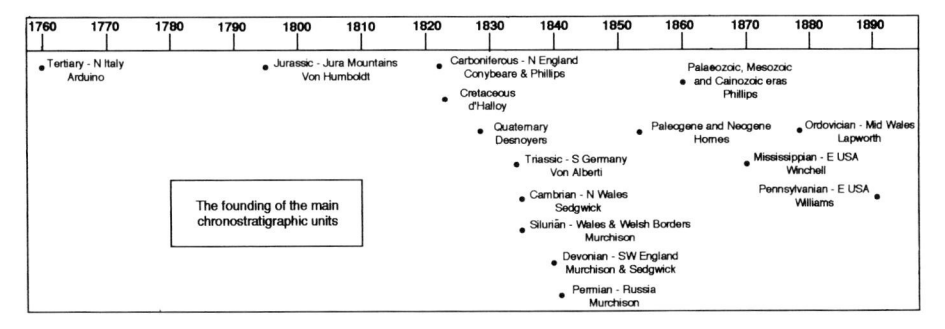

8.2 A timetable for the founding of the geological systems and some other major geological time units

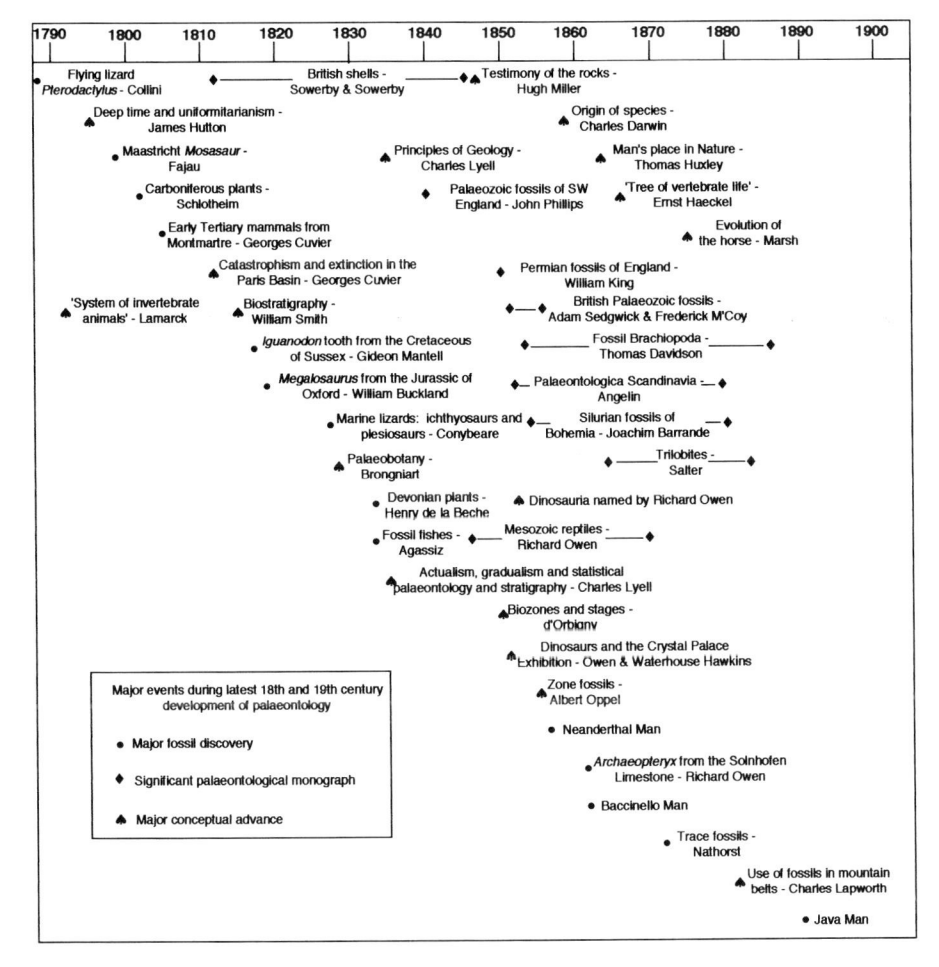

8.3 A timetable for some of the major discoveries and events during the nineteenth-century development of palaeontology

many amateur and professional collectors active in exploration; indeed fossil-collecting was an important part of Victorian culture. Magnificent collections were assembled not only by collectors but also during the active mapping programmes of the geological surveys, particularly in Britain and Ireland. The accurate description of fossil biotas based often on large and well-preserved samples was at last possible.

During the mid and late 1800s several major monographs, which remain the foundation of palaeontological research, dominated the development of the science. But against this background of discovery and description a number of more theoretical analyses and paradigms began to emerge which would establish palaeontology as a science.

The noted French anatomist, George Cuvier, had through his comparative anatomy of the extinct giant sloth *Megatherium* and the Eocene mammal faunas from Montmartre, demonstrated catastrophic changes through time in the Tertiary faunas of the Paris Basin and elsewhere. These studies were primary evidence for extinction events in the fossil record. The fact that fossil groups become extinct and new groups appear suggested that rocks of a particular age would be represented by a characteristic group of fossils.[17] William Smith used these temporal changes to develop biostratigraphy, the use of fossils for the correlation of rock strata. This technique underpinned the construction of the first geological map of England and Wales in 1815 only some twenty-five years ahead of the first geological map of Ireland published by Richard Griffith. Both were the first such maps produced anywhere in the world.

Classifications of animals and plants, whether living or fossil, must in some way reflect the evolution of the group. Palaeontologists use a modified version of principles established by Carl Gustav Linnaeus (1707–78) to name and categorise fossil taxa. Fossils, however, must then be classified by grouping together morphologically similar forms within a hierarchical system to develop an inclusive tree of life. Charles Darwin provided the essential evolutionary paradigm to classify organisms according to their history and mutual relationships. In fact Darwin's branching tree of life, demonstrating the divergence of characters from a common ancestor, is the only illustration in his *Origin of Species*.

During the 1850s the first undoubted evidence of fossil man was reported and from then until the end of the century the much scrutinized Neanderthal man, together with Baccinello man, and Java man, generated lively controversy on human origins, a debate bolstered by contributions from both Charles Darwin and Thomas Huxley.

Arguably King was not at the leading edge of these primary discoveries but he was not very far behind. Most new material would arrive on the desks and tables of the leading authorities of the moment usually researching with the financial support, staff, and facilities of large institutes and learned societies, and often dining with the great and good in the intellectual café societies of, say, London and Paris. King had none of these advantages. Nevertheless his contributions were formidable.

---

17 M.J.S. Rudwick, 'Cuvier and Brongniart, William Smith and the Reconstruction of Geohistory', *Earth Science History*, 15 (1996), pp. 25–36.

King's Research

William King's tenure spanned a heroic era of geological research. The founding of the geological systems together with the discovery and classification of many animal and plant groups were revolutionising the science. King's own research programme had quite incredible breadth, stretching from the taxonomy and shell structure of many invertebrate fossil groups, to a substantial monograph with Thomas Davidson on the bizarre trimerellid brachiopods,[18] to descriptions of the sediments and faunas from deep-sea cruises,[19] and to the anatomy of the lesser horse-shoe bat.[20] William King's early researches included a number of important taxonomic papers. Although many scientists had a rather vague idea of taxonomic procedure, King made advances with the systematics of the corals, brachiopods, and cephalopod molluscs, advocating the precise and proper definition of fossil genera and species. But his major investigations involved the Permian rocks of his native northeast England.

King's thesis on the Permian fossils of England is widely regarded as one of finest in the Palaeontographical Society's monograph series.[21] It described and illustrated the fauna of the Permian System that Roderick Murchison had already established in 1841 for sections in the remote Perm district of Russia. Nevertheless the editor for the Palaeontographical Society, Dr J.S. Bowerbank, first found it necessary to try to heal the rift between Richard Howse and King before publication.[22] On his departure from the Hancock Museum a bitter quarrel had erupted between King and his successor Howse, both claiming priority for their respective lists of the Permian fossils from the north of England. King had agreed to quote Howse where relevant while Bowerbank had in return felt his 'way with a leetle soft Sawder on his [Howse] services to science ... and he has nibbled like a sly old chub at a Fly'. Nevertheless Bowerbank found King's written style hard and crude but was apparently able to remove some of the rougher edges.

King continued his interest with the Permian System in Ireland, documenting sections in Cultra, Co. Down and Tullyconnell, Co. Tyrone and encouraging the search for Coal Measures beneath these sequences. However King was also turning his attention to the skeletal structure of shelled invertebrates.

In his work on the punctation of the brachiopod shell, King crossed swords with William Benjamin Carpenter FRS, the eminent Victorian physiologist and zoologist.[23] Carpenter was very critical of King's less than technical approach:

---

18 T. Davidson and W. King, 'On the Trimerellidae, a Palaeozoic Family of Palliobranchs or Brachiopoda', *Quarterly Journal of the Geological Society of London*, 30 (1874), pp. 124–73.

19 W. King, 'Notice of Some Objects of Natural History Lately Obtained from the Bottom of the Atlantic', *British Association Report*, 2 (1862), pp. 108–9. Also W. King, 'On Some Palliobranchiate Shells from the Irish Atlantic', *Proceedings of the Natural History Society of Dublin*, 5 (1868), pp. 170–3.

20 W. King, 'On the Occurrence of the Lesser Horse-Shoe Bat, *Rhinolophus hipposideros*', *Proceedings of the Dublin Natural History Society*, 1 (1859), pp. 264–8.

21 W. King, 'Monograph of the Permian Fossils of England', *Monograph of the Palaeontographical Society* (1850).

22 Sir Henry De la Beche correspondence, Archives of the National Museum of Wales, Cardiff.

23 W. King, 'Notes on Some Perforated Palaeozoic Spiriferidae', *Geological Magazine*, 4 (1867), pp. 253–66.

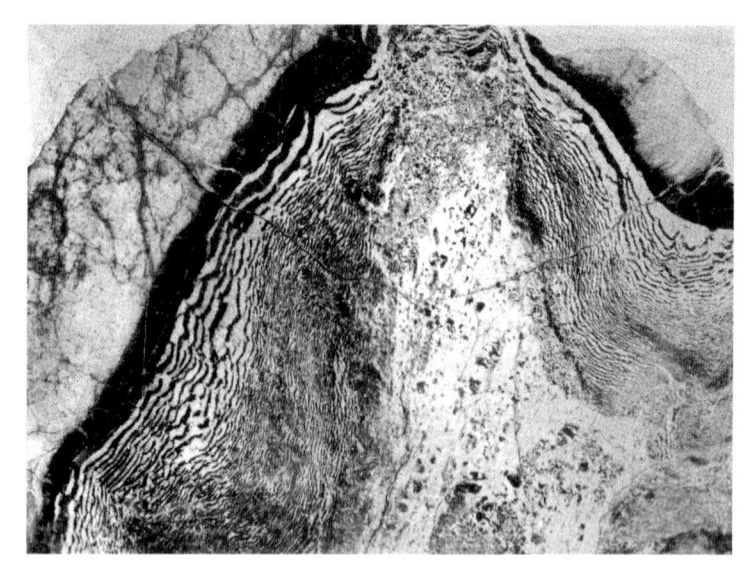

8.4 Photograph of a specimen of the typical so-called dawn creature *Eozoön*, based on a specimen of Precambrian marble from the Laurentian craton, prepared in the 1890s, approximately X3.

To myself personally it is a matter of entire indifference, whether Professor King does or does not, admit the correctness of my observations; but I would submit that the interests of science are not very likely to be promoted, by this easy setting-aside of my observations, made with every advantage of first-rate instruments and careful preparations of specimens, in favour of glances with a hand-magnifier at shells whose surfaces are peculiarly liable to present deceptive appearances, the examination being confined to their exterior, and no adequate means being taken to examine their intimate structure and arrangement.

Despite this severe reprimand King published a series of useful and quoted articles on brachiopod punctation. Carpenter and King were to cross swords again; next time the eminent physiologist was less fortunate.

Eozoön and the Origin of Life

During the latter part of the nineteenth century the search was on for the oldest fossil life forms on earth. Thomas Huxley and others had predicted that if life had evolved complexity and diversity over huge intervals of geological time then simple fossil organisms must be present in the rocks on the great Precambrian shield areas of the world. What then were these first organisms into which 'God breathed the first breath of life'? Professor J.W. Dawson had described laminar structures from the Laurentian Shield and amplified these finds in his text 'The Dawn of Animal Life';[24] he named these *Eozoön canadense*. These dawn creatures

---

24 J.W. Dawson, 'On the Structure of Certain Organic Remains in the Laurentian Limestone of Canada', *Quarterly Journal of the Geological Society of London*, 21 (1865), pp. 51–9.

were enthusiastically embraced by the nineteenth-century scientific community (fig. 8.4). William Carpenter was a strong advocate of eozoönism which again brought him into bitter conflict with King.

Eozoönism, and the eozoönists, formed a major Victorian cult that King and Rowney met head on. The Galway school comprising King and the Professor of Chemistry, Thomas Henry Rowney, convincingly demonstrated these structures were inorganic;[25] the association of these laminae with protozoans such as the foraminifera or parazoans such as sponges and stromatoporoids were dismissed and William Carpenter withdrew gracefully. This was a vigorous international debate bringing much credit to King and Rowney and of course to Queen's College Galway. Ironically nearly a hundred years later, the discovery of ancient stromatolites – sheets of calcium carbonate precipitated and trapped by Precambrian cyanobacteria – showed an uncanny resemblance to eozoöans.

Neanderthal Man

During 1856 a remarkable humanoid skull was discovered in a cave in the Neander Valley of northern Germany. This long skull had a large brain capacity but was distinguished by marked ridges above the eyes. King obtained a plaster cast of the skull cap from the Krantz family in Berlin and confirmed the anatomical features of the head (fig. 8.5).[26] Neanderthal Man was interpreted as an ugly, brutish form contemporary with *Homo sapiens*. Leading anatomists of the day sought a variety of bizarre explanations – Neanderthal Man was perhaps a Mongolian Cossack in the Russian Army with furrowed brows developed during the lengthy and uncomfortable horse ride from Moscow, or even an Old Dutchman with bow legs and rickets. Could the neanderthal have suffered rickets during childhood and

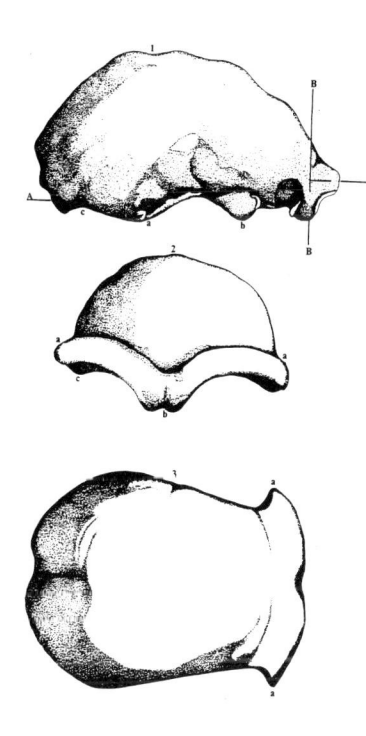

8.5 The plastotype of the Neanderthal skull cap reposited in the James Mitchell Museum, NUI, Galway, showing lateral (top), frontal (middle), and cranidial (bottom) views. Re-drawn by Sandra Minchin

---

25 W. King and T.H. Rowney, 'On "Eozoön Canadense"', *Proceedings of the Royal Irish Academy*, 10 (1869), pp. 506–51.
26 W. King, 'On the Neanderthal Skull; or Reasons for Believing It to Belong to the Clydean Period, and to a Species Different from that Represented by Man', *British Association Report*, 2 (1863), pp. 81–2.

arthritis in old age? King tested these theories against the available geological evidence. The cave sediments were probably over 30,000 years old; the hominid was not a contemporary with modern man, rather a fossil which he named *Homo neanderthalensis*; but in addressing the question of the skull, King plaintively admitted that in his opinion 'the thoughts and desires that once dwelt within it never soared above those of the brute'. Sadly Neanderthal Man, with his strong features, was an ancestor nobody wanted, although modern studies suggest the neanderthals formed civilised and sophisticated communities and probably shared a common African ancestor with *Homo sapiens*.[27]

These views promoting the antiquity of the neanderthals were strongly opposed by Darwin's 'bulldog', the eminent zoologist Thomas Huxley. In fact it was not until 1925 that Professor Raymond Dart, in discussing his Taung child from southern Africa and its descendants, enthusiastically supported King's position.[28]

Darwin's Origin of Species

The origin, development, and eventual publication of Darwin's *Origin of Species* has been widely documented.[29] Darwin's evolutionary paradigm was quite different from Lamarck's conveyor belt allowing transformations, or evolution, from rocks to angels. Natural selection was the key to evolution in Darwin's *Origin of Species*; evolution itself was already widely recognised in the scientific community but a mechanism had yet to gain acceptance. But King had his own viewpoint.[30] Perhaps evolutionary processes could be described in terms of two distinct mechanisms. Autotheogeny could create suites of characters isolated from all other groups; thus major groups of organisms must have been created, but in order, throughout geological time. On the other hand genetheonomy would permit a modification or fine-tuning of characters, not unlike the microevolutionary processes of phyletic gradualism now demonstrable in many fossil lineages. King's investigations of modern marine benthos clearly showed considerable phenotypic variation in populations probably related to environmental gradients. Small morphological changes were possible but large macroevolutionary jumps must be left to a creator.

King's publications have been listed and discussed elsewhere. But with a curriculum vitae containing over seventy publications there was always the probability that some papers might deviate from his usual high standards. Whereas much of his taxonomic research was sound, he was less fortunate with his explanations of the terraced limestones of the Burren and the development of cleavage in the Dalradian rocks of Donegal. Nevertheless his most classic misinterpretation was reserved for the enigmatic coral *Pleurodictyum problematicum*.[31] This tabulate coral, first described by Goldfuss, is common in the Devonian

27 R. Leakey and R. Lewin, *Origins Reconsidered* (London, 1992).
28 R.A. Dart, '*Australopithecus africanus*: The Ape-Man of South Africa', *Nature*, 115 (1925), pp. 195–9.
29 A. Desmond and J. Moore, *Darwin* (London, 1991).
30 W. King, 'On the Origin of Species', *Edinburgh Philosophical Journal*, 15 (1862), pp. 253–6.
31 W. King, 'On *Pleurodictyum problematicum*', *Annals and Magazine of Natural History*, 17 (1856), pp. 11–14.

shallow-water Rhenish magnafacies throughout Europe, where it occurs with coarse-ribbed brachiopods and highly-ornamented trilobites. King carefully studied specimens sent to him by the Krantz family. Each individual apparently had a honeycomb-like skeleton with a sigmoidal central canal. This morphology was clear evidence of a hitherto unknown organism perhaps intermediate between a lophophorate bryozoan and a cnidarian coral. This interpretation was the more remarkable in view of King's rejection of some of the main tenets of Darwinian evolution. Since the major, morphologically-discrete animal groups were created there could be no 'missing links' or intermediate forms connecting the main animal phyla. The real answer was much simpler; the coral *Pleurodictyum* consistently hosted a parasitic worm *Hicetes*. These papers were, however, uncharacteristic of King's research programme which, as a whole, remains impeccable.

King's Collections and the Museum

At an early stage the Queen's Colleges recognised the importance of a museum resource. Four areas of science and engineering were to be represented in the museum in Galway; but the Professor of Mineralogy and Geology would have overall responsibility for the collection, curation, and display of material. It did, however, take some years to establish the museum; the report of the museum committee of May 1852 listed acquisitions but noted the responsibility of the College to have representative collections of regional rocks, minerals and fossils together with flora and fauna.[32] Incidentally the museum appears to have purchased a substantial part of the King collections that probably originated in the Hancock Museum (fig. 8.6).

King was ideally suited to manage the museum and its collections. Firstly, he had experience, if controversial, from his curatorship in the Hancock Museum; secondly, he brought with him substantial amounts of material from the North of England and elsewhere; and, thirdly, he was a collector of some repute likely to continue with the acquisition of material during his tenure. Many years later D'Arcy Thompson jun. was to remark that 'Old King of Galway was a collector of some note, always boasting about the size of his *Turritella*'; the specimen in question is, in fact, extant in the James Mitchell Museum, a turretted gastropod, probably *Campanile giganteum* from the Eocene of the Paris Basin, measuring nearly a metre in length!

The bulk of the collection was assembled by King based on material collected in England and on the continent prior to his arrival in 1849, later supplemented by exchanges and gifts together with purchases from dealers, notably Dr Krantz of Berlin. The scope of the material reflects the nineteenth-century policy to acquire an adequate representation of a very wide variety of fossils. The core of the museum is the type and figured material for King's monograph on the Permian fossils of north-east England. Virtually all specimens relating to King's classic

---

32 D.A.T. Harper (ed.), *An Irish Geological Time-Capsule: The James Mitchell Museum, University College Galway* (Galway, 1996).

> Report of Museum Committee to the Council of Queen's College, Galway,
> 15 May 1852
>
> The museum committee in compliance with the request of the 24 April beg to inform the Council that the Museum at present contains the following series of Specimens of Natural History, Mineralogy and Geology supplied partly out of the funds allocated to the Chairs of Natural History and Geology and partly from donations.
>
> 1st A very complete collection of British shells principally consisting of specimens obtained by dredging in the bay of Galway and its inlets, to the formation of which the prize money allocated to the Natural History class in the year 1850–51 was devoted by the Prize Men Charles Duggan, Thomas O'Hara and Thomas Skilling.
> 2nd A collection of rarer fishes and Crustacea from the same localities a great portion of which, as well as of the former collection, has been presented by Dr. Melville.
> 3rd A collection of foreign fresh water shells presented by John Adamson Esq. of Newcastle upon Tyne through the Curator of the Museum.
> 4th A few Specimens of Skins of – and Birds not yet in a condition to be exhibited, but serviceable for the purpose of instruction, several of which were presented by P. Macauly Esq., Furbo.
> 5th An extensive collection of British plants in appropriate cases for their preservation.
> 6th A collection of Minerals, rock specimens and fossils purchased for the department of Mineralogy and Geology classified and arranged as completely as the limited furniture of the Museum will admit of. This collection is especially valuable, as containing the Types of the Invertebrata described in Professor W. King's Monograph of the Permian fossils of England and also a complete suite of fossil plants from the Coal Measures of the North of England, some of which are of great rarity.
> 7th A valuable collection of plaster casts of fossil Vertebrata from the Servalitki? Hills presented by the Honourable the Directors of the East India Company through Dr. Melville.
> 8th A valuable series of Tertiary and other fossils presented by Baron de Besterot of Duras, Kinvara.

8.6 Part of the 1852 report of the Museum Committee of Queen's College Galway

monograph are extant together with backup collections from the Sunderland area and some comparative Permian material from Germany. The collection is supported by eleven of Dinkel's original lithographs of the Permian fish illustrated in the monograph; all are of an exceptional quality and were restored by the staff of the National Gallery of Ireland. Additionally, figured material relating to King's pioneer paper on the problematic Devonian coral, *Pleurodictyum* has been located in the collections together with specimens of *Eozoön* which featured in the violent controversy surrounding the origin of the so-called dawn creature. Moreover King's original hand-written catalogues are available together with many of the original specimen labels.

Although apparently no formal practical classes were scheduled, it is probable that students could examine museum material in their own time. The walls were hung with a large plesiosaur, a giant crinoid, a small ichthyosaur, and a cast of Fajau's mosasaur. King had also arranged a series of fossils in chronological order through the geological systems and a long horizontal case extending the entire length of the gallery was dedicated to fossils and minerals from Galway including metal ores, granite, and marble together with Silurian and Carboniferous fossils.

With the appointment of Richard J. Anderson MD to the chair of Natural History, Geology, and Mineralogy in 1883, the Geology and Natural History collections were amalgamated to form the Natural History Museum; the collections were contained in five rooms, three for zoological specimens and accessories and two for fossils and minerals. Anderson summarised a number of the more significant specimens, for example the giant crinoid, the ichthyosaur, plesiosaur, mosasaur skull cast, and the alabaster models of vertebrates including a labyrinthodon.[33] The south-facing wall holds framed specimens of the large marine reptiles *Ichthyosaurus* from Holzmaden, Germany and *Plesiosaurus* from Lyme Regis, England. The Lyme Regis plesiosaur was purchased from the Damon family of Weymouth in the 1880s; the Holzmaden ichthyosaur was probably acquired later in the century during the 1890s, when over 300 specimens were extracted from the Holzmaden Quarry. A replica of the famous Cretaceous reptile *Mosasaurus* is mounted above these Jurassic animals. Fajau's mosasaur was excavated from late Cretaceous rocks at St Peter's Mountain near Maastricht in 1780. The 'Giant Animal of Maastricht' had an eventful history. Following disputes over ownership of the skull, the animal was found in a Maastricht cellar by invading French troops in 1795. The troops were rewarded with six hundred bottles of wine for its capture and the skull was delivered to the Paris Museum. Early identifications as a whale and then a crocodile were incorrect. Baron George Cuvier confirmed the reptilian features of the animal and Conybeare named the fossil *Mosasaurus*.

Equally striking is the plaster model of a pterodactyl, based on Richard Owen's reconstruction and probably modelled by Benjamin Waterhouse Hawkins following the re-opening of the Great Exhibition at Sydenham in 1854.[34] In addition Anderson noted a plaster replica of the Waterhouse Hawkins's Jurassic 'seascape' where a large, basking ichthyosaur is surrounded by relatively small plesiosaurs based on the models for the Great Exhibition and reproduced as plates in Buckland's textbook on Geology and Mineralogy published in 1858.

The College records have little data on the purchase of specimens for the museum and the Museum Minute Book is apparently no longer extant. Nonetheless, as noted above, the report of the Museum Committee to the Council of Queen's College Galway, dated 15 May 1852, recommended purchase of zoological, botanical, geological, and mineralogical specimens to the value of £300, a collection that included King's type and figured material from the Permian of England. The Academic Council thanked a number of individuals for donations to the museum: R.L. Franklin Esq. and Baron de Basterot (26 April 1850), Mr Wright for minerals and Edward L. Hunt for valuable contributions (24 April 1852). Bryce McMurdo Wright, also known as Bruce M Wright, Bryce M. Wright, and Bryce-Wright, traded in minerals and fossils from various premises from 1843 to 1894.[35] Between 1843 and 1855 Wright sold mineral specimens from Liverpool and was the probable supplier of minerals to the Museum in 1852. In the latter half of the century cheques were issued to individuals for purchases: Evelyn Oldham (2 June 1883, £18. 6s. 0d), Dr Robert Ball (27 November 1880, £50. 0s. 0d), R. Damon (13 April 1878, £44. 19s. 0d; 10 February 1883, £28. 15s. 4d; 15 December 1883, £5. 8s. 0d). College records

---

33 R.J. Anderson, 'The Natural History Museum, Queen's College, Galway', *Irish Naturalist*, 8 (1899), pp. 125–31.
34 M.J.S. Rudwick, *Scenes from Deep Time* (Chicago, 1992).
35 R.J. Cleevely, *World Palaeontological Collections*, British Museum (Natural History) (London, 1993).

suggest that of the payments to Damon, the first two were for the plesiosaur and the mosasaur replica, while the last covered a geological model of the south-east of England which interestingly shows the track of the Channel Tunnel, surveyed last century;[36] all three purchases are extant and are on display in the Museum. Robert Damon (1814–89) and Robert Ferris Damon (1845–1925) were both Weymouth dealers in fossils, shells, and minerals; one or both supplied the Museum with material from the Dorset coast.

On 19 December 1881, the college sanctioned payment of £12.19s.11d. to Dr Krantz of Berlin for a collection of Mesozoic fossils, mainly ammonites, from mainland Europe. The Krantz firm was established in Berlin in 1833, moving to Bonn after 1850; the company supplied fossils and minerals to collections throughout Europe. Payment was not always prompt; King had to intercede at least once on behalf of vendors and urge the Finance Committee to honour accounts.

The same records noted unsuccessful requests from Professor King for financial support for a visit to the South Kensington Museum in search of specimens for the geological museum (20 May 1876) and for the purchase of specimens whilst researching on the continent under the auspices of the Royal Society (12 May 1877).

Despite King's reputation as an avid and voracious collector there is remarkably little local material in the collections; but what is available is of high quality. Anderson however cited King's displays of local Silurian and Carboniferous fossils in the Natural History Museum, emphasising the excellent preservation of the latter presumably due to silicification.[37]

The close relationship between the Geological Survey in Ireland and the Queen's Colleges was also manifest in the gift of teaching materials to the Department and the Museum. Sir Henry De la Beche arranged for the Decades, together with copies of the one-inch, hand-coloured geological maps and also representative rock, mineral and fossil specimens, to be donated to the Mineralogy and Geology Departments in Ireland.[38] There were, however, delays. Although Thomas Oldham approached De la Beche for the authority to send these materials in 1849 for the opening of the colleges, these were not sent to the college Presidents for reposition in the geological museums until 1851 at the earliest by Joseph Beete Jukes. Nevertheless a small collection of Survey material has now been identified within the collections including specimens derived from Major General J.E. Portlock's mapping programme during the 1830s and 1840s.[39]

King's Teaching

The curriculum in Mineralogy and Geology initially serviced agricultural and engineering students. Science operated as a division of the Arts Faculty. Almost

---

36 *Report* of the President of Queen's College Galway, 1876–7.
37 Anderson, 'The Natural History Museum'.
38 Sir Henry De la Beche correspondence, Archives of the National Museum of Wales, Cardiff.
39 David A.T. Harper and Matthew A. Parkes, 'Geological Survey Donations to the Geological Museum in Queen's College Galway: 19th Century Inter-Institutional Collaboration in Ireland', *Geological Curator*, 6 (1996), pp. 233–6.

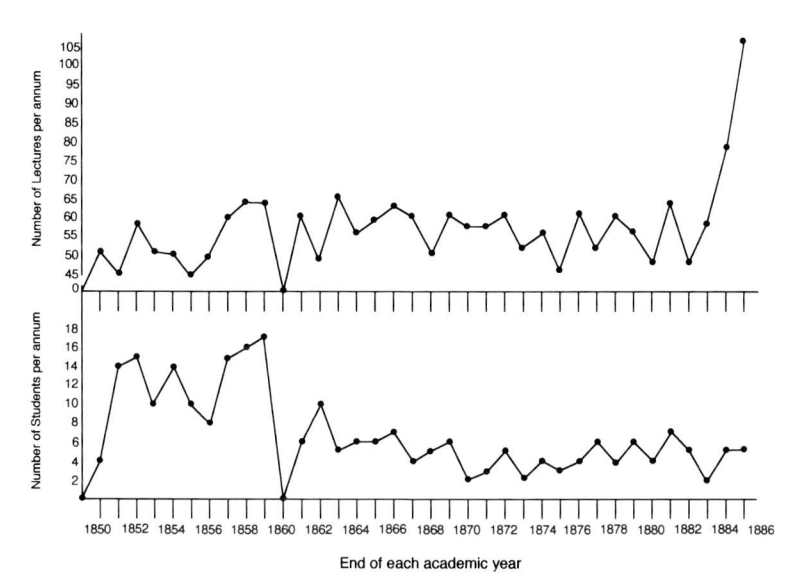

8.7 Frequency polygon of number of lectures per annum (upper) and number of students per annum in Mineralogy and Geology, Queen's College Galway during William King's tenure. Note the crash in the academic year 1860–1.

ten years into the working of the College, King was critical of these arrangements. A tripartite split of Arts to include the Natural Sciences as a further, separate division would strengthen his and related subject areas' representation on committees in the College. Moreover the overlap between his department and geography obviously promoted some rivalry in the teaching of physical geography, but, most seriously, his dual role as teacher and curator was far from satisfactory. King argued strongly for a separate full-time curatorship for the museum which would free him more time for research and teaching.[40]

During the mid 1850s the Local Director of the Geological Survey of Ireland, Joseph Beete Jukes, acted as examiner for the Queen's Colleges. Jukes and his family, contrary to Sir Henry De la Beche's assurances, found the cost of living in Ireland high and perhaps his fee of £50 per annum helped supplement his income from the survey. His examination papers were focused on the more applied aspects of geology with an emphasis on mapping, very relevant for the classes of agriculture and engineering students under King's instruction.[41]

Student numbers remained small with few Catholics attending classes, their faith and morals may indeed have been corrupted by the accumulating evidence for Darwin's paradigm of evolution through natural selection.[42] These students were encouraged to study philosophy, history, and science. Nevertheless, despite the relatively small numbers, there was a major crisis just over ten years into the teaching programme. In the academic year 1860–1 no students apparently followed courses in Mineralogy and Geology and no lectures were given. Prior to the 1860–1 academic year, class sizes were usually in the mid teens, dominated by agricultural and engineering students; after that year classes rarely exceeded six students (fig. 8.7). The reasons for the sudden and subsequent decline are unclear.

40 *The Queen's Colleges (Ireland) Commission: Report* (1858).
41 Queen's College Galway, *Calendar* (1855).
42 Ó hEocha, 'The Queen's College at Galway', in Ó Cearbhaill (ed.), *Galway*, p. 169.

AGRICULTURE
MINERALOGY, GEOLOGY and PHYSICAL GEOGRAPHY
22nd September, 1855, 2 o'clock p.m.
J. Beete Jukes, M.A., F.R.S.

1. What are the minerals entering into the composition of 'granite', 'syenite', 'greenstone', and 'basalt', respectively?
2. Mention the minerals which enter most abundantly into the composition of ordinary igneous and aqueous rocks in the British Islands.
3. If you found crystals of quartz, feldspar, and calcspar, how should you distinguish them from each another?
4. What are the mineral substances most essential to the formation of a fertile soil?
5. Give brief general descriptions of the following rocks:- 'granite', 'greenstone', 'limestone', 'shale', 'marl', 'gravel', and 'clay', stating which are igneous and which aqueous, which stratified, and which unstratified.
6. What do you understand by 'drift'?
7. State the general relations between 'drift' and other rocks, and show how far the agricultural value of land depends on one or the other.
8. What is the practical use of fossils in geology?
9. Give an abstract of the general series of stratified rocks, mentioning any characteristic fossils of each great formations that occur to you.
10. Of what great class of stratified rocks does Ireland principally belong?
11. Describe generally the course of the gulf stream and its effect on the climate of the British islands and Scandinavia.
12. What is the northern limit of the growth of wheat in the different countries of the northern hemisphere, and what remarkable deviations are there from the average course of this limit? State also the height above the sea at which wheat ceases to be productive in England and Ireland.

ENGINEERING
MINERALOGY, GEOLOGY and PHYSICAL GEOGRAPHY
28th September, 1855, 2 o'clock p.m.
J. Beete Jukes, M.A., F.R.S.

1. Describe in general terms the external characters and chemical composition of the following minerals:- Quartz, common feldspar, mica, hornblende, augite, olivine.
2. Define 'quaquaversal dip', 'anticlinal and synclinal line', 'contortion', 'inversion', and 'denudation'.
3. What are 'gneiss', 'mica schist', and 'primary limestone'? and how did they become what they are?
4. Give the chemical composition of 'serpentine'; state its use, and mention the principal localities where it occurs in the British Islands.
5. What is a mineral vein?
6. There is a general rule as to the inclination of faults, and the intersection of mineral veins, by which the direction of the 'shift' or 'throw' can be calculated on; state this rule, and explain it by means of diagrams.
7. What form will the angular blocks of basalt assume on weathering, and what is the origin of that form?
8. What are the subdivisions of the Carboniferous system of Ireland, as given by Dr. Griffith, in his geological map?
9. Explain the geological structure on which the possibility of artesian wells depends.
10. In travelling by railway from Cheshire or from Derbyshire to London, we meet with few or no tunnels till we pass Birmingham on the one line and Bristol on the other; but there are several large tunnels both between Birmingham and London and Bristol and London: describe the great feature in the geology and physical geography of that part of England which rendered these circumstances inevitable.
11. We pass by railway from Dublin, across Ireland, to Galway, to Limerick, and to Cork, without tunnels, and without any deep cuttings: describe so much of the geology and physical geography of Ireland as shall explain the possibility of thus crossing from sea to sea in Ireland, while it would be impossible thus to cross any part of England.

8.8 Examination papers in Mineralogy, Geology, and Physical Geography for Agriculture and Engineering students, Queen's College Galway for 22 and 28 September 1855, respectively

> M.A. NATURAL SCIENCE
> GEOLOGY
> 2nd October, 1875 – Morning
> Professors KING, SC.D.; HARKNESS, F.R.S.; and CUNNINGHAM, M.D.
>
> 1. What are the features which distinguish rocks deposited by fresh water?
> 2. What is the effect of pressure on fossils? In what rocks are such effects best displayed?
> 3. What relation do Doleritic and Trachytic rocks bear to each other in connection with Volcanic outbursts?
> 4. What is the geological position, and what are the characteristic fossils of the limestones of the Chair of Kildare?
> 5. What is the geological range of Trilobites?
> 6. In what strata have the earliest evidences of Sponge life been obtained? Under what conditions do these evidences occur?
> 7. In what respect do the Sea-urchins of the Palaeozoic rocks differ from those of later formations?
> 8. Where, and under what circumstances, have the earliest air-breathing Molluscs been found?
>
> B.A. with honours – NATURAL SCIENCE
> GEOLOGY
> 2nd October, 1875 – Morning
> Professors KING, SC.D.; HARKNESS, F.R.S.; and CUNNINGHAM, M.D.
>
> 1. How are Plutonic Rocks distinguished from Aqueous and Volcanic Rocks?
> 2. Describe the several kinds of Metamorphic Rocks; and give their mineral composition.
> 3. What is the difference between Stratification and Lamination?
> 4. What are the series of rocks which constitute the Cambrian group in the British Isles? Mention some of the characteristic fossils of these rocks?
> 5. Name some of the important fossils belonging to the Lower Ludlow strata.
> 6. What species of fossil plants characterise the Devonians?
> 7. What fossil Reptiles has the Permian formation afforded?
> 8. Where, in the continent of Europe, are the equivalents of the *Avicula contorta* beds best represented? In what respect do they differ from those of Britain?
> 9. By what means are the several portions of the Lower Lias divided into distinct horizons?
> 10. What important fossils have been obtained from the Stonesfield slate?
> 11. Where, in England, do the Wealden strata occur? How are they grouped? Under what circumstances have they originated?
> 12. What is the position of the Gypseous strata of Montmartre? What important fossils have been obtained from them and their associated strata?

8.9 Examination papers in Geology for the degrees of MA and BA with honours (below) in Natural Science, Queen's College Galway, 2 October 1875

Is it possible that King, ever up-to-date, rapidly introduced the substance of Darwin's *Origin of Species*, into his lectures, further alienating the Roman Catholic and the established church? A simple footnote in the calendar for the year, and subsequent years, explains that owing to an alteration of the Ordinances of the University no lectures in Mineralogy and Geology were delivered in Queen's College Galway during 1860–1.[43] The examiner in Mineralogy and Geology that year was Professor Wyville T.C. Thomson (Queen's College Belfast); the next year William King took up his post as examiner for the Queen's University.

By the mid 1870s, King and his fellow professors at the other colleges, Harkness and Cunningham, were together examining students in the Arts Faculty in a more typical geological syllabus. The papers quizzed students about Cambrian sponges,

---

43 Queen's College Galway, *Calendar* (1861).

Devonian plants, Permian reptiles, Jurassic dinosaurs, and the mammal faunas of the Montmartre that had signalled to George Cuvier the reality of extinction (figs 8.8 and 8.9).[44]

There is little evidence that fieldwork was an important part of the classes in Geology and Mineralogy. King did, however, advertise field or 'travelling geological' classes during the summer. The advertisement in the 1860 volume of the *Geologist* invited gentlemen to contact King at his home in Belmont; part of the course would be taught in the Geological Museum and the remainder in the field areas of Connemara together with counties Antrim and Kerry.[45] Professors and lecturers were usually only paid during term time for lectures; the travelling class would have provided King with additional finance.

Irish Geological Society

The Irish Geological Society of the mid-nineteenth century was a vigorous intellectual milieu, in terms of both characters and ideas. The community was exclusively male, dominated by the higher strata of Irish society, including titled gentlemen, Fellows of the Royal Society, and Members of the Royal Irish Academy.[46] Few were Roman Catholics, in fact the earl of Enniskillen was the Imperial Master of the Orange Order,[47] but most were Irish. William King was an exception; he was an English immigrant from a working-class background with little formal education.

The period 1845–75 included the golden years of Irish geology, attracting many major intellectual figures to the island. In the University of Dublin, John Phillips (1800–74) was the first Professor of Geology in the Museum Building of Trinity College. Phillips was a nephew of William Smith and an acolyte of Sir Henry De la Beche.[48] Sadly, his short tenure was marred by controversy, which forced his resignation. He was unable to secure the Local Directorship of the Geological Survey to add to his position in Trinity. By the mid 1850s he had been appointed to the chair of Geology in Oxford, where he remained. Frederick McCoy (1823–99) had already published lasting and substantial monographic works on the Carboniferous and Silurian fossils of Ireland, based mainly on collections accumulated during Richard Griffith's survey. One of Thomas Oldham's first tasks on succeeding Captain James at the head of the Geological Survey of Ireland was to reprimand McCoy for unsatisfactory mapping.[49] McCoy moved on,

---

44 Ibid., 1875.
45 W. King, 'Travelling Geological Class', a flier which appeared with either the April or July issue of the *Geologist*, vol. 3, 1860.
46 G.L. Herries Davies, 'The History of Irish Geology', in C.H. Holland (ed.), *A Geology of Ireland* (Edinburgh, 1980), pp. 303–15.
47 K.W. James, *'Damned Nonsense'! The Geological Career of the Third Earl of Enniskillen* (Belfast, 1986).
48 P. Wyse Jackson, *In Marble Halls: Geology in Trinity College, Dublin* (Dublin, 1994).
49 G.L. Herries Davies, *Sheets of Many Colours: The Mapping of Ireland's Rocks 1750–1890* (Dublin, 1983).

apparently unperturbed, to join the Revd Professor Adam Sedgwick at Cambridge; their joint monograph on the Palaeozoic rocks and fossils of Britain, published between 1851 and 1855, remains a formidable, much-quoted work of reference. In 1849, McCoy became the first Professor of Mineralogy and Geology in Queen's College Belfast. Although he was soon appointed examiner in Mineralogy and Geology for the Queen's Colleges, within five years he occupied the chair of Natural Science in the University of Melbourne; toward the end of his illustrious career in Australian science, he was knighted by Queen Victoria.[50]

James Nicol (1810–79) was appointed to the chair of Mineralogy and Geology in Queen's College Cork under the patronage of Sir Henry De la Beche. Two years later however, Nicol was already bored with the local geology and complained to Sir Henry, citing the problems between the President and his professors, together with the lack of adequate field sections for teaching, for his dissatisfaction. Nicol also communicated his wish to work under Sir Henry on the geological survey of Scotland much in preference to 'teaching geology to Irishmen in this remote corner'.[51] Soon he had left, returning to his native Scotland to occupy the chair of Geology in the University of Aberdeen.

All three professors established very short careers in the Irish universities before moving on; in contrast, William King held tenure for nearly 35 years. Nevertheless both Robert Harkness (1816–78) in Cork, and the Revd Samuel Haughton (1823–97) in Trinity, subsequently developed substantial careers in Ireland.

King attended relatively few meetings in Ireland or, indeed, elsewhere; he never joined the geological societies of Dublin or London and was never elected to the Royal Irish Academy or the Royal Society. It has been suggested King felt out of place with perhaps his north of England accent clashing with the nasal tones of the Anglo-Irish. But King was not without ambition; in 1873 he applied, unsuccessfully, for the vacant Woodwardian Chair in Cambridge.[52] Alternatively King's lack of participation may have reflected his financial situation. King had no private means and he regularly applied, unsuccessfully, to the college for travel funds. The tyranny of distance may have prevented King's active attendance at meetings and membership of societies.

Achievements

William King's long tenure set a standard for scholarship. Through his research and teaching programmes, together with the foundation and development of the Geological Museum, he established a platform of academic excellence in the geological sciences. King's research was recognised with a number of honours. He was elected to membership of the Geological Society of France and was a voting member of the Natural History and Medical Society of Dresden. Within the Irish

---

50 Frederick McCoy's father, Simon, was the first Professor of Materia Medica at QCG. Appointed in 1849, he occupied the chair until his retirement in 1873.
51 Sir Henry De la Beche correspondence, Archives of the National Museum of Wales, Cardiff.
52 Archives of the Sedgwick Museum, University of Cambridge.

system he was elected examiner in Geology, Mineralogy, and Physical Geology for the Queen's Colleges in 1859 and three years later he was appointed Lecturer in Geology by the Committee of Lectures, Dublin Castle for courses held in both Bandon and Galway. King's academic career was recognised by the award of the first Doctor of Science degree (*honoris causa*) by the Queen's University of Ireland. On the retirement of Professor Alexander Melville in 1882 he became Professor of Natural History, Geology and Mineralogy; following an attack of paralysis in 1883 he retired to an emeritus professorship.

King's Legacy

Following King's death the geological sciences in Galway remained in stasis for almost a century. King's successor, the colourful Richard John Anderson occupied the chair of Natural History, Geology, and Mineralogy from 1883 until his death in 1914. Anderson's research, and presumably teaching interests, were within the life sciences; with the exception of a useful description of and guide to the museum, he contributed virtually nothing to the geological sciences. Henry Brenan Cronshaw was an economic geologist and occupied the chair in Geology and Mineralogy during the turbulent period from 1915 to 1920. His interests in the mining industry coincided with the decline of base-metal mining in Connemara; nevertheless Cronshaw's interests in the Connemara marble and related rocks are preserved in the James Mitchell Museum as a series of polished slabs.

Professor James Mitchell's long tenure of the chair in Geology and Mineralogy (1921–66) was a post he held concurrently from 1934 with that of Secretary of the College. Mitchell was an outstanding administrator; however, mineralogy and geology remained very much in the service area of the curriculum, mainly assisting with courses in civil engineering. But through a mixture of foresight and neglect, the main gallery and collections of the Geological Museum remained virtually intact, while similar collections in the University Colleges of Belfast, Cork, and Dublin were already broken up for teaching material or even discarded entirely.[53] The Geological Museum was formally renamed the James Mitchell Museum in 1977 in recognition of his considerable contributions to the development of UCG.[54]

Mitchell's charismatic successor, David Skevington, initiated the BSc honours course in geology in 1968 together with an active research programme in the geological sciences and re-established the museum as a centre for the acquisition and preservation of display, research, and teaching material. The staff complement and class grant began to increase although class sizes remained small.

In the period from 1985–95 student numbers in geology have increased aided by the establishment of a four-year denominated degree course in the Earth Sciences and an increasing awareness and popularity of the geological sciences in

---

53 M.D. Fewtrell, 'The James Mitchell Geology Museum, University College, Galway', *Irish Naturalists' Journal*, 19 (1979), pp. 309–10.
54 M.D. Fewtrell and P.D. Ryan, 'Queen's College Museum, Galway', *GCG: Newsletter of the Geological Curators' Group*, 2 (1979), pp. 173–81.

Ireland through the school system, adult and distance learning, and the annual events associated with Irish Geology Day. A major renovation programme in the James Mitchell Museum, grant-aided by FÁS (Training and Employment Authority) and the National Heritage Council, has refurbished the main gallery and its exhibitions and, moreover, established a computer-based database for all the display, research, and teaching collections in both the museum and the department.[55] The Erasmus student mobility programme has provided new opportunities for both Irish and visiting students, adding a global dimension to the courses and research school in Galway. Moreover the introduction of Earth Science as a first-year option in the Strategic Plan for the evolving university has already attracted over a hundred students into the Department. Student numbers are set to escalate and at last geologists in Galway will be able to compete on more equal terms with their colleagues elsewhere in Europe. Research programmes in palaeontology and stratigraphy have come full circle.

The wealth of detailed monographic studies of the late nineteenth century and most of the twentieth century are now being complemented by models for large-scale evolutionary change and attempts to relate biological processes through time with the development of the planet as a whole, its atmosphere, hydrosphere, and lithosphere,[56] aspirations not so different from those of King and his better-known contemporaries in Britain, Henry De la Beche, Charles Darwin, Charles Lyell, Richard Owen, and Adam Sedgwick.

But one hundred and fifty years ago the future was probably very far from William King's thoughts as he prepared to put his own exciting vision of the developing geological sciences to small second-year classes of agricultural and engineering students. That vision established the geological sciences in Galway and helped set standards and an agenda for the next century.[57]

---

55 D.A.T. Harper, 'The James Mitchell Museum: A Museum of a Museum in University College Galway', *Geological Curator*, 5 (1992), pp. 292–7.
56 P.J. Brenchley and D.A.T. Harper, *Palaeoecology: Ecosystems, Environments and Evolution* (London, 1998).
57 I thank Mike Benton (Bristol), Euan Clarkson (Edinburgh), Tim Collins (Galway), and Tony Wright (Belfast) for useful discussions on the development of nineteenth-century geology and palaeontology and Paul Ryan for reading the final manuscript. Fiona Bateman and Matthew Parkes (Geoscapes) helped with archival material in Galway and Dublin, respectively, during the later stages of the project.

Melville, Hart, and Anderson: Early Teachers of Natural History, 1849–1914

TIMOTHY COLLINS

When Queen's College Galway (QCG) opened its gates to the first intake of sixty-eight students on the morning of Tuesday 30 October 1849, the Department of Natural History offered two overlapping courses, in the faculties of Medicine and Arts. Looking back at the syllabus and examination papers of this period, the subject appears quaint and unscientific, with a reliance on a classical education and a rather simplistic view of the diversity of animal and plant life. Much of this kind of study was based on the anatomical and morphological differences which could be seen between species, with the result that naturalists occasionally came to absurd conclusions when viewing specimens of hitherto unknown species for the first time.[1]

It must be taken into account that the publication of Darwin's *On the Origin of Species* in 1859, was still ten years away, so there were many schools of thought regarding the origins of the great biodiversity of life which existed on land and sea. Some people were developing theories of evolution and extinction based on the comparative anatomy of living and fossil animals and plants. Fossil bones were being collected in ever-increasing numbers and attempts were being made to make them 'fit in' with existing knowledge. Other people adhered rigidly to the strict biblical interpretation of Creation, dismissing the notion that living species had evolved from extinct species, and choosing to believe that they had been created

---

1 Two examples of absurd conclusions worth mentioning are cited by Lynn Barber, *The Heyday of Natural History 1820–1870* (London, 1980), pp. 40–1, and relate firstly to the arrival of specimens of the first Birds of Paradise to the British Museum, which had their legs cut off to facilitate packing. Leglessness thereupon became enshrined as a characteristic of the species and popular writers went into rhapsodies describing these little creatures spending all of their lives on the wing. Only the arrival of a Bird of Paradise complete with legs put paid to these fantasies. In the second example, John Edward Gray, Keeper of Zoology at the British Museum, made a similar mistake when reviewing a book on the fauna of India, published by naturalists attached to the Indian civil service. He dismissed as inaccurate, drawings of certain species of turtle because they showed no holes in the flippers, which could be seen quite clearly in the British Museum specimens. The authors replied icily and publicly that, as everyone in India knew, it was the custom for fishermen to make these holes after catching the turtles, in order to tie the flippers together to immobilise them. These incidents also highlight the huge gulf of knowledge that existed between the 'professional' naturalist who spent his time listing specimens in a museum and the 'amateur' naturalist, who went out into the countryside, collecting and noting how different species interacted with each other in nature.

whole and entire, for man's benefit. The fossils being found were accepted as being merely of antediluvian origin, serving as further proof that many species of animals had failed to survive the Noachian flood. Science, as we know it today, was still in its infancy and did not come of age until the final decades of the nineteenth century. Although botany and zoology had been defined as distinct sciences as early as the seventeenth century, it was only in the latter half of the nineteenth century that research in the biological sciences became more specialised. Indeed, biochemistry was only defined as a distinct science in 1869 and microbiology in 1888, while the term oceanography first appeared during the publication of the results of the now-famous world cruise of HMS *Challenger* which appeared in fifty volumes containing almost 30,000 pages, from 1880 to 1895.[2]

9.1 Alexander Gordon Melville, Professor of Natural History 1849–82

In 1849, there were no degree courses in the subject. Natural history was taught to medical students, almost as an optional extra. This provided a grounding in comparative anatomy and physiology and also in botany, which had been linked with medicine since the days of herbalism. As an Arts subject, it was meant to complement the courses in philosophy, so practical work in this case was nonexistent. Although agriculture was taught in Queen's College Galway, by Professor Thomas Skilling, it was quite separate from natural history.[3]

2 HMS *Challenger* was a Pearl class wooden-hulled steam-assisted screw corvette of over 2300 tons, commissioned at Woolwich in 1858. The three and a half year voyage of HMS *Challenger* from December 1872 to May 1876 has frequently been referred to as marking the birth of oceanography and has made her the most famous oceanographic research ship of all. Following this cruise, she was withdrawn from active service and re-commissioned in 1876 as a Naval Reserve and Coast Guard Drill Ship at Harwich. Subsequently becoming a stores hulk at Chatham Royal Dock Yard in 1880, HMS *Challenger* was sent for breaking up in 1921 when her hull became unsound. Anthony L. Rice, *British Oceanographic Vessels 1800–1950* (London, 1986), pp. 30–41, has given details of the contribution of HMS *Challenger* to marine research, while Margaret B. Deacon has written a wider account of developments in marine science at this time in *Scientists and the Sea 1650–1900: A Study of Marine Science* (London, 1971).
3 Thomas Skilling was Professor of Agriculture at Queen's College Galway from its opening in 1849 until his death in 1865. Before being appointed to this post he had worked with Lord Wallscourt, an eccentric aristocrat, who owned a farm of some 1,500 acres at Ardfry, near Oranmore where, according to John Cunningham ('Two Galway Utopias: Ardfry c. 1832–1849 (Lord Wallscourt); Toghermore 1930–1950 (Bobby Burke)', unpublished paper), a novel experiment in profit-sharing had been in progress from the early 1830s. Lord Wallscourt provided the initial capital, while Skilling and the tenants all shared in the profits, or losses, from each year's harvest. Details of this

The first person to be appointed to the Chair of Natural History was Alexander Gordon Melville MD, DL, DSc, MRCSE (fig. 9.1). With his own background in science and medicine, and considering the state of knowledge in the subject at this time, Melville was unusually well qualified for the post. He was also quite young, being only thirty years old when appointed. Prior to his arrival in Galway, Melville had already built up quite a reputation for himself as a comparative anatomist. The experience he gained as Demonstrator in Anatomy at the University of Edinburgh following his graduation there with the degree MD certainly stood him in good stead. Curiously enough, although he later gained his membership of the Royal College of Surgeons of England, he never practised, having, it was said, a constitutional dislike of surgical operations. This was not in the least unusual. Charles Darwin, Richard Owen, Thomas Henry Huxley, and many of the other great naturalists of this period started their careers in medical school, but it needed a strong stomach to assist in surgical procedures when operations were performed without anaesthetics and when cadavers used for dissection were frequently putrid and often stolen from the grave.

Melville moved to Oxford where his interest in comparative anatomy led to his appointment as an assistant to Sir Henry Wentworth Acland, an eminent anatomist who was Lee's Reader in Anatomy at the time and who later became Regius Professor of Medicine at the University of Oxford. While there, Melville developed his interests in art and architecture and also became something of an authority on bookbinding and book illustration. One of Melville's achievements as Acland's assistant was to set up a museum of zoology and comparative anatomy in Christ Church, Oxford, where he later gained his DSc. At the same time he began to make his ideas in comparative anatomy known to his professional colleagues, giving a number of lectures to the Fellows and Members of the Royal Zoological Society in London.

History has not been kind to Melville. Although quite active in many different spheres of endeavour, very little is known of him today. Perhaps because of his argumentative personality, his academic colleagues had little good to say about Melville or his work, so it would appear they chose to say nothing at all. That he was arrogant, there is no doubt, as it is reflected in his published work, yet he did enjoy a certain amount of respect from his peers elsewhere. For instance, Alexander Goodman More, the noted botanist, found Melville extremely helpful when compiling *Cybele Hibernica*, published in 1866, and said as much in his personal correspondence, which was edited by Moffat in 1898.[4] Ducker, who

---

experiment can also be found in James Caird *The Plantation Scheme; or, The West of Ireland as a Field for Investment* (Edinburgh, 1850), pp. 56–7. As farm manager, Skilling provided the scientific skill to improve farming practices and had published a number of texts based on his experiences, notably *The Science and Practice of Agriculture* (1846), *The Farmer's Ready Reckoner* (1848), and *The Turnip and Its Culture* (1857). After Skilling's appointment to QCG, project work at the Ardfry farm initially formed an important component of the courses taught, although it was discontinued after the deaths of both Lord Wallscourt and Skilling. Subsequent practical work by students of agriculture was carried out on land bought by the College at Dangan, where the Sports Grounds are located today.

4 Alexander Goodman More (1830–95) was one of the foremost botanists to work on the Irish flora in the nineteenth century. Although dogged by ill-health throughout most of his life, he

edited some of the letters of William Henry Harvey, cites one particular letter written by Harvey in 1844, which offers a telling insight into both Melville's personality and professional abilities:

> My *opponents* are both friends of mine – Dr Steele (who is '*not a scientific botanist*') & Dr Melville, author of the Dodo, who is very scientific, but very quarrelsome and opinionated. If I had a vote, & were not myself a candidate I should support Dr Melville, though *personally* I am much more attached to Steele. I do not think Steele however would add to the reputation of the Chair, & I know that Melville *could*, if he *would* – the only question in his case is '*would he*'? – If I do not get it I hope he will.[5]

As mentioned earlier, Melville was an excellent comparative anatomist, which ability had been developed as a result of his medical training. Looking again at his papers after more than a century, one is struck by his meticulous eye for detail. His conclusions are arrived at only after careful analysis of the facts. Indeed, in one paper on the variable anatomy of mammalian and reptilian vertebrae, he had the temerity to question the findings of Richard Owen, one of the foremost palaeontologists of the nineteenth century and best remembered today as the man who coined the term 'dinosaur' in 1842.[6] In this paper, originally read at a meeting of

---

nevertheless managed to complete an enormous amount of work himself and, by his efforts, spurred others on to complete similar work on the Irish flora. His greatest contribution to the literature was the publication of *Cybele Hibernica* in 1866, which he co-authored with David Moore. He died while compiling a second edition of this great work, which was completed by Nathaniel Colgan and Reginald Scully in 1898. Charles Bethune Moffat published a comprehensive biography which included his correspondence and a significant amount of his published work in *Life and Letters of Alexander Goodman More* (Dublin, 1898).

5 It would appear that, prior to his appointment to the chair of Natural History at QCG, Melville had been actively seeking a professorship in various colleges. The much sought-after appointment which Harvey is referring to in this letter is the chair of Botany at Trinity College Dublin which had become vacant in 1844 on the retirement of William Allman (1776–1846). In the event, the post was filled by Cork-born George James Allman (1812–98), whose contribution to the study of botany at TCD has been detailed by D.A. Webb, 'The Herbarium of Trinity College Dublin: Its History and Contents', *Botanical Journal of the Linnean Society*, 106 (1991), pp. 295–327. Of interest here is the fact that William Allman's son, George Johnston Allman (1824–1904), was a brilliant mathematician, being appointed Professor of Mathematics at QCG in 1853, a post he held until his retirement in 1893. As detailed by T.P. Foley '"A Nest of Scholars": Biographical Material on Some Early Professors at Queen's College Galway', *Journal of the Galway Archaeological and Historical Society*, 42 (1989–90), pp. 79–80, both men have frequently been confused with each other, because of the close similarity in their names. Professor George James Allman subsequently became Regius Professor of Natural History at Edinburgh University and went on to become a respected zoologist with an international reputation, gained from his work on marine invertebrates, including specimens collected during the HMS *Challenger* cruise. At various times he was President of the Linnean Society and the British Association for the Advancement of Science. He was elected a Fellow of the Royal Society in 1854 and received the Cunningham Medal of the Royal Irish Academy in 1878.

6 Richard Owen (1804–92) was, in his time, one of the most well-known palaeontologists of the nineteenth century. Prior to the publication of *On the Origin of Species*, Owen's name was frequently mentioned in the press and his public lectures were usually sell-out successes. His very

the Zoological Society in London, Melville was highly critical of the work done by Owen in reconstructing fossil reptiles from the enormous numbers of bones then being acquired by the British Museum. As the published discussion shows, Owen was considerably angered by Melville's comments on the evolution of the vertebra. Undeterred, Melville returned to the subject later, reasserting his conviction that vertebrae varied considerably between species as a result of function.[7] Popular opinion at the time favoured Owen, but recent palaeontological work at the Natural History Museum has shown that many of the dinosaur skeletons put together by Owen are, in fact, wrongly constructed.[8] To suit his own theories of evolution, Owen occasionally confused biped vertebrae with quadruped vertebrae and even herbivore skulls with carnivore skulls, something that should be obvious from the dentition, even to an untrained eye. Melville continually questioned Owen's conclusions regarding the evolution and extinction of dinosaurs at meetings while in London, so the realisation, over a hundred and fifty years later, that he was largely right all along is a belated vindication of his professional abilities.

William King, the first Professor of Geology and Mineralogy, worked closely and, it would seem, quite amicably with Melville. Details of King's life and

---

conspicuousness at this time makes him appear more important than Darwin as, in his lifetime, he was to popularise science and scientific thinking. With his ability to successfully badger government ministers for finance by skilful use of institutional power, science was given such a prominence in learning that its continued growth into the twentieth century was assured. Without Owen's work in the mid-nineteenth century, it is doubtful if science would have been accepted as a suitable subject for third-level education. Popularly known as 'the British Cuvier' because of his great work in comparative anatomy (publishing over 400 papers in the process), he was recognised as the leading authority in all matters relating to zoological or palaeontological classification. Barber, *The Heyday*, pp. 171–83, details Owen's contribution to science, in particular the setting up of the Natural History Museum using the specimens from the British Museum's collections in South Kensington London, in spite of the strong opposition of Darwin and his followers. His competitive treatment of rivals, coupled with his theistic theory of evolution which clashed with Darwin's, and his strategy of covert promotion of evolutionary thinking made Owen a controversial figure, both feared and hated by a substantial number of his fellow naturalists. One reason why Owen is relatively unknown today is that, even before his death, disciples of Darwin had commenced a campaign of character assassination by making his rather dogmatic personality the issue, thus undercutting his scientific credibility. In the one hundred odd years since his death, Owen has been systematically written out of Victorian natural history or, at best, remembered solely for his rejection of the theory of evolution by natural selection, by pro-Darwinian historians whose works have dominated this subject in the twentieth century. For a more sympathetic analysis of Owen's contribution to science, the recently-published biography by Nicolaas A. Rupke, *Richard Owen: Victorian Naturalist* (London, 1994) is recommended. Likewise, the published discussions of Rupke's work by Levere et al., 'Imposing Owen', *Metascience*, 7 (1995), pp. 56–76, further put Owen's scientific contribution into context. Most recently, Jane Camerini, 'The Power of Biography', *Isis*, 88 (1997), pp. 306–11, favourably compares Owen to Huxley as one of the greatest scientists of the nineteenth century.

7   A.G. Melville, 'On the Ideal Vertebra', *Proceedings of the Zoological Society London*, 16 (1848), pp. 145–50.
8   It is now generally accepted that the first dinosaur skeleton to be correctly reconstructed was *Hadrosaurus foulkii*, which was pieced together in 1876 by Joseph Leidy, the leading American palaeontologist of his time, and displayed as part of the celebrations which took place honouring the centenary of American Independence in Washington. This species was named by Leidy after William Parker Foulke, an amateur fossil hunter who had unearthed the bones in New Jersey in 1856.

academic achievements have been published by Harper, while his impact on Irish geology has been elucidated by Herries Davies.[9] Like Melville, King had a meticulous eye for detail and any anomalies seen while working on fossils would be noted rather than ignored. This characteristic led to him achieving international renown when he correctly described the bones of *Homo neanderthalensis* and interpreted their importance to the evolutionists as belonging to an early hominid. In collaboration with Thomas H. Rowney, Professor of Chemistry in QCG from 1856 until his retirement in 1889, King demonstrated in some detail the inorganic origin of the so-called fossil *Eozoön canadense*. These structures, found in strata from the Precambrian Laurentian Shield of Canada, the oldest rocks then known to exist, were thought, rather optimistically, to be the original life forms from which all other species of animals and plants were derived.[10] The name of the genus, *Eozoön*, was derived from the Greek for 'dawn animal'.

With assistance from Melville, King was one of the first to acknowledge that specimens of crinoids and other related echinoderms collected by deep soundings off the west coast from HMS *Porcupine* were, in fact, hitherto unknown deep-sea species and not shallow water species that had somehow got caught in the sounding cable while it was being deployed.[11] That life could exist at hitherto unheard of depths was becoming more obvious. Since the early decades of the nineteenth century, the Azoic Theory propounded by Edward Forbes, among others, was becoming more and more untenable. Based on Forbes's own limited findings, the Azoic Theory stated that, with increasing depth, the number of species and the number of individuals decreased to a point where, below 300 fathoms (1,800 feet), the seabed is devoid of life. Consequently, when HMS *Porcupine* called at Galway for regular coaling and re-victualling, King made sure to have access to the material which had been dredged up, before it was packed off to London and Oxford by mail-train. Later oceanographic cruises, in 1869 and 1870, by HMS *Porcupine* followed up and confirmed the findings of her earlier cruises and those of HMS *Lightning*, made during the years 1865–8 off the south and west coasts.

From the outset, the teaching facilities at QCG were inadequate. The lack of sufficient lecture theatres was commented on regularly in the early annual reports but, for the teaching of Natural History, the lack of adequate museum and

---

9   D.A.T. Harper (ed.), *William King D.Sc. (1809–1886). A Paleontological Tribute* (Galway, 1988), pp. 1–24. See also Gordon L. Herries Davies, 'William King and the Irish Geological Community', ibid., pp. 25–32; and Harper in this volume.
10   W. King and T.H. Rowney, 'On the So-called Eozoönal Rock', *Quarterly Journal of the Geological Society*, 22 (1866), pp. 185–218.
11   W. King, 'Preliminary Notice of the Organic and Inorganic Objects Obtained from the Soundings of HMS *Porcupine* off the West Coast of Ireland', *Nautical Magazine* (1862) pp. 600–2. HMS *Porcupine* was a wooden-hulled paddle powered gun-vessel of just under 500 tons, commissioned at Deptford in 1844. In 1856 HMS *Porcupine* became the Royal Navy's principal survey ship in home waters and, until she was succeeded by HMS *Triton* in 1881, completed a number of major surveys in the waters off the west of Ireland. Although these surveys were primarily to seek new routes off the continental shelf for transatlantic telegraph cables, the results of these deep-sea soundings also provided the impetus to develop new fishing grounds. The Porcupine Bank was so-named after its discovery by HMS *Porcupine* during one such survey.

laboratory facilities was an additional problem, as well as dampness.[12] In a recent paper detailing the origins of the geological museum in QCG, Harper states that William King was to have overall responsibility for the collection, curation, and display of material even though the museum was to encompass the physical sciences and engineering as well as the biological sciences and geology.[13] Although the college authorities never acceded to his frequent requests for a full-time curator, King managed to build up the geological specimen collection by availing of the strong links which existed in the early years between the Queen's Colleges and the Geological Survey of Ireland, itself set up in 1845. As detailed by Herries Davies, Thomas Oldham, local director of the Survey was instructed in 1846 to collect five representative sets of specimens.[14] Two sets were for the Geological Survey museums in London and Dublin and the other three were for the new museums which were to be established in the Queen's Colleges in Belfast, Cork, and Galway.

It would seem that, following King's lead, Melville set himself the task of building up a botanical and zoological specimen collection, something of which he would have had good experience from his time in Oxford. Again, it must be said that, as in other areas of overlapping responsibility, Melville appears to have worked quite satisfactorily with King in building up the museum collections. Within a few years the collection of zoological specimens was quite extensive and, by the turn of the century, Anderson was able to state that the museum in QCG ranked with the best teaching collections to be found in other universities.[15]

In spite of statements to the contrary, QCG was not an academic backwater. Visits by eminent persons were frequent, and according to the local press, these visitors were treated with all due respect and honours. When Queen Victoria's Consort, Prince Albert, visited Queen's College Galway in January 1856, he was met by Joseph O'Leary, Vice-President and Professor of History and English Literature, in the company of Professors Melville and King. As with all important visitors who came to the college at this time, Prince Albert was brought on a tour of the Departments of Natural History and Geology, the museum, and their library; and they also walked the grounds, including the President's Garden and botanical plot, before returning to the museum where Prince Albert presented a gift of a specially-inscribed copy of William Macgillivray's *Natural History of Deeside and Braemar*, edited by E. Lankester (London, 1855).[16] The Prince also

12 *Report on the Condition and Progress of the Queen's University of Ireland for the Year Ending June 19, 1852* (Dublin, 1852). See also James Mitchell, 'Queen's College Galway 1845–1858: From Site to Structure', *Journal of the Galway Archaeological and Historical Society*, 50 (1998), pp. 49–89; James Mitchell, 'The Appointment of Revd J.W. Kirwan as First President of Queen's College Galway and His Years in Office: 1845–1849', ibid., 51 (1999), pp. 1–23.
13 D.A.T. Harper and Matthew A. Parkes, 'Geological Survey Donations to the Geological Museum in Queen's College Galway: 19th Century Inter-institutional Collaboration in Ireland', *Geological Curator*, 6 (1996), pp. 233–6.
14 G.L. Herries Davies, *Sheets of Many Colours: The Mapping of Ireland's Rocks 1750–1890* (Dublin, 1983).
15 R.J. Anderson, 'The Natural History Museum, Queen's College Galway', *Irish Naturalist*, 8 (1899), pp. 125–31. Further details in the development of the geology museum, known today as the James Mitchell Museum, can be found in D.A.T. Harper, *An Irish Geological Time Capsule: The James Mitchell Museum University College Galway* (Galway, 1996).
16 A search of the bookstock of the James Hardiman Library has failed to find any trace of this book

complimented Melville and King on the completeness of the museum collection and its layout. Another royal personage who received similar treatment was Prince Louis Napoleon of France, whose visit in 1857, which fuelled the existing Francophobia of the time, has been detailed by Collins.[17]

Perhaps Melville's greatest contribution to the literature of natural history was the book, *The Dodo and Its Kindred*, published in 1848, which he co-authored with the geologist Hugh Edwin Strickland, whose early death in 1852 at the age of forty-two robbed Melville of the opportunity for further joint work. Although the title conjures up images reminiscent of the writings of Lewis Carroll, it is in fact a well-researched study of various species of recently-extinct flightless birds, based on a small number of incomplete skeletons, assorted bones, preserved skins, feathers, and contemporary illustrations, which had been acquired by various collectors. As Strickland and Melville pointed out, the book was aimed at 'rescuing these anomalous creatures from the domain of fiction'.[18] Central to the discussion was the involvement of man in the disappearance of these species and whether or not they would have become extinct anyway. An attempt was made to unravel folklore from fact in descriptive accounts going back to the sixteenth century, when the Dodo was still to be found on the island of Mauritius. In pursuing his own research, Melville had access to bones in the British Museum as well as Oxford. Due credit must be given for his painstaking work, noting the anatomical affinities to other species, yet at the same time highlighting rather than ignoring the anomalies. At the conclusion of his anatomical studies, Melville felt that the Dodo was more closely related to the dove and pigeon family than to any other avian group. Of course, this immediately placed him at odds, once more, with Richard Owen who, in an earlier study of just one Dodo bone in the British Museum collection, had concluded that this extinct group was related to the vulture family. Owen had previously published a paper in 1839 establishing a new genus *Dinornis* as a result of studying some bones from New Zealand of a hitherto unknown, but now extinct, giant flightless bird related to the Kiwi. As a result, he felt he was in a position of authority regarding all such animals. Following this, Strickland published a number of supplementary notes, based on further studies of new specimens and contemporary illustrations, to support the findings of the book.[19] Melville took no further part in this vigorous defence as, by this time, he had left Oxford for Galway. Again, it must be said that his relations with Strickland were

---

which, although absent from V. Steinberger, *Catalogue of the Library of University College Galway* (Galway, 1913), is listed in J.H. Richardson, *Alphabetical Catalogue of the Library of Queen's College Galway* (Dublin, 1864).

17 Timothy Collins, 'The Town Hall in 1857 – When Galway Hospitality Met Crimean Cannon', *Journal of the Galway Archaeological and Historical Society*, 48 (1996), pp. 137–42.

18 H.E. Strickland and A.G. Melville, *The Dodo and Its Kindred: or, The History, Affinities, and Osteology of the Dodo, Solitaire and Other Extinct Birds of the Islands Mauritius, Rodriguez and Bourbon* (London, 1848), p. 62.

19 H.E. Strickland, 'Supplementary Notices Regarding "The Dodo and its Kindred"', nos 1, 2, 3, *Annals and Magazine of Natural History*, 2nd series, 3 (1849), pp. 136–9; 'Supplementary Notices', nos. 4, 5, ibid., 4 (1849), pp. 259–61; 'Supplementary Notices', nos. 6, 7, 8, ibid., 4 (1849), pp. 335–9; 'Supplementary Notices', no. 9, ibid., 6 (1850), pp. 290–1.

always cordial, and in his memoirs, which were edited by Jardine in 1858, Strickland gives due credit to Melville for his expertise in avian anatomy and his support for a new theory on the phylogenetic importance of this group of birds which went against popular thinking. Indeed, a recent study, published by Quammen in 1996, on the continuing increase in the rate of extinctions globally in the twentieth century, cites the importance of Strickland and Melville's seminal work in identifying man as the prime cause for the depletion of the planet's biodiversity.[20]

After his appointment to the Department of Natural History, Melville became interested in the fauna of Galway Bay. This is reflected in his publications after 1850, which changed in subject matter from comparative anatomy to marine faunal studies. One paper, a list of ten species of crustacea dredged up from various stations around Aran and Bertraghboy Bay, published in 1851, gives an early indication of the kind of work he was willing to pursue. Another paper published in 1857, a list of the crustacea of Galway Bay, has served as a model for successive generations of marine researchers, and, in consequence, is frequently cited in the literature, most recently by Ó Céidigh in 1996, who puts Melville's pioneering work into its regional context.[21]

As can be seen from various sources, Melville was also very active as a field naturalist, collecting and noting the locations of many plant specimens from all parts of Connemara. According to Desmond, there are collections of plants made by Melville in the herbaria of the National Museum of Wales and Queen Mary College, London. Kent and Allen state that there are also specimens collected specifically in the Galway area (vice-counties H15, H16, and H17) in 1852, by Melville, to be found in the Warwick Archaeological and Natural History Society Museum. Scannell and Synott also give due credit to Melville for his work. Indeed, the accuracy of his observations has resulted in Melville being regularly cited in the literature, usually confirming the location of species noted during his time in Galway.[22]

---

20 William Jardine (ed.), *Memoirs of Hugh William Strickland, MA* (London, 1858); David Quammen, *The Song of the Dodo: Island Biogeography in an Age of Extinctions* (London, 1996).
21 A.G. Melville, 'Localities of Rare British Crustacea', *Annals and Magazine of Natural History*, 2nd series, 8 (1851), p. 236; A.G. Melville, 'Carcinological Notes: Being a List of the Crustacea Podophthalmia of Galway Marine Districts, Chiefly Made during the Summer of 1850', *Natural History Review*, 4 (1857), pp. 151–3; Pádraig Ó Céidigh, 'Marine Science on the West Coast of Ireland and the Contribution of University College Galway', in Brendan F. Keegan and Roseanne O'Connor (eds), *Irish Marine Science 1995* (Galway, 1996), pp. 21–36. For reasons of space, it has not been possible to append a full list of Melville's published work with this chapter although an annotated bibliography of his writings has been compiled by the author, T. Collins, *Annotated Bibliography of the Writings of A.G. Melville: First Professor of Natural History at Queen's College Galway 1849–1882* (Galway, 1999). Copies are available from the Secretary, Social Sciences Research Centre, Newman House, NUI, Galway.
22 Ray Desmond, *Dictionary of British and Irish Botanists and Horticulturists Including Plant Collectors, Flower Painters and Garden Designers* (London, 1994); D.H. Kent and D.E. Allen, *British and Irish Herbaria: An Index to the Location of Herbaria of British and Irish Vascular Plants* (London, 1984); Mary J.P. Scannell and Donal M. Synnott, *Census Catalogue of the Flora of Ireland*, 2nd ed. (Dublin, 1987). Recent examples are papers by Cilian Roden, '*Orchis morio* L. in the West of Ireland', *Irish Naturalists' Journal*, 24 (1993), pp. 220–2 and Don Cotton et al., 'On the Occurrence of *Pseudorchis albida* in Sligo (H28), Leitrim (H29), and Galway (H15, H16, and H17)', *Irish Naturalists' Journal*, 24 (1994), pp. 468–71.

More than most members of the staff in QCG at this time, Melville did much to bridge the gap between 'town and gown' by making himself available for public lectures which were given in his free time. He was a frequent guest lecturer at the Mechanics' Institute and advertisements appeared regularly in the local press announcing lectures on many aspects of natural history, at such venues as Mrs Carrigan's Large Room and Kilroy's Assembly Room. In the winter of 1860–1, for instance, Melville gave a series of public lectures each Tuesday and Saturday on geology to an enthusiastic audience at Mrs Carrigan's Large Room, which was situated at the north end of Eyre Square, near the present-day Imperial Hotel. The proceeds of these lectures were given to the St Vincent de Paul Society 'for the relief of the poor of the city' and, in consequence, Melville was usually introduced by Fr Peter Daly who, among his many interests, was deeply involved with the Society.[23] It says a lot for the literary life of Galway that such lectures were so well attended. Indeed, in his editorial on the subject in the *Galway Vindicator* (2 January 1861), John Francis Blake had nothing but praise for Melville's lectures:

> The ennobling part science plays in the enlightenment and amelioration of the human race has stamped it with an almost sacred character. When for the

---

23 Fr Peter Daly (c.1788–1868) played a key role in the commercial development and modernisation of Galway in the nineteenth century. A skilful entrepreneur, adept in local business development and property speculation, he was a man ahead of his time. With a flair for oratory and a personality that appealed to the ordinary person and resulted in massive popularity for all of his schemes, Fr Daly was especially successful at coercing local investors, as well as the government, into backing his many business ventures. While Chairman of Galway Town Commissioners, he successfully lobbied Parliament for grant aid to complete the programme of canal building in Galway, linking the Corrib system with the sea. He was Director of the Galway Gas Company which, from 1837 provided power and light in the town. Using his position on the Board of the Midland and Great Western Railway Company, he ensured that the railway was brought right into the centre of Galway, terminating at Eyre Square, and personally supervised the construction of the Railway Hotel (now the Great Southern Hotel), at its opening in 1851 and for many years afterward, the largest hotel in Ireland. Using his membership of the Galway Harbour Commissioners, Fr Daly ensured that a comprehensive programme of port development was undertaken, again with financial backing from parliament. As chairman of the Galway Bay Steam Navigation Company, he inaugurated the first regular steamship service between Galway and the Aran Islands in 1858. He was responsible for putting the first steamships on the Corrib to develop trade up the lake as far as Cong, while at the same time setting up a line of fast steamships to exploit the growing transatlantic trade. The short-lived Galway Line competed unsuccessfully for supremacy of the transatlantic trade with the Cunard and Allen Lines by offering a service to St Johns Newfoundland, Halifax Nova Scotia, Boston and New York in the early 1860s. Its history has been detailed by Timothy Collins, 'The Galway Line in Context: A Contribution to Galway Maritime History, pt i' and 'The Galway Line in Context: A Contribution to Galway Maritime History, Concluded', *Journal of the Galway Archaeological and Historical Society*, 46 (1994), pp. 1–42 and 47 (1995), pp. 36–86. Prime Minister Lord Palmerston lived in awe of Fr Daly and once said of him: 'He is the foremost politician in Ireland, though he be a Catholic priest'. Such complex, and frequently lucrative, business activities led to him clashing with his superiors Dr MacHale, archbishop of Tuam, Dr MacEvilly, bishop of Galway, and Cardinal Cullen, then archbishop of Armagh, on a number of occasions. For further details of this extraordinary man, the detailed biography by James Mitchell, 'Fr. Peter Daly (c. 1788–1868)', *Journal of the Galway Archaeological and Historical Society*, 39 (1983–4), pp. 27–114 is recommended.

while leaving the field of education and bringing its fertilising influences into the domain of charity, science becomes doubly sacred.[24]

The text of these lectures was usually reported in detail in the *Galway Vindicator* and gave the ordinary individual some idea of the level of knowledge of the subject at this time. For instance, in his lecture, which was reported in the *Galway Vindicator* on 19 January 1861, Melville spoke on submarine geology and the additional information being collected as a result of the deep-sea surveys then being conducted in association with the laying of transatlantic submarine cables. In summing up, Melville stated that 'all life appears to cease about 500 fathoms down and one then moves into a region of death and sterility'. In another lecture, Melville spoke about the process of fossilisation which, he said, occurred only in the ocean depths. With our present-day knowledge of the subject, it is easy to make light of Melville's erroneous pronouncements, but one can see how such lectures must have fired the imagination of those listening. Some of his public lectures also brought out the serious side of his subject. The *Galway Vindicator* (23 January 1861) reported that his lecture of the previous night on geochronology was remarkable in that it was attended by a considerable number of Catholic clergy. No doubt they were interested in exposing any possible conflict with the biblical interpretation of the theistic creation of the earth. However, on this occasion, he must have been uncharacteristically diplomatic, as it appears his lecture was 'frequently applauded, and at the close the plaudits were warm and general'.

The following winter, Melville was again prevailed upon to give another series of ten lectures, entitled 'Life and Organisation in Plants and Animals'. Commencing in December 1861 and running into 1862, this series was also remarkable in that it included two field trips and culminated in a written examination in botany, under the auspices of the Science and Art Department of the Council on Education Committee, which was responsible for funding these courses in cities and towns throughout Britain and Ireland. Indeed, more than any other single factor, these courses contributed to the explosion in interest in natural history which occurred at this time and resulted in the rise of the amateur naturalists' field clubs. Following the written examination in June 1862, which was taken by a large number 'of gentlemen and some of the most respectable ladies of the town', Melville was asked to run another course, commencing that same month and

24 The *Galway Vindicator and Connaught Advertiser*, to give it its full name, was quite an outstanding newspaper of the period, and the only one in the region to be published twice weekly, on Wednesdays and Saturdays. Owned at this time by John Francis Blake, the paper was proud of its Galway roots and its partisan style reflected Blake's judgement when answering criticisms about issues that were close to his own heart. Blake himself claimed that his paper was the best medium for advertising in the west of Ireland. His death in March 1864 saw a moderation in the tone of the paper which, in retrospect, can only be regretted as it gave an insight into the cut and thrust of Galway commercial, political, and academic life in the mid-nineteenth century. Apart from Toby Joyce, 'The *Galway American* 1862–63, part i: James Roche and the American Civil War' and 'The *Galway American* 1862–63, Concluded: Politics and Place in a Fenian Newspaper', *Journal of the Galway Archaeological and Historical Society*, 47 (1995), pp. 108–37 and 48 (1996), pp. 104–36, very few studies have been made of such local papers as historical sources of information by researchers.

including field trips, taking advantage of the summer season, to further study the flora and fauna of the vicinity. However, relations between Melville and the public seem to have soured somewhat at this point and he decided not to proceed with this planned course. It is not clear what exactly happened, but it would seem that his own personality led to him alienating himself from his audience at a most inopportune time. According to the *Galway Vindicator* (7 June 1862), Melville 'incurred the displeasure of the people of Galway by some indiscreet expressions made use of by him at the finish of his lectures. His reflections on the national character were as unjust as they were uncalled for'.

One can only surmise as to what Melville actually said, and even the publication of an abject apology some days later in the same paper did not help things. It is possible that the whole episode was blown out of proportion by John Francis Blake of the *Galway Vindicator*, as he had been prevented from attending a previous lecture on volcanism, which included details of a recent eruption of Vesuvius, because all tickets had been sold in advance. Blake demanded the right to report the lecture, invoking the freedom of the press, but was told personally by both Fr Peter Daly and Melville that there was no room for him. In a particularly vitriolic editorial, Blake later demanded an apology from both Fr Daly and Melville, but received no satisfaction. Considering the large audiences his lectures attracted, with the proceeds all going to charity, it seems rather extreme that Melville's good work for the poor of the town should have been so easily jeopardised. In an open letter published later in the *Galway Vindicator*, Joseph Semple, chairman of the Galway branch of the St Vincent de Paul Society at the time, asked for forgiveness on all sides in order that the next planned series of lectures could commence, but all to no avail. Again, one can only surmise as to the consequent effect on learning in Galway if those lectures and field trips had gone ahead, as elsewhere it was from such beginnings that many of the country's learned clubs and societies sprang up in the latter half of the nineteenth century. Indeed, it is this writer's opinion, that it was only with the arrival of the amateur naturalist and the setting up of the amateur naturalists' field clubs across the country, that the 'Golden Era' of Irish natural history began. Curiously enough, very little has been written about this aspect of Ireland's cultural heritage, although recently-published material collected by Foster is an attempt to rectify this.[25]

The first, and reckoned by some the greatest, amateur naturalists' field club was set up in Belfast in 1863 as a result of a similar series of winter lectures given by Joseph Beete Jukes, then Director of the Geological Survey of Ireland, and botanist Ralph Tate. Over the years other clubs were set up in various towns, often by ex-members of the Belfast Naturalists' Field Club and like-minded individuals. In response to popular demand, the Dublin Naturalists' Field Club was founded in 1886, although according to Bailey its survival was in doubt for the first five years of its existence.[26] This was, in part, due to the fact that some of the founding members were professional biologists who just had to devote more time to their

---

25 John Wilson Foster (ed.), *Nature in Ireland: A Scientific and Cultural History* (Dublin, 1997).
26 Desmond Bailey, 'History of the Dublin Naturalists' Field Club', in *Reflections and Recollections: 100 Years of the Dublin Naturalists' Field Club* (Dublin, 1987), pp. 6–29.

academic duties. Edward Perceval Wright, first President of the Dublin Club, was an ophthalmic surgeon and also Professor of Botany at Trinity College Dublin. Alfred Cort Haddon, first Vice-President, was Professor of Zoology at the Royal College of Science for Ireland. In the 1880s he was committed to organising the various expeditions which studied the deeper waters off the south and west coasts with regard to fisheries development.[27]

In common with the other clubs, the amateur naturalists' field clubs in Limerick and Cork owed their existence to a curious blend of the amateur and the professional. In 1892 the first President of the Cork Naturalists' Field Club was Marcus Manuel Hartog, at the time Professor of Natural History at Queen's College Cork and from 1909, Professor of Zoology at University College Cork. According to Reynolds and Scannell, the Limerick Naturalists' Field Club came into existence in December 1892 through the efforts of Francis Neale, an ex-member of the Dublin Naturalists' Field Club, who specialised in entomology, Dr George Fogerty, an ex-Royal Navy surgeon and his brother W.A. Fogerty, who read a paper at the inaugural meeting entitled rather enigmatically 'Some Low Forms of Animal Life'.[28]

In Galway one must look to the founding of the Galway Archaeological and Historical Society in 1900 for a similar grouping of like-minded individuals. The first President, the Hon. Robert E. Dillon, who later inherited the title Lord Clonbrock, was an active member of this Society, according to Townley.[29] As well as having an interest in antiquities, he had already made his mark as a gifted naturalist, with a keen interest in entomology. Dillon describes, in various publications, the extensive collection he had put together.[30] Throughout its existence, the Galway Archaeological and Historical Society has maintained close links with the College, a point made by Collins when noting the support given by the academic staff to community activities, and by people like Melville, who anticipated the kind of activities for which the Galway Archaeological and Historical Society is now noted.[31]

As has already been stated, Melville was an excellent field naturalist, and each year his students, whether of medicine or arts, took part in at least one major excursion. One such excursion, detailed in the *Galway Vindicator* (28 May 1864)

---

27 A fascinating account of these expeditions, using the steam yacht *Fingal*, the steam fishing vessel *Harlequin*, and the paddle steamer *Lord Bandon*, later known as the *Flying Falcon*, is to be found in Robert Lloyd Praeger, *The Way that I Went: An Irishman in Ireland* (Dublin, 1937). A concise summary, placing this work into context, has been published by Rice, *British Oceanographic Vessels*, while most recently a study of the research vessels themselves has been published by M.J. Gillooly, T. Collins et al., 'Vesselised not Fossilised: Irish Marine Research Vessels 1845–1995', in Keegan and O'Connor (eds), *Irish Marine Science*, pp. 49–61.
28 Sylvia P. Reynolds and Mary J.P. Scannell, 'A History of the Limerick Naturalists' Field Club 1892–1913', *Irish Naturalists' Journal*, 24 (1992), pp. 101–6.
29 Christopher Townley, 'The Galway Archaeological and Historical Society', *Journal of the Galway Archaeological and Historical Society*, 35 (1976), pp. 5–11.
30 Robert E. Dillon, 'Six Years' Entomology in Co. Galway', *Entomologist*, 27 (1894), pp. 88–91, 169–71, 190–1; 'Lepidoptera at Clonbrock, Co. Galway', ibid., p. 322; 'Lepidoptera', *Irish Naturalist*, 7 (1898), pp. 209–10; '*Colias edusa* in Ireland', ibid., 9 (1900), p. 246.
31 T. Collins, 'Dodos and Discord: A Biographical Note on A.G. Melville of Queen's College Galway', *Journal of the Galway Archaeological and Historical Society*, 50 (1998), pp. 90–111.

gives some idea of what was involved. With the PS *Pilot*,[32] under the command of Captain Paddy Reilly, chartered specially for the trip by the Academic Council of QCG, Melville, accompanied by George H. Kinahan of the Geological Survey of Ireland,[33] his brother John Robert Kinahan,[34] and a Dr Underwood of Loughrea, departed from Galway with a number of students and steamed out to Aran on the morning of Monday 23 May 1864. Both Kinahans were extremely interested in the flora and fauna of the region and were publishing papers on their respective excursions at this time. Arriving at Killeany Bay, the PS *Pilot* dropped anchor, and lunch was served before those on board went ashore, where

> Much time was spent examining specimens of plants, rare in Europe and Britain, which everywhere grew in profusion … Glasson Rock was studied and its geology commented on. Many seabirds were noted as they flew or swam in the vicinity of their nests. After some time spent admiring this splendid scene and shooting some of the rarer kinds of waterfowl the old fort of Duchar [*sic*] was visited.

A tour of other archaeological monuments and ruins was completed before the party returned to the PS *Pilot* for dinner. The following day, they steamed to Kilmurvey, where they were perfectly placed to tour other sites of archaeological interest culminating in a visit to Dun Aengus, at which an unusual ceremony took place:

32 The prefix PS before the name of a ship denotes that the vessel is a paddle steamer. This particular steamer had been bought by her two Masters, John McIntyre and Patrick Reilly, from the Galway Bay Steam Navigation Co., set up by Fr Peter Daly in 1858 to operate between Aran, Ballyvaughan, Newquay, and Galway and to act as tender for the transatlantic steamships of the Galway Line which, unfortunately ceased its service in January 1864. As a result the PS *Pilot* was sold off. Tragically, McIntyre succumbed to tuberculosis within weeks of purchasing the PS *Pilot*, leaving Reilly to operate the service alone. For further details of this period in the development of Galway port, see Collins, 'The Galway Line'.

33 Dublin-born George Henry Kinahan (1829–1908), was one of the greatest Irish geologists of the nineteenth century. Known as 'the big miner', Kinahan was a man of boundless physical and intellectual energy. As a geologist, his work of mapping took him to almost every part of Ireland, giving him an almost encyclopaedic knowledge of the country. Much has been written about his personality by Praeger, in *The Way* and Davies, in *Sheets*. His contribution to the Geological Survey of Ireland, which, like the Queen's Colleges, was also established in 1845, has been elucidated in a sesquicentennial history by G.L. Herries Davies, *North from the Hook: 150 Years of the Geological Survey of Ireland* (Dublin, 1995).

34 John Robert Kinahan (1828–65), brother of the aforementioned G.H. Kinahan was, like Melville, qualified in medicine but became more interested in natural history. Having obtained the degree MD in Trinity College Dublin, he lectured widely on botany and zoology under Science and Art Department. and was for many years Secretary of the Natural History Society of Dublin. Like his brother, John Robert was a man of exceptional energy and enthusiasm. He wrote extensively on Irish botany, geology, and zoology and was a leading figure in Irish scientific life, although he died at the age of thirty-seven before reaching his full potential. The following are two examples of the Kinahan brothers' publications detailing their work in the west of Ireland at this time: J.R. Kinahan, 'Notes on the Marine Fauna of the Coast of Clare', *Proceedings of the Dublin Natural History Society*, (1856–7), pp. 99–103 and G.H. Kinahan, 'The Seaweeds of Yar Connaught and their Uses', *Quarterly Journal of Science*, 6 (1869), pp. 331–41.

Dr Melville assembled the group at the centre of the fort and it being Her Majesty's Birthday, called for a cheer for the Queen, which was responded to with such good will that the very puffins forsook their native cliffs in sheer fright.

The next day, steam was got up and the PS *Pilot* proceeded for Greatman's Bay in Connemara, where some dredging was done and a large collection of specimens put aside for later identification. Later that day, the PS *Pilot* headed for Galway, steaming close to the coast and noting the geology along the way. Arriving off Mutton Island at 6 p.m. in a glorious sunset, the steamer was loudly cheered by the crew of HMS *Royal Charlotte*, a cutter stationed in Galway, as they still had a large amount of bunting and flags hoisted since the Queen's Birthday celebrations of the previous day. Other field trips to Aran and across Galway Bay to Ballyvaughan and Newquay, to study the flora, fauna, and antiquities of the Burren, were frequently made using the steamers SS *Vestal* and SS *Midge* of the Ballast Board, whenever these ships came to Galway on their tours of inspection.[35]

Melville had one son, Andrew, who, it would appear, inherited his father's outspokenness. While still a medical student at QCG, he was responsible for the Extraordinary Visitation which was convened in Dublin Castle in 1870, as a result of a formal complaint he had made against Professor Richard Doherty, first Professor of Midwifery, and his clinical tutor.[36] In essence, the complaint centred around the alleged failure of Professor Doherty to give clinical tuition which was an important component of the course. Doherty was at some disadvantage in that he did not have access to hospital patients at this time; a prior agreement, giving access to patients in the County Infirmary and the Union Workhouse, which had been in existence for ten years, had come to an end in 1859. Consequently, Doherty prevailed on the College Council to purchase the collection of post-mortem specimens and instruments of obstetrical and related interest which had been accumulated by the noted Dublin obstetrician, William Montgomery.[37] This collection, known as the Montgomery Museum, the remains of which are housed today in the Department of Obstetrics and Gynaecology, NUI Galway, was used extensively by Doherty for the benefit of his students. Andrew Melville was not happy with this, and tried, without success, to gain access himself to female patients in the County Infirmary. As a consequence of this failure to study

---

35 The Corporation for Preserving and Improving the Port of Dublin, set up in 1786 and better known as the Ballast Board, was one of a number of organisations in existence at this time for the express purpose of servicing the lighthouses, buoys, beacons, and other seamarks around the coast of Ireland, and in providing facilities for the surveying and examination of vessels needing repair. The Merchant Shipping Act of 1854 saw the creation of the Port of Dublin Corporation with two distinct areas of responsibility. This led ultimately, in 1867, to the Dublin-based responsibilities coming under a new corporation, the Dublin Port and Docks Board, and the responsibility for maintaining the aids to navigation in Irish waters being passed to the Commissioners of Irish Lights, whose excellent work down to the present day in maintaining this service has gone largely unnoticed and unrecognised by the general public.
36 James P. Murray, *Galway: A Medico-Social History* (Galway, 1994) gives some details of this episode.
37 Ibid., p. 120.

patients, he took action to seek a refund of that part of his College fees which related to clinical tuition, as he felt he had received none, by requesting a meeting with the Academic Council in order that they might listen to his complaint.

When he received no satisfaction from the College authorities, Andrew Melville decided to go public with his grievances in a detailed letter which was published in the *Lancet*.[38] Reaction to this publication was swift and unprecedented. Following a special meeting of the Academic Council, Melville was informed that he had been rusticated (that is, suspended) for a period of three years for bringing the College into disrepute. In a surprisingly public exercise in damage limitation, there followed a series of letters in the *Lancet* by members of the Academic Council, including Edward Berwick, President of QCG, William Lupton, Registrar, and various professors of medicine. Each letter was replied to in full by Melville, with other QCG students and even the editorial board of the Lancet, taking sides with their own comments. The result of this very public airing of his grievances and his subsequent treatment by the College was that Andrew Melville was granted his wish. The Queen's University of Ireland announced that an Extraordinary Visitation of Queen's College Galway would be held.

The Extraordinary Visitation was convened in Dublin Castle on 30 and 31 March 1870 to hear the complaint of Andrew Smith Melville against his College, as laid out in his original letter to the *Lancet*, and his appeal against rustication. The Visitors presiding were Sir Maziere Brady, Vice-Chancellor of the Queen's University of Ireland, Dr John T. Banks, President of the King and Queen's College of Physicians, and Dr Rawdon Macnamara, President of the Royal College of Surgeons. Queen's College Galway was well represented with President Berwick in attendance along with William Lupton who, besides being Registrar, was a barrister by profession, Professor Doherty, and a number of other members of the Faculty of Medicine. As statements were read out and witness after witness was called to testify, it became obvious that some academics had no doubt who was really at fault. In a written statement to Edward Berwick, defending Doherty's lectures and practicals and commenting on the *Lancet* correspondence, Professor James V. Browne claimed that:

> He (Andrew Melville) is set on by his father, who is always at war with his brothers and is not on terms of friendship with one of them; and this is nothing but an attempt to annoy the school, which he is always abusing … One of Dr Melville's great grievances is that he cannot get on the Council. I never saw his name on a voting slip; nobody could sit on a council with him. He is the real author of the letter bearing his son's signature – a most disrespectful, groundless, crotchety document, and of no further use than to annoy.[39]

38 Andrew Smith Melville, 'The Medical School of Queen's College Galway', *Lancet*, 2, 18 December 1869, p. 865.
39 *Report of an Extraordinary Visitation of Queen's College Galway Held in Dublin Castle on 30th and 31st March 1870* (Dublin, 1870), p. 53. James V. Browne was first Professor of Surgery at QCG. Appointed in 1849, he died in office in 1887. He also held the position of County Infirmary Surgeon and therefore was in a position to say who should, or as in this case, should definitely not, have access to patients in the County Infirmary. Like Melville, Browne was an arrogant man and,

In reply to such an extraordinary allegation, Andrew Melville was quick to point out that his father had taken no part in his action against the College and, indeed, there is no evidence to support Browne's allegation. Finally, in his own lengthy answer to the Visitors, Doherty contended that practicals using the Montgomery Collection were tantamount to clinical lectures. After deliberating on the evidence, the Visitors accepted Doherty's view. They also asked that Andrew Melville be refunded his clinical tuition fees, something that had already been done many weeks before in an unsuccessful effort to defuse the situation, and that he also be asked to further his medical education elsewhere.

Following this judgement, Andrew Melville moved to Edinburgh to continue his studies at his father's *alma mater*. To his credit, he had also inherited his father's interest in natural history, and he was invited to lecture part-time on botany and zoology at the Edinburgh School of Arts. Unfortunately, Andrew Melville died suddenly in Edinburgh before he could finish his studies. According to Desmond there are some plant specimens collected by Andrew Melville among the herbarium collections of the Royal Pharmaceutical Society of Great Britain.[40]

Melville himself retired in 1882, after thirty-three years of service but was not replaced immediately. This was because of a rather curious arrangement, agreed in 1867, by which both he and William King, Professor of Geology and Mineralogy, received an addition to their salaries on the understanding that when either chair became vacant, the surviving professor would take on the duties of both chairs. Accordingly, King was appointed Professor of Mineralogy, Geology, and Natural History. When Melville left QCG, he did not, according to Foley, quoting Moffett, 'leave behind a single friend in Galway'.[41] Melville sold his house in Shantalla and retired to Knockawn, Portlaw, Co. Waterford where he lived quietly, dying at the advanced age of 82 years on 8 June 1901. An anonymous obituary, which appeared in a local newspaper, neatly sums up Melville's personality:

> He was never popular with his students, as he was stern of manner, and maintained the most strict and unbending discipline in his classes. When, however, he accompanied the classes on botanical excursions, he laid aside all

according to Murray, his own relations with his academic colleagues were frequently acrimonious. At this hearing, his main cause for complaint was that Andrew Melville regularly refused to doff his hat when they met in public, and also that he once drove his pony and trap at speed past his carriage on Newcastle Road, causing his horse to panic! From the plaintiff's viewpoint, it could be construed that the real villain was Browne himself, whose antagonistic attitude towards an undergraduate provoked the submission of a formal complaint in the first place. Indeed, it can be seen from the published proceedings that Browne was the real cause of Doherty's problems, as it was he who had put an end to the agreed visits by undergraduates to the County Infirmary for clinical tuition in midwifery. The acquisition of the Montgomery Museum and its substitution for clinical visits was really only a stopgap measure brought in by Doherty. It is difficult to gauge the quality of the Montgomery Museum today as most of the organs, foetuses and sections have been disposed of in recent years, leaving only a small number of specimens that have somehow survived intact in their original preserving jars, while the specialist instruments are on permanent display in specially-made cases in the Department of Obstetrics and Gynaecology, NUI Galway.

40 Desmond, *Dictionary*.
41 Foley, 'A Nest', p. 77.

his sternness, and became a most genial and agreeable companion, interesting the students, not only in the flowers and plants, but in the archaeology of the district, with which he was well acquainted.[42]

Already suffering from ill health when he took on the extra duties of teaching Natural History, Professor King himself was forced to resign the dual chair in 1883 when he became paralysed. He died at his residence, Glenoir, Taylor's Hill, on 24 June 1886.[43]

On King's resignation, Dr Richard John Anderson was appointed Professor of Natural History, Geology, and Mineralogy (fig. 9.2). Like his predecessor Melville, Anderson came from a medical background. He was a native of Ballybought, Co. Antrim, and his date of birth, according to the 1915 volume of the *UCG Annual*, was 24 July 1848. He received his early education at Potterton's School, Newry before graduating from Queen's College Belfast with an MA and then an MD in 1872. He must have been an exemplary student as he won class scholarships each year as an undergraduate and received the College's Gold Medal in his final examinations for both degrees. After graduation he worked for a time in St Bartholomew's Hospital, London and gained, in the process, his membership of the Royal College of Surgeons of England. Subsequently he worked as a comparative anatomist in the Universities of Leipzig and Heidelberg, before moving on to work in the College de France in Paris and at the Zoological Station in Naples. Returning to Ireland in 1875, Anderson was appointed Assistant, then Demonstrator, of Anatomy at Queen's College Belfast (QCB), before accepting the post of Professor of Natural History, Geology, and Mineralogy at QCG in 1883.

Very little has been written about Anderson, other than what he himself published, but his own publications are substantial. His varied appointments before coming to Galway certainly gave him the necessary experience upon which to base his wide-ranging interests later in life. Even after coming to Galway, he continued to travel widely, regularly attending conferences and meetings in Britain, France, Germany, Switzerland, Spain, Portugal, and even the United States and Mexico, contributing papers on medicine, zoology, geology, and botany.

9.2 Richard John Anderson, Professor of Natural History, Geology, and Mineralogy 1883–1914

---

42 *Galway Express*, 15 June 1901.
43 A full account of King's contribution to science may be found in Harper (ed.), *William King*, and this volume.

9.3 Natural History Museum, Queen's College Galway in the late nineteenth century. Some of the specimens photographed here will be familiar to present-day students of zoology, as they are still being used in the teaching of camparative anatomy and evolutionary studies

He also kept up his contacts with professional colleagues by corresponding and acting as joint editor of the internationally-respected *Monthly Journal of Anatomy and Physiology* (often cited confusingly in the literature by Anderson under its German sub-title *Die Internationale Monatsschrift für Anatomie und Physiologie*).

Anderson was certainly very active in his chosen profession and was able to build on the foundations of the teaching of natural history laid down by Melville and King before him. His great collecting ability meant that he was able to further improve the collections of specimens already in the museum (fig. 9.3). It also meant that he was able to teach an excellent course of natural history, backed up by practical work in the museum and the adjacent laboratory. By this time, natural history was being taught as a science subject to degree level and, although comparative anatomy was still a major part of the syllabus, developments in evolutionary theory and heredity had led to an increased awareness that living animals and plants were not fixed entities to be collected, listed, and filed away in display cases, but were part of a changing, evolving pattern of life. The syllabus now placed an emphasis on physiology and microbiology, as the mechanisms by which animals and plants lived came under scrutiny.

Anderson ensured that the Natural History Museum was fully supplied with the latest equipment, including microscopes and lantern slide projectors for his courses. He employed the services of two specialist glassblowers from Germany to make the beautiful, and accurate, models of phytoplankton and zooplankton, as well as crustacean larvae and other invertebrates, which have been used by successive generations of students. In a detailed paper on the subject, Anderson describes the Natural History Museum and, from the text, it clearly ranks with the best working natural history museums to be found in any university at the time.[44]

44 Anderson, 'Museum'. The Department of Natural History, Geology, and Mineralogy was located in the corner of the Quadrangle presently occupied by the Department of Geology.

The extent and general completeness of the varied collections themselves can be gauged from what remains today and from the first two parts of a planned, but never completed, *Catalogue of Specimens* compiled by Anderson and published in 1911 and 1912.

Unlike Melville, Anderson was exceedingly well liked by his students and seems to have been able to communicate his subject with ease. Charles Conor O'Malley, a medical undergraduate of the time, who later became Professor of Ophthalmology in UCG, was a pupil of Anderson's and described him as follows:

> Professor Anderson of Zoology and Botany we called 'Dickie John' and he always dressed in black. He wore a coat to his knees, with great big pockets stuffed with papers of great scientific value. He wore a large sombrero hat, a goatee beard and carried a gamp. He liked his students to write a lot in answering exam questions, so I wrote a lot. I can see him now with a gleam in his eye as he balanced my answer books on his hand saying, 'Mr O'Malley, would you like me to mark them by weight'?[45]

In an earlier paper on the subject, O'Malley described a problem specimen which was regularly produced at practical examinations for identification:

> Some of the zoology specimens seemed antediluvian, unknown even to Sergeant Holland, the lab attendant, and apparently known only to the Professor. I recall one completely inspissated and dehydrated item. No one ever guessed what it was in a practical. Sergeant Holland thought it the gizzard of an ostrich, or the patella of a gorilla.[46]

Although he may well have been an excellent teacher, instilling into the minds of his students a healthy curiosity and a spirit of free enquiry, Anderson was not a good scientist himself. Fairley, who is the only researcher to have studied Anderson's work in any detail, accurately describes him as a scientific dilettante.[47] This is certainly reflected in his writings, an annotated listing of which has been compiled by Collins.[48] At first glance this list (191 items, including some half-dozen books and scores of privately-printed pamphlets) completely overshadows Melville's modest output, which, in comparison with the output of other early academics, was itself above average. As well as the subjects on which he was professionally qualified to write, Anderson wrote with self-appointed authority on bacteriology, genetics, agriculture, engineering, geography, politics, sociology, and even ancient classics.

In looking down through his list of publications, certain trends can be seen. His early papers on human anatomy were based on research done on cadavers in the

---

45 Charles Conor O'Malley, 'College Memories', *Galway Medical Annual*, 11 (1981–2), pp. 41–2.
46 O'Malley, 'Memories of UCG', *Galway Medical Annual*, 2 (1970–1), pp. 3–6.
47 James Fairley, *Irish Whales and Whaling* (Belfast, 1981), pp. 302–7.
48 Timothy Collins, *An Annotated Bibliography of the Writings of R.J. Anderson, Professor of Natural History, Geology and Mineralogy 1883–1914* (Galway, 1999). Copies are available from the Secretary, Social Sciences Research Centre, Newman House, NUI, Galway.

Anatomical Rooms of Queen's College Belfast. Published primarily in the *Journal of Anatomy and Physiology*, with occasional notes in the *Dublin Journal of Medical Science*, the *Lancet*, and the *British Medical Journal*, these papers show Anderson's keen eye for noting anything out of the ordinary.

Following his appointment to Galway in 1883, the publications on human anatomy became repetitive. This republishing of previous work was an unfortunate trait of Anderson's and it reduced the scientific value of any new material he produced. He regularly attended the annual British Association meetings, but his papers which were published year after year consisted of nothing more than anatomical anomalies which he had noted, and indeed had frequently published, previously. The same is true of the papers which he read at the annual meetings of the British Medical Association in which material previously submitted at British Association meetings would surface again, and be duly published in the *British Medical Journal*. Indeed, Michael George O'Malley, brother of Charles Conor O'Malley, who was also taught by Anderson and who later became Professor of Surgery in UCG, commented on his unique style of lecturing and reading of papers:

> He (Anderson) was a very loveable man and his absentmindedness was a joke. He sat facing his class with his hands in his trouser pockets, and read out from copious reams of notes. He had a diagram on the blackboard, and when he wished to indicate something on the board, he remained sitting and threw a piece of chalk at the diagram! He was a member of the Anatomy Society of Great Britain and Ireland, and afterwards when I became a member, the older men used to tell me all about him. He attended at least once a year to read some obscure paper. He was always put in at the tea interval, and his only audience was the presiding chairman![49]

Through the 1880s and 1890s his publications show that he was actively pursuing certain lines of research. His skills as an inventor, his ability to successfully improvise equipment to suit his work, are demonstrated in two papers. One, detailed in the *Philosophical Magazine* (1888), consisted of a framework with cords and weights which could be used to illustrate crystal forms to students of geology (fig. 9.4a). Another useful invention, described in the *Monthly Journal of Anatomy and Physiology* (1889), was a revolving microscope platform specially designed for viewing large numbers of slides with relative ease (fig. 9.4b).

As a further aid to his students, he began publishing the text of his lectures. He must have kept many a small printer happy, as these lecture notes, which were published privately in Galway, Belfast, London, Dublin, Portadown, and Newry (where he had a home address), gradually grew in size, number and in subject matter to cover virtually everything on which he had an opinion. Anderson's first booklet, *The Elephants*, published by the Belfast bookseller Erskine Mayne in 1895, was termed by the author a 'zoological mnemonic' and consisted of forty-one pages of verse on the anatomy and phylogeny of this group. In it Anderson puts

---

49 Michael George O'Malley, 'Memories of Queen's College Galway 1904–1909', *Journal of the Galway Archaeological and Historical Society*, 50 (1998), pp. 112–17.

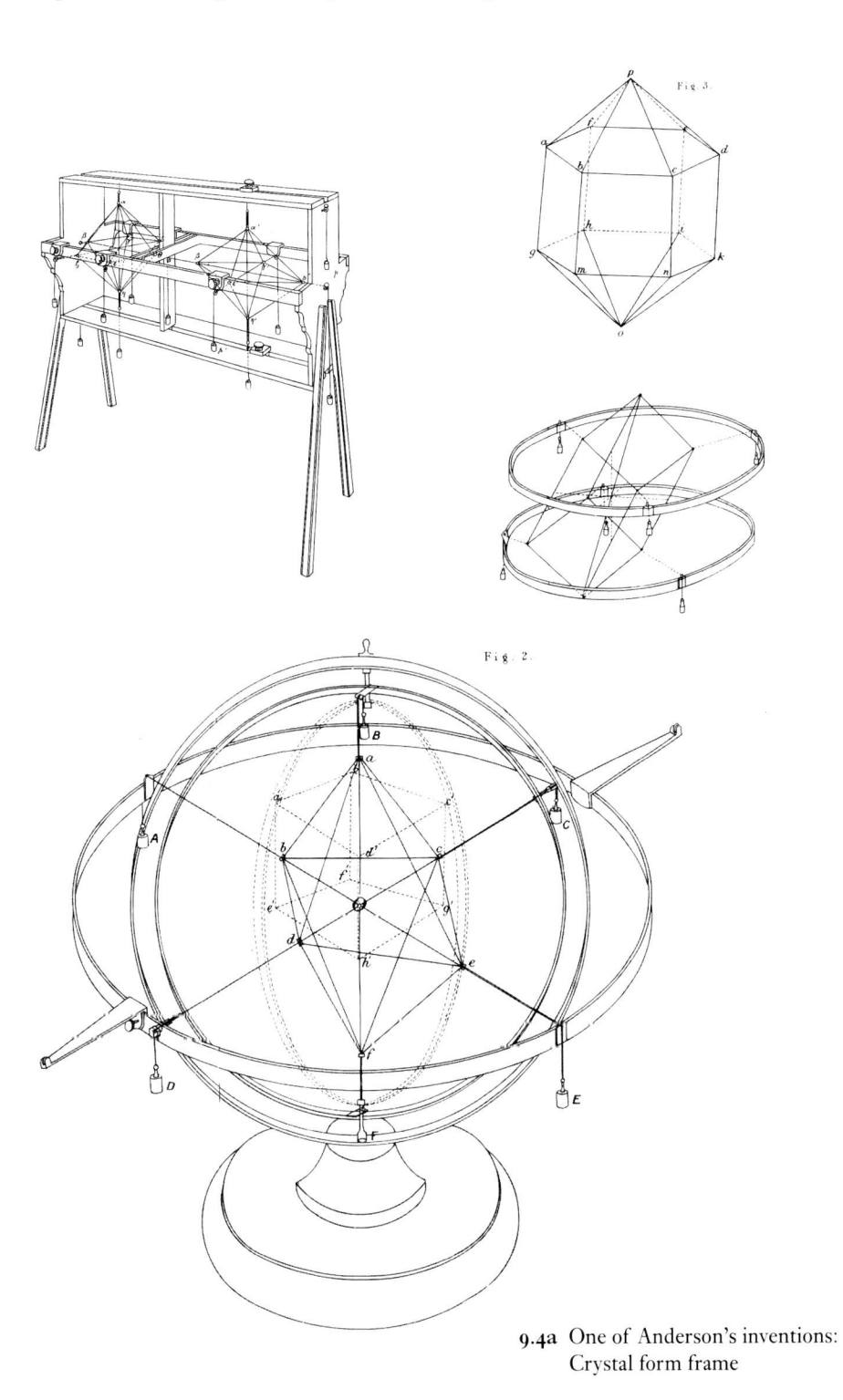

9.4a One of Anderson's inventions: Crystal form frame

forward the notion, tongue in cheek one hopes, that length of nose can be used as a measure of intelligence:

> Frederic and Bonaparte were one
> With the General Wellington
> In having noses large and long,
> Such as to mind and chest belong.
> George Washington did too disclose
> His character by length of nose.

He then takes this argument to its logical (!) conclusion:

> If what I've said has the effect
> Of showing nose proves intellect,
> Then you can judge by length of snout
> No beast an elephant can flout.

Whether or not he expected his students to be able to memorise his mnemonics, he continued publishing in verse. *The Whales and Dolphins* published, again, by Erskine Mayne in 1896, is one of Anderson's longest mnemonics, consisting of some 3,200 lines of verse describing their anatomy, physiology, and phylogeny. *The Chelonia*, which was published by the Portadown printer, J. Young, under the pen-name 'Vratsch', in 1912, continues the theme, describing the anatomy of turtles and tortoises in verse. *Ancient Hibernians and Others* (1912) traces the arrival of man in rhyming quatrains, but would be of little value to a present-day student of archaeology. *Heredity* (1912) is yet another study in verse on learning and instinct, but his *Prehistoric, Geographic and Geological Notes* (1912), written under the pen-name this time of 'Wratsch',[50] is by far the most vivid of his verses and, considering the advances of knowledge in the subject, is still largely accurate. In the opening lines he describes how the island of Ireland was formed:

> This Isle of Erin now so small
> Leagues sixty by one hundred,
> Is what one may a vestige call
> Of land sunk low or sundered.
> First over sea appeared the land
> No doubt 'tween Tomsk and Galway;
> To North and South of this the strand
> From Bombay stretched to Solway.

---

50 The origin of his pen-name, whether 'Wratsch' or 'Vratsch', is something of an enigma and was probably known only to Anderson himself. It has been brought to the author's attention (Professor Paul Mohr, personal communication), that it is remarkably similar to the word 'Ratschlag', which is a piece of advice in German. Considering Anderson's admiration for things German, and his fluency in the language, it is possible that his pen-name was chosen to reflect this.

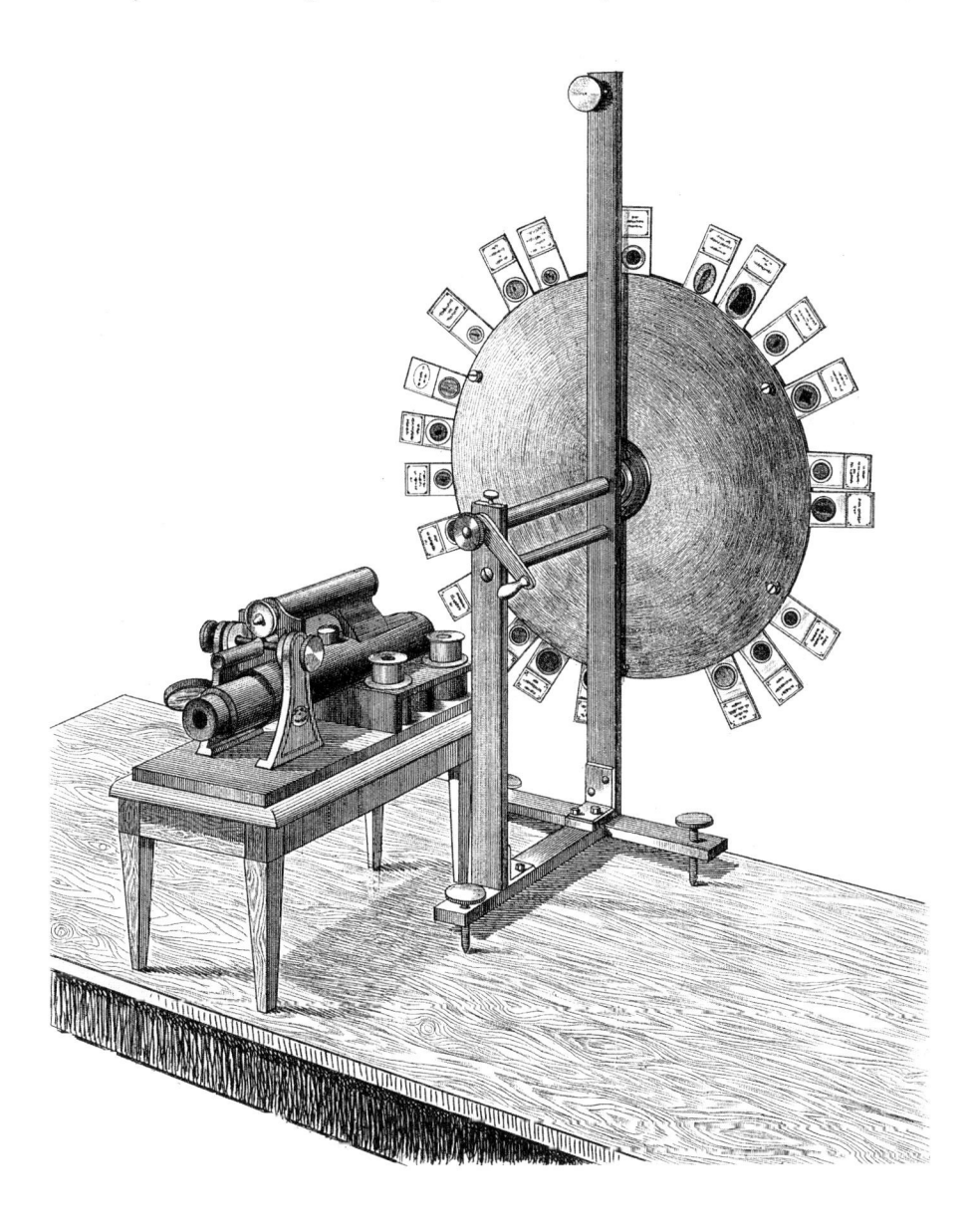

9.4b Another of Anderson's inventions: Revolving microscope platform

> Erin then had worms and weeds,
> Crustacea, lamp shells oddest.
> Nature through things like these proceeds
> To great! She's sure tho' modest.
> Mollusca, pterypods, bivalves
> In Cambrian rocks imbedded.
> Theca this system also salves;
> To Paradox 'tis wedded.
> This is the age of trilobites,
> Crustaceans intermediate,
> Between the King Crabs and the mites,
> The Apus did not lead yet.

In subsequent stanzas, Anderson describes the diversity of life in the sea and on land as well as the development of the earth's crust through geological periods of time:

> Trilobites, corals, fish came now
> The sea gave them protection.
> Ostracoderms one may allow
> To have with sharks connection.
> Vulcan, who in previous times
> His forge in Wales erected
> (He had some fires in Irish climes)
> For new ones Erin elected.
> Silurian thus gives us a single
> Volcanic Wenlock group at Dingle.

The work culminates with the arrival of man:

> No doubt in Erin large mammals roamed
> Or climbed in trees more sprightly,
> Rare ostriches perhaps here roamed
> And ran o'er grassland lightly.
> Man certainly first lived in trees
> Had grasping feet and supple,
> Climbing does e'en our infants please
> Soles make a grasping couple.
> These climbing men might well defy
> The beasts that held the lowlands.
> They could their clubs and axes ply
> Below the line of snow-lands.
> Palaeolithic man used caves
> In which some beasts sought refuge,
> The beasts fled from the hunters brave
> And many an outside deluge.

> Then neolithic man built huts
> On piles in lake mud driven.
> Their food was likely fish, fruit, nuts,
> Milk, too might have been given.

The question of heredity and acquired characteristics in man and animals also occupied much of Anderson's time and three of his early books dealt extensively with his interpretation of what were hereditary characteristics, such as hair and eye colour and handed down through successive generations; and what were acquired characteristics, such as calluses in the hands of tradesmen like tailors, or scars, which were also seen in the offspring. These latter were seen and noted by Anderson in two separate publications, 'A Note on the Persistence of Trade Impressions', published in the German medical journal *Anatomischer Anzeiger* in 1905 and 'Anatomical Anomalies' published in the *British Medical Journal* in 1899. Many of his later publications on this subject verge on racism and it would appear that Anderson would not have objected to this description. After his time in Heidelberg as a young man, Anderson regularly visited Germany. His pamphlet *Influence, Intellectual and Moral, Illustrated by Example of Germany* published by the Galway printer, Matthew Clayton, in 1896, is a thinly disguised paean of praise for all things Aryan, a theme he was to return to in *Heredity: Or, What Living Things Owe Their Ancestors and What They Do Not*, again printed by Matthew Clayton, in 1898, and in his 1910 essay 'Some Great Universities' in which he praises the Teutonic efficiency of Heidelberg and other German universities.

In keeping with this line of research, Anderson used what was termed the 'Index of Nigrescence', which scaled anatomical characteristics such as height, weight, and skull size as well as hair, skin and eye pigmentation, to calculate deviations from an accepted norm. He went on to publish a paper entitled 'Iberian Characters in West-Ireland (Including Connaught)', which he had presented at the 14th International Conference of Medicine in Madrid in 1903. In this paper, data from Britain was compared with his own measurements made on the students of the Claddagh Piscatory School, and on the members of the Royal Naval Reserve unit at Renmore Barracks. These findings, which he read again at the 15th International Conference of Medicine in Lisbon in 1906, entitled this time 'Racial Types in Connaught with Special Reference to the Basque Type', were published abroad. One can only guess at the furore which would have erupted locally were these papers made available to those whom he had been measuring and rating according to the Index of Nigrescence! Such considerations did not deter Anderson from publishing a pamphlet entitled *The Fate of the White Race* in 1910, in which he saw the unique qualities of whites being dissipated by mixing with other races. Presumably it was this kind of thinking, common enough at the time, which provided such fertile ground for sowing the seeds of Nazism in Germany and apartheid in South Africa, later in the twentieth century.

Anderson even committed some of these theories to verse in a rambling 546-line poem entitled *Heredity: A Mnemonic*, published by the Connacht Tribune Printing Works in 1912. Here is a sample:

> For soldiers, sailors, physicians, tailors,
> Chemists, blacksmiths, too, and the farming class;
> Lawyers and bakers, book model makers,
> Surveyors, painters, all before us pass.
> Thieves, too, and robbers, and various jobbers;
> The lewd and lustful, and the knavish kind;
> The felon, drunkard, the youthful dotard,
> Are made in childhood often one may find.

As if to compensate for this, Anderson's papers on comparative anatomy in the animal kingdom are well researched, although again he tended to republish his findings. Rib measurements of mammal skeletons in the museum collections are detailed in a paper in the *Monthly Journal of Anatomy and Physiology* in 1889 and the variations between duck-billed platypus, kangaroo, dog, horse, cow, whale, and some primates, including man, are duly noted. Other papers deal with the anatomy of limbs, noting the variation according to function, in a similar spread of mammals including man. He also published work on variations in skull anatomy in mammals. One paper, published in 1900, entitled 'Notes on the Comparative Thickness of the Skull as an Index of Brain Recession', was an attempt to confirm his own theories relating to intelligence and learning. In relation to this subject, Anderson published a number of papers in 1907 and 1908 on the usefulness of Pavlovian techniques in training animals, especially dogs. He was also of the opinion that such techniques could be applied to the teaching of children and could be used in military discipline for the training of soldiers!

Anderson, who, as previously mentioned, was known affectionately to all and sundry as 'Dickie John', differed from Melville in being largely uninterested in pursuing fieldwork of his own. He was certainly no botanist although he published a number of papers on plant physiology and anatomy. Anderson's only paper on the Irish flora was based on an address he gave at the 8th International Geographical Conference, held in Washington in July 1905 and entitled 'Flora of Connaught as Evidence of a Former Connection with the Atlantic Continent'. Anderson devotes much of the paper to the common landmass which had existed in the northern hemisphere in the earliest geological times, and which, under the influence of continental drift, evolved into the continents of America, Europe, and Asia. He makes no mention of the great advances then being made in the knowledge of the flora in Ireland at this time, but confines himself to general comments on its richness and diversity and notes, in passing, that various species of *Erica*, as well as *Potamogeton kirkii* and *Deschampia dicolor*, are 'peculiar' to the region.

In practice, Anderson really preferred to do his work in the museum and adjoining laboratory in the south-eastern corner of the College quadrangle, where he regularly spent whole days and nights, sleeping on a camp bed, while pursuing some line of inquiry which would entail poring over specimens and writing up his notes for publication. His wife, Hannah, would come to the campus during the day and prepare his meals in an adjoining kitchen, bringing the tray to the Museum. One story, possibly apocryphal, recounts an incident which occurred when he was

9.5 Henry Chichester Hart, botanist, explorer, and philologist. An occasional lecturer in the Departmentt of Natural History, Geology, and Mineralogy, he became acting Head of Department in 1886–7

bent over his workbench dissecting something that was very dead, which had been sent to him for identification. As his hands were full, Anderson asked his wife to leave the tray on one side. Returning later to find the tray untouched, Hannah asked him why he had not eaten, to which he replied in all innocence, 'Well, I've eaten something, dear'!

According to College records, Anderson fell ill in November 1886 and a request was received that a 'locum tenens' be appointed to discharge his duties.[51] Professor Joseph Pye took on the Natural History lectures for the rest of Michaelmas Term for an agreed fee while James Perry, Galway County Surveyor, gave the lectures in Geology without remuneration.[52] This may have been because Perry was actually

---

51 Dr Séamus Mac Mathúna, Secretary, NUI, Galway supplied this information to Professor M. Mitchell who, in turn, communicated it to the author.
52 Dr Joseph Patrick Pye (1847–1920), was appointed Professor of Materia Medica in 1873, but resigned on being appointed Professor of Anatomy and Physiology in 1877. Murray, in *Galway*

a brother-in-law of Anderson's (his wife Hannah was a Perry), and he would not have been happy charging for his services. In January 1887, Anderson was given leave of absence on the receipt of evidence that he would be unable to resume for at least two months. T.W. Moffett, President, was 'requested to procure a substitute for Dr Anderson during the remainder of this term, the remuneration to be provided by Anderson'. Thus the appointment of Henry Chichester Hart, described as a Lecturer in Natural History and Geology was approved (fig. 9.5).

QCG was extremely lucky to have the services of Hart, who was an excellent field naturalist and, according to Scannell, was one of a small band of botanists who laid the foundation of plant distribution studies in Ireland in the latter half of the nineteenth century.[53] Hart was a man of magnificent physique whose physical prowess and stamina were acknowledged by his contemporaries. This certainly stood him in good stead when 'botanising' across arduous terrain and was commented on when he took part in the British Arctic Expedition of 1875–6 as naturalist on board HMS *Discovery* which, along with HMS *Alert* and HMS *Valorous*, a wooden-hulled, paddle-powered frigate, were under the overall command of Captain G.S. Nares, one of the Royal Navy's ablest surveyors. Coincidentally, HMS *Valorous* later became quite well-known in Galway as she was used to distribute relief supplies along the west coast during the famine of 1879–80.[54] Nares had previously commanded HMS *Challenger* and was actually taken off her when she arrived at Hong Kong during her now-famous world cruise of 1872–6, to take command of the Arctic expedition. Nares' published account of the expedition became a best-seller and in it due credit is given to Hart for his efforts in collecting a significant number of plant specimens and for his contribution to the successful conclusion of the expedition, which included a final attempt by a sledge party, among them Hart, on the North Pole itself. This sledge party reached a record latitude of 83° 20'26", the most northerly point reached by any expedition up to that time. With most of the party weakened by scurvy, it was decided to turn back, but not before a cairn of stones, containing details of who had built it, was completed, largely by Hart, who was one of the few still fit enough to undertake such work.[55] Unusually for him, Hart fell ill after returning home from this expedition and as a consequence, his own detailed results were not published until 1880, when they appeared in eight parts in the *Journal of Botany*. Again, they showed that he had completed a surprising amount of botanical work in the most extreme conditions.

(and this volume), gives details of Pye's career as a popular teacher of medicine to successive generations of students. He was even Registrar of the College for a time and he died in office in 1920.

53 Mary J.P. Scannell, 'Henry Chichester Hart: Botanist, Explorer and Philologist', in Charles Mollan, William Davies, and Brendan Finucane (eds), *More People and Places in Irish Science and Technology* (Dublin, 1990), pp. 40–1 has put his work into context, while his various expeditions are synopsised by I. Higgins, 'Henry Chichester Hart', in Foster (ed.), *Nature in Ireland*, pp. 360–5.

54 T. Collins, 'HMS *Valorous*: Her Contribution to Galway Maritime History', *Journal of the Galway Archaeological and Historical Society*, 49 (1997), p. 122–42, gives details of the humanitarian role played by the Royal Navy in famine relief at this time.

55 G.S. Nares, *Narrative of a Voyage to the Polar Sea During 1875–6 in H.M. Ships* Alert *and* Discovery (London, 1878).

Visiting some forty stations in Greenland, between 68° 42'30" and 82° 50'30", he collected large numbers of specimens which were subsequently identified. Apart from his fieldwork, Hart concentrated on the area of Discovery Bay, where HMS *Discovery* and HMS *Alert* were based for almost a year, just north of the 80th parallel. As well as his studies of the local flora, Hart successfully grew a variety of vegetables including celery, beans, peas, mustard, cress, and wheat. He also dissected a variety of animals and birds to determine their diet, the results of which were published in four short papers in the *Zoologist*.

Hart was no stranger to the west of Ireland as, when he was not travelling on expeditions to places like the Sinai, he lived in Donegal where his family were landowners.[56] Although his father, Sir Andrew Hart, was a distinguished mathematician who became Vice-Provost of Trinity College Dublin, Hart himself was not interested in following his father's footsteps into academic life, preferring the countryside to the lecture hall, and occupying only the occasional teaching post, such as was offered to him in QCG. In Donegal, he concentrated on the family landholdings, becoming, in the process, high sheriff for the county in 1895. He published many papers on the flora of the west, based on his own findings, including an early list of plants found on the Aran Islands.[57] He is best remembered by botanists for his *Flora of Howth* (1887) and his *Flora of the County Donegal* (1898). Like many other eminent naturalists of this period, Hart was something of a polymath, publishing zoological papers on mammals, insects, molluscs, and birds as well as a book on the animals mentioned in the Bible.[58] He had an interest in dialects, especially those of Ulster, and his pioneering work in this area has been detailed by Traynor.[59] Hart was also an authority on English literature; he wrote critical papers on the works of Ben Jonson, John Marston, and Shakespeare. He spent his later years editing the Arden Shakespeare series, including *Othello, Love's Labours Lost*, and *The Merry Wives of Windsor*.[60]

It would appear that Anderson's illness was more serious than had been first thought, as towards the end of Hilary Term, Moffett was again requested to extend the arrangements for Hart's lectures to be continued through Trinity Term. Following letters from Anderson, the College Council resolved at its meeting of 5 April 1887 that:

---

56 H.C. Hart, *Some Account of the Fauna and Flora of Sinai, Petra, and Wâdy 'Arabah* (London, 1891).
57 H.C. Hart, *A List of Plants Found in the Islands of Aran, Galway Bay* (Dublin, 1875).
58 H.C. Hart, *The Animals Mentioned in the Bible* (London, 1888).
59 M. Traynor, *The English Dialect of Donegal: A Glossary Incorporating the Collections of H.C. Hart* (Dublin, 1953).
60 In recognition of his contribution to Irish botany, Professor David A. Webb (1912–1994), the noted botanist, named a species of saxifrage *Saxifraga hartii* in his honour. This species was first identified in west Donegal by Hart and recently featured on a commemorative postage stamp as part of An Post's Flora and Fauna series. Praeger gives many anecdotes about this extraordinary man. A detailed obituary was written by Richard Barrington, 'Henry Chichester Hart', *Irish Naturalist*, 17 (1908), pp. 249–54, from which the portrait used here is taken.

> Whereas Anderson is bound to pay to his substitute the whole amount of £75 due to the same, having authorised the President & Council to make provision for the discharge of his duties, Council nevertheless, in consideration that Anderson has been put to great expense by his illness, the amount due to his substitute for at least three months being the entirety of a quarter's salary, agrees to accept the proposal of Anderson that he should pay £40 out of the current quarter and the remaining £35 in July.

Permission was also sought, without success, to reimburse Anderson £35 out of College funds. Luckily, Anderson recovered his health and returned to his duties in time for the next academic year.

Curiously, Anderson took no part in any of the major biological surveys which had been going on throughout the final years of the nineteenth century and early years of the twentieth. With backing from the government and from the learned societies, individuals and groups had been busily engaged in completing a register of Ireland's known flora and fauna. One of the most gifted organisers of this kind of work was Robert Lloyd Praeger (1865–1953), who was classed as an amateur naturalist because, although he was a botanist by inclination, he was an engineer by qualification, and a librarian by profession. It was initially as a geologist, and later as a botanist, that he made his mark in Victorian Ireland, yet he is best remembered today for his many books and papers extolling the virtues of getting out into the countryside. Praeger was very active in the naturalists' field club movement which reached the peak of its popularity in the Edwardian era.[61]

In light of the fact that much fieldwork was done by such people in the west of Ireland, it seems strange that the facilities of the Department of Natural History were not availed of. This apparent enigma can be explained by the fact that, at this time, academic staff were paid only for the duration of the college year. With no salary during the summer months, those who were able, pursued their own personal research in Britain and the continent, or took part in government-sponsored expeditions to obscure parts of the world. Certainly there would have been nothing to keep any staff in the College during the summer and the campus would have effectively been shut down. As it was in the summer that most naturalists came to the west of Ireland to do their collecting, they would generally have made their own arrangements. From his writings, it would appear that Anderson himself travelled widely virtually every summer, and would not have been around to facilitate any visiting naturalists.

One example of such visits by groups of naturalists was the week-long first Irish Field Club Union Conference and Excursion which was held in Galway in July 1895. Organised by Praeger, over a hundred naturalists stayed in the Railway Hotel (now the Great Southern Hotel). They converted one of the first-floor smoking saloons into a makeshift laboratory for the duration of their stay and,

---

61 Praeger's impact in Irish natural history can be best assessed by reading his own partly-autobiographical books, especially *The Way that I Went* (Dublin, 1937). T. Collins has written a biography and compiled an annotated bibliography of his published work, listing almost 800 items: *Floreat Hibernia: A Bio-bibliography of Robert Lloyd Praeger 1865–1953* (Dublin, 1985).

apart from a tour of the grounds, they made no use of the facilities in QCG. The results, which were edited for publication by Praeger in 1895, proved extremely fruitful, and demonstrated the usefulness of having groups of specialists working together in one area to compile joint lists of their findings. This, and other excursions, which have been detailed by Collins, proved singularly useful in extending the knowledge of the flora and fauna.[62] Naturalists living and working in Galway, such as the entomologist Robert Dillon, and fisheries inspector E.W.L. Holt had their own facilities and, although they enjoyed cordial relations with Anderson, made no use of his departmental laboratories or expertise.[63]

The largest and most comprehensive biological survey to be undertaken in Ireland in the twentieth century, the Clare Island Survey of 1909–11, was also carried out without any input from Anderson. Again, it would appear that his omission from this major project was by mutual consent as, at this time, he was just too busy with his own projects to take on additional work. His relations with Praeger, who was responsible for the planning and organising of the Survey, were apparently quite good.[64] Anderson even published a number of notes on various topics in the *Irish Naturalist* at this time but they are not of any lasting scientific merit.[65]

Unwittingly, Anderson was also the cause of a flurry of correspondence between Dublin Castle and London which in hindsight is quite hilarious.[66] What

---

62 R.L. Praeger, 'Report of the Conference and Excursion of the Irish Field Club Union Held at Galway July 11th to 17th 1895, i: General Account', *Irish Naturalist*, 4 (1895), pp. 225–35; T. Collins, 'Praeger in the West: Naturalists and Antiquarians in Connemara and the Islands 1894–1914', *Journal of the Galway Archaeological and Historical Society*, 45 (1993), pp. 124–54.

63 Fairley, *Irish Whales*, and Noel P. Wilkins, *Ponds, Passes and Parcs: Aquaculture in Victorian Ireland* (Dublin, 1989), have assessed Holt's contribution to fisheries research in the west of Ireland, while Collins has also given details of his other interests, notably his links with the Galway Archaeological and Historical Society during its early years in 'Oysters and Antiquities: A Biographical Note on E.W.L. Holt', *Journal of the Galway Archaeological and Historical Society*, 43 (1991), pp. 157 66.

64 T. Collins, 'The Clare Island Survey of 1909–1911: An Early Multidisciplinary Success Story', in Keegan and O'Connor (eds), *Irish Marine Science 1995*, pp. 85–97, gives details of the successful multidisciplinary nature of the Clare Island Survey, which has been used as a model for other surveys by researchers ever since.

65 The *Irish Naturalist* was a monthly journal which commenced publication in 1892 to meet the information needs of the growing number of clubs and societies, as well as individuals, who needed a forum to publish their findings and communicate their ideas and theories. With Robert Lloyd Praeger as joint editor throughout its life, the *Irish Naturalist* published a significant amount of quality work, something that can be seen even today in the number of its papers which continue to be cited in the literature. Although the *Irish Naturalist* ceased publication in 1924, a victim of the times, it was succeeded by the *Irish Naturalists' Journal*, which commenced publication the following year. To the present day, the *Irish Naturalists' Journal* continues the work of publishing papers in botany, geology, and zoology along the lines originally laid down by the editors of the *Irish Naturalist*. In fact, these two journals form a link with the last century and the great advances in the knowledge of the subject in Ireland can be traced through their pages.

66 I am indebted to Fiona Bateman, Department of English, NUI, Galway, for bringing this material to my attention. National Archives, Chief Secretary's Office Registered Papers (CSORP) 1899/12583, Correspondence: R.J. Anderson to Chief Secretary, 3 March 1899 and other material, CSORP 1899/4261.

happened was that he was almost appointed President of Queen's College Galway by mistake! When T.W. Moffett, Professor of History, English Literature, and Mental Science, and President of the College since 1897, resigned in 1899, Anderson duly applied for the post of President and forwarded a detailed curriculum vitae of his achievements, together with glowing testimonials from a variety of academics, aristocrats, and politicians from Ireland, England, Germany, the United States of America, Russia, and Hungary, to Dublin Castle. Another applicant, ultimately successful, was Alexander Anderson, Professor of Physics in QCG since 1885. Whatever deliberations ensued, Alexander Anderson was the preferred candidate. However, someone subsequently confused the Christian names of the two Andersons. The result was that a dispatch dated 13 March 1899 was sent from the Chief Secretary's Office in Dublin Castle to the Home Office in London, asking that the necessary steps be taken to appoint Richard John Anderson as President of QCG. It would seem that the error was discovered within hours of this dispatch being sent and another was rushed off to London, dated 16 March, in a successful attempt to stop Dickie John's appointment being ratified by Queen Victoria. This later dispatch merely stated that, 'a mistake was unfortunately made in the Christian name. His Excellency's letter contained the name Richard John Anderson. It should have been Alexander Anderson. A fresh letter will be dispatched by this night's post'. In the event, Alexander Anderson had a lengthy tenure, retiring in 1934 after thirty-five years as President. History does not record how R.J. Anderson reacted to this news if, indeed, he ever found out.

As mentioned earlier, Fairley has evaluated Anderson's zoological publications, especially his papers on marine mammals, and he has found a wide variation in quality. Although Anderson diligently recorded anatomical details, such as specific dentition, he still managed to get facts wrong. According to Fairley, Anderson is credited with recording the first True's beaked whale in Irish waters, although this fact did not emerge for many years, as he had wrongly identified the specimen in question which had been stranded in Galway Bay, as a Hector's beaked whale, another equally rare species, but noted only from New Zealand waters.[67]

When the British Association met in Belfast in 1902, Anderson was, as usual, very much in evidence, reading papers in three different sections; comparative anatomy, in which he spoke on the importance of the parietal bone in relation to brain development in primates; plant physiology, where he detailed the results of experiments aimed at measuring fluid flow in various plant stems; and cetology, in which details were given of the stranding of a pilot whale with a deep harpoon wound. In this paper he mentioned his special interest in marine mammals, collecting any specimens that were washed ashore in Galway Bay and even on occasion forming what he termed 'shooting parties' when further specimens were needed! In 1904, he again got it wrong when he published a note in the *Irish Naturalist* on what he believed was another Hector's beaked whale stranded on the Aran Islands, the head of which had been sent to him for identification. This time, the specimen was later identified from an examination of the skull as a Cuvier's whale.

---

67 Fairley, *Irish Whales*, p. 106; R.J. Anderson, 'A Note on a Beaked Whale', *Irish Naturalist,* 10 (1901), pp. 117–19.

By this time he must have considered himself to be something of an authority on cetaceans, as he read a paper at the 6th International Conference of Zoology which was held at Berne, in August 1904. In the course of his paper, 'Some Notes on the Cetacea of the Irish Atlantic Coast', Anderson spoke about whales and whale strandings in general, making continuous unrelated anatomical comparisons with marsupials, crocodiles, oxen, and his obvious favourites, elephants. His final contributions to cetology were published posthumously in 1914 and were based on a paper read at two different conferences held in 1913, the British Association in Birmingham and the 9th International Congress of Zoology held in Monaco.

In some of his pamphlets and mnemonics, Anderson occasionally enlivened the text with illustrations. Drawn in what can only be termed a naive style, they confirm what is obvious from his writings, that he had a surrealistic view of the world. These drawings, which usually bear no relation to the text, depict numbers of his favourite animals (elephants, bears, whales, reptiles, marsupials) in various poses, frequently in the company of humans. What he is trying to portray can only be left to the imagination of the beholder, but in general they appear to be harmless juxtapositions of man and beast and are not disturbing, although a psychoanalyst would have plenty of material with which to work.

His final publications, a series of lecture notes on commercially-important animals such as the pig, goat, horse, ass, cat, ox, and including the flea, louse, and bed bug, culminated in each case with a number of proverbs relating to the animal in question.

Anderson died suddenly in July 1914 at the age of sixty-six, while still busily engaged in his various researches. In summing up, one can only agree with Fairley when he says that 'if there were more like him now it would be no bad thing for the universities. Genuine eccentrics are a lamentably scarce commodity there today and he must surely have been among the most stimulating of mentors'.[68]

Certainly his loss was keenly felt by the colleagues and friends he left behind, as can be seen in the obituary notice which appeared in the 1915 edition of the *UCG Annual*. In its opening paragraph, this loss is expressed:

> The loss our College has suffered by the death of Professor Anderson is one from which it never can fully recover. Good and distinguished men may fill the academic positions left vacant by his death, but we doubt if ever anyone can take possession of the hearts of his fellow Professors and students as he did. Never was a Professor more loved by all the members of his College as was Dr Anderson. College life is not the same since he left us. Something has gone out of our lives, and there remains but the memory of one of the finest men we can ever hope to meet.

Following his death, Anderson's widow, Hannah, who had met him while she was studying medicine in QCG, returned to College to finish her studies. O'Malley, who by this time had qualified in medicine, had this to say of her:

---

68 Fairley, *Irish Whales*, p. 107.

There was the annual outing to Gentian Hill to look at the flora and fauna, followed by tea, cakes and lemonade in the Anderson home in Salthill. When Dickie died, Mrs Anderson had to take up medicine again, where she had left off at Second Med. I was demonstrator in the anatomy room when Mrs Dickie studied there for hours and hours at a time. She used to carry the bones of the wrist in her pocket, getting familiar with all their joints. She passed the Finals in record time and got a good job in London.[69]

Another telling insight into the Andersons is to be found in the text of a lecture given by Professor Mary Donovan-O'Sullivan at a meeting commemorating the centenary of the opening of QCG, which has only recently been published:

A quiet retiring man (Anderson), he was just the type of Professor one reads about in books. He was always *distrait* and never seemed to come down to earth, or, if he did, he came down with a bang and was soon away in the clouds again. He seemed to wear several waistcoats at one time and his breast pocket always carried an amazing array of lead pencils – one could not help feeling that each one of them had a special function ... I knew his wife very well and greatly esteemed her. She was a Miss Perry of a previous generation – aunt to the Misses Perry of my day – who when a widow came back here to College at the age of 51 to do a medical course. She qualified quickly and had a full and useful life in practice in London for 20 years after that – an amazing example of grit and courage.[70]

Always an independent woman, Hannah Anderson is of interest for many reasons, not least because she was able to successfully complete her studies. According to Mary Clancy, Hannah was also an active suffragist, joining the Connaught Women's Franchise League when it was launched in Galway in January 1913. Indeed, Clancy points out that there was a notable UCG connection with this suffragist society.[71] Among the founders of the Connaught Women's Franchise League were the above-mentioned Mary Donovan-O'Sullivan, elected to the Governing Body in 1913 and later the first Professor of History in 1914; Emily Anderson, wife of Professor Alexander Anderson, President of the College, and his daughter, also Emily, who became the first Professor of German in 1917. Also involved were members of Hannah's own family, the Perrys, who lived in Wellpark. Her niece Alice Perry was the first woman to graduate in engineering from QCG, becoming the first woman in the world to hold such a qualification. Following the death of her father in 1906, Alice held his post of Galway County Surveyor for a time. Again, she was the first woman in Ireland to hold such a post,

---

69 C. O'Malley, 'Memories' (1971).
70 M.D. O'Sullivan, 'The Centenary of Galway College: The Text of a Centenary Lecture Delivered on 19th November, 1949, Prepared for Publication by Joe O'Halloran', *Journal of the Galway Archaeological and Historical Society*, 51 (1999), pp. 24–42.
71 Mary Clancy, ' "It was our joy to keep the flag flying": A Study of the Women's Suffrage Campaign in County Galway', *UCG Women's Studies Centre Review*, 3 (1995), p. 99.

although she was not made permanent, something which rankled with her. She had left Galway for America by 1913, but her sisters, Janet and Margaret, remained active suffragists in Galway.

It would appear that, in the Anderson household both husband and wife were politically aware, as Anderson himself had published a number of pamphlets on the benefits to Ireland of Home Rule, proportional representation, and nationalism, as well as on many local issues. One rather prophetic pamphlet published in 1912, entitled *A Rampart for Salthill*, advocated the construction of a breakwater out to Mutton Island and the construction of a sewage farm on the island to overcome the growing problem of pollution to the tourist beaches of Galway Bay![72] Another pamphlet, on the financial independence from Britain which would be one of the benefits of Home Rule, was even published in verse, again bringing Anderson's unique insight to the subject. The opening lines give us an indication of his ideas:

> John Bull and Sandy once arranged
> To club and work together.
> They took in Pat, a bit estranged,
> To save him from the weather.
> 'Now, Pat', said John, 'You'll let me say
> Good company you're keeping;
> We'll never part you, come what may,
> In sowing, rest, or reaping'.

Anderson's death in 1914 coincided with a period of rapid change, both in UCG and in the outside world. The world in which he, Hart, and Melville had grown up disappeared for ever with the outbreak of the First World War. In Ireland, the Easter Rising of 1916 was followed by a War of Independence and then a Civil War and it was just not possible for groups of people to pursue their interests in natural history in the countryside. Research in all areas suffered in the 1920s and 1930s as the fledgling Irish Free State government had little time or funding to devote to such activities. The 1940s brought another world war and the 1950s another post-war depression. Indeed, it was well into the 1960s before the government slowly began to make funds available for surveys of Ireland's rich and diverse flora and fauna. Like history repeating itself, work published throughout the 1970s and 1980s has shown the potential value of floral and faunal studies and

---

72 Since the 1980s, Mutton Island had been at the centre of a controversy concerning the siting of a badly-needed sewage treatment plant, which was actively opposed by a broad-ranging group of concerned Galway people, who did not accept the decision by Galway Corporation to build such a plant on the island. This group questioned the Corporation's decision to go ahead with such a scheme which would only be accessible by an as yet unbuilt causeway, in an area of scenic beauty, when alternative sites had not been examined. At one time the European Parliament ruled that such a project would get no funding because of the controversial location. Finally, following a High Court ruling, Galway Corporation was granted permission, in early 1998, to commence work on the construction of a sewage treatment plant on Mutton Island, and the work began in early 1999.

the importance of associated fieldwork. Although a sweeping generalisation, it would appear that in Ireland, as in Europe, the twentieth century has been mostly one of lost opportunity for researchers. In some disciplines the level of activity and investment is only now catching up with what it was prior to the outbreak of World War I and this has also been reflected in the ongoing development of the Department of Natural History after 1914.[73]

---

[73] Following Anderson's death in 1914, the chair of Natural History, Geology, and Mineralogy was again split. Dr H.B. Cronshaw was appointed Professor of Geology and Mineralogy, while Joseph Mangan was appointed Professor of Natural History. Upon his resignation in 1925, Mangan was succeeded by Thomas J. Dinan and upon his resignation in 1960, the statute relating to the Department of Natural History was extinguished and two new academic departments, Botany and Zoology, were established in 1962, to be followed by Microbiology and Biochemistry the following year. The museum collections were split in 1963, with the geological material being retained to form the basis of the James Mitchell Museum, itself officially opened in 1992. M.D. Fewtrell, 'The James Mitchell Geology Museum, University College Galway', *Irish Naturalists' Journal*, 19 (1979), pp. 309–10, gives a description, while Collins, 'The Museum, the College and the Community', in Harper (ed.), *Irish Geological Time Capsule*, pp. 58–67 and Harper in the same volume, describe the present impact of having such a collection available for consultation. The botanical and zoological collections, including the priceless glass models, have been incorporated into the collections of the Departments of Botany and Zoology.

I am indebted to Professor Michael Mitchell and to Professor James Fairley for reading an early draft of this work and making constructive criticisms which were exceedingly welcome. Professor Paul Mohr and Professor David Harper also provided additional information, as did Ms Fiona Bateman. My friend and former colleague, Ms Fionnuala Byrne, at the time Librarian-in-charge of the Hardiman Library's Special Collections, made my work much easier by ensuring that early College records were readily available for consultation.

From Political Economy to Economics and Commerce

TOM BOYLAN & TADHG FOLEY

On the occasion of the visit of the lord lieutenant to Queen's College Galway shortly after its opening, the President of the College, Edward Berwick, expressed the hope that 'this Institution may continue to merit your attention and approbation' and that 'through its means ... useful knowledge will be widely disseminated throughout this town and province'.[1] Berwick did not elaborate on his views as to what constituted 'useful knowledge', but we may surmise that political economy may have been envisaged as falling within this domain. From the foundation of the Queen's Colleges, political economy was conjoined with jurisprudence and both were assigned to the same professor. The chair of Jurisprudence and Political Economy was, during the course of the nineteenth century, occupied by a number of the most distinguished political economists of their time. In this chapter we will concentrate on the political economists, their lives and research, from the opening of the College until comparatively recent times, along with a brief outline of the development of the Faculty of Commerce following its establishment in the second decade of this century.

The conjoining of political economy with jurisprudence was a characteristic of the arrangements for this particular chair in each of the Queen's Colleges. This was in contrast with the arrangements in Trinity College Dublin, where the Whately Professorship of Political Economy was, from its inception, a dedicated chair in political economy.[2] However, the linkage of jurisprudence with political economy in the Queen's Colleges reflected the close ties between these domains of study, a feature which characterised, and arguably influenced, both the method, and to some extent, the content of political economy in the Irish universities during the nineteenth century.

The distinguished historian of Irish economic thought, R.D. Collison Black, has suggested that the fact that most of the holders of the Whately Professorship in Trinity College Dublin were lawyers by training explains their concentration on

---

[1] *Report* of the President of Queen's College, Galway for 1851–2, p. 7.
[2] The Whately chair of Political Economy is called after its founder, Archbishop Richard Whately, who was the Anglican archbishop of Dublin from 1831 to 1863. Whately had been Drummond Professor of Political Economy in Oxford from 1829 to 1831. See Thomas A. Boylan and Timothy P. Foley, *Political Economy and Colonial Ireland* (London, 1992), pp. 17–43.

the study of practical issues.[3] Black's explanation for this emphasis on practical problems is, he argues, 'partly accounted for by the economic circumstances of nineteenth-century Ireland', which made such studies 'almost a social duty on those who could perform them'. But it may also be attributed to the fact 'that virtually all the Whately professors were lawyers by training, if not also by profession', with the result that their attention was 'devoted to problems, such as the Irish land question, which had both a legal and an economic aspect'.[4] What was true of the Whately professors was, by extension, also true of the holders of the chairs of Jurisprudence and Political Economy in the Queen's Colleges. In the case of Queen's College Galway, out of the five holders of the chairs of Jurisprudence and Political Economy between 1849 and 1903, three were educated at Trinity College Dublin, and three held the Whately chair.

Denis Caulfield Heron (1824–81), the first Professor of Jurisprudence and Political Economy at Queen's College Galway, was born on 16 February 1824 in Dublin, the first son of William Heron of Newry, Co. Down, and Mary Maguire (fig. 2.1). He was educated at St Gregory's, Downside and in 1840 he entered Trinity College Dublin. He qualified for a scholarship in 1843, but as a Catholic was refused election. Heron appealed to the Visitors of the University and, though unsuccessful, his case achieved considerable notoriety. He graduated in 1845 and two years later, in one of his earliest and major publications, *The Constitutional History of the University of Dublin* (Dublin, 1847), he addressed the issue of the position of Catholics in the University of Dublin and demanded reform of their status and entitlements.[5] In 1848 Heron was called to the Irish Bar, and the following year he was appointed to the Professorship of Jurisprudence and Political Economy at Queen's College Galway, a position he held until 1859. In 1857 he was awarded the LLB and LLD.

Heron was also closely associated with the Dublin Statistical Society, being one of the original members.[6] He was also one of the first four Barrington Lecturers appointed in 1849.[7] He was appointed a member of the Council of the Society in 1850, and was a vice-president from 1871 until his death in 1881. After he resigned his chair at Queen's College Galway, Heron devoted himself to his legal career, becoming a Queen's Council in 1860, a Bencher of King's Inns in 1872, and third Serjeant-at-law in 1880. His legal career was interspersed with a short interlude in active politics. He was a Member of Parliament for Co. Tipperary between 1870 and 1874, having narrowly won the seat from Charles Kickham. Heron would most probably have been offered the presidency of the Dublin Statistical Society, or the Statistical and Social Inquiry Society of Ireland following its re-organisation

---

3   R.D.C. Black, 'Economic Studies at Trinity College, Dublin – I', *Hermathena*, 70 (1947), pp. 65–80
4   Ibid., p. 73.
5   R.D.C. Black, *The Statistical and Social Inquiry Society of Ireland: Centenary Volume 1847–1947* (Dublin, 1947), p. 67.
6   Mary E. Daly, *The Spirit of Earnest Inquiry: The Statistical and Social Inquiry Society of Ireland 1847–1997* (Dublin, 1997).
7   For an account of the Barrington Lectures, see Boylan and Foley, *Political Economy and Colonial Ireland*, pp. 100–15.

in 1862, but he died, while on a fishing trip on Lough Corrib, at the age of fifty-seven in April 1881.

Heron's major publications, in addition to the *Constitutional History of the University of Dublin*, included *Three Lectures on the Principles of Taxation, Delivered at Queen's College, Galway, in Hilary Term, 1850* (Dublin, 1850); *Should the Tenant of Land Possess the Property on the Improvement Made by Him?* (Dublin, 1852); *An Introduction to the History of Jurisprudence* (Dublin, 1860); and *The Principles of Jurisprudence* (Dublin, 1873). Heron also contributed a number of papers to the Statistical Society between 1851 and 1872. The two most significant papers were 'Historical Statistics of Ireland', delivered in January 1862,[8] and 'Ireland in 1864', delivered in that year.[9] The former paper caused considerable controversy, arising from its strident refutation of what was then the accepted view which interpreted the high levels of emigration during the 1850s as a positive development and an integral part of the adjustment of the post-famine economy. The more immediate reason was the depression in agricultural output in the late 1850s and early 1860s.[10]

Economists at the time were divided as to whether the agricultural depression was primarily caused by bad weather conditions, or by 'deep-seated defects in social organisation'.[11] The conventional view, as reflected in a number of papers delivered during the course of the 1850s, interpreted the negative developments of this period as a short-term phase of the longer-term adjustment process. Heron's paper of 1862 argued, in contrast, that there was evidence of a relentless decline in the economic and social condition of the country, which was attributable to serious defects in the land system. Heron's paper has been described as reading 'like a concise summary of what was to become the nationalist interpretation of Irish economic history, epitomised by the writings of George O'Brien',[12] and as a paper which would 'fully meet Brendan Bradshaw's plea for recognition of the "catastrophic dimension of Irish history" '.[13] Heron's ideas were quickly subjected to critical counter-arguments by a number of writers, including R.W. McDonnell and W.N. Hancock.[14] Black has

8 *Journal of the Dublin Statistical Society*, 3 (1861–3), pp. 235–57.
9 *Journal of the Statistical and Social Inquiry Society of Ireland*, 4 (1864–8), pp. 105–13.
10 James S. Donnelly, 'The Irish Agricultural Depression of 1859–64', *Irish Economic and Social History*, 3 (1976), pp. 34–54.
11 R.D.C. Black, *Economic Thought and the Irish Question* (Cambridge, 1960), p. 47.
12 Daly, *The Spirit of Earnest Inquiry*, p. 41. Here Daly is referring to the work of Professor George O'Brien (1892–1973), who was Professor of Political Economy and National Economics at University College Dublin from 1926 to 1961. He was the author of a number of works on the economic history of Ireland, covering the seventeenth, eighteenth, and nineteenth centuries. These works became the target of critical scrutiny during the 'revisionist' debate. For an interesting biography by his successor in UCD, see James Meenan, *George O'Brien: A Biographical Memoir* (Dublin, 1980). For an analysis of the revisionist debate, see Ciaran Brady (ed.), *Interpreting Irish History: The Debate on Historical Revisionism 1938–1994* (Dublin, 1994).
13 Daly, *The Spirit of Earnest Inquiry*, p. 41. This is a reference to Brendan Bradshaw's seminal paper in the more recent phase of the revisionist debate, 'Nationalism and Historical Scholarship in Modern Ireland', *Irish Historical Studies*, 26 (1988–9), pp. 329–51.
14 Randall William McDonnell, 'Statistics of Irish Prosperity', *Journal of the Dublin Statistical Society*, 3 (1861–3), p. 268–78; William Neilson Hancock, *Report on the Supposed Progressive Decline of Irish Prosperity* (Dublin, 1863). W.N. Hancock (1820–88) was one of the most prolific

perceptively noted, that while the debate was ostensibly conducted as a dispute over interpretations of different sets of statistical information, the substantive debate concerned two radically different positions on social and economic organisation. The official view, as represented by Hancock, measured prosperity in terms of increased net returns, albeit for a declining population. Heron, in contrast, gave priority to security on the land for the existing population over that of increasing productivity.[15] While the conventional view favoured Hancock rather than Heron, the issues raised in this dispute remain central to the debate on economic development and its implications. Much of Heron's argumentation on Irish land tenure was to be later defended, by his successor in the chair of Jurisprudence and Political Economy at Queen's College Galway, John Elliot Cairnes, and was ultimately vindicated in the passing of the Land Acts which Heron lived long enough to see enacted.

As the holder of the first chair of Jurisprudence and Political Economy, Heron occupied that unenviable position of launching the comparatively new university discipline of political economy.[16] The circumstances were hardly propitious. Edward Berwick, the President of Queen's College Galway, reporting on the first academic session, noted that the College opened on 30 October 1849, but 'under circumstances of a very discouraging nature'. For Berwick these circumstances included the fact that the town of Galway 'possesses a population of not more than 20,000 inhabitants, the greater portion of whom are in a state of the most abject poverty', and that the 'unfinished state of the building at the time of opening, led to a very general belief that its proceedings would not commence until the succeeding year'. Nor could Berwick avoid commenting on the difficulty which faced all of the Queen's Colleges, the opposition of a large part of the Catholic hierarchy to the attendance of Catholics at these Colleges. For Berwick, this represented 'the strange and almost unintelligible opposition of a portion of the clergy of that persuasion for whose benefit the Queen's Colleges were mainly founded'.[17] The difficulties facing Queen's College Galway was a theme that was to preoccupy the reports of the President on a recurring basis.[18]

Notwithstanding these difficulties, sixty-eight students were admitted in October 1849. The difficult circumstances and the modest number of entrants

---

Irish political economists in the nineteenth century. He was the fourth holder of the Whately chair of Political Economy in Trinity College Dublin (1846–51) and while holding that position he was also appointed to the first chair of Jurisprudence and Political Economy at Queen's College Belfast in 1849, a position he held until 1853.

15 Black, *Economic Thought and the Irish Question*, pp. 47–8.
16 For an analysis of the development of political economy in the universities in the nineteenth century, see Alon Kadish and Keith Tribe (eds), *The Market for Political Economy: The Advent of Economics in British University Culture, 1850–1905* (London, 1993).
17 *Report* of the President of the Queen's College, Galway for 1849–50, p. 56. For a perceptive profile of pre-famine Galway, see Gearóid Ó Tuathaigh, ' " ... the air of a place of importance": Aspects of Nineteenth-Century Galway', in Diarmuid Ó Cearbhaill (ed.), *Galway: Town and Gown 1484–1984* (Dublin, 1984), pp. 129–47. An excellent overview of pre-famine Ireland is provided in Gearóid Ó Tuathaigh, *Ireland before the Famine 1798–1848* (Dublin, 1972).
18 For extended analysis of these difficulties, see the *Report* of the President of Queen's College Galway for 1856 and for 1884–5; the latter *Report* was written by Thomas Moffett, who succeeded Berwick in 1877 and remained as President until 1899.

insured that no particular discipline or professor was going to be overwhelmed by large numbers of students. Jurisprudence and Political Economy was certainly not the most popular choice of discipline, recording a total of four students as attending the lectures of the professor in the first two academic years. For the duration of Heron's stay at Queen's College Galway, the largest number of students recorded as attending his lectures was seventeen, during his last academic session of 1858–9.[19] Over his ten-year period in the College, the average class size in Jurisprudence and Political Economy was ten students. Not that Heron need have felt particularly aggrieved or disappointed in failing to attract students to his discipline; if we take the fifty-one year period from 1849 to 1900, then the average class size in terms of attendance at lectures was a mere seven students, which was a forty-three per cent decrease in average class size compared with his period in office.

Heron's prescribed reading for his students included Smith's *Wealth of Nations*, Senior's *Treatise on Political Economy* (based on his contribution to *Encyclopaedia Metropolitana*), Burton's *Political and Social Economy*, Bastiat's *Popular Fallacies*, and his own *Three Lectures on Taxation*.[20] For the period, this reading must be regarded as safe rather than adventurous in orientation and content. Conspicuous by their absence was any material from John Stuart Mill or, more particularly, David Ricardo. Given Heron's interest in the land tenure issue as reflected in his papers to the Statistical and Social Inquiry Society in the 1860s, referred to earlier, it is hard to conceive of Heron not engaging the work of Ricardo and of the later Mill had he chosen to stay in an academic career as a teacher of political economy.

It was during Heron's term of office that Commissioners were appointed 'to inquire into the progress and condition of the Queen's Colleges at Belfast, Cork, and Galway'. The Commission was appointed on 6 February 1857 and held its first meeting in Dublin Castle later that month. The Commission completed its work during 1857–8 and its *Report* was published in 1858.[21] The three professors of jurisprudence and political economy in Belfast, Cork, and Galway gave evidence to the Commission and some interesting insights into the position and role of political economy in the Queen's Colleges can be gained from their submissions. From the outset it was evident that the effects and relative size of the three locations exerted considerable influence on the function and place of political economy, and of commercial education in general, particularly in relation to the perceived needs of the wider society.

In Belfast the holder of the chair of Jurisprudence and Political Economy, T.E. Cliffe Leslie,[22] was arguing for what he called another 'kind of education', which was based on the need to introduce the physical sciences into the practical operations of life. Leslie was arguing for an expanded commercial and mercantile

---

19 Ibid., 1870–71 and 1871–2, p. 5.
20 Ibid., 1850–1, p. 67.
21 *Report of Her Majesty's Commissioners Appointed to Inquire into the Progress and Condition of the Queen's Colleges at Belfast, Cork, and Galway; With Minutes of Evidence, Documents, and Tables and Returns* (Dublin, 1858), otherwise referred to as *The Queen's Colleges Commission*.
22 Thomas Edward Cliffe Leslie (1825–82), a native of Co. Wexford and a graduate of Trinity College Dublin. Leslie was appointed Professor of Jurisprudence and Political Economy at Queen's College Belfast in 1853, a position he retained until his death in 1882.

education, which would include the physical and mathematical sciences. He cited the arrangements at the Trade Institute of Berlin, which he clearly envisaged as a prototype.[23] Leslie later developed this theme when he submitted a supplementary statement to the Commission entitled 'The Demand for Scientific Industrial Instruction in the Queen's College Belfast'.[24] In this contribution Leslie argued in defence of two major propositions. Firstly, that there was a demand for this kind of education which the Queen's Colleges were not supplying and, secondly, that there existed ample evidence from continental countries of the kind of institutions which represented 'nearly complete models of the kind of additional instruction wanted'.[25]

In the development of this new 'kind of education', Leslie envisaged that political economy would be a significant part of the curriculum, taking its place among such subjects as mathematics, descriptive geometry, linear drawing, chemistry, experimental physics, mechanics applied to arts, botany, and modern languages. His defence of the inclusion of political economy, as part of a new type of industrial education, is an interesting account of how, on the basis of a judicious selection of topics, it could be made to serve the mercantile and commercial interest of society. Arguably Leslie's concerns with the issue of merging political economy with the interests of commercial society was greatly influenced by his location in Belfast which, at the time, was the undisputed industrial capital of Ireland.

The concerns expressed by Leslie with respect to political economy were also reflected in the evidence from his counterparts in Cork and Galway, but the general tenor of their contributions conveyed a gloomier picture to that prevailing in Belfast. In Queen's College Cork, Richard Horner Mills had been appointed Professor of Jurisprudence and Political Economy in 1849, a position he held for forty-four years until his death in 1893.[26] The position of political economy within the BA degree structure was similar in all of the Queen's Colleges, with jurisprudence and political economy constituting a third-year optional course to metaphysics. In Cork and Galway the number of students attending courses in law in general and jurisprudence and political economy was particularly small compared with Queen's College Belfast.[27] Apart from the problem of the opposition of the Catholic hierarchy to the Queen's Colleges, an influence more acutely felt in Cork and Galway than in Belfast, a more mundane, but nonetheless real, set of reasons for the low student numbers was provided by Mills and Heron in their evidence to the Commission.

23 *The Queen's Colleges Commission*, 1858, p. 100.
24 Ibid., pp. 325–7.
25 Ibid., p. 326.
26 Richard Horner Mills (1815–93), a native of Dublin and a graduate of Trinity College, where he obtained a BA in 1838, followed by an MA in 1841. He was called to the Irish Bar in 1847. He was appointed the first Professor of Jurisprudence and Political Economy at Queen's College Cork in 1849, a position he retained until his death in August 1893.
27 Students from both the Law and Arts Faculties could take the third-year course in Jurisprudence and Political Economy. In his evidence to the Commission, Heron indicated that from a total of nine students, four were from the Faculty of Law and five from the Faculty of Arts. Heron is referring to either the academic session of 1855–6 or 1856–7, when the total number of students attending his lectures was recorded as nine. When he gave his evidence to the Commission, the number of students had dropped to seven.

Both acknowledged that since candidates aspiring to the Irish Bar had, in any event, to attend either the Benchers' own law school in Dublin or the law school in Trinity College Dublin, the provision of legal education in the provincial cities was of little use to them, with its attendant implications for political economy. Neither, it was argued, did the other branch of the legal profession – the attorneys – appreciate the value of the faculties in the Queen's Colleges. Consequently, the only potential clientele were the apprentices to attorneys who were located in Cork or Galway, and even their attendance was not a necessary requirement. Therefore, both Mills and Heron argued that the small numbers studying in their respective faculties was a function of the number of attorneys practising in their respective cities.[28] This prompted Mills to recommend to the Commission that the law faculty in Queen's College Cork should be abolished, but that legal instruction should be retained on a more modest scale.[29]

Heron did not agree with Mills's suggestion in his evidence to the Commission, and expressed surprise at why either Belfast or Cork, given their relative size compared with Galway, should have experienced difficulty in acquiring students.[30] Both Leslie and Mills were firmly of the opinion that political economy suffered greatly by virtue of its association with jurisprudence, combined as they were in the one chair. Indeed Mills's motivation in seeking the abolition of the faculty of law was largely derived from his concern to develop the teaching of political economy, which he regarded as 'one of the most important branches of education'.[31] Heron, however, was more circumspect with respect to political economy, being more concerned to defend the retention of the faculties of law in the Queen's Colleges against Mills's suggestion for their abolition.[32] Heron argued that there would 'always be some three or four students, at least, in each of the Colleges going to the bar', and that these would 'be generally among the most distinguished students'. It was, he concluded, 'most important that they should be furnished with the best means of being educated, in both the Science and Practice of Law'.[33]

Heron did, however, propose in the course of his evidence that a number of new diplomas should be established by the Queen's University and should be offered in the Queen's Colleges. In this he struck a similar note to that of Cliffe Leslie in Belfast. One of the courses Heron suggested was a diploma in commerce which, as he envisaged its operation, would address the educational needs of a particular group in the commercial domain, that of the personnel from the various bank branches throughout the country. But, on reflection, he quickly conceded that this proposal 'would be more useful in Cork and Belfast than Galway –

---

28 It should be remembered that both Mills and Heron were located within the Faculty of Law. Heron was Dean of the Faculty of Law, which had two members, himself and Professor Hugh Law, who was Professor of English Law.
29 *The Queen's Colleges Commission*, 1858, pp. 228–9.
30 Ibid., p. 289.
31 Ibid., p. 230.
32 Mills's suggestion for the abolition of the faculties of law was primarily addressed to his own situation in Cork but, from his line of argument to the Commission, the same reasoning applied to Belfast and Galway, and particularly the latter.
33 *The Queen's Colleges Commission*, 1858, p. 289.

10.1 John Elliot Cairnes, Professor of Jurisprudence and Political Economy, 1859–70

especially in Belfast, because the system of banking is more extended in the North of Ireland than in any other part of Ireland'.[34] It is difficult to detect much optimism in Heron's evidence to the Commission. He was acutely aware of the difficulties within which the College was operating, well attested to by his reference in relation to the difficulties students had in procuring accommodation. The College, Heron contended, 'in this respect is just as if it was placed in a desert'.[35]

John Elliot Cairnes (1823–75), who succeeded Heron in 1859, was unquestionably the most renowned Professor of Jurisprudence and Political Economy at Queen's College Galway, arguably the most distinguished economist Ireland has produced, and generally considered to have been among the leading economists in the world at the time of his death at the early age of fifty-one (fig. 10.1). He was, in the words of his intimate friend John Stuart Mill, 'one of the ablest of the distinguished men who have given lustre to the much-calumniated Irish colleges'.[36]

---

34 Ibid., p. 290.
35 Ibid.
36 Review of *The Slave Power*, in *Westminster Review*, n.s. 22 (1862), p. 489.

Cairnes was born at Castlebellingham, Co. Louth, in December 1823 into a brewing family.[37] He declined to enter the family business, much to the displeasure of his father. He did, however, decide to enter Trinity College Dublin in 1842 and graduated in 1848 with a BA. Six years later, in 1854, he received his MA from the same university. He spent some time after graduation in an engineer's office in Galway, and it was while he was in Galway that he became acquainted with William Nesbitt, Professor of Latin and later of Greek at Queen's College Galway. Nesbitt became Cairnes's closest friend, a friendship that endured until Cairnes's death. In 1860 Cairnes married Eliza Alexander, a sister of Nesbitt's wife. It was Nesbitt who turned Cairnes's attention to the study of political economy and urged him to compete for the Whately professorship in Trinity College Dublin. Cairnes was successful and became the sixth incumbent of the chair in 1856, holding it for the full five-year tenure. In 1859 he was appointed to the chair of Jurisprudence and Political Economy at Queen's College Galway, an appointment he held until 1870. In 1866, however, he was appointed to the Professorship of Political Economy at University College London. Thus he held joint-professorships in Galway and Dublin between 1859 and 1861 and in London and Galway between 1866 and 1870. Due to ill-health he resigned his London professorship in 1872, having already vacated his Galway chair two years previously. Cairnes had been called to the Irish Bar in 1857, but never seriously practised law nor engaged in any other occupation. He was, from the beginning, a full-time academic economist; in fact he was one of the first professional economists in Great Britain and Ireland. In 1874 the University of Dublin conferred the honorary degree of LLD on Cairnes. He died, after prolonged suffering borne with great patience, at his home in London on 8 July 1875.

Cairnes's reputation rests largely on his two major works within the mainstream of economic analysis, respectively his first and last works, *The Character and Logical Method of Political Economy* (London, 1857, 2nd edition, expanded 1875), and *Some Leading Principles of Political Economy* (London, 1874). In particular, his *Leading Principles* is seen as the final restatement of classical political economy in the Ricardo–Mill tradition.[38] Notwithstanding the impeccably orthodox credentials of the *Leading Principles*, it is interesting to note that, according to Kaldor, among others, the theory of 'excess capacity', which was outlined in Sraffa's famous article in the *Economic Journal* in 1926, is to be found 'in essentials' in Cairnes's last work.[39] Cairnes's *Character and Logical Method of Political Economy*, according to Professor R.D.C. Black, 'stands as the definitive statement of the methodology of the English classical school'.[40] Such a work, wrote the historian, H.T. Buckle to

---

37 See entry in *Dictionary of National Biography* (*DNB*); Palgrave's *Dictionary of Political Economy* (London, 1874); *The New Palgrave: A Dictionary of Economics* (London, 1987); Black, *The Statistical and Social Inquiry Society of Ireland;* Adelaide Weinberg, *John Elliot Cairnes and the American Civil War* (London, 1967).

38 Joseph A. Schumpeter, *History of Economic Analysis* (Oxford, 1954), pp. 533–4.

39 Nicholas Kaldor, *Essays on Value and Distribution* (London, 1960), p. 63. See also E.H. Chamberlain, *The Theory of Monopolistic Competition* (Cambridge, MA and London, 1959), p. 106 and P. Sraffa, 'The Laws of Return under Competitive Conditions', *Economic Journal*, 36 (1926), pp. 535–50.

40 R.D.C. Black, 'Cairnes', *International Encyclopaedia of the Social Sciences*, vol. ii, 1968, pp. 257–8.

Cairnes, 'augurs well for the University of Dublin'.[41] Walter Bagehot, in his obituary of Cairnes in the *Economist* in 1875, wrote that in this work Cairnes 'defines better ... than any previous writer, the exact sort of science, which political economy is, the kind of reasoning which it uses and the nature of the relation which it, as an abstract science, bears to the concrete world'.[42] His substantial writings on Bastiat, Comte, and Herbert Spencer are best seen as contributions to this aspect of political economy.[43] Despite Cairnes's undoubted theoretical ability, and his commitment to a rigorous deductivist methodology, he was much preoccupied by the application of economic principles to practical economic and social problems, which is reflected in many of his writings collected in his *Essays in Political Economy, Theoretical and Applied* and *Political Essays*, both published in London in 1873.

Cairnes's writings on the gold question, in the years 1859–60,[44] have been described as 'among the most important works of the nineteenth century on monetary theory'.[45] His *Examination into the Principles of Currency Involved in the Bank Character Act of 1844*, published in 1845, and which was one of his earliest technical writings in political economy, was highly thought of by Thomas Tooke.[46] Jevons recognised that Cairnes's writings on gold both anticipated and corroborated his own later statistical work on this topic.[47] But the most influential of all Cairnes's works was *The Slave Power*, published in London in 1862 when he was Professor of Jurisprudence and Political Economy in Queen's College Galway, but the substance of which formed the subject matter of a course of lectures in Trinity College Dublin, a year or so previously.[48] This work was described by Leslie Stephen as 'the most powerful defence of the cause of the Northern States' in the American Civil War 'ever written' and which 'made a great impression both in England and America'.[49] Darwin was very impressed by *The Slave Power*,[50] while Jevons saw it as a 'nearly or quite irrefragable piece of reasoning'.[51] It exerted,

---

41 H.T. Buckle to Cairnes, 1 March 1858 (National Library of Ireland (NLI), Cairnes Papers, MS 8944 (5)).
42 Reprinted in R.H. Hutton (ed.), *Biographical Studies* (London, 1881), p. 362.
43 J.E. Cairnes, 'Bastiat', *Fortnightly Review*, n.s. 8 (1870), pp. 411–28; 'M. Comte and Political Economy', ibid., n.s. 7 (1870), pp. 579–602; 'Mr Spencer on Social Evolution', ibid., n.s. 17 (1875), pp. 63–82; and 'Mr Spencer on the Study of Sociology', ibid., n.s. 17 (1875), pp. 200–13.
44 J.E. Cairnes, 'The Laws, According to which a Depreciation of the Precious Metals Consequent upon an Increase of Supply Takes Place, Considered in Connection with the Recent Gold Discoveries', *Journal of the Dublin Statistical Society*, 2 (1859), pp. 236–69 (paper read to the British Association, September 1858); 'Essays towards an Experimental Solution of the Gold Question', *Fraser's Magazine*, 60 (1859), pp. 267–78; 'Essay towards a Solution of the Gold Question', ibid., 61 (1860), pp. 38–53; review of M. Chevalier, *On the Probable Fall in the Value of Gold: The Commercial and Social Consequences which May Ensue, and the Measures which It Invites* (London, 1859), *Edinburgh Review*, 112 (1860), pp. 1–33, reprinted in *Essays in Political Economy: Theoretical and Applied* (London, 1873), pp. 109–65.
45 'Cairnes', entry in *Encyclopaedia Brittanica* (Chicago, 1963) by T.W. Hutchinson.
46 Tooke to Cairnes, 27 March 1856 (NLI, Cairnes Papers, MS 8944 (4)).
47 See R.D.C. Black, 'Jevons and Cairnes', *Economica*, 27 (1960), pp. 214–32.
48 J.E. Cairnes, *The Slave Power* (London, 1862), p. vii. A second edition followed in 1863.
49 See Stephen's entry on 'Cairnes' in *DNB*.
50 F. Darwin (ed.), *The Life and Letters of Charles Darwin* (London, 1887), vol. iii, p. 11.
51 Quoted by Black, 'Jevons and Cairnes', p. 223.

wrote Henry Fawcett, 'a powerful influence on English public opinion in favour of the North' in the American Civil War.[52] Its 'practical object' was 'completely accomplished', wrote Cliffe Leslie, but its 'philosophic purpose' gave it 'a permanent value as an economic classic'.[53]

The ambitious 'philosophic purpose' of *The Slave Power* was 'to show that the course of history is largely determined by the action of economic causes'.[54] It is scarcely surprising that Marx should show an interest in this work, and it is not widely known that Marx's own analysis of the slave economy is very much indebted to Cairnes. In their controversial revisionist study of American slavery, *Time on the Cross*, the American economic historians, Fogel and Engerman, criticise Cairnes's work as representing a pre-cliometric, unreconstructed understanding of slavery.[55] Engerman writes that Marx drew largely on Cairnes in his analysis of the slave South, as indeed did subsequent Marxist scholars.[56] This remains true to recent times; Eugene Genovese, a leading post-war Marxist writer on slavery, was very much indebted to the work of John Elliot Cairnes.[57] Maurice Dobb, the late Marxist economist at Cambridge, claimed that Cairnes's analysis of a slave economy could be a fruitful model for an understanding of the economics of imperialism.[58]

In addition to his theoretical work, we have argued elsewhere that Cairnes's contribution to the area of economic policy has been of immense significance and more radical in orientation and content than that of his theoretical writings.[59] In particular, his attack on *laissez-faire* and his writings on the Irish land question represented seminal contributions to both areas. John Maynard Keynes, in his book, *The End of Laissez-Faire*, published in 1926, stated that Cairnes 'was perhaps the first orthodox economist to deliver a frontal attack upon *laissez-faire* in general'.[60] This was a lecture, 'Political Economy and *Laissez-Faire*', which he delivered at University College London in 1870. *Laissez-faire*, Cairnes argued, had 'no scientific basis whatsoever' and was 'at best a mere handy rule of practice'.[61]

---

52   Henry Fawcett, 'Professor Cairnes', *Fortnightly Review*, n.s. 18 (1875), p. 152.
53   T.E. Cliffe Leslie, 'Professor Cairnes', *Essays in Political Economy*, 2nd edition (Dublin and London, 1888), p. 61. Originally an obituary in the *Academy*, 17 July 1875.
54   *The Slave Power*, p. vii.
55   See R.W. Fogel and S.L. Engermann, *Time on the Cross: The Economics of American Negro Slavery* (Boston and Toronto, 1974).
56   S.L. Engermann, 'Marxist Economic Studies of the Slave South', *Marxist Perspectives*, 1 (1978), p. 49.
57   See E. Genovese, *Political Economy of Slavery: Studies in Economy and Society of the Slave South* (New York, 1967); see also Charles Post, 'The American Road to Capitalism', *New Left Review*, no. 133, 1982, pp. 33–4.
58   Maurice Dobb, *Political Economy and Capitalism* (London, 1964), p. 251.
59   T.A. Boylan and T.P. Foley, 'John Elliot Cairnes, John Stuart Mill and Ireland: Some Problems for Political Economy, *Hermathena*, no. 135, (1983), pp. 96–119, republished in Antoin E. Murphy (ed.), *Economists and the Irish Economy from the Eighteenth Century to the Present Day* (Dublin, 1984), pp. 96–119; 'John Elliot Cairnes on Land and *Laissez-Faire*: An Irish Challenge to Political Economy'?, paper presented to the British History of Economic Thought Conference, University of Surrey, September 1984.
60   J.M. Keynes, *The End of Laissez-Faire* (London, 1926), p. 26.
61   J.E. Cairnes, 'Political Economy and Laissez-Faire', *Fortnightly Review*, 10 (1871), pp. 80–97. The quotation is from p. 86.

Cairnes's more radical writings on the Irish land question are contained in a series of articles in the *Economist* in the mid-1860s, which represented a fundamental reconsideration on his part of the rights of private property and the status of contract. In his important paper on 'Political Economy and Land', published in 1870, Cairnes returned to this crucial topic. Even if Cairnes had not produced the corpus of theoretical work which he did, it is most likely that his writings on economic policy would have earned him an assured place in the history of nineteenth-century political economy.

In his first academic session at Queen's College Galway, Cairnes delivered thirty-four lectures in jurisprudence and civil law and fifteen lectures in political economy. He had a total of seven students in his law class and six attended his political economy class. His overall assessment was succinct, noting that 'the progress of the students was, on the whole, satisfactory, and their general deportment exceedingly good'.[62] Cairnes would have been a most conscientious and demanding teacher. He expanded the reading material on his course in political economy and by 1862–3 we find Mill, Ricardo, and Göschen represented on his required reading.[63] The inclusion of Mill and Ricardo is hardly surprising given Cairnes's life-long intellectual commitment to the Ricardo-Mill tradition in classical political economy. Cairnes never kept a house in Galway. He retained his house in Dublin, but spent a good deal of his free time at the family home at Stameen, outside Drogheda. His wife Eliza never moved to Galway, which in turn gave rise to an extensive correspondence (when he was away from home he wrote to her almost every day). During the last three years of his tenure at Queen's College Galway, Cairnes, who had moved to London in 1865 to the Professorship of Political Economy at University College London (which he took up in 1866), was allowed to appoint a deputy to lecture in his place.[64]

In his report for the academic session 1869–70, Edward Berwick, President of Queen's College Galway, on the occasion of Cairnes's resignation, noted with regret that, 'in consequence of his continued ill-health, the College has been deprived of the services of one of its ablest Professors – Mr J.E. Cairnes'. 'I cannot', Berwick added, 'conclude this report without bearing testimony to the zeal and the eminent ability manifested by him during his connection with the College'.[65] When Cairnes died five years later, similar sentiments were frequently expressed. The *Times* obituary described him as 'the most powerful and exact of our recent Political Economists', while Cliffe Leslie, in his obituary notice in the *Academy*, wrote: 'Professor Cairnes has been laid to rest with extraordinary honour. No other author's death in our time, save Mr Mill's, has called forth so strong and general an expression of feeling'. His 'moral as well as his intellectual qualities', concluded Leslie, 'won for him the reputation which has now become

---

62 *Report* of the President of Queen's College for 1859–60, p. 11.
63 Ibid., 1862–3, p. 22.
64 For an account of Cairnes's stay in Galway, see Thomas A. Boylan and Timothy P. Foley, 'Cairnes, Hearn and Bastable: The Contribution of Queen's College, Galway to Economic Thought', in Ó Cearbhaill (ed.), *Galway*, pp. 183–205.
65 *Report* of the President of Queen's College Galway for 1869–70, p. 8.

10.2 Students at Queen's College Galway, c.1870

historical'. He was, stated Edwin Cannan in his authoritative *Review of Economy Theory*, 'perhaps the most respected economist of the time in England'.[66]

William Lupton (1830–76) succeeded Cairnes at Queen's College Galway. He was educated at Queen's College Belfast, where he graduated with first-class honours in mathematics in 1852. The following year he obtained his MA in mathematics and mathematical physics with first-class honours. He was also a member of the Inner Temple. In 1853 he was appointed Registrar of Queen's College Galway, a position he held until 1870 when he was appointed to the chair of Jurisprudence and Political Economy, which he retained until his death in 1876. In the final year of his tenure as professor, Lupton's lectures were delivered by Thomas Maguire, Professor of Latin (1869–80) and 'Lecturer in Political Economy and Civil Law'.[67] Lupton was the author of *The Reform Bill and the Queen's University in Ireland* (Dublin, 1860) and a series of articles, 'Industrial Progress: Its Causes and Conditions', in the *Irish Industrial Magazine* (1866).

Robert Cather Donnell (1839–83), who succeeded Lupton, was completing his term of office as the ninth Whately Professor of Political Economy of Trinity

66 Boylan and Foley, 'Cairnes, Hearn and Bastable', in Ó Cearbhaill (ed.), *Galway*, p. 205.
67 *Report* of the President of Queen's College Galway for 1875–6, p. 19.

College Dublin when the chair of Jurisprudence and Political Economy became vacant following Lupton's death in 1876. Donnell was born on 25 June 1839, the second son of William Donnell and Isabella Cather, at Ballinamallard, Co. Tyrone. He was educated at Queen's College Belfast, where he had a distinguished academic career. He graduated with the BA in 1860 having been awarded the gold medal and first place in both jurisprudence and political economy and in English literature. In 1863 he was awarded the MA in Queen's College Belfast, achieving first place in political economy. The following year he was called to the Irish Bar. In 1871 he was appointed Whately Professor of Political Economy for the regulation five-year period, and between 1871–3 he held the Barrington Lectureship. While a Whately Professor he was also Examiner in Jurisprudence and Political Economy in the Queen's University during 1875.

In his application for the Professorship at Queen's College Galway, Donnell presented an impressive list of referees, which included the President of Queen's College Belfast, the Revd P. Shuldham Henry, Professor Moffett, who was later to become President of Queen's College Galway, Professors Cliffe Leslie and W.N. Hancock, the first and second holders of the chair of Jurisprudence and Political Economy at Queen's College Belfast respectively, Arthur Houston, the seventh holder of the Whately Professorship, and D.C. Heron, the first holder of the chair of Jurisprudence and Political Economy at Galway. Donnell faced considerable opposition in the list of candidates who applied for the chair in Galway. These included James Slattery, a former holder of the Whately chair in Trinity and later to become President of Queen's College Cork, one Mr S. Amos, Professor of Jurisprudence at University College London, and John Dockrill. Cairnes, incidentally, had an extremely high opinion of Dockrill. From a final list of six candidates Donnell was ranked first, followed by Dockrill and Amos.[68] Though having achieved a distinguished academic record in political economy, Donnell chose not to pursue his career within this discipline, and his main academic legacy is as a writer on legal matters, particularly issues related to land. His principal publications included: *Practical Guide to the Law of Tenant Compensation and Farm Purchase under the Irish Land Act* (Dublin, 1871); *Chapters on the Leaseholder's Claim to Tenant-Right, and Other Tenant-Right Questions* (Dublin, 1873); *A Scheme of Land Transfer for Small Proprietors, by Local Registry of Title* (Dublin, 1874); and *Reports of One Hundred and Ninety Cases in the Irish Land Courts* (Dublin, 1876).

In his *The Statistical and Social Inquiry Society of Ireland: Centenary Volume*, Professor R.D.C. Black claimed that 'If there are many distinguished names to be found amongst the lists of members of the Statistical Society, there are perhaps only two which are familiar to every student of Economics. One is John Elliot Cairnes, the other Charles Francis Bastable'.[69] It is gratifying to note that both were professors at Galway.[70]

---

68 Donnell's application for the Professorship of Jurisprudence and Political Economy, 16 August 1876, National Archives, MS CSORP 1876/16849.
69 Black, *Centenary Volume*, p. 80.
70 A distinction, it must be noted, that is shared with Trinity College Dublin, since both men had also held the Whately Chair of Political Economy at that University.

Charles Francis Bastable (1855–1945) was born in Charleville, Co. Cork, the son of a clergyman. His early education was obtained at Fermoy College. He entered Trinity College Dublin in 1873, and graduated in 1878 with first-class honours in the senior moderatorship in history and political science. After graduation he commenced his legal studies, and was called to the Irish Bar in 1881. He obtained the MA and LLD degrees in 1882 and 1890 respectively. In 1882, at the age of twenty-seven, Bastable succeeded in the competitive assessment for the Whately chair. The Whately chair, as prescribed by its founder, was to be held for a five-year period. Bastable, however, was to break with this rule when, in 1887, at the end of his first term, he was re-appointed for a second five-year period. In 1912, at the end of his sixth term, he was given a life tenure in the post. However, the stipend for the Whately chair was a fixed amount and Bastable supplemented his income by accepting the Professorship of Jurisprudence and Political Economy at Queen's College Galway in 1883, on the death of Robert Cather Donnell. Bastable held the position in Galway for twenty years. In 1902 the chair of Civil Law and General Jurisprudence was revived at Trinity College Dublin, and Bastable was appointed to the post. For a brief period, in 1902–3, he had the distinction of holding three professorships, but because of pressure of work he resigned from the chair in Galway in 1903. In 1908 he was appointed Regius Professor of Laws in the University of Dublin, a post he retained until his retirement in 1932, at the age of seventy-seven.

Bastable was an active member of the Statistical and Social Inquiry Society of Ireland.[71] He served as honorary secretary from 1886 to 1895, and vice-president from 1896 to 1915. He was also one of the original Fellows of the Royal Economic Society, and a member of its first council. In 1894 he was elected President of the British Association, section F, and in 1921 he was elected a Fellow of the British Academy. When the Irish Free State was established in 1921 he served on the Fiscal Inquiry Committee, which reported in 1923.

In contrast with his predecessor, Robert Cather Donnell, who concentrated primarily on legal issues, Bastable, though he trained as a lawyer and, as we have seen, held three different chairs of law, his reputation rests exclusively on his publications in economics. Bastable made important contributions in two major areas of economics, international trade theory and public finance. His major works appeared in book form between 1887 and 1892. In 1887 *The Theory of International Trade* was published, and ran to four editions by 1903. In 1892 his two most prestigious works were published, *The Commerce of Nations* and *Public Finance*. The former was an immediate success that ran to nine editions, and was translated into a number of European languages. For some commentators, however, *Public Finance* was deemed the more original of the two.

Bastable's contribution to international trade theory represents an extension of the free trade doctrines of the classical school of nineteenth-century economics. More specifically, his contributions provided major theoretical extensions to the existing Ricardo-Mill theory of trade, through the introduction of a number of

---

71 In Black's *Centenary Volume*, p. 88, Bastable is credited with presenting eight papers to the Society, while Daly, *The Spirit of Earnest Inquiry*, pp. 199–200, identifies nine papers.

important qualifications. In addition, Bastable also made a number of improvements and corrections to John Stuart Mill's analysis of the international payments system, particularly where the source of these payments did not originate in commerce. Reviewing the second edition of *The Theory of International Trade*, in 1897, for the *Economic Journal*, F.Y. Edgeworth, the distinguished Irish economist and pioneer theorist in mathematical economics, who was then the Drummond Professor of Political Economy at Oxford, referred to it as 'the best manual on the most difficult part of Economics'.[72] In the course of the same review Edgeworth generously conceded that Bastable was indeed correct when he disputed Edgeworth's earlier analysis of the impact of import and export taxes. Edgeworth wrote:

> For my part I at once admit that on one of the most important points on which we differed, Professor Bastable was right and I was wrong. I refer to my conclusion that there is an essential difference between the action of import and that of export taxes.[73]

Edgeworth continued to hold Bastable's work in the highest regard. Referring to a later edition of the same work, he stated that in the 'successive editions of this work Professor Bastable ... maintains his reputation as author of the best text book on the subject'. Edgeworth also paid Bastable the tribute of obtaining a 'new distinction by displaying in his replies to criticisms a candour and courtesy which are rare in economic literature'.[74]

Bastable's second book in international trade theory, *The Commerce of Nations*, was, when it was first published in 1892, described, by L.L. Price, as 'the most scientific volume which has yet come under our notice'.[75] This book presented a powerful critique of the economic arguments for protection. It was described as providing a 'fair but destructive account of the modern protectionist theory'.[76] Bastable did in fact provide explicit conditions that should be met to justify a restricted form of protection for a limited period of time to industry in the early stages of its development. This argument was referred to as the 'infant industry' argument for protection in the economic literature. John Stuart Mill had earlier argued a similar case in his *Principles of Political Economy*. Bastable's name has been enshrined in economic thought in the form of the 'Mill–Bastable condition', which has become an integral part of the analysis of protection.[77]

While acknowledging Bastable's significant contributions to international trade theory, Professor G.A. Duncan, who succeeded Bastable in the chair of Political

---

72 F.Y. Edgeworth, review of *The Theory of International Trade*, 2nd ed., in *Economic Journal*, 7 (1897), pp. 397–403. The quotation is from p. 397.
73 Ibid.
74 F.Y. Edgeworth, review of *The Theory of International Trade*, 3rd ed., in *Economic Journal*, 10 (1900), pp. 389–93. The quotations are from p. 389.
75 L.L. Price, review of *The Commerce of Nations*, in *Economic Journal*, 2 (1892), pp. 324–5. The quotation is from p. 324.
76 Ibid., p. 325.
77 Murray C. Kemp, 'The Mill-Bastable Infant Industry Dogma', *Journal of Political Economy*, 68 (1960), pp. 65–8.

Economy in the University of Dublin in 1932, has argued that Bastable's principal intellectual interest was not trade theory but public finance, 'a field in which, for the British Isles, he was a pioneer, and laid the foundations of a systematic study'.[78] This systematic study was contained in Bastable's *Public Finance*, which Duncan described as 'the best text-book in English for its organisation, synoptic treatment, and sense of proportion'.[79] L.L. Price, who reviewed *Public Finance* for the *Economic Journal*, argued that Bastable's work on public finance had been the most comprehensive treatment of the topic since Adam Smith's *Wealth of Nations* (1776), notwithstanding Ricardo's *Principles of Political Economy and Taxation* (1817) and McCulloch's *Taxation and the Funding System* (1845). He had produced, stated Price, 'a book which, we venture to think, will take its place among the permanent, as distinguished from the merely ephemeral, products of British economic inquiry'.[80] Likewise, Henry Higgs referred to it as 'a work of assured position, which seems destined to be revived again and again',[81] while Edgeworth, commenting on a later edition, referred to it as 'this now classical work'.[82]

Bastable displayed considerable foresight in anticipating as early as he did the increasing significance of the public sector. He articulated a pioneering schematisation of the contributing factors for the development of the public sector and analysed in detail the implications of these developments for taxation. Based on his major works, along with his contributions to the leading journals of the day, particularly the *Economic Journal* and the *Quarterly Journal of Economics*, Bastable is assured of a permanent and honoured place in the development of the subject.

On Bastable's resignation the chair of Jurisprudence and Political Economy was filled by John Henry Wardell (1878–1957). Wardell came from a Readership in History in the University of Dublin and his contribution to political economy was to be minimal. Wardell had been awarded First Prize in Political Economy and had won the Whately Memorial Prize and was also a Whately (Research) Prizeman. Bastable, who provided a testimonial for Wardell, thought highly of him and regretted very much Wardell's 'severing his connection with the teaching work in Dublin University'.[83] Bastable had also assured Alexander Anderson, President of Queen's College Galway, that 'he (Wardell) is likely to do original work and is quite an enthusiast in his subjects'.[84] J.P. Mahaffy of Trinity College Dublin, who also provided a testimonial for Wardell, was under the impression that Wardell was 'a candidate for the Chair of Political Science' in Queen's College Galway. Indeed, it

---

78 G.A. Duncan, 'Charles Francis Bastable 1855–1945', *Proceedings of the British Academy*, 31 (1946), p. 3.
79 Ibid., p. 2.
80 L.L. Price, review of *Public Finance*, in *Economic Journal*, 2 (1892), pp. 671–6. The quotation is from p. 673.
81 Henry Higgs, review of *Public Finance*, 2nd ed., in *Economic Journal*, 6 (1896), pp. 104–5. The quotation is from p. 104.
82 F.Y. Edgeworth, review of *Public Finance*, 3rd ed., in *Economic Journal*, 13 (1903), pp. 226–8. The quotation is from p. 226.
83 Wardell's application for the Professorship of Jurisprudence and Political Economy, 20 July 1903, National Archives, MS CSORP 1903/14383.
84 Ibid.

is hard to blame Mahaffy as Wardell actually applied for the chair of 'Jurisprudence and Political Science'. Mahaffy was happy to 'recommend him in every other way as a scholar and a gentleman, with a special turn for Irish History'.[85] The fact that Wardell was First Senior Moderator and Large Gold Medallist in History, Political Science and Jurisprudence in his degree in 1900 in Trinity College may account for Mahaffy's emphasis on Political Science and 'Irish History'. The year after his graduation, Wardell was appointed Lecturer to the Indian Civil Service School, and the following year, in 1902, he was appointed Reader in History in the University of Dublin.[86] Wardell's main publication was an edited work, *With the 'Thirty Second' in the Peninsula and Other Campaigns: Being the Memoirs of Major Harry Ross-Lewin of Ross Hill, in the Co. Clare* (Dublin, 1904).[87]

James Anderson (1881–1915), who was to be the last holder of the chair which carried the title of Jurisprudence and Political Economy, was a native of Derry. He was the eldest son of Thomas Anderson, a merchant in that city. James Anderson planned to pursue a career in banking, a profession which he entered at the age of fifteen. After a few years, and having reconsidered his career options, he matriculated in the Royal University of Ireland in 1902 and entered Queen's College Belfast.[88] He graduated in 1906 with first-class honours and first place, and was awarded the McKane Gold Medal and appointed the First Law Scholar. The following year he was awarded an MA along with a Studentship. During the academic year 1907–8 he was Acting Professor of Jurisprudence and Political Economy in Queen's College Belfast. He served as a barrister on the Connacht Circuit. In November 1910 he was appointed to the Professorship of Jurisprudence and Political Economy at Queen's College Galway. The year before he died, he was appointed to the Reid Professorship of Criminal and Constitutional Law in Trinity College Dublin, a position he held in addition to his position in Galway. He died on 19 June 1915. In his Presidential Report for that year, Alexander Anderson, President of Queen's College Galway, referred to the two 'very distinguished members Professor R.J. Anderson and Professor J. Anderson', who 'have been removed from us by death'.[89] Professor James Anderson, the President noted, 'was regarded by those who were best able to judge as a man who would rise to an eminent position in his profession'.[90] His premature death at the early age of thirty-four precluded the realisation of this possibility.

85 Ibid.
86 Wardell's appointment to this post arose from the resignation of J.B. Bury from the Professorship of Modern History and his appointment as Regius Professor of History at Cambridge.
87 It should be noted that Wardell was appointed Director of Military Studies at Dublin University in 1904. He won the Whately Prize in Political Economy for his essay, 'The Economic Aspects of Modern Colonization'. Presumably he published this as 'Certain Aspects of Colonial Democracy (with Especial Reference to Australasia)', *Hermathena*, no. 29, 1903, pp. 383–427.
88 The Royal University of Ireland was established in 1879 as an examining body. The Queen's University was abolished, but the three Queen's Colleges retained their original titles. See T.W. Moody and J.C. Beckett, *Queen's Belfast, 1845–1949: The History of a University*, 2 vols (London, 1959), vol. i, pp. 293–5.
89 *Report* of the President of University College Galway, for the sessions 1913–14, 1914–15, and 1915–16, p. 4. The R.J. Anderson referred to was Professor of Natural History, Geology, and Mineralogy from 1883 until his death in 1914.
90 Ibid., pp. 4–5.

By 1915, at the time of James Anderson's death, the institutional arrangements had changed dramatically. The National University of Ireland had been established in 1908 under the Irish Universities Act (1908). This Act, which was introduced into the British House of Commons on 31 March 1908 and received the royal assent on 1 August of the same year, represented the very considerable achievement of Augustine Birrell, chief secretary for Ireland in Asquith's first administration. Birrell's predecessors, in the previous half century, had failed to find a solution to the difficult problem of responding to the demands of Irish Catholics for university education.[91] The bill introduced by Birrell in 1908 faced opposition from two principal sources. One was from the Ulster Unionists in parliament and the other from the parliamentary representatives of the University of Dublin. Birrell's solution found acceptance with both of these formidable sources of opposition. Opposition from the University of Dublin was deflected by assurance that their status and privileges would not be interfered with under the proposed new arrangements. The Ulster Unionists' opposition was assuaged by the establishment of a new University in Belfast, the Queen's University of Belfast. The Catholic demand for university education was met by the establishment of a non-denominational university with three constituent colleges, University College Dublin (the former Catholic University) and the two Queen's Colleges of Cork and Galway, which were now to be known as University College Cork and University College Galway respectively.[92]

The 1908 Act provided for the formation of two statutory bodies, which were given the task of establishing the two new universities, the Queen's University, Belfast and the National University of Ireland. The bodies became known as the Belfast Commissioners and the Dublin Commissioners respectively.[93] As part of their work the Dublin Commissioners undertook an extended examination of the need to make provision for new areas of study in the new National University of Ireland. This entailed extended and detailed interviews with various representatives from universities, chambers of commerce, professional institutes such as those of architects and bankers, and others. In the commercial area, interviews were held with such representatives as the Dean of the Faculty of Commerce, University of Manchester, the Director of the London School of Economics, along with representatives from the Chambers of Commerce in Dublin and Cork. The issue under examination was the need for the establishment of Faculties of Commerce in the National University of Ireland.[94]

---

91 For an extended account of these developments, see Moody and Beckett, *Queen's Belfast*, vol. i, pp. 381–413.
92 These arrangements pertained until the passing of the Universities Act, 1997 under which University College Galway was reconstituted as a University with the title of National University of Ireland, Galway, and is now a constituent University of the National University of Ireland (together with National University of Ireland, Dublin, National University of Ireland, Cork, and National University of Ireland, Maynooth).
93 For a profile of the members of the Dublin Commissioners, which included Alexander Anderson, President of Queen's College/University College Galway, see Cyril M. White, 'The 80th Anniversary of the National University of Ireland', *UCD News*, November 1988, pp. 4–7.
94 Dublin Commission (Irish Universities Act, 1908). Report of Conferences with University Authorities and Representatives of Chambers of Commerce, Institutes of Architecture and

In the event the decision was taken to proceed with their establishment and a new chair of Commerce and Accountancy was established at University College Galway with Professor B.F. Shields as the first incumbent.[95] Under Statute IV of the new University College Galway, there was provision for the amalgamation of economics with commerce and accountancy into one professorship.[96] On the death of James Anderson in 1915, the provisions of this statute were availed of and Shields was appointed to the reconstituted Professorship of Economics, Commerce and Accountancy. He was also the first Dean of the newly-established Faculty of Commerce, and his term as Dean, which lasted until 1918, coincided with the first cycle of Bachelor of Commerce students, who graduated in 1918.[97]

Francis McBryan, who succeeded B.F. Shields, was to hold the chair of Economics, Commerce, and Accountancy and the Deanship of the Faculty of Commerce for a thirty-four year period from 1918 until 1952. When McBryan applied for the professorship he had already been appointed to a temporary position, in October 1918, as a substitute for the Professors of Economics, Commerce, and Accountancy. Prior to this he had spent seven years teaching in the Omagh Technical School, Co. Tyrone, and six years as Chief Commercial Instructor with the Co. Mayo Technical Instruction Committee. For the last two years of that period he had served as Principal of the Ballina Technical School. In 1910 he was awarded a Scholarship from the Department of Agriculture and Technical Instruction, tenable for two years, at the London School of Economics. He was awarded a Diploma in Higher Commercial subjects from the London School of Economics, graduating with distinction in 1912. On his return, he registered for the BA degree in University College Dublin as an external student, where he studied political economy and national economics of Ireland. He graduated in 1915 and proceeded to a Higher Diploma in Education at University College Dublin, which he obtained in 1916, again as an external student. He also obtained a diploma from the University of Lille and a certificate from Queen's University Belfast.[98]

McBryan's term as Professor and Dean of the Faculty of Commerce was marked by continuity of content and structure. The configuration of the Bachelor of Commerce and the one-year Certificate in Commerce were essentially the same at the end of McBryan's term of office as he had inherited them from Shields. But

---

Music, and other Persons as to Provision for Technological, Commercial, and other Studies in the National University of Ireland (Dublin, 1909).

95 'Editorial', *U.C.G. A College Annual*, no. 3, 1 (1915), p. 4. This issue also contains an article by Professor Shields, 'Landmarks of Ireland's Economic Position in the 19th Century', pp. 24–32.

96 *Report* of the President of University College Galway, for the sessions 1913–14, 1914–15, and 1915–16, p. 5.

97 *The National University Handbook 1908–1932* (Dublin, 1932), p. 143. Apart from Professor Shields, the other members of the Commerce Faculty in 1918 were : Professor Liam Ó Briain (Romance Languages), Professor William A. Byrne (English), Professor M.J. D. O'Sullivan (History), Professor R.J. Sheedy (Commercial Law), Professor T. Ó Máille (Irish), Professor Seaghán P. Mac Énrí (Modern Irish – Mac Énrí was Professor of Ophthalmology and Otology and Lecturer in Modern Irish), Professor H.B. Cronshaw (Geography).

98 McBryan's Application for the Professorship of Economics, Commerce, and Accountancy, 15 November 1918, NUI, Galway Archives.

the circumstances were not particularly conducive to positive change, much less to experimentation. The period in question was one of the most difficult in the history of the College; it included specific threats to its long-term viability, a harsh economic environment, along with having to cope with the difficulties arising from the circumstances of the Second World War. McBryan witnessed the numbers of students in the Commerce Faculty decline by more than half between the mid-1930s and the end of the Second World War, from 106 in the academic year 1934–5 to 46 in 1944–5.[99]

When McBryan retired in 1952, at the age of seventy,[100] he was replaced by Liam Ó Buachalla who had already been in University College Galway since 1927 as Lecturer in Economics, Commerce, and Accountancy. This Lectureship was carried out through the medium of Irish, a development which was later enshrined in the University College Galway Act of 1929. Ó Buachalla was extremely committed to, and actively pursued, the promotion of teaching through Irish.[101] He was a native of Drogheda, where he acquired his early education and industrial work experience in the cooperage department of the Irish Packing Company and later with the Guinness company in Dublin. He graduated from University College Dublin in 1927 with first-class honours and the following year he received the Higher Diploma in Education. He completed a Master of Commerce degree in University College Galway for which he was awarded first-class honours.

During the tenure of his lectureship he contributed extensively to local and national organisations in the educational and political sphere. He was a Barrington Lecturer in Economics for many years, a member of the Commission of Inquiry on Agriculture (1939), a member of the Senate of the National University of Ireland, President of the Gaelic League, an examiner in Economics, Commerce, and Accountancy for the Civil Service Commissioners, and he was a member of various boards under the Civil Service and Local Appointments Commissions. In 1939 he became a member of Seanad Éireann; he was nominated by the Taoiseach to that body on two occasions and he was twice elected. He was later elected Cathaoirleach of the Seanad. In Galway he was a member of various committees, including the Co. Galway Vocational Education Committee, the Co. Galway Libraries Committee, and the Galway Co. Council Scholarships Committee. During the period of his lectureship, Ó Buachalla devoted a considerable amount of his time to the preparation of textbooks in Irish on Economics, Commerce, and Accountancy.[102] He also published in journals such as *Studies* and presented a number of papers to the Statistical and Social Inquiry Society of Ireland.[103]

---

99 *Report* of the President, 1934–45.
100 Not at seventy-three, as claimed by Ronan Fanning, 'Economists and Governments: Ireland 1922–52', in Murphy (ed.), *Economists and the Irish Economy*, p. 142.
101 Ó Buachalla was also listed as Assistant in Geography (through Irish) from 1930–1 until his appointment as professor.
102 These included: *Bunadhas na Tráchtála agus Eagras Gnótha* (Baile Átha Cliath, 1944); *Cuntais agus Cuntasaíoch* (Baile Átha Cliath, 1954); *Bunadhas an Gheilleagair* (Baile Átha Cliath, 1956); *Ard-Cuntasaíoch* (Baile Átha Cliath, 1959); *Forás Teoricí an Gheilleagair: Anall go dtí 1800* (Baile Átha Cliath, 1968).
103 His papers published in the *Journal of the Statistical and Social Society of Ireland* were: 'Some

In his application for the professorship he was provided with testimonials from two of his predecessors in the position, B.F. Shields who, on leaving Galway in 1918, had become Professor of Commerce and Dean of the Faculty of Commerce in University College Dublin, and Francis McBryan, his immediate predecessor and former colleague. George O'Brien, Professor of Political Economy and National Economics in University College Dublin, and his former teacher, and Professor T.A. Smiddy, former Professor of Economics and Commerce at University College Cork, who had served with Ó Buachalla on the Commission of Inquiry on Agriculture, also acted as referees.[104] The non-academic who provided a testimonial on his behalf was T.J. Kiernan, who was then the Irish Ambassador to Australia. For the circumstances of the time this was an impressive array of referees, all of whom spoke very positively of Ó Buachalla's ability, wide experience, and accumulated practical knowledge of business and economic affairs.[105]

As in the case of his predecessors, Ó Buachalla, from his appointment in 1952 to the Professorship of Economics, Commerce, and Accountancy until his retirement in 1964, was also Dean of the Faculty of Commerce. He would have witnessed the steady growth in student numbers in the faculty from a low of forty-six in 1945 to one hundred-and-sixty by 1960. The 1960s was to be a decade of substantial growth at both Faculty and College levels. When Ó Buachalla retired in 1969, the Faculty of Commerce had over two hundred students, a growth of 33 per cent over the decade, while the total student population had grown by 161 per cent in the same period to almost three thousand. During his tenure of office, a number of appointments were also made. In 1953, Ó Buachalla's vacant lectureship was filled by Labhrás Ó Nualláin, while in 1967 two new staff were appointed; Diarmuid Ó Cearbhaill as Lecturer in Economics and Commerce and Leon Ó hAichín as Lecturer in Accountancy. These appointments represented the emergence of an identifiable core group of academic staff in the Commerce Faculty which would form the basis for major expansion during the 1970s and 80s.

From a longer-term future perspective, the years 1970–1 will be viewed as a major watershed in the development of the Commerce Faculty at Galway. A crucial development in this process was the appointment of Labhrás Ó Nualláin to a reconstituted Professorship of Economics, which was now separated from Commerce and Accountancy. In 1965 Ó Nualláin had succeeded in changing his statutory position from Lecturer in Economics, Commerce, and Accountancy to Lecturer in Applied Economics. Ó Nualláin was by training, interests, and commitment an economist, and on acceding to the chair of Economics set about the process of restructuring the teaching of economics in both the Arts and Commerce Faculties. In this he was greatly assisted by a distinguished external

---

Reflections on the Social and Economic Organisation of Connemara', 15 (1936–7), pp. 31–46; 'Unemployment: Broadcast Discussion', 16 (1939–40), pp. 94–102; 'Symposium on the Report of the Commission on Emigration and Other Population Problems', 19 (1955–6), pp. 117–20.

104 Smiddy was in fact the chairman of the Commission of Inquiry on Agriculture (1939). For a brief profile of Smiddy's career, see Ronan Fanning, 'Economists and Government: Ireland 1922–52', in Murphy (ed.), *Economists and the Irish Economy*, pp. 143–4.

105 Ó Buachalla's application for the Professorship of Economics, Commerce, and Accountancy, 25 March 1952, NUI, Galway Archives.

examiner, the late Sir John Vaizey of Brunel University.[106] He also sought additional staff and one of the first appointees to the restructured Department of Economics was Michael Cuddy, who had just completed his doctoral studies in the United States, and who succeeded Ó Nualláin in 1982 as Professor of Economics.

Ó Nualláin had an outstanding academic career at both University College Dublin and Trinity College, where he had graduated with a BComm and a BA (Mod) in 1943 and 1945 respectively. In 1953 he was awarded the DEconSc for his book *Ireland: The Finances of Partition* (Dublin, 1952). He also had an extensive and respected career in the Civil Service from the 1930s to the early 1950s, serving in various branches of the Department of Industry and Commerce and, between 1947 and 1953, he served as Secretary-Accountant to the Institute for Industrial Research and Standards. Ó Nualláin was a pioneer in developing an academic interest in Ireland in development economics and the study of less developed regions. He had spent the academic year 1959–60 on a Research Fellowship at Yale pursuing the study of economic development, and later spent periods at the University of Michigan, Ann Arbor, and the University of Chicago. He was awarded Fellowships and study-tour grants by the Council of Europe and the Organisation for Economic Co-operation and Development (OECD) to undertake studies of regional development in Europe, and wrote extensively on these issues in both English and Irish at both popular and academic levels. Notwithstanding a vibrant and active research agenda, Ó Nualláin devoted enormous energy to the restructuring of both the Department of Economics and the Faculty of Commerce, for which both owe him a very considerable debt of gratitude.

The growth and changes that were to follow in the course of the 1970s and 1980s were both rapid and substantial. In 1971, James Doolan, a graduate of Galway and the Harvard Business School, was appointed to the new Professorship of Business Studies, which led to the establishment of a new academic department.[107] This was to be followed by a new Chair in Marketing, originally funded by the Bank of Ireland, and later a Chair in Accountancy and Finance, with their accompanying academic departments. The Faculty of Commerce now revolves around the four core departments of Accountancy and Finance, Economics, Management, and Marketing. It is the third largest faculty in the University with extensive undergraduate and postgraduate teaching programmes, and provides courses to five of the seven faculties of the university. When Denis Caulfield Heron, the first provider of 'commercial and mercantile education' at Queen's College Galway, proposed a Diploma in Commerce to the Queen's Colleges Commission of 1858 to meet the needs of the bank clerks in Galway, he could not have envisaged the growth in student numbers, and in the range in expertise and professionalism of his heirs and successors.

---

106 Personal discussions with Professor Ó Nualláin.
107 Professor Doolan retired in 1995 and the Professorship of Business Studies has been renamed the Professorship of Management as has the academic department.

Classics in Victorian Galway

ARTHUR KEAVENEY

The first Professor of Greek at Queen's College Galway was William E. Hearn (1826–1888; fig. 11.1).[1] Born in Co. Cavan, the son of a Church of Ireland clergyman, he had a distinguished career in Trinity College Dublin (TCD), and was first senior Moderator in Logic and Ethics. He graduated in 1847 and went on to take his MA and LLD degrees in 1863. Before coming to Galway he had already achieved fame in the wider world by winning the Cassell prize of 200 guineas offered by a London publisher, John Cassell, for the best essay on the moral, social, and political condition of Ireland. This was eventually published in London, in 1851.

Hearn did not remain long at Galway; in 1854 he resigned his chair to become one of the first four professors in the new University of Melbourne. What informed his decision I cannot say but salary may have had something to do with it. At Galway Hearn earned £150 per annum, whereas Melbourne offered £1,500 per annum.

Hearn's new chair was not a classical one but rather was in Modern History and Literature, Political Economy, and Logic. Such a title must surely entitle Hearn to a place among the many polymaths who flourished in the high Victorian age. Moreover his assumption of the Galway chair at the age of twenty-three would not have been regarded as absurdly young at that time.

At any rate, Hearn soon shed Literature and Logic and eventually settled for a Professorship in Modern History. After this he had little to do with Classics except as a substitute teacher. When the original professor of Classics died within a

---

[1] The result of an earlier trawl through the source material may be found in my paper, 'Classics in a "Godless College": Galway in the 19th Century', given at the Greenbank Colloquium: Nineteenth-Century Classical Scholarship in English, Liverpool, September 1990. See also T.P. Foley, '"A Nest of Scholars": Biographical Material on Some Early Professors at Queen's College Galway', *Journal of the Galway Archaeological and Historical Society*, 42 (1989–90), pp. 72–86. Of all our professors he has probably attracted the most interest as his fairly extensive bibliography shows: D.B. Copland, *W.E. Hearn: First Australian Economist* (Melbourne, 1935). See T.A. Boylan and T.P. Foley, 'Cairnes, Hearn and Bastable: The Contribution of Queen's College Galway to Economic Thought', in D. Ó Cearbhaill (ed.), *Galway: Town and Gown 1484–1984* (Dublin, 1984), pp. 183–205; T.A. Boylan and T.P. Foley, '"Tempering the Rawness": W.E. Hearn, Irish Political Economist and Intellectual Life in Australia', in S. Grimes and G. Ó Tuathaigh (eds), *The Irish-Australian Connection: An Caidreamh Gael-Astrálach* (Galway, 1988), pp. 99–119; T.A. Boylan and T.P. Foley, 'W.E. Hearn's Irish Writings: A Pattern Established', in P. Bull, C. McConville, and R. McLachlan (eds), *Irish Australian Studies* (Melbourne, 1990), pp. 1–16. Hearn is mentioned in *The Presidents, Vice-Presidents, and Professors of Queen's College Galway* (Dublin, 1902), p. 5, and he has articles dedicated to him in vol. i of *Modern English Biography* and vol. iv of *Australian Dictionary of Biography*.

month of reaching Australia, Hearn took his place for a time and again in 1871–2 he doubled for a colleague who was absent. As may be guessed from his obtaining the Cassell prize, Hearn had a special interest in economics and, we may add, the law (he was called to the Bar in 1853) and it is in these areas that he published extensively.[2] I am not competent to comment on Hearn's standing as an economist but it may be said that in his own time he was treated with respect and, to this day, his name is invoked by practitioners of the discipline.

After 1878 Hearn took an active interest in public life. He was a member of the Victoria Bar (admitted 1860), a QC and a member of the Legislative Council for Central Province. He also played a full part in university politics with the inevitable consequence that he made a host of enemies. Although these rose up in a swarm, Hearn beat off the lot of them to become first Dean of the Law Faculty in 1872 (after resigning his chair) and then Chancellor of the University of Melbourne (1886).[3] Later he received an honorary DLitt from the Queen's University of Ireland and an LLD from the University of Melbourne.

11.1 William E. Hearn, Professsor of the Greek Language, 1849–54

As this was an age in which every gentleman aspired to a classical education and expected in consequence to receive positions of considerable emolument, it was but natural that Galway, at its foundation, should have separate chairs of Greek and Latin. Its first Professor of Latin was William Nesbitt (1824–81; fig. 11.2).[4]

---

2 His main publications are: *Plutology or the Theory of the Effort to Satisfy Human Wants* (Melbourne, 1863; London, 1864); *Payment by Result, in Primary Education* (Melbourne, 1872); *The Aryan Household. Its Structure and Its Development* (London, 1879); *The Theory of Legal Duties and Rights* (Melbourne, 1885); *The Government of England: Its Structure and Its Development* (London, 1867; 1887).

3 The British Library catalogue lists a pamphlet which Hearn issued in reply to his foes. Unfortunately it does not seem to be available. Even before he left Galway, Hearn showed he was well able to look after himself. The *Galway Vindicator* of 6 April 1853 contained a letter from Hearn, in his capacity as Secretary of the Royal Galway Institution, complaining that in its issue of 2 April it had misreported the proceeding of a meeting addressed by Cornelius Mahony, Professor of Celtic Languages in the Queen's College. How exactly the *Galway Vindicator* had sinned is not altogether clear and, sad to record, the editor appears to have remained unmoved by Hearn's grave rebuke. See also the *Galway Mercury* and the *Galway Express* of 9 April 1853.

4 See *The Presidents and Vice-Presidents*, pp. 5–6; *Modern English Biography*, vol. ii; *Belfast Newsletter*, 28 November 1881; Keaveney, 'Classics'; Boylan and Foley, 'Cairnes', pp. 194–5; and Foley, 'Nest', pp. 77, 82–3.

11.2 William Nesbitt, Professor of the
Latin Language, 1849–54, Professor of
the Greek Language, 1854–64

11.3 Richard Blair Bagley, Professor
of Latin, 1854–69

Nesbitt was born in Enniskillen, the son of a Wesleyan minister. After a period teaching at Raphoe Royal School he entered TCD and received his BA in 1845. He was scholar, first senior moderator in Classics, and first Berkeley Gold medallist in Greek. When Hearn vacated the chair of Greek, Nesbitt took his place before moving, in 1864, to Belfast where he held the chair of Latin until his death.

One of his obituarists in the *Belfast Newsletter* describes Nesbitt as a man of wide intellectual interests, being well versed in Latin, French, and German literature. Apparently he could lay claim to being something of a Shakespeare scholar as well. He also had a deep interest in political economy and it was he who urged the famous J.E. Cairnes (1823–75) to embark upon those studies in which he was to win renown.

Like Hearn, Nesbitt came young to the job but he seems to have been in uncertain health for a number of years. He did publish some classical material in *Hermathena*, which was (and is) the learned journal of Trinity College Dublin, but the bulk of his publications deal with education and, as their titles would suggest, are really only likely today to interest the student of the controversies of the time.[5]

5   *The Irish Education Question* (London, 1860); *Irish National Education* (Dublin, 1864); *Remarks on Dr Corrigan's Letter on University Education in Ireland* (Dublin, 1866). Another pamphlet called *A Reply to the Rev. Dr McCosh on the Recent Ordinances of the Senate of the Queen's University*, was written in 1860 but appears never to have been published.

Nesbitt was an advocate of higher education for women and was one of those responsible for their being admitted to examinations in the Royal University. He helped to found the Ladies' Institute and lectured to it for several winters. He took particular interest in the development of state education. He was influential in shaping the Intermediate Education Act and acted as one of its superintendents. Under this legislation schools were to receive government grants, but the amount would depend on pupils' success at examinations set by a Board of Intermediate Examiners. J.C. Beckett's judgement on this particular enterprise is worth quoting, 'for generations to come secondary education was dominated (and some would say, bedevilled) by these "intermediate examinations" '.[6]

Out of all of this, very little trace of a personality emerges but Nesbitt seems to have been that kind of high-minded Victorian who wished to be of public service and who held a strong belief in the ability of education to improve people. He was certainly not without honour in his own time for, shortly before his death, he received an honorary DLitt from the Queen's University in recognition of his services to education.

Nesbitt's successor to the chair of Latin in 1854, Richard Blair Bagley (1822–69), was not a graduate of TCD but one of the first graduates of Queen's College Cork (fig. 11.3). A Corkman and a Protestant, he took a BA there with first-class honours in Classics and Continental Languages, winning many prizes and scholarships. In the year preceding his appointment to Galway he received an MA with first-class honours in Classics. He had spent a year or so in Cambridge prior to the opening of the Queen's Colleges, but his father had been unable to afford to keep him there. His application for the Galway chair was supported by references from some of the most eminent Classical scholars in Ireland, Professors Charles MacDouall, described by Berwick as 'if not the first, certainly among the first classical scholars and linguists in the empire'; Bunnell Lewis, 'the best classical scholar the London University had ever sent out'; and John Ryall, an 'eminent Greek scholar'.[7] In a letter to Larcom, under secretary at Dublin Castle, Robert Kane, President of Queen's College Cork, mentioned the importance for the Queen's Colleges of employing a graduate of the Queen's University:

> I think his being appointed to the Galway Chair would prove of the most important service to the Queen's Colleges System altogether. At present the great weakness of the system is that no body [sic] is identified with it. It affords no career; all our good men look to leaving the Colleges not to advancement in them. Hence the promotion of Bagley would have a very important moral effect.

He adds: 'Of course I would not meddle in an affair of Galway College but that Berwick who thinks with me perfectly, requested me'. Bagley had previously applied for a Classical post to the new University of Melbourne, but had been unsuccessful.[8]

---

6   J.C. Beckett, *The Making of Modern Ireland* (London, 1966), p. 387.
7   National Archives, Official Papers 1854/51, letter from Edward Berwick, President of QCG, to Colonel Larcom, Under Secretary, Dublin Castle, 11 September 1854.
8   Ibid., letter dated 9 September.

The poor standard of Latin and Greek amongst the students entering Queen's College Galway was an ongoing problem due to the low number of Classical schools in the west of Ireland. Bagley, however, was inclined to defend the standard of Latin with which the students arrived at College, remarking that they were not so deficient in Latin as in Greek. He did not consider that many were excluded from the College due to the requirement of Latin and insisted on its importance 'even in a mercantile or commercial education'.[9] In this he differed from other professors who felt that modern languages might be more appropriate and more useful for many of the students. His premature death in 1869, along with that of Professor Bensbach, was mentioned with sadness in the President's Report that year and it was noted that the College 'has thus been deprived of two conscientious and energetic teachers, the body of Professors of two loved and faithful colleagues'.[10]

We may at this point say something of two men who left a mark in the field of Classics, even though the chairs they held were in Mathematics and in History, English Literature, and Mental Science respectively. I refer to G.J. Allman (1824–1904) and W.J.M. Starkie (1860–1920).

Allman was born in Dublin in September 1824, the younger son of William Allman, Professor of Botany in TCD. He himself graduated from Trinity in 1844 as Senior Moderator and gold medallist in Mathematics. He was also a Bishop Law's mathematical prizeman. He received an LLB in 1853 and an LLD in 1854. In 1853 he was appointed to the chair of Mathematics at Galway, a post he held until he retired in 1893.[11]

Allman was one of the few Irish people to be attracted to the doctrine of positivism of Auguste Comte. Allman corresponded with the master and even went to Paris to sit at his feet (1852–4) but, as the *Dictionary of National Biography* puts it dryly, 'his position at Galway prevented his taking any public part in the positivist movement'.

Allman contributed some articles on mathematicians ancient and modern to the *Encyclopaedia Brittanica*. His fame, however, rests on his one and only book, which first appeared as a series of articles in *Hermathena*. This was his *History of Greek Geometry from Thales to Euclid* (London and Dublin, 1889).[12]

The President of the College between 1897 and 1899 was W.J.M. Starkie. He was obviously one of the Brazen Guts of the age because he combined this position with the Chair in History, English Literature, and Mental Science. I have been able to discover little about what he did at Galway but an obituary in *Hermathena* in 1922 delicately hints he might have been a difficult colleague. He probably owes a certain amount of his fame to the fact that he was the father of the French scholar Enid (died 1970) and Walter (1894–1976), the author of *Spanish Raggle-Taggle* (London, 1935). However he does not need to bask entirely in

---

9 *The Queen's Colleges (Ireland) Commission Report* (Dublin, 1858), pp. 257–8.
10 President's *Report*, 1868–9, p. 7.
11 He became Bursar in 1864. As we shall see, he was not the only nineteenth-century professor to combine an academic with an administrative post.
12 W.B. Stanford, 'Articles on Classical Subjects in *Hermathena*', *Hermathena*, 115 (1973), p. 7; Foley, 'Nest', pp. 79–80.

reflected glory. To this day his editions of three plays of Aristophanes – *Wasps* (London, 1897), *Acharnians* (London, 1909), and *Clouds* (London, 1911) – are still treated with respect and consulted with profit.[13]

The next inhabitant of the chair of Greek, D'Arcy Wentworth Thompson (1829–1902),[14] was probably its most fascinating (fig. 11.4). He served in that capacity from his appointment in 1864 until he died a scholar's death, dropping dead in the street one day in January 1902 as he returned home from giving his students a lecture on Thucydides.[15]

Thompson's father, John Skelton Thompson, was a ship's master who had contracted to take convicts to Australia and hence it happened that Thompson was born on 18 April 1829 in a ship off Van Diemen's Land. He grew up, however, in Maryport in Cumberland and attended school (1835–47) at Christ's Hospital in Sussex. From here he went to Cambridge attending first Trinity and then Pembroke College, where he took an MA. Two explanations are advanced for his failure to gain a fellowship there. According to one account he damned himself by appearing one Sunday in chapel in a dressing gown. According to another he failed to show the necessary proficiency in Greek and Latin verse composition.[16] I could not pretend to say for definite which story is true but I suspect the latter may be for, as we shall see, it may have helped shape his philosophy of education.

As the family was in straitened circumstances, Thompson was obliged to find work, and became, in 1852, first Classical Master at the Edinburgh Academy. Among his pupils, in the years 1861–62, was Robert Louis Stevenson. Although Stevenson later mentioned him in a poem, neither master nor pupil made much of an impression on each other. A lesser literary figure, Andrew Lang (1844–1912),

11.4 D'Arcy W. Thompson, Professor of Greek, 1864–1902

---

13   *The Presidents*, p. 9. His son mentions Galway in his autobiography but unfortunately was too young to remember anything worthwhile. See also the note on Starkie on pp. 395–6 below.

14   Apart from his own writings, listed below, the principal sources for Thompson are the biography of his son by his granddaughter Ruth D'Arcy Thompson, *D'Arcy Wentworth Thompson: The Scholar – Naturalist, 1860–1948* (Oxford, 1958), and *The Presidents*, p. 6. See also Keaveney 'Classics'.

15   This also ended his acting librarianship which he had assumed in 1877. I wonder if this is some kind of record for a temporary post? I suspect that the excellence of the NUI, Galway library holdings in nineteenth-century classical texts must be due to him.

16   Even though he won a prize for Latin verse composition in 1849.

was more impressed and called Thompson 'a friend of literature' and 'a graceful scholar'.[17]

In 1859, in Edinburgh, he married Fanny Gamgee but she died within a year of puerperal fever after the birth of their only child also named D'Arcy Wentworth Thompson. In other ways too things were beginning to go wrong for Thompson in Edinburgh. The evidence for this is found mainly in his own writings and it is an unfortunate fact that when his style does not clunk it can become somewhat allusive. Nevertheless it is possible to gather what was happening. Thompson had devised some kind of *viva voce* or direct method for teaching Greek and this was regarded with suspicion by Edinburgh purists as being dangerously progressive. It would also seem that by this time he had formed his life-long aversion to corporal punishment and this too was thought odd by those who felt a Classical education could not be acquired except at the price of periodic physical assault. Indeed it is worth remarking that many of Thompson's views were fairly progressive. He felt the contemporary method of teaching classics to be stultifying and in need of remedy. He expressed a particular hatred – possibly rooted in personal experience – for the Cambridge practice of granting fellowships to those who showed proficiency in verse composition. He also advocated introducing modern languages, mathematics, and science into the curriculum in order to produce his ideal well-rounded man. When he got to Ireland, we might add, he became an advocate of a secular system of education in order to remedy the country's ills.

So it may have been with some relief that Thompson came to Ireland in 1864. Certainly Galway never found any difficulties with his way of teaching Greek. In fact, he was soon regarded with mingled awe and affection and people pointed to him – his bulky figure clad in a long coat and his hat well pulled down on his head – as he took his daily walk accompanied by a small dog with whom he held regular colloquy. In Galway he remarried, his bride being Amy Drury, daughter of the Recorder of the Court of Chancery, Dublin. Thompson's happiness was summed up by one of his pupils, the Nationalist MP, T.P. O'Connor: 'he ate freely of the lotus flower which grows so abundantly on the banks of the Corrib'. This, of course, was meant as a compliment, pointing out how well Thompson had adapted to a strange land. However, when I first heard this remark college wit had been to work and it was held to be a sarcastic verdict on Thompson's alleged indolence and his failure to produce works of scholarship. To both of these matters I shall return in due course.

As a profound student of Greek literature, Thompson would have known well that you should 'count no man happy until he is dead'. He certainly experienced personal tragedy. By his second marriage he had four daughters and two sons but he lost both of these sons by drowning. William, who had followed his grandfather's vocation, was lost in the Pacific. His brother, John Skelton, died in a boating accident on Lough Corrib in August 1887.[18]

---

17 Ruth D'Arcy Thompson, *D'Arcy Wentworth Thompson*, p. 5.
18 There is a memorial in the grounds of the Collegiate Church, dedicated to him and the two others who were also drowned in that accident, one of whom was the son of Professor Kinkead, Professor of Midwifery, 1876–1928.

There was one occasion when it looked for a time as if Thompson might lose his position because of his outspokenness. In May 1867 Thompson wrote letters to the *Scotsman*, the London *Daily News*, and (for good measure) the *Galway Vindicator*, advocating clemency for two Fenians, Burke and Doran, who had been sentenced to hang in Dublin. The inevitable then happened: an MP from Dungannon asked a question in the House of Commons the essence of which was, whether such a person should be allowed to hold a chair in a Queen's College. There then followed a lively debate in both the Irish and English newspapers. In the meantime, however, the government had moved and the Lords Justices asked Edward Berwick, the President of QCG, to provide an explanation for his colleague's actions. By this time Thompson was beginning to feel rather uncomfortable and Berwick was able to bring home to him the seriousness of the position. Thompson then wrote a letter which Berwick submitted to the government and received a reply from the lord lieutenant, Lord Naas, declaring the matter closed.[19] Angry letters to the press form only a fraction of D'Arcy Thompson's published output. His work could be categorised into textbooks, nursery rhymes, translations, and essays and lectures.

The textbooks are principally of interest to us in that they illustrate, in a concrete fashion, the development of D'Arcy Thompson's teaching methods. His *Latin Grammar for Elementary Classes* (Edinburgh, 1857) is a conventional textbook which deals with grammar in the descriptive manner usual then, and now. *Scalae Novae or a Ladder to Latin* (London, 1866), written, so Thompson himself tells us, during a rainy holiday in Connemara, is altogether different. Here Thompson attempts to apply to Latin the *viva voce* methods he used to teach Greek and the book itself is designed to be used for any course which teaches Latin in this way. The nursery rhymes were first written for D'Arcy Thompson jun. Although the original audience is unlikely to have been very critical, it has to be said that on the whole these rhymes read rather awkwardly and the chief charm of the books is, I think, the illustrations by the talented Charles Bennett (1829–67).[20] The translations from Greek are equally uninspiring. The occasional felicitous rendition is to be found but the overall impression is wooden.[21]

D'Arcy Thompson was, at one time, in much demand as a public speaker and the topics he covered ranged over literature, history, education, and philanthropy.[22]

---

19 The detailed study of this episode by T.P. Foley, 'D'Arcy Wentworth Thompson: Classical Scholar and Fenian Sympathiser', *Journal of the Galway Archaeological and History Society*, 45 (1993), pp. 90–121, also contains a great deal of information on other aspects of Thompson's career.
20 *Nursery Nonsense, or, Rhymes without Reason* (London, 1864) and *Fun and Earnest, or, Rhymes with Reason* (London, 1865). A third volume, *Rhymes Witty and Whymsical* (Edinburgh, 1865) was cancelled before publication.
21 *Ancient Leaves or Translations and Paraphrases from Poets of Greece and Rome* (Edinburgh, 1862) and *Sales Attici or the Maxims Witty and Wise of the Athenian Drama*, collected, arranged and paraphrased (Edinburgh, 1867).
22 *English Oration on the Benefits of the Royal Hospitals Delivered in the Great Hall of Christ's Hospital on St Matthew's Day 1848* (London, 1848); *Day Dreams of a Schoolmaster* (Edinburgh, 1864); 'On History and Progress', in *The Afternoon Lectures on English Literature Delivered in the Theatre of the Museum of Industry, St Stephen's Green, May and June, 1865*, 3rd series (London and Dublin,

Reading these productions today is, however, a rather painful experience. The style, it has to be said, is often leaden and the humour almost invariably heavy-handed. As I read them, there were times when I wished he had spent a little more time in the company of his pupil Stevenson, and here we hit a paradox or contradiction. The universal testimony of his time is that D'Arcy Thompson was a powerful and attractive speaker. Whether he chose to deploy his talents – and we do know he had a most melodious voice – in the classroom or on the public platform he was able to keep his audience enthralled. The only conclusion is that Thompson was a consummate performer and could, at will, hold his hearers spellbound whether in college or further afield. Indeed, I like to think of him as a kind of Magus, who, master of his art, could set dross before those who came to listen and persuade them it was spun gold.

The list of D'Arcy Thompson's publications is a long one indeed but there is little or nothing in it which could be described as scholarly. He cannot match the output of TCD scholars at this time, let alone those in Germany or England. We could best describe his work as *belles lettres* and he himself would be the first to agree since he made no secret of his distaste for exact scholarship. He tells us he once started to write a commentary on a book of Homer but desisted after a couple of months and burnt what he had written. He did give his son D'Arcy Thompson jun. some help with a translation of Aristotle's *Historia Animalium* but it is a fact that when classicists speak now of D'Arcy Thompson it is this son they mean, whose glossaries of Greek birds and fish have not been superseded to this day.

Yet, for all their faults, D'Arcy Thompson's essays must engage the historian's attention. In the first place, he affords us a valuable glimpse of the nineteenth-century professor at work.[23] On arriving in Galway, Thompson discovered that all his pupils were attending classes in mathematics, French, German, and English. Some of the more advanced also attended, over a two-year period, lectures in logic, metaphysics, natural history, law, and political economy.[24] This left only three hours a week for Greek and Thompson soon found there was another

---

1866); 'History and Philosophy of Story Telling', in *The Afternoon Lectures on English Literature Delivered in the Theatre of the Museum of Industry, St Stephen's Green, 1866* (London and Dublin, 1867); *Wayside Thoughts of an Asophophilosopher* (Edinburgh, 1864); *Wayside Thoughts: Being a Series of Desultory Essays on Education* (New York, 1868); 'The End of the World', originally delivered in Black's Assembly Rooms, was published in the *Galway Vindicator*, 24 March 1866, and reissued as a pamphlet by Philip O'Gorman in 1945; 'What Are the Best Means for Improving the Status of Teachers, and for Securing for the Public Sufficient Guarantees for the Efficiency of Their Teaching', in *Transactions of the National Association for the Promotion of Social Science*, 1867, pp. 326–37. 'Galway: Or the City of the Tribes', in *Macmillan's Magazine*, 12 (1865), pp. 411–19.

23 Further glimpses are to be found in the reports of two royal commissions which I have freely drawn on in preparing this paper, *Queen's College (Ireland) Commission: Reports*. Both were published in Dublin, the first in 1858, the second in 1885. One should also consult T.P. O'Connor, *Memoirs of an Old Parliamentarian* (London, 1929), vol. i, especially pp. 20, 25–6; vol. ii, p. 98 for a student's view.

24 In fact it was even more difficult than that. As Nesbitt told the Royal Commission of 1858 (pp. 251–6), a student had to pass in fourteen subjects in all in order to gain a BA in Galway, while the number in Trinity was six. There was no such thing as a BSc and so the curriculum embraced both the humanities and the natural sciences.

complication. Many of his students knew no Greek when they came up to university. Such a lamentable state of affairs is, of course, virtually the norm today but in those times it was highly unusual. Nothing daunted, Thompson set to work with his *viva voce* methods and laid heavy emphasis on translation. It is worth adding in parentheses, perhaps, that a special care over translation has always been a feature of classics at Galway. My generation is unlikely to forget Professor Margaret Heavey assuring us that all translators are traitors and then embarking on a search for the *mot juste*. Unique – so far as I know – to Galway was the translation criticism question set in Finals, in our time. A slab of Greek or Latin was printed along with three or four different translations and the student was invited to sit in judgement on them.

But to return to Thompson. He declared that after two years in his hands his pupils were reasonably competent in Greek. Once elementary grammar had been mastered, Plato's *Apology* was read together with a book of Homer. After this the student was ready to tackle Demosthenes' *De Corona*. On the whole this is a pretty ambitious programme. Homeric dialect can be daunting and the convoluted periods of Demosthenes often baffle. His pupils, however, do not seem to have been put off. In later years they remembered him with affection and sometimes awe.

D'Arcy Thompson also had something to say about how TCD regarded the new Queen's Colleges:

> It is ill with the stream when the water at the spring is bitter. A very few years ago the London University was almost invariably mentioned with epithets of a foolish and ungenerous contempt by members of the more ancient foundations. The Ancient College of Dublin has, until a very recent date, exhibited a jealousy, unworthy of herself, towards the recently-founded Queen's Colleges. Indeed on one occasion some six professors of the latter were treated with a marked rudeness at her hall table, simply and obviously on account of the new connection they had formed; simply and obviously so, as every one of them had been a highly distinguished Alumnus of the old foolishly jealous Alma Mater.

Probably the best reason we have for reading these essays is that we meet D'Arcy Thompson himself, for he makes no effort at concealment. J.E. Cairnes may have found his conversation 'disturbing' but the modern reader will find himself in the presence of a most attractive character. On occasion he may be overly sentimental, but that is no more than the expression of a warm and kindly nature. Generous is another word which readily springs to mind, as does noble, and high-minded. In sum, D'Arcy Thompson seems to have been a thoroughly decent person. I have alluded earlier to Thompson's alleged indolence but there is nothing to support the charge, no evidence to suggest he was in any way neglectful of his pupils. In fact, the warmth of their admiration argues otherwise. His distaste for pure scholarship we have discussed, but perhaps this alone does not explain his failure to publish anything after the Fenian debacle. It may very well be, as some have suggested, that this experience totally unnerved him, for paranoia is the occupational illness of the academic. Ultimately, however, we shall only understand D'Arcy Thompson if we grasp that all his life he remained a schoolmaster at heart. When he left Edinburgh to come to Galway he found that, in many ways, his duties had not changed and he does not seem to have been greatly disturbed by this. We may measure the concern he had for the teaching of the young when he tells us he even offered to help the Jesuits teach their charges if they would be happy to have a heretic like himself near them. The answer, if there was any, is not recorded.

Now we return to the Latin chair and to the man, Thomas Maguire (1831–89), who held it between 1869 and 1880.[25] Like D'Arcy Thompson he was to be involved in political controversy but, unlike Thompson, he was a scholar of some distinction. His articles in *Hermathena* ranged over Greek philosophy, metrics, and grammar, as well as Latin and Greek authors. His more substantial work was in ancient and modern philosophy, and also textual criticism.[26] The list below does not exhaust Maguire's energies or the list of his publications. We may note, first of all, that he contributed to *Kottabos*. This was a magazine for TCD men when they were in an unbuttoned mood and wished to display their skill in the now almost forgotten arts of Latin and Greek verse composition.[27] Nor is that all. Maguire's philosophical bent led him into the realms of theological speculation and thus, sometimes, to religious controversy. In 1889 he produced a treatise on 'The Existence of Purgatory' for the *Weekly Freeman* which he afterwards suppressed. The theme however, seems to have exercised a fascination for him for we find that prior to this he had reviewed the Revd Mr Barlow's *Eternal Punishment* for the *Christian Examiner*.[28] In 1888 he gave the world *Proteus: A Layman's Reply to Sir James Stephen on Mr Mivart's Modern Catholicism* published in Dublin.

Thomas Maguire was born in Dublin on 24 January 1831. His father was a merchant who afterwards emigrated to Mauritius to become a stipendiary

---

25 For Maguire, consult Keaveney, 'Classics' and the obituary in the *Classical Review* for 1889 by Philip Sandford. His periodical publications are listed by R.G. Hayes, *Sources for the History of Irish Civilisation: Articles in Irish Periodicals* (Boston, 1970), vol. iii, p. 572. T.P. Foley's 'Thomas Maguire and the Parnell Forgeries', *Journal of the Galway Archaeological and Historical Society*, 46 (1994), pp. 173–96 covers far more than the title would suggest.

26 In chronological order, his publications included: *An Essay on the Platonic Idea* (London and Dublin, 1866); *Notes on the Agamemnon of Aeschylus: Chiefly in Defence of the MSS* (London and Dublin, 1868); *The External Worlds of Sir William Hamilton and Dr. Thomas Brown: A Paper Read before the Dublin University Philosophical Society 1857* (Dublin, 1868); *Essays on the Platonic Ethics* (London and Dublin, 1870); *The Parmenides of Plato* (ed.), (Dublin and London, 1882); *The Will in Reference to Dr. Maudsley's 'Body and Will': An Opening Lecture, Michaelmas Term, 1883* (Dublin, 1883); *Agnosticism: Herbert Spencer and Frederic Harrison. A Lecture Delivered in Michaelmas Term, 1884* (Dublin, 1884); *Lectures on Philosophy: First Series* (London, 1885) (there was no second series); *Mr Balfour on Kant and Transcendentalism: A Lecture Delivered in Michaelmas Term, 1888* (Dublin, 1889).

27 When they were not busy inventing philosophy the Greeks liked to play a game called kottabos which had its origins in Sicily. Essentially it was a kind of distant ancestor of darts. A saucer or other object was placed in the middle of the floor and diners would try and hit it by flicking the lees of their wine. The widespread popularity of this witless exercise prompts the reflection that at least some of the ancient Greeks are a bit overrated but, at any rate, the adoption of the name for a light-hearted magazine now becomes explicable.

28 This, along with reviews of J.S. Mill's *Utilitarianism* and *Hamilton* which had appeared in the *Examiner* between 1863 and 1864, was issued later in book form (Dublin, 1867).

magistrate. The younger Maguire joined him there in 1846 but returned in 1851 and entered TCD. He took a BA in 1855 and became a Scholar in the same year.[29] In 1861 he obtained a Law studentship at Lincoln's Inn and in the following year was called to the English Bar. He returned to Ireland in 1866 to be made an LLD of Dublin University. From the time of his return until his appointment at Galway he took private pupils at TCD. The reasons for this latter circumstance will be explained shortly.

Contemporary estimates of Maguire's character differ but, in view of how he ended his days, those who branded him as 'guileless' may not be too wide of the mark. In weighing him up we must ever remember that his political views, which we shall deal with in due course, were of a sort to make him a host of enemies and they, being chiefly Irish, would not, of course, use one good word where they might use a dozen bad. However, bearing these cautionary remarks in mind, I still think it safe to believe those reports which claim he was negligent of his duties at Galway and, in fact, rather given to drink. The measure of Maguire's unhappiness may be gauged from the fact that a lot of his energies seem to have been absorbed in his treatise on the existence of Purgatory. Now, as we grow older, no doubt we all, from time to time, ponder this question if only because it is the best deal we are likely to get. In Maguire's case however, there seems to have been a more immediate stimulus. For the man who once declared that 'TCD was the only thing in Ireland Irish men need not be ashamed of', to languish in the place even D'Arcy Thompson affectionately called 'The End of the World', cannot have been a pleasant experience and will be likely to have dampened the spirits.[30] The validity of this hypothesis is underlined, I believe, by the fact that when TCD summoned, Maguire answered the call with alacrity and apparently, once more, became a model of industry.

In the period 1866–9 Maguire could only take private pupils at TCD because Catholics were not allowed to hold scholarships or fellowships. In 1873 this disability was removed by what is known as 'Fawcett's Act', and Maguire had the distinction, in 1880, of being the first Catholic to be elected to a fellowship.[31] He became a lecturer in Greek and Latin composition until 1882 when he became Professor of Moral Philosophy, a post he held until his death in 1889.

For all his scholarly attainments and love of religious controversy, Maguire, I suspect, would, like many of our nineteenth-century professors, be a half-forgotten figure were it not for his political views, or to be pedantic about it, where those views ultimately led him, conferring an undying, if slightly dubious fame upon him. Maguire was what was known at the time as a 'Castle Catholic' or, as his *Times* obituarist flatly put it, 'a zealous and uncompromising Unionist'. When he first formed these views I cannot pretend to say, but they certainly would seem to inform his pamphlet of 1869, *The Maynooth Resolutions Considered: On the*

---

29 He won the Wray prize in metaphysics in 1853 and the Berkeley medal in Greek literature and composition in 1857.
30 A lot of students, it may be said, seem to have shared this attitude. It was hard to attract people to Galway when a place like Belfast was so much better equipped with places of amusement.
31 He produced a pamphlet, *Professor Fawcett's Bill Considered* (Dublin, 1873).

Ecclesiastical Control of University Education in Ireland which, despite its admirable opposition to clerical involvement in politics and education, was also the result of Maguire's own experience. He had, it would seem, neither forgiven nor forgotten having been twice an unsuccessful candidate for the chair of Greek in the Catholic University.[32]

In 1886 Maguire returned to the charge. Worried, I suspect, by an alliance between Parnell and Gladstone which had then been forged, he fired off in that one year three pamphlets with self-explanatory titles: *Reasons why Britons Should Oppose Home Rule*, *The Effects of Home Rule on the Higher Education*, and *England's Duty to Ireland as Plain to a Loyal Irish Roman Catholic*. These, as may be expected, are vehemently opposed to Home Rule and virulently anti-Parnellite. They are also vigorous, well-written pieces, shot through from time to time with a mordant and sarcastic wit. Perhaps one should blush to say this, but if it can sometimes be a trial to read the kindly D'Arcy Thompson, there is a great deal of low enjoyment to be derived from the more pugnacious Maguire.[33]

Ultimately, it was to be his hatred of Parnell, which caused Maguire to overreach himself. On 18 April 1887 the *Times* published what purported to be letters of Parnell's which allegedly showed him to be sympathetic to the Phoenix Park murders of May 1882. A Special Commission was set up to investigate the matter. It soon emerged that the letters were a forgery by a journalist, Richard Pigott, who bolted for the Continent and committed suicide on 1 March in Madrid. By this time, however, certain other embarrassing details had come to light. The man who passed the letters to the *Times*, Edward Caulfield Houston of the Irish Loyal and Patriotic Union – a unionist organisation – testified that when he had gone to Paris to buy the letters from Pigott, he had not only been accompanied by Maguire, but the professor had lent him £850 to complete the transaction. Maguire himself was by now in London waiting to testify but on the night of 25 February (the very day Pigott fled) he died in his lodgings without ever taking the stand.

His death left three mysteries unsolved but, as it happens, we can offer reasonably certain solutions to two of them. Despite claims at the time to the contrary, Maguire's death was from natural causes. Rumours of suicide or murder seem to have rested on nothing more than the coincidence of Pigott's death shortly after. Again, we may say with some confidence that, to his dying day, Maguire believed the letters to be genuine even if we have to concede that his judgement was partially warped by his fierce hatred of Parnell.

What is less easy to account for is where he got the money to pay for the letters. If we accept the disclaimer of the Irish Loyal and Patriotic Union that they had never given any money to Maguire or Houston for the letters, then we have to assume that the money came from Maguire himself. But we must then reckon with

---

32 D'Arcy Thompson had also beaten him to the Greek chair in Galway.
33 Of course not everybody at the time found these pamphlets so funny. Among those who replied was an Englishman resident in Ireland, called James Pearse, who issued *A Reply to 'England's Duty to Ireland' as It Appears to an Englishman*. James was the father of the rather better known Patrick Pearse.

the fact that £850 was rather a large sum and academics, then as now, were not particularly well paid. Maguire was not married but he had two spinster sisters to support on a professorial salary. Houston claimed that Maguire's bank account contained £900 in 1886 before he received his loan. The problem is, where did that money come from? Did somebody else pay it in, or was it the result of prudent housekeeping by Maguire?

When Maguire departed for Dublin in 1880, the chair of Latin at Galway was given to John Fletcher Davies (1831–89; fig. 11.5).[34] Like so many professors of this time, Davies was a graduate of TCD. He became a scholar in 1858 and a gold medallist in Classics in 1859, the year he took his BA. He received an MA in 1869 and subsequently an honorary DLitt of the Queen's University and became a Fellow of the Royal University. Between 1860 and 1878 he was Classical Master at Kingston School where (and surely this evokes the time and the place) he had, among other duties, charge of the India Civil Service Class.[35] He had also taught at Portora and Stonyhurst College as well as Downside.

Davies' work can be divided into three categories: his contributions to *Hermathena*, to *Kottabos*, and his critical edition of the *Oresteia*. Whatever their scholarly value, what strikes the reader most forcibly about some of the contributions to *Hermathena* is their somewhat bizarre style. Long ago when writing an article about this journal, W.B. Stanford could not resist quoting a specimen and I propose to follow him:

> ... ye lucifer matches, ye sulphurless, nonphosphorous, only – igniting-on-the-box and non pareil Tandstickor, useful but not beauteous beings, shall I keep you, or Homer? I shall miss you, to be sure, but how much more miss Homer! Ye must go and the greater two-headed continent that Columbus discovered shall go along with you to swell the precious pile.

He is saying – I think – that the safety match is a wonderful thing in its way and so is America but, if he had to choose between these two great modern discoveries and Homer, he would settle for Homer. As Stanford aptly remarked this looked like something out of Lever or Peacock rather than a serious academic discussion. It comes from the first volume of *Hermathena* and is in an article dealing with the meaning of certain words in Homer. It is perhaps superfluous to add that Davies takes rather a long time in coming to the point. His other contributions to *Hermathena* dealt with Cicero and the Greek tragedians. Davies' contributions to *Kottabos* were of such an order as to win him a mention in O'Donoghue's *The Poets of Ireland* (London, 1892–3).[36] Lest there should be any rush to rescue from oblivion the works of a forgotten genius, it should perhaps be stated that O'Donoghue listed virtually everybody in Ireland who had ever attempted verse composition. Throughout his life Davies worked on his edition of the *Oresteia*. A

---

34 For Davies, see *The Presidents*, pp. 7–8; *Modern English Biography*, vol. v; Hayes, *Sources*, vol. ii, p. 29; Stanford, 'Articles'; and Keaveney, 'Classics'.
35 He himself described this position as a 'grinder'.
36 D.J. O'Donoghue, *The Poets of Ireland* (London, 1892–3), pt i, p. 52.

11.5 John Fletcher Davies, Professor of Latin, 1880–9

11.6 Philip Sandford, Professor of Latin, 1890–1903

critical edition of the *Choephorae* (with the scholia or ancient commentaries) was issued in London in 1862. The *Agamemnon* followed in 1868 and *Eumenides* in 1885, both published in London.

Like D'Arcy Thompson, John Fletcher Davies has left us a glimpse of himself at work in the classroom. Indeed, like Thompson, he found many of his freshmen – even those awarded gold medals – were ill equipped for university. So he remedied the deficiency with classes in Latin grammar. Armed only with blackboard and chalk he expounded the mysteries and, from the very start, set his pupils exercises in composition. Davies interpreted his brief to teach Roman history as being fulfilled by providing a commentary on whatever text he happened to be studying with his students. There is a suspicion that he was ahead of his time in that he seems to have favoured what we would call continuous assessment. On one occasion he admitted to having passed a student in his subject even though he had failed the examination. The justification Davies offered was that the candidate had performed well all year and the examination result was obviously some kind of aberration which did not reveal his true abilities.[37]

Before leaving Davies I propose to draw attention to what seems to be a certain quirk in his character. Most scholars, I suspect, view with distaste the purely mechanical aspect of their craft. They regard the job of preparing a work for the

37 *Queen's Colleges (Ireland) Commission Report*, 1885, evidence 5613.

publishers with its proof-reading, index-compiling, and so on as drudgery. Necessary but still drudgery. Textual critics however are a breed apart who seem to relish such things. Davies, as we saw, was a textual critic and he appears to have gone out of his way to undertake this kind of task. We happen to know that he helped Allman prepare his book for the press and Maguire thanked him in the preface for reading the proofs of his *Parmenides*.

Perhaps his greatest achievement though, was seeing Henry's *Aeneidea* through the press. This book was written by a Dublin doctor James Henry (1798–1876) who abandoned medicine to wander, mostly on foot, throughout Europe. Undeterred by the deaths of both his wife and daughter on the road he sought out manuscripts and editions of Vergil which he eventually brought back to Dublin where he committed the fruits of his research to paper. Unfortunately he died before completing the work and hence Davies' intervention. 'Diffuse' is a word often applied to the *Aeneidea* and it is difficult to escape the conclusion that in Davies it had a sympathetic editor.

In succession to Davies, Philip Sandford (died 1903) became Professor in 1889 (fig. 11.6).[38] He was born in Clonmel, the son of a Church of Ireland clergyman. He had a brilliant academic career at TCD, where he distinguished himself in classics, English, and metaphysics and won numerous prizes, distinctions, and scholarships. After that he spent some time in South Africa and was headmaster of the High School in Durban. In 1886 he became a Fellow of TCD and was later a member of the Senate of the University of Dublin and a Fellow of the Royal University.

Sandford contributed papers on Latin authors, both prose and verse, to *Hermathena* and the *Classical Review*. He also edited a number of school editions of the Classics. For the 'Intermediate Education Series' he edited Homer's *Iliad*, 22 and 24 (Dublin, 1879 and 1880) and Books 1 and 2 of Xenophon's *Hellenica* (Dublin, 1886). These are slight works which contain brief introductions and a minimum of notes. The author says he worked in haste and the skimpy nature of the editorial matter seems to be due to the fact that they were prepared for Trinity undergraduates.[39]

Rather more ambitious in scope are Sandford's editions of Vergil's *Aeneid*, Books 2 and 3 which were published (London, 1900 and 1901) in Blackie's 'Illustrated Latin Series'. These are typical school books of the time. Lavishly illustrated and soundly annotated, they may still be consulted with profit. One interesting feature of the notes is the constant references to other literatures. They also include – and here again the Galway concern with elegant translation can be seen – appendices where translations of part of the text by various hands are to be

---

38 See *The Presidents*, p. 8; *QCG*, no. 3, 1 (1903), p. 89 and no. 1, 2 (1903), pp. 5–8, 35; and Keaveney, 'Classics'.
39 This prompts the reflection that it would seem, in what is usually described as the golden age of Greek at Trinity, men who had matriculated there had scarcely reached a standard to surpass D'Arcy Thompson's neophytes. Lest however I be accused of partisan zeal, I should add that Professor Nesbitt was of the opinion that the standard of Greek at Galway was so low as to allow a man to gain the BA in Greek even though he had only commenced the subject at university. Which, perhaps, puts a certain gloss on D'Arcy Thompson's activities.

found. Other appendices illustrate the way in which other writers, both classical and modern, handled the themes treated by Vergil.

If we believe his obituarists, Sandford was a lively and athletic man. He had once been tennis champion of Natal and, putting his expertise to good use, he also became tennis champion of the College. He was also a keen member of the Debating Society and a regular attender at its Saturday night meetings. Like many others who indulge in violent exercise, Sandford became an easy prey to disease and died rather suddenly of rheumatic fever in 1903.

Charles Exon (died 1966) had won a gold medal, held a senior moderatorship and made a considerable name for himself as a scholar in TCD before becoming Professor of Latin at Galway in 1903, in succession to Sandford. His chief interests lay in the field of Latin grammar, philology, and metrics. Between 1901 and 1926 he published extensively in *Hermathena*.[40] In the classical world today Exon is chiefly remembered for the metrical law he discovered and which is named after him, 'Exon's Law of Syncope'. In Galway he is remembered for a different reason. He resigned his chair in 1916 on the grounds of ill-health and retired to Brighton, presumably to die. He continued, however, to draw his pension up until 1966.[41]

With the departure of Exon the chairs of Greek and Latin were amalgamated. Paucity of Greek students to which reference is often made in our sources, would seem to be the simple explanation for this move.[42] The first Professor of Classics was Thompson's successor in the chair of Greek, R.K. McElderry (died 1949).[43]

As professors of history are never tired of assuring their pupils, any stopping point in a historical narrative is, of its very nature, arbitrary, since some men live beyond it and events continue to develop after it. Not everybody who knew Louis XIV died with him. On the other hand, they usually go on to assure their charges that the cut-off point they personally have chosen is less arbitrary than most others as there are clear differences between what went before and what was to come after. The France of the Regent is not the France of Louis XIV.

I propose to invoke this formula which has been honoured by time and reputation if nothing else. With hindsight we can see that by now the Irish Free State is but a few years away. The Ireland of Queen Victoria is not the Ireland of

---

40 One or two titles will give an idea of the kind of thing which evidently fascinated him: 'The Contracted Cases of Deus', *Hermathena*, 14 (1907), pp. 338–59; 'The Latin Genitive in-ai', *Hermathena*, 13 (1905), pp. 955–74.
41 See Keaveney, 'Classics'.
42 We should remember that even in D'Arcy Thompson's day there had been problems and cold statistics (kindly supplied by T.P. Foley) bear out our suspicions. Between 1849 and 1884 there is roughly parity between the two languages, about thirty students each. However after 1884, through to 1900, the picture changes radically. Latin numbers still hold steady at around thirty, but Greek now rarely has more than twenty and there are some particularly bad years such as 1891, when there are only fourteen students, and 1899 when numbers sink to twelve.
43 He was an authority on the Flavians and Roman Spain. On a more convivial note he seems to have indulged in the Edwardian practice of singing after dinner to entertain the guests at college functions. In 1924 he moved to Belfast to take up the Chair of Greek at the Queen's University. See *QCG*, 1 (1902), 2 (1904), 3 (1905), and 5 (1906); The *Times*, 14 July 1949.

de Valera. D'Arcy Thompson is plainly a very different figure from Professor Thomas Fahy (1887–1973).[44] Thompson, like the others we have described, is plainly an individual but he also recognisably belongs to a definite period in history. For the rest, I can only hope for myself that I have been able to do justice to those classicists who laboured in a college which now seems so far away and so long ago.[45]

---

[44] Professor of Classics between 1927 and 1957.
[45] I should like to thank Professor Tadhg Foley for asking me to try.

Irish: A Difficult Birth

BREANDÁN Ó MADAGÁIN

When the Queen's Colleges were established, a professorship in 'the Celtic Languages' was included among the chairs to be set up in each College.[1] The term Celtic here is misleading as it conjures up what we understand today by Celtic Studies, which as an independent academic discipline was as yet unborn in 1845. The foundation stone of modern Celtic Studies was the monumental *Grammatica Celtica*, by Johann Caspar Zeuss, published in two volumes in Leipzig in 1853. The first Professorship of Celtic was that at the University of Oxford (and attached to Jesus College), not established until 1876, with John Rhys as the first incumbent. The first chair in Scotland was established in Edinburgh in 1882, and the second in Glasgow as late as 1956, although Celtic was regularly taught there since it was introduced by the ubiquitous Kuno Meyer in 1903. In Germany, to whom we owe so great a debt, the first ordinary professorship of Celtic was that established in Berlin in 1901, with Heinrich Zimmer as first professor, to be followed by Kuno Meyer. Prior to that, the Celtic languages were studied by individual scholars under the aegis of comparative philology. The two venerable journals of Celtic Studies also commenced publication in the later decades of the nineteenth century: the *Revue Celtique*, established in 1870 with D'Arbois de Jubainville as editor, and the *Zeitschrift für Celtische Philologie*, which had its first issue in 1896, edited by Kuno Meyer and Ludwig Stern. The word Celtic in the titles of the professorships established in the original Queen's Colleges was simply a deliberate euphemism for Irish, a word politically incorrect and unacceptable to the government. They felt compelled to use the same euphemism when they eventually conceded a place to Irish in the Intermediate Education (Ireland) Act of 1878; again they called it Celtic, despite the recommendation of the O'Conor Don.

In the half-century or so before the establishment of the Queen's Colleges, largely through the antiquarian bent of the Romantic movement, some of the more enlightened of the Anglo-Irish were beginning to discover that Ireland had a past and a culture. General Charles Vallancey began collecting Irish manuscripts, at the instigation of Edmund Burke.[2] In 1789 Charlotte Brooke published her *Reliques of*

---

[1] This chapter is the text of a lecture delivered (in Irish) in October 1995 to the annual conference, Litríocht agus Cultúr na Gaeilge, Áras na Gaeilge, UCG, commemorating the 150th anniversary of the establishing act of parliament for the Queen's Colleges.

[2] Caerwyn Williams, *Traidisiún Liteartha na nGael* (Dublin, 1979), p. 316. For Burke's Gaelic background and interest see Conor Cruise O'Brien, *The Great Melody* (London, 1992), pp. 19–23 *passim*.

Irish Poetry with originals and translations, the first ever of its kind. Edward Bunting published his three collections of *Ancient Irish Music*, between 1796 and 1840, and Tom Moore's *Irish Melodies*, issued in ten folio instalments from 1808 to 1834, popularised Irish music in Anglo-Irish and English drawing-rooms. In 1808 the Revd William Neilson, a Presbyterian, published *An Introduction to the Irish Language*. Native Irish scholars began to emerge who would combine their own inherited tradition with the new learning. The new awakening among the ascendancy was largely responsible for providing the funding for publication. These scholars included such men as Eugene O'Curry, John O'Donovan, John O'Daly, and James Hardiman who as early as 1831, nearly twenty years before his appointment as librarian in Queen's College Galway, published, in London, the two large volumes of his *Irish Minstrelsy or Bardic Remains of Ireland*, originals and translations. And it was Hardiman who provided the twenty-one year old O'Donovan with an education in Irish manuscripts by employing him as a copyist in his house on Taylor's Hill from 1827 to 1830.[3]

This new awakening was reflected and fostered by new societies. The Royal Irish Academy was founded in 1785, with people like General Vallancey and Charles O'Conor of Belanagare as members. The Gaelic Society of Dublin was established in 1807 and the Iberno-Celtic Society in 1818 but both were short-lived. Perhaps most pertinent to our subject was the Irish Archaeological Society, established in 1840 by the Revd James Henthorn Todd, which employed O'Donovan to edit a series of Irish texts, which he later continued with the Celtic Society, founded in 1847. The Irish Archaeological Society sought its membership from the ranks of 'Noblemen and Gentlemen'.[4] The list of members for 1843 is quite revealing. The Patron was no less a personage than His Royal Highness Prince Albert. The President was the Duke of Leinster. The members included the lord lieutenant (Earl de Grey), a host of other establishment dignitaries of the highest rank, as well as a number of scholars such as Hardiman, George Petrie, and Todd, all three council members, and O'Donovan.

It is no surprise that some of the prominent members of this society would be involved in the establishment of the professorships of Celtic in the new Colleges. Furthermore it is likely that it was some of its high-ranking members who overcame the reluctance of the Government to establish professorships of Irish. It may well be significant that when the chair of Celtic in Galway became vacant in 1854 and Edward Berwick, then President of the College, proposed to the government that it be left unfilled, its retention was largely due to the influence of Thomas Larcom, one of the original Council members of the Irish Archaeological Society, by then under-secretary and acting in this matter against the recommendation of his senior civil servants.[5] It may be said that the attitude of the latter,

---

3 In 1852, while O'Donovan was Professor of Celtic Languages in Queen's College Belfast, he applied unsuccessfully for the Vice-Presidency of QCG. See Patricia Boyne, *John O'Donovan* (Kilkenny, 1987), p. 94.

4 Report of Irish Archaeological Society for year ending 27 June 1843, p. 18, printed (with list of members, etc.) with John O'Donovan, *The Tribes and Customs of Hy-Many*, published by the Society in Dublin in 1843.

5 'Larcom, taking an Archaeological [*sic*] view of the question, is all for maintaining the Celtic

in contrast to Larcom's, was in keeping with the age-old and deep-seated prejudice of the government and establishment against the Irish language. The language was allowed no recognition in the schools until many years later, neither as a school subject nor as a medium of instruction, even in Irish-speaking districts (nearly half the entire population in 1845 being Irish speakers).[6] Trinity College Dublin, the only Irish university before the Queen's Colleges, had only very recently (1838) allowed the establishment of an Irish chair in the College, with great reluctance and after many years of agitation, and then only by public subscription without any cost to the College, and without any academic aim but for the service-teaching of some students for the Church of Ireland ministry, or as McDowell and Webb put it, out of 'concern ... for the need to rescue the Connaught peasantry from the bonds of Popish superstition'.[7] Likewise in the Royal College of Maynooth, which did not yet have university status, the Irish language was taught at that period for purely practical purposes such as preaching.

That Her Majesty's Government should establish professorships of Irish *(de facto)* in the new Queen's Colleges was, then, quite a remarkable development. That it was not to be expected was emphasised at the time by William Smith O'Brien, writing to C.M. Sweeney on 1 July 1845: 'Any proposal to establish a professorship of Irish in the new colleges would only be laughed to scorn in the house of commons'.[8] For some time now scholars have been speculating on how such an unlikely event came about. I believe that the credit for the initiative can safely be attributed to Fr Joseph W. Kirwan, first President of Queen's College Galway. The general situation is outlined in an *aide memoir* preserved among the papers of Thomas Larcom in the National Library of Ireland:

Chair' – Germans to Young (both of them against), 7 October 1854, National Library of Ireland (NLI), MS 7667, item 44. Larcom had a close involvement with the Queen's Colleges scheme from the beginning. He had served as one of the commissioners for taking evidence regarding the choice of location of the Queen's College in Ulster, and in 1851 was nominated a member of the Senate of the Queen's University by the Royal Charter of that year. His interest in Irish survived his early unsuccessful efforts to learn the language from John O'Donovan and, in 1852, he was appointed one of the commissioners for directing the transcription and translation of the Ancient Laws of Ireland. See Cyril M. Cawley, 'Thomas Larcom, Irish Under-Secretary, 1853–1868', MA thesis, UCG, 1980, pp. 10, 13, 130–2. Prince Albert also took a particular interest in the university question – see T.W. Moody and J.C. Beckett, *Queen's Belfast, 1845–1949 The History of a University*, 2 vols (London, 1959), vol. i, p. 51.

6   Donnchadh Ó Súilleabháin, *Cath na Gaeilge sa Chóras Oideachais 1893–1911* (Dublin, 1985).
7   R.B. McDowell and D.A. Webb, *Trinity College Dublin, 1592–1952: An Academic History* (Cambridge, 1982), p. 190. The first holder of the professorship (appointed 1840) was the Revd Thomas Coneys of the Clifden family of that name, who published in 1849 *Focloir Gaoidhilge-Sacs-bearla or An Irish-English Dictionary*, intended, in his own words, 'to help missionaries who needed to preach to an Irish-speaking population'. See Catherine Jennings, 'Thomas Coneys: First Professor of Irish in T.C.D.', *Connemara*, no. 1, 2 (1995), pp. 78–95.
8   Smith O'Brien to C.M. Sweeney, in Moody and Beckett, *Queen's Belfast*, vol. i, p. 51. William Smith O'Brien, MP, was a keen collector of Irish manuscripts – see B. Ó Madagáin *An Ghaeilge i Luimneach 1700–1900* (Dublin, 1974), pp. 78–81 – and he was a member of the Irish Archaeological Society who favoured Irish professorships. (National Archives, Official Papers 1845/111). My thanks to Fiona Bateman for this reference.

> Before the opening of the Colleges a Committee of the Presidents was appointed [in accordance with the law] to frame rules allocations and bye laws for the government of the Colleges. They recommended a larger number of Professors than the framers of the Act of 1845 contemplated. The recommendation was adopted and the charter amended accordingly in 1850 ... the emolument provided for the smaller number had to be divided among the greater, somewhat reducing all the salaries.[9]

There was no reference to professorships of Celtic in the original list from the government. But in the Letters Patent, published in 1850, a Professorship of Celtic Languages appeared among the extra professorships to be established in each College on the recommendation of the Board of Presidents.[10] Shortly after the Act of 1845, in January of the following year when the Board of Presidents was already at work, Father Kirwan wrote (from Dublin) to his friend James Hardiman concerning the new Colleges. His letter (preserved in the Royal Irish Academy) includes the following:

> There is another [subject] also upon which I would much desire to obtain your advice – The Colleges Act makes no provision for a Professorship of Irish – Yet knowing as I do the importance of this language, I am very anxious to have it introduced in some way into our course of General Education. I think therefore by the allocation of our funds we might by economy in other departments be enabled to fund a Supplemental professorship for Irish with a salary not under a hundred per annum with fees of pupils. His duties would be light – say two or three Lectures in the week – Do you think you could be able to procure for this small sum a man of name and talent? – for I am happy to tell you that none but such will be admitted into our Colleges in every Department.[11]

Kirwan speaks in a singularly personal voice all through this passage and makes it clear that his proposition is a personal one. Even the 'small sum' he mentioned turned out to be the parsimonious salary of £100 per annum allowed for the Professorships of Celtic in the Letters Patent later on (when £250 was allocated for the Professorship of Latin and other subjects, and £800 for the Presidency). Apart from the personal tone of Kirwan's letter to Hardiman, it is unlikely that the proposal would have come from either of the other Presidents: some years later, when Kirwan's successor, Berwick, was making a case for leaving the professorship of Celtic vacant in QCG he declared: 'I have consulted the Presidents of the Cork and Belfast Colleges on the step I am now recommending: both those Gentlemen fully concur in its propriety'.[12] Kirwan, 1796–1849, a native of Galway city, had at

---

9 NLI, MS 7667, introductory.
10 *Letters Patent for Increasing the Number of Professors in Each of the Queen's Colleges, Belfast, Cork and Galway* (HM Stationery Office, 1850).
11 Royal Irish Academy (RIA), MS 12 N 21, 330, 27 January 1846. (Letters out of place – at beginning of MS.)
12 Edward Berwick to Hon. Major Ponsonby, 26 September 1854. See longer extract below. NLI, MS 7667, no. 40.

that time been, for about twenty years, parish priest of Oughterard, then an Irish-speaking district.[13]

In the absence of Hardiman's reply we can only surmise that he offered Kirwan his own support for the idea, his opinion that there were available enough scholars to fill the posts, and, significantly, his own commitment to solicit political support, from his friends in high places, for such a recommendation. In any case the proposal was made and accepted and two years later Kirwan's concern was to find a suitable person to fill the Galway post, in anticipation of the Letters Patent as yet unpublished. Another letter from Kirwan to Hardiman, dated November 1848, offered him the Professorship of Irish [sic] – not for the first time, it seems – and urged him to accept:

> The Board of Presidents is now engaged in selecting Professors for the several Chairs. Allow me again to press on your attention the Chair of Irish for the Galway College – It will have no severe duties attached to it – only an occasional lecture which will be an amus[e]ment to yourself whilst it will be of much advantage to the youth of Ireland. The salary will be only One Hundred p[er] annum, but, I know, the remuneration is but a secondary consideration with you. Allow me to name you for that Chair in our college and thus confer an additional honour on our native Town.[14]

Hardiman declined. And Kirwan replied:

> I have received your favor of the 13th inst. in which I am sorry to see that you decline the Chair of Irish Literature – but it may be all for the better as happily there are but few applications for the Library – and I shall have much pleasure in naming you for that office (£150 p.a.) ... I am afraid you will have much more trouble than would devolve upon you in the Chair of Irish.[15]

It is quite clear what he understood by Celtic Languages in the title of the chair: Irish and Irish Literature.

Kirwan added a postscript to that letter, asking Hardiman 'to suggest some person to fill the Chair of Irish', adding, 'You know the person must be such as we would not be ashamed of – it would be well to consult your friend'. A few weeks later he reminds Hardiman of this request. It is unlikely that Hardiman was involved when a young Munsterman, Cornelius Mahony, was appointed as first Professor of Celtic Languages in Galway the following year. Little is known of his background. He matriculated in 1840 (so that he was unlikely to have been born before 1820) and entered Maynooth College in that year as a clerical student for the diocese of Cloyne (which for the most part is in Co. Cork where the surname is abundant). He left Maynooth College before he had completed his second year.[16] The *Galway Vindicator*, announcing his appointment, declared that he had 'obtained

---

13 My thanks to Fr J. Mitchell for these personal details.
14 RIA MS 12 N 21, no. 333, 11 November 1848.
15 Ibid, no. 332, 14 November 1848.
16 My thanks to Professor Ruairí Ó hUiginn for these personal details.

the highest distinction in the Irish Language during his collegiate course at Maynooth College', adding that he had 'lectured in the Irish Language in St Vincent's Seminary, Cork'.[17] The Queen's Colleges Commission took evidence from him years later, when he was an inspector of schools, referring to him as 'one of the best Irish scholars in Ireland'.[18] Notwithstanding these plaudits there is no indication that Mahony had any academic training in Irish. In Maynooth College, where he spent less than two years, a course in Irish was essential for students of Rhetoric and Philosophy, but its aim was purely pastoral. Fr James Tully, from Mountbellew, Co. Galway, then a Gaeltacht area, was Professor of Irish at that time, a post he held for almost half a century (1828–76), 'but without enthusiasm for either teaching or the Irish language'.[19] Mahony was probably a native Irish speaker, as one might expect of a student for the diocese of Cloyne at that time, and had some familiarity with the later literature.

When the teaching sessions got under way there was scarcely any demand for Irish in the Galway College, any more than there was in the other Colleges and for the same reasons: there was no Irish in the schools at either primary or secondary level, there were no employment prospects following from its study, and the subject had marginal status in the university courses (as will be explained later). Cornelius Mahony had no student in his first year in the College and consequently did not deliver his inaugural lecture until November of the following year, 1850, when he had three students (the largest class he was ever to have!). He lectured in English as would be his practice, and that of his successor. The *Galway Vindicator* printed a summary of the inaugural lecture 'Celtic Languages and Literature', but which focused not so much upon 'Celtic languages as [upon] a vindication of their dignity and importance from the unmerited imputations which prejudice and ignorance have cast upon them'.[20] The syllabus followed in the Irish lectures was given in the President's *Report* for the session 1850–1 as follows:

CELTIC LANGUAGES
The class is open to all students, but chiefly recommended to students of the second year.
    The following is the course of instruction and examination:
        Selections from the Gospel of St Matthew.
        Haliday's edition of Keating's History of Ireland [Dublin 1811; original and translation, vol. 1 only].
        Select portions of O'Donovan's Annals of the Four Masters [Dublin 1848–51 with translation].
        Selections from Hardiman's Irish Minstrelsy [London 1831, with translation].
        Grammar and composition.
    Prizes are awarded to the best answerers provided they shall have attended the Professor's lectures during the terms of the session.

17 *Galway Vindicator*, 11 August 1849.
18 *Report of the Queen's Colleges Commission* (Dublin, 1858).
19 Patrick J. Corish, *Maynooth College, 1795–1995* (Dublin, 1995), p. 485.
20 *Galway Vindicator*, 30 November 1850.

This was a course in the Irish language with some literary texts from the seventeenth to the nineteenth centuries (all with translation), without mention of any other Celtic language.

Ironically we know a little more of Mahony's extra-mural activities than of his College work. The present Galway Chamber of Commerce and Industry takes its distant origin from a society founded in 1791 calling itself the Amicable Society of Galway. This society obtained a royal charter in 1839 and became the Royal Galway Institution which in turn evolved into the Royal Galway Institution and Chamber of Commerce, and finally (1955) the present Galway Chamber. A letter from the Institution to James Hardiman, dated 6 March 1839, acknowledges his major role in its creation: 'At your suggestion the members of the Amicable Society of Galway undertook with your assistance to create an Institution in this town for the promoting, the cultivation and diffusion of Science. The result is – the Royal Galway Institution by Her Majesty's patent'. Its council, to which Hardiman was elected, was divided into two committees, one of Science, Polite Literature, and Antiquities (of which he was a member), and the other of Finance. Hardiman presented the Institution with a thousand volumes towards the foundation of a library.[21] When QCG was founded very many of its staff became members of the Institution. Cornelius Mahony was elected to membership on 8 February 1850, in the company of the President (Edward Berwick) and Vice-President (J.P. O'Toole) of the College, and played a prominent role in the Institution during the next few years, being elected to the council and to the offices of Secretary and later Librarian. He read at least two papers to the Institution, on 'The Social Past and Present of Ireland' and 'The Early Practise [sic] of Mesmerism in Ireland', both reported in the *Galway Vindicator*.[22] But by the end of 1853 he had resigned from the Council and possibly from the Institution as his name does not occur again in the Minute Books.

His academic life must have been very unsatisfactory, with the frustration, if not the humiliation, of having virtually no students. There is a slightly pathetic tone to his report to the President for the session 1850–1:

> I have to report that my Lectures commenced about three weeks after the opening of the Session, and were continued twice a week until the close of the Session.
>   The number of Students in attendance has been only three. They have attended very regularly, and have made considerable progress, which is the more meritorious as their attendance was entirely voluntary.

This last phrase indicates the marginal position of Irish in the Colleges: it was not a general degree subject (see below, p. 351), a fact which further undermined the position of the professor.

---

21 Minutes ('General Meeting Book'), Royal Galway Institution, preserved by Galway Chamber of Commerce and Industry. The Institution decided to express its appreciation of Hardiman's gift by having his portrait painted for display on its premises. But although the minutes of a later meeting record three quotations from leading Irish portrait painters, there is no further mention of the portrait.
22 *Galway Vindicator*, 7 April 1852, 2 April 1853.

Mahony remained at the College for a further three sessions: 1851–2 when he had two students, 1852–3 when he had again two students, and 1853–4 when once more he had none.[23] In 1854, not surprisingly, he applied – successfully – for a post as Inspector of National Schools, and his appointment in QCG was terminated. An indication of his good standing in the university is the fact that he was appointed Examiner in Celtic Languages in the Queen's University, which examined candidates from all three Colleges, for autumn 1854 and again for 1855.[24]

When the Professorship of the Celtic Languages became vacant on Mahony's departure, the President suggested to the government that,

> as notwithstanding all our efforts to encourage the study of those Languages no class had ever been formed, the sum allocated to it might be given for other purposes ... But the Government [which reserved to itself the appointment of professors and officers in the Colleges] was determined to uphold the study of the Celtic Languages, and they filled up the vacancy.[25]

As mentioned earlier, its main defender was Thomas Larcom. Berwick, however, would have another day before very long.

After a two-year vacancy, John O'Beirne Crowe, a young graduate of Queen's College Belfast, was appointed to the vacant professorship in 1856. The registration records at Belfast tell us that he entered college in 1850, at the age of twenty-six, the son of Thomas Crowe of Creevaugh in the parish of Cong, Co. Mayo.[26] He was a native speaker of Irish, as we would expect of one coming from that district.[27] It seems that he had gone to Belfast with the express intention of taking a degree in the Celtic Languages, probably attracted by the reputation of O'Donovan, the professor (now aged forty-four and with many learned publications to his name). It is recorded that Crowe made this proposal at registration. This however was not an option, as is clear from the *Calendars*, Celtic not being among the subjects leading to the general degree in Arts (AB), but only for prizes and, at degree level, for Honours. The system for the award of Honours in Arts in the Queen's Colleges was as follows: students who had passed the general degree examination, with recommendation (for entry to Honours) from the Examiner in a particular subject, might then present themselves for examination for Honours (and a prize) in that subject. In the case of Celtic the qualification for entry to Honours was a pass in the general degree examination (in any subjects).[28] And so

---

23 *Report of the President* 1856–7, which corrects the often-quoted figures given in the *Report* of the previous year. During the 1851–2 session he also helped out with the English class (apparently in place of the Vice-President, the Revd Dr O'Toole), giving 25 lectures on the English language to sixteen first-year and three second-year students, *Report* of the President, 1851–2, p. 9.

24 The Examiners in Celtic in the Queen's University were as follows: 1852 and 1853, O'Donovan; 1854 and 1855, Mahony; 1856 and 1857, O'Donovan; 1858, 1859, and 1862, Connellan; 1860 and 1861, O'Beirne Crowe. Mahony died 1875 (my thanks to Diarmaid Breathnach for date).

25 *Report of the Queen's Colleges Commission* 1858, p. 238. Original proposal of Berwick to Lord Lieutenant (through Major Ponsonby), 26 September 1854, NLI, MS 7667, no. 40.

26 My thanks to Professor G. Stockman for these details.

27 *Report of the Queen's Colleges Commission*, 1858, evidence 3888.

28 On Professor Mahony's proposal (President's *Report*, 1852–3) the qualification was widened by

in 1853 we find O'Beirne Crowe taking a degree in Latin, Greek, and Ancient History, but also gaining an 'Honor – an Exhibition, value £10, and a Gold Medal' in the Celtic Languages. The University Examiner for that year was O'Donovan, and the rather formidable examination paper is printed in the Queen's University in Ireland *Report* for 1853–4.[29] But when asked later by the Queen's Colleges Commission whether he had *studied* under Professor O'Donovan, he replied, 'No: I have studied Celtic myself. I have spoken it from childhood ... I studied Irish for Philological purposes, and for facilitating my study of Sanskrit'.[30] O'Donovan did not give course lectures. Crowe remained on in QCB for at least another year: in August 1854 he wrote a pamphlet entitled *The Catholic University and the Irish Language*, describing himself on the title-page as 'Senior Scholar of Queen's College, Belfast'. In it he decries the omission of Irish from the subjects to be taught in the new Catholic University, and shows an awareness, at least, of the works of Pictet and Zeuss (newly published) on the Celtic languages.[31]

The names of the examiners for Crowe's appointment to QCG are of interest. They were the Revd Dr James Henthorn Todd, Irish scholar and founder of the Irish Archaeological Society, the Revd Dr Charles Graves, at whose instigation the government established the commission to edit the Brehon Laws, and Professor John O'Donovan.[32] Unfortunately O'Beirne Crowe's tenure of the professorship was no more successful than that of his predecessor, and suffered from a similar lack of students (1856–7, none; 1857–8, three; 1858–9, none; 1859–60, three; 1860–61, six; thereafter, none). Three lectures per week were given 'on the History of the Celtic Languages and Literature. Practical instruction also is given in these languages in both their ancient and modern forms, but especially in the Hiberno-Celtic'.[33] The meaning is clear enough: it was a course in Irish as a Celtic language. Crowe's own main interest lay in the literature of the earlier language, as is clear from his publications (all of which are subsequent to his period at QCG). For the most part, they are editions (originals with translation) of texts from the great medieval manuscripts, printed for the first time. Two are in book form – *Scéla na Esérgi. A Treatise on the Resurrection* (Dublin, 1865) and *The Amra Choluim Chilli* (Dublin, 1871), both from *Lebor na hUidre* (Book of the Dun Cow) – and the others in the learned journals, such as 'Táin Bó Fraích' from the *Book of Leinster*,[34] or 'The Dindsenchus of Erin' from the *Book of Ballymote* and the *Book of Lecan*.[35] Two notebooks,

---

the University to include graduates in degrees other than Arts (President's *Report* 1853–4). And so it was that George Sigerson, who gained the degree of MD in QCG in 1859, also got a first in Celtic Languages in that year, when Connellan was Examiner.

29 *Report on the Condition and Progress of the Queen's University in Ireland, from September 1st, 1853, to August 31st, 1854*, examination paper on pp. 56–7 (erroneously among the general papers).
30 *Report of Queen's Colleges Commission* 1858, evidence 3888, 3895. A different version of the refusal received by O'Beirne Crowe – if he is the student referred to – is given by a writer in the *Nation* 6 November 1858, but it is not in accord with the College *Calendars*, as explained above.
31 Adolphe Pictet, *De l'Affinité des Langues Celtiques avec le Sanscrit* (Paris, 1837); Johann Caspar Zeuss, *Grammatica Celtica* (Leipzig, 1853).
32 *Report of Queen's Colleges Commission* 1858, evidence 3896.
33 President's *Report* 1858–9.
34 RIA *Proceedings* 1870.
35 Royal Historical and Archaeological Association of Ireland, 1872. For a list of his publications, see R.I. Best, *Bibliography of Irish Philology and of Irish Printed Literature* (Dublin, 1913).

dating from his Galway years, indicate his interest in philology (Greek, Latin, and Irish) and also contain communication with O'Donovan.[36]

O'Beirne Crowe departed the professorship in 1862 on health grounds. He was employed for some time by the Royal Irish Academy in Dublin assisting O'Curry (on the latter's recommendation) with the cataloguing of the Irish manuscripts in the Academy library. But in 1868 he fell foul of the Academy and was excluded from its library.[37] He died, in poor circumstances, in Dublin on 13 December 1874.[38] After his death the Royal Irish Academy purchased his papers (1875) mainly transcripts from Irish manuscripts, some used by him in subsequent publications.[39]

The commission set up by the government to examine the progress of the Queen's Colleges issued its *Report* in 1858, having taken evidence from the officers and professors and from others. It recommended the abolition of the Professorships of the Celtic Languages. The recommendation was severely criticised in the press: as one writer put it, 'If the Government attempt their abolition, it will be after giving them a most unfair trial, after having given positive discouragement to their success according to the evidence of Professors Connellan and Crowe'.[40] The proposed abolition was put into effect as soon as a vacancy occurred in each college: in Belfast, in 1861, with the death of O'Donovan, in Galway, in 1862 with the departure of O'Beirne Crowe, and in Cork, in 1863, with the departure of Connellan.

Subsequently the Colleges ignored the growing interest in Celtic Studies, mainly abroad, and in Irish, both language and literature, at home. By the last decade of the century the founding and wildfire spread of the Gaelic League was symptom as well as cause of the rapidly changing public attitude to Irish. A Galway graduate, Mícheál Breathnach, recalling that period, wrote, 'Is deacair do lucht na haimsire seo a thuiscint cén draíocht a bhain le gluaiseacht na Gaeilge sna laethanta sin'.[41] The tide was turning, and would soon reach the university. In 1897 Queen's College Cork appointed a young scholar, Osborn Bergin, as Lecturer in Celtic. The *Gaelic Journal* for September of that year says that

> The credit of this important concession is due, in the first place, to the students' organisation, which pressed the matter on the attention of the visitors last year, and secondly, to the agitation raised by the Gaelic League on the subject some months ago.[42]

36 RIA, Irish MS 873 and 877.
37 Minutes of RIA Council meetings, 1 September 1868, 3 February 1873. My thanks to Siobhán O'Rafferty, Librarian, for references.
38 In Johnson's Court, Great Britain St – according to P.J. O'Donoghue, *The Poets of Ireland* (Dublin, 1912), p. 90. My thanks to Dr Seán Ó Lúing for this reference. The date of death is from the obituary in *Revue Celtique*, 3 (1876–8), pp. 147–8, which gives his date of birth as 1833, probably incorrectly; the obituary says that his being afflicted with a chronic alcoholic problem prevented the realisation of his great potential as a scholar.
39 *Catalogue of Irish MSS in RIA*, MSS 860–82, where the cataloguer commends the transcriptions.
40 *Nation*, 6 November 1858.
41 Mícheál Breathnach, *Cuimhne an tSeanpháiste* (Dublin, 1966), p. 88. Translation: 'It is difficult for people today to understand the magic that pertained to the Irish movement in those days'.
42 *Irisleabhar na Gaedhilge (Gaelic Journal)*, no. 89, 8 (1897). My thanks to Seán Mac Mathúna, Ard-Rúnaí an Chonartha, for this reference. Cornelius G. Buttimer, 'Celtic and Irish in College

In the other colleges old prejudices yielded more tardily. In Trinity College Dublin, the chair of Irish was not separated from the Divinity School until 1919, when Thomas F. O'Rahilly was appointed professor. In Queen's College Galway as from 1898 it was possible to take 'Celtic' for the 'First Year's Literary Scholarship' examination.[43] But when, in 1903, a young freshman from Co. Galway – who had gained an entrance scholarship taking Irish as one of his subjects – proposed taking Irish as a subject towards a BA degree he was rebuffed. This was Mícheál Breathnach.[44] With the new confidence of the time he wrote remonstrating with the College authorities and threatening unwelcome publicity. The College compromised allowing him to take Irish for his university examinations but without providing any tuition in the subject. When Breathnach reached the third year (1905–6), still without tuition, he and a second-year student in the same situation successfully appealed to the College to provide them both with tuition in Old Irish (required for the Royal University examination). A postgraduate student, Stiophán Mac Donnchadha, a native speaker of Irish who had studied Old Irish in the School of Irish Learning in Dublin, was employed for the purpose.[45] After several decades of pressure and negotiation by the Catholic Church for equal university opportunity for Catholics as for Protestants,[46] and having had the reports of two Royal Commissions on the subject (1901, 1906), the British Government finally passed the Irish Universities Act of 1908. During the years of deliberation which led up to this, the Gaelic League (funded by Hyde's American tour) mounted a strong public campaign demanding that Irish be given its due place in the new universities. Their main objectives were achieved: the establishment of chairs of Irish (and of Irish history) in each of the Colleges of the National University of Ireland, as well as a lectureship (rather than a professorship as demanded) in Celtic at Queen's University Belfast and, from 1913, Irish became a requirement for matriculation in the colleges of the NUI. With little support from the Catholic bishops, at least on the matriculation requirement, their main backing came from the members of the County Councils.

1849–1944', *Journal of the Cork Historical and Archaeological Society*, 94 (1989), pp. 92–4. It seems that Bergin had to depend upon the students' fees, an insecure income.

43 The College accounts for that year record three guineas to be paid to Mr John McNeill for his services as examiner. For 24 November 1903 there is a record of two guineas paid to Joseph J. O'Neill, MA among 'Sums voted for Assistants, Demonstrators and Examiners in this Session'. My thanks to Dr Séamus Mac Mathúna, Secretary for Academic Affairs NUI, Galway, for this information. O'Neill is named as 'lecturer' (Celtic) in the Calendar of 1903–4, probably in error (for 'examiner') as it seems from what follows here that no tuition was given. O'Neill (1878–1952) was from Aran and a graduate of QCG, who later studied at the School of Irish Learning. In 1923 he became Secretary of the Department of Education. See Diarmaid Breathnach and Máire Ní Mhurchú, *Beathaisnéis*, vol. i (Dublin, 1986), pp. 92–3, sv Seosamh Ó Néill.

44 Breathnach, *Cuimhne an tSeanpháiste*, pp. 102, 120–1, 129. He later became Secretary of the Department of Education.

45 Mac Donnchadha graduated BA in 1905, with a Senior Exhibition in English and Modern Languages in 1906, and in Metaphysics, Political Science, and History in 1907. He is listed as Lecturer in Celtic in the QCG *Calendar* for 1906–7. Breathnach tells us (ibid., p. 114) that he himself was employed as 'léachtaí le Gaeilge' while still a student (1907) but this is not recorded in the Calendar.

46 David Kennedy, *Towards a University* (Belfast, 1946), pp. 60–1.

12.1 Tomás Ó Máille, Professor of Irish Language, Philology, and Literature, 1909–38

Initially two Irish chairs were instituted in University College Galway: the Professorship of Modern Irish Language and Literature, to which Tomás Ó Máille was appointed on 28 October 1909 (fig. 12.1), and the Professorship of Celtic Philology, which was never filled. In the following year both professorships were replaced by the Professorship of Irish Language, Philology, and Literature to which Tomás Ó Máille was automatically appointed, and a part-time Lectureship in Modern Irish Language to which Seaghan Mac Énrí was appointed.[47]

Tomás Ó Máille was born and reared in the townland of Munterowen near Maum in the Joyce Country, Co. Galway, on the border with Co. Mayo.[48] The year on his birth certificate is 1880.[49] When he was appointed professor in the year 1909

47 My thanks to Dr Séamus Mac Mathúna for this information.
48 Dónall Mac Giolla Easpaig of the Placenames Office of the Ordnance Survey tells me that it is more commonly called Béal Átha na mBreac by the local people. For a fuller account of Ó Máille see Ruairí Ó hUiginn, 'Tomás Ó Máille', *Léachtaí Cholm Cille*, 27 (1997), pp. 83–122.
49 Thomas O'Maley was born on 3 March 1880 according to a birth certificate in the NUI, Galway Archives. My thanks to Dr Séamus Mac Mathúna for this information. The *Census Report* of

he was a very young man with a doctorate in Celtic Studies from the University of Freiburg. People are sometimes puzzled by this apparently overnight flowering – fás aon oíche – on an unpromising landscape. But this is to underestimate the tradition from which Ó Máille came. When a brother of his – Mícheál (c.1879–1911) – died as a young man, Seán Mac Giollarnáth wrote an obituary in *An Claidheamh Soluis* in which he described him as descended

> ó sheanbhunadh Gaelach nár scar lena dtréartha ná lena dteangain ariamh. Tógadh é i ngleann fá bhun beann iarthair na Gaillimhe i measc daoine nár labhair go dtí le fíorghairid ach an Ghaeilge. Bhí a mhuintir ariamh – agus tá i gcónaí – ar na daoine ba fiúntaí san mbarúntacht, agus ní raibh aon ghlún acu le na céadta bliain gan suim acu i léann agus i seanchas agus i litríocht na Gaeilge.[50]

Notwithstanding its pious tone, this eulogy can be largely substantiated with evidence. According to the *Census Report* of 1901 all members of the Ó Máille household (including Tomás) spoke both Irish and English, with the exception of a servant boy who spoke Irish only. Later on Tomás declared: 'I have spoken Irish as my native tongue from childhood'.[51] Tomás was the second youngest of the large family (of whom nine survived) born to Mícheál Ó Máille (1830–1918) and his wife Sorcha Sheoighe (1845–1916). The Ó Máilles were an old-established family in the district, as strong sheep farmers for the most part, who held large tracts of land, much of it mountain, on lease from Lord Leitrim.[52] They traced their genealogy back to Éamonn Saighdiúir ('the Soldier') who fought on the Jacobite side at the battle of Aughrim. Tomás's grandfather Peadar (1800–81), who held the large family farm at Kilmeelikin, had to cope with the problem of providing education for his family in the absence of schools. The real situation had changed very little for him from that of his father's youth when the Penal Laws were still on the Statute Book, and according to a Connacht account 'people were not allowed by law to have schools, either public or private ... Richer people [kept] religious and scholars in their homes to teach their children'.[53]

1901 gives his age as 20. But on a *curriculum vitae* which he submitted to the University of Freiburg he gave the date 1882. My thanks to Professor Gearóid Mac Eoin for this information.

50 *An Claidheamh Soluis*, 9 Nollaig 1911, obituary of Mícheál Ó Máille ('Diarmaid Donn') by Maine [Seán Mac Giollarnáth]. The spelling has been standardised in this excerpt. Translation: 'From an old Gaelic family who had never parted with their traditions or their language. He was reared in a glen at the foot of the peaks of west Galway among people who until very recently spoke nothing but Irish. His family were always – and still are – among the most respectable people in the barony, and there was no generation of them for centuries without an interest in Irish learning and tradition and literature'.

51 Application of Tomás Ó Máille for professorship in UCG. My thanks to Dr John Nolan, Registrar NUI, for a copy of this application.

52 My thanks to Dr Sheila Mulloy (Ní Mháille) and to the late Dónall Ó Máille (son of Tomás) for general information on the family.

53 Written of the diocese of Elphin, 1753. Quoted by James Coombes, *A Bishop of Penal Times* (Cork, 1981), p. 42.

Peadar Ó Máille, together with a couple of his neighbours, hired the services of a resident schoolmaster, by the name of Siúrtán (Jordan).[54] One of Siúrtán's charges from this group became a professor in Maynooth College,[55] and Mícheál Ó Máille (father of Tomás) had a reputation of having a very good knowledge of Latin and Greek, although he had no other teacher. The Kilmeelikin patrimony was inherited by Mícheál's eldest brother, Peter James, and Mícheál set up on a farm at nearby Munterowen, also Lord Leitrim property, but, although substantial, without a lease. Like their father before them, Mícheál and his two brothers, Peter James and Tomás, hired the services of a schoolmaster to teach their children. This was Pádhraic Ó Máille, known as Peaitsín Pheige. Something of a rough diamond, it would seem, who had got an education as a poor scholar in Co. Tipperary and had a knowledge of Latin, Greek, and English, and was a native speaker of Irish, for which he had scant regard.[56] The Ó Máille brothers are said to have each paid him £10 a year, and he stayed a week in turn in each of their houses.[57] Later, however, Lord Leitrim ordered Mícheál to give up the services of the schoolmaster, and Mícheál, unlike his lease-holding brothers, was in no position to defy him.[58] It would seem that it was the first half of the family that was taught by Peaitsín Pheige, and that Mícheál, the brother immediately preceding Tomás, was the last one to be taught by him. However, Tomás no doubt benefited from the family education provided by Peaitsín Pheige, which is not to be underestimated, as is clear from their achievements and those of their cousins. An elder sister, Caitlín, was certainly a pupil of his, and when a 'national school' was established in Seanadh Charracháin, not far away on the shores of Loch na Fuaiche, in 1884, she was appointed teacher. If Tomás was born in 1880, as seems most likely, he was then four years old, and we are told that it was Caitlín who taught him. But as four other older members of the family became teachers – all taught by Peaitsín Pheige – it is likely that some or all of them had a hand in Tomás's education.[59] One of these was Mícheál ('Diarmaid Donn'),[60] closest to him in age, and, it would seem, an exemplar to him. In the obituary which Seán Mac Giollarnáth wrote on the occasion of Mícheál's death – as a young man full of promise – he said:

54 Brighid Bean Uí Mhurchadha, *Oideachas in Iar-Chonnacht sa Naoú Céad Déag* (Dublin, 1954), p. 45. Siúrtán had spent some years as a student in Maynooth.
55 Dr Ó Ruairc (Uí Mhurchadha, ibid.) also known as Hugh O'Rourke (1837–85), who became Professor of English and French in 1862. See Corish, *Maynooth College*, p. 479.
56 Uí Mhurchadha, ibid., p. 46; Ó hUiginn, 'Tomás Ó Máille', p. 84; Mulloy, 'Memories of a Connemara Man', *Connemara: Journal of the Clifden and Connemara Heritage Group*, pt 1, 2 (1995), pp. 33–46.
57 Uí Mhurchadha, ibid.
58 Uí Mhurchadha, ibid.; Peaitsín Pheige taught school for a time in the Catholic chapel of Kilmeelikin (ibid., from Sinéad Ní Mháille, sister of Professor Tomás; it would seem that she was the main source of Bean Uí Mhurchadha's information on the Ó Máilles). Peter James and his wife Mary (Ní Mháille) had a large family. Five of them became doctors (including two professors in the Medical Faculty in UCG, Michael and Charles Conor). There is a window by Evie Hone in Kilmeelikin church to the memory of John Francis who greatly distinguished himself in the medical profession in England.
59 As well as Caitlín (later Sr Ita in the Presentation Order) the following were teachers: Sinéad (b. 1871), Sorcha (b. 1873), Peadar (b. 1878), and Mícheál (born *c*. 1879).
60 For whom see Breathnach and Ní Mhurchú, *Beathaisnéis*, vol. iii (Dublin, 1992) p. 120.

An léann do bhí ag a mhuintir ariamh bhí gean agus grá aige dó. Thosaigh sé go luath ag bailiú seaniarsmaí an léinn sin. Thosaigh sé ag cruinniú na scéalta agus na filíochta agus an bhéaloidis ó na daoinibh. Tá beagán den mhórchnuasach do rinne sé le feiceáil in *Amhráin Chlainne Gaedheal*.[61]

We may take it that that was how Tomás commenced his own life's work, in partnership with Mícheál in the work of collection and preservation. Hence it was under their joint names that they published what was intended to be the first instalment of their collection, *Amhráin Chlainne Gaedheal* (1905), a small but important collection of song-texts which they had collected for the most part in Corr na Móna where Mícheál had spent some time teaching. Mícheál was already engaged in scholarly and editorial work, being one of the people who assisted Fr Dinneen with the proofing of his Dictionary.[62] He was an active member of the Gaelic League as was, more prominently, his older brother Pádraig.[63] Tomás was to follow this example also and become the centre of some controversy in the League.[64] Tomás is said to have spent some time in the school at Béal Átha na mBreac, beside home,[65] and probably to have acted as a monitor there.[66] By 1904, at the latest, he was in Dublin and attending the School of Irish Learning which providentially had been established the previous year by Kuno Meyer. There he studied Old Irish with John Strachan in the summer of 1904 and the following years. He was now preparing himself for the BA examination of the Royal University (an examining institution only) where he graduated in 1905 in English, Irish, Mathematics, and Mathematical Physics.[67] He continued his studies in Old Irish with Professor Edmund Hogan SJ in University College Dublin, where he was also employed to lecture in Irish,[68] and he was also an Irish columnist with the *Freeman's Journal*.[69] In 1906 he competed with Osborn Bergin for a travelling studentship. Bergin was awarded first place, but because of the excellence of Ó Máille's performance Mrs Alice Stopford Green, who was personally funding the studentships, agreed to provide a second one for him.[70] This is an indication of the urgency felt by a small group of visionary intellectuals of providing Irish scholars – especially natives – for the cultural revolution they were striving to bring about.

61 *Claidheamh Soluis*, 9 Nollaig 1911, by 'Maine', spelling standardised. Translation: 'The learning that his forebears always had was a matter of love and affection for him. He began early collecting the remains of that learning. He began collecting the stories and the poetry and the folklore from the people. A little of the great collection he had made is to be seen in *Amhráin Chlainne Gaedheal*'.
62 Patrick S. Dinneen, *Foclóir Gaedhilge agus Béarla* (Dublin, 1904).
63 Breathnach and Ní Mhurchú, *Beathaisnéis*, vol. iii, pp. 120–2.
64 Ó hUiginn, 'Tomás Ó Máille', pp. 86 seq.
65 Muiris Ó Droighneáin, *Taighde i gcomhair Stair Litridheachta na Nua-Ghaedhilge ó 1880 anuas* (Dublin, 1936), p. 221.
66 Breathnach and Ní Mhurchú, *Beathaisnéis*, vol. iii, p. 122.
67 My thanks to Dr John Nolan for these particulars.
68 Application for professorship.
69 Not without controversy. See Ó hUiginn, 'Tomás Ó Máille', pp. 91 seq.
70 R.B. McDowell, *Alice Stopford Green* (Dublin, 1967), p. 79; Seán Ó Lúing, *Kuno Meyer 1858–1919: A Biography* (Dublin, 1991), p. 64. Mrs Green had helped establish the School of Irish Learning, was one of its original governors, and 'contributed generously to its funds'. (McDowell, ibid.)

Ó Máille used his studentship to go first to the University of Manchester to Professor Strachan for Old Irish, Celtic Philology, Sanskrit, Greek, and other subjects. He was awarded an MA in 1908 for a thesis on 'The Language of the Annals of Ulster' which he later published as a book.[71] Between 1907 and 1909 he spent periods in Germany at the University of Freiburg with the great Thurneysen, and in Berlin with Zimmer, studying Old Irish, Breton, and Welsh as well as Philology. He also spent some time with Kuno Meyer at the University of Liverpool.[72] He gained his doctorate from the University of Freiburg in 1909.

The establishment just at this time of professorships of Irish in the new Colleges of the NUI was most timely, or perhaps the greater timeliness was the availability of trained young scholars ready to fill those professorships: Ó Máille in UCG and Bergin in Old Irish in UCD.[73] Ó Máille concluded his application for the Galway post with a statement of aim:

> If appointed to the Professorship I should be able to impart to my students the knowledge of Celtic Philology necessary to enable them to study Irish Literature and Philology on a thorough basis. In this way I should hope to develop the natural advantages for Modern Irish of the situation of the University College in an Irish-speaking district so as to make it a great centre of Irish learning and Celtic Studies.[74]

He was a young man full of vision and enthusiasm and energy, confident of his own capacity, and ready to take on the building of a lofty edifice from its foundations. He became a scholar of importance, as well as being a man of action fully *engagé* in the cultural and political revolution of his time. With the appointment of Ó Máille, Irish in UCG can be said to have at last been put on a secure footing, in contrast with the difficulties of the previous century. Some ninety years on, the full-time staff of the School of Irish consists of two professors (Modern Irish, and Old and Middle Irish and Celtic Philology), two associate professors, two statutory lecturers, two college lecturers, two junior lecturers (including one – a Scot – in Scottish Gaelic), and two lecteurs/lectrices (native speakers, respectively of Welsh and Breton). Current student numbers are: first year 180, second year 90, BA 90, as well as numerous postgraduate students and visiting students from foreign universities. The School of Irish, as well as Bord na Gaeilge, is housed in Áras na Gaeilge, a recent building in the centre of campus, with excellent facilities, specially provided by the government in 1993. A more extensive account of the history of the discipline and its development since 1909 must await another occasion.

---

71 Manchester University Press, 1910.
72 Application for professorship.
73 A post for which Ó Máille was also an applicant, to the irritation of Mrs Green and her friends in the School of Irish Learning. See Ó hUiginn, 'Tomás Ó Máille', p. 106. With his application for the UCG post, Ó Máille provided testimonials from Hogan, Zimmer, Thurneysen, and Hereford (Professor of English in the University of Manchester). Two other applicants competed for the post, Fr Tomás Ó Ceallaigh and Dr Seaghan P. Mac Énrí, both of whom were subsequently connected with the Irish Department in UCG.
74 Application for professorship.

Modern Languages

ROSALEEN O'NEILL

In January 1846 the Board of Presidents and Vice-Presidents of the planned provincial colleges that were to become Queen's Colleges Belfast, Cork, and Galway, met in Dublin Castle to consider their submission to Sir James Hugh Graham, Home Secretary, and Sir Robert Peel, Prime Minister, on 'the Statutes, the System of Education, and other elements of the Collegiate Plans'. In the course of their deliberations they developed a proposal which was, as they were well aware, 'a distinct deviation from the practice of most colleges'.

The Board recommended that two of the twelve professorships allowed to each College be allocated to modern languages: one in German and a cognate language, and another in French and Italian. The proposed course of study in Arts, while making Latin obligatory, offered a choice between Greek and German in the first year, Greek and modern languages in the second, and Classical Literature, Modern Foreign Literature, and Rural Economy in the third. In accordance with the curriculum outlined, candidates for admission to the Colleges were to choose between Greek and French at the entrance examinations.

Defending what it regarded as 'the most important step as yet adopted', the Board stressed its unanimity on this matter, stating that all members felt that

> although the Ancient languages are certainly of the Highest Value in a liberal Education, yet that for the practical wants of the Middle Classes, too much has been hitherto sacrificed to their Exclusive Study, and that for a Community busily occupied with practical Science, with Commerce, with Agriculture and with Manufactures the study of Modern Languages should hold an important place.

The board emphasised that the proposed regulations would allow the student who chose to study Greek to become 'a really good Greek scholar'. But

> if his tastes or his probable mode of life turn him to Modern Languages then he must learn French and German thoroughly, and the Board considers that a knowledge of the tongues of the two most important Modern Continental Nations may be considered equivalent in Education to an acquaintance with the language of Ancient Greece.[1]

---

[1] National Archives, Dublin, MS CSORP 1846, O. 1052.

Although these proposals were questioned by Graham and were later abandoned, it is important to record the principle that underlay them: that rather than simply imposing the traditional curriculum of the older universities, the Colleges should seek to adapt to the perceived needs of the social classes and geographical locations they were to serve. The challenge of reconciling the principle of 'usefulness' with established academic standards and practice was often to present itself, as here, in approaches to the study of modern languages.

While the revised provisions of 1847 and 1848 allowed for only one professorship in modern languages (from a new total of twenty for each College), they included a chair of Celtic languages, and this was to meet with the approval of successive holders of the modern languages chair. No continental language was to be required in the matriculation examination (for Arts, Law, and Medicine), but both Greek and Latin were obligatory here, as also in the first year of the Arts course. This course prescribed the subjects English language, Greek, Latin, Mathematics, and *one* of French, German and Italian in the first year. The second year was to be devoted to Logic, Chemistry, the principles of Zoology and Botany, and *either* Higher Mathematics *or* Greek and Latin. In the third and final year the subjects were Natural Philosophy, History and English Literature, Physical Geography, and *either* Metaphysics *or* Jurisprudence and Political Economy. Students who had passed College examinations in this three-year course were entitled to sit, in Dublin, the BA examination of the Queen's University. Only after successful completion of this could they present for honours in a further examination. Options for the MA degree included the combination of Latin, Greek, and a modern language. All students in the Faculty of Medicine were obliged to attend and to be examined in a course in modern languages and, from 1859, a modern language (in practice French) became an obligatory first-year subject in the course for Civil Engineering.

The first Professor of Modern Languages in Queen's College Galway (QCG) was Augustus Bensbach MD, a graduate of the University of Heidelberg (fig. 13.1). In his inaugural lecture, published in full in the *Galway Vindicator* of 15 December 1849, he traced the development of Europe's languages from Indo-European, and gave an outline of European literature since the Middle Ages, concentrating on the Italians but including quotations in English from Provençal poetry, from Ben Jonson (on Shakespeare), from Schiller and Goethe, and from 'the patriotic bard Thomas Moore'. He praised the wisdom that had regulated that the study of at least one modern language be obligatory 'at this our University', comparing this favourably with the situation in the then recently-founded Taylor Institute in Oxford. At that 'excellent College' students could attend the lectures of the Professor of Modern Languages and the teachers of French and German, but there was 'one drawback: the lectures are optional, and thus fewer students attend than if they were made a portion of the general education'. (He might have added that the situation was similar in Trinity College Dublin, where modern languages were not an essential part of any degree course until 1871.[2])

---

2 R.B. McDowell and D.A. Webb, *Trinity College Dublin 1592–1952: An Academic History* (Cambridge, 1982), p. 58.

13.1 Augustus Bensbach, Professor of Modern Languages, 1849–68

Bensbach stressed the usefulness of a knowledge of French, 'and especially German', not only to students of classical literature but to those engaged in Medicine and in every branch of the physical sciences. He spoke of the advantage of languages to the merchant and to the European traveller who, now that the railways had made Europe one country, must be able to converse with, and learn from, his continental neighbours. He concluded his lecture with some remarks on the moral education to be derived from the study of literature, and the reminder to his audience that they were called upon to become 'useful members to society': 'Let us all strive and exert ourselves to forward this noble work, and let it be our pride, our glory, to be numbered among the benefactors of this country'.

Of the sixty-eight students who entered QCG in the year of its opening, 1849–50, fifty-four attended lectures in modern languages. In spite of the drop in total student numbers following the condemnation of the Queen's Colleges by the synod of Thurles in 1850, modern languages remained relatively strong because they formed an integral part of first-year courses in Arts and Medicine. However, Bensbach was to find that his students, with very few exceptions, had no previous knowledge of French or German – no classes were formed in Italian. The courses in French and German involved grammar, composition, and an outline of the respective literatures. In French, students also read Mignet's *Revolution Française* and Racine's *Athalie*; in German, Goethe's *Iphigenie auf Tauris* and Liebig's *Chemische Briefe*. (The latter was an unusual choice, but was probably selected because students from Arts and Medicine attended these courses together and Bensbach was, after all, a medical doctor.) Candidates for College prizes were examined on additional literary texts and also had to present for 'a catechetical examination' on Corneille, conducted in French, or for 'conversation in German'. This recognition of the importance of the spoken language, especially in the form of the financial incentive of a prize, is perhaps the most interesting feature of the early syllabus, at a time when modern languages as part of university courses were taught, if at all, as 'dead languages' in Dublin and in Britain (Cambridge, for example, did not introduce 'optional conversation' until 1909).[3]

As well as the obligatory first-year courses, Bensbach offered voluntary advanced classes to students of the second and third years, but was clearly disappointed by the attendance at these. Indeed one of the main complaints voiced to the Queen's Colleges Commission of 1857 was that students for the BA degree were obliged to study too many subjects, fourteen in all (compared with six in Trinity College Dublin), and that new subjects were introduced each year, none of these being examined by the *University* until the BA examinations, held in Dublin Castle in the October after the final academic year. William Nesbitt, Professor of Greek at QCG, told the Commission that he believed the College curriculum was based on 'a vicious principle – the principle of admitting all the new studies without excluding any of the old', and that, given the deficient preparatory training and immature age of the students, it was absurd to attempt to teach them 'the whole circle of the sciences'. He felt that students of Greek, Latin, and modern languages were induced by this 'ill-arranged' curriculum to 'break off their grammatical studies just when they have got over the drudgery, and are beginning to pursue them with some advantage'. Nesbitt did not think that there was 'anything magical' about the study of Latin or Greek and believed that a competent knowledge of modern languages was equally deserving of high reward and literary distinction.[4]

Augustus Bensbach, in his evidence to the Commission, drew from his knowledge of continental and English universities and suggested that it had been a mistake to model the new Colleges on the system of general education applied in Trinity College Dublin, and in the English universities, rather than on the specialist education offered on the continent. It had been forgotten that 'we have a different class of persons to deal with'. He believed that the Arts course made 'a poor man a poor gentleman, that is a man not fit to earn his bread'. Bensbach proposed the introduction of a first-year matriculation class for those whose schooling had not prepared them adequately for university, and the subsequent subdivision of the three-year Arts course into three specialisms, one of which the student would choose to pursue: literature and philology, physical science, and natural science. 'In this way, instead of giving a man merely the fine title of BA,

---

3 Michael Sanderson, *The Universities and British Industry 1850–1970* (London, 1972), p. 208.
4 *The Queen's Colleges Commission Report*, 1858, pp. 251–2.

you would fit him for life; and that, in my opinion, is the object of the Queen's University'.[5]

While the recommendations of the Commission did not lead to any revision of the matriculation system they did result in some important changes. Second-year courses in modern languages were introduced as an option with Greek, Latin and mathematics, thus allowing for a certain level of specialisation. A First Arts examination in the Queen's University was introduced after the second academic year. A further development was that those sitting the BA honours examination in modern languages were to present in at least two of French, German, and Italian.

From the beginning, the BA examinations in modern languages consisted of translations from and into the target language, with more difficult passages and some grammatical, philological, and literary questions for honours candidates. The literary section ranged from a series of questions on the writings of Voltaire which included the rather loaded 'Was any good accomplished by them'? (from an early paper set by the Revd J.G. Abeltshauser of Trinity College Dublin), to the somewhat safer 'Say what you know of the life and works of Metastasio', and 'Try a parallel between Klopstock and Milton'. All examinations for Junior and Senior scholarships had a strong literary component and included original composition in the relevant language. Candidates for the degree of MD were examined in the translation of medical texts, with questions on medical terminology in the respective language supplementing the standard grammar and literature on the honours paper.

In his report to President Berwick in 1860, Bensbach was happy to note that the three highest honours in modern languages in the previous year's degree examinations had been obtained by students from QCG. Among those who benefited from their modern language studies in Galway were many later appointees to the civil service in China, Ceylon, and especially India. (Modern European languages formed part of the examinations for applicants for these posts.) These included, for example, Michael McAuliffe, who was to become a judge in the Punjab and translated *Guru Granth Sahib*, the Sacred Book of the Sikhs; and Sir Anthony P. MacDonnell, who, after a distinguished career in India, was appointed under secretary to the lord lieutenant of Ireland and became involved with the Irish Reform Association.[6] George Y. McMahon, one of the students who entered QCG in 1849, became Professor of Modern Languages at the Royal College, Mauritius, while William A. Browne, who took his BA degree in 1853, later founded a scholarship in modern languages in the College. The most famous of Bensbach's students was undoubtedly T.P. O'Connor, who graduated in 1866, winning a Senior scholarship in Modern Languages and Modern History. After working as a journalist in Dublin he moved to London, where he secured a post with the *Daily Telegraph* which allowed him to combine his twin passions, politics and journalism:

---

5 Ibid., pp. 258–9.
6 For an account of the 'devolution crisis', in which MacDonnell played a central part, see F.S.L. Lyons, *Ireland since the Famine*, 2nd ed. (London, 1973), pp. 220–3.

I found myself in London at the very beginning of the Franco-German War, and it was just the moment, in some respects, for me. I had been an eager student of French and German during my University career, and the first job I got in London was to read through the French, German, and Austrian papers, where one could now and then supplement the very brief messages from the correspondents of the paper, most of whom broke down during the war.[7]

O'Connor, a supporter of Parnell, was later to become MP for Galway and then Liverpool, becoming eventually the 'father' of the House of Commons, and the first film censor in Great Britain. Equally well-known as a journalist, he founded and edited the *Star* and the literary *T.P.'s Weekly*. The *UCG Annual* of 1929–30 contains an obituary of O'Connor and mourns him as 'one of the most loyal of the Alumni of the College'.

It is probable that O'Connor gained at least part of his political and social education from his former teacher. Bensbach, who was the author of a *Sketch of German Literature*, believed in the 'diffusion of knowledge' as an essential element in the social and moral progress of humankind. He became Vice-President of the Royal Galway Institution and, in a lecture to that body published in the *Galway Vindicator* of 15 January 1851, proposed several measures aimed at improving the lot of the poor of Connacht and the 'toiling classes' of the towns. These measures included the establishment of a savings' bank, a public library, and evening classes which might be taught by QCG professors. It was largely at his urging that the College later opened its library, with certain restrictions, to members of the public. Augustus Bensbach died in 1868, and he was remembered by the College President as a 'conscientious and energetic' teacher, a 'loved and faithful' colleague. Given his enthusiasm for Europe's new rail system it is sadly ironic that Bensbach died, suddenly, at a railway station in Belgium.[8]

Eighteen sixty-eight, the year of Bensbach's death, was also the year in which Oxford University abolished the chair of modern languages it had established in 1845, and which had been held by Max Müller, the Indo-European scholar.[9] The decision may have been taken in the light of thinking similar to that of John Stuart Mill, who, in his inaugural lecture at the University of St Andrews in 1867, stated that he did not agree with 'those reformers who would give a regular and prominent place in the school or university course to modern languages', not because he thought them unimportant, but because they were 'so much more easily acquired by intercourse with those who use them in daily life'.[10] One of the principal functions of the Queen's Colleges, however, was to serve those who had

---

7 T.P. O'Connor, *Memoirs of an Old Parliamentarian*, 2 vols (London, 1929), vol. i, p. 1.
8 Timothy P. Foley, ' "A Nest of Scholars": Biographical Material on Some Early Professors at Queen's College Galway', *Journal of the Galway Archaeological and Historical Society*, 42 (1989–90), p. 77.
9 Eda Sagarra, 'The Centenary of the Henry Simon Chair of German at the University of Manchester', *German Life and Letters*, no. 4, 51 (1998), p. 513.
10 Quoted in C.W. Proescholdt, 'The Introduction of German Language Teaching into England', *German Life and Letters*, no. 2, 44 (1991), p. 97.

neither the means nor the leisure to acquire such knowledge through travel or private instruction, and QCG immediately set about appointing a successor to Bensbach's chair. The new Professor of Modern Languages was Charles (Karl) Geisler PhD (fig. 13.2).

The appendix to the *Report* of the President of QCG for 1874–5 includes statements from each of the professors on their year's work. Geisler's report gives an insight into his methodology and practice. First-year students, who with rare exceptions took up their study of French or German in QCG, were first introduced to grammar, using *Otto's French* (or) *German Conversational Grammar*. With the help of exercises 'made at home' they could then begin to 'enter upon a critical reading of easy prose extracts from classical writers'. By the end of the third term, having translated and analysed Scribe's *Le Verre d'Eau* and three acts of Schiller's *Maria Stuart*, they had some knowledge of the 'literary merits' and 'idiomatic peculiarities' of these texts. Second-year students engaged in translations from 'easy modern English historians' with an emphasis on 'idiomatical phraseology and the niceties of syntax'. In German, Graeser's *Thesaurus of German Poetry* was used, and Schiller's *Wilhelm Tell* and the first two acts of Goethe's *Tasso* were read; in French, Ponsard's *L'Honneur et L'Argent* and Pellissier's *Morceaux Choisis*. Also, we are told, 'occasional lectures on literature were given'. The courses of the third year, which essentially prepared students for the Senior scholarship examinations, centred upon the history of the respective language and literature, with additional texts by Goethe, Racine, and Molière. 'Free essays on a given subject were', he informs us, 'handed in every fortnight, even during the summer vacations'. Geisler also offered lectures in Sanskrit, but no class was formed. Nor had he any students in Italian in this period, although the College examination papers do include a third-year Italian paper for 1872–3. In general, Geisler's examination papers reflect his interest in idiom; they also contain useful exercises such as the translation of a verse passage from Racine into 'good French prose'. There was an oral component in the Senior scholarship examination in French, but not in German.

One of Professor Geisler's students, James Mullin, published an autobiography in which he gives a vivid account of his years at QCG.[11] A Catholic from Cookstown, Co. Tyrone, living in very poor circumstances with his widowed mother, Mullin served his time as a cart-maker but, at the age of twenty-two, was encouraged to attend classes at Cookstown Academy by its headmaster, T.G. Houston MA, a graduate of QCG. Houston's successor, another QCG graduate, persuaded Mullin to try for the matriculation and scholarship examinations in Galway. Successful in these, Mullin proceeded to take a BA in QCG, living frugally on annual College scholarships and spending his summers working as a carpenter with the new telegraph works in Cookstown. He studied French and German with Geisler and remembered him as 'an extraordinary character' and a humorous and lively teacher. Geisler had worked as a teacher in St Petersburg and advised Mullin to go as a teacher of English to Russia, promising him letters of introduction,[12] but Mullin chose to study medicine, graduating MD in 1880, and then moving to Cardiff where he worked as a general practitioner.

11 James Mullin, *The Story of a Toiler's Life* (Dublin and London, 1921).
12 Ibid., p. 106.

The evidence of Albert Meissner, Professor of Modern Languages at Queen's College Belfast (1865–1902), to the Royal Commission on University Education in Ireland in 1902, gives a curious account of Professor Geisler's final years in office. Meissner, 'a difficult, touchy, pugnacious man',[13] had a falling-out with the Senate of the newly-established Royal University in 1884 over the election of Geisler to a University Fellowship to which Meissner believed himself to be more entitled. This 'scandal' was brought to the attention of the House of Commons, where T.M. Healy questioned the authenticity of Geisler's academic qualifications, in particular his doctorate from Göttingen. (James Mullin mentions that Geisler had a PhD from Heidelberg.) President Moffett of QCG was asked to investigate 'the alleged fraud' and the government reported itself satisfied

13.2 Charles Geisler, Professor of Modern Languages, 1868–86

that Professor Geisler did not obtain his appointment at Galway on the strength of a degree which he did not possess, but because he was thought by the Government of the day to be the best candidate for it, and that he subsequently obtained a degree at Vienna in the usual way, and not on the strength of his holding a professorship in the Queen's College, Galway.

In spite of requests from Healy no original documents were produced in the House as these were stated to be confidential, but it was pointed out that Geisler was highly thought of by 'men competent of judging of his qualifications', and was a man of 'estimable character' who had 'faithfully discharged all the duties of his post'. And there the matter rested. According to Meissner, however, Geisler 'retained his Fellowship and Professorship but never returned to Ireland, the Senate and Dr Moffett appointing substitutes for him. After two years spent partly in Germany, partly in London, Professor Geisler died'.[14]

Whatever the situation at the time of his initial appointment, Charles Geisler would appear to have held both a PhD and a DLitt. His library borrowings show him to have had a scholarly interest in Celtic philology and in Sanskrit as well as in

---

13 T.W. Moody and J.C. Beckett, *Queen's Belfast, 1845–1949: The History of a University*, 2 vols, (London, 1959), vol. i, p. 168.
14 *Report of the Royal Commission on University Education in Ireland*, 1901–3, pp. 46–7; *Hansard*, vol. 291, cols 1350–1; vol. 292, col. 91; vol. 293, cols 900–1.

the modern languages he taught. He died in Halle on 18 May 1886, and NUI, Galway archives contain correspondence about his salary with solicitors in London and with his brother Wilhelm, whom the royal court in Halle had appointed guardian to Geisler's two daughters. The outstanding sum was duly transferred after subtraction of payments to a Mr Dacus for lecturing and examining duties in QCG. President Moffett's report for 1885–6 laments the premature death of 'a respected and eminently learned professor, Dr Geisler, who for eighteen years occupied the chair of modern languages in the College'.

With the establishment of the Royal University in 1881–2, the Queen's University ceased to exist, and the Queen's Colleges retained 'no bond of connexion but mutual good-will'.[15] The Royal University was an examining body only, and candidates who had satisfied the matriculation requirements (which now included a modern or classical language plus Latin) could prepare themselves for subsequent examinations in any educational institution or indeed by private study. (Only medical students had to attend a named institution.) The new BA examination required Latin and Greek and any *one* of French, German, Italian, Spanish, Celtic, Sanskrit, Hebrew, and Arabic, with *two* of these being necessary for honours. All examinations were open to women but there were separate examination halls for women and men, and it was not until 1887 that women began attending as full-time students in QCG. The immediate effect of the dissolution of the Queen's University on the Queen's Colleges was a marked drop in student numbers. The number of new entrants to QCG fell from 105 in 1880–1 to 34 in 1882–3. In modern languages this was reflected in a falling-off from a total of 101 attending lectures in 1880–1 to a total of 33 in 1882–3. The latter decline is chiefly due to the fact that students of Engineering and, primarily, Medicine, who under the Queen's University system had been obliged to take a modern language, were now required to sit, although not to attend courses for, the First Arts examination of the Royal University in addition to their own studies. As the Professor of Modern Languages in Queen's College Cork, Owen O'Ryan, stated to the Queen's Colleges Commission in 1884: 'Students are anxious, even to their own disadvantage, to avoid all lectures if they can'. Thus many of the medical students in the Queen's Colleges decided, 'as if they had held a meeting',[16] to avoid the requirements of the Royal University by going elsewhere for their degrees, for example, to Surgical Corporations or to Scottish licensing boards.[17] The minutes of evidence to the Queen's Colleges Commission, which reported in 1886, include the views of several professors on the desirability of a familiarity with modern languages for practitioners of medicine, from Dr Richard Anderson's doubts about the advantage of a doctor's knowing German if he did not know how to set a leg, to Dr Marston's question as to whether a knowledge of French and German might not make someone 'a known as compared with an unknown man'.

In spite of a certain confusion regarding the status of the Colleges after the dissolution of the Queen's University and the subsequent decline in student

---

15 President's *Report*, 1881–2, p. 3.
16 Evidence of Professor Owen O'Ryan, *Queen's Colleges (Ireland) Commission*, 1885, pp. 95–6.
17 James P. Murray, *Galway: A Medico-Social History* (Galway, 1994), p. 123.

13.3 Valentine Steinberger, Professor of Modern Languages, 1886–1916

numbers, there were thirty-nine applicants for the vacant modern languages chair in Galway, 'many of them men of high character and ability'.[18] The new appointee was Valentine Steinberger, a native of Alsace, who had studied in Munich, Rome, Naples, and Paris (fig. 13.3). He had been headmaster of the Modern Languages Department of the Royal Belfast Academy from 1880 to 1886 and had taken, through private study, an MA in the Royal University in 1885. He was to serve the College as professor, and from 1902 also as Librarian, until his death in 1916.

In 1887, the year after Steinberger's appointment, Charles Colbeck published a study on the teaching of modern languages in which he welcomed a slight improvement in their status while pointing out that there were still traces of the 'contempt' in which they had been held. 'The living languages, we have been told, are too trivial to be scholarly, too easy to be learned, too useful to be dignified'.[19]

18 President Moffett in a letter to Dr Allman, Professor of Mathematics and College Bursar, 24 July 1886. NUI, Galway Archives.
19 Charles Colbeck, *On the Teaching of Modern Languages in Theory and Practice* (Cambridge, 1887). Quoted in Proescholdt, 'The Introduction of German', p. 95.

This last criticism, with its opposition of usefulness and dignity, was typical of an attitude to education in general which the founders of the Queen's Colleges in Ireland had consciously sought to counter. Their utilitarian ethos was further developed in the Royal University, which aimed to encourage a high standard of education among as broad a constituency as possible. To avoid what was perceived as the danger of 'mere memory work' and 'cramming', there was an emphasis on the testing of oral and practical skills. Oral examinations were introduced in all Arts subjects at honours level, and at Second Arts (honours) and higher examinations in modern languages the examiners could choose to conduct the oral in the respective language. In addition to questions on the history of the language and literature, the written examinations emphasised grammar, 'unprepared' passages for translation from English, and composition in the foreign language on a literary or historical topic. This emphasis was soon to develop into the regulation that no candidate should be allowed to pass any examination in modern languages and literature who had not exhibited a competent knowledge of the language in question, a regulation which remains with us to the present day. (Unfortunately, we have had to dispense with the 'special merit' given to candidates in German for 'handwriting in the German characters'!) Italian was included in the regular examinations but candidates presenting in Spanish were required to give notice of their intentions three months before the examination date.

A further impetus to the development of French and German (but, indirectly, a disincentive to students who might otherwise have selected Italian or Spanish) was the foundation, in 1899, of annual awards in these languages in QCG and in the Royal University. William A. Browne LLD, a native of Co. Monaghan, who had taken his BA in QCG in 1853 and was a member of the War Office Headquarters staff from 1856 to 1897, founded, in memory of his wife, Caroline Charlotte Browne FZS, a generous annual scholarship in QCG for proficiency in French and German, 'a competent colloquial knowledge of both languages being required'. At the same time he provided that a gold medal (to the value of £10 in 1902, when it was first awarded) and a prize of £5 be granted to the first and second candidates in the BA degree examinations in the Royal University who had satisfied the same requirement. (Any or all of these awards could be withheld if the examiners considered that sufficient merit had not been shown.) The 'Browne', as the QCG scholarship became known, doubtless encouraged students who might have studied only French to take up German too, and it certainly promoted keen competition among students of both languages. The scholarship is still awarded today, although its actual monetary value has diminished with time.

Professor Steinberger, who became a Fellow of the Royal University and one of its examiners, was ideally suited to a system which laid stress on competence in the living language. Indeed, in his evidence to the Royal Commission in 1902, he stated his belief that the University had not gone far enough in this direction and that, contrary to the general impression, the system of higher education in Ireland had 'far less elasticity in it' than had that of Germany. There were too many examinations and too little time was left for developing the intellect; in his hurry to work through a programme the professor's own individuality – 'a most valuable asset in a lecture room' – was lost. He spoke of the growing recognition of the importance of modern languages in scholarship, science, and business, but deplored their 'backward condition' in Ireland, a condition due to faulty early training. The conclusion had been drawn that 'the gift of tongues' had not been bestowed upon the Irish, but this 'hastily formed and widely accepted theory' was, in his experience, erroneous. Everything depended on the method followed, especially with beginners in a language, and the introduction of a written examination in the first stages of Intermediate schooling had been a great mistake. Steinberger believed that early language instruction should be oral and practical and carried out only by qualified teachers; it should also be interesting and enjoyable. Few of the students he had encountered who had begun their language learning at school were able to pronounce 'foreign sounds' properly, with the result that the modern language, 'which ought to be a *living* and *spoken* one', became for them a dead one and 'practically valueless'. This was an example of what he saw as a lack of cohesion between the secondary and university systems. While he agreed that the examinations in the Royal University had become more practical, he felt that the final proof of a candidate for the BA ought to be 'that he possesses absolute command in writing and speaking these languages in their *present* state of development'. The BA examination ought to consist of an oral examination and two essays, one written in class and the other researched and written at home, with absolute freedom given to the student in the composition of the latter; the more literary and historical side of the language should be left to a postgraduate course. Since there was at the time a danger that Galway might lose its medical school, he proposed that the usefulness of the College could be greatly increased by its establishing a high-class training college for secondary teachers – 'the greatest educational want in Ireland'. Steinberger declared that it was impossible to perform the work of his chair properly according to the contemporary development of linguistic science and that at least six professors would be required to do the same work 'according to Continental ideas'. He was, however, proud to have gradually built up the first laboratory for experimental phonetics in Ireland.[20]

Much of what Steinberger had to say is still of relevance today, although there is sadly no trace of the instruments he bought for his laboratory. The purchase of one of these, 'an *appareil inscripteur* as used by Professor Rousselot of the Collège de France', is mentioned in the President's *Report* for 1899–1900. This was a kymograph, an instrument for recording sound waves and speech curves. Rousselot (1846–1924) was the founder of experimental phonetics and his work was very influential in the early twentieth century, when laboratories were established in many universities in Europe and the US. The instruments used were considered especially helpful to adult learners. According to Micheál Breathnach, a former student, Steinberger believed that speakers of Irish should have no difficulty with the pronunciation of any other language, and he regularly asked Breathnach to pronounce difficult French words for the benefit of the other students, particularly those from the North who found the French accent challenging (and who must on occasion have welcomed the inanimate kymograph).[21] Throughout

---

20 *Report of the Royal Commission on University Education in Ireland*, 1901–3, pp. 145–7.
21 Micheál Breathnach, *Cuimhne an tSeanpháiste* (Baile Átha Cliath, 1966), p. 119.

his career Steinberger conducted his historical and literary lectures to third-year honours students 'in the vernacular of the language being studied'. In the 1890s he published two annotated editions of French texts, Arago's *Histoire de ma Jeunesse* and Lamartine's *Guillaume Tell* and *Bernard de Palissy*. In 1902 he took on the additional post of Librarian and produced, in 1913, a printed catalogue of QCG's collection, which then consisted of over 30,000 volumes as well as numerous miscellaneous papers and reports, a phenomenal task which he carried out single-handed.

During all of this period Steinberger's efforts in his professorial capacity were rewarded with extraordinary success. The first Dr and Mrs W.A. Browne gold medal in French and German in the Royal University (1902) was awarded to his daughter Cécile L.M. Steinberger, who also won the first Browne scholarship in QCG in 1899 and held it for the following two years. Her sister, Lilian Blanche Steinberger, won this each year from 1904 to 1906. The Browne gold medal was won again by Galway students Janet H. Perry in 1908, Katharine Tennant in 1913, and Margaret Cooke in 1916. The Browne prize was won by Samuel Minnis in 1903, James Johnston in 1913, and Julia Walsh in 1914. Cécile Steinberger obtained a PhD from the University of Paris in 1908 and was possibly the first Irishwoman to receive this degree. Her thesis, *Étude sur William Dunbar*, was published in 1908. Janet H. Perry, one of the well-known Perry sisters of Wellpark, Galway, became a Lecturer in Spanish studies in King's College, London and was the translator and editor of several Spanish texts, including *The Harrap Anthology of Spanish Poetry* (London, 1953).[22] Katharine Tennant and Julia Walsh became temporary assistants to Professor Steinberger, and Margaret Cooke (later Shea) was to become Professor of German in UCG. Thomas Rea (MA 1902) became a Junior Fellow of the Royal University and was appointed Lecturer in German and Teutonic Philology in the University of Bangor. In 1906 he published *Schiller's Dramas and Poems in England*, the product of a research degree taken in Cambridge. Edward McGrath (MA 1902) became Modern Language Master in King's College, Wimbledon, and Nathaniel Irwin-Brown (MA 1913) was later a Professor of Languages in Syria. The first official teacher of Spanish in the College was Richard J. Conroy, who graduated with a first-class honours degree in French and Spanish in 1913 and an MA in 1914; he then continued his studies in Spain. He was Assistant in Spanish in UCG in 1916 and 1917 and later became Lecturer in Spanish at the University of Birmingham, publishing an annotated edition of selected readings from Juan de Mariana's *Historia de España* in 1929. A fascinating connection between QCG in the first years of the century and NUI, Galway into the new millennium, was initiated by Samuel Minnis and Mary Eakin, both students of Steinberger's between 1901 and 1904. Minnis, who was a founding editor of the student magazine *QCG*, a Literary and Debating Society speaker, the winner of the President's Medal for Oratory, and a member of the athletics club, was placed first in French and German in the Royal University in 1901 and 1902 and won the Browne prize in 1903. He obtained a high place in the

---

22 The dedication in this book is to 'Miss Bel Chestnut of the High School Galway who guided my first steps in Spanish. In affectionate remembrance'.

Home Civil Service examinations and took up a post in Somerset House. Eakin, a keen member of the College tennis club and a contributor of articles on English literature to *QCG*, studied for a year at the University of Grenoble after completing her degree. Both became active members of the QCG Alumni Association, founded in 1904. The May 1906 issue of *QCG* announced their forthcoming marriage. Their grandson, Professor Moray McGowan of the University of Sheffield, is currently external examiner to the Department of German, NUI, Galway.

Mention should be made of two important developments in the later Steinberger years. One was the establishment, in 1908, of the National University of Ireland, of which QCG became a constituent College, changing its name to University College Galway. The other was the gradual feminization of modern language studies, a phenomenon that was not peculiar to Galway or to Ireland. As growing numbers of women students successfully took up modern languages, their male counterparts began to direct their energies elsewhere. QCG had not opened its internal scholarships and prizes to women until 1896 and the first Senior 'lady scholar' in modern languages was Margaret Aimers, who later taught in Odessa. A glance at the lists for honours and scholarships as well as for the three Browne awards from that point forward shows that women were high achievers in this area and that modern languages were increasingly perceived as 'women's subjects'.

The *UCG Annual* of 1913, in a series of comical sketches of the idiosyncrasies of the various professors, has Professor Alzzo (as the students called Steinberger) remark that there should be 'a few extra schols. for the lady students'. It is unclear whether this was meant to encourage them further or to leave some scholarships for the gentlemen. (His own daughters were no longer in UCG.) The sketch goes on to poke fun at Steinberger's passion for oranges and for his bicycle, and at his, by then probably old-fashioned, insistence that every student should apply for a post in the Indian Civil Service. Certainly Steinberger's 'own individuality' was not lost on his students, and his involvement in their extra-curricular activities included the presidency, at different periods, of the cricket, cycling, and hurling clubs, as well as the choral and orchestral society. He also directed, on at least one occasion, a student drama production in French.

The First World War was to bring about many changes for modern language students in UCG. The author of the 'Ladies Notes' in the *UCG Annual* of 1915 lamented the fact that the war had put an end to all dreams of 'going out au pair' and reminisced about those of 'our sisters' who used to go to Germany every summer and would 'come back to Erin filled with the spirit of the Fatherland'. Much more serious were the stirrings of anti-German sentiment in Galway, especially after the sinking of the Lusitania. The window of Faller's Jewellers was smashed because Stephen Faller was German, although 'naturalised'. The *Tuam Herald* of 9 October 1915, without naming Steinberger, drew attention to his nationality and position. 'There is, I hear, some comment in loyalist circles as to why any German in such times should be not only Librarian but Professor of Modern Languages'.[23] The writer claimed that the

---

23 Micheál Breathnach's *Cuimhne an tSeanpháiste* is, I believe, a reliable source for Steinberger's origins in Alsace. However, that would have made him, at the time of his birth, a French citizen, and there is no evidence that he was ever considered anything other than German.

matter was exciting 'some interest in some circles'. Whatever the truth of this report, Steinberger was to experience far greater ignominy. On 27 April 1916, four days after the start of the Easter Rising, he was taken from his home in Rockbarton and imprisoned, first in Galway and then in Queenstown (Cobh), to where he and the other prisoners were brought by ship in overcrowded and insanitary conditions. Steinberger was then over seventy, and the harsh treatment he endured during the weeks of his internment cannot but have contributed to his subsequent illness. He died of pneumonia on 3 November 1916. The *UCG Annual* of 1917 mourns the loss of 'one of our oldest and most distinguished professors' and remembers 'the kind, fatherly interest he displayed in each of us'. It also contains an obituary (signed 'Simplicissimus') by a former student of his who was interned with him and who describes his cheerfulness and his kindness to others throughout his ordeal, which he insisted on treating as a kind of adventure. It is sad that Valentine Steinberger, whose interest in politics and society was manifest in essay topics such as women's suffrage, the conflict between labour and capital, and the Hague Conferences on arms limitation, should have become a victim of a turbulence in which he was in many ways an innocent abroad.

In Steinberger's case it was the Easter Rising and the fear of German involvement that led to his arrest, but, throughout Britain, Germans and German-speakers were being ostracised and imprisoned. While British Germanists were taken prisoner of war in Germany, German academics were being dismissed from their posts in Britain and Ireland. Max Freund, Professor of Modern Languages in Queen's University Belfast, was in Germany at the outbreak of the war and was peremptorily deprived of his post, as were professors and lecturers in Aberystwyth, Birmingham, and Leeds.[24] Yet the resolution of condolence adopted by the Senate of the National University of Ireland after Steinberger's death was much more than a formality, and placed on record the Senate's high appreciation of the services he had rendered to education in Ireland;[25] and the position of German was consolidated by the decision to replace the chair of modern languages with two new professorships, one in German and the other in Romance Languages. In the academic year 1916–17, before these appointments were made, the Professor of History, Mary Donovan-O'Sullivan, acted in French and German, and Richard Conroy in Spanish; Katharine Tennant and Julia Walsh continued their work as Assistants. Mary Donovan-O'Sullivan had been an Assistant in modern languages in 1907–8.

Not long after Steinberger's death, the feminist republican, Hanna Sheehy Skeffington, whose husband, Francis, had been murdered during the Easter Rising and who wished to move out of Dublin with her young son, wrote to UCG to inquire about the vacant chair. She had studied French and German in Dublin, and after periods spent in Paris and Bonn had obtained a first-class honours MA in the Royal University in 1902. In the response she received from the Revd John Hynes, then the College Secretary and Registrar, she was told that 'a Galway

---

24 Sagarra, 'The Centenary of the Henry Simon Chair', p. 515. This article gives further details and references on the impact of the First World War on German Studies in Britain and Ireland.
25 The National University of Ireland, *Minutes of Senate*, vol. v, 8 December 1916.

graduate would almost certainly be awarded any such post'.[26] In the event the new posts went to graduates from Galway and UCD. There were seven candidates for the Chair of German, and ten for that of Romance Languages, and the new professors were Emily Anderson BA and Liam Ó Briain (William O'Brien) MA.

Emily Anderson (1891–1962) was a daughter of Alexander Anderson, the College President and Professor of Physics, and was educated privately before taking up her studies at UCG. In 1909 she gained first place and first-class honours in English, French, German, and Latin, winning a Literary scholarship. In her second year she obtained a scholarship for her performance in English, French, and German. She was the Browne scholar in 1909 and 1910 and took her BA in 1911. Unfortunately the student magazine *QCG* ceased publication in 1907 and the *UCG Annual* was not founded until 1913, so there is no College record of her other interests or pursuits during her undergraduate years. She was, however, active in the women's suffrage movement in Galway at this time.[27] After further study at the Universities of Berlin and Marburg, she taught for two years at Queen's College, Barbados before returning to Galway in 1917 to take up her post as first Professor of German in UCG. In 1918 she radically revised the German programme, prescribing additional literary texts at all levels (including works by Kleist, Hebbel, and Grillparzer), emphasising a theoretical knowledge of phonetics as related to German, introducing the study of Middle and Old High German, and expanding existing courses on German literature in the eighteenth and nineteenth centuries to include, for BA honours students, 'a detailed knowledge of the history of German literature from the twelfth to the sixteenth century, inclusive'. This revised course of studies was to be Emily Anderson's legacy to UCG, as she resigned from the professorship in 1920.

The reasons for her resignation are unknown. It may be that she found Galway stifling after her travels abroad, especially as she most likely lived with her family, and therefore in the Quadrangle building where she also worked. Student numbers in Arts were exceptionally low, with a total of five First Arts students in 1916–17 and eight in 1917–18, her first year in office, and she must have found her work unchallenging, although she had some good students, notably Browne scholars Bridget Dermody and Margaret Curran. The *UCG Annual* of 1919–20 bemoans the state of apathy into which the students had fallen and mentions that the dramatic, and choral and orchestral societies were 'beyond renascence'. Perhaps Emily Anderson's thinking was similar to that of James Mullin forty years earlier. In his autobiography he describes how 'the atmosphere of pleasant indolence' which pervaded Galway almost tempted him to stay there, 'plucking the small flowers that grew within my reach, and never hoping for anything bigger or better', but that he resisted this, opting instead for 'the tormenting cant of the strenuous life'.[28] Certainly, as her subsequent career was to show, her resignation was an incalculable loss to UCG.

26 Margaret Ward, *Hanna Sheehy Skeffington: A Life* (Cork, 1997), p. 176.
27 Mary Clancy, ' "It was our joy to keep the flag flying": A Study of the Women's Suffrage Campaign in County Galway', *UCG Women's Studies Centre Review*, 3 (1995), p. 99.
28 Mullin, *The Story of a Toiler's Life*, pp. 140, 144.

Anderson moved to London, where she entered the Foreign Office. In 1923 she published an English translation of Benedetto Croce's book on Goethe. From 1940 to 1943 she was seconded to the War Office and was awarded an OBE for intelligence work carried out in the Middle East (her obituary in the *Times* states that she was 'one of those rare scholars who was completely at home in the world of action').[29] She then returned to the Foreign Office where she remained until her retirement in 1951. But it was in the world of music that she was to achieve international distinction. In 1938 she published *The Letters of Mozart and His Family*, in three volumes, a work she edited and translated single-handed. She devoted her retirement to *The Letters of Beethoven*, published in three volumes in 1961. The *New Grove Dictionary of Music and Musicians* describes these achievements as follows:

> Her tireless, world-wide search for original sources of the text was complemented by scrupulous accuracy and thorough annotation. She developed a style of timeless English which she handled in as lively and readable a manner as was consistent with fidelity to the German ... Of the two, the Beethoven was perhaps the more remarkable because his illegible handwriting had produced so many inaccurate readings in earlier texts that Miss Anderson, besides mastering his orthography, had either to inspect personally all the extant autographs or else procure photographs. Of the 1750 Beethoven letters, she published 250 for the first time.[30]

The Federal Republic of Germany awarded Emily Anderson the Order of Merit (First Class) for her work on the Beethoven letters. While she must have valued this, the *Times* obituary claims that she did not welcome publicity and that she treated her celebrity with a mixture of genuine modesty and disdain for 'anything that seemed likely to divert attention from her work to her personality'. She refused to live 'on the trivial level at which music and scholarship could be put aside' for gossip and chatter, but 'relaxed into warmth and cheerfully alert wisdom when she felt secure upon her own ground'. Curiously neither the author of this obituary, who would appear to have known her well, nor any of the other sources (including the short biographies in her books and *Who Was Who*) mentions the fact that Anderson was a graduate of UCG or that she had been Professor of German there, although almost all record that her father was President of the College. She is variously described as having taught or been a lecturer in German in UCG after studies in Berlin and Marburg. She died on 26 October 1962, having made provision in her will for the foundation, in the Royal Philharmonic Society, of an international prize for violin playing.

Liam Ó Briain (1888–1974), who held the chair of Romance Languages from 1917 to 1958, was, like Anderson, a person of great energy and commitment whose publications consisted mainly of translations and who was 'at home in the world

---

29 Frank C. Roberts (ed.), *Obituaries from The Times 1961–1970* (London, 1975), p. 23.
30 Stanley Sadie (ed.), *The New Grove Dictionary of Music and Musicians* (London, 1980), vol. i, p. 399. Entry by Alec Hyatt King.

of action'. But there the similarities end. Ó Briain's passion was not for music but for the Irish language and its revival, and he was gregarious and loquacious and very much a public figure. From his membership of the committee that organised the demonstrations at the funeral of O'Donovan Rossa to his appearances as a regular panellist on the Late Late Show in the 1960s, he witnessed, and participated in, many of the major developments in Irish society in his lifetime. It would be impossible to do justice here to the full range of his activities and achievements.

He was born in Dublin and educated at O'Connell Schools before winning a scholarship to UCD. One of the last cohort to take a degree in the Royal University, he gained a first-class honours BA in Irish, English, and French in 1909, and an MA (NUI) in 1910. From 1910 to 1911 he was an Assistant in French in UCD, and, on winning the first Travelling Studentship of the NUI in Irish Language and Literature, he left Dublin and spent three years studying Old Irish in Berlin, Bonn, Freiburg, and Paris. The First World War broke out as he was returning to Ireland. From 1914 to 1916 he worked again as an Assistant in French in UCD, but was to lose this post because of enforced absence.

Ó Briain's own account of the period from 1914 to 1917 and in particular of the Easter Rising, in which he participated as a member of the Volunteers (although finding himself, in the confusion, in Stephen's Green and the College of Surgeons with the Citizen Army), is contained in his lively and even heroi-comical *Cuimhní Cinn*.[31] He was imprisoned in Wandsworth (where he and others set up Irish classes) and in Frongoch internment camp, which he always considered the best university he had attended. Some months after his release in 1917 he was appointed to the UCG chair. The early years of his tenure were interrupted by further periods of imprisonment: three months in Belfast in 1919–20 for organising the Michael Collins-inspired National Loan in Co. Armagh, where Ó Briain had been a Sinn Féin candidate in 1918, and thirteen months in Galway Gaol, Galway Town Hall, and the Curragh, in 1920–1. In the second instance, shortly after Bloody Sunday (1920), he was taken from the College dining-room by a troop of Black and Tans who had surrounded the entire Quadrangle building.

During Ó Briain's imprisonment in Belfast the College appointed Professor Emily Anderson as examiner in French for the Browne scholarship, and Margaret Cooke as lecturer and examiner for the period. Cooke, a native of Tourlestrane, Co. Sligo, had entered UCG on a County Council scholarship and had been a student of Steinberger's. She won first place in the NUI in her BA examinations and was awarded the Browne gold medal. She had also studied Italian for two years. After Steinberger's death she obtained permission from the University Senate to study for an MA at Newnham College, Cambridge under the supervision of Karl Breul, who was the first Professor of German in Cambridge and was, at that time, external examiner in the NUI. She gained a first-class honours

---

31 Liam Ó Briain, *Cuimhní Cinn, Cuid i: Cuimhní an Éirí Amach* (Baile Átha Cliath, 1951). Part ii never appeared, but Ó Briain published further accounts of these and later events in regular contributions to *Comhar*, notably between 1943 and 1950. Most of the details of his life are taken from these and from Diarmuid Breathnach and Máire Ní Mhurchú, *Beathaisnéis*, vol. iii (Baile Átha Cliath, 1992), pp. 65–8.

MA in the NUI in 1918. In 1921, during Ó Briain's second and longer absence from UCG, Margaret Cooke was appointed to the Chair of German vacated by Emily Anderson. In addition to her own duties she, together with Margaret Curran and Thomas F. Heneghan, substituted for Ó Briain, their remuneration being deducted from his salary. In an act that was both generous and courageous Professor Cooke wrote to the College authorities, returning a cheque she had already received and waiving all payment for any lecturing she would do on Professor Ó Briain's behalf.[32] The *UCG Annual* of 1919–20 had welcomed her return to the College, praising 'her undoubted ability and charming personality'. The 1920–1 volume congratulates her on her appointment to the chair: 'It is gratifying to have on the University staff one who has at all times evinced such a keen and lively interest in the student life of the College'. Margaret Cooke married Stephen Shea, who was Professor of Anatomy from 1921 until 1967. She retired in 1965 and died in 1981. Liam Ó Briain married Helen Lawler in 1921. Their daughter, Eileen, was for many years a journalist with the *Irish Times*.

While Professor Shea only very gradually changed the German programme which had been so thoroughly revised by Emily Anderson, Liam Ó Briain expanded the existing French courses but left the Italian and Spanish of Steinberger and Conroy unchanged. On the first-year pass course in these languages, Goldoni's *Il Vero Amico* and Calderon's *El Principe Constante* waited, faithful and constant, for over thirty years for the occasional student who would come their way. The changes made by Ó Briain and Shea in French and German clearly reflect their own academic interests. Ó Briain was passionate about French literature and introduced works by La Fontaine, La Bruyère, Le Sage, Marivaux, Rousseau, Hugo, de Vigny, and de Musset, and, later, Baudelaire and the other Symbolist poets. Shea's main interest was in the historical development of German literature and in German history and she prescribed Tacitus' *Germania* and Cramer's *Deutschland in römischer Zeit*, and asked students to examine, for instance, the differences between the historical and the literary Wallenstein. This interest is also manifest in her fondness for Heine. (She regularly set topics for composition in German such as 'A stroll through Galway with Heine' or 'A conversation with Heine about Galway', as well as, on one occasion, 'A journey through Ireland with Taugenichts'.)

The *UCG Annual* of 1928–9 contains a contribution by Ó Briain which is a reprint of an article published in the *O'Connell Schools Centenary Record*. Entitled 'The Irish Revival and Modern Languages', it is an impassioned expression of his credo: that far from hindering the progress of the Irish language, modern languages should play a vital part in the revival process. The primary aim of the revival was de-Anglicisation, and a familiarity with, especially, the language and culture of France, 'a sister Celtic race whose most fundamental qualities are largely identical with the most fundamental of our own', could help Ireland to recover its 'true mental poise' and express the depths of its own soul. The study of German philosophy and music and of the cultures of Italy and Spain would provide further

---

32 UCG Finance and Standing Committee minutes, 11 February 1921. For this, and for other valuable archival references, I am indebted to Fiona Bateman.

enrichment. The following year's annual includes what can only have been intended as a counterbalance to this essay. In 'A few words about Continental languages', Margaret Shea writes that while 'a knowledge of modern languages is not essential to intellectual development' it is 'an exceedingly valuable asset'. She describes English as 'the most useful and popular tongue in the world today' and while accepting the validity of the study of Irish, argues that continental languages should be studied by all those seeking 'to keep abreast of new tides of knowledge'.

Ó Briain's commitment to modern languages as part of the Gaelic revival was given practical expression in his work with An Taibhdhearc, Galway's Irish-language theatre. He was one of its founders and it was he who asked Micheál MacLiammóir and Hilton Edwards to establish the theatre and refused to take no for an answer, 'looking at me', as MacLiammóir recalled, 'with fierce anticipation much as the lions must have regarded the fanatic Early Christian half eager to be devoured'.[33] Their first production, in 1928, was MacLiammóir's *Diarmuid agus Gráinne*, with Ó Briain in the role of Fionn MacCumhail. He was to take part in many Taibhdhearc productions, including the famous Galway and Dublin performances, in 1950 and 1951, of the translation by his former student, Siobhán McKenna, of Shaw's *Saint Joan*, *San Siobhán*, the direction of which she took over when Ian Priestley Mitchell became ill. McKenna herself took the leading role and Ó Briain played Cauchon, bishop of Beauvais, but the Professor of English at UCG, Jeremiah Murphy, was dropped from the cast by McKenna because he had not learned his lines by the dress rehearsal.[34] Ó Briain also tried to win for An Taibhdhearc the services of a young American who had arrived in Ireland at the age of fifteen, travelling around Connemara with a donkey and cart before presenting himself to MacLiammóir and Edwards in the Gate Theatre as just the man they were looking for; this was Orson Welles. Ó Briain promised Welles the hastily-invented sum of £4 a week if he would spend six months in the Gaeltacht learning Irish and then join the Taibhdhearc company, but Hilton Edwards thwarted this attempt to poach his new star.[35] Ó Briain's principal involvement in An Taibhdhearc was as a member of the Board of Directors, and as a provider of plays which he translated from French, Italian, and English, including Henri Gheon's *La Parade du Pont du Diable* and *Le Chat Botte*; Molière's *Le Dépit Amoureux*; Jean-Jacques Bernard's *Nationale Six*; Diego Fabbri's *Processo a Gesù*; an adaptation of Shakespeare's *Coriolanus*; and plays by Pearse, Synge, and Lady Gregory.

Ó Briain had a genuine interest in theatre as art and was a regular visitor to the Comédie Française in Paris. (The first conversation he ever held in Irish, as a youth, was with Sean O'Casey, although not about theatre.) He clashed with other board members in his insistence that the Taibhdhearc was to be essentially a *theatre*, presenting the best of European drama in Irish, rather than an Irish-

---

33 Micheál MacLiammóir, *All for Hecuba: An Irish Theatrical Autobiography* (Dublin, 1961), pp. 53–4.
34 Micheál Ó hAodha, *Siobhán: A Memoir of an Actress* (Dingle, 1994), p. 41.
35 Proinsias Mac Aonghusa, 'Liam Ó Briain. Scoláire, Réabhlóidí agus Pearsa Phoiblí', *Feasta*, Meán Fomhair 1988, p. 7; MacLiammóir, *Hecuba*, pp. 127–34.

language institution which would produce home-grown, often propagandist plays.[36] What Paul Durcan wrote in his poem, 'Micheál MacLiammóir',

> I dreamed a dream of Jean Cocteau
> Leaning against a wall in Killnamoe

could equally apply to Liam Ó Briain.[37] The ideological disagreements were such that Ó Briain resigned from the board in 1938. It had been his hope that An Taibhdhearc would awaken new writers in Irish, inspired by the theatrical traditions of Europe, but his dream of a Taibhdhearc school of dramatists was never fulfilled.

There was, however, no shortage of boards and committees that required Ó Briain's attendance, including the Censorship of Publications Appeal Board, the Gaelic League, An Club Leabhar, the Radio Advisory Committee, and the Cultural Relations Committee of the Department of Foreign Affairs. He also played an important part in the founding of Galway city's first all-Irish primary school, Scoil Fhursa. In 1945 he was a candidate for the Presidency of UCG, but having sided with the pro-Treaty forces and being a Fine Gael supporter, he could not win against Monsignor Pádraig de Brún, who had de Valera's backing. (De Brún was another great linguist and conversationalist.) Early in his career in UCG, Ó Briain established a French-speaking Cercle Français for his students, and, in the fifties, ran French 'soirées' every Sunday in the old Coffee Shop (now Áras Fáilte). The best account of his teaching is that given by Dr Seán Mac Réamoinn, and is worth quoting in full:

> As students, we found him at first garrulous and lacking in high seriousness on matters of national importance: he spoke little of principles and a great deal of people and events. But, gradually the picture formed, and the colours were warm and clear and true.
>
> It was, of course, as a university teacher that Liam played his most important part of all, although God will have forgiven him if he often thought he was wasting his time there. A chair of 'Romance Languages' in a small, underfinanced college gave little scope to his scholarship, his creative humanism or his taste for academic politics. But to his students he was a godsend. I was one of them during the doldrum years of the second World War, and, at a time when the doors and windows were bolted, he was a one-man Open University. And he was magnificent proof that a love of tradition could live with an openness to new and radical ideas, that an Irishman could be a European, that a Jackeen could be a Gael.[38]

---

36 Pádraig Ó Siadhail, *Stair Dhrámaíocht na Gaeilge 1900–1970* (Indreabhán, 1993) pp. 103–4 and elsewhere.
37 Paul Durcan, *A Snail in My Prime: New and Selected Poems* (London, 1993), pp. 47–8.
38 Seán Mac Réamoinn, *Irish Times* 13 August 1974. Mac Réamoinn's own language skills are immortalised in the student magazine, *An t-Irisleabhar*, of 1939–40, where he is given these lines to speak:

Ó Briain's library borrowings show that he was conversant with seven languages, excluding their older forms, but French and Irish were the most important to him. In 1951 the French Government elected him a Chevalier de la Légion d'Honneur for his long service in the cause of good relations between France and Ireland. After his retirement from UCG he returned to Dublin. A few months before his death he was awarded an honorary doctorate in literature by the NUI. He died on 12 August 1974 and was buried with what amounted to a state funeral, with a military guard of honour, and Taoiseach Liam Cosgrave and former President, Éamon de Valera, attending. The lesson was read by Siobhán McKenna and Micheál MacLiammóir delivered a graveside oration. The funeral was also attended by representatives from UCG.

From 1936 to 1953 Professor Ó Briain had had the assistance of Dr Louis Evers in the teaching of French. Dr Evers was a Belgian who had studied at Louvain. He taught music in Galway city and was, for a time, organist in the Pro-Cathedral.[39] In 1949 Máire O'Reilly (Máire Ní Raghallaigh) MA was appointed to a Lectureship in Romance Languages. She was a first-class BA graduate of UCG in French and Irish, gained a first-class honours MA and the French Government Medal, and won the first NUI Travelling Studentship in Modern Languages to be awarded to a candidate from UCG. After studies in Paris she returned to Galway. While she did excellent work with students of French her main achievement was to bring Spanish studies to life. She was a very popular teacher and set high standards. For a brief period in the 1960s student numbers in Spanish exceeded even those in French: in 1963–4, by 175 to 168, and in 1964–5, by 205 to 194. Máire O'Reilly was appointed Associate Professor of Spanish in 1968. She died in 1977.

Liam Ó Briain's successor was Proinnsias Mac Giollarnáth (Frank Ford) MA, LLB, BL. A fluent Irish speaker, he maintained many of the connections established by Ó Briain. He was a Galway graduate and had won the French Government Medal in 1948. He expanded the French course considerably, as also that of Italian which began to attract more students in the 1960s. (The first full-time appointee in Italian was Dr Ottavio di Fidio, who taught from 1969 until his retirement in 1991.) Mac Giollarnáth was a regular contributor to *Comhar* on aspects of French literature. He had a remarkable command of French and many of his former students recall his inspirational readings of French poetry. He died in 1987.

In the early 1960s German had fewer students than any of the other languages. There were many years during Professor Shea's tenure when German, like Italian and Spanish, had no students at all. The principal reason for this is that Professor Shea, like Max Müller in Oxford in the 1860s, did not see it as her responsibility

Léighim-se Spáinnis, Laidean, Eabhrais is Gréigis,
Fraincís, Duit, agus trí shórt Béarla,
Gaedhilge na Mumhan a chuireann's Mhicí 'un suain
Agus Gearmáinis bhinn bhlasta Uí Shéaghdha.

Translation: 'I read Spanish, Latin, Hebrew and Greek, French, Dutch, and three kinds of English, Munster Irish that sends Micky to sleep, and the sweet fluent German of Professor Shea'.

39 My thanks to Fr James Mitchell for details on Dr Evers.

to teach German to beginners, and there was then very little German in the schools. Where Max Müller had the Taylorean, Margaret Shea had the 'Tech', as the Technical School was known, where modern languages were taught in evening classes. On occasion, when students were especially keen, she did take beginners' classes but they were not offered on a regular basis.[40] During the Second World War the linguist and scholar of folklore, Dr Heinrich Becker, taught German classes to students of Chemistry under an arrangement agreed between Séamus Delargy, Director of the Irish Folklore Commission, Professor Dillon of the Chemistry Department, and the College President, Monsignor Hynes. Needless to say, Professor Shea did not approve of this development, but it lasted while Dr Becker was in Galway.[41]

The James Hardiman Library, NUI, Galway holds a bound typescript in two volumes, 'A Guide to the Study of German Literature', and 'A Survey of German Literature from 1800–1950', written by Margaret Shea. They are based on a series of lectures she gave to students of German in UCG from 1950 to 1954. A note at the beginning of the first volume states that if these lectures were available in book form they would help students to appreciate the development of German intellectual life from Roman times to the beginning of the nineteenth century, 'or possibly until 1950'. It is not known if she sought a publisher for these works. The content is learned but remarkably opinionated for a survey, and much of the German literature dealt with is discussed in terms of a strict Catholic morality. Former students say that Professor Shea was formidable until closer acquaintance, when she proved friendly and exceptionally helpful to individual learners.

Professor Shea's successor in office was Timothy J. Casey MA, DPhil (Bonn), who held the Professorship of German from 1966 until his retirement in 1992. He quickly built up student numbers, introducing a formal beginners' class which the Department still runs, and gradually appointing permanent staff. He seldom taught language courses, although he has an astounding command of German, but he was a very fine teacher of literature, with a modest, almost conversational lecturing style which never quite managed to conceal his learning. The teaching of twentieth-century literature came into its own under Professor Casey. He is a Rilke scholar and has been described as the most sensitive and percipient reader of German poetry outside of Germany itself. Together with his wife, Erika, a skilled translator, he published a critical edition of selected readings from Jean Paul in English in 1992.

Too little space remains for further detail. Professor Casey was succeeded by Eoin Bourke DPhil (Munich), and Professor Mac Giollarnáth's chair of Romance Languages was replaced, over a period of years, by chairs of Spanish, French, and Italian. The first Professor of Spanish was Derek Harris PhD (Hull), who was appointed in 1979 and who resigned in 1990. He was succeeded by Diarmuid Bradley, a Cambridge graduate. Pádraig Ó Gormaile, Doc Trois Cyc (Toulouse), first Professor of French, continues the links between the Irish and French

40 My thanks to Professor (Emeritus) Gearóid Mac Eoin, who was one of those keen students, for this information.
41 Interview conducted with Dr Becker, November 1995.

languages. In Italian, the first professor was Áine O'Healy PhD (Wisc.); she was appointed in 1996 and resigned in 1998. The new Professor of Italian, Dr Catherine O'Brien, from University College Cork, is to take up office later this year. Colm Luibhéid, Professor of Ancient Classics, has been Acting Head of Italian at different periods. Curricular developments include the teaching of the history of art in Italian studies, the introduction of media courses in German, and the broadening of the French and Spanish programmes to include Francophone literatures and Latin-American studies respectively. There are also new courses on theoretical linguistics, and several staff members participate in women's studies programmes. In addition to the core Arts curriculum, the modern language departments provide service courses to students of Commerce, Law, Science, and Engineering. Staff of modern languages have formed a Modern Language Board and meet regularly. The work of the departments is greatly assisted by the Embassies and Cultural Institutes of the countries whose languages they teach and by bodies such as Alliance Française and the DAAD. The language departments have over fifty Socrates agreements with universities abroad and most students now study for a BA International. Valentine Steinberger's long-vanished kymograph was replaced in the 1960s by An Teanglann, the Language Laboratory, under the direction of Seán Mac Íomhair, who has continued to guide us in the technology of language teaching and the development of Computer Assisted Language Learning (CALL).

We are confident that the year 2000 will see NUI, Galway's modern language departments happily housed in the new Regional Centre for Modern Languages, with an excellent view of the old Quadrangle and the windows of the room which was Augustus Bensbach's office, class-room, and lecture-hall a century and a half ago.

14

English, History, and Philosophy

TADHG FOLEY & FIONA BATEMAN

When the Queen's Colleges opened in 1849, Arts degrees were less specialised than they are today. A broad range of twelve subjects was studied by all Arts students including subjects from both the Literary and Scientific divisions of the Arts Faculty. Initially, in 1846, the Board of Presidents and Vice-Presidents of the Provincial Colleges named in the first Letters Patent, which had the task of drawing up Statutes for the new Colleges, proposed twelve chairs, six in a Department of Science and six in a Department of Literature. English was one of six chairs in the Department of Literature, the chair of Logic and Mental Philosophy was another. By 1847 the proposed number of chairs had increased to twenty, and the chair of English had become 'History and English Literature', within the Literary division of the Arts faculty. English was a compulsory subject of study, and was divided into 'English Language' and 'History and English Literature' for teaching purposes. History, while listed alongside English as a core part of the degree, was not examined for several years in the University. Logic and Metaphysics, as it had become, was now in the Scientific division of the Arts Faculty.

Despite the *Galway Vindicator*'s enthusiastic welcome for the new Galway college, '[w]hat an advancement from the Gothic barbarism and presumptive ignorance of the *hedge*, to the bright polish and intellectual refinement of the University',[1] public reaction to the scheme for the new Colleges was mixed; the essential difficulty being the 'non-sectarian' nature of the institutions, which many believed to be a euphemism for non-Christian, hence the appellation 'Godless'. The certainty with which this newspaper asserted that '[e]ducation is the sword and shield of freedom' was in direct contrast with a popularly-held belief that the colleges were intent on proselytising and would ultimately pervert the morals of Catholic students. At a conference held by the Catholic prelates to consider the bill, the proposed amendments designed to protect the faith and morals of Catholic students included a clause that there be Catholic professors for a number of subjects: history, logic, metaphysics, moral philosophy, geology, and anatomy. While this was never given serious consideration at an administrative level, there was general agreement that the demand was justified in regard to history, logic and metaphysics, but not for the other 'secular' subjects. Sir James Graham, the home secretary, acknowledged that the teaching of history in a mixed college might present a difficulty, but maintained that he would rather have had no chair in

---

1 *Galway Vindicator*, 8 September 1849.

history at all than to have been obliged to fill it with a professor of one particular denomination. The option of a dual chair, which may have been the intention of the bishops, was not considered at all.[2] On 8 August 1849 the *Freeman's Journal* pondered the impact of Protestant history lecturers on Catholic students:

> the chairs specially named by the *unanimous* resolutions of the Catholic Bishops as chairs *requiring separate professors for the Protestant and Catholic youth* – the chairs of history – have one and all been filled with Protestants who must *Protestantise* their pupils, if they do not *indifferentise* them.

In the same month the *Cork Examiner* contained an impassioned attack on the choice of history professors:

> Amongst all the appointments to the colleges, none required a greater amount of deliberation and care, as well as honesty, on the part of those with whom the power of appointment lay, than the appointments to the chairs of history. To anyone who for a moment reflects how fatal has been the influence of the unscrupulous, dishonest, bigotted, and narrow minded historian in this country, the necessity for the deliberation, care, and honesty of which we speak, must be clearly obvious. History has been to the youth of Ireland an impure fountain, in whose waters no life or health existed. No language can be too strong in its reprobations of that abominable tissue of lies and exaggerations which went by the name of history, and which was placed in the hands of the youth of this country at a time when the mind was most elastic, the memory most tenacious, and the heart most susceptible of impressions for good or evil. The youth of Ireland have been deliberately poisoned by the writings of base literary hacks who sacrificed truth and honour at the shrine of Mammon and prostituted their talents to gain the short-lived patronage of some designing minister or rabid faction. Instead of being a calm, unimpassioned and instructive narrative of great events, and an enlightened biography of those who played an eminent or infamous part upon the great stage of public life, history – the history of the schools – has been nothing better than a deliberate distortion of facts; and either a disgraceful caricature of one class of remarkable personages, or a more disgraceful daubing of another class. What could the youth who drank at such a fount imbibe, but bigotry, illiberality, stupid intolerance and active ill-will? That such teaching has had its bitter results in this unhappy country, it is needless for us to say.[3]

Such debate never raged with regard to the teaching of English although there is no doubt that within the educational system, literature was being employed as a means of moral and social education, both in the colonies as well as in the

---

2 See T.W. Moody and J.C. Beckett, *Queen's Belfast 1845–1949: The History of a University*, 2 vols (London, 1959), vol. i, p. 27.
3 *Cork Examiner*, 18 August 1849.

education of the potentially disaffected lower classes in Britain. In the *Queen's University of Ireland Report* for 1868-9, the Duke of Abercorn rejoiced 'to see that English literature and English classical works hold their fitting place, and that Milton and Shakespeare are honoured as they deserve'. He went on to suggest that the poetry and prose of Moore and Burke showed some 'national defects' and that the 'study of the best models will act as a corrective'. A theme running through the addresses to public meetings of the University depicts the Irish (especially Catholics) as brilliant but undisciplined. Eloquence, impetuous valour, and unflinching courage were all very well but the Queen's University saw its role as pointing out the 'ways of success in the more tranquil fields of learning' and to give 'native genius ample aids to its development and progress'.[4] The liberal arts were seen as a civilising force and literature was a powerful weapon in that armoury. The ideological implications of the choice of texts to be studied were never questioned. The whole issue of the canon and who initially established the curriculum to be studied is unclear, probably it was the Board of Presidents and Vice Presidents. It seems that there was little disagreement about what a 'selection of good authors' might be. Examination questions confirm that the whole approach to the study of literature was quite different to the methods employed today.

From the foundation of the Queen's Colleges, both History and English Literature were assigned to the same professor who was also the Vice-President of the College in the case of the first three incumbents in Galway. The Vice-Presidency was a position of responsibility imbued with an aura of objectivity and apolitical by implication, and so its incumbents were chosen to lecture in this, the most sensitive subject area. In 1863 'Logic and Metaphysics' (now styled 'Mental Science') were added to an already demanding brief, the holder successively becoming Registrar and President. His successor was the last professor of these subjects to hold either the Presidency or the Vice-Presidency. And finally, in 1914, the chair was split into English, History, and Philosophy. This paper will concentrate almost totally on the lives and research of those who taught in these areas from the opening of the College until relatively recent times.

EDWARD BERWICK (1804-77), who was nominally Professor of History and English Literature from the foundation of the College in 1845 until its opening in 1849, was the son of the Revd Edward Berwick, rector of Esker, Lucan, Co. Dublin. He entered Trinity College Dublin on 5 July 1819, at the age of fifteen, and graduated with a BA degree in 1827. He was called to the Irish Bar in 1832. He was Vice-President of Queen's College Galway (QCG), as well as Professor of History and English Literature, from 1845 until 1849 when he became President, a post he held until his death on 7 March 1877. As English language classes were scheduled for the second term of the first session (according to the 1851 QCG *Calendar*), it seems likely that Berwick did not actually teach at all as he assumed the Presidency after Kirwan's death, which occurred on Christmas Eve 1849, not long after the official opening of the College. Although he may not have had the opportunity to teach, he was involved in the structuring of the BA and the position

---

4 Public Meeting of the Queen's University, Vice Chancellor, Maziere Brady, 12 October 1886.

14.1 Very Revd John Paul O'Toole, Professor of History and English Literature and Vice-President, 1850–2

of English and history in the curriculum because, as Vice-President, he had been Secretary of the Board of Presidents and Vice-Presidents of the Provincial Colleges (1846–50). As one who was mainly an administrator, his publications were few, apart from his *President's Reports*.[5]

JOHN PAUL O'TOOLE (1804–76), was Professor of History and English Literature from 1850 until 1852 (fig. 14.1). He was born in Galway in 1804. He studied in the Irish College in Paris and he was ordained in the church of Saint Sulpice on 18 December 1830. He obtained the degree of Doctor of Divinity and was appointed Professor of Logic and Metaphysics in the Irish College. He returned to Ireland in 1843 and the following year he set up St Mary's College, Galway, a secondary

---

5   Among his publications were: [Edward Berwick], 'Speech of the Earl of Mulgrave on the State of Ireland, in the House of Lords, Monday, 27th of November, 1837', *Edinburgh Review*, 66 (1838), pp. 450–61 and 'Reports of the Commissioners Appointed to Consider and Recommend a General System of Railways for Ireland', *Edinburgh Review*, 69 (1839), pp. 156–88 (with the novelist Marmion W. Savage).

school for boys. According to the prospectus of the College, the system of education was based upon

> a solid religious education. No expense has been spared to secure the best masters in the various departments of Literature and Science, and whilst sufficient attention is directed to the study of the classics, peculiar care is taken to give the students the refined and polished manners of the gentleman.[6]

Doubtless to achieve the more fully this supreme accolade, music, dancing, drawing, and fencing were available at an extra charge.

He was held in high esteem by the people of Galway, though not presumably by those who cast a cold eye on his well-known ability to win converts. On the opening of Queen's College Galway, O'Toole decided to apply for a position. He forwarded testimonials from a number of bishops, the Galway Town Commissioners, and from several prominent citizens. He was considered for the Presidency but, as the chief secretary informed the prime minister in a letter on 28 October 1845, the authorities in Dublin decided that, since he was not sufficiently well known in Ireland because of his long absence abroad, they could not appoint him to that office. His friend, Dr J.W. Kirwan, parish priest of Oughterard, was preferred and he expressed a wish that O'Toole would accept a position in the new College. Father O'Toole wound up his school and early in January, following the premature death of Kirwan, he was appointed Vice-President and Professor of History and English Literature at QCG. His appointment was quite likely an effort to appease the critics of the 'Godless colleges'. In the 1851–2 President's *Report*, history was delicately alluded to as '[t]he science of History, occupied with matters which occasionally intertwine themselves with religious considerations'. It was reported that O'Toole, the Vice-President, had been given the responsibility of teaching history, as the one who had 'a perfect and constant insight into the working of the entire Establishment'. It was felt that 'if any danger could, by possibility, accrue to the religious or moral principles of any class of the Students, it must be with his entire cognizance', and this was clearly unimaginable.[7] The synod of Thurles, which met in August 1850, issued a decree which, having been approved by the Vatican, and becoming operative on 23 May 1851, forbade priests to accept or hold office in the new colleges. O'Toole, who had been appointed before the Thurles decree, went to Rome on the spring of 1852 and was received by Pope Pius IX who

---

6 James Mitchell, 'The First Saint Mary's: Father John Paul O'Toole, D.D. 1804–1876', *Altra: Jubilee Book of Saint Mary's College* (Galway, n.d.) and *The Mantle*, no. 3, 5 (1962), pp. 27–32. According to Uinsionn B. Mac Eoinín, 'Coláistí na Bainríona', *Galvia*, 7 (1960), p. 23, 'Ní raibh ach beirt ollún Caitliceach i gColáiste na Gaillimhe, Seán Ó Maolchatha, A.B., Ollamh le Matamaitic, agus an tAthair S.P. Ó Tuathail, Ollamh le Stair agus Litríocht an Bhéarla'. He cites W.K. Sullivan, *University Education in Ireland* (Dublin, 1866), p. 17, in support of this erroneous statement. But Sullivan is here referring only to the Arts Faculty. Translation: 'There were only two Catholic professors in the Galway College, John Mulcahy, A.B., Professor of Mathematics, and Fr J.P. O'Toole, Professor of History and English Literature'.

7 QCG President's *Report* 1851–2

expressed sympathy with him but who felt that he should abide by the ruling of the synod. O'Toole, while still in Rome, announced his acceptance of the papal decision and, on his return to Ireland, tendered his resignation on 21 December 1852.[8] He took up parochial work in the diocese of Southwark, in the south of England and in 1854 he was appointed the first parish priest of Abingdon, in Oxfordshire. He died in Abingdon on 21 December 1876, on the twenty-fourth anniversary of his resignation from Queen's College Galway. He was seventy-two years of age. He is buried in the cemetery attached to his church, with a Celtic cross marking his grave.[9]

JOSEPH O'LEARY (1792–1864) was Professor of History and English Literature from 1852 until 1864. He was born in Cork in 1792; he graduated from Trinity College Dublin in 1818 and was called to the Bar in 1825. According to John S. Crone's *Concise Dictionary of Irish Biography* (Dublin, 1928), O'Leary was frequently confused with a namesake who was a songwriter who wrote 'Whiskey Drink Divine'. When O'Toole resigned subsequent to the ruling of the synod of Thurles, O'Leary replaced him in the chair of History and English Literature and as Vice-President of QCG. His appointment was seen as political and it provoked editorials in two local newspapers, the *Galway Vindicator* and the *Galway Packet*, on 28 December 1849. The *Packet* described O'Leary as an 'obscure stranger' whose career at the bar was 'a notorious failure'; making him a professor because of his legal qualifications was like making someone a 'Professor of German because he played the German flute'! It appeared that O'Leary, who was over sixty, could teach anything. If a veterinary chair was established in Galway, he would be an ideal incumbent, as 'law, literature, and horse-doctoring are all alike to him'. If Lord Eglington, who patronised the turf, 'selected Mr. O'Leary upon his merits alone … it must be on the principle of the donkey race, in which the last is declared the winner'. Indeed, QCG was becoming a kind of Chelsea Hospital, 'a refuge for worn-out veterans'. The *Packet* quoted an unnamed QCG person as saying that it used to be a College but was now 'about to be converted into an asylum for the crippled and decayed intellects of fogies from the camp of Toryism'. The *Galway Packet* of 1 January 1853 remarked that O'Leary was 'totally unknown in science and literature', and on 8 January it further condemned his appointment 'when the merits and services of able and deserving men are ignored, to make way for political jobbing and faction'.[10]

---

8 Thomas Moffett, Professor of Logic and Metaphysics and Cornelius Mahony, Professor of the Celtic Languages, lectured to his class in his absence.
9 O'Toole's only publication appears to be a lecture which he delivered on the English language, to 'a crowded and fashionable audience', which was reproduced in full in the *Galway Vindicator* of 24 April 1850 and the *Galway Mercury* of 27 April 1850.
10 Canvassing for academic positions was quite normal in the nineteenth century. John Elliot Cairnes, for instance, in his successful quest for the Professorship of Jurisprudence and Political Economy, reported the progress of his 'canvass' to his friend William Nesbitt: Cairnes to Nesbitt, 16 October 1859, National Library of Ireland, Cairnes Papers, MS 8941 (2). For evidence of J.W. Kirwan's canvass for the Presidency in 1845, see James Mitchell, 'The Appointment of Revd J.W. Kirwan as First President of Queen's College, Galway and His Years in Office: 1845–1849',

When O'Leary began teaching, the criticism continued regarding the content of his course and the books he recommended. The *Galway Packet* of 16 February 1853 noted that he recommended Hume's *History of England*, and Pinnock's edition of Goldsmith's *History* to be read by the class, which included a majority of Catholic students. O'Leary was himself a Catholic, and in the Commission of 1858 he asked that the Commissioners should 'recommend to the Government to make an effort to obtain for the Colleges the sanction and co-operation of the Roman Catholic prelates'. He also mentioned that History was not examined, and was in fact ignored and he stated that he was in favour of examining it. The textbook he used in class was Lingard, and the topics studied were Henry VII and the Protectorate.[11] O'Leary's main publications were in the area of law: *The Law of Statuable Composition for Tithes in Ireland* (Dublin, 1834), *Rent-Charges in Lieu of Tithes* (Dublin, 1840), and *Dispositions for Religious and Charitable Uses in Ireland* (Dublin, 1847). The *Dublin University Magazine* published a very long review of his first book, praising it for its account of the existing law

> in language remarkable for accuracy. The style is far better than that of most law books, and would of itself, furnish strong evidence of the clearness with which the author thinks. It is free from the pedantry of an affected use of technical language, and from the worse affectation of avoiding such language, where the subject seems to require it.[12]

SIR THOMAS W. MOFFETT (1820s–1908) was Professor of Logic and Metaphysics from 1849 until 1863 and Professor of History, English Literature, and Mental Science from 1863 until his retirement in 1897 (fig. 14.2). He was also Registrar from 1870 until 1877 and President of the College from 1877 until 1897. Moffett was born in Dublin in the 1820s and he was educated at Trinity College Dublin from which he graduated in 1843 as Senior Moderator in Ethics and Logic. He won gold medals for Logic, Metaphysics, and Greek and he was prizeman in Divinity and Modern History. In 1852 he took the LLD degree in Dublin University and he later received the DLitt (*honoris causa*) both from the Queen's University and his *alma mater*. At the time of his application to the Queen's

---

Journal of the Galway Archaeological and Historical Society, 51 (1999), pp. 2–3. To give another example, Daniel Owen Madden, of Mallow, Co. Cork, was a candidate for one of the chairs in the Queen's Colleges (it was a common practice before the Colleges opened to make a general application of this kind, and indeed to apply for chairs in more than one academic area) and Fr Theobald Mathew wrote a letter on his behalf to Thomas N. Redington, under-secretary for Ireland, as it transpired, unsuccessfully. See Gearóid Ó Tuathaigh, 'A Letter from Fr. Mathew to Thomas N. Redington', *Journal of the Galway Archaeological and Historical Society*, 36 (1977), pp. 85–7.

11 *Report of Her Majesty's Commissioners Appointed to Inquire into the Progress and Condition of the Queen's Colleges at Belfast, Cork, and Galway, with Minutes of Evidence, Documents, and Tables and Returns* (Dublin, 1858), pp. 247, 250–1. Lingard was John Lingard (1771–1851), an English Catholic priest and author of the enormously successful work to which O'Leary referred, *The History of England from the First Invasion of the Romans to the Accession of William and Mary*, published in eight volumes between 1819 and 1830. There were many subsequent editions.

12 *Dublin University Magazine*, no. 25, 5 (1835), p. 81.

14.2 Sir Thomas Moffett, Professor of Logic and Metaphysics, 1849–63, Professor of History, English Literature, and Mental Science, 1863–97, and President, 1877–97

Colleges, he was Headmaster of the Classical Department and Professor of Logic and Belles Lettres in the Royal Academical Institution, Belfast, an office to which he had been appointed in May 1848. In 1849 Moffett came to Galway as the first Professor of Logic and Metaphysics and in 1863 this chair was combined with that of History and English Literature. Thereafter Moffett was styled Professor of History, English Literature, and Mental Science. He was appointed Registrar in 1870, vacating that office when he became President in 1877. In the *Report of the Treasury Commissioners Appointed to Inquire into Certain Matters Connected with the Queen's Colleges at Belfast, Cork and Galway* of the previous year it was recommended that professors be appointed to the Presidency of the Queen's Colleges and that both offices be combined.[13] This policy was first put into effect with Moffett's appointment. He retired in 1897 having been President of the College for twenty years and a professor for forty-eight. He was appointed a Senator of the Royal University at its foundation and he was knighted in 1896. He was President

13 Moody and Beckett, vol. i, p. 216.

of the Royal Galway Institution and he was the last High Sheriff for the Borough of Galway. He died on 6 July 1908.

His evidence to the Royal Commission in 1858, while Professor of Logic and Metaphysics, provides some insights into his views. His opinion that Latin should be an optional subject was not unique, but it was a radical view at that time. In Galway, particularly, there had been quite a debate on the subject, as due to the scarcity of classical schools, few students had achieved a high standard of Latin at matriculation and some felt that it would be more advantageous to these students to learn a modern language than struggle to learn basic Latin to which they might never have recourse after leaving college. As Berwick, the President of QCG, stated at the same Commission, 'I think a knowledge of Classics is useless, unless it is in some degree profound'.[14] Berwick also maintained under close questioning that while it would be a new approach for a university in the empire, foreign universities already gave degrees without a knowledge of classical languages. From Moffett's evidence it seems that he had had extensive consultation with Professors Nesbitt (Latin, 1849–54 and Greek, 1854–64) and Allman (Mathematics, 1853–93) regarding alternative approaches to the curriculum. He appears to have been keen to build a closer relationship with the professors in Cork and Belfast, and refers to the fact that they had not been 'altogether able to arrive at a common understanding with reference to Psychology and Metaphysics'. Expressing his anxiety that a uniform series of textbooks be adopted, he suggests Locke's *Essay Concerning Human Understanding* and Sir W. Hamilton's edition of Thomas Reid, whether of his *Works* (1845) or his *Essays on the Intellectual Powers of Man* (1853), is not clear. He states that he encourages students to write essays, and he was clearly a popular teacher, his voluntary course being nearly as well attended as his compulsory course.

An ordinance of the Queen's University of Ireland (QUI) in 1860 made history a degree subject for the first time.[15] The subject received a great deal of attention during the parliamentary debate on the University Education (Ireland) Bill in 1873. It was proposed to exclude from the examination Moral Philosophy and Modern History (a recommendation commonly known as the 'gagging clauses') and it was pointed out that effectively this would mean the exclusion of the subjects from the whole University curriculum 'as students would study only those subjects which were imperatively required'.[16] During the same debate, Lord Robert Montagu colourfully depicted the difficulties inherent in the teaching of history, describing how 'one lecturer in history might tell the students in his class that Henry VIII was one of the jolliest of kings, and had patted Robin Hood on the back, and another might give that monarch a very different character'. He also reminded the assembled body that 'all disputes and differences of opinion in Ireland did not relate to theological subjects, but had references to historical events also, such as the battles of the Boyne and of Aughrim'.[17] The 'gagging clauses',

---

14 *Royal Commission* 1858, evidence 3643.
15 Moody and Beckett, vol. i, p. 250.
16 Mr Osborne Morgan in the *Parliamentary Debate on the University Education (Ireland) Bill* (London, 1873), p. 24.
17 Ibid., Lord Robert Montagu, p. 29.

it was variously opined, would make the University 'the laughing stock of Europe', and would be 'a sentence of capital punishment upon liberal education in Ireland'.[18] They would 'put aside those studies which make man acquainted alike with his outward actions and his internal constitution'. The University would be 'a *monstrum cui lumen adeptum*, deprived of the light of religion, ethics, and historic knowledge'.[19] It was also suggested during the debate that if Modern History and Moral Philosophy were to be excluded because of their indirect connection with Theology, that modern Literature might as well be excluded too on the the basis that 'as deep offence can be given in a lecture on literature as in a lecture on history'.[20] However this argument did not attract much attention. No doubt the academic staff in QCG had an interest in the gagging clauses and opinions on the teaching of modern history and moral philosophy (particularly Professor Moffett), but their interest in this debate would have been focussed on another element of this bill – the proposal to shut down the Galway College. The bill was narrowly defeated (Ayes 284, Noes 287), unfortunately for Gladstone whose government fell as a result, but fortunately for all connected with QCG. A letter from Gladstone in the University Archives, dated 21 February 1873, which was apparently written in response to a letter from the President and Professors of the College, reassures them regarding the 'protection of [their] personal interests in the event of the dissolution of the College'. It states that,

> this question will undoubtedly be dealt with in an equitable spirit, especially since all appear to be sensible that the governing and teaching body at Galway have done themselves much honour by the way in which under great difficulties they have performed their arduous duties.

By the time of the next Royal Commission in 1885, Moffett was President of QCG, and gave his lengthy evidence in that capacity but also as Professor of English, History, and Mental Science. Much of his evidence on this occasion involved defending the Galway College, particularly as the replacement of the Queen's University by the Royal University in 1883 had already had the effect of dramatically reducing student numbers in Galway and the College was yet again under threat of closure. Regarding his classes, Moffett referred to his own education in Trinity College Dublin and maintained that the logic and metaphysics lectures he was giving to students were up to the standard of those given by Dr Butcher, and that his history lectures were equivalent to Dr Toleken's. He seems not to have studied English literature himself as he comments that there was no class for English literature in Trinity at the time he was there.[21] He is careful to

---

18 Ibid., Mr Pim, p. 72; Mr W. Johnston p. 75.
19 Ibid., Mr Gathorne Hardy, pp. 104–5.
20 Ibid., Sir Rowland Blennerhassett, p. 78.
21 *Queen's Colleges (Ireland) Commission: Reports of the Commissioners Appointed by his Excellency John Poyntz, Earl Spencer, K.G., Lord Lieutenant of Ireland, to Inquire into Certain Matters Affecting the Well-being and Efficiency of the Queen's Colleges in Ireland together with the Minutes of the Various Meetings of the Commission, Minutes of Evidence, Documents, Returns, and Tables* (Dublin, 1885), evidence 4977.

mention that he does not interpret his role as merely preparing the students for examination, but that he endeavours to 'develop the intellectual powers of students, and to exercise their judgement, and cultivate their taste'.[22] His only complaint regarding the students was that he had 'on many occasions to restrain their excessive interest to learn'! Matriculation in English was essential for a candidate's acceptance; it was examined both by written examination and orally and Moffett made it clear in no uncertain terms that mis-spelling was grounds for rejection.[23]

The numerous testimonials which accompanied Moffett's application for the professorship, testified to his literary attainments, his teaching ability, and his good character. John Kells Ingram commented that Moffett had 'always won the respect and esteem of everyone who knew [him], by [his] honourable, manly, and consistent conduct'. William Neilson Hancock referred to his 'zeal and energy' and his 'diligence and ability'. The Revd Thomas Luby remarked 'His character, both moral and religious, I have always found most unexceptionable', and in the context this can be read as a compliment. It was noted with satisfaction by William Masson that Moffett displayed 'an equal devotedness to Classical learning and Intellectual Philosophy' and that, 'though an ardent admirer of the genius of Bacon', he had a due appreciation of the 'transcendent merits of Aristotle'. And while Moffett was 'fully aware of the services rendered to mankind by the Scottish Philosophy', he did not undervalue Whately and Mill.[24]

It seems likely that in applying to the Queen's Colleges, he was expecting to be appointed to a position in the Belfast College; however Robert Blakey took the chair of Logic and Metaphysics there, a man who, though largely self-educated and holding no degree, had been able to submit eight volumes of philosophical work with his application. He was, however, dismissed for 'neglect of his duty' in 1851.[25] When the QCB professorship of Greek fell vacant in 1850, Moffett was quick to apply for the position which would bring him 'home' to Belfast. In a long letter to the President of QCB applying for the post, he expressed the deep respect and regard he had for the President of QCG and the great kindness he had had shown to him, but he mentioned his anxiety to return to Belfast where his relatives and friends resided and where his 'personal character' was 'pretty generally known', which he suggested might be of advantage to the College. He reminded the reader that his initial application was for either the Chair of Classics or that of Logic and Metaphysics. A letter of support from parents of some of his former pupils at Royal Academical Institution described how their references were given from a sense of duty 'not to him, but to the cause of literature' and they mentioned the 'varied useful information which he so largely and luminously communicated' to their sons.[26]

22 Ibid., evidence 4952.
23 Ibid., evidence 6924.
24 Moffett's application for the Professorship of Greek at QCB, 20 August 1850, National Archives, MS OP 1850/50.
25 Moody and Beckett, vol. i, pp. 116, 164.
26 Moffett's application to QCB.

Sir Thomas published *Selections from the Philosophical Works of Bacon, with Translation and Notes* (London, 1847) and some essays, lectures, and reviews on literary, philosophical, and economic topics. His inaugural lecture at Queen's College Galway was published in the *Galway Vindicator* on 19 December 1849 and in the *Galway Mercury* on 22 December 1849.[27] He had a life-long interest in social and economic questions and in 1849 he joined the Dublin Statistical Society (later to become the Statistical and Social Enquiry Society of Ireland). Perhaps his most important contribution in this area was as Barrington Lecturer between 1849 and 1856. These lectures were funded by the Dublin businessman, John Barrington, for the purpose of teaching the principles of political economy to the lower classes. Moffett lectured in Dublin (on a number of occasions), Clonmel, Galway, Ardee, Armagh, Dungannon, Coleraine, Lisburn, Holywood, Downpatrick, Derry, Belturbet, Lurgan, Dundalk, Kilkenny, Garvagh, Trim, and Waterford. According to the various Reports of the Council of the Dublin Statistical Society, Moffett was a very popular and successful lecturer. He also lectured frequently to the Royal Galway Institution and to similar literary, philosophical, and scientific societies

WILLIAM JOSEPH MYLES STARKIE (1860–1920) was President of QCG and Professor of History, English Literature, and Mental Science from 1897 to 1899. He was born in Sligo on 10 December 1860, the fifth son of William Robert Starkie JP, RM, Cregane Manor, Rosscarbery. He was educated at Clongowes Wood, Shrewsbury, Trinity College, Cambridge, and Trinity College Dublin. He was a foundation scholar at Trinity College, Cambridge (apparently the first Roman Catholic to win such an award since the reformation) and he achieved first-class honours in the Classical Tripos. He was First Scholar and First Senior Moderator at Trinity College Dublin, winning a classical scholarship, the Berkeley Gold Medal for Greek, and the Madden Prize. In 1890 he became a Fellow and Tutor of Trinity College Dublin, a position he resigned to become President of Queen's College Galway in 1897. With the unexpected death of the Honourable Christopher Redington in 1899, Starkie left Galway to become the new Resident Commissioner of National Education, a post he retained until the end of his life. In 1911 he was appointed Chairman of the Board of Intermediate Education. He was a member of the Royal Commission on University Education (Ireland), 1901–2, a Senator of the Royal University of Ireland, and a member of the Academic Council of Dublin University. He was President of the British Empire Shakespeare Society (Dublin Branch) and he was President of the Classical Association of Ireland, of which he was a founder member, in 1911. In 1914 he became a member of the Irish Privy Council. He was awarded honorary doctorates by both Trinity College Dublin and the Royal University of Ireland. He was the father of the scholar and critic Enid Starkie and of Walter Starkie, academic, linguist, musician, founder of the British Council, a former director of the Abbey Theatre, and the author of *Spanish Raggle-Taggle* (London, 1935).

---

27 Moffett published an article, 'Queen's College, Galway' in the *New Liberal Review*, 3 (1902), pp. 488–98.

Despite a very busy life, Starkie retained a close interest in classical studies. He was an Aristophanes scholar and his translations of *Wasps* (London, 1897), *Acharnians* (London, 1909), and *Clouds* (London, 1911) are still respected by classicists. He was by profession an educationalist and his publications in this field include *Recent Reforms in Irish Education* (1902), *History of Irish Primary and Secondary Education during the Last Decade* (1911), and *Continuation Schools* (1912). He wrote for several journals including the *Classical Review*, *Quarterly Review*, *Hermathena*, and *Kottabos*.

According to the obituary in *Hermathena*, the 'key-note' of Starkie's character was 'frankness; he was downright' and 'incapable of subterfuge'. 'Less courageous men could criticize his impatience as imprudent', we are told, and 'discomfited opponents might protest against the rudeness of his attacks on their particular prejudices, but no one could deny that Starkie was sincere, free from self-interest, and eminently fair as a fighter'.[28] He died, unexpectedly, at Cushendun, Co. Antrim, on 21 July 1920.

WILBRAHAM FITZ-JOHN TRENCH (1873–1939) was Professor of History, English Literature, and Mental Science from 1899 until 1912. He was born in Dublin in 1873, the only son of John Alfred Trench and Janetta, the eldest daughter of Wilbraham Taylor. In 1903 he married Mary Alicia (who died in 1930), eldest daughter of Edward Cross, and they had two sons and two daughters. Trench was educated at Trinity College Dublin and Christ's College, Cambridge. He received MA degrees from the Universities of Dublin and Cambridge and the degree of LittD from Dublin. He was also a member of the Royal Irish Academy. Having served as Professor of History, English Literature, and Mental Science at Galway from 1899 until 1912 (he was the first holder who was neither President nor Vice-President), he retired, at the youthful age of thirty-nine, to Co. Wicklow. However, his *otium cum dignitate* terminated the following year when he was appointed Professor of English Literature in Dublin University in succession to Edward Dowden. Trench, who lived at Grianblah, Palmerston Park, Dublin, died on 14 July 1939.

Prior to his appointment in 1899, Trench's only connection with Galway was his ownership of a small property near New Inn which, in 1905, he sold to the tenants 'in terms satisfactory to all parties'.[29] His grandfather was brought up at Woodlawn but the family later left Galway. Trench, according to a valedictory article in the *Connaught Tribune* of 28 December 1912, was 'rather a litterateur than a historian, rather a man of broad, and even generous human sympathies than of mouldy statistics and dates'. Though an 'avowed Conservative, he was a personality possessed of more than ordinary interest to the class from whom the wide gulf of politics would seem to separate him'. He was a particular favourite with students and he was a frequent contributor to the Debating Society. In 1906 he formulated a plan for the future of Queen's College Galway which was quite similar to the settlement reached in 1908 with the foundation of the National

---

28 *Hermathena*, no. 43, 19 (1922), pp. v–vi.
29 *Connaught Tribune*, 28 December 1912.

University of Ireland. There were widespread fears that the proposals of James Bryce, the then Chief Secretary, would lead to the closure of QCG. On 5 February 1907, Trench and Stephen Gwynn MP organised a great public meeting in Galway, at which the archbishop of Tuam, among others, protested against the treatment of the Galway College. Eventually, Bryce was replaced and his successor, Augustine Birrell, a minor poet and essayist, introduced the 1908 Act which saved QCG, transforming it into UCG.

Trench, a Conservative politically, was something of an economic nationalist after the fashion of Sir Horace Plunkett. Largely through the efforts of Captain John Shawe-Taylor, the Industrial Development Association of Galway was formed in 1906. The following year, Trench succeeded him as President, an office he held for several years. In 1908, the Association, under his leadership, organised a large and successful Industrial Conference in Galway, which was accompanied by an important Exhibition of Irish manufactures. Trench was an enthusiastic supporter of the Irish industrial movement. Industrialism, he said, 'has gone too far in England for the welfare of the community, but not anything like far enough in Ireland'.[30] He was a zealous supporter of buying Irish goods. Our purchases, he said, were 'commercial dealings, but if besides seeking to get what we want we seek to do a little benefit to our needy country, then our purchasing is raised into a sphere that is higher than that of purely commercial dealings',[31] a view shared by Moffett.

When the Galway Archaeological and Historical Society was founded in 1900, Trench was appointed Honorary Secretary and Editor of the Society's *Journal*, a position he held for eight years. In 1909, he was appointed President of the Society and remained in office until his departure from Galway. He was a member of the executive committee of the Co. Galway Association for the Promotion of Temperance, the aim of which was to establish restaurants or other means for the supply of temperance refreshments at fairs throughout the county. Trench was also involved in some commercial ventures in Galway. He was a shareholder in the Galway Granite Company and, thinking that regular communication by water between Galway and Maam might be profitable as well as beneficial, he bought, in 1903, for £500, the SS *Cliodhna*. The service, which was afterwards subsidised by the Department of Agriculture, continued regularly until 1907 when, for economic reasons, it was discontinued and the boat was sold.

While in Galway, Trench lived at Ardmore, Taylor's Hill. On his departure from UCG, he was presented with a piece of Irish-made silver by the students at a meeting in the Greek Hall, with President Anderson in the chair. In losing his services, declared the President, 'the College was being deprived of one of its greatest ornaments'. Speaking on behalf of the students, M.J. Fogarty, mentioned the names of some of the students which were taught by Trench and who were beginning to distinguish themselves in various fields. He mentioned Tom Rea who had become a Junior Fellow of the Royal University and a Lecturer in the University of Bangor, Joseph O'Neill of Galway city, and Sam Minnis who had

30 Ibid.
31 Ibid.

achieved great success as a higher civil servant and who had 'set a good example to us all by marrying a student of Q.C.G., Miss Eakin'. Fogarty also mentioned Tom Jack, the 'pride of Q.C.G.', who achieved a double-first and a high place in the Higher Civil Service examination and one whose name reflected 'a lustre on our Arts School'. His list included Mary J. Donovan, who formally made the presentation to Professor Trench, and who, the following year, became Professor of History in UCG. To this list, Trench himself added the names of two Galwaymen of note, Philip Fogarty and Jack Donovan.[32]

When Synge's *Riders to the Sea* was staged for the first time, in 1904, every effort was made to be faithful to the Aran Islands setting of the play. Trench supplied Synge with samples of cloth and, in a letter preserved in Trinity College Dublin, Synge thanked him for his help.[33] Trench's relations with Yeats were less cordial. In his Preface to Lady Gregory's *Cuchulain of Muirthemne*, Yeats wrote that if 'we but tell these stories to our children the Land will begin again to be a Holy Land, as it was before men gave their hearts to Greece and Rome and Judea'. Trench strongly disapproved of this sentiment and he wrote to Lady Gregory (15 May 1902) complaining that Yeats

> regrets the giving of the heart to 'Judea' & the setting of Christ before the soul instead of faery-men. That Mr Yeats has his eyes closed to the eternal Truth & dreams of shadows instead is the greater pity for him. But to many of us – even if we appreciate Cuchulain or Homer – this neo-paganism is a hateful thing, and Christ & his doctrine are as dear as life . . . I have just cut the stupid Preface out of my copy & without it the book is perfect. If I give away some copies the Preface shall come out of them too.

Lady Gregory replied to Trench vindicating Yeats's Preface.[34] According to R.F. Foster (who refers to Trench as 'Wilberforce' Trench), Yeats considered Trench 'a Protestant bigot with reactionary teaching ideas'.[35] Perhaps Trench got a measure of revenge when he succeeded to Dowden's chair at Trinity College Dublin. One of the unsuccessful candidates was William Butler Yeats.

Trench published two books, *A Mirror for Magistrates: Its Origin and Influence* (1898) [printed for private circulation], *Shakespeare's Hamlet: A New Commentary with a Chapter on First Principles*, (London, 1913) and many pamphlets, essays, addresses, and articles of various kinds.[36]

---

32 *Galway Express*, 22 February 1913.
33 Ann Saddlemyer (ed.), *The Collected Letters of John Millington Synge*, vol. i, 1871–1907 (Oxford, 1983), pp. 76–7.
34 Cited in John Kelly and Ronald Schuchard (eds), *The Collected Letters of Yeats*, vol. iii, 1901–4 (Oxford, 1997), pp. 184, 188.
35 R.F. Foster, *W.B. Yeats: A Life i: The Apprentice Mage 1865–1914* (Oxford, 1997), p. 484.
36 Among his pamphlets are: *An Inaugural Lecture Entitled an Introduction to the Study of the Renaissance in Its Relation to English Literature* (1914); *Christian Unity in Ireland* (1918); *The Way to Fellowship in Irish Life* (1919); *The Spirit of Shakespeare's Approach to Tragedy ... to which the Author Has Appended A Shakespearean Sonnet* [1925]; *Contacts with Reality* (1930); and *Tom Moore: A Lecture*, (1934). Among his published articles are the following: 'William Baldwin',

At the 1902 Royal Commission, Frederick Boas, Professor of History and English Literature in Belfast, gave evidence as to why it was his opinion that the subjects of English and History should be divided into two chairs. Acknowledging that in 1849 it had been 'natural' that the subjects should be combined, he argued that due to the progress made in each area there was now a far greater area of knowledge to be addressed than previously and that it was too much for a single person 'to keep himself abreast of the advance in knowledge in such varied spheres'. He also claimed that English Language, and Literature, and Modern History, form so important a part of the intellectual equipment not only of specialists, but of the whole body of educated citizens, particularly those who are qualifying for any branch of the public service, or for an educational career in Intermediate or Elementary Schools, that it is most desirable in the general national interest that they should be liberally encouraged by the State.[37]

Philip Sandford, Professor of Latin at QCG (1889–1903), enjoyed the experience of acting as substitute for the Professor of English, History, and Mental Science to such an extent that when the chair was advertised in 1899, he applied for the post, suggesting to the under secretary that 'this chair be attached to the chair of Latin'.[38] His proposal was rejected by the President of QCG, Alexander Anderson, who argued that 'it would weaken the position of the College as a Centre of University Education' and that he was of the opinion 'that the work would be far too much for one man'.[39] In light of the fact that at this time most other interested academics were arguing that the chair should be divided rather

Modern Quarterly of Language and Literature, 1 (1898–9), pp. 259–67; 'Some Thoughts on the Cork Exhibition', *Q.C.G.*, February, 1903, pp. 68–74; 'Our College Buildings', *Q.C.G.*, November, 1905, pp. 65–70; 'The Union of Hearts', *Q.C.G.*, November, 1906, pp. 35–8; 'Industrial Development', *Galway Express*, 8 February 1908; 'Law and Liberty', *Irish Church Quarterly*, April 1914, pp. 109–18; 'The Doctrine of Resurrection: Its Value in Relation to Apologetics', *Church of Ireland Gazette*, 11 December 1914, p. 985; 'St. Patrick', *Irish Times*, 17 March 1916; 'Shakespeare: The Need for Meditation', in *A Book of Homage to Shakespeare* (1916), pp. 135–6; 'A Common Ground: Prof. Trench, T.C.D. and Irish Conference Committee: Settlement Scheme', *Evening Herald*, 14 April 1917 [an interview with Trench]; 'The Church and the Future', *Irish Times*, 26 November 1918; 'The Church and the Future (ii)', *Irish Times*, 3 December 1918; 'The Function of Poetry According to Aristotle', *Studies*, no. 76, 1930, pp. 549–63; 'Mimesis in Aristotle's Poetics', *Hermathena*, 23 (1933), pp. 1–24; 'A Note on Five Dramatic Interruptions; Being a Contribution to the Textual Criticism of Shakespeare', *Hermathena*, 23 (1933), pp. 85–92; 'The Renaissance as Interpreted by the Donnellan Lecturer', *Church of Ireland Gazette*, 21 February 1936; 'The Astronomer and the Renaissance', *Church of Ireland Gazette*, 6 March 1936, p. 141; 'The Ethiopian', *British Weekly*, 4 June 1936; 'The Christian Shakespeare', *British Weekly*, November 19 and 26, 1936; 'The Place of Katharsis in Aristotle's Aesthetics', *Hermathena*, 51 (1938), pp. 110–34; 'On Swift's Marginalia in a Copy of Macky's Memoirs', *Transactions of the Bibliographical Society*, December 1938, pp. 354–62 (with K. B. Garratt). He also wrote an introduction to the pamphlet by 'Unificus', *Ireland's Opportunity: A Plea for Settlement by Conference* (1916).

37 *Royal Commission on University Education in Ireland, Appendix to the Third Report, Minutes of Evidence Taken in April, May and June 1902*, evidence 7482.
38 Letter of application dated 9 May 1899, National Archives, CSORP 1899/8551.
39 Letter from Anderson to the under secretary reporting on applications for chair of English, History, and Mental Science dated 29 May 1899, National Archives, CSORP 1899/9800.

than that further subjects be added, his proposal seems quite extraordinary. The difficulty of finding someone with expertise in three separate subject areas was difficult enough – of the nineteen candidates for the chair in 1899, Anderson considered only five to be properly qualified in all three subjects. One applicant was acknowledged to have qualifications of the very highest order in English Language and Literature, but his testimonials gave 'no evidence of ability to lecture in Mental Science, or indeed of any acquaintance with the subject'.[40] In 1914 the chair of English, History and Mental Science was split into three distinct chairs, those of English, History, and Philosophy.

English

C[HARLES] MAX[WELL] DRENNAN (1870–1935) was the last Professor of History, English, and Mental Science (1913–14) and the first Professor of English Language and English Literature (1914–17). Max Drennan, as he was known, was born at Sandwich, Kent on 9 June 1870 and educated privately. He received an MA in Classics from London University and he graduated from the University of Cambridge, where W.W. Skeat was one of his teachers, in the Mediaeval and Modern Language Tripos, achieving first-class honours with double distinction. He was a scholar of Emmanuel College, Cambridge and a Lecturer in English for the Special Board of Cambridge University from 1910 until he was appointed to the Professorship of History, English, and Mental Science in Galway in 1913, the last person to hold the combined chairs. Following the division of the chair, in October 1914, he became Professor of English Language and English Literature. Drennan, who resided at Milleen, College Road, resigned in 1917 and moved to South Africa to become Professor of English and Philosophy at the School of Mines, Johannesburg and later Professor of English Language and Literature at the same institution, now renamed the University of Witwatersrand. He died on 14 January 1935.

Drennan published *The Spirit of Modern Criticism* (London, 1922), *The Writing of English* (Johannesburg, 1926), (with J. Gurney Lawrie), and editions of Chaucer's *Parlement of Foules* (London, 1914), *Pardoner's Tale* (London, 1910), (with A.J. Wyatt), *Prioress's Tale* (London, 1914), *Prioress's Tale, Tale of Sir Thopas, Monk's Tale* (London, 1933), (with A.J. Wyatt), and *Hous of Fame* (London, 1921), as well as an edition of Langland's *Piers Plowman* (London 1915). The *Intermediate Text-Book of English Literature* (London, 1926–7), pts i and ii, by A.J. Wyatt and W.H. Low, was 'Revised and Partly Rewritten' by Drennan. He published a novel, *The Adventures of Ali Ben* (London, 1931) and also apparently some poems, though Roy Campbell did not think much of them, if we are to judge by his quatrain, 'On Professor Drennan's Verse':

> Who forced the Muse to this alliance?
> A Man of more degrees than parts—

---

40 Ibid.

> The jilted Bachelor of Science
> And Widower of Arts.[41]

In his satire, 'The Waygoose' (1928), a philippic against dullness in the manner of Dryden's 'Mac Flecknoe', Campbell says, with reference to 'Fair Pyorrhoea, the Colonial Muse':

> Inspired by Her the lofty Drennan sprung
> To write his poems—yet remain unhung;
> 'Twas due to Her—a couple rather odd,
> That Drennan in the garden walked with God.
> 'Twas She who breathed the Theory Holistic,
> And turned a general into a mystic.[42]

The general referred to here is Smuts, and in his notes, Campbell quotes Drennan as saying that 'Nobody ought to deny that General Smuts is a *great poet*'.[43]

According to Bruce K. Murray, the historian of the University of Witwatersrand, Drennan, 'an accomplished mediaevalist', was one of the original Arts appointments in 1917. He became Head of the English Department in 1922 and was assisted by J. Gurney Lawrie, with whom he collaborated on *The Writing of English*. He retired in 1931. According to Murray, Drennan

> was noted for his vivid sense of humour, and was particularly popular as a lecturer. He had a gift for conveying the zest as well as the learning of his subject. An important contribution he made to the University was in establishing links with the local community, mainly through his columns in the *Rand Daily Mail* and *Sunday Times*.[44]

While in Galway he wrote a series of articles entitled 'The Short Story: A Literary Chat', for the *Irish Monthly*.[45] It is worth noting that Thomas MacDonagh, one of

---

41 Roy Campbell, *The Collected Poems* (London, 1949), p. 197. We are grateful to Mr Joe O'Halloran, formerly of the James Hardiman Library, NUI, Galway, for this information.
42 Campbell, *The Collected Poems*, p. 262.
43 Ibid., p. 293.
44 Bruce K. Murray, *Wits: The Early Years. A History of the University of the Witwatersrand, Johannesburg and Its Precursors, 1896–1939* (Johannesburg, 1982), p. 148. We are very grateful to Dr David Attwell, of the Department of English, University of Natal, Pietermaritzburg, South Africa, for this reference.
45 *Irish Monthly*, 44 (1916), pp. 494–9, 568–72, 640–7, and 800–6; 45 (1917), pp. 159–67. He reviewed Thomas MacDonagh's book, *Literature in Ireland: Studies in Irish and Anglo-Irish*, for the *Irish Monthly*, 'The Irish Mode: A Review of Thomas Macdonagh's Last Book', 44 (1916), pp. 706–11. In the same periodical Drennan produced his last article for an Irish publication, the cautionary tale, 'The Cinema and Its Dangers', 45 (1917), pp. 74–82. Drennan also contributed several articles to *Punch*, including several 'Irish' pieces: 'Meditations of Marcus O'Reilly', 148 (1915), p. 442; 'Meditations of Marcus O'Reilly', 149 (1915), pp. 9–10; 'Our School', 149 (1915), p. 121; 'Chatto and the Pessimist', ibid., p. 127; 'In His Own Defence', 149 (1915), p. 154; 'The Recruiting of Poppett Minimus', 149 (1915), pp. 329–30; 'Meditations of Marcus O'Reilly:

the leaders of the 1916 Rising, was a candidate for the professorship to which Drennan was appointed. Indeed there is a letter, written in Irish, in the MacDonagh collection in the National Library of Ireland, from his friend and Gaelic League activist, Seaghan P. Mac Énrí, Professor of Ophthalmology and Otology and Lecturer in Modern Irish in UCG (1910–30), giving details of the Faculty of Arts meeting which considered the applications for the vacant post. According to Mac Énrí:

> Rinne Steinberger agus mé féin troid ar do shon ach bhí an dream Gallda agus an Máilleach ar thaobh an Droighneánaigh. Bhí an Máilleach níos nimhnighe in d'aghaidh ná an dream Gallda agus bhí sé ghá iarraidh a chur n-a luighe ortha nach bhfuil aon mhaitheas in do leabhar. *Eadrainn féin* ní raibh an Paorach chomh láidir ar do thaobh is badh chóir agus thug guthanna n-ár n-aghaidh go minic.[46]

The other main candidate was Mary J. Donovan who the following year became Professor of History (1914–57).

WILLIAM A. BYRNE (1872–1933), Professor of English from 1917 until his death in 1933, was born in Rathangan, Co. Kildare in January 1872, though according to some authorities he was not born until 1876 (fig. 14.3).[47] His father was a national teacher in Rathangan. According to Kathleen Benson (and *Ireland's Own*), he was reading at the age of three and at the age of nine he was writing his first poem, 'a

---

Lucy', 150 (1916), p. 88; 'Why Go to Germany'? 151 (1916), p. 178; 'The Literary Touch', 151 (1916), p. 281; 'The Organiser of Victory', 151 (1916), p. 296; 'The Recent Truce', 152 (1917), p. 112; 'Meditations of Marcus O'Reilly: The Great Dog Fight', 152 (1917), p. 372; 'Meditations of Marcus O'Reilly: On the Danger of Popularity', 153 (1917), pp. 402–3; 'Our Ballybun Lottery', 158 (1920), pp. 42, 44; 'Little Tales for Young Plumbers', 158 (1920), p. 86; 'The Rise and Fall of an Amateur Examiner', 158 (1920), pp. 424–5; 'Remarkable Experiences with a Medium', 163 (1922), p. 342; 'Our Boys', 165 (1923), p. 366; and 'Civilizing Ubongo', 167 (1924), pp. 68–9.

46 Mac Énrí to MacDonagh, 21 February 1913, National Library of Ireland, MacDonagh Papers, MS 20,642. Valentine Steinberger was Professor of Modern Languages and Librarian (1886–1916); Tomás Ó Máille was Professor of Irish (1909–38); and Michael Power was Professor of Mathematics (1912–55). Translation: 'Steinberger and I fought on your behalf but the anti-Irish group and Ó Máille were on Drennan's side. Ó Máille was more poisonous in his opposition to you than they were and he tried to convince them that your book had no value. *Between ourselves* Power did not support you as strongly as he should have and he voted against us frequently'.

47 He was born in 1872 according to Donnchadh A. Meehan, 'Forgotten Singer', *Irish Bookman*, no. 11, 1 (1947), p. 3; Kathleen Benson, 'The Forgotten Poet of Co. Kildare', *Journal of the Co. Kildare Archaeological Society*, no. 1, 14 (1964–5), p. 54; and 'Hall of Fame', *Ireland's Own*, Halloween Annual [November, 1988], p. 38 (which derives its information, without acknowledgement, from Benson's short piece, who in turn silently borrows from Meehan's article). But he was born in 1876 according to K. Donnellan (Catherine Donnellan, BA 1930; MA 1933), an Assistant Lecturer in English at UCG and the editor of the anthology, *The College Book of Poetry: English and Anglo-Irish* (Dublin, n.d.). This volume was published by the Educational Company of Ireland, and dedicated to Byrne's memory. The biographical note on Byrne is on p. 239. James Flynn, 'Sweet Singers Gone', *Capuchin Annual*, 1958, p. 218 also gives Byrnes's date of birth as 1876.

source of great wonder to family and friends', in the words of *Ireland's Own*.[48] However, James Flynn has our young genius composing poetry at the age of five.[49] According to Benson, in his college days he won many exhibitions 'and no student passed through college halls with higher marks or greater distinction'.[50] Benson claims that, in 1915, he went to Cambridge University and took his degree 'with such brilliance' that he was selected for the chair of English at Freiburg University.[51] But Byrne's degree was an external one from London University, not a degree from Cambridge. Because of the war, the Freiburg post was not filled and Byrne was, we are told, '*entitled* to become Tutor to the Royal family', but he nobly declined to accept this distinction because of his Catholicism.[52] But God never closes one door but he opens another, for, on the execution of his friend, the republican, Thomas MacDonagh in 1916, an Assistant Lectureship in English in University College Dublin became vacant and Byrne was unanimously elected. The following year virtue was further rewarded for Byrne was successful where McDonagh had earlier failed: he became Professor of English at University College Galway, a post he was to retain until his death, of a heart attack, in 1933.

14.3 William A. Byrne, Professor of English, 1917–33

In her obituary in the *U.C.G. Annual*, Catherine Donnellan remembered him as a 'brilliant scholar and singer of sweet songs', with 'talents amounting to genius'. She continued: 'Studious, intelligent sensitive and gifted with the gift of poetry, life seemed to hold more in store for him than a professorship in a provincial town'. Ill-health and the Great War combined to frustrate his ambition. When at Maynooth he took the examinations of the Royal University of Ireland (RUI), becoming an exhibitioner and a gold medallist, and achieving a first-class honours degree. So exceptional was his performance, we are told, that W.F. Trench, formerly of Galway, in his capacity as examiner for the RUI, remembered Byrne, though he had never met him, 'as being the only candidate to whom he had ever awarded full honours marks'.[53]

48 Benson, 'The Forgotten Poet', p. 54 and 'Hall of Fame', *Ireland's Own*, p. 38.
49 Flynn, 'Sweet Singers Gone', p. 218.
50 Benson, 'The Forgotten Poet', p. 55.
51 Ibid., p. 54.
52 Ibid.
53 'Kay Don', 'The Late Professor W.A. Byrne', *U.C.G. Annual*, no. 9, 8 (1933–4), p. 15. 'Kay Don' was, presumably, K. (or Catherine) Donnellan.

After his time in Maynooth, Byrne spent two years in Switzerland for reasons of health. On his return to Ireland, he taught for ten years in Knockbeg College and in St Kieran's College, Kilkenny (where a future Professor of English in UCG, Thomas Kilroy, was to study) where his colleagues included Thomas MacDonagh and Francis Sheehy-Skeffington.[54] In order to compete for a Junior Fellowship in the Royal University of Ireland, he entered Emmanuel College, Cambridge, where his tutor in English was A.J. Wyatt (Drennan's collaborator), best known as the editor of *Beowulf*. But before he could compete, the RUI ceased to exist and Byrne presented himself for a degree at London University. He took his BA degree as an external student of London University, with first-class honours in English and French. According to Donnellan, 'he passed with such distinction' that his name was selected for the Chair of English at Freiburg University. His selection 'lay mainly in the hands of Professor Max Drennan', Byrne's predecessor in Galway. Byrne was also offered other appointments, including the Professorship of English at St Xavier's College, Bombay University, 'but he declined all to enter University College London [where John Elliot Cairnes of Galway had, many years previously, taught political economy], and there study the methods of the foremost teachers of Germanic Philology, as a final preparation for the promised appointment in Fribourg [*sic*]'.[55] Prior to beginning this postgraduate work, Byrne had taught for a short while at the Grocers' Company School, Hackney Downs, London.[56]

In 1901 Byrne published, under the pseudonym 'William Dara' (doubtless in homage to his native place and perhaps also to his illustrious predecessor, Michael of Kildare), his only book, a volume of poetry entitled *A Light on the Broom*. The publishers were Sealy, Bryers and Walker. A second edition, under his own name, was published in 1904 by M.H. Gill in Dublin and Benziger Bros in New York. This edition was arranged differently and it included some new poems while omitting some previously published pieces. While he was attending Maynooth (he had hoped to become a priest but he abandoned the idea) he wrote, in 1895, the 'Maynooth Centenary Ode'.[57] According to Donnellan, *The Light on the Broom* was his only other poetic production, apart from 'a few poems in the annual magazine of University College, Galway'. She found the poems of *The Light on the Broom* 'characterised by sweetness, sadness, and a haunting music, for he agreed wholly with W. Pater that all great art tends to the condition of music'.[58] 'The

---

54 Ibid.
55 Ibid., p. 16.
56 Meehan, 'Forgotten Singer', p. 34.
57 Published in [John Healy] (ed.), *A Record of the Centenary Celebrations Held in Maynooth College in June, 1895* (Dublin, 1896), pp. 111–13.
58 Donnellan, *The College Book of Poetry*, p. 239. Among the poems he published in the *U.C.G. Annual* was 'Ballade of Golden Girls', no. 1, 3 (1924–5), p. 57, which was reprinted in no. 3, 4 (1926–7), pp. 42–3, according to the editor, 'at the express request of its author, who has been so beset for copies by his many admirers, that the demand for a second issue was imperative' (p. 43). He also published in the *U.C.G. Annual*, 'The Grail-Song!' no. 5, 5 (1929–30), p. 25; 'Spring', ibid., p. 31; 'Overture', ibid., p. 48; and a short essay, 'Recollections of Father O'Growney', ibid., pp. 35–8.

Purple Heather' is Byrne's best-known poem and, according to Donnellan, it was 'specially singled out for praise' when his volume appeared. The poem, which Donnellan reprinted, was frequently anthologised and is familiar to many people from school readers.[59] If we are to believe Flynn, he was only nine years old when he wrote this poem.[60]

Donnellan found in Byrne's verse that infallible sign (for many a Galway academic) of the poetic, 'a love of nature equal to Wordsworth's', though he was not merely a nature poet but one whose work was inspired by 'a deeply religious feeling and a love of Ireland'.[61] James Flynn found in Byrne an authentic exponent of the Celtic note as successfully marketed by Matthew Arnold: his nature poetry had Celtic charm and magic and he was a prime exemplar of what Arnold had called the 'Titanism' of the Celts.[62] When *The Light on the Broom* appeared, T.P. O'Connor (himself a Galway graduate) spoke of the 'general purity of tone and the intense human and national sympathy' which was diffused throughout the volume.[63] According to Hannah Sheehy-Skeffington, the appearance of the book 'at once placed Dara in the front rank among the poets of the day'.[64] One enthusiast contrasted Yeats's 'ramshackle' philosophy unfavourably with Byrne's who saw 'Rathangan as a parable of the divine reality'.[65] In like manner, Swords wondered if, in the 'Song of a Turf Sod', Byrne 'was anticipating those racial archetypes at which Carl Jung was to arrive years afterwards in his groping into the "Collective unconscious of the Race"'.[66] But even Yeats himself ('the other great Willie', as Kathleen Benson admiringly calls him),[67] whom, apparently, Byrne met only once, in Galway, seemed not unappreciative of his worth.[68] Yeats wrote to him as follows: 'Lady Gregory has just read to me your charming lines on bringing back the old Gaelic music heard in a dream'.[69] In her autobiography, *Life and the Dream*, Mary Colum, describing what authors Irish people were reading in the early years of the twentieth century, wrote that, among others, 'there was William Dara, whose verses the students read, and probably other people, though I never met them'. Colum, who did not seem to realise that 'William Dara' was a pseudonym, then added: 'Long afterwards, in the 1930s, James Joyce, who had been a student some years before me, recalled so much of William Dara, as did I, that, sitting in a Paris café, we were able to repeat his verses line by alternative line'.[70] Indeed Joyce,

---

59 Donnellan, *The College Book of Poetry*, pp. 193–5.
60 Flynn, 'Sweet Singers Gone', pp. 218–9.
61 Donnellan, 'The Late Professor W.A. Byrne', p. 16.
62 Flynn, 'Sweet Singers Gone', pp. 221, 222.
63 Cited in Donnellan, 'The Late Professor W.A. Byrne', p. 18.
64 In an article in the *Irish Press*, the week of Byrne's death in 1933, cited in Meehan, 'Forgotten Singer', p. 34.
65 L.F.K. Swords, 'How to Read the Poems of William Byrne', *Vexilla Regis*, 1956, p. 106.
66 Ibid., p. 109.
67 Benson, 'The Forgotten Poet', p. 54; Meehan, who was Benson's source, had said that Byrne possessed 'a genuine organ for what is true and excellent', 'Forgotten Singer', p. 33.
68 Information supplied to Meehan by Peter Byrne, the poet-professor's brother. William Byrne found Yeats 'very talkative and very absent-minded', Meehan, 'Forgotten Singer', p. 35.
69 Cited in Donnellan, 'The Late Professor W.A. Byrne', p. 18.
70 Mary Colum, *Life and the Dream*, revised edition, with additional material (Dublin, 1966), p. 100.

if we are to believe him, intended to write about 'Dara'. In a letter to his brother Stanislaus on 13 November 1906, Joyce wrote: 'You remember the book I spoke to you of one day in the Park into which I was going to put William Dara and Lady Belvedere'. The editor, Richard Ellmann, was unable to identify Dara and did not realise that it was a pseudonym. In a footnote he remarked that 'Dara is said to have owned a house near Belvedere College on Great Denmark Street'.[71]

The distinguished medievalist, W.P. Ker (later to become Professor of Poetry at Oxford), whom he must have known from his time at University College London, wrote a testimonial in support of Byrne's application for the Galway chair in which he found his candidate exhibiting qualities rarely to be found consorting together, accuracy and inspiration.[72] His obituarist tells us that Byrne knew all his students and took a personal interest in them and that his kindness won their lasting affection.[73] This interest sometimes took peculiar forms. According to Tomás Ó Broin, who took his BA in English and Irish in 1932 and was later to become Professor of Modern Irish Literature in UCG, 'Billy Byrne', as the students called him, had a curious habit:

> Dhéanadh sé tagairt do chuid de na mná sciamhacha agus mná meabhracha a bhí mar mhic léinn aige. Bhí pictiúirí na mban sin ar an matal taobh thiar den ollamh. Bhí a fhios ag an saol nach raibh caidreamh ceart riamh aige le bean ar bith; ba bhaitsiléara críochnaithe é. Grá i gcéin a bhí i gceist, grá éagmaise.[74]

According to Michael Power, Professor of Mathematics at UCG from 1912 to 1955, who has been a student of Byrne's for a short period around 1901 at St Kieran's College, Kilkenny, his 'lady students had a particular affection for him, of which he showed appreciation in his own whimsical way by writing a poem to them in the College Magazine'.[75] Byrne also published a number of critical articles in the *Carlovian*.[76] He is buried in the New Cemetery, Bohermore, Galway.

JEREMIAH MURPHY, or Diarmuid Ua Murchadha (1895–1966), who was Professor of English Language and English Literature, from 1934 until 1965, was born at Ballincollig, Co. Cork in 1895. His mother was a teacher and his father was a builder. He received his primary education locally and he attended secondary school at the Christian Brothers, North Monastery in Cork city. Having obtained

---

71 Richard Ellmann (ed.), *Letters of James Joyce* (London, 1966), vol. ii, p. 193.
72 Cited in Donnellan, 'The Late Professor W.A. Byrne', p. 18.
73 Ibid.
74 Personal communication to authors from an tOllamh Tomás Ó Broin, Ollamh Emeritus le Litríocht na Nua-Ghaeilge, NUI, Galway. Translation: 'He used to refer to some of the good-looking women and the intelligent women who were his students. There were photographs of these women on the mantelpiece behind the professor. But everyone knew that he never had a proper relationship with any woman, for he was a confirmed bachelor. It was all fantasy'.
75 M[ichael] P[ower], 'William Dara (William A. Hayden Byrne)', *Vexilla Regis*, 1956, p. 103. This was the 'Ballade of Golden Girls', *U.C.G. Annual*, no. 1, 3 (1924–5), p. 57 and reprinted no. 3, 4 (1926–7), pp. 42–3.
76 Meehan, 'Forgotten Singer', p. 44.

the BA degree in English from University College Cork (where he studied with Professor W.F.P. Stockley), he went on to achieve his MA, in 1926, for a thesis entitled 'The Spirit of Anglo-Saxon Literature as Reflected in Later English'. He was granted a PhD in 1932 for his translation into Irish of the Anglo-Saxon Chronicles. From 1931–3 he was an assistant to Professor Daniel Corkery at Cork. Murphy had also taught at primary level for three years but his main experience was as a secondary teacher for fifteen years. His first teaching post was at the Christian Brothers, Carlow (1915–16) and he spent ten years on the staff of Christian Brothers' College, Cork (1923–33). According to the testimonial of Dr Edward J. Thomas of the University of Cambridge, the external examiner for the PhD degree, Murphy had produced

> an Irish translation of independent value both from the point of view of language and of history. In it the Irish students of the English language and Irish historical students have a scientific work more reliable than anything that exists in English.[77]

Under the name Diarmuid Murphy, he wrote a work of fiction, *Hewn of the Rock*, published by Talbot Press, Dublin in 1933 and consisting of two novellas, 'The Bare Place' and 'Kato'. He also wrote a number of short stories for various periodicals. However, his main interest was drama and the theatre. As a young man he was associated with St Aidan's amateur theatre group in his native Ballincollig. This group was the first to stage Patrick Pearse's play, *The Singer*, in Dublin, at the Peacock Theatre, with Murphy as producer. He was deeply involved in amateur drama in Cork and was associated with the Cork Shakespearean Company ('The Loft'). He wrote several plays, both in English and in Irish, and won a prize and received a commendation for two plays which he entered for the Tailteann Literary Competition in 1931. When he moved to Galway he soon became closely involve with Taibhdhearc na Gaillimhe, as actor, director, writer and, for twelve years, Chairman of the Board of Directors. He wrote several plays which were staged at An Taidhbhearc, and many of the annual pantomimes. He also composed two 'saga dances', which he described as a sort of precursor of Irish ballet. At UCG, he founded the Dramatic Society (its predecessor had been defunct for a number of years), the Arts Society, as well as the Boat Club. He was a founder member, and the first President, of the Galway Literary Society which was set up in 1944, and he also became a member of the Board of the Abbey Theatre.

Jeremiah Murphy was very much as Christopher Townley described him in an obituary, 'a students' man'.[78] He produced no scholarly or critical work, apart from what Townley called his 'yearly *pot-pourri*' for the *Capuchin Annual*.[79] Murphy retired in 1965 and died within a year.

77 Application for chair of English Language and Literature, NUI, Galway Archives. We are grateful to Professor Murphy's daughter, Mrs Mary Rose MacNamara, Bankyle House, Corofin, Co. Clare, for information on her late father.
78 Christopher Townley, 'Tribute to a Scholar Friend', *Capuchin Annual*, 1967, pp. 270–2. The reference is on p. 270.
79 Ibid., p. 272. The following is a complete listing of Murphy's writings for the *Capuchin Annual*:

PATRICK M. DISKIN (1914–94) was an Assistant in English from 1938 until 1962 and Lecturer in English Language and Literature from 1962 until his retirement in 1983. He was born in Milltown, Co. Galway on 7 August 1914 and educated at St Jarlath's College, Tuam to which he won an entrance scholarship in 1927. He also won scholarships at UCG as well as the Blayney Exhibition in Classics. He graduated in 1935 with first-class honours in English and Irish. He was awarded the MA degree in 1952, also with first-class honours, for a thesis entitled 'The Poetry of Thomas Moore'. Diskin lectured frequently to clubs and societies in the west of Ireland and he was a founder member of the Galway Literary Society. In terms of his research, he was particularly interested in nineteenth-century Irish literature in the English language. He was especially accomplished in the identification of literary sources and many of his publications are in this area.[80] He retired in 1983 and died on 23 April 1994.

On the retirement of Jeremiah Murphy, the Professorship of English Language and English Literature was divided into two, Modern English, to which Lorna T. Reynolds was appointed (1966–77) and Old and Medieval English, which was

---

'The Choice of Circumstance: A Mediaeval Selection', 1958, pp. 379–89; 'Reflections and Refractions: Theatrical Cogitations', 1960, pp. 73–83; 'Meandering Meditations Mainly Theatrical', 1961, pp. 247–58; 'Great Literature: Philosophical Musings Thereon', 1962, pp. 195–205; 'Sporadic Sanities Regarding Literary Criticism in the Green Fields of the Sacred Cows', 1963, pp. 372–83; 'Sentiment and Sentimentality in Ballad, Song and Lyric', 1964, pp. 224–36; Comment on Desmond Fennell, 'The Failure of the Irish Revolution – and Its Success', 1964, pp. 347–9; 'The Poet and the Theatre: An Inquiry', 1965, pp. 257–69; 'Donal: Reflections upon the Personality and Work of Daniel Corkery, M.A., D.Litt.', 1967, pp. 83–97.

80 The following is a list of Patrick Diskin's main publications: Letter on Capt. Edward P. Doherty, the 'Avenger of Lincoln's Death', *The Bell*, no. 2, 14 (1947), pp. 85–8; 'Galway's Literary Associations', *Galway Reader*, no. 3, 1 (1948), pp. 32–5; 'Irish-American Writers', *Iarlaith*, 1957, pp. 106–8; 'The Poetry of James Clarence Mangan', *University Review*, no. 1, 2 (1958), pp. 21–30; 'Moore's Irish Melodies', *University Review*, no. 8, 2 (1960), pp. 34–40; 'A Source for Yeats's "The Black Tower"', *Notes and Queries*, 206 (1961), pp. 107–8; 'Irish Scholars and Language Workers in the West, 1800–1900', *Iarlaith*, 1961, pp. 88–92; 'Replies', *Notes and Queries*, 210 (1965), pp. 278–9 [an addition to 'The Black Tower' note above]; 'Joyce and Charlotte Brontë', *Notes and Queries*, 211 (1966), pp. 94–5; 'Poe, Le Fanu and the Sealed Room Mystery', *Notes and Queries*, 211 (1966), pp. 337–9; 'The Gaelic Background to Anglo-Irish Poetry', *Topic: A Journal of the Liberal Arts*, no. 24, Fall, 1972, pp. 37–51; 'The Literary Background of "The Old Curiosity Shop"', *Notes and Queries*, 219 (1974), pp. 210–13; 'Some Sources of "Wuthering Heights"', *Notes and Queries*, 222 (1977), pp. 354–61; 'Yeats's "Purgatory" and Werner's "Der Vierundzwanzigste Februar"', *Notes and Queries*, 224 (1979), pp. 340–2; 'Joyce's "The Dead" and Hardy's *The Woodlanders*', *Notes and Queries*, 228 (1983), pp. 330–1; 'Eliot, Dickens, and *The Waste Land*', *Notes and Queries*, 229 (1984), p. 511; 'Galway's Literary Associations', in Diarmuid Ó Cearbhaill (ed.), *Galway Town and Gown 1484–1984* (Dublin, 1984), pp. 206–22. He also wrote a number of articles, based on original research, for the *Connacht Tribune*, including the following: 'M.J. Logan and *An Gaodhal*', 'Eva of *The Nation*', 'Young Irelanders and Fenians in Queen's College, Galway', 'The Author of *Mick McQuaid*', 'Francis A. Fahy', 'A County Galway Astronomer – John Birmingham'. He published several reviews in *Notes and Queries* and many reviews and articles, on a wide variety of literary topics, in 'Writing in the West' (*Connacht Tribune*), *West Magazine*, and elsewhere. We are grateful to his widow, Mrs Máire Diskin, for her kind assistance, and to John Cunningham, Department of History, NUI, Galway and Dr Riana O'Dwyer, Department of English, NUI, Galway for their help in locating material.

filled by P. Leo Henry (1966–87). Thomas Kilroy (1978–89) succeeded Lorna Reynolds as Professor of Modern English and was, in turn, succeeded by Kevin Barry in 1991.[81]

14.4 M.J. Donovan-O'Sullivan, Professor of History, 1914–57

History

MARY J. DONOVAN-O'SULLIVAN (1887–1966), was Professor of History at UCG from 1914 until her retirement in 1957 (fig. 14.4). Mary Donovan, the daughter of William and Bridget Donovan from Co. Cork, was born in Fairhill, Galway in 1887. Her father had been in the Royal Navy and, during the First World War, she became president of the Galway Ladies Recruiting Committee. She was educated by the Dominican nuns at Taylor's Hill, Galway and at QCG, where she received the BA in 1908 and the MA in 1909, both with first-class

---

81 Declan Kiberd is listed in the *Calendar* of 1990–1 as Professor of English but he did not take up the position.

honours, having been the recipient of many prizes on the way. On Trench's resignation in 1912, she was a candidate for the Professorship of History, English Literature, and Mental Science. At the meeting of the Governing Body (6 March 1913), of which she was the only woman member, she discussed the report of the Academic Council on the candidates and then withdrew from the contest. In the subsequent vote, Max Drennan received thirteen votes and Thomas MacDonagh received seven. Both names were submitted to the Senate and Drennan was appointed. Donovan then became Drennan's assistant in English. In October 1914 Drennan became Professor of English Language and English Literature. At a meeting of the Governing Body (25 June 1914), Professors Robert McElderry (Ancient Classics) and Joseph Pye (Anatomy and Physiology) proposed that the appointment to the Professorship of History, 'with special reference to Irish History', be postponed but the proposition was not adopted. Donovan received eighteen votes, with McElderry and Pye not voting. No other candidates received votes but it was decided to also submit the names of Bryan A. Kelly and Miss Monckton Jones to the Senate. Donovan was appointed, becoming the first woman professor in Galway, and she served until her retirement in 1957.[82]

She had been a student of Professor Trench and she formally made a presentation to him, on behalf of the students of the College, at a ceremony to mark his departure from Galway. In his address, M.J. Fogarty, representing the students, spoke about some of the distinguished recent graduates of the Department, among them Donovan. 'I cannot refrain from mentioning', he concluded, 'one other name which reflects a lustre on our Arts School – Miss Donovan – on whom her fellow graduates have recently conferred so high an honour'.[83] She was a member of the Connaught Women's Franchise League and wrote an article in the *Galway Express* (10 May 1913) on 'Why I am a Supporter of Woman's Suffrage'. In the area of work, women had to overcome 'a world of prejudice' and although 'probably better qualified than most men' received 'something like half the salary for the crime of being a woman'.[84]

Donovan-O'Sullivan, who lived at Liosgorm, Rockbarton, in Galway, is mainly remembered for her *Old Galway: The History of a Norman Colony in Ireland*, published by W. Heffer and Sons, Cambridge in 1942. She was the editor of the *Galway Archaeological and Historical Journal* from 1932 until 1951 and she wrote many articles for this publication.[85] Two articles which she published in the 'Tory

---

82 Governing Body Minutes, Archives, NUI, Galway.
83 *Galway Express*, 22 February 1913.
84 Mary Clancy, 'On the "Western Outpost": Local Government and Women's Suffrage in County Galway', in Gerard Moran and Raymond Gillespie (eds), *Galway: History and Society: Interdisciplinary Essays on the History of an Irish County* (Dublin, 1996), p. 544.
85 The following is a list of her publications in the *Journal of the Galway Archaeological and Historical Society*: 'The Lay School at Galway in the Sixteenth and Seventeenth Centuries', 15 (1931–3), pp. 1–32; 'Glimpses of the Life of Galway Merchants and Mariners in the Early Seventeenth Century', 15 (1931–3), pp. 129–40; 'Notes on the Lives of Aedanus Burke and John Daly Burke', 15 (1931–3), p. 165; 'The Fortification of Galway in the Sixteenth and Early Seventeenth Centuries', 16 (1934–5), pp. 1–47; 'Obituary of The Right Hon. the Earl of Westmeath', 16 (1934–5), p. 92; 'Barnabe Googe Provost-Marshal of Connaught, 1582–5', 18 (1938–9), pp. 1–39; 'Note on the St. Nicholas Mss', 18 (1938–9), pp. 69–71; 'The Use of Leisure

and Conservative' *Quarterly Review* in 1930 ('Eight Years of Irish Home Rule') and 1932 ('Minorities in the Irish Free State'), were vigorously attacked by one Stephen Quinn in the conservative and pugnacious *Catholic Bulletin*.[86]

GERARD A. HAYES-MCCOY (1911–75), who was born in Galway, was appointed Professor of History in 1958, in succession to Donovan-O'Sullivan, a position he held until his death in 1975. He was, according to Charles Petrie,

> a most painstaking scholar, and the original research which he did, particularly in the sixteenth century period, threw a great deal of light upon an area which had hitherto been the playground of religious and political prejudice to which Hayes-McCoy was a total stranger.[87]

His appointment to the chair at Galway was the 'culmination of a brilliant academic career' and his work had 'advanced our knowledge in many spheres, for his information was little short of encyclopaedic'.[88] Speaking of his 'prodigious' output, Nicholas Canny stated that *Scots Mercenary Forces in Ireland* established his reputation, a monograph which was followed by 'a series of stimulating and original papers on military affairs in sixteenth century Ireland'. According to Canny, when taken together, these publications 'constitute a reappraisal of Irish history of the sixteenth century in a European context, and they established G.A. Hayes-McCoy as one of the leading Irish scholars of his generation'.[89]

Hayes-McCoy was, for many years, the editor of the *Irish Sword*, the journal of the Military History Society of Ireland, of which he was a founding member. He was also one of the longest-standing members of the Galway Archaeological and

---

in Old Galway', 18 (1938–9), pp. 99–120; 'Some Documents Relating to Galway', 18 (1938–9), pp. 170–82; 'An Inquiry Concerning Polychrome Jugs', 20 (1942–3), p. 85; 'The Wives of Ulick 1st Earl of Clanricarde', 21 (1944–5), pp. 174–83; 'Italian Merchant Bankers and the Collection of Papal Revenues in Ireland in the Thirteenth Century', 22 (1947), pp. 132–63; 'The Centenary of Galway College', 51(1999), pp. 24–42 (introduced and edited by Joe O'Halloran). Among her other publications are the following: 'Sea Wrack: An Appreciation', in *U.C.G.: A College Annual*, no. 2, 1 (1914), pp. 6–8; 'Matthew de Oviedo, Archbishop of Dublin and the Counter-Reformation', *Studies*, 17 (1928), pp. 94–107; 'Eight Years of Irish Home Rule', *Quarterly Review*, no. 504, 254 (1930), pp. 230–49; 'Minorities in the Free State', *Quarterly Review*, no. 512, 258 (1932), pp. 312–26; 'The Exploitation of the Mines in Ireland in the Sixteenth Century', *Studies*, 24 (1935), pp. 442–52; 'Some Italian Merchant Bankers in Ireland in the Late 13th Century', *Royal Society of Antiquaries of Ireland Journal*, series 7, 19 (1949), pp. 10–19.

86 Stephen Quinn, 'Our Academic Flower Show, 1930', *Catholic Bulletin*, no. 9, 20 (1930), pp. 857–62, and Stephen Quinn, 'The Western Professor Again', *Catholic Bulletin*, no. 6, 22 (1932), pp. 437–43.
87 Charles Petrie, 'An Appreciation', *Irish Sword*, no. 47, 12 (1975), p. 81.
88 Ibid.
89 Nicholas Canny, 'G.A. Hayes-McCoy: An Appreciation', *Journal of the Galway Archaeological and Historical Society*, 35 (1976), p. 157. Canny (ibid.) lists the following papers as being the most notable: 'Strategy and Tactics in Irish Warfare, 1593–1601', *Irish Historical Studies*, 2 (1941), pp. 255–79; 'The Army of Ulster, 1593–1601', *Irish Sword*, 1 (1951), pp. 105–17; 'The Early History of Guns in Ireland', *Journal of the Galway Archaeological and Historical Society*, 18 (1938), pp. 43–65.

Historical Society and he was a frequent contributor to its *Journal*. His reputation as a professional historian rests overwhelmingly on his contributions to military history, but he also wrote on other aspects of history, on the history of his native Galway city, on ships, on historical figures in fiction, and on Robert Louis Stevenson. He also wrote poems, radio and pageant scripts, and even a cartoon strip for the *Cork Examiner*. There is an exhaustive listing of his works by Harman Murtagh, in the *Irish Sword* issue of winter 1975.[90] Among his main publications are: *Scots Mercenary Forces in Ireland, 1565–1603* (London and Dublin, 1937); (ed.), *Historical Studies* iv (London, 1963); (ed.), *The Irish at War* (Cork, 1964); *Ulster and Other Irish Maps c. 1600* (Dublin, 1964); *Irish Battles* (London, 1969); (ed.), *Historical Studies* x (Galway, 1976); and the posthumously-published *A History of Irish Flags from Earliest Times* (Dublin, 1979).

SÍLE NÍ CHINNÉIDE (1901–80), was Lecturer in History (through Irish), 1927–65 and Associate Professor of History, 1965–70 (fig. 14.5). She was born into a republican family in Waterford in 1901. She entered University College Cork in 1920 and graduated with a BA degree in 1923. In 1925 she was awarded the MA in History by UCC for a thesis on the origins and results of the plantation of Ulster in the seventeenth century. In the same year she received the Higher Diploma in Education. Having spent some time in continental Europe, she taught for a while in schools before being appointed, in 1927, to a Lectureship in History (through Irish), at University College Galway, becoming one of the first to be appointed to teach subjects through the Irish language in the university system. She was promoted to Associate Professor of History in 1965, a position she retained until her retirement in 1970. She died in 1980.[91]

In her research she concentrated on eighteenth and nineteenth-century Irish history, being especially interested in Franco-Irish relations in this period. She edited the accounts of various French visitors on the state of Ireland in the late eighteenth century and she was particularly interested in the historical connections between Ireland and Europe. According to an tOllamh Gearóid Ó Tuathaigh, 'Bhí scoláireacht chruinn, intleacht scóipiúil, agus breithiúntas meáite ag baint lena saothar foilsithe ar fad'.[92] She was a founder and, from 1954 to 1965, the co-editor of the Irish-language historical journal, *Galvia*. She was also, for many years, a joint editor of the *Journal of the Galway Archaeological and Historical Society*. She published a textbook, *An tSean-Eoraip* (Dublin, 1947) as well as numerous scholarly articles and reviews in a wide variety of journals and periodicals.[93] She

---

90 Harman Murtagh, 'The Historical Writings of G.A. Hayes-McCoy', *Irish Sword*, no. 47, 12 (1975), pp. 83–9. This listing excludes over two hundred book reviews as well as his purely journalistic writings.
91 Application for Associate Professorship, UCG, 1965, NUI, Galway Archives.
92 M.A.G. Ó Tuathaigh, 'Obituary: An tOllamh Síle Ní Chinnéide, M.A. (1901–1980)', *North Munster Antiquarian Journal*, 22 (1980), p. 79. Translation: 'Her scholarship was careful, her intellect expansive, and all her published work was characterised by a measured judgement'.
93 The following is a list of her main academic publications: 'Some Dangers Threatening Bilingual Education in Ireland', *Irish Monthly*, 60 (1932), pp. 689–92; 'The Foundations of Modern Ulster', *Ireland To-Day*, no. 2, 1 (1936), pp. 21–9; review of Nicholas Mansergh, *The Government*

wrote many reviews of historical works, as well as special articles, for the national newspapers, as well as broadcasting on historical subjects. Most of her summer holidays were spent on the continent working on documents of Irish interest in French and German archives. In 1953 she was appointed by the Department of External Affairs to represent Ireland at the Round Table Conference in Rome, a conference convened by the Council of Europe to formulate plans for closer co-operation between the universities of Western Europe. She was a member of various public boards, such as the Cultural Relations Committee of the Department of External Affairs, the Military History Bureau, and the Television Commission.

TOMÁS P. Ó NÉILL or Thomas P. O'Neill (1921–96) was born in Co. Carlow and educated at Knockbeg College (as was William A. Byrne) and at University College Dublin. In 1942 he received the BA degree with first-class honours, winning a postgraduate scholarship. In 1946 he was awarded the MA degree, with first-class honours, for a thesis entitled 'The Organisation and Administration of Relief during the Great Famine'. This work, which formed the basis for his chapter in Edwards and Williams's *The Great Famine*, is, according to an tOllamh Gearóid Ó Tuathaigh,

14.5 Síle Ní Chinnéide, Lecturer in History (through Irish), 1927–65, Associate Professor of History, 1965–70

of Northern Ireland: A Study in Devolution, in *Ireland To-Day*, no. 7, 1 (1936), pp. 77–8; 'Irish in the Schools', *Ireland To-Day*, no. 3, 2 (1937), pp. 58–60; 'Our Western Seaboard', *Ireland To-Day*, no. 12, 2 (1937), pp. 13–19; 'A Frenchman's Impression of Limerick, Town and People, in 1791', *North Munster Antiquarian Journal*, 5 (1946–8), pp. 96–101; 'Cathair na Gaillimhe sa Bhlian 1791', *Fír*, 3 (1948–50), pp. 39–44; 'Coquebert de Montbret, in Search of the Hidden Ireland', *Journal of the Royal Society of Antiquaries of Ireland*, pt 1, 82 (1952), pp. 62–7; 'Coquebert de Montbret's Impression of Galway City and County in the Year 1791', *Journal of the Galway Archaeological and Historical Society*, 25 (1952), pp. 1–14; 'Dhá Leabhar Nótaí le Séarlas Ó Conchubhair', *Galvia*, 1 (1954), pp. 32–41; 'Luke Wadding, 1588–1657', *Journal of the Galway Archaeological and Historical Society*, 26 (1955–6), pp. 81–93; 'Dialann Í Chonchúir', cuid a dó, *Galvia*, 4 (1957), pp. 4–17; review of Patrick K. Egan, *The Parish of Ballinasloe*, in *Journal of the Galway Archaeological and Historical Society*, 29 (1960), pp. 39–40; 'The Gaelic Contribution to Irish Nationalism', *University Review*, no. 9, 2 (1960), pp. 67–76; *Napper Tandy and the European Crisis of 1798–1803*, O'Donnell Lecture Delivered at University College, Galway, July 1962 (Dublin, [1962]); 'Burgairí agus Buirgéisí', review of Gearóid Mac Niocaill, 'Na Buirgéisí XII–XV Aois', *Galvia*, 10 (1964–5), pp. 41–5; review of Aubrey Gwynn, *The Twelfth Century Reform*, vol. ii, pt i of *A History of Irish Catholicism* (ed.), P.J. Corish, *North Munster Antiquarian Journal*, 11 (1968), pp. 88–9.

'an outstanding piece of work' which has 'stood the test of time very well'.[94] In 1948 he was appointed Assistant Librarian in the National Library of Ireland and he was promoted to the post of Assistant Keeper of Printed Books in 1952. From 1949–51 he was seconded by the government to do historical research on the question of Irish partition. From 1963 to 1967 he was granted leave of absence, without pay, to write the authorised biography of Éamon de Valera. Jointly with Pádraig Ó Fiannachta, he published the two-volume work in Irish (Dublin, 1968, 1970) and with Lord Longford the single-volume English version (Dublin and London, 1970). In 1967 he was appointed Lecturer in History, a post he held until 1982 when he was promoted to Associate Professor of History. He retired in 1987 and died in Dublin in 1996.

O'Neill's professional life was extraordinarily full and varied. He was a member of the consultative committee of the Irish Historical Society, an editorial director of Irish University Press, a historical adviser on documentary films on Irish history, *Mise Éire* and *Saoirse*, and on various television programmes on Irish history. He lectured to many learned societies but he was also an extremely popular speaker with non-specialist audiences. He published very extensively, in English and in Irish, in many journals and periodicals and on a wide variety of subjects, such as the Great Famine, the economic and political ideas of James Fintan Lalor, bookbinding, printing, paper currency, paper-making, and Irish radical journals. From 1942 until 1945 inclusive, he was mainly responsible for compiling 'Writings on Irish History' for the journal *Irish Historical Studies*. These were comprehensive annual bibliographies of books and articles on Irish history. He wrote several articles on Fintan Lalor and published a biography, in Irish, *Fiontán Ó Leathlobhair* (Dublin, 1962). He also published a well-known booklet, *Sources of Irish Local History* (Dublin, 1958), a reprint of eight articles which had appeared in *An Leabharlann* from 1955 to 1957. He had, according to Gearóid Ó Tuathaigh, 'a formidable knowledge of the sources for the history of modern Ireland' and he was 'unfailingly generous' in sharing it with others.[95]

JOHN G. BARRY (1926–89), was born in Conna, Co. Cork and educated at Mount Mellary Seminary and University College Cork. He was awarded the BA degree in 1947, with first-class honours in History and English. In 1949 he received the MA degree, with first-class honours, for a thesis entitled 'Survivals of Early Irish Church Organisation in Late Medieval and Early Modern Times'. In 1952 he received the PhD degree, for a thesis entitled 'The Function of Coarb and Erenagh in the Irish Church'. In 1950 he became assistant librarian at the National Library of Ireland. In 1962 he was appointed Lecturer in History (with special reference to Medieval History), a position which he held until his appointment to

---

94 Gearóid Ó Tuathaigh, 'Professor T.P. O'Neill: An Appreciation', *Connacht Tribune*, 8 March 1996. T.P. O'Neill, 'The Organisation and Administration of Relief, 1845–52', in R. Dudley Edwards and T. Desmond Williams (eds), *The Great Famine* (Dublin, 1956), pp. 205–60. Details of O'Neill's life and work, for the early period, are taken from his application for the Lectureship in History in 1967, NUI, Galway Archives.
95 Ibid.

the newly-created Professorship of Medieval History in UCC in 1965. He died on 6 August 1989. He contributed articles to various journals, including the *Irish Ecclesiastical Record*, the *Journal of the Cork Historical and Archaeological Society*, and the *Irish Sword*. He also contributed to the *New Catholic Encyclopaedia*.[96]

Thomas Bartlett was appointed Junior Lecturer in History in 1978, a position he retained until his promotion to Lecturer in 1985. He was made Associate Professor of History in 1993; he resigned in 1995 to become Professor of Modern Irish History at UCD. Gearóid Mac Niocaill was appointed Lecturer in History in 1971 and Professor of History in 1977, following the death of Hayes-McCoy. He retired in 1997 and was succeeded by Professor Nicholas Canny as Head of the Department of History.

Philosophy

JOHN F.W. HOWLEY (1866–1941), Professor of Philosophy from 1914 until 1936, was the eldest son of Richard Irwin Howley, and was born in Sligo in 1866 (fig. 14.6). He was educated at Summerhill College, Sligo, St Stanislaus's College, Tullabeg, and University College Dublin. He received the BA degree in 1888, majoring in Philosophy and Physics and Chemistry. He received the MA in Philosophy in 1889, and the DLitt in 1925 for his book, *Psychology and Mystical Experience*. He was appointed Professor of Psychology and Pedagogy at St Patrick's Training College, Drumcondra, Dublin in 1908 and in 1914 he moved to Galway to become Professor of Philosophy. He was selected as Examiner in English to the Intermediate Board in 1912 and he was substitute professor and internal examiner in English at UCG in 1917, during the interregnum between Professors Drennan and Byrne. He also served for a period as Dean of the Faculty of Arts. He was Librarian from 1917 until his retirement in 1936. He became a member of the Governing Body in 1928 and he represented the College at the Catholic Emancipation celebrations of 1929 (he was a canopy-bearer) and at the Eucharistic Congress in 1932. He was President of the Library Association of Ireland in 1941 and he was a member of the Hospitals Library Council from 1937 until his death. He was President both of the Arts Society and the Dramatic Society in the College and he was President of the St Vincent de Paul Conference in UCG and according to an obituary in *Irisleabhar Choláiste na hIolsgoile, Gaillimh*, (signed 'C. T.', presumably Christopher Townley, later to become Librarian at UCG), 'níor staon sé ó bheith ag obair le cruadhchás bochtán na Gaillimhe do laghdú'.[97]

According to a tribute in the *U.C.G. Annual* on his retirement from the College (signed by 'M. H.', presumably Margaret Heavey, or Mairéad Ní Éimhigh, then

---

96 We are grateful to an tUasal Aoife Ní Bhraoin, College Archives, University College Cork for providing us with material on the late Professor Barry.
97 C[hristopher] T[ownley], 'In Memoriam Sheáin Uí Amhluidhe M.A., D.Litt. (1866–1941): Ard-Ollamh agus Leabharlannaidhe', no. i, 3 (1941–2), p. 51. Translation: 'He never ceased to work to alleviate the hardship of the poor of Galway'.

14.6 John F. Howley, Professor of Philosophy, 1914–36

Lecturer in and later Professor of Ancient Classics in UCG), Howley was a very impressive public speaker and there was a brisk demand for his services intra and extra murally. He spoke at debates in the College and addressed the Aquinas study circle; he gave public lectures in Galway but reached a larger audience through his allocutions to the Congresses of the Catholic Truth Society of Ireland.[98] Indeed, he had been the Auditor of the Literary and Historical Society at University College Dublin for the year 1889–90 and his inaugural address to that body was published, in 1889, by Browne and Nolan in Dublin. It was entitled *Prussian Education a History and a Lesson*.

He published one book, *Psychology and Mystical Experience* (London, 1920). He was a frequent contributor to periodicals such as the *Month*, *Monthly Review*, *Macmillan's Magazine*, *Contemporary Review*, *New Ireland Review*, *Catholic Bulletin*, and *Studies*[99]. He was in great demand as a reviewer, particularly of

98 M[argaret] H[eavey], 'Dr John Howley: His Work for U.C.G.', *U.C.G. Annual*, 1936–7, pp. 20–1.
99 The following is a list of most of Howley's contributions to periodicals: 'Family and Faction', *Contemporary Review*, 88 (1905), pp. 53–9; 'The Scylla and Charybdis of the Living Wage', *New*

Catholic books. He also took part in various broadcasts on Radio Éireann between 1937 and 1940.[100] As Librarian, Howley had occasion to deal with no less a personage than James Joyce. Michael Healy, Joyce's uncle-in-law, had asked Joyce to send a prospectus concerning the facsimile manuscript edition of his booklet *Pomes Penyeach* (Paris, 1932) which he had offered to the UCG library and which Howley had the 'graciousness' to accept.[101] Howley, who was unmarried, lived at 11 The Crescent, Galway. On his retirement, he moved to 'Cepeda', Goatstown Road, Dundrum, Co. Dublin. He died in September 1941, aged 75 years, and his funeral was attended by An Taoiseach, Éamon de Valera, the Minister for Education, and the Lord Mayor of Dublin.[102]

FELIM Ó BRIAIN (1895–1957), Professor of Philosophy from 1937 until his death in 1957, was the son of Diarmaid (or Dermot) Ó Briain and Catherine Moran, and was born at Cong, Co. Mayo on 4 November 1895. He was baptised Thomas and he was educated locally and at the Franciscan College, Multyfarnham, Co. Westmeath. He entered the Franciscan Order on 16 September 1921 and made his profession on 17 September 1922 and 1925. He studied at the Gregorianum in Rome (graduating with the degree of Doctor of Divinity) and he was ordained priest on 3 July 1927. He then continued his studies at the Catholic University of Louvain (Leuven), Belgium, graduating with the LicScHist. He had chosen for his doctoral thesis the life of St Brigid and he had already engaged in extensive research in the area when he was recalled by his superiors to teach philosophy to Franciscan students at the newly-opened St Anthony's College in Galway. He later received the PhD degree from the National University of Ireland. He was a much-

---

Ireland Review, 29 (1908), pp. 129–43; 'The Paradox of the Politician', *New Ireland Review*, 30 (1908), pp. 155–64; 'A Sermon on a Store List', *Catholic Bulletin*, 3 (1913), pp. 73–9; 'Notes on the Psychology of Religious Experience. Conversion and the New Birth', *Irish Ecclesiastical Record*, 5th series, 4 (1914); 5 (1915); 13 (1919); 14 (1919); 'The Psychology of Religious Experience', *Studies*, no. 6, 2 (1913), pp. 117–31; 'The Psychology of Religious Experience: Conversion and the New Birth', *Studies*, no. 8, 2 (1913), pp. 441–55; 'Notes on the Psychology of Religious Experience: Conversion and the New Birth', *Studies*, no. 10, 3 (1914), pp. 41–63; ''Twas a Decade Ago in Babylon', *U.C.G.*, no. 4, 1916, pp. 8–11; 'Humanism and Mystical Experience', *Studies*, no. 55, 14 (1925), pp. 459–75; 'Humanism and Mystical Experience', *Studies*, no. 58, 15 (1926), pp. 285–98; 'St John of the Cross a Doctor of the Church', *Studies*, 16 (1927), pp. 91–8; review of Joseph A. Glynn, *Life of Matt Talbot*, *Studies*, 17 (1928), pp. 317–9; '"The Lyceum": Some Student Recollections', *U.C.G.*, no. 1, 6 (1928–9), pp. 45–8; review of Mrs Thomas Concannon, *At the Court of the Eucharistic King*, *Studies*, 19 (1930), pp. 132–3; 'The Encyclical "Mens Nostra" and a Recent Controversy on Prayer', *Studies*, 19 (1930), pp. 45–54; 'Fiction and Culture', *An Leabharlann*, no. 4, 1 (1931) and *U.C.G. Annual*, 1931, pp. 42–5; Editorial Letter, *An Leabharlann*, no. 4, 3 (1933); Presidential Address (Cork Conference), *An Leabharlann*, no. 4, 3 (1933); 'Henri Bremond 1865–1933', *Studies*, 23 (1934), pp. 71–6; 'Father Joseph Darlington, S.J., 1850–1939: An Appreciation', *Studies*, 28 (1939), pp. 501–4.

100 There are fair copies of some of these talks (1936–7) in typescript (*c.* 160 pages) in the NUI, Galway Archives, Other Resources Special Collection, MS 3.
101 Ellmann (ed.), *Letters of James Joyce*, vol. iii, p. 371.
102 See 'Dr John F.W. Howley, M.A.: President, Library Association of Ireland', *An Leabharlann*, no. 1, 8 (1941), pp. 7–9; 'Dr Howley', *An Leabharlann*, no. 1, 8 (1941), pp. 3–4; and Stephen J. Brown, S.J., 'John Howley 1866–1941', *Studies*, 30 (1941), pp. 601–4.

admired student master in St Anthony's College, where he also taught Franciscan history and he was a Franciscan definitor or councillor to the minister provincial. He was appointed to the chair of Philosophy in UCG in 1937. He enjoyed philosophical and historical debates and he frequently wrote letters to the newspapers on moral and theological questions. He engaged in a celebrated confrontation with Owen Sheehy-Skeffington on the question of liberalism, and, in 1950, the *Irish Times* published the proceedings in a collection called *The Liberal Ethic*. He was, according to an obituary in the *University Review*, 'one of those rare characters who follow, one might say, almost ruthlessly, the promptings of their own spirit, and pass through life with small distraction to the right or the left'.[103] Certainly, his distractions to the left were not numerous. In later years, Ó Briain gave up the teaching of speculative philosophy and devoted himself to the social sciences, lecturing widely throughout the province of Connacht. The unsigned obituary in the *University Review* concluded as follows:

> Not always, indeed, easy of approach, perhaps from a shyness which he strove to conceal. Not always too patient of those with whom he was engaged in discussion, for which St. Francis must have felt tempted at times to tweak his ear. Still too near for us to be able to appreciate his great qualities. Near enough for us to know how well we shall miss him.[104]

He died in hospital in Dublin on 24 January 1957 and was buried in Galway.[105]

Ó Briain published very little in philosophy but he produced many articles on Celtic Studies, the early Irish Church, and the history of the Irish Franciscans. He founded the *Catholic Survey*, an ambitious periodical which did not survive his death. There is an exhaustive list of his historical writings, compiled by Anthony Lynch, which includes details of the vast number of contributions he made to the *Dictionnaire d'Histoire et de Géographie Ecclésiastiques* and to *De Katholieke Encyclopaedie* (Amsterdam).[106]

EDWIN RABBITTE (1916–92), Professor of Philosophy from 1958 until 1985, who was baptised Michael, was the son of Patrick Rabbitte and Anne Allen. He was born in Galway on 23 December 1915. He was the oldest of six children and his father died when he was very young. He entered the Franciscan Order on 7 September 1932 and made his profession on 8 September 1933 and 1936. He graduated from UCG with a BA degree in 1936. He had studied logic with John Howley whom he remembered with affection. He then went to Rome where he was ordained priest on 9 July 1939 and where, in 1943, he successfully completed his thesis on the theology of Alcuin of York for the Doctor of Divinity degree. He returned to Ireland (via Portugal) in 1943 and taught dogmatic theology in St

---

103 *University Review*, no. 11, 1 (1957), p. 71.
104 Ibid., p. 73.
105 See also obituary by M[ichael] P[ower], *Vexilla Regis*, 1957, pp. 75–6.
106 Appendix 2 in B. Millett and A. Lynch (eds), *Dun Mhuire Killiney 1945–95* (Dublin, 1995), pp. 219–22.

Anthony's College, Galway for the next six years. In 1949 he went to Louvain to further his philosophical studies and, in 1953, he was awarded the PhD degree for his work on the 'argument from design'. He returned to Ireland in 1951 and the following year he began teaching in UCG. In 1958 he was appointed Professor of Philosophy. He retired from the post in 1985 and he died in the Regional Hospital, Galway on 14 November 1992. He is buried in the Franciscan grave in the New Cemetery, Bohermore, Galway. His funeral oration, by his fellow Franciscan and Department of Philosophy colleague at UCG, Dr Colin Garvey, was published in *Seanchas na mBráithre*, no. 175, Christmas, 1992.[107]

CHARLES H. NOLAN (1908–56) was a Lecturer in Philosophy from 1947 until his early death in 1956. Hyacinth Nolan, his name in religion, was born on 10 June 1908, at Cummer, Co. Galway to Michael Nolan and Margaret Kemple. He entered the Franciscan Order on 7 September 1929 and made his profession on 8 September 1930 and 1933. He studied in Louvain and later in Rome, where he was ordained in 1935. He then returned to Louvain for postgraduate studies (he was awarded the PhD in Philosophy in 1938) and he was there when the German army forced the community to leave in 1940. He moved to St Anthony's College, Galway where he taught theology to the Franciscan students during the war. He was appointed to a Lectureship in Philosophy in UCG in 1947. He died, having undergone a hip operation in England, on 10 July 1956, at the age of forty-eight.

Celsus O'Brien, whose baptismal name was William, received the BA degree from UCG in 1936 and he taught in the Philosophy Department from 1945–50. Eustás Ó hÉideáin was a Lecturer in Philosophy from 1959 until 1968, when he became Professor of Education at UCG. He retired in 1987. Colmán Ó hUallacháin, whose baptismal name was Liam, was a student at UCG in the late 1940s and he taught in the Philosophy Department from 1953 until 1956. In 1953 he obtained the PhD degree from Louvain for a thesis on 'Dun Scotus and the Philosophers According to the Opening Question of the *Ordinatio*'. He became Professor of Ethics at St Patrick's College, Maynooth and he was the first Director of Institúid Teangeolaíochta Éireann. He was appointed Lecturer in Modern Languages (Irish) at the New University of Ulster, Coleraine in 1973. He died unexpectedly

---

107 Among his publications are a 'popular' book on philosophy, *Cosmology for All* (Cork, 1956) and the following articles: 'The "Motive" of the Incarnation: Was Scotus a Scotist'? *Irish Ecclesiastical Record*, 65 (1945), pp. 117–25; 'The Debt of Contracting Original Sin in the Blessed Virgin Mary', *Irish Ecclesiastical Record*, 70 (1948), pp. 402–12; 'The Primacy of Christ: A Study in Speculative Theology', *Irish Ecclesiastical Record*, 70 (1948), pp. 878–89; 'Kerk en Staat in Ierland', *De Nieuwe Mens*, 1949, pp. 105–8; 'Eternity', *Terminus*, 1953, pp. 225–6; 'The Argument from Design', *Catholic Survey*, 1953, pp. 18–38; 'Mother and Son', *Catholic Survey*, 1953, pp. 301–16 [This article is based on a lecture given at Rome and which was published in *Alma Socia Christi. Acta Congressus Mariologici-Mariani Romae Anno Sancto MCML Celebrati* (Rome, 1952), vol. iii, pp. 27–33]; 'John Duns Scotus', *Assisi*, 1954, pp. 71–4; 'Hume's Critique of the Argument from Design', *Philosophical Studies*, 5 (1955), pp. 100–17; 'The Subjective Norm of Morality', *Philosophical Studies*, 7 (1957), pp. 43–55; 'Liberty, Personality, Morality', *Philosophical Studies*, 9 (1959), pp. 36–48. He also published some book reviews, for example in *Philosophical Studies*, 2 (1952), pp. 136–9; 4 (1954), p. 132; and 7 (1957), pp. 213–16.

in Gormanston College on 20 October 1979. In 1958 he published, in Dublin, *Foclóir Fealsaimh*, a dictionary of philosophical terms in Irish.[108] On 1 January 1987 Markus H. Wörner was appointed Professor of Philosophy at UCG in succession to Edwin Rabbitte.

---

[108] Among his philosophical publications are: 'A Scotist Criticism of St Thomas on the Necessity of Revelation', *Irish Theological Quarterly*, 1949, pp. 264–7; 'On Recent Studies of the Opening Question in Scotus's *Ordinatio*', *Franciscan Studies*, 15 (1955), pp. 3–31; 'An Chonspóid faoi Dhúchas Duns Scotus', *Galvia*, 3 (1956), pp. 30–46; 'Duns Scotus and 13th Century Philosophy', *University Review*, no. 10, 1 (1956), pp. 38–43; and 'Scotus's Ordinatio on Certain Knowledge', *Philosophical Studies*, 8 (1958), pp. 105–14. Most of his other publications were on the teaching of language, especially Irish. We are extremely grateful to Ignatius Fennessy OFM, Franciscan Library, Killiney, Co. Dublin for providing us with details on the lives and works of the Franciscans who taught philosophy in UCG.

Notes on Contributors

FIONA BATEMAN is a Social Science graduate from University College Dublin and has the MA in Culture and Colonialism from Galway. She is currently a Government of Ireland Scholar engaged in research for a PhD in the Department of English, NUI, Galway.

TOM BOYLAN is Associate Professor of Economics and currently Dean of Research at NUI, Galway. He is a graduate of UCD and Trinity College Dublin. He has published widely in development economics, applied econometrics, methodology, and the history of Irish economic thought. He is the author (with Tadhg Foley) of *Political Economy and Colonial Ireland* (1992) and (with F.P. O'Gorman) of *Beyond Rhetoric and Realism in Economics* (1995).

R.N. BUTLER was educated at UCC and did post-doctoral research at the University of Leicester. He won the 1851 Exhibition Scholarship for Ireland in 1967 and was awarded the Boyle-Higgins Medal of the Institute of Chemistry of Ireland in 1998. He is also a Member of the Royal Irish Academy. He is Professor of Chemistry at NUI, Galway.

TIMOTHY COLLINS is a chartered librarian in the James Hardiman Library, NUI, Galway. He is a science graduate from Galway with a special interest in the history of Irish science. His first book, *Floreat Hibernia: A Bio-Bibliography of Robert Lloyd Praeger 1865–1953*, was published in 1985 by the Royal Dublin Society. His edited volume, *De-Coding the Landscape*, was published by the Social Sciences Research Centre, NUI, Galway in 1994, with a second edition in 1997. His forthcoming work includes a history of the Clare Island Survey, to be published by the Royal Irish Academy, and a history of the Galway Steamship Line, to be published by Collins Press, Cork.

PAUL DUFFY a graduate in Engineering and Law from NUI, Galway, is currently working as a forensic engineer. He has published widely on the history of Irish engineering and industrial archaeology.

TADHG FOLEY a native of Donoughmore, Co. Cork, is Associate Professor of English at NUI, Galway, and a graduate of Galway and of the University of Oxford. He is the author (with Tom Boylan) of *Political Economy and Colonial Ireland* (1992). He is the co-editor of *Gender and Colonialism* (1995) and of *Ideology and Ireland in the Nineteenth Century* (1998).

DAVID A.T. HARPER is Professor of Palaeontology in the University of Copenhagen. He is a graduate of Imperial College, London (BSc), Queen's University Belfast (PhD), and he is a chartered geologist. Following post-doctoral fellowships in Norway and Scotland, he lectured in University College Galway for fourteen years where he was also keeper of the James Mitchell Museum.

ARTHUR KEAVENEY a graduate of Galway and of the University of Hull, is a Senior Lecturer in Classical Studies at the University of Kent at Canterbury. He is the author of a number of books and papers on ancient history.

JAMES P. MURRAY was Lecturer in Radiology (1967–78) in Galway and Professor of Radiology from 1978 until his retirement in 1987. He was a graduate of NUI, Galway. He had a particular interest in the history of medicine and was the author of *Galway: A Medico-Social History* (1994). He died in 1999.

TOM O'CONNOR a native of Naas, Co. Kildare, studied Physics at UCD and the Dublin Institute for Advanced Studies and received the PhD from Galway. He began teaching in UCG in 1956 and was appointed Lecturer in Experimental Physics in 1962. He developed a research school in the Physics of aerosols and set up the atmospheric research station on Mace Head, near Carna, in 1958. He initiated studies in occupational hygiene and health and safety at work in 1985. He continues to take an interest in these subjects and in the historical aspects of Physics.

BREANDÁN Ó MADAGÁIN a graduate of the NUI, is Professor Emeritus of Irish, NUI, Galway. He is a Member of the Royal Irish Academy and Chairman of the Governing Board of the School of Celtic Studies of the Dublin Institute for Advanced Studies.

LIAM O'MALLEY a graduate of Galway and of Trinity College Dublin, and a Barrister-at-Law, is Professor of Business Law at NUI, Galway. He is a former Dean of the Faculty of Law.

ROSALEEN O'NEILL studied in UCG and the Universities of Freiburg and Basel. A Browne gold medallist in French and German, she is a Lecturer in the German Department, NUI, Galway. Her publications include *Geschichten aus der Geschichte Nordirlands* (Darmstadt, 1977), with Peter Nonnenmacher.

GEARÓID Ó TUATHAIGH is Associate Professor of History in NUI, Galway. Educated at Galway and at Peterhouse, Cambridge, he has been a Visiting Professor at many universities, including the University of Toronto, Boston College, the University of Barcelona, and the University of Missouri. He is widely published, principally in 19th and 20th-century Irish and British history. He is consulting editor for several journals and special series, a member of the Senate of the NUI, of the Governing Authority of NUI, Galway, and of the National Economic and Social Forum. He was also a member of the Ireland-US Fulbright Commission, 1996–8. Professor Ó Tuathaigh is a Fellow of the Royal Historical Society.

SEÁN TOBIN a graduate of Galway (BSc and MSc) and Manchester University (PhD), was a Lecturer in Mathematics (1956–61) and Professor of Mathematics and Head of the Department in UCG from 1961 until his retirement in 1995. He was a Visiting Professor at the Institute for Advanced Studies in Canberra and at the California Institute of Technology in Pasadena. His specialist interest is in the Theory of Groups.

Index

Abdey, Professor, 41
Abel, Sir F.A., 220, 222
Abeltshauser, Revd J.G., 364
Abercorn, Duke of, 386
Academic Council, 174, 257, 281–2
Academic Staff Association, 171
Accountancy and Finance Department, 325
Acland, Sir Henry Wentworth, 268
agriculture, 267
Agriculture, School of, 23, 35–6
Aiken, Frank, 173, 190
Aimers, Margaret, 373
air pollution, 208–9
Albert, Prince Consort, 272–3, 345
Alexander, Eliza, 83–4, 311
Alexander, George Henry Minto, 83–4
Algar, Joseph, 228
Allman, Professor George Johnston, 160–1, 162–5, 167–8, 170, 171, 330, 341, 392
Allman, William, 162
American Civil War, 312–13
American Medical Association, 152
Amicable Society of Galway, 350
Amos, Professor S., 316
anatomy, 267
Anatomy, Department of, 144–5, 150, 151, 157
Anderson, Professor Alexander, 166–7, 169–70, 195, 198, 202, 206, 207, 224, 300, 375, 397
  academic career, 164–5, 187–9
  four-year report, 169–70
  Latin Department, 399–400
  President, 298, 319, 320
  research, 203–4
  X-rays, 205
Anderson, Professor Emily, 188, 300, 375–6, 377, 378
Anderson, Hannah, 291–2, 299–300
Anderson, Professor James, 19, 113, 320, 322
Anderson, Professor Richard J., 256–8, 264, 283–94, 296–300, 320, 368
  death of, 299–300
  illness, 293, 295–6
  inventions, 286, 287, 289
  politics, 301
  Presidential appointment, 297–8
  publications, 285–91

Anderson, William, 128
Anschutz, Professor, 225
antiquarianism, 344–6
Applied Physics, Department of, 190–1, 212–13
Aran Islands, 279–80, 295, 298, 398
archaeology, 345–6
Arduino, Giovanni, 246
Aristotelian Society, 224
Arkins, Professor Patrick A., 19, 20, 116
Arnold, Matthew, 405
Arnold-Forster, Florence, 65, 70, 100
Arts Faculty, 16, 23, 31, 112, 182, 384–420
  Deans, 24
  difficulty of degree, 82–3
  and Law Diploma, 36, 37
  natural history, 266
  and Natural Philosophy, 191
  Science division, 245, 258–9
Arts Society, UCG, 407, 415
Ashbourne, Lord, 109
Atkinson, Lord, 20, 86, 88, 89–90, 164
Atmosphere-Ocean Chemical Experiment (AEROCE), 211–12
Attfield, Professor, 224
Austin, Percy C., 225, 226

Bacon, Lord, 72
Baer, Reinhold, 179
Bagehot, Walter, 74, 312
Bagley, Professor Richard Blair, 328, 329–30
Bailey, Desmond, 277–8
Balfour, Gerald, 90
Ball, Dr Robert, 257
Ballinasloe Canal, 126
Bank of Ireland, 325
Banks, Dr John T., 281–2
Barlow, Revd Mr, 336
Barrington, John, 395
Barrington Report on Safety, Health and Welfare at Work, 210–11
Barry, Charles Robert, 60, 67
Barry, Professor John G., 414–15
Barry, Professor Kevin, 409
Barry, Vincent C., 230–1, 232, 234
Bartlett, Professor Thomas, 415

Bastable, Professor Charles Francis, 19, 108–12, 316–19
Basterot, Baron de, 257
Bateman, Richard C., 193
Becker, Dr Heinrich, 382
Beckett, J.C., 329
Belfast, 10, 13, 82, 105, 157
Belfast Commissioners, 321
Belfast Naturalists' Field Club, 277
Bennett, Charles, 333
Bensbach, Professor Augustus, 55–6, 84, 330, 361–5, 383
Benson, Kathleen, 402–3, 405
Bent, A.J., 180
Bergin, Osborn, 353, 358, 359
Bermingham, Thomas, 132
Berwick, President Edward, 18, 55, 87, 281, 306, 329, 364
    academic career, 386–7
    Cairnes resignation, 95, 314
    and Celtic chair, 345, 347, 351
    commission of enquiry, 1857, 80, 81–2, 83
    Lord Lieutenant's visit, 303
    Royal Galway Institution, 350
    supplementary charter issue, 93
    and Thompson, 333
Binns, Emily, 188
biochemistry, 267
Biochemistry, Department of, 153, 155, 156, 207, 236, 238
Birr Castle, Co. Offaly, 185
Birrell, Augustine, 321, 397
Black, Professor R.D. Collison, 303–4, 305–6, 311, 316
Blake, Sir Henry, 98–9
Blake, John Francis, 275, 277
Blake, Martin Joseph, 13
Blake, Sir Valentine, 13
Blakey, Professor Robert, 394
Blood, Bindon, 128, 129
Blood, Professor William Bindon, 128–30, 135
Board of Intermediate Education, 395
Board of Presidents, 347
Board of Works, 135, 198
Boas, Professor Frederick, 399
Boat Club, 407
Bodkin, John James, 13
Boole, Professor George, 161, 164
Bord na Gaeilge, 359
botany, 267, 294–5, 296
Botany, Department of, 208, 361
Bourke, Professor Eoin, 382
Bowen, John E., 205, 216
Bowerbank, Dr J.S., 251
Boyd, Dr Chris, 182

Boyle, Professor Kevin, 20, 116
Boyne Viaduct, 129
Bradley, Professor Diarmuid, 382
Bradley, Professor D.J., 191
Bradshaw, Brendan, 305
Brady, Sir Maziere, 21, 41–2, 160, 161, 281–2
Brady, Sir Thomas, 109
Breathnach, Mícheál, 353, 354, 371
Breathnach, Pádraig, 214
Brennan, Michael, 139–40
Brereton, Professor William W., 147, 150
Breul, Professor Karl, 377
Bright, John, 56
British Academy, 317
British Army, 135–6, 143
    Medical Services, 143, 148
British Association, 129, 192–3, 286, 298, 299, 317
British Medical Association, 286
British Museum, 270
Bromwich, Professor Thomas John l'Anson, 166–8, 224
Brooke, Charlotte, 344–5
Brougham, Lord, 25
Brown, Lois, 174, 176
Brown, William H., 20
Browne, Caroline Charlotte, 370, 372
Browne, Professor James V., 146, 147, 281–2
Browne, William A., 364
    scholarship, 370, 372
Brunel, I.K., 128
Bryce, James, 397
Buckle, H.T., 311–12
Buckley, Thomas, 20
Bühler, Dr J.G., 99
buildings
    Áras Fáilte, 380
    Áras na Gaeilge, 359
    Árus de Brún, 175
    modern languages, 383
    physics department, 198
    Queen's College, 16–17
Bunting, Edward, 345
Burke, Edmund, 344
Burke, Mrs J.J., 216
Burns, John, 180
Burnside, W., 164, 166
Burnside Groups, 176
Business Studies Department, 325
Butcher, Dr, 393
Butler, Professor R.N., 237
Byrne, Geraldine, 180
Byrne, Professor William A., 402–6, 415

Index

Cahill, Cathy, 216
Cairnes, Professor John Elliot, 19, 66, 96, 108, 306, 328, 335, 404
   academic career, 76–8, 83–4, 310–15
   death of, 314–15
   later career, 92–5
   publications, 311–14
Cairns, Lord, 45
Callagy, James, 181
Campbell, Roy, 400–1
Campion, Professor William B., 19, 56, 76, 78–80, 102, 103, 104, 108–9
   death of, 113–15
   QCG career, 84–5
Cannan, Edwin, 315
Canny, Professor Nicholas, 411, 415
Cardiology, Department of, 153, 156
Carlisle, Earl of, 87
Carpenter, William Benjamin, 251–2, 253
Carroll, William, 237, 239
Casey, Erika, 382
Casey, Br J.F., 206
Casey, Professor Timothy J., 382
Cassell, John, 326
Catholic Bulletin, 411, 416
Catholic Emancipation, 2, 4, 6
   centenary, 415
Catholic hierarchy, 354
   Charitable Bequests Act, 8–9
   national education system, 6
   and O'Connell, 4
   opposition to Queen's Colleges, 11–13, 18–19, 81, 105, 308
   priests in politics, 6
   and Union, 2
   university education, 60–1, 73, 93
Catholic School of Medicine, Dublin, 142
Catholic Truth Society of Ireland, 416
Catholic University of Ireland, 19, 60, 93, 94, 105, 337–8
   Irish language, 352
   and Royal University, 106–7
Catholic University School of Medicine, 226
Celtic languages, 361
Celtic Philology, Department of, 355
Celtic Studies, 344–6, 353
Censorship of Publications Appeal Board, 380
Central Hospital, Galway, 150–1, 152
Centre for Study of Digestive Diseases, 156
Chaloner-Smith, 134
Chancery (Ireland) Regulation Act 1850, 79
Chapman, Richard, 131
Charitable Donations and Bequests Act (Ireland), 1844, 8–9

Chemistry, Department of, 198, 218–41, 361
   1845–1895, 219–22
   1895–1945, 222–32
   1945–1999, 232–8
   degrees by research, 239–41
   German language, 382
   Irish language, 237
   number of students, 237
   premises, 236
   publications, 231–2, 235
Christofides, Dr Anthony, 177, 178, 179, 182
Church of Ireland, 46, 109
   disestablishment, 56–8
City Waterworks, Galway, 137–8
Civil Engineering, School of, 23, 196, 361
Civil Service Commissioners, 323
Civil War, 301
Claidheamh Soluis, An, 356, 357–8
Clancy, Mary, 300
Clare Grand Jury, 129
Clare Island Survey, 297
Clarendon, Lord, 21, 31
Clarke, Dr Laurence P., 212
Clarke, Dr Rosalind, 224–5, 226, 228–9, 232
Classical Association of Ireland, 395
Classical Languages, Department of, 199
classics, 326–43, 360
Clayton, Matthew, 291
Cleland, Professor John, 144, 147
Clements, Henry, 125
Clifden Railway, 130, 131–2, 139
Clinical Sciences Institute, 154
Cliodhna, SS, 397
Club Leabhar, An, 380
Colaiste Éinde, Galway, 181, 233
Colahan, Professor Nicholas W., 103–4, 147
Colbeck, Charles, 369–70
College Council, 22, 24, 91, 109, 112, 280
   Anderson illness, 295–6
   and law programme, 114
   Law School resolutions, 55
Colleges (Ireland) Act, 1845, 8, 9–15, 21, 30
Collins, Michael, 377
Collins, Timothy, 273, 297
Colum, Mary, 405
Commerce and Accountancy, Department of, 322
Commerce Faculty, 321–5
Commission of Inquiry on Agriculture, 323, 324
Commissioners of National Education, 395
Common Law Procedure Act, 91
Compton, Arthur, 148, 226
Computer Assisted Language Learning (CALL), 383

Computing Studies, 197
Comte, Auguste, 330
Concannon, Fionnuala, 180
concrete technology, 138–9
Connacht Tribune Printing Works, 291
Connaught Women's Franchise League, 300, 410
Connellan, Professor, 353
Connolly, D., 139
Connolly, Seán, 182
Conroy, Carol, 180
Conroy, Richard J., 372, 374, 378
Conservative Party, 3, 9, 60–1
Conybeare, W.D., 257
Cooke, Margaret. see Shea, Margaret
Coote, Catherine, 179–80
Cork, 10, 13, 78, 157
Cork Naturalists' Field Club, 278
Corkery, Professor Daniel, 407
Corley, Anthony, 142
Corrib Navigation Trustees, 135
Corrib Viaduct, 130
Cosgrave, Liam, 381
Cosgrave, W.T., 228
Costello, Lt Augustine, 68
Costello, Karen, 239
Council for Postgraduate Medical and Dental Education, 155
Council on Education Committee, 276
Courtney, L.H., 95
Cowdy, Henry Lloyd, 112–13
Crofton, Professor Morgan William, 184–5, 191–2
Croker King, Professor and Mrs Charles, 84
Crolly, Dr, Archbishop of Armagh, 6, 12
Cromwell, Oliver, statue of, 103
Crone, John S., 389
Cronshaw, Henry Brenan, 264
Crookes, Sir William, 220
Cross, Edward, 396
Cross, Mary Alicia, 396
Crowe, Professor John O'Beirne, 351–3
Cruikshank, J.A., 180
Cuddy, Professor Michael, 325
Cullagh, Bridget, 215
Cullen, Cardinal Paul, 12, 93–4, 105
Cultural Exchange (Fulbright) scholarships, 210
Cumann Ceimicí na hÉireann, 232, 234
Cummins, R.J., 214
Cunnane, Professor Con, 138
Cunningham, Professor 261
Cunningham, D., 237
Cunningham, John, 216
Curran, Margaret, 375, 378

Curran, Michael P.J. (Bobby), 178, 179
Curtis, Professor Arthur Hill, 186–7, 194, 201, 207
Cuvier, Baron George, 250, 257, 262

Daly, James, 101
Daly, Fr Peter, 275, 276
Damon, Robert, 257–8
Damon, Robert Ferris, 258
Dara, William. see Byrne, William
Dark, Dr Rex, 179
Dart, Professor Raymond, 254
Darwin, Charles, 242, 250, 259, 261, 265, 266, 268, 312
Origin of Species, 254–5
Davidson, Thomas, 251
Davies, Professor John Fletcher, 339–41
Davis, Thomas, 12–13
Davitt, Michael, 20, 101
Dawson, Professor J.W., 252–3
de Brún, Monsignor Pádraig, 171–2, 175, 380
De la Beche, Sir Henry, 245, 258, 259, 262, 263, 265
de Valera, Éamon, 228, 380, 381, 414, 417
de Valera, Professor Máirín, 236
Debating Society, 342, 396
Deignan, J.P., 207
Delany, William SJ, 106
Delargy, Séamus, 382
Dermody, Bridget, 375
Derry, 10
Desmond, Ray, 274
Devon commission, 8
di Fidio, Dr Ottavio, 381
Dicey, A.V., 74
Dillon, John Blake, 226
Dillon, Robert, 297
Dillon, Robert E., 278
Dillon, Professor Thomas, 226–32, 234–5, 238, 382
Dillon, Valentine, 226
Dinkel, ?? 256
Dinneen, Father, 358
diplomas, 34–6
Diskin, Patrick M., 408
Disraeli, Benjamin, 61
Dissenters, 4, 9, 46–7
Divers, Edward, 143, 220, 221–2
Dixon, Professor Alfred Cardew, 165–6, 167–8
Dixon, Professor Augustus E., 222–3
Dobb, Maurice, 313
Dockrill, John, 316
Dodo, the, 273
Doherty, Professor Richard, 144, 145, 147, 163
Visitation, 280–2

Donegan, Professor Joseph, 150, 151
Donnell, Professor Robert Cather, 19, 96–7, 107, 108, 109, 315–16, 317
Donnellan, Catherine, 403, 404–5
Donovan, John T., 20, 398
Donovan, Mary J. *see* O'Sullivan, Mary J. Donovan –
Doolan, Professor James, 325
Dowden, Professor Edward, 396, 398
Downing, Samuel, 129
Dowse, Richard, 60
Dramatic Society, 407, 415
Drane, Professor Thomas, 128
Drennan, Professor Charles Maxwell, 400–2, 404, 410, 415
Driscoll, Dennis, 116
Drummond, Michael, 20, 99, 103–4
Drury, Amy, 332
Dublin, 7, 60, 98
 transport, 135
Dublin Castle administration, 2, 4–5, 169, 171
 Catholics in, 5
 Committee of Lectures, 264
 Extraordinary Visitation, 280–2
 Law Advisers, 56–61, 69
 Presidential appointment, 297–8
Dublin Commissioners, 321–2
Dublin Institute for Advanced Studies, 171, 174, 208, 216
Dublin Journal of Medical Science, 286
Dublin Law Institute, 29
Dublin Naturalists' Field Club, 277–8
Dublin Statistical Society, 22, 45, 48, 69, 70, 72, 75, 304–5, 395. *see also* Statistical and Social Inquiry Society
Dublin University Magazine, 390
Duce, Professor Bob, 211
Dugan, Charles W., 193
Duncan, Professor G.A., 318–19
Dundalk RTC, 177
Durcan, Paul, 380

Eakin, Mary, 372, 373, 398
Earth Sciences, 264, 265
Easter Rising, 1916, 226–7, 301, 374, 377, 401–2
Eastman-Kodak Company, 205
Ebrill, George, 228
economics, 73, 75
Economics, Department of, 325. *see also* Jurisprudence and Political Economy
Edgeworth, F.Y., 318, 319
Education, Department of, 154, 175
Edwards, Hilton, 379

electoral corruption, 60
Electricity Supply Board, 138, 210, 212
Electronic Engineering, Department of, 197
Elementary Law, Diploma of, 34–8
Ellis, Dr Graham, 180, 182
Ellmann, Richard, 406
Engermann, S.L., 313
engineering, 135, 172, 368
 private schools, 125, 126–7
Engineering School, 23–4, 112, 125–41, 191
 Diploma in, 35–6
 women in, 139
English, Department of, 400–9
 divided, 408–9
English language, 361, 379, 384
English literature, 361, 385–6. *see also under* History
Enniskillen, earl of, 262
ENT Department, 153
EOLAS, 216
Eozoön, 242, 252–3, 256, 271
Erasmus programme, 265
Erasmus Smith Grammar School, 162
Erin's Hope, 67–8
Eucharistic Congress, 415
European Commission, 155, 156, 216
European Regional Development Fund, 212
Evers, Dr Louis, 381
Exhibition scholarships, 1851, 147, 195, 215
Exon, Professor Charles, 342
Experimental Medicine and Practical Pharmacology, Department of, 153, 156, 199
Experimental Physics, Department of, 184, 189–90, 195–6
External Affairs, Department of, 413
Extramural Studies, Diploma in, 197

Fagan, Olivia M., 180
Fahy, Gerard, 239
Fahy, Professor Thomas, 156, 343
Fairley, James, 285, 298, 299
Faller, Stephen, 373
Fannin, Thomas, 126–7
Fanning, J.D., 180
FÁS, 265
Fawcett, Henry, 95, 313
'Fawcett's Act,' 1873, 337
Fegan, Professor D.J., 179
Fenians, 64, 67, 69, 333
Finan, Dr Tony, 234, 235, 236, 239
Finance, Department of, 134
Fine Gael, 380

First World War, 143, 235, 301, 373–4, 377, 403, 409
   German academics, 374
Fiscal Inquiry Committee, 317
Fisher, Joseph R., 20, 99
FitzGerald, Charles William, Marquis of Kildare, 80
Fitzgerald, Emily, 66
Fitzgerald, Joseph, 136–7
Fitzgerald, Margaret T., 221
Fitzgerald, M.J., 180
Fitzgerald, Turlough, 157
Fitzgibbon, John, 1
Flanagan, Thomas P., 137
Flanagan, V.P., 208
Flannery, Dr Dane, 180, 182
Flannery Bridge, 138
Flood, D.T., 230
Flood, Mr, 115
Flynn, James, 403, 405
Flynn, John, 154, 155
Fogarty, M.J., 397, 410
Fogarty, Philip C., 20, 398
Fogel, R.W., 313
Fogerty, Dr George, 278
Fogerty, W.A., 278
Foley, T.P., 282
Forbairt, 216
Forbes, Edward, 271
Ford, Frank. *see* Mac Giollarnáth, Proinnsias
Foreign Affairs, Department of, 380
Forster, W.E., 64, 65, 70
fossils, 247–50, 266–7, 270, 271
Foster, R.F., 398
Fox, Professor, 178
Franciscan Order, 417–19
Franklin, R.L., 257
French, 360, 361, 362–3, 374, 378
   awards, 370
   Department of, 382
   Ó Briain, 380–1
Freudenberg, Professor, 233
Freund, Professor Max, 374
Freyer, Peter, 104, 143, 147, 148
Friel, N.P., 180

Gaelic League, 323, 353, 354, 358, 380, 402
Gaelic Society of Dublin, 345
Gaffney, Frank, 214, 215
Gallagher, Professor Patrick J., 19–20, 116
Gallagher, Séamus, 216
Galvia, 412
Galway, 10, 13–15, 18
   anti-German sentiments, 373–4
   water supply, 137–8

Galway, County, 247, 323
Galway Archaeological and Historical Society, 278, 397, 411–12
Galway Chamber of Commerce and Industry, 350
Galway Clinical Club, 150
Galway Corporation, 208
Galway County Council, 154
Galway County Infirmary, 280
Galway Express, 410
Galway Grand Jury, 129
Galway Granite Company, 397
Galway Hospitals Act, 1892, 144
Galway Ladies Recruiting Committee, 409
Galway Literary Society, 407, 408
Galway Mercury, 395
Galway Model School, 199
Galway Packet, 161, 389, 390
Galway Technical School, 382
Galway Town Commissioners, 388
Galway University Press, 209
Galway Vindicator, 127, 159, 245, 333, 365, 384, 389, 395
   Celtic Languages chair, 348–9
   and Melville, 275–6, 277, 278–9
Gamgee, Fanny, 332
Gannon, William J., 195
Garry, Tom, 148
Gartside, Dr Paul, 182
Garvey, Dr Colin, 419
Gastroenterology, Department of, 153, 154
Geisler, Professor Charles, 366–8
General Medical Council, 144, 147, 152, 153, 158
General Practice, Department of, 157, 158
Genovese, Eugene, 313
geography, 361
Geological Museum, QCG, 245, 255–8, 263
geological sciences, 242–65
Geological Survey of Ireland, 245, 258, 259, 262, 272, 277, 279
Georgi, Brendt, 216
Geraghty, N.W.A., 237
German, 360, 361, 362–3, 374, 378, 381–2
   Academic Exchange Service, 179
   awards, 370
   Department of, 374, 375
Gibson, James, 48, 80
Gill, Mrs, 83
Gillanders, Dr Gary, 213
Gillen, P.J., 180
Gilligan, Patrick, 134
Given, Fred, 156
Gladstone, W.E., 3, 63, 64, 69, 242, 338
   Irish policy, 56, 57

QCG dissolution bill, 393
university question, 60, 61, 92, 94
Global Atmospheric Gases Experiment (GAGE), 211
Global Atmospheric Watch (GAW), 212
Glynn, John P., 139
Glynn, Professor Thomas J., 191, 207
Goode, John, 215
Gordon, Judge John, 20, 99–100, 104
Gordy, Professor Walter, 206
Governing Body, 175, 209
Graben, Wil, 216
Graham, Sir James Hugh, 360–1, 384–5
Graham, Thomas, 219
Grand Canal, 131–2
Grant, Professor Lou, 209
Graves, Revd Dr Charles, 352
Great Exhibition, 1851, 219, 257
Great Famine, 15, 18, 192
Greek, Department of, 326–7, 331–6, 360, 361
Green, Alice Stopford, 358
Gregory, Lady, 398, 405
Gregory, Mr, 126
Grey, Earl de, 5, 345
Grey, Sir George, 93
Griffin, Fr Michael, 228
Griffith, Arthur, 228
Griffith, Richard, 250
Griffith, Professor William G., 216
'Groups in Galway,' 179
Gruenberg, Dr Karl, 182
Guinness family, 109
Gúm, An, 172
Gupta, Narain, 157
Gwynn, Stephen, 397

Haddon, Professor Alfred Cort, 278
Haematology, Department of, 157
Hall, J.B., 98
Hall, Professor Marshall, 174
Hall, Philip, 174, 176
Hall, Thomas, 220
Hamilton, Judge, 71
Hancock, Professor William Neilson, 305–6, 316, 394
Hancock Museum, 242, 245, 251, 255
Hannah, Dr John, 180
Hardiman, James, 125, 345, 347–8, 350
Hardy, G.H., 166, 167, 175
Hare, William, 205, 214
Harkness, Robert, 261, 263
Harper, D.A.T., 271, 272
Harris, Professor Derek, 382
Harrison, John H., 104

Harrison, T.H., 104, 164
Hart, Sir Andrew, 295
Hart, Henry Chichester, 293, 294–5, 301
Hartog, Professor Marcus Manuel, 278
Harvey, William Henry, 269
Haughton, Revd Samuel, 263
Hawkins, Benjamin Waterhouse, 257
Hayes-McCoy, Professor Gerard A., 411–12, 415
Head, Sir Francis B., 16
Health, Department of, 152, 153
Health Act, 1953, 152
Health Promotion, Department of, 157, 158
Healy, Maurice, 98
Healy, Michael, 214, 417
Healy, T.M., 63, 367
Heaney, F., 237
Hearn, Professor William E., 74–5, 326–7
Heavey, Professor Margaret, 335, 415–16
Henchy, Séamus, 20
Heneghan, Thomas F., 378
Henry, Dr James, 341
Henry, John, 195, 205, 216
Henry, Professor P. Leo, 408
Henry, Revd Pooley Shuldham, 30–1, 316
Hermathena, 162, 328, 330, 336, 339, 341, 342, 396
Heron, Professor Denis Caulfield, 19, 32, 40, 77, 83, 85, 316, 325
  academic career, 21–2, 38, 44, 45–54, 304–10
  contribution to QCG, 71–4
  death of, 70–1
  on Jurisprudence, 72–3, 74
  later career, 66–71
  on legal education, 40, 91–2
  number of students, 90–1
  Parnell trial, 61, 62
  publications, 305
Herries Davies, Gordon L., 271, 272
Hess, V.F., 189
Heytesbury, Lord, 31
Higgins, Dr Bryan, 218
Higgins, T., 237
Higgins, William, 218–19
Higgs, Henry, 319
Higher Education Authority, 154, 181
Higman, Dr Graham, 174
Histopathology, Department of, 156, 157
history, 390, 392–3
  'gagging clauses,' 392–3
  teaching of, 384–5
History, Department of, 361, 384, 409–15

History, English Literature, and Mental Science, Department of, 386–400
Hofmann, A.W. von, 220, 222, 224
Hogan, Pat, 215
Hogan, Professor Edmund, SJ, 358
Holland, Sergeant, 285
Holt, E.W.L., 297
Home Rule, 3, 301, 338
Hooke, Robert, 248
Hooker, Sir William Jackson, 244
Horgan, Jim, 216
Hospitals Library Council, 415
Houghton, C.J., 180
Houston, Professor Arthur, 316
Houston, Edward Caulfield, 338–9
Houston, T.G., 366
Houston, Professor W.A., 168–9
Howley, Professor John F., 415–17, 418
Hughes, Dr David, 180
Hugo, Victor, 238
Hume, George A., 20
Hunt, Edward L., 257
Hurley, Dr Donal, 179
Hurley, Professor Thaddeus C., 180, 181, 182
Huxley, Thomas Henry, 250, 252, 254, 268
Hyde, Douglas, 354
hydrology, 138
Hynes, Michael, 210, 237, 239
Hynes, Monsignor John, 374–5, 382

Iberno-Celtic Society, 345
Ievers, Robert W., 104
Imbusch, Professor George F., 190, 196, 206, 207
Immunology, Department of, 156
Incorporated Law Society of Ireland, 26
Industrial Development Association of Galway, 397
Industry and Commerce, Department of, 135, 325
Inglis, Sir Robert, 11
Ingram, John Kells, 394
Inns of Court, London, 25, 26, 79
Institiúid Teangeolaíochta Éireann, 419
Institute for Industrial Research and Standards, 216, 325
Institute of Chemistry of Ireland, 232, 234, 238
Institution of Civil Engineers, British, 129
Institution of Civil Engineers of Ireland, 127, 128
Institution of Engineers of Ireland, 131, 134
Intermediate Education Commissioners, 187

Intermediate Education (Ireland) Act, 1878, 106, 329, 344
Irish Archaeological Society, 345, 352
Irish Field Club Union, 296–7
Irish Folklore Commission, 382
Irish Free State, 188, 301, 317, 410–11
Irish Geological Society, 262–3
Irish Geology Day, 265
Irish Historical Society, 414
Irish Hospitals Sweepstakes, 199
Irish language, 189, 190, 345–6
   chemistry, 232, 237
   lectureships, 172
   mathematics, 175
   and modern languages, 378–9
   physics, 196
   revival movement, 377
Irish Language, Philology, and Literature, Department of, 344–59, 355–9
   fight to establish, 346–8
   lack of students, 349, 350–1, 352
Irish Linen Board, 218
Irish Loyal and Patriotic Union, 338
Irish Reform Association, 364
Irish Republican Army (IRA), 137, 227
Irish Universities Act, 1908, 110, 321, 354
Irish University Press, 414
Irish Volunteers, 228, 377
Irwin-Brown, Nathaniel, 372
Italian, 360, 361, 362, 370, 378, 381–2
   Department of, 383

Jack, Tom, 398
James Hardiman Library, 382 see Library
James Mitchell Museum, 243, 255–8, 264
   renovation, 265
Jennings, Professor Stephen G., 191, 208, 209
Jesuit Order, 107, 336
Jevons, William Stanley, 75, 312
J.L. Kier, contractors, 139
Johnson, Solicitor-General, 64
Johnston, John, 372
Johnstone, R. O'D., 180
Jones, Dr Mark, 180
Jones, Miss Monckton, 410
Joyce, Arthur E., 132
Joyce, James, 405–6, 417
Joynt, Christopher, 143
Jukes, Joseph Beete, 258, 259, 277
Jung, Carl, 405
Jurisprudence and Political Economy, Department of, 50–1, 72–3, 91–2, 303–21, 361
   number of students, 307

Index

Kaldor, Nicholas, 311
Kane, Sir Robert, 329
Kavanagh, Arthur, 106
Keane, J.B., 17
Keatinge, Justice Richard, 46
Kekulé, August, 220
Kelly, Bryan A., 410
Kelvin, Lord, 205
Kemple, Margaret, 419
Kennedy, Professor John, 152
Kennedy, Michael, 228
Kennedy, Tristram, 29, 30
Kenny, Colum, 29
Kenny, Professor John, 210, 216
Keogh, Sir Alfred, 143, 148
Keogh, Judge, 60, 67
Ker, Professor W.P., 406
Kerr, Donal, 11
Keynes, John Maynard, 313
Kickham, Charles J., 67, 69, 304
Kiernan, T.J., 324
Kildare Canal, 131
Killeen, T., 239
Killen, James Bryce, 20, 101
Kilroy, Professor Thomas, 408–9
Kim, In-Ho, 216
Kinahan, George H., 279
Kinahan, John Robert, 279
King, Aelian Armstrong, 20, 86, 88
King, Professor Charles Croker, 144
King, Professor William, 242–65, 272–3, 282–4
    achievements of, 263–4
    collections of, 255–8
    Darwin's theory, 254–5
    early life, 244
    Hancock Museum, 245
    legacy of, 264–5
    and Melville, 270–1
    origins of life, 252–4
    in QCG, 245–8
    research of, 251–2
    teaching of, 258–62
King, William jun., 244
King and Queen's College of Physicians, 281
King's Inns, Dublin, 25, 26, 29, 35, 309
    Benchers, 60, 69
    Law appointment, 56
    and legal education, 80
    student privileges, 42, 110–11
Kinkead, Professor Richard J., 147
Kirwan, Revd Joseph W., 346–8, 386, 388
Kirwan, Páraic, 182
Kirwan, Richard, 218–19
Kottabos, 336, 339, 396

Krantz family, 253, 255, 258
Kyne, M.F., 210

Ladies' Institute, 329
Laffey, Professor Tom, 177
laissez-faire, 313–14
Lalor, James Fintan, 414
Lamarck, Chevalier de, 254–5
Land Acts
    1870, 58–60, 69, 97
    1881, 63–4
    1896, 90
Land League, 20, 61–2, 101
land reform, 8, 56, 96–7, 306, 313–14
Lang, Andrew, 331–2
Lang, Dr Mark, 213
Language Laboratory, The, 383
Larcom, Thomas, 329, 345–6, 351
Larkin, Professor Declan M., 190, 196, 206
Larkin, Jim, 206–7
Larmor, Professor Sir Joseph, 165, 169, 185, 187, 194–5, 198, 202
    research, 203
Late Late Show, 377
Latin, Department of, 327–9, 336–42, 361, 399
Lavelle, Professor Seán, 153, 156
Law, Ellen Maria, 66
Law, Professor Hugh, 19, 21, 35, 79, 94
    academic career, 44–5, 49, 54
    contribution to QCG, 71–2
    death of, 65–6
    on legal education, 26–8, 33
    subsequent career, 55–66
Law, Hugh Alexander, 66
Law, John Jnr, 66
Law Faculty
    first full-time professor, 20, 116
    graduates, 116–24
    under Queen's University, 16–116
        Civil Law, 51–2, 91–2
        Colonial Law, 52–3
        Elementary Law Diploma, 34–8
        first professors, 21–4, 71–5
        Jurisprudence, 50–1, 72–3, 91–2
        LLB and LLD, 38–42
        non-resident professors, 48
        programme, 32–4
    under Royal University, 105–16
    salaries, 23
    scholarships, 112
    students, 54, 85–90
    success of, 97–104
Lawler, Helen, 378
Lawrie, J. Gurney, 400, 401

Lawson, Henry, 143
Lawson, James A., 38
Lederman, Professor, 177
Lee, Dr Elizabeth, 234, 235, 236, 237
Lee, George, 137
Lee, Richard, 216
Leech, Dr Donal P., 239
Leeny, Dr Mark, 180
legal education, 24–8, 42–3, 108, 309
  apprenticeship, 26–8, 91
  low student numbers, 90–2
  in Queen's Colleges, 28–30
Leinster, Duke of, 345
Leitrim, Lord, 356, 357
Leonard, Professor Brian, 156
Leslie, Professor T.E. Cliffe, 36, 40, 307–8, 309, 313, 316
  on Cairnes, 314–15
  on legal education, 50–3
Lewis, Professor Bunnell, 329
Lewis, Sir Walter Llewellyn, 20, 99, 100
Liberal Party, 4–5, 60–1
Library, 415, 417
  catalogue, 372
  scientific journals, 203
Library Association of Ireland, 415
LIDAR project, 212–13
Liebig, Baron von, 219–20, 222
Lightning, HMS, 271
Limerick, 10
Limerick Naturalists' Field Club, 278
Lindley, Lord, 89
Linnaeus, Carl Gustav, 250
Literature, Department of, 384
Littledale, W.F., 26–7
Local Area Network (LAN), 197
Local Government Act, 1898, 90
Lodge, Sir Oliver, 205
Loftus, Professor Gerry, 156
Logan, Michael, 125–6
Logic, 361
Logic and Mental Philosophy, Department of, 384
Logic and Metaphysics, Department of, 386
Longfield, Dr, 91
Longford, Lord, 414
Louis Napoleon, Prince, 273
Lovelock, J.E., 211
Low, W.H., 400
Lowie, Revd Morgan, 127
Lowther, James, 106
Luby, Revd Thomas, 394
Luibhéid, Professor Colm, 383
Lupton, Professor William, 19, 95–6, 108, 281, 315

Lyell, Charles, 265
Lynch, Anthony, 418
Lynham, Professor John Isaac, 147, 150
Lyons, F.W., 166

McArdle, P., 237
McAuliffe, Michael, 20, 86, 88, 364
McBryan, Professor Francis, 322–3, 324
McCall, Robert A., 20, 104
MacCana, Alasdar, 216
McCann, Dr Brendan, 180
McCarthy, Caroline M., 180
McCarthy, Ciarán, 155
Mac Cionnaith, Professor Eoghan, 172, 189–90
McClelland, Professor John A., 188–9, 195, 215–16
McCluskey, Dr Aisling, 180, 181, 182
McCoy, Frederick, 262–3
McCoy, Professor Simon, 33, 145
McCrea, W.H., 173
MacCullagh, Professor James, 162
McCurtin, J.G., 208
McDermott, Aidan, 182
McDermott, J.J., 180
McDermott, John P.J., 176, 179
McDermott, Richie, 215
McDonagh, Francis, 62
McDonagh, Dr Seán, 177
MacDonagh, Thomas, 401–2, 403, 404, 410
Mac Donnchadha, Stiophán, 354
McDonnell, R.W., 305
MacDonnell, Sir Anthony P., 364
McDonough, Mary A., 180
McDonough, Dr Thomas P., 176
MacDouall, Professor Charles, 329
McDowell, R.B., 346
Mace Head research station, 208, 211–12
McElderry, Professor Robert, 342, 410
Mac Énrí, Professor Seaghan, 150, 402
MacEvilly, Dr, Bishop of Galway, 93
McGann, Brendan, 216
McGill, Dr Paul, 180
Mac Giollarnáth, Professor Proinnsias, 381
Mac Giollarnáth, Seán, 356, 357–8
McGovern, J.G., 210
McGowan, Professor Moray, 373
McGrath, Edward, 372
McGreevy, Revd T.P.G., 207, 208
MacHale, Professor Des, 177, 183
MacHale, Dr John, Archbishop of Tuam, 6, 8, 13, 14, 93
McHenry, Professor J.J., 189, 205–6, 207, 216
McIlwaine, Sir Robert, 20

McInerney, D.P., 180
Mac Íomhair, Seán, 383
McKane, Professor John, 20, 86, 87–8
McKenna, J., 232
McKenna, Keelin, 239
McKenna, Siobhán, 172, 379, 381
McLaughlin, D.G., 207
McLaughlin, Dr Thomas A., 134, 216
MacLiammóir, Micheál, 379, 381
McMahon, George Yielding, 39–40, 364
MacMahon, Dr James, 180
McManus, P.R., 180
Macnamara, Dr Rawdon, 281
McNena, Séamas, 181
McNicholl, Brian, 154, 155
Mac Niocaill, Professor Gearóid, 415
McQuillan, Dr Donald L., 176
Mac Réamoinn, Dr Seán, 380
McSwinney, Robert F., 20, 104
Magee College, Derry, 60
Maguire, Professor Thomas, 96, 315, 336–9, 341
Maguire, Thomas M., 21, 104
Mahaffy, J.P., 319–20
Mahon, Professor Ralph Bodkin, 150
Mahoney, Tess, 215
Mahony, Professor Cornelius, 348–51
Malone, Dr James F., 212
Management Department, 325
Manning, Robert, 138
Manpower programme, 197
Mansion House Committee, 228
Manufacturing Research Centre, UCG, 212
Mapother, Edward Dillon, 142, 148
Marketing Department, 325
Marriott, Sir John, 74
Marshall, Alfred, 75
Marston, Dr, 368
Martin, Dr Joseph, 197
Martin, Peter, 126
Martin, Thomas Barnewell, 13
Martin Ryan Institute of Marine Science, 209
Marx, Karl, 313
Masson, William, 394
Materia Medica Museum, 145–6
Mathematical Academy, Galway, 126
Mathematical Physics, Department of, 184, 189–90, 195–6
Mathematics, Department of, 159–83, 177, 180, 361
   Aiken Scholars, 173
   group theory, 179
   Irish language, 172, 174–5, 181
   number of students, 164, 169–70
   rotating headship, 182
   secretariat, 179–80
   statistics, 178
matriculation, 34
Maxwell, William H., 104
Maxwell, James Clerk, 187
Mayne, Erskine, 286, 288
Maynooth College, 12, 81, 110, 169, 171, 207, 357, 404, 419
   Irish language, 346, 349
Maynooth College Act, 1845, 8, 9
Medical Alumni Association, 149
medical education, 150, 152, 157, 368
Medical Faculty, 16, 23, 31, 111, 112, 142–58, 191
   Anatomy Department, 144–5
   expansion of, 153–4
   hospital training, 150–1, 152–3
   modern languages, 361
   natural history, 266
   and Natural Philosophy, 193, 194
   number of graduates, 158
   overseas students, 151–2
   postgraduate education, 154–5
   publications, 147–8, 151, 155, 157
   training hospitals, 146–7
   under UCG, 149–58
   Visitation, 152, 281–2
Medical Museum, 145
Medical Research Council, 155, 156
Medical Therapeutics, Department of, 153
Meehan, Maria G., 180, 182
Meissner, Professor Albert, 367
Melbourne, Lord, 5, 6
Melville, Professor Alexander G., 264, 267, 268–77, 281–5, 291, 301
   Dodo studies, 273–4
   field trips, 278–80
   on Owen, 269–70
Melville, Andrew, 146, 280–2
Mental Science. see History
Meredith, Richard Edmund, 20, 97
Merlin Park Hospital, 153
Metaphysics, 361
Meyer, Professor Kuno, 344, 358, 359
Microbiology, Department of, 156, 267
Midland Great Western Railway, 131, 137–8
Midwifery, Department of, 144, 147, 280–2
Military History Bureau, 413
Military History Society of Ireland, 411
Mill, John Stuart, 75, 95, 307, 310, 314, 318, 365
Millar, William John, 20
Mills, Professor Richard Horner, 50, 91–2, 308–9

Mineralogy and Geology, Department of, 242–4, 245–8
  King's legacy, 264–5
  King's teaching, 258–62
Minnis, Samuel, 372–3, 397–8
Mitchell, Ian Priestley, 379
Mitchell, Professor James, 175, 264
Mitchell, William, 68–9
Modern English, Department of, 408–9
Modern Irish Language and Literature, Department of, 355
Modern Language Board, 383
modern languages, 360–83
  feminization, 373
Modern Languages, Department of, 362, 366
Moffat, C.B., 268
Moffett, Sir Thomas W., 74, 101, 103, 104, 282, 397
  academic career, 390–5
  Anderson illness, 294, 295
  and Campion, 109
  on Dixon, 165–6
  and Geisler, 367, 368
  and Hearn, 75
  resignation, 298, 316
  Royal University Charter, 106, 107
Molloy, Constantine, 61
Molyneux, Professor Echlin, 35, 38–9, 92
Monaghan town, 68–9
Monroe, John, 20, 85–6, 101
Montagu, Lord Robert, 392
Montgomery, William, 280
Montgomery Collection, 145, 280, 282
Moore, Charles, 67
Moore, Tom, 345
Moorehead, James, 104
Moorhead, John, 193
Moran, John, 21
More, Alexander Goodman, 268
Morgan, G.P., 207
Morris, Professor Dennis, 150
Morrison, H.N., 207
Moynihan, P., 230
Mulcahy, Professor John, 159–61, 162, 171
Muldoon, John, 20, 237
Mulhern, Colette, 176
Mulhern, Dr John F., 176
Mulholland, William, 20, 86, 88, 89
Müller, Professor Max, 365, 381–2
Mulligan, James, 20, 104
Mullin, James, 145, 148, 366, 375
Municipal Corporations Act, 1840, 14
Murchison, Roderick, 251
Murnaghan, F.D., 174
Murphy, Professor Jeremiah, 379, 406–7, 408

Murray, Bruce K., 401
Murray, Dr, Archbishop of Dublin, 6, 8, 12
Murtagh, Harman, 412
Mutton Island, 301
Myles, Michael, 214

Naas, Lord, 333
Nagle, W.J., 67–8
Nares, Captain G.S., 294
Nash, Professor J.E., 138
Nation, 7, 12
National Authority for Occupational Health and Safety, 211
National Breast Cancer Research Institute, 156
National Centre for Laser Applications, 207
National Diagnostics Centre, UCG, 156
national education system, 5
National Exhibition, Cork, 1852, 129
National Gallery of Ireland, 256
National Heritage Council, 265
National Irish Safety Organisation, 211
National Library of Ireland, 346, 402, 414
National Science Council, 216
National Science Foundation, US, 211–12
National University of Ireland (NUI), 23, 110, 169, 171, 188, 224, 396–7
  established, 321–2, 373
  honorary degrees, 381
  Irish language, 354
  sciences, 195
  Senate, 323, 374
natural history
  amateur field clubs, 277–8
Natural History, Department of, 266–302
  field trips, 296–7
  inadequate facilities, 271–2
Natural History, Geology, and Mineralogy, Department of, 256–7
Natural History and Medical Society, Dresden, 263
Natural History Museum, QCG, 257–8, 284–5
Natural Philosophy, Department of, 165, 184–9, 191, 193–4, 195, 200–2, 361
Naughton, Mary, 214
Neale, Francis, 278
Neanderthal Man, 242, 250, 253–4, 271
Neilson, Revd William, 345
Nesbitt, Professor William, 76–7, 83, 311, 327–9, 392
Neumann, Professor Bernard, 177
Newell, Doreen, 176
Newell, Professor Martin L., 179
Newell, Professor Martin J., 161, 172–6, 175–6, 181, 199

Newman, Cardinal John Henry, 19
Newman, Michael, 157
Newman, Professor M.H.A., 170–1
Ní Chinnéide, Síle, 412–13
Ní Dhireáin, Máire, 215
Nicholson, Jane, 244
Nicol, Professor James, 263
Nimmo, Alexander, 125
Nolan, Charles H., 419
Nolan, J.J., 189
Nolan, Michael, 419
Nolan, Professor P.J., 189, 207, 208
Norton, Bernard Gustavus, 20, 86, 88
NUI, Cork, 177
NUI, Dublin, 177

Ó hAichín, Leon, 324
O'Beirn, Séamas, 148
Ó Briain, Professor Felim, 417–18
Ó Briain, Professor Liam, 228, 375, 376–81
O'Brien, Professor Catherine, 383
O'Brien, Celsus, 419
Ó Brien, Eileen, 378
O'Brien, George, 305
O'Brien, William Smith, 10, 12, 346
Ó Broin, Professor Tomás, 406
Ó Brolcháin, Professor Cilian, 189–90, 200, 207, 215, 216
Obstetrics, Department of, 154, 150, 156
Ó Buachalla, Professor Liam, 323–4
O'Casey, Sean, 379
Ó Catháin, S., 180
occupational hygiene, 211
oceanography, 267
Ó Cearbhaill, Diarmuid, 324
Ó Céidigh, Pádraig, 274
Ó Cinnéide, Professor Seán, 232, 236–7
Ó Cochláin, B., 237
Ó Coisdealla, Máirtín Davey, 214
Ó Colla, Professor Proinnsias S., 230, 232–4, 236
O'Connell, Daniel, 4–5, 6–8, 15
  and Queen's Colleges, 11, 12–13
O'Connell, John, 11, 12, 13
O'Connor, H.G.L., 137, 138
O'Connor, Professor Kieran, 138
O'Connor, Dr Tom, 196, 207, 208, 210
O'Connor, T.P., 332, 364–5, 405
O'Conor, Charles, 345
O'Conor Don, the, 106, 344
O'Curry, Eugene, 345, 353
O'Daly, John, 345
O'Dea, J.J., 208
O'Donnell, Charles, 99, 104
O'Donnell, Frank Hugh, 20, 99, 100–1

O'Donnell, Jack, 214
O'Donoghue, Daniel, 'The O'Donoghue', 93
O'Donoghue, D.J., 339
O'Donoghue, Niall, 143
O'Donoghue, Professor Pádraic, 140–1
O'Donovan, Professor John, 345, 352, 353
O'Donovan, Dr P.P., 208
O'Donovan Rossa, Jeremiah, 67, 69, 377
Ó Droighneáin, Pádraic, 214
Ó hÉideáin, Eustás, 419
Ó hEocha, Professor Colm, 153, 222, 230, 235–6, 239
Office of Public Works, 127, 132
Ó Fiannachta, Pádraig, 414
Ó Gormaile, Professor Pádraig, 382–3
O'Hagan, Chief Justice, 64
O'Halloran, Anne F., 180
O'Hara, Charles, 193
O'Hara, Colonel, 84
O'Healy, Professor Áine, 383
O'Healy, John, 237
O'Healy, Ronan, 237
O'Kane, Peter, 215
O'Keeffe, Professor John Declan, 138–40
O'Kinealy, James, 20, 86
O'Kinealy, Peter, 20
Old and Medieval English, Department of, 408–9
Oldham, Evelyn, 257
Oldham, Thomas, 258, 272
O'Leary, John, 67
O'Leary, Professor Joseph, 272, 389–90
Ó Lochlainn, Professor Pádraic, 138, 216
Ó Máille, Caitlín, 357
Ó Máille, Mícheál ('Diarmuid Donn'), 356, 357–8
Ó Máille, Pádhraic (Pcaitsín Pheige), 357
Ó Máille, Pádraig, 358
Ó Máille, Professor Tomás, 228, 355–9, 402
O'Malley, Professor Charles Conor, 285, 286, 299 300
O'Malley, Professor Michael George, 147, 150, 286
Ó Muircheartaigh, Iognáid, 178, 181
O'Neill, Joseph, 397
O'Neill, Professor Thomas P., 413–14
Ó Nualláin, Professor Labhrás, 324–5
Ophthalmology and Otology, Department of, 150, 153
Optronics Ireland, 207
O'Rahilly, Professor Thomas F., 354
Orange Order, 2, 68–9, 262
O'Regan, Dr Donal, 180, 182
O'Reilly, Máire, 381

Organisation for Economic Co-operation and Development, 325
O'Riordan, J.A., 134
Ó Rodaighe, Dr A.F., 208–9
O'Ryan, Professor Owen, 368
O'Shaughnessy, Sir Thomas Lopdell, 20, 97
O'Sullivan, Denis, 216
O'Sullivan, Professor Mary J. Donovan, 300, 374, 398, 402, 409–11
O'Sullivan, Dr Niamh, 182
Ó Tnúthail, Máirtín. *see* Newell, Professor Martin J.
O'Toole, Revd Professor John Paul, 350, 387–9
Ó Tuathaigh, Professor Gearóid, 412, 413–14
Otway, John Hastings, 79
Ó hUallacháin, Colmán, 419
Owen, Richard, 257, 265, 268, 269–70, 273

Paediatrics, Department of, 153, 154, 155, 156
Palaeontographical Society, 251
palaeontology, 248–50
Palles, Christopher, 60, 61
parliament, Irish, 1–2, 6, 26
Parnell, Charles Stewart, 100, 338–9, 365
  trial, 61–2
Pathology, Department of, 150, 151, 152, 156, 199
Pearse, Patrick, 407
Peel, Sir Robert, 1, 3, 6, 157, 220, 245, 360
  and O'Connell, 4–5
  policy on Catholics, 8–9
  Queen's Colleges, 10, 13–14, 14
Peel, Sir Robert (3rd baronet), 105
Peel Prize, 172
Penal Laws, 356
Perkin, W.H., 220
Perry, Agnes M., 167
Perry, Alice, 139, 140, 300–1
Perry, James, 293–4
Perry, Janet H., 301, 372
Perry, Margaret, 301
Petrie, George, 345
Pfeiffer, Dr Götz, 180, 182
Pharmaceutical Society, 224
Pharmacology, Department of, 156
Phillips, John, 262
Philosophy, Department of, 386, 415–20
physics, 208–10
Physics, Department of, 184–217
  equipment and apparatus, 200–3
  Irish language, 196
  premises, 198–200
  research, 203–13
  students and courses, 191–8
  support staff, 213–16

physiology, 267
Physiology, Department of, 150, 151, 157
Pigott, Richard, 338–9
Pius IX, Pope, 388–9
Plastic Surgery, Department of, 156
Plunkett, Count, 228
Plunkett, Geraldine, 226–7
Plunkett, Sir Horace, 397
Plunkett, Joseph, 227
Political Economy Department. *see* Jurisprudence
Pollak, Professor L.W., 208
Porter, Sir George, 65
Porters' Office, 214
Portlock, Major General J.E., 258
Power, John, 169
Power, Professor Michael, 169–72, 173, 174, 402, 406
Power, Patrick, 171
Power, Sheila, 171
Praeger, Robert Lloyd, 296–7
Prendergast, Professor William Hillary, 130, 135–6
Presbyterians, 10, 104
Preventative Medicine, Department of, 153
Price, Bonamy, 32, 80
Price, L.L., 318, 319
Privy Council, Irish, 61
Psychiatry, Department of, 154, 156
Pye, Professor Joseph P., 103–4, 104, 145, 146, 150, 293, 410

QCG, 103, 114, 373, 375
Queen's College Belfast, 23, 95, 110, 272, 283, 316, 392. *see also* Queen's University Belfast
  Celtic languages, 347, 351–2, 353
  English and history, 399
  geology, 263
  Latin, 76
  legal education, 20, 28, 30–1, 38–9, 43, 50–2, 91, 92, 97, 320
  logic and metaphysics, 394
  mathematics, 166, 315
  modern languages, 367
  political economy, 307–8, 309–10
Queen's College Cork, 43, 60, 82, 110, 161, 272, 316, 392. *see also* University College Cork
  Celtic languages, 347, 353
  classics, 329
  legal education, 28, 50, 52, 91–2, 97
  modern languages, 368
  political economy, 307, 308, 309
  residency requirements, 81

Queen's College Galway. *see also* buildings;
    University College Galway
  beginnings, 306–7
  difficulties of, 81–2
  established, 13–15
  Extraordinary Visitation, 280–2
  mixed education, 104
  not in University Bill, 60
  under Queen's University, 97–104
  residency requirements, 81
  under Royal University, 105–16, 149
  royal visit, 272–3
Queen's Colleges, 1, 6, 8–15, 157, 370
  Arts degrees, 384
  geology, 272
  history, 384–5
  legal education, 28–34, 42–4
  modern languages, 360–1
  supplementary charter debate, 92–4
Queen's Colleges Commission, 1857–58, 391
  Celtic Languages, 353
  classics, 392
  Irish language, 349
  legal education, 28, 32, 35, 48, 49, 50–3, 72, 90–2
  mathematics, 162–3
  modern languages, 363–4
  physics, 185, 213–14
  political economy, 307–10, 325
  report, 1858, 80–3
Queen's Colleges (Ireland) Commission, 1884, 107–8, 163–5, 194–5, 202, 368, 393
Queen's University Belfast (QUB), 170, 191, 322
  established, 110, 321
  First World War, 374
  geological collection, 264
  Irish language, 354
Queen's University of Ireland, 80, 142–3, 184, 264, 327, 329, 339
  Celtic languages, 351
  commission report, 1858, 80–3
  dissolution, 165, 193, 194, 393
  established, 23, 24
  history, 392–3
  legal education, 33, 41–2
  medical education, 147, 149
  modern languages, 368–9
  physics, 187, 215
  QCG Visitation, 281–2
  report, 1868–69, 386
  Senate, 162
  supplementary charter issue, 93–4
  syllabus, 361
Quinn, Stephen, 411

Rabbitte, Professor Edwin, 418, 420
Radio Advisory Committee, 380
Radio Éireann, 417
Radiology, Department of, 153, 154, 156
railway engineering, 125, 126–7, 130–2, 135–6
  water supply, 137–8
Razymyslov, Y., 176
Rea, Thomas, 372, 397
Redfern, Dr Michael, 197, 212–13
Redington, C.T., 215
Redington, Sir Thomas, 80
Redmond, William, 103
Reed, Sir Andrew, 20, 86, 87
Regional Centre for Modern Languages, 383
Regional Hospital, Galway, 152–3, 154, 199
Regional Laboratory, Galway, 152, 153
Regional Technical Colleges, 177, 178
Reilly, Captain Paddy, 279
Reilly, Paddy, 215
Reist, Professor Parker C., 210, 216
Renewable Energy Research Group, 210
Rentoul, James Alexander, 20, 98, 99, 101–4, 104
Repeal movement, 5, 6–8, 15
Respiratory Medicine, Department of, 154
Reynolds, John, 126
Reynolds, Professor Lorna, 408–9
Reynolds, S.P., 278
Rheumatology, Department of, 153
Rhys, Professor John, 344
Ricardo, David, 75, 307, 314, 319
Richardson, Thomas, 221
Richey, Alexander G., 59
Rishworth, Professor Frank Sharman, 132–5, 136, 139
road engineering, 139–40
Roberts, Samuel U., 135, 137–8
Robertson Commission, 1903, 108
Roe, William, 142
Romance Languages, Department of, 374, 375, 376–81, 382
Ronalds, Professor Edmond, 220–1, 222
Röntgen, Professor W.C., 205
Rooney, F.J., 180
Rosse, earl of, 185
Rowney, Professor Thomas Henry, 220, 222, 223, 237, 242, 253, 271
Royal Academical Institution, Belfast, 391, 394
Royal Belfast Academy, 369
Royal College of Physicians of Ireland, 146
Royal College of Science for Ireland, 278
Royal College of Surgeons in Ireland, 142, 143, 146, 147, 281
Royal College of Surgeons of England, 268

Royal Commission on University Education in
    Ireland, 1902, 110, 367, 370–1, 395, 399
Royal Dublin Society (RDS), 109, 185, 218
Royal Economic Society, 317
Royal Galway Institution, 129, 197, 350, 365,
    392, 395 see Amicable Society of Galway
Royal Galway Yacht Club, 151
Royal Irish Academy (RIA), 174, 179, 262,
    263, 345, 347, 353, 396
Royal Irish Constabulary (RIC), 20, 87, 98–9
Royal Navy, 294–5
Royal Pharmaceutical Society, 282
Royal Society, 147, 162–4, 167–8, 185–6, 187,
    218, 222, 262, 263
Royal University of Ireland, 94, 97, 132, 162,
    187, 222, 320, 339, 341, 370
    awards, 215
    dissolved, 169
    English, 403, 404
    established, 105–7, 193, 194, 393
    examinations, 165
    Irish language, 354, 358
    mathematics, 164, 167
    medical education, 142, 146, 147, 149
    modern languages, 368–9, 371, 374, 377
    physics, 202
    QCG in, 75
    sciences, 195
    Senate, 367, 391, 395
Royal Yacht Club, 199
Royal Zoological Society, 268, 270
Ryall, Professor John, 329
Ryan, D.M., 180
Ryan, Dominick Daly, 40
Ryan, E. Ralph, 135, 172, 177
Ryan, Professor Hugh, 226, 227, 228
Ryan, J. Oliver, 216
Ryan, J.H., 130, 132
Ryan, Dr Ray, 180, 182

sabbaticals, 177
St Andrews Colloquium, 174
St Anthony's College, Galway, 417–18, 419
St Joseph's School, 216
St Mary's College, Galway, 387–8
St Patrick's College, Maynooth. see
    Maynooth College
St Vincent de Paul Society, 275, 277, 415
Sandford, Professor Philip, 340, 341–2,
    399–400
Savage, Dr Angela, 237, 239
Scallan, P.G., 180
Scannell, M.J.P., 274, 278, 294
Schawlow, Arthur, 190
School of Irish Learning, 354, 358

Science and Art Department, 276
Science Faculty, 23, 157, 190, 193, 209, 215,
    219, 229, 236
Scoil Fhursa, Galway, 380
Scott, Michael, 175
Scott, Peter, 216
Scott Tallon Walker Architects, 200
Seanad Éireann, 323
seaweed research, 228, 229–31, 236
Second World War, 136–7, 174, 190, 222,
    301, 323, 382
    chemistry, 235
    intelligence work, 376
    Polish students, 151
    'Turf Campaign,' 137
Sedgwick, Revd Professor Adam, 263, 265
Select Committee on Foundation Schools
    and Education in Ireland, 29
Select Committee on Legal Education. see
    Wyse Committee
Semple, Joseph, 277
Senier, Professor Alfred, 222–3, 225, 226, 228
Shannon Hydro-Electric Scheme, 134, 135,
    139
Sharkey, W.P.F., 208
Shawe-Taylor, Captain John, 397
Shea, Professor Margaret, 372, 377–8, 379,
    381–2
Shea, Professor Stephen, 150, 151, 378
Sheahan, Dr Jerome, 178, 182
Sheehy, Professor Richard J., 19, 115
Sheehy-Skeffington, Francis, 404
Sheehy-Skeffington, Hanna, 374–5, 405
Sheehy-Skeffington, Owen, 418
Sheil, Dr John, 180
Shell Factory, 137
Shepheard, F.G., 226
Shiel, Joseph, R., 104
Shields, Professor B.F., 322, 324
Siemons, Dr Johannes, 180
Silverman, Professor Leslie, 210
Simmie, J., 237
Simmonds, Dr Peter G., 211
Simpson, Maxwell, 223
Sinn Féin, 228
Skelton, John, 332
Skevington, David, 264
Skilling, Professor Thomas, 267
Slattery, James, 316
slavery, 92, 312–13
Smiddy, Professor T.A., 324
Smith, Adam, 319
Smith, Henry, 147, 148
Smith, J.F., 101
Smith, Nicholas, 126, 131

Index

Smith, William, 246, 250, 262
Smylie, Archibald, 20–1
snowballs, 104
Society of St Vincent de Paul, 171
Socrates agreements, 383
soil mechanics, 138
Solar Energy Society of Ireland, 210
Sothman, J.F., 134
South Kensington Museum, 258
Spanish, 370, 372, 374, 378, 381
    Department of, 382
Spillane, W.J., 237
Sputnik satellite, 196
Stack, Dr Cora, 180
Stanford, W.B., 339
Stanley, Dr Gertrude, 180
Starkie, Enid, 330, 395
Starkie, Walter, 330, 395
Starkie, Professor W.J.M., 188, 330–1, 395–6
Statistical and Social Inquiry Society of
    Ireland, 304–5, 307, 317, 323, 395
Steinberger, Cecile L.M., 372
Steinberger, Lilian Blanche, 372
Steinberger, Professor Valentine, 369, 370–4, 377, 378, 383, 402
Stensen, Niels, 246, 248
Stephen, Leslie, 92, 95, 312
Stern, Ludwig, 344
Stevenson, Robert Louis, 331, 334
Stockley, Professor W.F.P., 407
Stoker, William Thornley, 142, 147
Stoney, Bindon, 129
Stoney, Professor George Johnstone, 185–6, 192–3, 197, 213–14
stratigraphy, 246–7, 248–50
Strickland, Hugh Edwin, 273
Stuart, Thomas, 167, 169, 170
Studies, 323, 416
Sullivan, A.M., 63, 68, 69
Sullivan, Sir Edward, 58, 64–5
Sullivan, Professor Helen, 180
Sullivan, W.K., 226
supplementary charter issue, 92–4
Surgery, Department of, 150, 154, 156
Sweeney, C.M., 346
Sweeney, Professor J.M.G., 20, 116
Sweeney, Maurice, 137
Sweetman, Professor James M., 19, 115
Swords, L.F.K., 405
Sylvester, Professor J.J., 185
Synge, J.M., 398
Synnott, D.M., 274
Synod of Thurles, 388–9

Taibhdhearc na Gaillimhe, 148, 379–80, 407
Tailteann Literary Competition, 407
Tate, Ralph, 277

Teanglann, An, 383
temperance association, 397
Tennant, Katharine, 372, 374
Tennent, Barbara, 221
Tennent, John, 221
Thomas, Dr Edward J., 407
Thompson, D'Arcy jun., 255–8, 334
Thompson, Professor D'Arcy Wentworth, 103, 104, 244, 331–6, 337, 338, 340, 343
    publications, 333–5
Thompson, William, 332
Thompson, William H., 143
Thomson, J.J., 187, 188
Thomson, William, 142
Thomson, Professor Wyville T.C., 261
Thurneysen, Rudolf, 359
Thynne, Andrew Joseph, 86–7
Thynne, Sir Henry, 20, 86, 87, 193
Tinney, Eithne, 171
Tinney, Hugh, 171
Tobias, Theodore C., 89–90
Tobin, P.J., 138
Tobin, Professor Seán, 173–4, 175–80
Todd, Andrew, 20
Todd, Revd Dr James Henthorn, 345, 352
Toleken, Dr, 393
Tooke, Thomas, 312
Townley, Christopher, 172, 278, 407
Townsend, Professor Edward, 103, 104, 125, 130–2, 135, 139, 193, 201
Townsend, Sir John, 132
Traynor, M., 295
Trench, Professor Wilbraham Fitz-John, 396–8, 403, 410
Trinity College Dublin (TCD), 18, 60, 94, 184, 231, 295, 303–4
    Catholics in, 9, 46–7, 93, 105, 159, 304, 337
    curriculum, 161, 361, 363, 393
    Engineering School, 127
    geology, 262
    Irish language, 346, 354
    legal education, 22, 25, 43, 53, 80, 91, 109–10, 113, 309
    physics, 184
    prestige of, 81
    and Queen's Colleges, 335
    Young Ireland, 7
Tuam, 10
Tuberculosis Prevention Act, 1908, 148
Tully, Fr James, 349
Twomey, Tadhg, 230

Ua Murchadha, Diarmuid. *see* Murphy, Jeremiah
UCG Annual, 188, 283, 299, 365, 373, 374, 375, 403
    modern languages, 378–9

Ulster custom, 96–7
Underwood, Dr, 279
Union Workhouse, 280
University Bill, 1873, 56, 60–1, 92, 94
University College Cork (UCC), 139, 170, 206, 412
    economics, 324
    English, 407
    established, 110, 321
    geology collection, 264 (*see also* NUI, Cork)
    science, 235
University College Dublin (UCD), 105, 107, 171, 176, 182, 208, 322, 323, 324, 325, 377, 415. *see also* NUI, Dublin
    chemistry, 226, 231, 232, 235
    established, 110, 321
    geology collection, 264
    Irish language, 358, 359
    L&H, 416
    physics, 179, 184, 188–9, 208, 213
University College Galway Act, 1929, 172, 232
University College Galway (UCG), 20, 23, 149, 170, 187, 397
    established, 321, 373
    Irish language, 355
    'Misery Index,' 178
University College Hospital, Galway, 156
university education, 9–15
University of Cambridge, 25, 187, 332
    Catholic foundation scholar, 395
    mathematics, 165
    modern languages, 363
    physics, 184
University of Dublin, 9, 43, 60, 73, 108, 311, 317, 395, 396
    history, 319, 320
    and NUI, 321
    political economy, 319
    Senate, 341
University of London, 25, 111
University of Mainz, 208
University of Manchester, 170, 176
University of Oxford
    Celtic Professor, 344
    legal education, 25
    modern languages, 365
University of Ulster at Coleraine, 210, 419

Vaizey, Sir John, 325
Vallancey, General Charles, 344, 345
Verzar, Professor, 208
Victoria, Queen, 263, 298
Vinrace, Felix, 143

Walker, Graham, 216
Walsh, Colm, 214

Walsh, Julia, 372, 374
Walsh, P.J., 215
Walsh, Professor Thomas, 150, 224
Walton, Professor Philip W., 190–1, 196, 197, 212
War of Independence, 137, 228, 301, 377
Ward, James, 180, 181
Ward, J.J., 180
Wardell, Professor John Henry, 19, 109, 113, 319–20
Warren, Colonel John, 67–8
Webb, D.A., 346
Welles, Orson, 379
Wellington, Duke of, 4–5
West, Sir Raymond, 20, 99
West of Ireland Cardiology Foundation, 156
Western Health Board, 155
Western Skin Cancer Registry, 156
whales, 298
White, Ellen Maria, 56
White, Sinclair, 143, 147, 148
Whittaker, E.T., 166
Williamson, Dr Alan, 180
Wilson, C.T.R., 188
Wilson, Miss, 84
Wims, Mai, 215
women
    chemistry, 224–5
    engineering, 139
    examinations, 23, 165–6
    higher education for, 329
    mathematics, 173
    medicine, 151
    suffrage movement, 300, 375, 410
Wood, Dr Martin, 180
Woods, Anne, 139
Wörner, Professor Markus H., 420
Wright, Bryce McMurdo, 257
Wright, Edward Perceval, 278
Wright, J.E., 169–70
Wright, Mr, 257
Wyatt, A.J., 400, 404
Wyse, Thomas, 10, 12, 29, 30
Wyse Committee, 25, 29, 30, 33, 35, 44

X-rays, 205

Yeats, W.B., 398, 405
Young, J., 288
Young Irelanders, 7, 12–13, 226

Zappa, Franco, 216
Zeuss, Johann Caspar, 344, 352
Zimmer, Professor Heinrich, 344, 359
zoology, 267, 361

President of the
declaration before
Galway that I wi
faithfully discharg
taken and acknow
the twenty sixth da

*Extract of the declaration signed by Edward Berwick,
President of Queen's College Galway,
26 March 1852*